THE RUSSIAN RESEARCH CENTER

The Russian Research Center of Harvard University is supported by a grant from the Carnegie Corporation. The Center carries out interdisciplinary study of Russian institutions and behavior and related subjects.

How *RUSSIA* is *Ruled*

How *RUSSIA* is Ruled

By Merle Fainsod

HARVARD UNIVERSITY PRESS · CAMBRIDGE · 1956

Distributed in Great Britain by
GEOFFREY CUMBERLEGE, Oxford University Press, London

This volume was prepared under a grant from the Carnegie Corporation of New York. That Corporation is not,
however, the author, owner, publisher, or proprietor of this
publication and is not to be understood as approving by
virtue of its grant any of the statements made or views
expressed therein.

Library of Congress Catalog Card Number 53–6029
Printed in the United States of America

For Johnny, Elizabeth, and Mary

Preface

The aim of this book is to analyze the physiology, as well as the anatomy, of Soviet totalitarianism and to communicate a sense of the living political processes in which Soviet rulers and subjects are enmeshed. This is an ambitious undertaking — perhaps too ambitious to be fully realized as long as many important areas of Soviet life are closed to scholarly investigation. Although Soviet secretiveness does not make the task easy, there is more to be learned from the flow of criticism in Soviet publications than is commonly recognized. In recent years Soviet official sources have been supplemented by a wealth of material derived from careful interviewing of Soviet refugees. The testimony of these "living witnesses" provides a reservoir of fresh data which have been of great importance in enriching our comprehension of Soviet realities. This study draws heavily on such testimony, and the author can only regret that the understandable desire of the refugees to protect their anonymity renders it impossible to make proper personal acknowledgments.

The plan of this volume can be briefly summarized. Part One presents a historical analysis of the forces and factors that produced the Bolshevik Revolution and transformed its character once power had been attained. Part Two is concerned with the Party and its changing role in theory and practice. In Part Three other instruments of rule are examined — the Constitution and the hierarchy of Soviets, the bureaucracy, the police, and the armed forces. Part Four portrays the impact of the Soviet pattern of controls on factory and farm, analyzes the tensions which they produce, and concludes with an appraisal of the strengths and weaknesses of the Soviet political system.

A draft of this study was completed before the death of Stalin. Although the changes which occurred in the first months after Stalin's death have been incorporated in the revised text, the basic scheme of organization and analysis around which the volume was originally constructed has been retained. Important as recent developments are, they are unlikely to effect any fundamental metamorphosis in the nature of Soviet totalitarianism in the immediate future.

A book of this character necessarily relies on the contributions of a wide company of scholars in the Slavic field. How much I owe to them only they will realize, although the ultimate responsibility for the views which I express here is my own.

I am profoundly grateful to Professor Clyde Kluckhohn, the Director of the Russian Research Center at Harvard, both for the generous support which made this volume possible and for constructive criticism of the manuscript. Professor Frederick C. Barghoorn of Yale University and Drs. Barrington Moore, Jr. and Alex Inkeles, my colleagues at the Russian Research Center, were also kind enough to read the manuscript and made many very valuable suggestions which are reflected in the final revision. Mr. Paul W. Friedrich was particularly helpful in providing background material for the chapter on the Komsomol. I am deeply indebted to Colonel R. S. Sleeper and his Air Force associates for facilitating interviews with Soviet refugees in Germany and Austria during the summer of 1949. I have also been able to draw upon the unique interview data and illuminating reports of the Russian Research Center's Refugee Interview Project, which is supported, under Contract AF No. 33(038)–12909, by the Human Resources Research Institute, Air Research and Development Command, Maxwell Air Force Base, Montgomery, Alabama.

I should like to express my gratitude to Mrs. Helen Parsons for helpful assistance, to Mr. Harvey Fireside, Mr. Mark Neuweld, and Mrs. Vera Spoerry for aid in research, and to Mrs. Sally Mead, Miss Muriel Levin, and Miss Rose DiBenedetto for an accurate typescript. Mrs. Chase Duffy of the Harvard Press has made me appreciate anew how much an author can learn from an able editor. Finally, I should like to record my deep obligation to Mrs. Jeane Olson, who has borne the major burden of preparing this manuscript for the Press and who has cheerfully undertaken the tedious but essential chore of indexing its contents. Her initiative and intelligence have been this author's constant joy.

A word of explanation is due on the vexing problem of rendering Russian words and titles into English. An effort has been made to strike a balance between the needs of the general reader and the Russian specialist. For the convenience of the general reader the plurals of most Russian words are Anglicized in the text, and the English style of capitalization is adhered to in transliterating titles of books and articles in the notes and bibliography. The system of transliteration follows that of the Library of Congress, with some minor exceptions. Ligatures have been eliminated, and the sounds $\widehat{iu}$ and $\widehat{ia}$ are transliterated as *yu* and *ya*. Established English usage has been observed in the spelling of familiar Russian proper names.

Grateful acknowledgment is made to the following publishers for permission to reprint excerpts from copyrighted materials:

George Allen and Unwin Ltd., London: Klaus Mehnert, *Youth in Soviet Russia.*
Current Digest of the Soviet Press.
The Dial Press: Bertram D. Wolfe, *Three Who Made a Revolution.*

Gerald Duckworth and Company, London, B. H. Sumner, *Survey of Russian History.*

E. P. Dutton and Company, James Mavor, *An Economic History of Russia,* Volume II.

Harcourt, Brace and Company: Leon Trotsky, *The Real Situation in Russia.*

Harper and Brothers: Markoosha Fischer, *My Lives in Russia.*

The Macmillan Company: W. H. Chamberlin, *The Russian Revolution, 1917–1921,* Volumes I and II; E. H. Carr, *The Bolshevik Revolution, 1917–1923,* Volumes I and II; W. R. Batsell, *Soviet Rule in Russia;* Andrei Y. Vyshinsky, *The Law of the Soviet State;* G. T. Robinson, *Rural Russia under the Old Regime;* P. I. Lyashchenko, *History of the National Economy of Russia to the 1917 Revolution;* B. H. Sumner, *Peter the Great and the Emergence of Russia.*

Public Affairs Press, Washington, D. C.: Virginia Rhine (translator), *Young Communists in the USSR.*

Routledge and Kegan Paul Ltd., London: Anton Ciliga, *The Russian Enigma.*

Charles Scribner's Sons: Leon Trotsky, *My Life.*

Martin Secker and Warburg Ltd., London: Eric Wollenberg, *The Red Army.*

Simon and Schuster: Leon Trotsky, *The History of the Russian Revolution,* Volume III.

The Viking Press: F. Beck and W. Godin, *Russian Purge and the Extraction of Confession.*

MERLE FAINSOD

25 MAY 1953

Contents

Charts

Tables

PART ONE
The Pursuit of Power

Chapter *1*

The Seedbed of Revolution

Every revolution bears the stamp of its own distinctive genius. It is a product of the historical forces that go before, of the leaders who shape its course, and of the problems with which they are confronted. It is a shallow view of Russian history which sees Bolshevism as an alien excrescence grafted on the Russian body politic by a handful of power-lusting conspirators without roots in the past. The triumph of the Bolshevik Revolution was in no sense inevitable, but Bolshevism as a movement was an indigenous, authoritarian response to the environment of Tsarist absolutism which nurtured it. Autocracy generates its own authoritarian antibodies and endows them with its own peculiar contours.

To insist that Bolshevism has an organic connection with the Russian past is not to say that the Russian is congenitally destined to be governed despotically or that there is some mystic substance in the Russian soul which breeds submission before authority. There is a fashionable but equally shallow view of Russian history that sees the Soviet regime as an inevitable outgrowth of the Russian past and as an expression of a need for domination which is deeply imbedded in the national character. To those who hold this view, the mounting struggle for freedom during the last century of Tsardom represents an aberration which is outside the main stream of historical development. To them, the miscarriage of the struggle is proof of the Russian lack of genius for self-government. While sweeping formulations of this type share the attractiveness of all simple solutions for highly difficult problems, the simplicity is delusive. Cultural determinism carries the same dangers as other forms of determinism. "Totalitarianism," George F. Kennan has wisely observed, "is not a national phenomenon; it is a disease to which all humanity is in some degree vulnerable." [1]

The problem of the origins of Communist totalitarianism is too complex to be disposed of by impressionistic judgments of Russian national character. The frame of analysis must include as well those distinctive characteristics of the Russian historical legacy that have left the Russian people badly prepared for self-government. It must give due weight to the profound social and economic dislocations which attended the abolition of serfdom, the beginnings of industrialization, and the efforts to modernize the Russian economy. It must embrace the armory of ideas which the Bolsheviks borrowed from the West and adapted to their own purposes. And it must recognize the cataclysmic importance of the First World War, which precipitated the Revolution of 1917 and gave Lenin his golden opportunity to bid for power.

The Heritage of Autocracy

On the eve of the First World War, Russia was still ruled by a Tsar-Emperor whose conception of the plenitude of autocratic power dated back to the fifteenth century. The system of autocracy was in process of erosion. Its foundations had been rudely shaken in the aftermath of defeat in the Crimean and Russo-Japanese Wars. But the more its moral authority was undermined, the more insistently it clung to the substance as well as to the semblance of its power. Nicholas II, forced by the 1905 revolution to convoke a Duma, nevertheless proclaimed that "the Supreme, Autocratic power belongs to the All-Russian Emperor" and repeated the ancient formula: "Obedience to his authority, not only for wrath but also for conscience sake, is ordained by God Himself." [2] The words of Nicholas II rang like an atavistic echo of Ivan the Terrible, who pronounced that "the Rulers of Russia have not been accountable to any one, but have been free to reward or chastise their subjects," [3] and of Peter the Great, who wrote, "The autocratic monarch has to give an account of his acts to no one on earth, but has a power and authority to rule his states and lands as a Christian sovereign according to his own will and judgment." [4]

The dominating role of the Autocrat was institutionalized through a highly centralized but far from efficient bureaucracy, whose uncertain dominion extended into the farthest reaches of the Empire. The army and the police provided the cohesive force which sustained the authority of the Autocrat. The social pillars that supported him were chiefly the church and the majority of the landowning gentry. The populace had no active part in this system of government; the duty of the people was to serve the Autocrat by yielding implicit obedience to his dictates. Directive authority was largely reserved for the representatives of the autocracy; their commandments were to be obeyed as the paternal expression of the supreme wisdom of the Autocrat. In the words of Pobedonostsev, tutor and adviser of the last two Romanovs:

The history of mankind bears witness that the most necessary and fruitful reforms — the most durable measures — emanated from the supreme will of statesmen, or from a minority enlightened by lofty ideas and deep knowledge, and that, on the contrary, the extension of the representative principle is accompanied by an abasement of political ideas and the vulgarisation of opinions in the mass of the electors.[5]

This was not a conception calculated to give scope to popular initiative or to test the capacity of the citizenry for self-government. Concessions had to be made in the face of popular restiveness as they were made after the Crimean and Russo-Japanese Wars. But concessions were followed by reassertions of bureaucratic power. The mood of the autocracy was to yield reluctantly under irresistible pressure and, at the first opportunity, to reassert absolutist pretensions.

Insistence on maintaining the full range of autocratic authority helped to radicalize the opposition. If Communism became, in Herzen's phrase, Tsarism turned upside down, not the least of the contributing causes were the conditions of combat which Tsarism imposed. The policies pursued by the Tsar-Autocrats alienated substantial sections of the vital and creative forces in society. They denied these forces experience in self-government, and where they could not deny, they limited such experience to the narrowest possible range. By damming up the constitutional channels for the expression of social grievances, they helped create a situation in which popular disaffection overflowed into revolutionary turbulence.

One of the characteristic features of Tsarist Russia was the separation of state and society. With a few striking exceptions, the higher offices of the public service were largely a monopoly of the nobility and landowning gentry. Until the creation of the *zemstvos*, or local government assemblies, in 1864 and the Duma reforms after the 1905 revolution, other social classes were for all practical purposes excluded from participation in state affairs, and even after these reforms, their activity was constrained in a tightening circle. But while opportunities were limited, appetites were growing. Klyuchevsky's pithy summation of Tsardom, "The state became swollen while the people shrank," needs to be modified for the nineteenth and early twentieth centuries. The state, to be sure, continued to swell, but the people refused to shrink. The history of nineteenth-century Russia is more than a history of autocratic power and its exercise; it is also a record of a great awakening.

Even earlier, Peter the Great had, as Pushkin said, cut a window into Europe. But Peter's interests were thoroughly practical and technical, and no Western liberal philosophical currents were permitted to pass through his window. Catherine the Great opened the window wide, and strange winds of Western doctrine began to blow. Voltaire, Montesquieu,

Adam Smith, and the Encyclopedists became the possessions of a newly awakening intellectual class in Russia, and other Western thinkers were eagerly read and discussed. But the peasant rising of Pugachev and French revolutionary excesses frightened Catherine and brought an abrupt stop to the journalistic activity and discussions stimulated by Western ideas. The intellectual ferment which Catherine herself had done so much to inspire was forced underground, where it largely remained through much of the reign of Alexander I.

New winds carrying the Western doctrine came in the wake of the Napoleonic campaigns; returning officers brought back in their baggage liberating ideas as well as trophies of war. The explosive force of these ideas was manifest in the abortive Decembrist revolt (1825), and though Nicholas the Gendarme disposed of the conspirators, he was unable to stamp out the ideas they represented. Russia's iron age of repression was also its golden age of literature, and literature, despite all the force of censorship, was the great outlet "for an oppressed people's dreams and aspirations." [6]

The Great Awakening

The first stirrings of the awakening were visible among the nobility and landed gentry. Most members of this class, to be sure, identified their interests with that of the autocracy. They staffed the higher ranks of the administration and the army. They looked to the state to protect their privileges. Though some among those who sought state service were prepared to press for modernization of the governmental apparatus and even for far-reaching social and economic reforms, the great majority were content with the *status quo*. They supported the autocracy because the autocracy supported them.

Yet all was not well with this privileged group. The literature of the golden age is a barometer of their discontents. A whole generation of "superfluous men" — Griboyedov's Chatsky, Pushkin's Onegin, Lermontov's Pechorin, Herzen's Beltov, Turgenev's Rudin — register the gathering disillusionment. Repelled by the atmosphere of servility that permeated the state service, rejecting the obscurantism and smug self-satisfaction of high society, cut off from the people by a deep, unbridgeable social chasm, weighed down by a feeling of uselessness on their estates, they agonized their sick consciences without being able to find a constructive outlet for their energies. Their tragedy of frustration was unresolved, but, like the lightning that precedes the storm, their dissatisfaction signaled a loss of faith and an alienation of confidence within the inner citadel of the autocracy itself.

Their ranks were soon to be supplemented by more determined men, aware of the evils with which they had to contend and ready to act on their convictions. Again it is literature that sounds the call. Belinsky, writing his famous denunciatory letter to Gogol, proclaims:

> Russia sees her salvation not in mysticism, nor asceticism, nor pietism, but in the successes of civilization, enlightenment and humanity. What she needs is not sermons . . . or prayers (she has repeated them too often!), but the awakening in the people of a sense of their human dignity lost for so many centuries amid the dirt and refuse; she needs rights and laws conforming not with the preaching of the church but with common sense and justice, and their strictest possible observance.[7]

The search for the new man is the keynote of Dobrolyubov's striking article, "What is Oblomovism?" Reviewing Turgenev's *On the Eve*, Dobrolyubov had written, "We are seeking, thirsting, waiting. We are waiting for somebody or other to explain to us what to do." [8]

Foreshadowed by the enterprising and self-reliant burgher figure of Stolz in Goncharov's novel *Oblomov*, the new hero of his time is practical, hard-working, and devoted to a life of order and reason. He finds expression in the protagonist of *On the Eve*, the Bulgarian revolutionary Insarov, who consecrates his life to the liberation of his people from the Turks; and again more brilliantly in the hero of Turgenev's *Fathers and Children*, the nihilist Bazarov, who dedicates his life to science and the destruction of illusions that others may build firmly on fact. With Chernyshevsky's novel *What Is to Be Done?* the circle is complete. The new man (and woman) claims the center of the stage, and overshadowing the main characters of the novel is Rakhmetov, the professional revolutionary, portent of the Bolshevik to come. Rakhmetov, to be sure, is a Narodnik, or Populist, but he is above all a man of action devoting the whole of his life to the revolutionary cause. It is a conception to which Lenin was to return again and again; indeed, it is not without significance that the title of the famous essay in which Lenin developed the organizational principles of Bolshevism was borrowed from Chernyshevsky's novel.

Literature was the laboratory of society. Just as the generation of "superfluous men" had their prototypes in the life around them, the activists mirrored in the novels of Turgenev and Chernyshevsky reflected the aspirations of the new intelligentsia which were beginning to assert their claims to shape the destiny of Russia. After the middle of the nineteenth century, the composition of the intelligentsia underwent rapid change. Their social roots were no longer overwhelmingly in the nobility and landed gentry. Infusions of new blood from the *raznochintsy* (the men of different classes) gave the intelligentsia an increasingly plebeian character. Belinsky was the son of a country doctor. Dobrolyubov came from a clerical family. Chernyshevsky, also a priest's son, was originally destined for a clerical career. There was an increasingly large number of professional men — physicians, lawyers, teachers, and journalists — who "belonged to the people by birth and . . . to the intellectual group by higher education." [9] Some of the more pliable and enterprising made very successful careers in the state service. For most, the road to bureaucratic power was closed, sometimes because of personal distaste for this type of activity, more often because of the court's preference for scions of the aristocratic families.

The new intelligentsia harbored some of the most active, energetic, and restless spirits of Russian society. Many of them were increasingly critical of the existing social and political structure — an attitude to which the autocracy responded by developing a sharp distrust of the group. The resulting estrangement of state and intelligentsia turned out to be a tragedy for both sides. The autocracy was unable and unwilling to harness the reforming zeal of the intelligentsia to state purposes. The rebels among the intelligentsia in turn were denied an opportunity to acquire experience in the arts of responsible government and were condemned to pursue their dream of justice in loose word-spinning or conspiratorial violence. Deprived of the chance to share in power, they placed themselves at the head of all the forces of discontent in Russian society and ended by releasing a Pandora's box of unintended consequences which represented a tragic betrayal of the dreams of freedom on which their revolt was nourished.

The Miscarriage of Reform

The tragedy of the estrangement was underlined by disillusionment with the belated concessions which the autocracy was forced to yield. The local government reforms which followed in the wake of the Emancipation Edict of 1861 had potentialities which, if developed, could have given important sectors of Russian society experience with self-rule. The Zemstvo Statute of 1864, for all of its limitations in the form of high franchise qualifications and divisions of the electorate into discriminatory colleges, opened the way to popular participation in the affairs of local government. The work of the zemstvos in the fields of popular education, medicine, and sanitation forms one of the brightest pages of Russian history between the Emancipation reforms and the Revolution of 1917. It is a page that could not have been written without the devoted work of the rural "intelligents," school teachers, doctors, and zemstvo clerks, who gave themselves unstintingly to the cause of popular enlightenment. They labored in the face of great difficulties — the apathy of the villages, the suspicions of the more reactionary landowners, and the frustrations imposed by the central bureaucracy. But the concessions granted in 1864 were whittled down in the reaction that followed the attempt on the Tsar's life in 1866 by the student Karakozov. The stunting of zemstvo institutions alienated and drove away the more liberal zemstvo workers, who, cut off from creative participation in zemstvo work, became ripe for more drastic, revolutionary alternatives. Harassment and persecution bred their antidotes.

A somewhat similar fate befell the great judicial reforms of 1864. The legal edifice erected by the Act of 1864 was imposing, even by advanced Western standards. The judicial system was made independent of administration, with judges subject to removal only for judicial misconduct; trial by jury was introduced in criminal cases; justices of the peace were to be elected by zemstvo and town assemblies; legal proceedings were to be public. These and other reforms, modeled on the best Western practices, promised to carry Russia far along the road to constitutionalism and due process. But like the zemstvo reforms, their continued existence depended on the favor of the Supreme Autocrat, and what the Autocrat could give, he could also take away. In the reaction which followed the acquittal in 1878 of Vera Zasulich, who shot the governor of St. Petersburg for ordering the flogging of a student revolutionary, much was taken away. Again the dashing of high hopes produced disenchantment. The professional bar created by the Act of 1864 might have become one of the strongest pillars of a constitutional order, but instead it found its position undermined and its dependence on the autocracy emphasized. Like other sections of the intelligentsia, it began to look elsewhere for its protection. Its professional attachment was to legal processes, but many of its members became convinced that in an autocracy even the struggle for legality could be carried out only through illegal means.

The revolution of 1905 ushered in a new wave of reforms and offered a fresh opportunity for the Tsar-Autocrat to conciliate public opinion. But once more the opportunity was passed by. The majority of the marchers who followed Father Gapon to the great square opposite the Winter Palace on Bloody Sunday (January 9, 1905 — Old Style) * came in a mood of humble petition.

We, working men and inhabitants of St. Petersburg of various classes, our wives and our children and our helpless old parents, come to Thee, Sire, to seek for truth and defense.

. . . Destroy the wall between Thyself and Thy people, and let them rule the country together with Thyself. Art Thou not placed there for the happiness of Thy people? But this happiness the officials snatch from our hands. It does not come to us. We get only distress and humiliation. Look without anger, attentively upon our requests. They are directed, not to evil, but to good for us as well as for Thee.[10]

* For the convenience of the reader, events occurring after January 1, 1917, are dated in accordance with the Western (Gregorian) calendar, which was adopted officially by Russia on February 14, 1918. Dates prior to 1917 follow the Old Style Julian calendar which is thirteen days behind the Gregorian. Both styles are given in the notes in cases where both were included in the primary source.

The petition was answered by a volley of bullets; hundreds were killed
and wounded. The letter which Father Gapon sent the Tsar after the
demonstration displays a different spirit. Addressed to "Nicholas Romanov, formerly Tsar and at present soul destroyer of the Russian
Empire," it reveals bitter disillusionment.

> With naive belief in thee as father of thy people, I was going peacefully to
> thee with the children of these very people. Thou must have known, thou didst
> know, this. The innocent blood of workers, their wives and children, lies forever
> between thee, O soul destroyer, and the Russian people. Moral connection be-
> tween thee and them may never be any more.[11]

In the initial panic inspired by general strikes, land seizures, and the
burning of manor houses, the Tsar and his advisers prepared to make
large-scale concessions. A commission was set up to draft labor legislation.
The Tsar promised a representative assembly, though the first proposal
incorporated in the Imperial Manifesto of August 6, 1905, limited the
functions of the Duma to that of an advisory body which could merely
discuss laws, the budget, and the report of the state auditor. The popular
disorders continued and were followed by wider concessions. The Manifesto of October 17, 1905, promised universal suffrage, freedom of speech,
assembly, conscience, and organization. It pledged that no law would
become effective without the approval of the Duma and gave assurances
that the Duma would have authority to investigate the legality of all
actions of governmental authorities. The October Manifesto was supplemented by measures designed to placate the peasantry. The redemption
payments which the peasants were still making for the land which they
received when serfdom was abolished were at first reduced and then
canceled. Purchase of land through Peasant Land Banks was facilitated.

The policy of concessions paid rich dividends. The revolutionary tide
began to ebb, and the solid ranks of the opposition were broken. The
rural gentry and the wealthier merchants and manufacturers rallied
around the government as a symbol of law and order, while the uprising
of Moscow workers in December alienated liberals and moderates who
sought to direct the energies of the nation into constitutional channels.

Once the moment of supreme danger had passed, the autocracy again
began to qualify its concessions. The Fundamental Law promulgated by
the Tsar on April 23, 1906, sought to make the Duma as innocuous a
legislative body as possible. Though the electoral law provided for the
representation of workers, peasants, and intellectuals as well as the
landed gentry, the latter were heavily overrepresented; the class
character of the suffrage provisions was designed to dilute the force of
the opposition to autocracy. Despite these provisions, the first electoral
campaign yielded a great victory for the opposition in general and the

Kadets (Constitutional Democrats) in particular. For the first time, organized legal political parties assumed a role on the Russian political stage.

The history of the Dumas is largely a record of the frustration of parliamentary hopes. The First Duma (1906) was quickly dissolved after a bitter struggle in which the Kadet majority refused to bow before the will of the government. The Second Duma (1907), with strengthened radical representation, proved even less tractable than its predecessor, and it too was soon dissolved. Stolypin, the Tsar's first minister, was prepared to work with the Duma, but only on his own terms. Since he held himself accountable solely to the Tsar, the fabric of collaboration with the forces of popular representation became irreparably strained. Repression replaced concession as the reactionary "ruling spheres" around the throne consolidated their dominant position. The new electoral law proclaimed on the occasion of the dissolution of the Second Duma greatly increased the influence of the wealthier categories of the electorate, and the composition of the Third and Fourth Dumas reflected their increased power. The reconstruction of the Duma provided a pliant and accommodating majority for the government, and the Third Duma was permitted to serve out its full term (1907–1912). The elections to the Fourth Duma (1912–1916) resulted in a victory for the conservative nationalist groups, but even these groups were pushed into opposition to the government by the incompetence of the autocracy in grappling with the problems presented by the First World War.

Despite the government's measures to restrict the effectiveness of the Duma and to emasculate its representative character, its substantive accomplishments were impressive. Owing largely to its initiative, and in the face of the deep-rooted opposition of the so-called Ministry of Public Instruction, the expenditures for education grew steadily from 44,000,000 rubles in 1906 to 214,000,000 rubles in 1917. On the eve of the war in 1914, 8,000,000 pupils, or approximately half of the eligible child population, were enrolled in primary schools.[12] The plans of the educational committee of the Duma contemplated universal instruction by 1922. Under pressure from the Duma, the civil rights of peasants were equalized with those of other citizens, and the centrally designated Land Captains were displaced in judicial matters by local justices of the peace. These and other achievements testified to the continuing vigor of the progressive forces in the Duma, held back though they were by the dead weight of the autocracy. Even though the Duma became increasingly conservative over the years, it remained a sounding board of ameliorative reform. Unfortunately, the ears that should have listened were closed, and the appeals of the shriller voices that came afterwards were addressed to a different audience.

The frustration of the constitutional impulse which the Duma sought to provide prepared the way for revolution and the ultimate triumph of Soviet totalitarianism. Constitutionalism in its inception is a tender plant; it needs a favorable environment in which to grow and prosper. The environment of the last decades of Tsardom was not favorable. To be sure, many members of the Russian intelligentsia were deeply attracted by Western parliamentary models and did their utmost to transplant these constitutional conceptions to Russian soil. But in the vastness of Russia, they were a pathetic fragment doomed to defeat by the recalcitrant forces of ignorance, apathy, and blind opposition that surrounded them. Confronted with a system of autocratic power that could not assimilate Burke's lesson of preservation through reform, the constitutionalists saw the ground slipping from under them. The rebuffs they received led many of their potential followers to embrace more extreme leadership. The political arrangements they preached had little support in native tradition The demands they made on the electorate could not be realized without a generation of widespread popular education. The parliamentarians were themselves the victims of their own parliamentary inexperience. Their only secure social support was a weakly developed middle class; their moderate programs fell far short of meeting the extreme grievances of a substantial part of the peasantry and industrial labor force. In the race between reform and revolution, the constitutional forces found themselves handicapped at every turn.

The hour of the autocracy was rapidly running out. It found itself increasingly isolated from the society which precariously sustained it. The power that was escaping from the hands of the autocracy had many potential claimants. Besides the intelligentsia, there was the vast inert mass of the peasantry and a new working class in process of creation. Their aspirations were diverse, but they were united by a common sense of grievance. The march of events was to insure that each would be compelled to test his claim in the crucible of revolution.

The Peasant's Claim to Power

In a country as predominantly agricultural as Russia, it was perhaps inevitable that many would look to the peasantry to become the residuary legatees of power. The orientation of the pre-Marxian Russian revolutionaries was based overwhelmingly on the peasantry, for the peasant, in their eyes, was a "socialist by instinct and a revolutionary by tradition." They tended to idealize the *mir*, or village commune, as an embodiment of coöperative fellowship, and they saw the risings of Stenka Razin, Pugachev, and other eruptive peasant *jacqueries* as a verification of the revolutionary potential of the peasantry. For many of them, Western Europe had little to offer by way of example. At first attracted by its atmosphere of freedom, luxuriant after the stifling confinement of Russia, they found themselves increasingly repelled by the bourgeois tone of European society, by capitalism with its slogan "Enrichissez-vous!" and by the ugly cancer of the urban industrial proletariat. Parliamentary institutions seemed to them little more than a cloak for business domination. Russia had to find another and better path of social development.

Herzen, in his post-1848 phase, illustrates this trend of thought. Repudiating the whole apparatus of parliaments and representation, he called on Russia to throw off serfdom, the nobility, the bureaucracy, and the Byzantinized church and to seek her destiny in a coöperative federation of free communes founded on the peasant's partnership in the mir. This dream may seem fantastic in the light of later developments, but the system of agrarian socialism and free federation which Herzen adumbrated supplied the staple ideas of the Narodniks, or Populists, and their successors, the Socialist-Revolutionaries, until they were crushed by the Bolsheviks.

The pre-Marxist revolutionaries differed in the strategies which they espoused, but they were at one with Herzen in looking to the peasant for salvation. For Bakunin, the peasantry was ripe for revolt; all that was required was that the flames be ignited by determined groups of professional revolutionaries skilled in conspiratorial tactics. For Tkachev, writing in the 1870's, the seeds of capitalism in Russia were already discernible; his theory of "preventive revolution" involved seizing power before the bourgeoisie could become strong in order to insure an agrarian path of development for Russian socialism.

The Russian Intelligentsia and the Peasantry

Maximalist tactics had a powerful fascination for many members of the Russian intelligentsia. The conditions of repression under which they worked and the inadequate and pitiful crumbs of reform thrown their way by the autocracy inspired an impatience with gradualism in any form. Their reaction to the Act of Emancipation of the Serfs (1861) provides a vivid illustration. When it appeared that the peasants were being condemned to impoverishment as a result of the smallness of the land allotments and the excessive redemption payments, a strong current of disillusionment set in, and insurrectionist and terrorist elements among the intelligentsia began to come to the fore. Great hopes were placed in the revolutionary potential of the peasantry. A secret organization, *Zemlya i Volya* (Land and Freedom), planned a peasant rising for the summer of 1863, but nothing came of it, and a number of the leaders were executed. An attempt was made to assassinate the Tsar in April 1866, but this also failed. The societies which had helped plan the assassination were discovered, and many of their members were exiled to Siberia.

Russian revolutionaries during this period, however, were by no means united on terrorist and insurrectionary tactics. An important segment of the intelligentsia during the seventies was much attracted to the doctrines of Peter Lavrov, who preached education and propaganda among the masses. Lavrov's *Historical Letters*, written for the most part between 1867 and 1869, emphasized the duty of the "critically thinking individual" to devote himself to the welfare of the masses. No revolution was possible, argued Lavrov, without preparatory education of the *Narod*, the people. The obligation of the intelligentsia was to stop talking among themselves and go out into the villages to help awaken the peasant masses. Lavrov's idealistic message had a striking response, the famous movement of "going to the people," which assumed the proportions of a crusade. Students, teachers, lawyers, physicians, officers, and "repentant noblemen" joined in, and from the summer of 1872 to the summer of 1874 the countryside swarmed with crusaders and evangelists.

What happened is depicted in unforgettable fashion in Turgenev's *Virgin Soil*. The "dark forces" of the village could make nothing of the invaders. The gulf that divided what the Russians call "people" and "persons" was too deep. Most of the intelligentsia did not know how to talk to the people when they met them. The peasants could not understand what they were driving at. Some of the missionaries were confused with antichrist, and many were turned over to the police. For the intelligentsia, the experience was sobering and disillusioning. A few responded by committing suicide. Others, for the first time brought up against hard realities, were forced to recognize that vague idealism was not enough, that the task of educating the peasant was more than a weekend in the country, that patient devotion was required, and that a whole life had to be lived together.

A few — too few — digested the lesson and settled down in the countryside to undertake the long, disagreeable task of overcoming suspicion and proving their usefulness. Many — too many — flocked back to the towns and cities to torture their consciences in endless conversation and, when the pressure became too great, to break out with heroic acts of terrorism which brought the police down on town and countryside alike. As one of the best of the organizers who stayed behind in the country said, "As soon as we have started something going, bang! — the intellectuals have killed somebody, and the police are on us. Why don't they give us a chance to organise?" [13]

The history of the Narodnik movement during the late seventies and early eighties is one of increasing dedication to terror. The triumph of the extremists found expression in the organization in 1879 of *Narodnaya Volya* (the People's Will), perhaps the first tactically unified and tightly organized Russian revolutionary party. Like its predecessors, Narodnaya

Volya was primarily concerned with the liberation of the peasantry. Liberation, its members felt, could not be secured without constitutional reforms. Indeed, as the famous letter of its Executive Committee to Alexander III upon his accession makes clear, its aim was a constituent assembly composed overwhelmingly of peasant representatives who could be trusted to put a program of agrarian socialism into effect. Denied constitutional channels of expression, Narodnaya Volya turned to terror instead, hoping through a series of key assassinations to disorganize and intimidate the government into concessions, to arouse the people, and perhaps to seize power at the center. From the fall of 1879 to the spring of 1881, the terrorists waged a relentless duel with the government. A number of important officials were killed, and finally in March 1881 Narodnaya Volya accomplished its chief aim, the assassination of Alexander II. Instead of ushering in a constituent assembly, the revolutionists only succeeded in intensifying the repression. The peasants were deaf to the revolutionary signal, and after a short-lived panic in court circles, reaction consolidated its hold. The Narodnik groups were broken to pieces by the authorities; revolution was reduced, in the words of one boasting official, "to a cottage industry." [14] The Narodniks dwindled in effectiveness, although many of their ideas were to enjoy a remarkable revival with the organization of the Socialist-Revolutionary Party in the opening years of the twentieth century.

Meanwhile, the land was ominously quiet. The rumbling land-hunger of the peasant world was still muffled, though the condition of the *muzhik* was far from good. Grievances were repressed, and peasant resentment smoldered just below the surface of the deceptively peaceful countryside.

Land-Hunger and Revolution

The Emancipation Edict was deeply disappointing to the peasantry. Limited allotments and high redemption payments meant, in the words of Professor Geroid T. Robinson, that "the scales were weighted against the peasant; he was coming forth from the Emancipation with limited rights and little land, but abundant obligations." [15] During the decades following Emancipation, the position of the peasantry worsened. The growth of the village population was prodigious. Although the amount of land available to the peasantry increased between 1877 and 1905, it failed to keep pace with the muzhik's fecundity. The average size of household allotments declined from 13.2 *desyatins* (one *desyatin* equals 2.7 acres) in 1877 to 10.4 in 1905. [16] The shrinkage in the size of household allotments was not offset by more intensive cultivation of allotment land. The agricultural practices of the mir retained their primitive character, and as a result the yield per *desyatin* was far below the average in Western Europe.

Rural distress was aggravated by the long agrarian depression of 1875 to 1895. The peasant who had grain to sell had to operate in a market in which the prices were fixed by international competition; the manufactured goods which he bought were purchased at prices maintained at a high level by the protectionist policies of the government. As a result, redemption payments became an intolerable burden to the average peasant. Arrears accumulated, and the situation became so critical that the government was forced to pare down the total redemption debt. Beginning in 1881, a series of laws was enacted deferring some of the redemption payments and canceling portions of the debt. In 1886 the poll tax on all peasants was abolished. But even these concessions turned out to be half-measures; the arrears continued to accumulate and redemption payments remained a running sore.

The efforts of the government to grapple with the land problem during the post-Emancipation period were at best palliatives which left the land-hunger of most of the peasantry unappeased. In 1883 a Peasant Land Bank was established to provide credit for the peasantry in purchasing land. In the period from 1887 to 1903, peasants bought more than five and a half million *desyatins* with the help of the Bank.[17] These purchases helped to create a small class of more substantial peasants (seeds of the later *kulaks*), but they hardly touched the basic peasant mass.

The government also utilized resettlement and colonization to relieve the land pressure. The completion of the Siberian railroad in 1893 gave a powerful impetus to emigration; during the years from 1894 to 1903, new settlers aided by grants of state lands and state loans moved into the Siberian domain at an average rate of nearly 115,000 a year.[18] Even this by no means inconsiderable stream of colonization did little to relieve the overcrowded villages. The natural increase of the rural population in forty *guberniyas* (provinces) during the years from 1897 to 1900, when the Siberian immigration was at its height, was nearly fourteen times as great as the net loss incurred through emigration.[19]

Given the basic factors of rural congestion and agrarian distress, it was perhaps inevitable that an exodus from the village should take place. With the growth of industry and commerce, the muzhik swarmed into the industrial centers in search of work and livelihood. The first general census of the population in 1897 disclosed more than five million "villagers" in the cities of European Russia.[20] The five million undoubtedly included many temporary migrants from the villages, but as time passed, the number of peasants who settled permanently in the towns increased. Their connections with the villages became increasingly attenuated but were not completely broken. Indeed, the industrial workers who periodically returned to the villages after exposure to agitation in the factories became one of the most effective conduits through which urban heresies were communicated to the countryside. The peasants who abandoned the villages for the cities undoubtedly provided some relief from rural overpopulation, but their outward flow could not keep pace with procreation, and those who remained behind continued to nurse their grievances and sharpen their land-hunger.

The dissatisfactions which had been accumulating in the villages in the decades after Emancipation finally erupted into active violence. In 1902 peasant disorders broke out in the Kursk, Poltava, and Kharkov provinces in the wake of a crop failure. The movement gave every evidence of being spontaneous; as a rule, villagers simply banded together to seize grain to feed themselves and their animals.

The movement, however, coincided with a renewal of organized revolutionary activity. The Socialist-Revolutionary Party was founded as a united party in 1902. Like its progenitor Narodnaya Volya, it adopted terroristic tactics and called for nationalization of the soil. The Socialist-Revolutionaries carried on considerable agitation in the villages, but there is little evidence to indicate that their agitation exercised much influence in stimulating the initial disorders. As one of the peasants involved in the disturbances of 1902 testified when brought before a magistrate, "No rumors came to me about any little books. I think that if we lived better, the little books would not be important, no matter what was written in them. What's terrible is not the little books, but this: that there isn't anything to eat." [21]

In the years preceding the Russo-Japanese War, peasant restlessness continued to manifest itself in occasional burnings of manor houses and attacks on landlords and their stewards. But the disturbances were scattered and disorganized. The defeat at the hands of the Japanese unleashed the whirlwind. The revolution spread from city to countryside. The rural disturbances began deep in the Black Soil Region, in the province of Kursk, in February 1905, and rapidly extended to neighboring provinces. Initially the peasants confined their defiance to illicit timber cutting and pasturing and to rent and labor strikes. Instances of estate pillaging and land seizure were at first uncommon.

As the disorders spread, the peasants became bolder. The Constitutional Assembly of the All-Russian Peasants' Union, which met secretly in Moscow on July 31–August 1, 1905, declared: "Private property in land should be abolished . . . The land should be considered the common property of the whole people." [22] On November 3, 1905, the government announced the cancellation of all redemption dues. Even earlier, arrangements had been made to expand the facilities of the Peasant Bank and to transfer some crown and fiscal lands to the bank for distribution among the peasants.

But these belated sops could not quell the peasant uproar. The disturbances widened, became more violent, and reached a climax in November 1905. Looting, burning, and land seizures were common, and the local authorities showed themselves impotent in the face of the anarchic violence. During the winter there was a lull, but in the spring the peasants returned to the attack. By the end of the summer of 1906, the revolt began to show signs of exhausting itself. As the fury died down, the government recovered its nerve and dispatched punitive military expeditions to deal with the rebels. In the face of overwhelming force, the peasants usually submitted, and a holocaust of summary executions, floggings, and other punishments followed.

The striking quality of the peasant uprising of 1905–06 was its elemental, unplanned, and largely unorganized character. Unlike the great revolts of Pugachev and Stenka Razin, it gathered around no dramatic personal symbol of leadership. Its fires were fed by misery and land-hunger, and its leaders were scattered in the villages and merged in the crowds' grievances. Its spokesmen at the Peasant Congresses and the Duma were usually sober men with a single-minded absorption in the problems of the land and an earthy common-sense quality that frequently distinguished them from their more fluent colleagues among the intelligentsia. But these peasant delegates followed the revolution rather than led it. They gave voice to its demands, but they did not know how to organize to make their demands effective. The professional revolutionaries, on the other hand, were prepared to supply leadership, but they lacked a vital connection with the peasantry. The Socialist-Revolutionaries were particularly active in carrying on agitation in the villages; as the disturbances spread, they did their utmost to fan the revolutionary flames. Their activities, however, were scattered and sporadic, and they too gave the impression of being caught up and swept along by the elemental force of the uprising rather than of directing its energies in disciplined channels. The appeal of both the Bolshevik and Menshevik factions of the Social-Democrats was primarily to the urban proletariat rather than to the peasant mass; their rural agitation was largely confined to the agricultural laborers of the Baltic regions where the capitalistic organization of agriculture was most advanced. On the whole, the influence of the revolutionaries on the course of the uprising was slight. The momentum came from the isolated villages, and the movement dissipated itself in hundreds of uncoördinated outbreaks doomed to be crushed by the centralized military force of the autocracy.

The Stolypin Reforms

The peasant uprising of 1905–06 forced the government to reëxamine the basis of the agrarian policy which it had been pursuing for many decades. That policy had been to maintain the mir with its system of mutual responsibility and repartitional holdings on the assumption that the mir nurtured conservatism in the villages. The agrarian disorders challenged the old faith that the mir was a stabilizing force in the countryside. Instead, the landholding nobility now denounced the mir as "based upon socialistic foundations" and as "the nursery of socialist bacilli." [23] The First Congress of Representatives of the Nobles' Societies, meeting in St. Petersburg in May 1906, called on the government to break up the mir into private peasant holdings. The Most Humble Address which they forwarded to the Tsar stated:

> The recognition and confirmation of the full property-right of the peasants in respect to the lands in their possession is a primary need of the national life. The strengthening of property-rights among the peasants . . . will increase their attachment to that which is their own, and their respect for that which belongs to others. [24]

Expropriation of the holdings of the nobility was categorically rejected.

This program won acceptance from the government and became the basis of Stolypin's agrarian reforms which were incorporated in a ukase of November 6, 1906, and approved by the Third Duma in 1910. The legislation was inevitably complex since it had to provide for many different varieties of land tenure, but its essential purpose was to facilitate the separation of the individual peasant from the mir and ultimately to reconstruct Russian agriculture on a basis of individual peasant holdings. The latter, however, was a long-term goal. The incredible tangle of village legal relationships and the drag of peasant inertia made certain that the readjustment of the land system would be a long drawn-out process. As a result of World War I, the process of dissolution was virtually suspended, and even before the outbreak of the war, the number of separators showed a steady decline after the substantial exodus of 1908-09.

> By January 1, 1916 [according to the economic historian Lyashchenko], requests for acquisition of land in personal ownership were submitted by 2,755,-000 householders in European Russia. . . Altogether, 2,478,000 householders owning an area of 16,919,000 *dessyatins* left the communes and secured their land in personal ownership. This constituted about 24 per cent of the total number of households in forty provinces of European Russia. [25]

The available data give no precise picture of the character of the separators, but the indications are that the more prosperous layer of the peasantry who saw its interests and welfare impeded by the mir was substantially represented. At the same time, the reform also made it possible for households owning little land to withdraw, sell their land, and break their ties with the village. Undoubtedly, some of the land thus disposed of found its way into the hands of the more well-to-do peasant separators.

The objective of the Stolypin reform was to create a class of trustworthy small proprietors who could be counted on to provide a bulwark against revolution. Prime Minister Stolypin supplied an unforgettable statement of his purposes in an address to the Third Duma. "The government," he said, "has placed its wager, not on the needy and the drunken, but on the sturdy and the strong — on the sturdy individual proprietor who is called upon to play a part in the reconstruction of our Tsardom on strong monarchical foundations." [26]

The "wager on the strong" was a bold conception which even Lenin recognized as a serious effort to create a new class backing for the autocracy.[27] As it turned out, the wager was lost, not because of what the Stolypin reform did, but because of what it left undone. While the landholdings of the nobility declined steadily in the post-Emancipation period, in 1905 they still accounted for 53,200,000 *desyatins*.[28] The Stolypin reform left these large holdings more or less intact. The exodus of the separators from the mir sharpened social stratification in the villages and created antagonisms between "the sturdy and strong" and "the needy and drunken," but the villages still faced the manor houses with a hunger for land unappeased. The peasant deputy Sakhno, addressing the Second Duma, spoke for the village poor and the landless when he said:

When they are in great need, when they are poor, when they are hungry, when there is nothing with which to heat their huts, nothing with which to cook soup to feed their children, when they hear the priest who says: "Look first for the kingdom of heaven, for your home is in the heavens," they forsake the priest and begin to grumble. Why can the *pomiestchik* [large landowner] have so much land and to the lot of the peasant there falls only the kingdom of heaven? [29]

It was a question which would be heard again in 1917.

Russian Industrial Development

The changes taking place in the villages were paralleled by even more striking developments in the cities. The Industrial Revolution came late to Russia, and precisely because it came late and to Russia, it displayed peculiarities which differentiated it sharply from its Western counterparts.

Mid-eighteenth-century Russian industry, despite popular impressions to the contrary, was not hopelessly backward compared with the rest of Europe. The industrial structure, however, was primarily oriented toward the fulfillment of the military requirements of the state.[30] The great lag in Russian economic development was essentially a phenomenon of the late eighteenth and early nineteenth centuries. The technological revolution that gave such powerful impetus to English industrial productivity was slow to penetrate Russia. While England, and later the United States and Western Europe, shifted to machine methods of production and reliance on the steam engine and coal, Russia clung tenaciously to traditional techniques. Between 1800 and 1861, the production of pig iron in Great Britain increased twenty-four fold; in Russia it barely doubled, and Russia was reduced to eighth place among the nations producing pig iron.[31] The vision of Peter the Great in building his power on a heavy-industry base was denied his successors. The backwardness of industry reflected the backwardness of the court on whose impetus and initiative Russian economic development so largely depended.

One of the peculiarities of the Russian industrial system prior to Emancipation — a peculiarity which may go far to explain its backwardness — was its heavy dependence on serf labor. The state factories were almost exclusively manned by ascribed serfs, state peasants who were assigned to work in the factories. The so-called "possessional factories," though owned by private merchant-manufacturers, operated with "possessional serfs" who were attached to the factory and could be employed only in it. There were also so-called "manorial factories," owned by landowners and operated on their estates by serfs belonging to them.

Even before the Emancipation Edict of 1861, the trend was in the direction of increasing reliance on free labor. The "manorial factories" declined in importance. Many of the owners of "possessional factories" were quick to take advantage of a law of 1840 which permitted them to liberate their serf workers. While forced labor continued to predominate in the mines and Ural ironworks until Emancipation, the textile industries turned increasingly to free labor. It was perhaps not accidental that the cotton industry, which by 1840 was based entirely on free labor and which enjoyed relatively little government patronage, was also the industry which made most rapid technical progress. After removal of the British ban on the export of spinning machinery in 1842, a number of cotton factories were built and equipped with British assistance. Although their expansion was handicapped by the limited domestic market which serfdom imposed and they faced serious problems in recruiting needed skills, their equipment reflected the advanced techniques of the day. By 1850–1860, the Russian cotton industry had mastered the whole cycle of cotton production from the spinning of yarn to the output of finished fabrics, though it still depended on imported machinery and foreign technical direction. The notable industrial progress which took place in the textile industry should not, however, be exaggerated. In 1866 in all of Russia there were only forty-two mechanized cotton mills, and the number of employees working in textile factories amounted to 94,600 persons.

In other areas, the mid-nineteenth-century Russian economy appeared even more hopelessly backward. The metallurgic industry remained stagnant. Railroad construction, although begun as early as the 1840's, had only token achievements to its credit, and water and road transportation were still organized on a primitive basis. A modern system of credit institutions was lacking; privately-owned credit institutions were virtually nonexistent; and the first joint-stock commercial bank was not founded until 1864. No stable currency existed, and the depreciated paper currency in circulation did not inspire business confidence. All this hardly established a promising base for industrial expansion.

The effect of the Emancipation Edict was to make part of the peasantry available for industrial employment. Peasant mobility, however, was limited. Under the system of mutual guaranty, the village assembly was held responsible by the government for the payment of taxes and redemption payments by its members. Permission to leave the village depended on the consent of the assembly and was granted only when assurances were forthcoming that the continuing obligations of the departing peasant would be discharged. One class of peasants, however, the so-called "household serfs" who received no land allotments and who were not retained as domestic servants by their former masters, were practically forced to resort to the towns for employment. Many were destined to become part of the new labor force which industrialization called into being.

Emancipation helped clear the way for industrial modernization, but its effects were not immediately felt. A whole battery of measures had to be launched to prepare the ground for industrial advance. State investments, as in previous periods of industrial advance, played a major formative role. State policy was also designed to create favorable conditions for industrial investment by both domestic and foreign capital. The reversal of the high-tariff policy, which began in the fifties and lasted until the eighties when protection was once again adopted, was an important step in opening the door to the West. Although it dealt a serious blow to the obsolete Ural ironworks, it gave a considerable stimulus to railroad construction by permitting the importation of rails and other equipment either duty-free or under very low rates. Reutern, who served as Minister of Finance from 1862 to 1878, gave every encouragement to commercial and industrial development. Financial administration was reorganized. By increasing the treasury's reserve, preliminary steps were taken to place Russia on a gold standard, though it was not until 1897 that this policy was finally successful. The State Bank was reformed and the establishment of commercial banks encouraged. The organization of joint-stock companies was permitted; a rash of company promotions, financial speculation, and stock-exchange activity introduced new westernizing elements into Russian commercial life. Through a system of concessions, subsidies, and guaranties, the state gave substantial assistance to industrial development; both domestic and foreign capital benefited by the government's fostering care.

The first surge of industrial progress manifested itself in railroad construction. During the decade from 1866 to 1875, 14,083 *versts* (one *verst* equals 0.66 English miles) of new railroad lines were opened compared to 3,543 *versts* completed in all the years up to 1866. Although most of these lines were constructed by private companies, government assistance was extensive. After 1880 a number of them were purchased by the government, and the major share of new construction was undertaken by the state.

During the 1860's and 1870's, capital flowed chiefly into railroads and banking, attracted by prospects of quick returns. The large influx of foreign capital came later; in this period Russian industry still depended heavily on native capital.[32] But foreign investments were growing, and Russia was deeply indebted to foreign technicians and entrepreneurs for modernizing her textile industry and laying the basis for the emergence of new industries such as coal, steel, and petroleum. The Welshman John Hughes founded the southern iron and steel industry in the Donets basin in 1869, although it was not until the eighties that, thanks to Belgian and French capital, its tremendous expansion began. The visit of Robert Nobel to Baku in 1874 served as the prelude to the phenomenal oil development which, by the beginning of the twentieth century, raised Russia to second place in the world production of petroleum. During the seventies, however, these developments were still in the womb. Important beginnings were made toward creating a modernized heavy-industry base, but they were only a start, and the advance was very small in comparison with that of Western Europe and of the United States.

The economic depression which spread from Europe to Russia in 1873 and continued with minor interruptions until the nineties administered a sharp setback to Russia's rate of industrial growth. The boom of the early seventies was followed by a long period of decline. Railroad construction, for example, after adding 7,400 *versts* of new lines during 1871–1875, dropped to only 3,074 *versts* in 1881–1885 and to 2,864 *versts* during 1886–1890.[33] Capital investment slackened; business activity languished; a number of less efficient enterprises, established in the earlier period, were forced to the wall. The prolonged stagnation gave an impetus to concentration. It was also a period when the working class began to stir in sporadic outbursts of discontent and poorly organized strikes.

The long depression was followed by an industrial upsurge. During the nineties, Russia entered on a decade of intensive industrialization. Between 1891 and 1900, 21,396 *versts* of railroad were added, over three times the construction of the previous decade. Oil production increased 132 per cent, pig iron 190 per cent, coal 131 per cent, and cotton manufactures 76 per cent.[34] While the textile industry was still in the forefront in terms of value of output, heavy industry was rapidly overtaking light industry. Railroad construction and new investment in heavy industry operated as the spearhead of the industrial boom.

Governmental policy supported and stimulated industrialization. The guiding genius of the decade was Count Witte, Minister of Finance from 1892 to 1903. Under Witte the gold standard was finally introduced. The construction of the great Trans-Siberian Railroad was largely his achievement. While a shift, chiefly for fiscal reasons, from free trade to higher tariff duties began in 1877, during the nineties Witte became the firm supporter of a protectionist policy designed to safeguard the newly established "native" industries from foreign competition. Government contracts reinforced this protectionist policy. Government orders were reserved for domestic firms, and the prices paid by the treasury frequently represented a form of outright subsidy to the beneficiary. Not atypical was the rejection of the offer of English manufacturers to deliver rail for the Siberian railway at seventy-five kopecks in favor of a payment of two rubles to Russian producers.[35] The iron and steel industry in effect became a dependent of the treasury. The "protecting" hand of the government guided industrial development.

The striking industrial advance of the nineties was interrupted by the severe commercial crisis of 1900–1903 and the revolutionary disturbances of 1905–1906. By 1909, however, progress was resumed, and in the years before World War I there was a steady growth of production, particularly in the textile, metallurgic, and mining industries.[36] Although the over-all rate of growth was impressive, Russia remained backward by Western standards. Coal production in Russia in 1913 amounted to 36 million tons, compared with the German production of 190.1 million tons and the United States total of 517.1 million tons. The Russian pig-iron production of 4.6 million tons was far below the German production of 16.8 million and the United States total of 31.5 million tons.[37] Russian machine-building industries were in the most rudimentary stage of establishment, and almost all machinery was imported. The automotive industry was nonexistent. Chemical industries were poorly developed, and the production of electric power was markedly deficient. Despite striking gains since the nineties, Russia lagged far behind the most advanced industrial nations of the West.

The Weakness of the Russian Bourgeoisie

The auspices under which the belated Russian industrialization drive was conducted were not such as to stimulate a modernization and liberalization of its political institutions. Russian economic development was intimately intertwined with the state and heavily dependent on bureaucratic guidance and tutelage. Industrial growth was based on sustained intervention by the government. By 1913, two-thirds of the total railroad mileage was owned and operated by the government; the private lines that remained were subject to strict state supervision. Government enterprise was extensive. The state owned valuable mines and processed their ores in state plants. It operated a liquor monopoly. It controlled vast tracts of land and 60 per cent of the country's forests. Through the State Bank and other credit institutions, it financed private enterprises. It extended protection through the tariff. It granted concessions and subsidies. Government orders and contracts largely sustained heavy industry and were important in other areas as well. Private industry operated within the framework of governmental direction and supervision. While there was a noticeable tendency on the part of some Russian industrialists to seek release from bureaucratic restrictions and to develop a nongovernmental market, the dominant metal and fuel industrialists were not among them. In the words of their representatives, "The idea of building up our metallurgical industry on the basis of the horseshoes, axles, forged wheels, plows, and iron roofs needed by the Russian peasant will not appeal to practical people." [38]

Russian industrialists were accustomed to lean on the state for sustenance. However much they might resent bureaucratic stupidity or arrogance, they could find no easy escape from the shelter and confinement of government paternalism. Because of the belated industrialization of Russia, the bourgeois stratum of society was still weakly developed and was hampered in its aspiration for independent power by its excessive dependence on the state.

Native business leadership was also handicapped by its large-scale reliance on foreign capital to finance industrial activity and expansion.[39] Foreign investment played a particularly important role in the strategic areas of banking and heavy industry and inevitably influenced the course of business management. Russian entrepreneurial decisions in these fields were conditioned not only by bureaucratic direction but by dependence on representatives of foreign investors. It was not a setting calculated to stimulate bold initiative. In the years before World War I, native Russian business leadership showed many signs of restlessness and self-assertiveness, but the economic and bureaucratic fetters which bound it operated as a serious barrier to full emancipation.

Limited though Russian industrial development was, a highly important role was played by large-scale enterprise. This factor, too, operated to limit the spread of business influence, to facilitate labor organization, and to prepare the way for a revolutionary seizure of power. As early as the nineties, the degree of concentration of Russian industry exceeded that of Germany.[40] By 1910 Russian industrial establishments with over five hundred workers employed 53.5 per cent of the total working force. The comparable figure for the United States in 1910 was 33 per cent.

During the first decade of the twentieth century, nine metallurgic plants accounted for more than one-half of the total pig-iron production. By 1912 six large enterprises produced 65 per cent of the total petroleum output. Seven plants accounted for 90 per cent of the total rail production. [41] The heavy industries, supported by substantial pools of foreign capital and huge government and railroad orders, became centers of large-scale production and concentration. The predominance of the giant enterprises and their geographic concentration in the St. Petersburg, Moscow, Donets, and Baku areas paved the way for labor organization and, even more significantly, provided a fulcrum for revolutionary action.

At the same time, the organization of employers was also stimulated. After the turn of the century, a number of syndicates were formed for market control, such as *Prodomet* in the metallurgic industry and *Produgol* in the coal industry. Employer associations became quite common and were utilized not only to combat labor unions and stabilize markets but also as a sounding board for political aspirations. As might be expected, big business continued to call for state support of "the industries of the fatherland." During the Duma period, leading industrialists were attracted to the Octobrist Party, a conservative alliance of businessmen and landowners who anchored their hopes for a constitutional monarchy in the guaranties of the Manifesto of October 17, 1905. Frightened by the revolutionary temper of the workers in 1905–06, business leaders turned to the government for protection against strikes and revolutionary demands for social change.

The ambivalence of their role was to plague them to the end. They were anxious to modernize the autocracy but not to destroy it. As yet too weak to become a significant independent political force, they were reluctantly drawn into the system which sustained the autocracy, since they were threatened by the same revolutionary challenge and were dependent on the state for their privileges and perquisites. The uneasy alliance was broken only when the autocracy collapsed of its own incompetence. By that time, Russian industry was too compromised by its identification with the old regime to gather up the power which the Tsardom had dissipated. By one of those paradoxes in which history delights, the mantle of the succession was to fall not on those business leaders who had contributed so much to initiate Russia's belated industrialization but on those who were able to exploit the grievances of the industrial labor army which Russia's newly developing capitalism had called into being.

The Grievances of the Proletariat

The formation of the modern Russian industrial proletariat was essentially a post-Emancipation phenomenon. It has been estimated that approximately four million peasants of both sexes were rendered landless by the Reform.[42] They constituted the great labor reservoir on which the new factories drew. Industrialization was accompanied by a steady flow from the village to the cities. The link with the village remained a characteristic feature of Russian industrial development not only up to 1917 but even into the period of Soviet industrialization. As time passed, connections with the village became strained and then broken; a proletariat with its own "factory genealogy" appeared. The enlarging nucleus of "true" proletarians tended to develop class consciousness and to take leadership in articulating the grievances of their fellow workers, while the fresh arrivals brought with them the backwardness of the village and a passive endurance of the misery of their lot.

In the early phase of industrialization, during the seventies and early eighties, labor exploitation was at its worst. The working day for men, women, and children rarely ran less than twelve to fourteen hours and sometimes extended to sixteen or eighteen hours. Wages were miserably low and were frequently reduced by fines pocketed by the factory owner, and payments in kind were valued at prices well above the market. Sanitary conditions in the factories were unsatisfactory, and workers were often crowded together in huge factory barracks without distinction as to age or sex. For the most part workers bore what they could not change, though beginning in the mid-seventies there were occasional outbursts of protest, sporadic strikes, and even the elemental germs of labor organization.

The government made some effort to ameliorate conditions. In 1882 children under twelve were excluded from employment, and the working hours of adolescents from twelve to fifteen were limited to eight hours a day. In 1886 payment in kind was prohibited, and wages were required to be paid at least once a month. Although factory inspectors were appointed to prevent the evasion of these regulations, enforcement was weak, and ukases were frequently honored in the breach. Indeed, in 1890 the government, at the insistence of some manufacturers, relaxed the regulations to permit night and holiday work for children in some industries and to sanction the employment of children from ten to twelve, provided the Ministries of Finance and Interior approved. After this retreat, a forward step was taken in 1897 when day work of adults was limited to eleven and one-half hours and night work to ten hours. In 1903 a social insurance law was enacted, but its scope was limited and its benefits meager. In 1912 the law was amended and much improved. By 1914 over two million workers were enrolled in sick benefit funds.[43] While the record of Tsarist social legislation was one of slow progress over the years, as in so many other fields the concessions were belated and largely extorted under pressure. Advances were interrupted by retreats, and enforcement was uncertain. The credit that might have accrued to the autocracy was dissipated by the impression it left of intransigent opposition to the very reforms which it was reluctantly sponsoring.

Perhaps the most effective contribution made by the autocracy in preparing the way for Bolshevism consisted in its unwillingness to tolerate moderate trade unionism. Not until 1906 were unions finally legalized; even then, only local unions were permitted, and indeed most of them were wiped out in the reactionary period following the dissolution of the Second Duma. In 1907, at the height of union development in the period before the First World War, the total union membership was 250,000.[44] Under these circumstances, it was perhaps inevitable that factory labor would offer an inviting field for revolutionary agitation.

The history of Tsarist policy toward labor organization is a tragic story of wasted opportunities. In the early spontaneous strikes of the seventies and eighties, the demands of the workers were moderate. Ordinarily they struck against reduction of wages, and occasionally they demanded freedom to elect a "headman" to negotiate with the employers in behalf of the workers. The answer of the authorities was to crush these incipient organizations by arresting the leaders and more active workers and condemning them to prison or exile. Labor organizations were consequently forced into conspiratorial channels, and the hostility of the government helped to divert the grievances of the workers from economic to political programs.

During the late eighties, the groups among the revolutionary intelligentsia who were later to organize the Russian Social-Democratic Labor Party utilized such opportunities as were available to them to implant socialist political consciousness in the scattered workingmen's "circles" which they were also instrumental in organizing. Although their zeal was great, their influence was limited. The wave of strikes which broke out in the period 1895–1898, though more aggressively led than earlier disturbances and more responsive to Social-Democratic leadership, was essentially a "spontaneous" movement inspired primarily by economic grievances. A number of strikes led to concessions by employers, and this period witnessed the enactment of the law of 1897 limiting the working day to eleven and one-half hours.

In this relatively favorable atmosphere, an influential group of Social-Democratic leaders and workers began to call for the cessation of revolutionary activity and political agitation and concentration on "pure and simple" trade-union activity dedicated to winning immediate material advantages for the workers. The movement which this group led became known as Economism. Its leading doctrines were expounded in the "Credo" drafted by Madame Kuskova in the late nineties. The "Credo" was greatly influenced by Eduard Bernstein and the reformist and revisionist currents running strong in the European socialist movement around the turn of the century; indeed, its orthodox Marxist critics dubbed it "Russian Bernsteinism." Essentially, the "Credo" summoned the workers to fight for economic positions and the Marxian intelligentsia to join with the liberals in the struggle to reform the state.

> The Marxism which is negative, the primitive, intolerant Marxism (which employs in a too schematical way its division of societies into classes) must give way to democratic Marxism, and the position of the party in contemporary society will thereby be greatly changed. The party will find its *narrow corporative* and mostly sectarian aims changed into a tendency to reform contemporary society in the democratic direction adapted to the contemporary state of affairs, with the aim of more successfully and completely defending the rights . . . of the labouring classes.[45]

The doctrines of the "Credo" had considerable attraction for the Marxist intelligentsia of the day. Lenin sought to demolish Economism in his celebrated pamphlet *What Is to Be Done?* (1902), but the real work of destruction was performed not by Lenin but by the police absolutism which refused to permit trade unionism to take root.

The curious episode of Zubatovism, or police socialism, mirrored the dilemma of the autocracy in dealing with the rising challenge of illegal labor organization. Deeply suspicious of an independent trade-union movement and yet fearful of rising labor unrest, the political police in the years 1900–1904 developed an ingenious scheme by which they hoped to control the labor movement, insulate it from revolutionary propaganda, and concentrate its energies on purely economic aims. The originator of the scheme was one Zubatov, the chief of the political department of the Moscow police. His plan was to have labor organized by carefully selected agents of the political police whose identification would be unknown to the workers. For several years Zubatovism flourished, and societies of workingmen were widely organized. But as the movement spread, it passed beyond the control of Zubatov and the police. The disorders which broke out in Odessa in 1903 in the wake of activity by Zubatov agents expanded into a general strike which had to be suppressed with much bloodshed. Zubatov was held responsible and banished to the north of Russia. Although the associations which he had sponsored were discredited and disbanded, Zubatovism left a double legacy. It discouraged further efforts by the autocracy to outbid the socialists at the expense of employers. At the same time, it taught wide circles of workingmen how to combine, a lesson that was to be more effectively applied when instructors from the political police were unavailable.

The 1905 revolution demonstrated that the lesson was beginning to be learned and that the objectives of labor organization could no longer be contained within narrow trade-union demands. The year 1905 witnessed the greatest strike movement in Russian history; at some point in the year practically every worker was involved. While the eight-hour working day figured very largely in the workers' economic demands, political strikes became commonplace, and many ordinary workingmen joined with the radical intelligentsia in calling for the abolition of the autocracy and the convocation of a constituent assembly to establish a democratic republic. At the height of the crisis, the autocracy appeared to be shaken to its foundations, but it soon regained a partial equilibrium by policies which combined concession and repression. The concessions of 1905–06 were followed by increasing resort to repression. The trade unions which had been legalized in 1906 remained objects of suspicion and were subjected to the closest police supervision in the ensuing years. Although strikes declined markedly during the so-called prosperous years up to 1912, beginning in that year there was an ominous upsurge in labor unrest which reached a climax during the first seven months of 1914 and was interrupted only by the outbreak of war. The industrial workers remained a festering pocket of discontent in Russian society. An independent trade-union movement patterned on Western European and American models and dedicated to immediate improvements in wages, hours, and working conditions might have contributed greatly to stabilize industrial relations and to give Russian workers a stake in the community. Such a movement was never permitted to strike roots. The grievances which might have found an outlet and a remedy in collective bargaining became the fertile soil for extremist appeals. State policy barricaded the road to reform and opened the flood gates to revolutionary upheaval.

History is movement, and rulers who ride its whirlwinds must learn to bow before storms which they cannot control. The unyielding quality of Tsardom incapacitated it for survival in an era of rapid change. The downfall of the Russian autocracy was ultimately attributable to its inability to comprehend the forces which were shaping its course. The tragedy of its failure lay not in its own disappearance but in the creative energies of Russian society which it could not utilize, the frustrations which it engendered, and the maximalist temper which it imposed on Russian political life. Its most disastrous blunder was that it prepared the seedbed out of which Bolshevism grew.

Chapter 2

Bolshevism before 1917

An *acute observer* of Russian society in the late nineteenth and early twentieth centuries might have found the potential of revolution in every corner of the realm. Had he predicted that it would be the Bolsheviks who would ultimately inherit the Tsar's diadem, most of his contemporaries would probably have dismissed him as mad. Until 1917, the tiny handful of revolutionaries who followed the Bolshevik banner appeared to be swallowed in the vastness of Russia. Lenin, in a speech before a socialist youth meeting in Zurich on January 22, 1917, expressed strong doubts that he would "live to see the decisive battles of this coming revolution." [1] The sudden rise of Bolshevism from insignificance to total power was as great a shock to the Bolshevik leaders as it was to those whom Bolshevism displaced.

Yet it would be the height of superficiality to treat the triumph of Bolshevism as a mere accident. The great crises of history are rarely accidents. They have their points of origin as well as their points of no return. The doctrine, the organizational practices, and the tactics which Bolshevism developed in its period of incubation enabled it to harness the surge of revolutionary energy released by deeper forces of social unrest and war. If in the process Bolshevism also succeeded in replacing the lumbering, inefficient police absolutism of Tsardom and the short-lived democratic experiment of the Provisional Government by the first full-scale venture in modern totalitarianism, that result too was implicit in the doctrinal, organizational, and tactical premises on which the structure of Bolshevism was built.

The Development of Doctrine

Until the 1880's the Russian revolutionary movement, as was natural in a country so predominantly agricultural, revolved around the peasant and his fate. Whatever may have been the tactical divergences among Narodnik intellectuals — whether they dedicated themselves to agitation or terror — their whole orientation was toward Ilya of Murom, the peasant hero of the folk poems (*byliny*), who, as Masaryk puts it, "when the country is in straits . . . awakens from his apathy, displays his superhuman energy, and saves the situation." [2] Even the industrial awakening of the seventies did little to disturb this fundamental preoccupation with the peasant and his destiny.

Narodnik philosophers from Herzen to Lavrov and Mikhailovsky were not unaware of Marx and Engels; indeed, the Narodniks were largely responsible for translating Marx and Engels into Russian and introducing them to a wide audience of the intelligentsia. For the Narodniks, however, the stages of industrialization and proletarianization which Marx and Engels described were dangers to be avoided rather than paths to be traversed. Nor were Marx and Engels themselves at first certain that the course of economic development in Russia would have to recapitulate that of the West. In a letter which Marx wrote in 1877 to a Russian publication, *Notes on the Fatherland,* he referred to his theory of capitalist development as not necessarily everywhere applicable and spoke of Russia as having "the best opportunity that history has ever offered to a people to escape all the catastrophes of capitalism." [3] By 1882 Marx and Engels began to qualify their views on the possibility of Russian exceptionalism. In an introduction to a new Russian translation of the *Communist Manifesto,* they saw the capitalist system in Russia "growing up with feverish speed." They still thought, however, that the mir might "serve as a starting-point for a communist course of development" but only "if the Russian revolution sounds the signal for a workers' revolution in the West, so that each becomes the complement of the other." [4]

By 1892 Engels had in effect written off the mir as a Narodnik illusion. In a letter to Danielson, the Narodnik translator of *Capital,* Engels commented, "I am afraid that we shall soon have to look upon your mir as no more than a memory of the irrecoverable past, and that in the future we shall have to do with a capitalistic Russia." [5] In a brief reference to earlier hopes, he continued, "If this be so, a splendid chance will unquestionably have been lost." To the end of their lives, Marx and Engels remained warm admirers of the Narodnaya Volya and its courageous revolutionary Narodnik successors. Terror, for Marx and Engels, had a special justification in the struggle against Russian absolutism, and they deplored the efforts of their own Russian Marxist followers to discredit the Narodnik revolutionaries. Indeed, one of the last interventions of Engels in Russian affairs was his attempt in 1892 to arrange a merger of Narodniks and Marxists into a single party.[6] The effort, needless to say, failed.

The Beginnings of Russian Marxism

Russian Marxism as an independent political movement originated in the split in 1879 of the Narodnik organization *Zemlya i Volya* (Land and Freedom). The seceders, who stood for propaganda and agitation as opposed to terrorism, established a rival organization, the *Chërnyi Peredel* (Black Repartition), to propagate their doctrines. One of their leaders was Plekhanov, soon to be known as the father of Russian Marxism, but then still clinging to the Narodnik belief in the peasant as the driving force of revolution. The roundup of revolutionaries which followed the assassination of Alexander II in 1881 caused Plekhanov to flee abroad. His break with Zemlya i Volya on the issue of terror, the apparent bankruptcy of Narodnik policies in the reaction which followed 1881, and the manifest failure of the peasantry to respond either to agitation or terror impelled Plekhanov to reëxamine his views. The search for a new faith led him to Marxism. In 1883 Plekhanov, Paul Axelrod, Leo Deutsch, and Vera Zasulich, all of whom had been members of the Chërnyi Peredel, joined in establishing the first Russian Marxist organization, the group known as *Osvobozhdenie Truda* (Emancipation of Labor). Plekhanov from the beginning was the intellectual leader of the group. In a series of brilliantly written polemical works,[7] he laid the doctrinal foundations for Russian Marxism.

Russian Marxism thus emerged out of disillusionment with the Narodnik infatuation with the peasantry. As a result, it quickly took on a strong anti-peasant orientation. "The main bulwark of absolutism," argued the 1887 program of the Emancipation of Labor group, "lies in the political indifference and the intellectual backwardness of the peasantry."[8] In a later pamphlet by Plekhanov, *The Duty of the Socialists in the Famine*, the point was put even more strongly:

> The proletarian and the muzhik are political antipodes. The historic role of the proletariat is as revolutionary as the historic role of the muzhik is conservative. The muzhiks have been the support of oriental despotism for thousands of years. The proletariat in a comparatively short space of time has shaken the "foundations" of West European society.[9]

Since peasant worship still exercised a powerful hold on the minds of the Russian revolutionary intelligentsia, the task of Plekhanov, and later of Lenin,[10] was to undermine this faith and to turn the attention of the intellectuals from the village to the city, where capitalism was taking root and a new industrial proletariat was in process of creation. There, argued Plekhanov, was the coming revolutionary force. The challenge to the Narodniks was summed up in his famous dictum: "The revolutionary movement in Russia can triumph only as a revolutionary movement of the working class. There is not, nor can there be, any other way!"[11]

The sharp antithesis which Plekhanov made between revolutionary worker and backward peasant had great polemical value in combating the influence of Narodnik ideology. But it also meant that the Social-Democratic movement turned its back on the countryside. Its long-term legacy was an attitude of suspicious distrust toward the peasantry which affected both the Bolshevik and Menshevik wings of Russian Social-Democracy and was never altogether extirpated. Even so perceptive and skillful a revolutionary engineer as Lenin did not really sense the revolutionary potential of the peasantry until the peasant risings of the 1905 revolution forced him to reëxamine the tenets of his faith.

The first problem of the early Russian Marxists was to win acceptance for their proposition that Russia was launched on an irreversible course of capitalist development and that the Narodnik dream of skipping the stage of capitalism and leaping directly from the mir to socialism was nothing but a mirage. The struggle in its inception was a battle of books and pamphlets. The polemic of the Marxists against the Narodniks was even welcomed by the government, since in its eyes the Narodniks were still dangerous revolutionaries and the Marxists were viewed as essentially a rather harmless literary group.

The diffusion of Marxism among the intellectuals of the nineties was also attended by confusion about its content and significance. For many of the "fellow-travelers" of the Legal Marxist period, "Marxist" was hardly more than a generic name for the protagonists of the industrial development which appeared to be in full triumph in the early nineties. Even Peter Struve, who counted himself a Marxist in that period and drafted the manifesto of the First Congress of the Russian Social-Democratic Labor Party, held in Minsk in 1898, could end his "Critical Remarks on the Problem of the Economic Development of Russia" (1894) with the appeal: "Let us recognize our backwardness in culture and let us take our lessons from capitalism." [12] For still others, the so-called Economists of the late nineties, Marxism meant little more than "bread and butter" trade unionism, bargaining with employers for that extra kopeck on the ruble for which Lenin had such fierce contempt.[13] Other professed Marxists — and by 1899 Struve had become one of them — responded to Bernstein's challenge to orthodox Marxism by establishing a Russian branch of Critical Revisionism, a movement which was to lead them from Marxism to idealism and to an eventual break with the Social-Democratic Party.[14]

In the face of these divergent trends (later to be described as deviations), the doctrinal problem which Plekhanov and Lenin faced in the nineties was to buttress the orthodox Marxian analysis and to reassert its revolutionary content. In the international socialist controversies of the period, Plekhanov and Lenin took their stand with Kautsky, the guardian of the true faith, against the heterodoxies of Bernstein. In Russia they denounced the objectivism of the Legal Marxists and the reformist tendencies of Economism and Critical Revisionism. For both Plekhanov and Lenin, Marxism was a revolutionary creed not to be diluted by opportunistic waverings.

During this period, Plekhanov was still the master and Lenin the pupil. Both considered themselves orthodox Marxists. Marx's panorama of capitalist development seemed to imply that the socialist revolution stood its greatest chance of success in those countries in which the processes of industrialization were most highly advanced and in which the working class formed a substantial part of the population. How apply such a recipe for a successful socialist revolution to Russia with its nascent industrialism, its weakly developed proletariat, and its overwhelmingly peasant population? Confronted with Russia's industrial backwardness, both Plekhanov and Lenin agreed that the first order of business was to achieve a bourgeois-democratic revolution in Russia. With the further development of Russian capitalism, Russia would become ripe for a successful proletarian revolt. In this analysis they merely followed the familiar two-stage sequence laid down in the *Communist Manifesto*. Plekhanov, the theorist, was to remain loyal to this formulation for the rest of his life. Lenin, the activist, was to find it increasingly uncongenial, and though he continued for many years to pay it verbal tribute, his whole revolutionary career was essentially an escape from its confines.

The Problem of Industrial Backwardness

The question of the shape and pace of the Russian revolution was to produce furious controversies among Social-Democrats of all shades. The heart of the problem was Russia's industrial backwardness and the political consequences to be drawn from it. The Social-Democratic Labor Party based itself on a weak and still-undeveloped industrial proletariat. What was the role of the party to be? Should it attempt to seize power at the first promising opportunity or would it have to wait patiently until Russia's industrialization matched that of the most advanced Western nations? If it limited its immediate activities to organizing the proletariat and helping the bourgeoisie to overthrow the autocracy, would the party not be strengthening its most dangerous enemy by surrendering to it the power of the state? If, on the other hand, the party emphasized its hostility to the bourgeoisie and its role as capitalism's gravedigger, would the bourgeoisie not be driven to unite its fortunes with those of the autocracy? Questions such as these might be argued in terms of Marxian exegesis, but the answers that were evolved depended more on temperament than on theory.

The Menshevik wing of Russian Social-Democracy, with which Plekhanov was finally to ally himself, saw the arrival of socialism in Russia as the climax of a long process of development. The Menshevik response to the challenge of industrial backwardness was to preach the postponement of the socialist revolution until industrial backwardness had been overcome. Strongly influenced by orthodox Western Marxism and impressed by the weakness of the Russian industrial proletariat, the Mensheviks concluded that a socialist Russia was a matter of the distant future and that the immediate task was to clear the way for a bourgeois, middle-class revolution. Their first charge as good Marxists was to help the bourgeoisie to carry out its own historical responsibilities. They were therefore prepared to conclude alliances with liberal bourgeois forces who opposed the autocracy and to join them in fighting for such limited objectives as universal suffrage, constitutional liberties, and enlightened social legislation. Meanwhile, they awaited the further growth of capitalism in Russia to establish the conditions for a successful socialist revolution. Essentially, the Mensheviks had their eye on Western European models; they expected to march to power through legality and to be the beneficiaries of the spontaneous mass energy which the creation of a large industrial proletariat would release.

At the opposite extreme from the Menshevik conception was the theory of "permanent revolution" developed by Parvus and adopted by Trotsky during and after the 1905 revolution.[15] For Parvus and Trotsky, the industrial backwardness of Russia was a political asset rather than a liability. As a result of backwardness and the large role played by state capitalism, the Russian middle class was weak and incapable of doing the job of its analogues in Western Europe.* Thus, according to Parvus' and Trotsky's dialectic of backwardness, the bourgeois revolution in Russia could be made only by the proletariat. Once the proletariat was in power, its responsibility was to hold on to power and keep the revolution going "in permanence" until socialism was established both at home and abroad. The Russian revolution, Trotsky thought, would ignite a series of socialist revolutions in the West. This "permanent revolution" would offset the resistance which developed. Thus Trotsky's prescription for Russia's retarded economy was a new law of combined development. The two revolutions — bourgeois-democratic and proletarian-socialist — would be combined, or telescoped, into one. The working class would assert its hegemony from the outset and leap directly from industrial backwardness into socialism. Implicit in the Trotsky-Parvus formula was

* For an interesting anticipation of this view, see the following passage in the program drafted by Peter Struve for the First Congress of the Russian Social-Democratic Labor Party, held in Minsk in 1898: "The further east one goes in Europe, the weaker in politics, the more cowardly and meaner becomes the bourgeoisie, and the greater are the cultural and political tasks which fall to the lot of the proletariat" (*VKP[b] v Rezolyutsiyakh* [4th ed.], I, 2).

a clear commitment to the theory of minority dictatorship for Russia. An industrial proletariat which was still relatively infinitesimal in numbers was called upon to impose its will and direction on the vast majority of the population. Out of such theoretical brick and straw, the edifice of Soviet totalitarianism was to be constructed.

The position of Lenin and the Bolshevik wing of the Russian Social-Democratic Party was much closer in spirit to Trotsky than to the Mensheviks, though the verbal premises from which Lenin started seemed indistinguishable from the Menshevik tenets. Like the Mensheviks, Lenin proclaimed that Russia was ripe for only a bourgeois-democratic revolution. His *Two Tactics of Social-Democracy in the Democratic Revolution* (1905) contained at least one formulation which Mensheviks would wholeheartedly have endorsed:

> The degree of economic development of Russia (an objective condition) and the degree of class consciousness and organization of the broad masses of the proletariat (a subjective condition inseparably connected with the objective condition) make the immediate complete emancipation of the working class impossible. Only the most ignorant people can ignore the bourgeois nature of the democratic revolution which is now taking place. . . Whoever wants to arrive at socialism by a different road, other than that of political democracy, will inevitably arrive at absurd and reactionary conclusions, both in the economic and the political sense. If any workers ask us at the given moment why not go ahead and carry out our maximum program we shall answer by pointing out how far the masses of the democratically disposed people still are from socialism, how undeveloped class antagonisms still are, how unorganized the proletarians still are.[16]

Again, in the same pamphlet, Lenin reiterated: "We Marxists should know that there is not, nor can there be, any other path to real freedom for the proletariat and the peasantry, than the path of bourgeois freedom and bourgeois progress." [17]

While dicta such as these can be and have been cited to establish a basic area of agreement between Mensheviks and Bolsheviks on the two-stage perspective of the Russian revolution, the kinship was more illusory than real. Plekhanov summed up one of the important differences when he observed to Lenin, "You turn your behind to the liberals, but we our face." [18] For Lenin, as for Trotsky, the bourgeois liberals were a weak and unreliable reed. Like Trotsky, Lenin came to believe that the proletariat would have to take leadership in completing the bourgeois revolution; but unlike both Trotsky and the Mensheviks, Lenin looked to an alliance with the peasantry to provide the proletariat with a mass base.

In this rediscovery of the strategic significance of the peasantry, Lenin reclaimed the Narodnik heritage which both he and Plekhanov had done so much to repudiate in the nineties. In the essay on *Two Tactics*, Lenin declared:

Those who really understand the role of the peasantry in a victorious Russian revolution would not dream of saying that the sweep of the revolution would be diminished if the bourgeoisie recoiled from it. For, as a matter of fact, the Russian revolution will begin to assume its real sweep . . . only when the bourgeoisie recoils from it and when the masses of the peasantry come out as active revolutionaries side-by-side with the proletariat.[19]

The first task was to consolidate "the revolutionary-democratic dictatorship of the proletariat and the peasantry." After this was achieved, the socialist revolution would become the order of the day.[20] Lenin's formula thus envisaged two tactical stages: first, the alliance of proletariat and peasantry to complete the democratic revolution, and second, an alliance of the proletariat and village poor to initiate the socialist revolution.

Given Lenin's activist temperament, it was inevitable that he should feel greater affinity for Trotsky's revolutionary dynamism than for the Mensheviks' passive fatalism. As the excitement of the 1905 revolution mounted, we find him speaking the language of Trotsky: "From the democratic revolution we shall at once, and just in accordance with the measure of our strength, the strength of the class-conscious and organized proletariat, begin to pass to the socialist revolution. We stand for uninterrupted revolution. We shall not stop half way." [21] Despite many intervening conflicts, the bond with Trotsky was to be sealed by the experiences of 1917. The dialectic of backwardness was "resolved" by the Bolshevik seizure of power.

Out of that adventure a new theory of revolution was to be developed with world-wide applications. Stalin has given it authoritative exposition:

Where will the revolution begin? . . .

Where industry is more developed, where the proletariat constitutes the majority, where there is more culture, where there is more democracy — that was the reply usually given formerly.

No, objects the Leninist theory of revolution; *not necessarily where industry is more developed*, and so forth. The front of capitalism will be pierced where the chain of imperialism is weakest, for the proletarian revolution is the result of the breaking of the chain of the world imperialist front at its weakest link; and it may turn out that the country which has started the revolution, which has made a breach in the front of capital, is less developed in a capitalist sense than other, more developed, countries, which have, however, remained within the framework of capitalism.[22]

Thus Marx, who turned Hegel on his head, was himself turned on his head. Industrial backwardness was transformed from obstacle to opportunity. The concept of the dictatorship of the proletariat shifted from a weapon of the majority into a tool of minorities. Consciousness triumphed over spontaneity, and the way was cleared for the organized and disciplined revolutionary elite capable of transmuting the grievances of a nation into a new formula of absolute power.

Organization: The Elite Party

The organizational conception embodied in Bolshevism was essentially an incarnation of this elitist ideal. "Give us an organization of revolutionaries," said Lenin, "and we shall overturn the whole of Russia!" [23] It was Lenin who forged the instrument, but the seeds of his conspiratorial conceptions were planted deep in Russian history and were nurtured by the conditions of the revolutionary struggle against the autocracy. Pestel among the Decembrists, Bakunin, Nechayev, Tkachev, and the Narodnik conspirators of the seventies and early eighties, all provided organizational prototypes of the professional revolutionary as the strategic lever of political upheaval. It was a tradition from which Lenin drew deep inspiration even when he found himself in profound disagreement with the particular programs which earlier professional revolutionaries espoused. His works are filled with tributes to the famous revolutionaries of the seventies (figures like Alekseyev, Myshkin, Khalturin, and Zhelyabov).[24] In developing his own conceptions of party organization in *What Is to Be Done?* he refers to "the magnificent organization" of the revolutionaries of the seventies as one "which should serve us all as a model." [25] Lenin's conviction that Russian Marxism could triumph only if led by a disciplined elite of professional revolutionaries was reënforced by his own early amateur experiences as a member of the Petersburg League of Struggle for the Emancipation of the Working Class. This organization was easily penetrated by the police, and the first effort of Lenin and his collaborators in 1895 to publish an underground paper — "The Workers' Cause" — resulted in the arrest of Lenin and his chief associates and a quick transfer of domicile to Siberia.[26]

It is against this background that the organizational conceptions of Lenin took shape. By 1902, with the publication of *What Is to Be Done?* they were fully developed. In this essay, the seminal source of the organizational philosophy of Bolshevism, Lenin set himself two main tasks: (1) to destroy the influence of Economism with its repudiation of revolutionary political organization and its insistence on trade unionism as the basic method of improving the welfare of the working class, and (2) to build an organized and disciplined revolutionary Marxist party which would insure the triumph of socialism in Russia.

The polemic against the Economists clearly revealed Lenin's elitist preconceptions. More than a quarter of a century earlier Tkachev had written: "Neither in the present nor in the future can the people, left to their own resources, bring into existence the social revolution. Only we revolutionists can accomplish this. . . Social ideals are alien to the people; they belong to the social philosophy of the revolutionary minority." [27] Now Lenin was to repeat:

The history of all countries shows that the working class, exclusively by its own effort, is able to develop only trade union consciousness. . . This [Social-Democratic] consciousness could only be brought to them from without. . . The theory of socialism . . . grew out of the philosophic, historical, and economic theories that were elaborated by the educated representatives of the propertied classes, the intellectuals . . . quite independently of the spontaneous growth of the labor movement. . .

Our task, the task of Social-Democracy, is to *combat spontaneity*, to *divert* the labor movement from its spontaneous, trade unionist striving to go under the wing of the bourgeoisie, and to bring it under the wing of revolutionary Social-Democracy.[28]

To accomplish this objective, Lenin sought to weld together a disciplined party of devoted adherents, "a small, compact core, consisting of the most reliable, experienced and hardened workers, with responsible agents in the principal districts and connected by all the rules of strict secrecy with the organization of revolutionaries." [29] "I assert," Lenin continued in a passage which laid bare his basic faith:

(1) that no revolutionary movement can endure without a stable organization of leaders that maintains continuity; (2) that the wider the masses spontaneously drawn into the struggle, forming the basis of the movement and participating in it, the more urgent the need of such an organization, and the more solid this organization must be. . . (3) that such an organization must consist chiefly of people professionally engaged in revolutionary activity; (4) that in an autocratic state the more we *confine* the membership of such an organization to people who are professionally engaged in revolutionary activity and who have been professionally trained in the art of combating the political police, the more difficult will it be to wipe out such an organization, and (5) the *greater* will be the number of people of the working class and of other classes of society who will be able to join the movement and perform active work in it.[30]

Democratic management, Lenin held, was simply inapplicable to a revolutionary organization.[31] *What Is to Be Done?* disclosed the profoundly elitist and anti-democratic strain in Lenin's approach to problems of organization. It also made clear that in Lenin's new model party, leadership would be highly centralized, the central committee would appoint local committees, and every committee would have the right to coöpt new members. But it still left a precise blueprint to be worked out. This was the task which Lenin undertook to perform at the Second Party Congress of the Russian Social-Democratic Labor Party, which met in Brussels and then in London in the summer of 1903. Lenin prepared for this Congress with a meticulous attention to detail of which he alone among his revolutionary contemporaries was capable. His one desire was to construct a compact majority which would dominate the Congress and build a party willing "to devote to the revolution not only their spare evenings, but the whole of their lives."

The foundations seemed to be well laid. The rallying point of the "compact majority" was *Iskra* (The Spark), a journal which had been established abroad in 1900 largely on Lenin's initiative. Wisely, Lenin and his young associates, Martov and Potresov, enlisted the coöperation of Plekhanov and other members of the Emancipation of Labor group as co-editors. The association generated its own sparks; Lenin has provided a vivid record of the conflict in his "How the Spark Was Nearly Extinguished." [32] But the quarrels for supremacy were composed; Lenin still needed the prestige of the older generation of revolutionaries in mobilizing adherents to the *Iskra* platform. Meanwhile, Lenin retained control of the secret agents who smuggled *Iskra* into Russia and maintained the closest connections with the underground organizations which distributed the journal. This organization of *Iskra* men was to provide the core of Lenin's majority at the Second Congress.

When the Second Congress assembled in Brussels in 1903, thirty-three votes, a clear majority of the fifty-one official votes, belonged to the *Iskra* faction. The remaining eighteen delegates represented a collection of Bundists (members of the All-Jewish Workers' Union of Russia and Poland), Economists, and miscellaneous uncommitted representatives, whom the Iskraites described contemptuously as "the Marsh" because they wallowed in a quagmire of uncertainty. The Iskraites appeared to be in full control. They named the presidium and easily pushed through their draft program and various resolutions on tactics.

The next order of business was the adoption of the party rules, and here trouble developed. The Iskraites were no longer united; Lenin and Martov offered rival drafts. The initial issue was posed by the definition of party membership. Lenin's draft of Paragraph One read: "A Party member is one who accepts its program and who supports the Party both financially and *by personal participation in one of the Party organizations.*" Martov's formulation defined a party member as "one who accepts its program, supports the Party financially and renders it regular personal assistance under the direction of one of its organizations." [33] To many of the delegates, the difference in shading between the two drafts appeared slight, but as the discussion gathered momentum, the differences were magnified until a basic, and ultimately irreconcilable, question of principle emerged.

The issue was the nature of the party. Lenin wanted a narrow, closed party of dedicated revolutionaries operating in strict subordination to the center and serving as a vanguard of leadership for the masses of workers who would surround the party without belonging to it. Martov desired a broad party open to anyone who believed in its program and was willing to work under its direction. Martov conceded the necessity of central leadership, but he also insisted that party members were entitled to have

a voice in its affairs and could not abdicate their right to think and influence party policy.

As the debate raged, the *Iskra* group fell apart. Plekhanov rallied
to Lenin's defense; the Leninist formula seemed to him admirably
adapted to protect the party against the infiltration of bourgeois individ-
ualists.[34] Axelrod and Trotsky supported Martov. To Axelrod it seemed
that Lenin was dreaming "of the administrative subordination of an entire
party to a few guardians of doctrine." [35] And after the Congress had
adjourned, Trotsky, in a sharp attack on Lenin, provided the classic
formulation of the opposition. In Lenin's view, he pointed out, "the
organization of the Party takes the place of the Party itself; the Central
Committee takes the place of the organization; and finally the dictator
takes the place of the Central Committee." [36] It was to turn out a more
somber and tragic vision of things to come than Trotsky realized at the
time.

At the Congress, Martov's draft triumphed by a vote of twenty-eight
to twenty-two. But Lenin had not yet shot his last bolt. He still retained
the leadership of a majority of the Iskraites, though his group was now
a minority in the Congress. This minority was soon transformed into a
majority by a series of "accidents" to which Lenin's parliamentary
maneuvering and planning contributed. When the Congress rejected the
Bundist claim to be the sole representative of the Jewish proletariat, the
five delegates of the Bund withdrew from the Congress. Their departure
was followed by the withdrawal of the delegates from the League of
Russian Social-Democrats, an Economist-dominated organization, which
the Congress voted to dissolve on Lenin's motion. With the exit of these
two groups, the *Iskra* majority became the Congress majority and proceeded to elect its representatives to the central party organs. It was this
triumph which gave Lenin's caucus the title of Bolsheviks (the majority
men), while his defeated opponents became known as Mensheviks (the
minority men).

But the triumph was short-lived. The central party institutions elected
by the Second Congress consisted of the editors of *Iskra*, the Central
Committee in Russia, and a Party Council of five members (two representing *Iskra*, two the Central Committee, and a fifth elected by the
Congress). The Board of Editors of *Iskra* was given power equal to and
indeed above that of the Central Committee. Disputes between *Iskra*
and the Central Committee were to be settled by the Party Council. Lenin,
Plekhanov, and Martov were elected as editors of *Iskra*. Martov refused
to serve unless the original editorial board, which included Axelrod,
Zasulich, and Potresov, was restored. Lenin and Plekhanov were thus
left in exclusive control. The Central Committee in Russia was composed
entirely of Bolsheviks, and they were given power to coöpt other mem-

bers. The party apparatus appeared to be safely in Bolshevik hands when Plekhanov, out of a desire to heal the breach with his old associates, acceded to Martov's conditions and insisted on the restoration of the original *Iskra* board. Lenin promptly withdrew, and at one stroke *Iskra* was transformed into an organ of Menshevism.

Differences now began to develop in the Bolshevik Central Committee in Russia; a majority group emerged which advocated a policy of conciliation toward the Mensheviks. Three Mensheviks were coöpted into the Central Committee, and in the summer of 1904 this strategic power position, which Lenin had regarded as impregnable, passed over to the opposition. After all his careful planning and apparent triumph, Lenin was left isolated and alone, betrayed by his own nominees in Russia, alienated from the leading figures of the emigration, and the chief target of abuse in the party organ which he had been primarily instrumental in establishing.

After a temporary fit of utter discouragement, Lenin rallied and began once more to gather his forces. The remnants of the faithful in the emigration were welded into a fighting organization. Connections were reestablished with the lower party committees in Russia, and a new body, the Bureau of the Committee of the Majority, was established to coordinate the work of Lenin's supporters. Toward the end of 1904 a new paper, *Vperëd* (Forward), was founded as the organ of the bureau. A second effort to capture control of the party organization was now in the full tide of preparation. But this time the Mensheviks were wary and refused to attend the so-called Third Congress of the Social-Democratic Labor Party, which assembled on Lenin's initiative in London in May 1905.[37] The Mensheviks met separately in Geneva.

The 1905 revolution brought Bolsheviks and Mensheviks closer together. Responding to the *élan* of the uprising, Mensheviks became more militant and Bolsheviks seemed to abandon their distrust of uncontrolled mass organization. As Lenin put it, "The rising tide of revolution drove . . . differences into the background . . . In place of the old differences there arose unity of views." [38] Joint committees were formed in many cities, and finally a Joint Central Committee was created on a basis of equal representation to summon a "Unity" Congress. Both parties were flooded with new members for whom the old quarrels were ancient history and the practical tasks of the moment were paramount. The misgivings of the leaders were swept aside in a widespread yearning for unity.

The Fourth so-called "Unity" Congress, which took place at Stockholm in 1906, reflected this surge from below.[39] Thirty-six thousand workers took part in the election of delegates. Menshevism flourished on legality, and of the one hundred eleven voting delegates selected, sixty-two were Mensheviks and forty-nine Bolsheviks.[40] As a result, the Mensheviks dominated the proceedings. They wrote the program and resolutions and controlled the leading party organs. The Central Committee elected by the Congress was composed of seven Mensheviks and three Bolsheviks; the editorial board for the central party newspaper (which never appeared) was composed exclusively of Mensheviks. Perhaps the most important organizational action taken at the Congress was the admission of the Bund and the Polish and Latvian Social-Democratic parties as constituent units in the united party. The Polish and Latvian parties joined as autonomous organizations operating in their respective territorial areas; the Bund renounced its claim to be the sole representative of the Jewish proletariat on the understanding that it would be permitted to retain its program of national cultural autonomy and to organize Jewish workers without respect to territorial boundaries. The admission of these groups introduced an additional complication into the power structure of the party. Given the relatively even distribution of strength between Mensheviks and Bolsheviks in this period, the balance of power now shifted to the Bund and the Polish and Latvian Social-Democrats, and their votes became of crucial significance in shaping the party's future course.

Although Lenin suffered defeat at the Stockholm Congress, he continued to maneuver for ascendancy. The Bolshevik factional apparatus was maintained, and funds to finance the apparatus were partly obtained through "expropriations" (robberies and holdups). The effort to capture local organizations was continued, and Menshevik policies were attacked with relentless ferocity. As a result of this activity, the Bolsheviks registered marked gains at the Fifth Congress, held in London in 1907. While the precise strength of the Bolshevik and Menshevik blocs is still in dispute, all accounts agree that the Bolsheviks achieved a slight preponderance over the Mensheviks at the Congress.[41]

This did not mean, however, that the Bolsheviks controlled the Congress. The real power of decision rested with the Bund and the Polish and Latvian Social-Democrats, who exercised a role of balance between the conflicting Russian factions. On the whole, the Mensheviks attracted Bundist support, while the Bolsheviks were dependent on the Poles and Latvians for such majorities as they obtained.[42] While the Bolsheviks failed to secure the support of the national delegates in their efforts to condemn the work of the Menshevik Central Committee and of the Duma fraction of the party and were themselves condemned for their sponsorship of "expropriations," they were able to defeat the Mensheviks on a number of important resolutions. The Menshevik policy of cooperating with the Kadets was repudiated. The proposal of Axelrod and other leading Mensheviks to call a non-party labor congress and to transform the Social-Democratic Party into a broad, open labor party was denounced by Lenin as "Liquidationism" and decisively rejected by the Congress.

But the Bolsheviks were unable to achieve a dependable, monolithic majority, and the elections to the Central Committee yielded five Bolsheviks, four Mensheviks, two Bundists, two Polish Social-Democrats, and one Latvian Social-Democrat.

During the period of reaction and repression which accumulated momentum after the London Congress, both Menshevik and Bolshevik segments of the party underwent a serious crisis. Party membership crumbled away, and police spies penetrated such remnants of the organizational apparatus as remained. The crisis was particularly acute for the Mensheviks. Potresov, in a letter to Axelrod toward the end of 1907, reflected an almost hopeless despondency:

> Complete disintegration and demoralisation prevail in our ranks. Probably this is a phenomenon common to all parties and fractions and reflects the spirit of the times; but I do not think that this disintegration, this demoralisation have anywhere manifested themselves so vividly as with us Mensheviks. Not only is there no organisation, there are not even the elements of one.[43]

The situation within Bolshevik ranks was not much better. "In 1908," notes the Bolshevik historian Popov, "the Party membership numbered not tens and hundreds of thousands, as formerly, but a few hundreds, or, at best, thousands." [44] The plight of the Moscow organization was not atypical. From the end of 1908 to the end of 1909, membership declined from five hundred to one hundred fifty; in the next year the organization was completely destroyed when it fell under the control of a police spy.[45] The Bolsheviks, by virtue of their conspiratorial traditions and tight discipline, made a better adjustment than the Mensheviks to the rigors of illegal existence, but even Bolshevik vigilance could not prevent the secret agents of the police from penetrating the underground hierarchy and rising to high places in the party apparatus. Meanwhile, the leaders of both the Bolshevik and Menshevik factions fled abroad once more where they were soon engaged in resurrecting old quarrels and giving birth to new differences.

Both factions fell victim to internal dissension. The Mensheviks divided between the "Liquidators" (as Lenin dubbed them), who counseled the abandonment of the underground party and concentration on legal work in the trade unions and the Duma, and the "Party" Mensheviks, who continued to insist on the necessity of an illegal organization. Bolshevism spawned in rapid succession a bewildering series of controversies. First, there were the "Duma Boycotters," led by Bogdanov, at that time one of Lenin's closest associates. On this issue Lenin joined with the Mensheviks and supported party participation in the election of the Third Duma. Then there were the "Otzovists" and "Ultimatumists," the former demanding the immediate recall or withdrawal of the Duma party delegation and the latter insisting that an ultimatum be dispatched to the delegation with the proviso that its members should immediately be recalled if the instructions contained in the ultimatum were rejected. Lenin again opposed both tendencies. Next came the philosophical heresies, the Neo-Kantian "Machism" of Bogdanov and the "God-Creator" religionism of Lunacharsky and Gorky. These were heresies that Lenin endured as long as the heretics were enrolled in his political camp; they became intolerable only when Bogdanov and the rest challenged his control of the party faction. Finally, there were the Bolshevik "Conciliators" who insisted that peace be made with the Mensheviks after Lenin had determined that a final split was essential.

In the parlance of latter-day Bolshevism, each of these "deviations" had to be "liquidated" if Lenin was to build the party in his own image. He was determined to accomplish precisely that task. The first act took place in the summer of 1909 at an enlarged editorial conference of *Proletarii*, the organ of the Bolshevik caucus. Again Lenin made careful advance preparations, and equipped with the necessary votes, he carried a resolution declaring that Boycottism, Otzovism, Ultimatumism, God-Construction, and Machism were all incompatible with membership in the Bolshevik faction. Over bitter protest, Bogdanov was ousted from the Bolshevik central leadership where he had been second only to Lenin, and he and his associates were declared "to have placed themselves outside the faction." Expelled from the fold, the dissidents proceeded to declare themselves "true Bolsheviks," established a new journal utilizing an old name, *Vperëd*, and became known during the next years as Vperëdist Bolsheviks.

Having disposed of the Vperëdists, Lenin confronted the new opposition of the so-called Conciliators, or Party Bolsheviks, who called for reconciliation with the expelled faction and unity with the Mensheviks. At a plenary session, held in January 1910, of the Central Committee elected by the London Congress, Lenin received a sharp rebuff when the Conciliators turned against him. The conference voted to discontinue the Bolshevik paper *Proletarii* as well as the Menshevik *Golos Sotsial-Demokrata* (Voice of the Social-Democrat) and to replace both with a general party organ, *Sotsial-Demokrat*, which would have two Menshevik editors, Martov and Dan, two Bolshevik editors, Lenin and Zinoviev, and one representative of the Polish Social-Democrats, Warski, to break any deadlocks that might develop.

Again the attempt at "unity" miscarried. With the support of Warski, Lenin won control of the new party journal and denied the Menshevik editors the right to publish signed articles in what was supposed to be the organ of the united party. Martov replied by attempting to discredit Lenin through an exposure of the seamy side of Bolshevism — the holdups, the counterfeiting, and "expropriations" which Lenin had allegedly sanctioned and defended.

Lenin now moved toward an open and irrevocable break. Despite the protest of the Bolshevik Conciliators, he summoned an All-Russian Party Conference which met in Prague in January 1912 to ratify the split. Although the conference was dominated by a carefully selected group of Lenin's most reliable supporters, the uneasiness of the delegates in the face of Lenin's ruthless determination to move toward schism manifested itself in a belated decision to invite Plekhanov, Trotsky, and others to attend. To Lenin's great relief, both Plekhanov and Trotsky refused on the ground that the conference was too one-sided and imperiled party unity. Martov and the Menshevik Liquidators were not invited. The Bund and the Polish and Latvian Social-Democrats also stayed away.

The "Rump Parliament" proceeded to assume all the rights and functions of a party congress (indeed, Lenin called it The Sixth Congress of the Russian Social-Democratic Labor Party). The old Central Committee created by the London Congress was declared dissolved, and a new "pure" Bolshevik Central Committee was elected from which all Bolshevik Conciliators were excluded. The Prague Conference marked the decisive break with Menshevism and the turning point in the history of Bolshevism as an independent movement. There were to be many subsequent attempts to bring the Bolsheviks back into the fold of a united party, but all were doomed to failure. The last effort, sponsored by the International Socialist Bureau of the Second International, was slated to take place at the Vienna Congress of the Second International in August 1914. War intervened, and the congress was never held. By an ironical turn of events, the International which attempted to close the breach in the Russian party was itself split by the Bolsheviks whom it tried to bring to heel.

The early organizational history of Bolshevism, which has been briefly summarized here, holds more than historical interest. The experience of the formative years left an ineradicable stamp on the character and future development of the party. It implanted the germinating conception of the monolithic and totalitarian party. The elitism which was so deeply ingrained in Lenin, the theory of the party as a dedicated revolutionary order, the tradition of highly centralized leadership, the tightening regimen of party discipline, the absolutism of the party line, the intolerance of disagreement and compromise, the manipulatory attitude toward mass organization, the subordination of means to ends, and the drive for total power — all these patterns of behavior which crystallized in the early years were destined to exercise a continuing influence on the code by which the party lived and the course of action which it pursued.

The Tactics of Bolshevism

The organizational and doctrinal attributes of Bolshevism were supplemented by great tactical flexibility. The history of Bolshevism is a record of willingness to make sharp adjustments in the party line when circumstances appeared to require such adaptation, realism in appraising the actual configuration of power forces at any given moment, and the determination to make tactics serve the grand design of arousing and mobilizing the revolutionary potential inherent in Russian society. Perhaps it is more accurate to speak of these qualities as attributes of Lenin rather than of Bolsheviks in the mass, but Lenin's leadership in revolutionary engineering played such a decisive role in determining the tactical decisions of Bolshevism that the two became virtually indistinguishable. An analysis of changing attitudes toward the peasantry, the Soviet of 1905, the Duma, and nationality policy will serve to illustrate the flexible nature of Leninist tactics.

The Appeal to the Peasant

Lenin, like his master Plekhanov, at first underestimated the revolutionary potential of the peasantry. In their desire to discredit the Narodniks and to emphasize the industrial proletariat as the prime revolutionary force, both men turned their backs on the peasantry. Lenin, however, was to try to correct his errors; Plekhanov remained essentially indifferent to the problem. At the 1903 Party Congress, Lenin, alert to peasant restiveness, succeeded in incorporating an agrarian plank into the party program. In terms of peasant appeal, the plank left much to be desired, but it did call for the return to the peasants of the *otrezki* (the land cut off from their allotments by the landlords at the time of the Emancipation), for the abolition of redemption payments and the return of those already made, and for the repeal of all laws restricting the peasants in disposing of their lands.

As the peasant disorders mounted and land seizures and the burning of manor houses spread, Lenin began to realize that what the muzhik wanted was not merely the return of the otrezki but all of the land. The immediate problem for Lenin in 1905 was the overthrow of the autocracy. The bourgeoisie could not be trusted as allies. Peasant support was essential. Hence Lenin's slogan calling for a "democratic dictatorship of the proletariat and the peasantry." But how cement an alliance with the peasantry? What was the price of its support? If the land were simply turned over to the peasantry for redivision, would not that immediately create a class of bourgeois peasant proprietors who would solidly oppose a socialist revolution?

The problem was a painfully difficult one, both for Lenin and for all Marxists who tried to find a place in their thinking for the peasant. At the London Bolshevik Congress in 1905, Lenin pushed through a resolution which was designed to meet all contingencies. To attract peasant backing, the Bolsheviks pledged the "most energetic support of all the revolutionary measures undertaken by the peasantry that are capable of improving its position, including confiscation of the land belonging to the landlords, the state, the church, the monasteries, and the imperial family." At the same time, party workers were instructed "to strive for the independent organization of the rural proletariat, for its fusion with the urban proletariat under the banner of the Social-Democratic Party, and for the inclusion of its representatives in the peasant committees." [46]

The first proposition appeared to be an explicit endorsement of peasant land seizures. But Lenin quickly introduced qualifications.

> We are in favor of confiscation. . . But to whom shall we recommend that the confiscated land be given? On this question we have not tied our hands. . . What we do say is that this is a question we shall fight out later on, fight again, on a new field, and with other allies. Then we shall certainly be with the rural proletariat, with the entire working class *against* the peasant bourgeoisie. In practice, this may mean the transfer of the land to the class of petty peasant proprietors — wherever big estates based on bondage and feudal servitude still prevail, where there are as yet no material prerequisites for large-scale socialist production; it may mean nationalization — provided the democratic revolution is completely victorious; or the big capitalist estates may be transferred to *workers' associations.*[47]

This parade of alternatives could scarcely have been very meaningful to peasants hungering for land. If Lenin expressed uncertainty about how agriculture would ultimately be organized under Bolshevik auspices, he made it altogether clear that the alliance with the peasantry in general was a transitory phase and that the peasant bourgeoisie would be treated as a class enemy. This too was hardly a program calculated to rally a united peasantry to the banner of Bolshevism. Indeed, Bolshevism in this period had virtually no support among the peasantry, and such influence as it exerted was largely limited to landless agricultural workers on a few large estates.

At the Stockholm "Unity" Congress of 1906, Lenin sharpened, but did not substantially change, his agrarian program. Again he called for confiscation, with the understanding that the disposition of the land would be left to local peasant committees pending the establishment of a constituent assembly. After the triumph of a democratic republic, the party would support the nationalization of all the land. What would happen after nationalization was left vague. Lenin's formula of nationalization was rejected by the Menshevik majority in favor of "municipalization," that is, the transfer of ownership to official local government bodies which would presumably rent or lease the land to the cultivators. From the point of view of the muzhik who coveted the landlord's land, the debate over nationalization versus municipalization was a rather meaningless pastime of the intellectuals, but Lenin at least approached nearer the peasants' heart's desire with his proposal of local peasant committees to superintend the land seizures.

During the period of reaction which set in with the ebb of the 1905 revolution, Lenin made no important modifications in his land program. He watched the Stolypin agrarian reforms with the greatest interest and respected Stolypin as a dangerous and redoubtable enemy whose effort to create a peasant bourgeoisie might operate to add real strength to the counterrevolution. At the same time, he insisted that the result of Stolypin's policy would be to accentuate class difference in the village and thus make it all the more necessary for the Bolsheviks to address their primary appeal to the agricultural laborers and the village poor.[48]

The Revolution of 1917 found Lenin and the Bolsheviks with their old peasant program essentially intact. The Resolution on the Agrarian Question of the Bolshevik April Conference repeated the demands for confiscation and nationalization of the land. The immediate transfer of the land was to be organized under "Soviets of Peasants' Deputies, or under other organs of local government elected in a really democratic way and entirely independently of the landlords and officials." [49] The Resolution also advised "the rural proletarians and semi-proletarians to strive to organize on all landed estates fair-sized model farms to be conducted for the public account by the Soviets of Agricultural Laborers' Deputies under the direction of agricultural experts and with the application of the best technique." [50]

Although this program, compared with the Bolshevik starting point in 1903, represented a striking advance in its awareness of peasant grievances, it still failed to come to terms with the basic peasant demand — the desire to seize and divide up the landlords' estates. Lenin was still too powerfully dominated by Marxian categories and habits of thought to be able to meet the peasant on the least common denominator of his primeval land-hunger. The 1905 revolution had impelled him a long step forward. The Revolution of 1917 provided the final push.

Through the spring and summer of 1917 the peasants were on the move, seizing land without benefit of legal sanction and brushing aside all pleas of government leaders to postpone a land settlement pending the decision of a constituent assembly. "Too often it has happened," observed Lenin in this period, "that, when history has taken a sharp turn, even advanced parties have been unable for a fairly long time to adapt themselves to the new situation and have continued to repeat slogans which had formerly been true, but which had now lost all meaning." [51] Lenin now moved to rectify his agrarian tactics and condensed the whole Bolshevik program to one phrase, "Land to the Peasants." Thus Lenin capitalized on the grievances of the peasants and won their neutrality, or at least passive acquiescence, in a march to power which many of them were to live to regret bitterly. Subsequently they were to be reminded that in the Bolshevik lexicon "nationalization," "estates operated collectively," and "model state farms" were slogans with more continuing content than "Land to the Peasants."

The Soviet of 1905 and Duma Tactics

Leninist attitudes toward the 1905 Soviet and the Duma illustrate another facet of Bolshevik tactics. Bolshevism has traditionally sought to attack, boycott, or slander any agency which it believes it cannot effectively utilize or control. It has regarded every outside organization or legislative body in which it participates as a field of battle where it might carry on agitation, infiltrate into leading positions, discredit every competitor for mass support, and win sole ascendancy as the spokesman for the proletariat. This tactical instrumentalism is brought out sharply by the shifts in Bolshevik attitudes toward both the Soviet and the Duma.

The Bolsheviks were at first extremely cool toward the whole idea of the Soviet. As a spontaneous organization of factory labor delegates which had sprung up during the 1905 revolution without visible leadership from the Bolshevik faction, it appeared to be a potentially dangerous competitor. The local Bolshevik leaders in St. Petersburg at first boycotted the Soviet and then confronted it with an ultimatum that it recognize their program and "join" the party. Lenin was more realistic. Writing from Stockholm before his return to Russia and with only fragmentary reports of the activities of the Soviets before him, he rebuked the local leaders: "Comrade Radin . . . is wrong to pose the question: 'The Soviet of Workingmen's Deputies or the Party.' It seems to me that the solution ought to be: *Both* the Soviet of Workingmen's Delegates *and* the Party." [52]

Impressed by the mass support which the Soviet rallied, Lenin saw in it both a field of activity for the expansion of Bolshevik influence and "the germ of a provisional revolutionary government" to replace the autocracy. As it turned out, the Mensheviks, and especially Trotsky, played a far more active role in the life of the Soviets than the Bolsheviks; the latter found it much more difficult to make a quick readjustment from underground existence to open political activity. For Lenin, the lesson of this experience was not to boycott the Soviets but to intensify Bolshevik activity within them in order to establish control. It was a principle which Lenin would apply again in 1917, on that occasion more successfully than in 1905.

The Duma tactics of the Bolsheviks revealed a similar instrumental approach. The Bolsheviks, like other revolutionary parties, began by boycotting the elections to the First Duma on the assumption that the revolutionary tide of 1905 was still running high and that the Duma was at best a sop designed to placate unrest and to divert the energies of the revolt into pseudo-parliamentarianism. Indeed, at a Bolshevik conference held at Tammerfors, Finland, in December 1905, the assembled delegates asserted "that Social-Democracy must strive to disrupt this police Duma, rejecting all participation in it." [53] At this conference, Lenin astonished his colleagues by declaring himself against the boycott, but then, according to Stalin's report, "he saw his mistake and took his stand with the faction." [54] Lenin's uneasiness arose out of his fear that the boycott tactics would be self-defeating. By surrendering electoral leadership to the Kadets and *Trudoviks* (Party of the Peasant Union), the Bolsheviks ran the danger of isolating themselves from the masses. Officially, however, Lenin took his stand with the faction and defended its decision as "the only correct tactics at that time," given "the temper of the revolutionary proletariat." [55]

As the revolutionary tide receded, Lenin became convinced that the boycott tactics would have to be reversed. At the Stockholm "Unity" Congress in April 1906, he joined with the Mensheviks against most of his own faction in a decision to give up the boycott. By that time, most of the elections to the First Duma had been concluded. Only the Transcaucasian elections remained. There the Social-Democratic Party participated and won a sweeping victory, returning seventeen deputies, all Mensheviks.

At this time and for a considerable period afterwards, Lenin found himself in a peculiar position. A substantial element among his own followers insisted that the boycott tactics should not have been abandoned; Lenin had to persuade them that participation in the elections provided a useful platform for revolutionary agitation. While he voted with the Mensheviks against the boycott, at the same time he disagreed violently with their conception of parliamentary tactics. Their willingness to enter into electoral agreements and to make parliamentary "deals" with the Kadets seemed to him a betrayal of the revolutionary position. In Lenin's view, the Menshevik eagerness to use the Duma to advance reform legislation could only breed harmful constitutional illusions. Lenin sought to expose the "parliamentary comedy," to undermine faith in the Duma, and to use the opportunities which it afforded to impress the masses with the necessity for revolutionary action. The Mensheviks too were competitors for working-class support. Their influence had to be destroyed if Bolshevik ascendancy were to be insured.

Lenin consequently was forced to conduct his battle on a double front.

The struggle within his own faction ended with the purge of the Boy-
cottists, Otzovists, and Ultimatumists at the *Proletarii* Conference in the
summer of 1909.* The war with the Mensheviks was more protracted.
After the dissolution of the First Duma, the Mensheviks expressed their
willingness to enter into electoral agreements with the Kadets. Lenin
denounced this policy on the ground that the interests of the liberal
bourgeoisie and the proletariat were fundamentally incompatible and
that the Kadets had proven themselves traitors to the revolution. Lenin
called instead for alliances with the representatives of the peasantry, the
Socialist-Revolutionaries and Trudoviks, whom he termed real bourgeois
democrats as opposed to the Kadet "renegades."

In the elections to the Second Duma, the Bolsheviks and Mensheviks
maintained a precarious unity that constantly threatened to, and in St.
Petersburg did, spill over into open warfare. When the returns were in,
sixty-five partisans and adherents of the Social-Democratic Party had
been elected. Of these, thirty-six were Mensheviks (including four
sympathizers), eighteen were Bolsheviks (including three sympathizers),
and eleven took no definite stand, although they joined more often with
the Mensheviks.[56] As a result, the Mensheviks organized the party Duma
group, though not without the most bitter conflict with the Bolsheviks.
The differences between the two factions persisted throughout the
session, with the Bolsheviks insisting that parliamentary working agreements be limited to the Socialist-Revolutionaries and the Trudoviks,
while the Mensheviks, as earlier, were also willing to work with the
Kadets. Their running battle with each other and their joint battle with
the autocracy were brought to an abrupt end when Stolypin insisted on
the expulsion of the Social-Democratic fraction from the Duma. While
the Duma hesitated, Stolypin dissolved it.[57]

The dissolution of the Second Duma provoked a new outburst of boy-
cottist sentiment among the Bolsheviks, but again Lenin proved himself
master of the situation. Both Bolsheviks and Mensheviks participated in
the elections to the Third and Fourth Dumas, though as a result of the
new electoral law, their representation was greatly reduced. The total
Social-Democratic fraction in the Third Duma was thirteen. In the Fourth
Duma, Social-Democratic representation increased to fourteen, of whom
seven were Mensheviks, one a Polish Socialist who supported the Mensheviks, and six were Bolsheviks. These six, the Bolsheviks never tired of
pointing out, were elected in workers' districts, while the majority of the
Menshevik delegates came from mixed constituencies of workers and
other social categories. The internecine warfare between the factions,
which had already manifested itself in the Second Duma, intensified and

* See pp. 45–46.

finally led on October 25, 1913, to a complete break. After that, the
Bolsheviks operated as an independent fraction.

The reminiscences of A. E. Badayev, who served as a Bolshevik
deputy in the Fourth Duma, provide a somewhat naïve but very revealing
account of Bolshevik Duma tactics.[58] As Badayev makes clear, the
Bolshevik leadership took steps to ensure that its Duma representatives,
in contrast with the Mensheviks, would all be workers from the bench.
This was done in order to dramatize the notion that the Bolsheviks were
the party of the proletariat with workers as spokesmen for workers. At
the same time, as Badayev points out, the Bolshevik Duma group operated
under the most intimate supervision of the party leadership.

As the activity of the fraction developed the connection of our "six" with
the Central Committee and above all, with Lenin, became closer. Material,
information, etc., was sent to Cracow, and from Cracow the Bolshevik deputies
received literature, theses for speeches, instructions on separate questions
which arose in the course of their work.[59]

The main duty of the Bolshevik Duma deputy was to use his Duma
privileges to conduct revolutionary agitation. In the election campaign,
the Duma candidates were instructed to hammer home the three "whales,"
the demands for a democratic republic, an eight-hour working day, and
the confiscation of all landlords' estates.

The problem of relationships with the Mensheviks was more complicated. When Bolshevik and Menshevik candidates confronted each
other in elections in workers' districts, no stone was to be left unturned
to destroy the influence of the Mensheviks among the working class. At
the same time, as long as a common Duma group was preserved, a show
of outward unity was to be maintained in Duma work. But the Bolshevik
deputies were also instructed to do their utmost within the Duma group
to secure the adoption of Bolshevik slogans and programs. When these
efforts were thwarted by the Menshevik majority, the Bolshevik deputies
were enjoined to split the group and operate independently — at the
same time attempting in their propaganda among the workers to pin
responsibility for the split on the Mensheviks. These guide lines continued to shape the work of the Bolshevik deputies until their arrest in
1914, after which, of course, the parliamentary rostrum ceased to be
available as a sounding board for Bolshevik agitation.

The experience in the Duma dramatized a basic Leninist strategy to
combine legal with illegal forms of struggle and to utilize even the most
reactionary instruments if Bolshevik purposes could be advanced through
such action. It was a conception to which the Bolsheviks were to return
after their seizure of power, when they assumed the task of providing
guidance through the Comintern for other Communist parties facing the
same problem of combining illegal with parliamentary forms of struggle.

Nationality Policy

The development of Lenin's nationality policy illustrates still another aspect of Bolshevik tactics. It dramatizes his determination to exploit and mobilize every possible source of minority discontent in order to undermine the power of the autocracy, while at the same time preserving the integrity of the party itself against the danger of disintegration into its nationality components.

During the late nineteenth and early twentieth centuries, the Tsarist effort to cope with the minority problems of its multi-national Empire emphasized stubborn Russification, suppression, and the divide-and-rule strategy of deliberately provoking national, racial, and religious antagonisms. While the stress on Great Russian nationalism was intended to, and in a measure did, build support for the autocracy among the people of the dominant nationality, the reaction among other nationalities, particularly in the borderlands, was only to kindle separatist aspirations and to unleash centrifugal tendencies which threatened the disintegration of the Empire. Moreover, while the leadership of the national movements among the minorities tended to gravitate into the hands of the upper stratum of the native society, the national movements themselves united all classes of society against the common Great Russian enemy and thus served to blur or obfuscate class antagonisms within the minorities themselves.

The rising tide of nationalism, both among the Great Russians and the minorities, posed a difficult series of questions for the Russian Social-Democratic Labor Party with its aim of organizing the proletariat of the entire Russian Empire. As a class party, it cut across national lines. Should the party modify its internal structure in order to adjust to the wave of nationalisms that threatened to engulf the working-class masses of the Empire? What attitude should the party take to the separatist strivings of the borderlands? What position should be adopted toward the demands for federation and autonomy within the Empire?

The first tendency of Lenin and most Russian Social-Democrats was to withdraw from and underestimate the importance of the national question. Following the text of the resolution adopted at the London Congress of the Second International in 1896, the Second Congress of the Russian Party declared itself in favor of the full right of self-determination for all nations. But the formula still had vague connotations for most of the party.[60] As one member of the Committee on the Party Program stated at the Second Congress:

So far as the national question is concerned, our demands can only be negative ones, that is to say, we are against all restrictions imposed on nationalities. But whether this or that nationality will be able to develop as such, is none of our business as Social-Democrats. That will be decided by an elemental and spontaneous process.[61]

When a spokesman for the Bund moved an amendment to the "right of self-determination" resolution providing for the establishment of "institutions guaranteeing full freedom of cultural development" to national minority groups, the Congress overwhelmingly rejected it.[62] A second Bund amendment that minorities should be guaranteed "freedom of cultural development" was similarly defeated. The Bund next proposed that the Congress endorse "the right of every citizen to use his language everywhere — in government institutions and schools." [63] This time the Congress made a concession. It endorsed:

the right of a people to acquire an education in its mother tongue, which right is to be guaranteed by the establishment of such schools as are necessary therefor, at the expense of the state and the organs of self-government; the right of every citizen to use his mother tongue in public meetings; the use of the mother tongue in all local, public and governmental agencies together with the official language of the state." [64]

But the Congress refused to sanction the transfer of jurisdiction over minority groups to autonomous institutions of the minorities themselves. Its only major departure from centralism was a resolution advocating "regional self-government for those border areas in which the way of life and composition of the population differ from those in genuinely Russian areas." [65] Even this amendment offended Lenin's centralist predilections; his proposal to substitute "local" for "regional" self-government was, however, defeated.

At the Second Congress, the party also faced the problem of the impact of nationality on its own internal structure. The issue was precipitated by the Bund, which had been admitted into the party as an autonomous organization in 1898 and which now pressed for a recognition of its claims to be the "sole representative of the Jewish proletariat in whatever part of Russia it lives." When the Congress refused to accede, the Bund withdrew. In the debate, Lenin was particularly insistent in rejecting national autonomy as a basis for party organization.

Up to this point, Lenin had revealed himself as a centralist on issues of both party and state organization. He rejected all demands for a federated party or a federal republic. The proposals of the Austro-Marxists, Renner and Bauer, from whom the Bund had drawn inspiration for its national program, were utterly repugnant to him. Renner and Bauer had developed a theory of nonterritorial cultural autonomy by which members of different nationalities in the Austro-Hungarian Empire were to be organized, regardless of their place of residence, under national councils with exclusive jurisdiction over educational and cultural affairs. By making this concession to nationalism, the Austro-Marxists hoped to preserve the economic and political unity of the Empire. At the same time, they also applied their theory of national autonomy to party organization, and the Austrian Social-Democratic Party was reorganized (1899) into a federation of six autonomous national parties — German, Czech, Polish, Ruthenian, Italian, and South Slav.

To Lenin, this was no solution for the national problem. As his protégé, Stalin, said in his attack on the Austro-Marxists (*Marxism and the National Question*):

> In this way a united class movement is broken up into separate national rivulets. . . Nay more, it only serves to aggravate and confuse the problem by creating a soil which favours the destruction of the unity of the working-class movement, fosters national division among the workers and intensifies friction among them.[66]

What then was Lenin's "solution" for the problem? How exploit the genuine upsurge of national discontent among the oppressed minorities? Lenin's answer was breathtakingly simple — by holding out to the minority nationality the right to secede from the metropolitan area. To Rosa Luxemburg and the Polish Social-Democrats who faced the problem of combating native chauvinism in Poland, Lenin's slogan seemed tantamount to a surrender to Polish bourgeois nationalism and an abandonment of working-class unity. Lenin's reply made it clear that the significance of the slogan of secession was largely tactical.

> The right of self-determination [secession] is an *exception* from our general policy of centralism. This exception is absolutely necessary in view of Great-Russian arch-reactionary nationalism, and the slightest renunciation of this exception is opportunism — it is a simple-minded playing into the hands of Great-Russian arch-reactionary nationalism.[67]

If the Social-Democrats of the oppressing nations find it tactically necessary to emphasize the freedom to secede, this need not prevent the Social-Democrats of the oppressed nations from insisting on the freedom to unite.

> No Russian Marxist [said Lenin] even thought of blaming the Polish Social-Democrats for being opposed to the secession of Poland. These Social-Democrats err only when, like Rosa Luxemburg, they try to deny the necessity of including the recognition of the right to self-determination in the program of the *Russian* Marxists.[68]

At the so-called August (1913) Conference[69] of the Central Committee and leading party workers, the Bolsheviks summed up their nationality tactics in a five-point resolution: (1) they demanded a democratic republic with full equality of rights for all nations and languages, school instruction in the local language, and a wide measure of local self-government; (2) they repudiated the Austrian principle of "cultural-national" autonomy on a countrywide scale; (3) they rejected any division of working-class organizations on national lines; (4) they supported the right of all the oppressed nations of the Tsarist Empire to self-determination, which they defined as the right to secede and form an independent state; (5) they pointed out that the right to take such steps should not be confused with the expediency of such action.[70] Whether the right should be exercised in any particular case had to be decided by the party "from the point of view . . . of the interests of the class struggle of the proletariat for socialism." [71]

While points one and four of this program were designed to provide guide lines for Bolshevik agitation among the oppressed minorities and points two and three were intended to protect the party against the danger of national disintegration, it was point five which was to become of crucial significance after the Bolshevik seizure of power, when the party at last confronted the problem of preserving the Tsarist patrimony which it had inherited. Stalin, in 1913, had in a sense anticipated the problem when he wrote:

The Transcaucasian Tatars as a nation may assemble, let us say, in their Diet and, succumbing to the influence of their beys and mullahs, decide to restore the old order of things and to secede from the state. According to the meaning of the clause on self-determination they are fully entitled to do so. But will this be in the interest of the toiling strata of the Tatar nation? Can Social-Democrats remain indifferent when the beys and mullahs take the lead of the masses in the solution of the national problem? Should not Social-Democrats interfere in the matter and influence the will of the nation in a definite way? [72]

By 1918, when the borderlands began to secede under non-Bolshevik auspices, the answer of Stalin was clear:

All this points to the necessity of interpreting the principle of self-determination as a right not of the bourgeoisie, but of the working masses of the given nation. The principle of self-determination must be an instrument in the struggle for socialism and must be subordinated to the principles of socialism.[73]

In other words, the proletariat of the borderlands had to be "assisted" in exercising their right of self-determination against the bourgeoisie; self-determination was a right to unite as well as to secede, and the supreme test was the interest of the toiling masses as interpreted by the party.

In the grand strategy of Bolshevism, "self-determination," like so many other slogans, turned out to have almost exclusively tactical significance. It was useful in stirring up the forces of minority unrest and in winning supporters among the oppressed nationalities. As such, it justified itself.

But it always remained a formula with which Bolshevism was fundamentally uneasy. For, to the extent that it fed the flames of nationalism, it
set in motion fissiparous tendencies which would ultimately have to be
harnessed and bridled. The doctrinal and organizational premises of
Bolshevism were, after all, profoundly centralistic. Exceptions would be
tolerated only when, and only as long as, they served the purpose of
smoothing the road to power.

Toward this larger end Bolshevik doctrine, organization, and tactics
were all directed. The period before 1917 was a proving ground in which
doctrine was elaborated, organization tempered, and tactics tested. In
this crucible the strategy of 1917 was developed, and Bolshevism as a
system of governance took form. Still later, the experiences of this period
were to provide a set of precedents on the basis of which decisions would
be defended and attacked, orthodoxies would harden, and heresies be
condemned. History would be rewritten in the language of the victors; the
tale of the defeated would be twisted beyond recognition. Out of the
totalitarian embryo would come totalitarianism full-blown.

Chapter 3

The Road to Power

On the eve of the Revolution of March 1917, the total membership of the Bolshevik Party was generously estimated as 23,600.[1] The forces of the party were scattered and disorganized. Lenin was marooned in Switzerland and out of touch with his adherents in Russia. Oppressed by the staleness of *émigré* life, he immersed himself in a ceaseless round of literary and political activity, editing the journal *Sotsial-Demokrat* with Zinoviev, carrying on polemics with other socialists, working on his treatise on *Imperialism,* and participating in a series of meetings and conferences with antiwar socialists at which he called for the transformation of the war between the nations into an international civil war.

In Russia itself, most of the better-known Bolshevik leaders like Kamenev and Stalin languished in prison or in Siberian exile. Such remnants of the Bolshevik underground organization as survived the severe wartime repression functioned under the general supervision of the Russian Bureau of the Central Committee, which was then located in Petrograd [2] and consisted of two workingmen, Shlyapnikov and Zalutsky, and a twenty-seven-year-old student at the Polytechnic Institute, Molotov.

The Collapse of the Autocracy

The Revolution to which all the revolutionary parties had looked forward took them all by surprise. The collapse of the Romanov autocracy occurred with a catastrophic suddenness which stunned even those who had done most to bring it about. The dynasty had survived the 1905 revolution because in the hour of decision it could still count on the allegiance of the army, the police, the bureaucracy, the majority of the landed gentry, and the leading figures of the business and financial world. By 1917 these sources of support were melting away. The Grand Duke Alexander Mikhailovich was not far wrong when he wrote to the Tsar in

February of that year, "Strange though it may be, the government itself is the organ that is preparing the revolution." [3] The war — with its vast losses in men, territory, and resources, its revelation of impotence, incompetence, and degeneration in the highest court circles, its mounting weariness, its deprivations and hunger — stretched loyalty to Tsardom to the final breaking point. All that was needed was a precipitating incident to reveal the real weakness of the ties which sustained the autocracy.

The incident was provided on March 8, 1917, when bread riots and strikes occurred in Petrograd. During the next few days, the disorders expanded into a general strike. The decisive step toward revolution was taken when mutiny spread to the garrison and the soldiers of the regiments refused to obey the commands of their officers to fire on the crowds. The power was in the streets, but it was still formless, anarchic, and without clear direction. The fate of the Revolution turned on who would rush in to fill the vacuum of leadership which had been created.

The Dual Power

Out of the chaos of the early days two centers of initiative began to take shape. One was the Soviet of Workers' and Soldiers' Deputies; the other was the State Duma. The Soviet of Workers' and Soldiers' Deputies, which was modeled on its 1905 prototype, began its activities on March 12 when a miscellaneous group composed of left-wing Duma deputies, members of the labor group of the War Industries Committee, and representatives of trade unions and coöperatives constituted a Temporary Executive Committee and invited delegates from factories and regiments to assemble that same evening in the Tauride Palace to organize the Soviet. In the absence of any other authority, the Soviet quickly assumed such governmental functions as the regulation of the food supply and the organization of a workers' militia as a temporary substitute for the police. Perhaps the most famous of its early decrees was "Order Number One" (March 14) which, in effect, transferred control of the military forces to elected committees of soldiers and sailors by entrusting them with the disposition of all forms of arms. The same decree was also designed to make the armed forces subject to the paramount jurisdiction of the Soviet. From the beginning, the Soviet was far closer to the workers and soldiers than was the Duma; its decrees carried a persuasive power that no official body could command. Yet the members of the Soviet gave no indication of any eagerness to proclaim themselves the supreme rulers. They groped their way in the confusion, assumed authority by default, and took such action as the moods of the marching soldiers and workers seemed to dictate. [4]

Meanwhile, the more conservative leaders of the Duma moved to

bring order out of confusion. Their first hope was to persuade the Tsar
to concede a ministry responsible to the Duma. The Tsar's response was
to dissolve the Duma. The Duma leaders still cherished the dream of
saving the monarchy by securing the abdication of Nicholas II in favor
of his son or his brother Michael. This dream exploded when Michael, in
whose favor Nicholas II had abdicated, refused the throne. Nothing was
left except to establish a provisional government; for, as V. V. Shulgin,
one of the Duma leaders, put it,"If we don't take power, others will take
it, those who have already elected some scoundrels in the factories." [5]

No government with any pretension to authority could be formed at
this juncture without the support, or at least the acquiescence, of the
Soviet. The Duma leaders consequently negotiated an arrangement with
representatives of the Soviet by which the latter agreed to give con-
ditional support to a provisional government, provided that it met
certain conditions designed to guarantee the establishment of civil
liberties and democratic institutions.[6] The first Provisional Government,
which was headed by Prince G. E. Lvov, the head of the Union of
Zemstvos, was predominantly Kadet and Octobrist in composition. An
effort to broaden the political base of the cabinet by including several
Soviet leaders met with a rebuff. The only member of the Soviet in the
cabinet was the Socialist-Revolutionary Kerensky, who, despite a resolution of the Soviet Executive Committee declaring against the participation of its members in the new government, accepted the portfolio of
Minister of Justice.

Thus began the system of dual power under which the formal
authority of government was vested in a cabinet which rested on the
support of a relatively narrow stratum of articulate society while much of
the actual power of veto and decision reposed in a body of unofficial
Soviets which appeared to enjoy the confidence of the masses.[7] The
arrangement between the first Provisional Government and the Soviet
was a fragile truce rather than a solid agreement. The Soviet Executive
Committee promised support only "in the measure in which the newborn
government will act in the direction of fulfilling its obligations and
struggling decisively with the old government." [8]

The silences of the arrangement were eloquent of future difficulties.
There was no mention of the land question, no allusion to the organization of industry, no reference to peace or foreign policy. On issues such
as these, a cleavage was to develop which could not be bridged. The task
of Bolshevism was to deepen the chasm.

Bolshevik Waverings and Leninist Intransigence

During the first months of the Revolution, the Bolsheviks played a
minor role. Elections to the Soviets yielded a heavy preponderance of

Mensheviks and Socialist-Revolutionaries (SR's). In the general upsurge of revolutionary sentiment, sectarian political distinctions among the rank-and-file tended to be obliterated. Until the appearance of Lenin on the scene, the Bolshevik leadership responded to the mass mood by pursuing a relatively conciliatory policy toward other left-wing parties in the Soviet. While the first manifesto issued by Molotov and his associates called for the creation of a provisional revolutionary government [9] and the Provisional Government itself was subsequently denounced as "a class government of the bourgeoisie and the large landlords," [10] the Bolsheviks did not demand that the Soviet take power. Instead, as a Bolshevik resolution submitted to the Soviet phrased it, "The Soviet of Workers' and Soldiers' Deputies must reserve for itself complete freedom of action in the selection of means of realising the fundamental demands of the revolutionary people, and in particular in the selection of means of influencing the Provisional Government." [11]

With the return of Kamenev, Stalin, and Muranov from Siberian exile on March 25 and their assumption of the direction of the party in Petrograd, the policy of conciliation and compromise won strong reinforcement. Kamenev, in an article published in *Pravda*, the Party journal, on March 28 took a position on the war with which many Mensheviks and SR's would have fully agreed. He wrote:

> Our slogan is — pressure on the Provisional Government with the aim of forcing it openly, before world democracy, and immediately to come forth with an attempt to induce all the belligerent countries forthwith to start negotiations concerning the means of stopping the World War.
>
> Up to that time, however, each remains at his post.[12]

Kamenev was by no means alone. His position reflected the dominant view of the party leadership in Petrograd at that time.[13]

Meanwhile, Lenin, still in Zurich, was plotting a different course. In a letter to Madame Kollontai (March 16, 1917) he wrote, "We, of course, retain our opposition to the defense of the fatherland." [14] The next day, he wrote again,

> In my opinion, our main task is to guard against getting entangled in foolish attempts at "unity" with the social-patriots . . . and to continue the work of *our own* party in a consistently *internationalist* spirit.
>
> Our immediate task is . . . to prepare the seizure of power by the *Soviets of Workers' Deputies*. Only this power can give bread, *peace*, and freedom.[15]

"Bread, peace, and freedom" — these slogans were to be endlessly reiterated and emphasized, and they were to lift Bolshevism to power. "We shall see," wrote Lenin to Madame Kollontai, "how the People's Freedom Party [the Kadets] . . . will give the people freedom, bread, and peace . . . We shall see!" [16]

On the evening of April 16, Lenin arrived at the Finland Station in Petrograd. There he was coolly greeted by Chkheidze, the President of the Soviet. "We suppose," said the Menshevik Chkheidze, "that the main problem of the revolutionary democracy is the defense of our Revolution against any attacks on it, whether from without or from within. We suppose that for this end not disunion but consolidation of the ranks of the whole democracy is necessary. We hope that you will pursue these objectives along with us." [17]

It was to be a vain hope. Lenin's plan of campaign had already matured, and coöperation with the Chkheidzes had no place in it. His first words to Kamenev were a sharp rebuke for the tone of *Pravda*. In a speech delivered to his own followers on the day after his arrival, he demanded a complete break with the old line of "revolutionary defensism" and a repudiation of the Provisional Government. He called for "a republic of Soviets of Workers', Agricultural Labourers' and Peasants' Deputies throughout the land, from top to bottom, . . . abolition of the police, the army, the bureaucracy," and an arrangement by which "all officers [were] to be elected and to be subject to recall at any time, their salaries not to exceed the average wage of a competent worker." He proposed "confiscation of all private lands, nationalization . . . immediate merger of all the banks in the country into one general national bank, over which the Soviet of Workers' Deputies should have control . . . control of social production and distribution of goods . . . immediate calling of a party convention . . . changing the party programme . . . changing the name of the party," and "rebuilding the International." [18]

Lenin's intransigence was at first almost completely unacceptable to his own party. At a meeting of the Petrograd committee of the party, his theses were rejected by thirteen votes to two, with one abstention.[19] Kamenev, in an article in *Pravda* entitled "Our Differences," referred to these theses as Lenin's "*personal* opinion"; "as regards Comrade Lenin's general line," he wrote, "it appears to us unacceptable inasmuch as it proceeds from the assumption that the bourgeois-democratic revolution *has been completed* and it builds on the immediate transformation of this revolution into a Socialist revolution." [20]

The controversy between Lenin and Kamenev exposed a deep fissure within Bolshevik ranks which was to continue right up to the seizure of power, and even beyond. To Bolsheviks of Kamenev's persuasion, Russia was simply not ripe for a socialist revolution. Like the Mensheviks and like Lenin up to the 1905 revolution, these Bolsheviks made a sharp demarcation between the successive stages of bourgeois-democratic and socialist revolution. The first stage had to be completed before one could embark on the second, and the tactics suitable for the first stage excluded a Bolshevik *coup d'état* and the assumption of supreme power. In the perspective of Kamenev and his followers, the Russian revolution still had to run a long bourgeois course. The agrarian revolution had to be completed. The bourgeois-democratic revolution would culminate in the establishment of a revolutionary dictatorship of the proletariat and the peasantry, and only then would the socialist revolution become the order of the day.

To Lenin this perspective was now anathema. Impatient to take power, he brushed aside Kamenev's delaying formula. "Our doctrine," he quoted Marx, "is not a dogma, but a guide to action." [21] "The peculiarity of the present situation in Russia," Lenin declared, "is that it represents a *transition* from the first stage of the revolution, which, because of the inadequate organisation and insufficient class-consciousness of the proletariat, led to the assumption of power by the bourgeoisie — to its second stage which is to place power in the hands of the proletariat and the poorest strata of the peasantry." [22] "To that extent," Lenin insisted, "the bourgeois, or the bourgeois-democratic, revolution in Russia is *completed*." [23] Kamenev's use of the formula of "the revolutionary-democratic dictatorship of the proletariat and the peasantry" seemed to him "antiquated." " 'The Soviet of Workers' and Soldiers' Deputies,' — here," Lenin argued, "you have 'revolutionary-democratic dictatorship of the proletariat and peasantry' already realised in life." "Theory, my friend," Lenin goaded Kamenev, "is grey, but green is the eternal tree of life." The orthodox theory of the "Old Bolsheviks" that "the rule of the proletariat and peasantry, their dictatorship, can and must follow the rule of the bourgeoisie" had to be discarded as no longer corresponding with "living reality." [24]

Instead, Lenin offered his conception of dual power, "the fact that by the side of the Provisional Government, the government of the *bourgeoisie*, there has developed *another*, as yet weak, embryonic, but undoubtedly real and growing government — the Soviets of Workers' and Soldiers' Deputies." [25] To Lenin it appeared incontrovertible that such a combination could not endure. "There can be no two powers in a state." [26] For the moment, the two powers were interlocked; the Provisional Government rested on the support of the Soviet, and the Soviet yielded such support because it was still under the spell of "petty-bourgeois" delusions implanted by the SR and Menshevik leaders of the Soviet. These delusions had to be destroyed if the Provisional Government was to be overthrown. "The only way it can and must be overthrown," Lenin insisted, "is by winning over the majority in the Soviets." [27] Thus the slogan "All Power to the Soviets" merged into the recipe of all power to the Bolsheviks in the Soviets.

Despite the opposition of Kamenev and others whom Lenin described contemptuously as "Old Bolsheviks," Lenin carried the day. His program was approved first at the Petrograd City Conference of the party, which took place from April 27 to May 5, 1917, and then at the even more important All-Russian Conference of the party (described in party histories as the "April Conference"), which lasted from May 7 to May 12, 1917. The resolutions adopted by the conferences represented a great personal triumph for Lenin. Although the opposition continued to smolder and, at critical moments, even erupted into open defiance, henceforth Lenin's ascendancy in the party was never effectively challenged.

The End of the Honeymoon and the Rise of Bolshevik Influence

Meanwhile, events were moving in a direction which the Bolsheviks could only welcome. The honeymoon period of revolutionary exaltation and camaraderie was drawing to a close. The issues and the problems of state which the March Revolution had inherited could no longer be evaded. The economic situation continued to deteriorate, and the workers in the factories were increasingly rebellious in the face of higher living costs and food shortages. While the Provisional Government temporized with the land problem, peasant restiveness mounted and encroachments on the estates of landlords grew bolder. Discipline in the armed forces steadily deteriorated, particularly among the inactive garrisons in rear areas such as Petrograd. Military units resisted assignment to the front, and insubordination and desertion were on the rise.

If the Provisional Government was aware of the pressing character of these problems, it showed itself either unable or unwilling to come to grips with them. Blinded by the patriotic resurgence of the early days of the Revolution and determined not to betray its self-imposed mandate of fulfilling Russia's international obligations and safeguarding Russia's position as a great power, it insisted on fighting the war to a finish in the face of patent evidence that the war was becoming increasingly unpopular.

The first major crisis developed with the publication on May 3 of Foreign Minister Milyukov's note to the Allies emphasizing Russia's determination to carry on the war and fulfill its obligations to the Allies. Soldiers, sailors, and workers marched in demonstrative protest under banners bearing such inscriptions as "Down with Milyukov," "Down with the Provisional Government," and "Down with the War." As a result of the storm of disapproval which Milyukov's note had aroused, the government issued "an explanation" which was designed to square its war aims with the demand of the leaders of the Soviet for a peace without annexations and indemnities. Guchkov, the Minister of War, and Milyukov resigned from the cabinet. After protracted negotiations with the leaders of the Soviet in the course of which the Executive Committee first pronounced against participation in the cabinet and then reversed itself, Prince Lvov announced a new cabinet on May 18 which included three SR's — Kerensky as Minister of War, Chernov as Minister of Agriculture, and Pereverzev as Minister of Justice; two Mensheviks — Tseretelli as Minister for Posts and Telegraphs, and Skobelev as Minister for Labor; and the Populist-Socialist Peshekhonov as Minister for Food. This coalition cabinet, in which the moderate socialist parties which dominated the Soviet participated and for which they necessarily assumed responsibility, insured an exit from the immediate crisis, but it still left the aspirations for peace, land, and bread to be fulfilled.

Indeed, the moderate socialist parties of the Soviet, by shouldering formal governmental responsibility for the continuing crisis, were maneuvered into a position in which they inevitably became a target for mass frustration and dissatisfaction. The sobering complexities of the problems which the government faced were not conducive to hasty action. Delay, on the other hand, only strengthened the force of extremism. Caught in the tangles of coalition in a period when revolutionary zeal was still intensifying, the moderate socialists found themselves compelled to dampen the revolutionary ardor of the dissatisfied and were condemned to lose influence even with their own supporters.

This process did not take place all at once. At the National Congress of Soviets of Peasant Deputies, held in Petrograd from May 17 until June 10, the Bolsheviks mustered an insignificant minority of fourteen out of a total of 1,115 delegates.[28] The congress was dominated by the SR's who wrote the resolutions and elected a heavy majority of the Executive Committee. By late summer, as a result of the failure of the Provisional Government to come to grips with the agrarian problem, the SR Party itself divided into a right and left wing, the former still giving support to the Provisional Government while the latter called for the transfer of power to a government "responsible to the Soviets." At the meeting of the Council of the SR Party in late August 1917, the left wing mobilized thirty-five votes to fifty-four for the right wing majority.[29] The next month, the left wing captured control of the party's strategically important Petrograd committee.[30] The steady growth of left-wing influence in the SR Party served as an index of growing peasant disenchantment with the policy of the Provisional Government. It was to lead the Left to break away in November to form an independent party of Left Socialist-Revolutionary-Internationalists and even to join the Bolsheviks in a coalition which did much to sustain their regime in its early precarious days.

The rise of direct Bolshevik influence was more evident in the key cities. As early as June 13, the Workers' Section of the Petrograd Soviet, by a vote of 173 to 144, passed a resolution endorsing the Bolshevik formula of "All Power to the Soviets." Meeting at about the same time, June 12–16, a Conference of Factory Committees in Petrograd yielded a Bolshevik majority.[31] At the first All-Russian Congress of Soviets, which met in Petrograd on June 16, the Bolsheviks were still in a definite minority. Of the 777 delegates who declared their political affiliations, 285 were SR's, 248 Mensheviks, 105 Bolsheviks, and 32 Menshevik-Internationalists. The remainder belonged to various minor parties and groupings.[32] At this stage of revolutionary development, Bolshevik support was largely concentrated among the workers of the larger industrial centers; the military formations had yet to be effectively penetrated.

Meanwhile, the Bolshevik Party continued to gather its forces and strengthen its organization. At the so-called All-Russian April Conference (May 7–12), the 151 assembled delegates represented 79,204 party members,[33] over three times the membership figure on the eve of the March Revolution. At the party's Sixth Congress (August 8–16), the 157 voting delegates who participated represented 112 organizations with a membership of 177,000.[34] Sverdlov, who delivered the organizational report of the Central Committee at the Congress, claimed a total membership of 200,000 distributed among 162 organizations. Almost half of the membership was concentrated in the Petrograd and Moscow areas. Other strong points were the industrial areas of the Urals and the Don Basin and the Finnish and Baltic areas where Bolshevik influence was particularly powerful among the sailors of the fleet.[35] At this Congress, the *Mezhraiontsy* (Interborough Organization of the United Socialist-Democrats), some four thousand strong, merged with the Bolsheviks. This group, which numbered among its leaders such well-known figures as Trotsky, Lunacharsky, Uritsky, and Volodarsky, shared the Bolshevik attitude toward the war and had coöperated closely with the Bolsheviks on tactical matters in the preceding months. The accession of the Mezhraiontsy was especially important because of the talents of its leadership. Trotsky, in particular, was to play a dominant and crucial role in organizing the insurrection in the November days.

The flooding of the party by new members and the proliferation of new local party units inevitably created serious problems of direction and control. The sheer mass of the fresh forces which inundated the party in the 1917 days carried an implied threat of swamping the old leadership. The Bolshevik Party of 1917 was far from being the monolithic organization of which Lenin had dreamed in 1903 or which it later became. Lenin tried, so far as it lay in his power, to keep the threads of control in the hands of the seasoned underground veterans who had been closely associated with him in the pre-Revolutionary days. The Central Committee, except for the new recruits from the Mezhraiontsy, was constituted almost entirely of such elements. Of the 157 voting delegates at the Sixth

Congress, 149 had worked in the party organization since 1914 or earlier.[36]

Responsibility for the organizational work of the party was concentrated in Lenin's faithful lieutenant, Sverdlov, who officiated as the one-man secretariat of the Central Committee and gave the party machine such coherence as it was able to attain. Through Sverdlov, communication was maintained with the local party units, workers were dispatched where needed, and visits to or from the center were arranged. The Central Committee as a body devoted itself chiefly to broad policy and tactical matters; most of its energies were concentrated on developments in the capital, Petrograd. The guidance it provided for the party was exerted largely through *Pravda* and other party publications. Relationships between the Central Committee in Petrograd and adjoining party organizations in the Baltic, in Finland, and Moscow were fairly close. Communications with the peripheral areas, despite the strenuous efforts of Sverdlov, remained tenuous and adventitious. The new recruits who formed the party base were frequently illiterate, sometimes turbulent, badly disciplined, and unreliable.

The authority of the party leadership rested largely on its capacity to persuade and convince rather than to direct and dictate. In 1917, agitation and propaganda were the keys to party leadership; many who emerged from the ranks to become leaders in this period were precisely those who showed themselves gifted agitators and propagandists. If some semblance of order and homogeneity was imposed on the heterogeneous elements that flocked to the Bolshevik banner, it was due less to the perfection of the organizational instrument than to the party leadership's ability to articulate slogans and improvise tactics which rallied the support of the rank-and-file. It is symptomatic of this stage of development in Lenin's career that, under the influence of the revolutionary ferment, he temporarily abandoned the distrust of mass spontaneity which characterized so much of his earlier outlook. "Do not be afraid," he now cried, "of the initiative and independence of the masses." [37] The transformation of the Bolshevik Party from a small conspiratorial band into a mass revolutionary organization was a visible expression of this change of outlook, although Lenin, as always, took precautions to insure that control of the organization which he had created would not gravitate into other hands.

The Bolshevik march to power can, for purposes of analysis, be conveniently divided into three periods. During the first period of upsurge, which ended with the July uprising of soldiers and workers in Petrograd, the Bolsheviks gathered their forces, sought to increase their strength in the Soviets, and called for a transfer of "All Power to the Soviets." During the second period of reaction, which lasted from the repression of the party in mid-July until the collapse of the Kornilov plot in September, the slogan of "All Power to the Soviets" was withdrawn. The Soviets were denounced as "fig leaves of the counterrevolution," and the party was called upon to prepare its forces for the decisive struggle while avoiding the danger of premature outbreaks.[38] For a brief moment, when the danger of the Kornilov coup was at its height, Lenin returned to "the pre-July demand of all power to the Soviets, a government of S.-R.'s and Mensheviks responsible to the Soviets." [39] But this slogan quickly disappeared with the evaporation of the Kornilov danger. The third period began in mid-September with a resurgence of Bolshevik strength and the attainment of majorities in the Petrograd and Moscow Soviets. During this period, the slogan of "All Power to the Soviets" was again revived,[40] and the summons went out to prepare the insurrection.

The First Phase: Caution the Motto

During the first period, the Bolsheviks moved relatively carefully. They were still a small minority. When the Petrograd Bolshevik Committee issued the slogan of "Down With the Provisional Government" during the May demonstrations, Lenin rebuked the committee for its premature adventurism.[41] During the next few months, the Bolshevik leaders concentrated their major energies on winning a dominant position in the Petrograd factories. By mid-June their efforts had been crowned with considerable success; they won control of the Workers' Section of the Petrograd Soviet and carried a resolution embodying the Bolshevik formula of transfer of power to the Soviets. As their mass support increased, the Bolsheviks grew bolder. The party leadership voted on June 21 to stage a large street demonstration two days later. There is evidence to indicate that some of the more aggressive and adventurous spirits among the Bolsheviks anticipated a clash with the authorities and were laying their plans for a seizure of power in Petrograd. But this was a design not shared by the responsible leadership of the party, who at this point were all too conscious of their relative weakness in the provinces and in the army. Indeed, the leaders themselves were divided about the wisdom and risks of the demonstration. When both the Executive Committee of the Petrograd Soviet and the All-Russian Soviet Congress joined in prohibiting it, the Bolshevik Central Committee decided at the last moment to call it off.[42]

A week later the Bolsheviks had their revenge when the Congress of Soviets authorized a demonstration, held July 1, which was intended to be a vote of confidence in the Congress. Instead, it was transformed into a triumphal procession for Bolshevism, with the Bolsheviks' banners demanding "Bread, Peace, and Freedom" and "All Power to the Soviets" dominating the demonstration.

The First of July demonstration coincided with the launching of the ill-fated Kerensky offensive on the Galician front. The announcement of early successes kindled a brief flare-up of patriotic ardor. When the offensive turned into a debacle, it became crystal clear that the army had lost its will to fight. Many of the peasant soldiers began to vote against the war "with their feet" by deserting in droves and rushing back to their villages to participate in the partition of the landed estates which was beginning unofficially to gather momentum.

The failure of the offensive seriously weakened the position of the Provisional Government and its Menshevik and SR supporters. They could offer the country neither victory nor peace. Meanwhile, the influence of the Bolsheviks was obviously mounting, particularly in the Petrograd area among the factory workers, the soldiers of the inactive garrison, and the sailors of Kronstadt and the Baltic fleet. The only potentially effective counterpoise to Bolshevik power was the officer corps and such loyal regiments as it could command. The moderate socialists thus faced a painful dilemma. The deepening Revolution polarized the forces of revolution and counterrevolution. If the moderate socialists invoked the support of the army generals to suppress the Bolshevik threat, they faced the hazard of being themselves displaced by a dictatorship of the generals from the Right. If they joined with the Bolsheviks to ward off the threat of a rightist *coup d'état*, they faced an even more certain danger that the Bolsheviks would attempt to dump them on the "dust heap of history" at the first favorable opportunity.

The moderates began by temporizing with the first of these unpalatable alternatives. The July risings raised the specter of a Bolshevik seizure of power. Soon after the launching of the Kerensky offensive, discontent and unrest spread among the military units and factory workers of Petrograd. The Bolshevik leadership, not yet ready to try to take power, sought at first to prevent street manifestations. When that proved impossible, the Central Committee issued a call for "a peaceful organized demonstration" to demand the assumption of power by the Soviets. The movement of July 16–18 quickly got out of control.[43] Masses of soldiers and workers poured through the streets shooting aimlessly, breaking into houses and stores, and looting their contents. For two days both the government and the Soviet were powerless to deal with the rioting mobs; order began to be restored only on July 18 when reliable troops were brought in to patrol the streets of the capital.

The July rising represented one of the most curious episodes of the Revolution. The Bolshevik Central Committee — believing that the rising was premature but feeling that it could not dissociate itself from the elemental activism of the demonstrators – assumed the leadership reluctantly. The crowds marched to the Soviet demanding that the moderate socialists who still controlled the Executive Committee take power; the leaders of the Executive Committee replied by calling on the demonstrators to disperse. With both the Bolsheviks and the Executive Committee unprepared to assume the reins of government, the rising was deprived of a political objective. The soldiers and workers were left no alternative except to trickle back to the barracks and factories with a sense of frustration and bewilderment.

The government, relying on the loyal regiments which were available to it, now moved to the counterattack. The Ministry of Justice released documents designed to prove that Lenin was a "German spy." On the morning of the eighteenth, the offices of *Pravda* were raided and a newly established Bolshevik printing plant destroyed. The next day, an order was issued for the arrest of Lenin, Zinoviev, and Kamenev. Lenin and Zinoviev succeeded in avoiding arrest by going into hiding; but during the next few weeks Kamenev, Trotsky, Lunacharsky, Madame Kollontai, and many lesser Bolsheviks were apprehended and imprisoned. Some of the more turbulent regiments were dissolved. On July 25, four days after Kerensky replaced Prince Lvov as Premier, the death penalty at the front was restored.

This display of firmness by the Provisional Government was more fictive than real. Trotsky and other prominent Bolsheviks, to be sure, were confined to prison, but they were released in mid-September after the failure of the Kornilov coup. The second level of the party apparatus remained largely intact, and Lenin continued to direct its operations from his various hideouts. Agitators were still at work in the factories and the garrisons, and Petrograd and the Baltic fleet remained Bolshevik strongholds. The Sixth Congress of the party, which met *sub rosa* in August, registered a striking increase in party membership. Despite repression, the party continued to flourish, and the policy of striking at a few leaders left their roots of support still intact.

The Second Phase: Preparation of Forces

The lesson which the Bolshevik leadership drew from the July rising was embodied in the resolutions of the Sixth Congress. The slogan "All Power to the Soviets" was temporarily withdrawn.[44] The party was warned that power had passed "into the hands of the counterrevolutionary bourgeoisie" and that it was necessary to organize to wrest power from it.

The Congress appeared to commit the party to the path of insurrection, but it set no time schedules, and indeed, with the experience of the July days fresh in mind, it warned against the danger of premature outbreaks. The party was still waiting for the revolutionary tide to come to full flood.

Meanwhile, Kerensky sought to strengthen the position of the Provisional Government by invoking the support of "the live forces of the country," as the current phrase had it. The Moscow State Conference, which assembled from August 25 to August 28 at the call of the Provisional Government, included representatives of every class, profession, and shade of political opinion in Russia except Bolshevism. The conference had no legislative mandate; it was intended to be an advisory, consultative body which would provide a sounding board of national sentiment.

This effort to rally "the flower of the nation" behind the Provisional Government turned into a dismal fiasco. To begin with, the absence of the Bolsheviks gave all references to national unity a somewhat specious ring. Despite a dramatically staged reconciliation in the course of which the Soviet leader Tseretelli and the prominent industrialist Bublikov exchanged handshakes, the conference revealed a deep and tragic chasm between the Right, which was heavily overrepresented, and the moderate socialists of the Left. While the conference was in session, preparations for a right-wing military *coup d'état* were already far advanced. The speeches of such military leaders as Kornilov and Kaledin bordered on open defiance of the government and inspired a bitter taunt from Lenin: "Kaledin mocked the Mensheviks and S.-R.'s who were compelled to keep silent. The Cossack general spat in their faces, and they wiped themselves off, saying: 'Divine dew!'" [45] Kerensky's efforts to pour oratorical oil on the troubled waters were in vain. His speeches, as Trotsky noted later, "were merely a sumptuous pounding of water in a mortar." [46] The basic alignment of forces was left undisturbed.

With the conclusion of the conference, the military plot to seize power and install General Kornilov as dictator moved toward its climax. Kornilov's plan involved an envelopment and march on Petrograd by Cossack, Caucasian, and other supposedly loyal divisions. Before the plot could be executed, Kerensky got wind of it and ordered the immediate dismissal of Kornilov as Commander-in-Chief of the Army. Kornilov ignored the order and, in a mood of high confidence, gave the word for the "promenade" to proceed to Petrograd. Difficulties quickly developed — railroad workers sabotaged trains carrying the troops of the expedition; telegraph operators refused to dispatch the messages of the staff; agitators penetrated Kornilov's picked divisions and, without too great difficulty, persuaded them not to fight against the legal government.

The collapse of the Kornilov expedition marked an important turning point in the Revolution. It revealed the emptiness of the power of the generals and the weakness of the appeal of traditional conservatism. When troops regarded by the general staff as its most reliable support were no longer willing to obey the commands of their officers, it became patently clear that the officer corps had lost the power to determine the destiny of the Russian Revolution. Who would inherit the loyalties which the generals had forfeited? With the elimination of Kornilov, the ground was prepared for the final battle between the moderate socialists and the Bolsheviks.

The first temporary effect of the Kornilov scare, however, was to throw the moderate socialists and the Bolsheviks into each others' arms. On Menshevik initiative, the Central Executive Committee (VTsIK) of the Congress of Soviets created a Committee for Struggle with Counter-revolution in which Bolsheviks, Mensheviks, and SR's were represented by three members each. For a brief moment at the height of the Kornilov crisis, Lenin played with the idea of a compromise, an arrangement by which the Mensheviks and SR's would organize a government responsible to the Soviets and "the Bolsheviks . . . would refrain from immediately advancing the demand for the passing of power to the proletariat and the poorest peasants." [47]

But this idea was abandoned almost as quickly as it was conceived. In a letter to the Central Committee of the Bolshevik Party written on September 12, Lenin made his own position clear: "We will fight, we are fighting against Kornilov, even *as Kerensky's troops do,* but we do not support Kerensky. *On the contrary,* we expose his weakness. There is the difference. It is rather a subtle difference, but it is highly essential and one must not forget it." Lenin called on his cohorts to intensify their propaganda among the workers, soldiers, and peasants involved in the struggle with Kornilov: "Keep up their enthusiasm; encourage them to beat up the generals and officers who express themselves in favour of Kornilov; urge *them to* demand the immediate transfer of the land to the peasants; give *them* the idea of the necessity of arresting Rodzyanko and Milyukov, dispersing the State Duma, shutting down the *Ryech* and other bourgeois papers, and instituting investigations against them. The 'Left' S.-R.'s must be especially pushed on in this direction." [48] The rise in mass militancy which accompanied the frustration of the Kornilov coup worked to the advantage of the Bolsheviks. By mid-September a strong shift of sympathy toward them was apparent. For the first time, Bolshevik resolutions commanded majorities in both the Petrograd and Moscow Soviets.[49]

Meanwhile, the position of Kerensky and the moderate socialists was visibly deteriorating. The defeat of Kornilov had eliminated one contender for power, but, with Bolshevism resurgent, a far more formidable antagonist confronted the government. After the Kornilov affair, the officer corps spared no love for Kerensky; in any case, its support by this time had become an asset of dubious value. With defeatism rampant in the army and many units in a state of mutinous disintegration, the determination of Kerensky and the moderate socialist leaders to carry on with the war was hardly calculated to make them very popular with the rank-and-file soldier or sailor.

Even in the countryside, where the SR Party had its strongest support, the position of the government was perceptibly weakening. Faced with the autumn upswing of peasant violence and land seizures, Kerensky countered on September 21 by issuing a military order forbidding the peasants to take other people's land or property and threatening them with dire legal penalties if they persisted. Since there was no power capable of enforcing the order, the peasants paid no attention to it. Its only effect was to serve as an irritant and drive the peasants into the arms of the Left SR's and, sometimes, into the arms of the Bolsheviks, who were willing to bless what the peasants in any case were determined to do. In the cities, industrial disorganization spread and intensified. The government was powerless either to restore worker discipline or to check the rise in living costs which helped undermine it. The Bolsheviks, with their call for workers' control, intensified the chaos and were themselves the beneficiaries of the chaos which they helped create.

The political coalition which supported the Provisional Government showed many signs of strain and weakness. After the resignation of the four Kadet ministers from the coalition cabinet on July 15 as a protest against the government's concession to Ukrainian demands for autonomy, and particularly after the Kornilov affair, many Kadets of the Right hardly scrupled to conceal their distaste for Kerensky. They gave him grudging and reluctant support only because Bolshevism appeared to them so much the greater evil. Nor were the Mensheviks united in their approval of the Provisional Government. A substantial group of Menshevik Internationalists led by Martov was sharply critical of Kerensky's foreign policy; the backing which they extended was at best wavering and hesitant.

The situation within Kerensky's own SR Party was, if anything, even more critical. The resignation of Chernov, perhaps the most respected of SR leaders, from the Kerensky government on September 13 in protest against the postponement of a land settlement, did much to undermine the position of Kerensky within his own party. The party divided into a right-wing minority which supported Kerensky, a growing left wing which moved close to the Bolsheviks, and a large center group led by Chernov, which occupied an intermediate position. On every side, Kerensky's support seemed to be melting away.

Toward the end of September, Kerensky made a last desperate effort to cement the coalition which was so obviously falling apart. On September 27, the so-called "Democratic" Conference assembled in Petrograd; the twelve hundred odd delegates represented Soviets, coöperatives, trade unions, and municipal and county dumas. The Conference first passed a resolution to exclude Kadets from the coalition, and then added a final touch of absurdity to the proceedings by overwhelmingly defeating the formula of "coalition without the Kadets." When the SR orator Minor made his plea for a coalition government with the warning that otherwise "we will begin to cut to pieces," voices from the floor inquired, "Whom?" Minor's reply, "We will cut each other to pieces," [50] had more than a touch of prophetic vision.

The Democratic Conference was succeeded by the so-called Council of the Republic, or Pre-Parliament, a much smaller body which gave more substantial representation to the nonsocialist groups which had been meagerly represented in the larger Conference. The Pre-Parliament was intended to serve as a stop-gap consultative and deliberative body until the convocation of the much-delayed Constituent Assembly which was scheduled to open December 11. The first session of the Pre-Parliament was marked by a mass walkout of the Bolshevik delegation.[51] The departure of the Bolsheviks removed a discordant element from the council's deliberations, but it left the same old problems to be resolved and the same inability to come to grips with them.

The Third Phase: Insurrection

Meanwhile, the Bolsheviks debated the question of insurrection. Lenin, who was still in hiding, precipitated the issue in two letters to the party's Central Committee. The first letter, dated September 25–27, began "Having obtained a majority in the Soviets of Workers' and Soldiers' Deputies of both capitals, the Bolsheviks can and must take power into their hands." [52] "To 'wait' for the Constituent Assembly," Lenin insisted, "would be wrong. . . It would be naïve to wait for a 'formal' majority on the side of the Bolsheviks; no revolution ever waits for *this*. . . History will not forgive us if we do not assume power now." [53] The second letter, dated September 26–27, continued:

Victory is assured to us . . . we must *push* our whole fraction *into the factories and barracks*: its place is there; the pulse of life is there; the source of saving the revolution is there. . .

And in order to treat uprising in a Marxist way, *i.e.*, as an art, we must at the same time, without losing a single moment, organise the staff of the insurrectionary detachments; designate the forces; move the loyal regiments to the most important points; surround the Alexander Theatre; occupy Peter and Paul Fortress; arrest the general staff and the government; move against the military cadets, the Wild Division, etc., such detachments as will die rather than allow the enemy to move to the centre of the city; we must mobilise the armed workers, call them to a last desperate battle, occupy at once the telegraph and telephone stations, place *our* staff of the uprising at the central telephone station, connect it by wire with all the factories, the regiments, the points of armed fighting, etc.

"Of course," Lenin concluded, "this is all by way of an example, to *illustrate* the idea that at the present moment it is impossible to remain loyal to the revolution *without treating uprising as an art*." [54]

The Central Committee took up Lenin's letters at its meeting on September 28.[55] They exploded like bombshells. Some four years later, Bukharin, at an evening of reminiscences, described the meeting of the group:

> We all gasped. Nobody had posed the question so abruptly. . . At first all were bewildered. Afterwards, having talked it over, we made a decision. Perhaps that was the sole case in the history of our party when the Central Committee unanimously decided to burn a letter of Lenin. . . Although we believed unconditionally that in Petersburg and Moscow we should succeed in seizing the power, we assumed that in the provinces we could not yet hold out, that having seized the power and dispersed the Democratic Conference we could not fortify ourselves in the rest of Russia.[56]

The actual minutes of the meeting of the Central Committee are more laconic and provide a somewhat contradictory version of the affair. They merely record that by a vote of six to four, with six abstentions, the Committee voted to preserve only one copy of the letters.[57] Kamenev, as in earlier days, emerged as one of the leaders of the opposition to Lenin. His resolution, which proposed an outright repudiation of the conclusions contained in Lenin's letters, failed of approval. The vote was not recorded.[58]

While the Central Committee hesitated and busied itself with such questions as the party's attitude toward the Democratic Conference and the Pre-Parliament, Lenin grew more and more impatient. From the beginning, he demanded a boycott of both bodies on the ground that the pressing task before the party was the preparation of the insurrection. The decision of the party led by Kamenev and Rykov went in favor of participation, although the Bolshevik delegation did withdraw at the first meeting of the Pre-Parliament.[59] In his diary on October 6 Lenin noted, "Not all is well at the 'parliamentary' top of our party. . . There is not the slightest doubt that in the 'top' of our party we note vacillations that may become *ruinous*." But he reserved a plaudit for Trotsky: "Trotsky was for the boycott. Bravo, Comrade Trotsky!" [60]

Faced with substantial opposition in the Central Committee, Lenin sought to mobilize his supporters in the local organizations. While the Central Committee continued to temporize, Lenin grew desperate. In a letter of October 12, he tried to shock the party leaders into action by proffering his own resignation from the Central Committee.[61] No action was taken on the offer of resignation, and Lenin followed up his implied threat of war against the Central Committee by firing a volley of letters at the Petrograd and Moscow committees and the Bolshevik participants in the Northern Regional Congress of Soviets. With these letters,[62] Lenin sought to build a fire under the Central Committee.

The tactics were effective. On Lenin's initiative, the Petrograd City Conference, held October 20–24, passed a resolution which "insistently" requested "the Central Committee to take all measures for the leadership of the inevitable insurrection of the workers, soldiers and peasants." [63] The denouement came at a meeting of the Central Committee on October 23 in Petrograd, to which Lenin journeyed in disguise from his hiding place in Finland. Present at the meeting besides Lenin were Zinoviev, Kamenev, Trotsky, Stalin, Sverdlov, Uritsky, Dzerzhinsky, Kollontai, Bubnov, Sokolnikov, and Lomov. The minutes record that Lenin reproached his colleagues for "a certain indifference toward the question of uprising" [64] and that his restatement of the case for insurrection was apparently powerful enough to win the support of all committee members except Kamenev and Zinoviev. By a vote of ten to two, the Central Committee placed "the armed uprising on the order of the day." "Recognizing therefore," the resolution read, "that an armed uprising is inevitable and the time perfectly ripe, the Central Committee proposes to all the organizations of the party to act accordingly and to discuss and decide from this point of view all the practical questions." [65]

The issue was still not finally resolved. Kamenev and Zinoviev were adamant in their opposition to the Central Committee's decision. Following the example set by Lenin earlier, on October 24 they sent a letter to the Petrograd and Moscow city committees, the Moscow and Finnish regional committees, and the Bolshevik fractions of the Central Executive Committee (VTsIK) and of the Northern Regional Congress of Soviets, in which they stated the case for postponement of the insurrection. The arguments of Kamenev and Zinoviev reduced themselves to three: [66] (1) the majority of the people of Russia were still not with the Bolsheviks; (2) the international proletariat was not yet ready to come to the assistance of the Russian revolution; (3) the likelihood of a successful uprising was remote.[67] Proceeding from this analysis, Zinoviev and Kamenev argued that it would be suicidal to stake the entire game on one card. Instead, they called for a continued buildup of strength through the Soviets and the Constituent Assembly. "The Constituent Assembly plus the Soviets — this is that combined type of state institutions towards which we are going. It is on this political basis that our party is acquiring enormous chances for a real victory." [68]

The stubborn opposition of Kamenev and Zinoviev to the insurrection was again made manifest at an enlarged meeting of the Central Committee on October 29 in which key leaders of the Petrograd party organization also participated. At this meeting, Lenin's resolution calling for the most energetic preparation of the armed uprising carried by a vote of nineteen to two, with four abstentions. The lack of unanimity in the group was more sharply brought out by the vote on Zinoviev's resolution, which stated: "Without delaying the reconnoitering preparatory steps, it is considered that such uprisings are inadmissable until a conference [is held] with the Bolshevik part of the Congress of Soviets." This time the vote was six for and fifteen against, with three abstaining. At the conclusion of the meeting, Kamenev announced his resignation from the Central Committee with a warning that the party had embarked on the road to disaster.[69] On October 31, Kamenev published a statement in *Novaya Zhizn'*, a nonparty paper of the Left, in which, speaking in his own name and in that of Zinoviev, he declared himself "against any attempt to take the initiative of an armed uprising." [70]

The hint in the declaration that the party had taken its stand for insurrection and the violation of party discipline involved in the disclosure sent Lenin into a towering rage. In an angry letter addressed to party members that same day, he demanded the immediate expulsion of Kamenev and Zinoviev from the party. "I say outright that I do not consider them comrades any longer, and that I will fight with all my power both in the Central Committee and at the congress to expel them both from the party." [71] Meanwhile, the party faced the problem of undoing the damage of Kamenev's revelation. At a meeting of the Petrograd Soviet, also on October 31, Trotsky stated that no immediate uprising was planned. Kamenev, who spoke after Trotsky, blandly associated himself with Trotsky's statement. To Lenin, this added insult to injury. In a letter to the Central Committee dated November 1, he again reiterated his demand for the expulsion of the "strike-breakers" from the party.[72]

The issue came to a head at a meeting of the Central Committee on November 2 from which Lenin was absent. That morning before the meeting, there had appeared in the party's central organ, *Rabochii Put'* (Workers' Road), side by side with Lenin's attack on Kamenev and Zinoviev, a letter from Zinoviev announcing that his views were "very far" from those which Lenin combatted and that he subscribed to Trotsky's declaration in the Soviet. Appended to Zinoviev's letter was an editorial note prepared by Stalin in which he expressed the hope that the declaration of Comrade Zinoviev (as well as the declaration of Comrade Kamenev in the Soviet) could be considered as closing the debate. "The sharpness of the tone of Comrade Lenin's article," Stalin continued, "does not change the fact that basically we remain of one mind." [73]

Stalin's effort to play the role of peacemaker had only modified success. Though Kamenev and Zinoviev were not expelled from the party, Kamenev's resignation from the Central Committee was ratified by a vote of five to three, with Stalin in the minority. At the same time, the Central Committee voted to impose on Kamenev and Zinoviev "the obligation not to make any statements against the decision of the C.C. and the line of work laid out by it." [74] It also approved "the proposition of Milyutin that no member of the C.C. shall have the right to speak against the adopted decisions of the C.C." [75] Kamenev and Zinoviev suppressed their dissatisfaction and refrained from further outbursts against the uprising. A last-minute truce was arranged, and Kamenev reappeared as a member of the Central Committee at its meeting of November 6.[76] At the moment of insurrection, the unity of the top command was restored. It was not to be long-lasting.

While the battle raged in the Central Committee, preparations for the uprising were going forward. The military forces on which the Bolsheviks relied were (1) the Red Guard recruited from factory workers; (2) the sailors of Kronstadt and the Baltic fleet; and (3) the units of the Petrograd garrison which were favorably inclined. Of these, the most dependable was the workers' Red Guard, approximately twenty thousand strong. Compared with professional soldiers, they were poorly trained and equipped, but what they lacked in arms they made up in morale and dedication to the Bolshevik cause. The sailors were unruly and undisciplined, but their fighting spirit was high, and they too could be counted on to play an active role in the insurrection. Bolshevik influence in the fleet was strong, though it had to dispute for supremacy with units of Left SR's and Anarchists. The most dubious quantity was the Petrograd garrison. While the major part of the troops could probably be depended on not to oppose the insurrection, they could not be relied on to give it vigorous support. The struggle to gain control of the garrison constituted the last stage preparatory to the insurrection itself.

The medium through which the Bolsheviks organized their forces for the final coup was the Military Revolutionary Committee of the Petrograd Soviet. With the Bolsheviks in full control of the Soviet, a resolution to create the committee was carried on October 29, and the committee itself was named on November 2, four days before the insurrection. The staff of the committee was composed only of Bolsheviks and sympathetic Left SR's. Trotsky, the President of the Soviet, also served as chairman of the committee and surrounded himself with a core of reliable Bolsheviks who, in effect, comprised the general staff of the insurrection. Liaison with the Bolshevik Central Committee was maintained through a secret "military revolutionary center," consisting of five members of the committee, Sverdlov, Stalin, Bubnov, Uritsky, and Dzerzhinsky.[77]

The party's role in directing the insurrection was camouflaged behind the façade of the Soviet. This shrewd strategem provided a measure of pseudo-legality for the organizers of the insurrection. It was of particular value in mobilizing the support of the wavering and hesitant who were ready to respond to an appeal of the Soviet when they would have been unwilling to follow the naked leadership of the Bolsheviks. It was of outstanding importance in dealing with the Petrograd garrison which early in the Revolution had formed the habit of looking to the Soviet as its protector against transfer to the front and refused to take orders not countersigned by that body.

In its preparations for the insurrection, the Military Revolutionary Committee relied heavily on the Bolsheviks' Military Organization, which counted approximately a thousand members in the Petrograd area — among them a number of young officers as well as others with military experience. Through this organization, commissars were assigned "for observation and leadership" to the garrison's combat units, as well as to arsenals, warehouses, and other institutions of military importance.[78] Arrangements were made through the commissars, who were in charge of issuing arms, to prevent the arming of the *Junkers,* or cadets in the military schools, and at the same time to divert rifles and other equipment to the Red Guard. Kernels of resistance developed. The Bolshevik commissar was unable to establish his authority in the important Fortress of Peter and Paul which commanded the Winter Palace. On the afternoon of November 5, this obstacle was overcome when Trotsky appealed to the soldiers of the fortress. With this peaceful surrender went a prize of one hundred thousand rifles, no mean contribution to future success.

On the evening of the fifth, the Provisional Government made a belated attempt to fight back. The decision was made to close the Bolshevik newspapers, *Rabochii Put'* and *Soldat* (Soldier), to initiate criminal proceedings against the members of the Military Revolutionary Committee, to arrest leading Bolsheviks, and to summon reliable military units from the environs of Petrograd. The first tests of strength augured badly for the government. The Bolshevik printing plants were raided by government troops at 5:30 A.M. on November 6 and copies of the newspapers confiscated; by eleven o'clock that morning the newspapers reappeared. The government ordered the cruiser *Aurora,* manned by a Bolshevik crew and moored in the Neva uncomfortably close to the Winter Palace, to put to sea on a training cruise; the order was effectively countermanded by the Military Revolutionary Committee.

On the morning of the sixth, Kerensky appeared before the Pre-Parliament, proclaimed a state of insurrection in Petrograd, and asked for unqualified support in suppressing the Bolsheviks. After prolonged debate, with the Kadets and Cossack delegates in opposition, a resolution drafted by Martov, a Menshevik Internationalist, was adopted by the close vote of 113 to 102, with twenty-six abstentions. The resolution condemned the insurrection, but it pointed the finger of responsibility at Kerensky by calling on him "first of all, to pass immediately a decree transferring the land to the land committees and to take a decisive stand on foreign policy proposing to the Allies that they announce the conditions of peace and begin peace negotiations." The resolution concluded by recommending the creation of "a Committee of Public Safety comprised of representatives of municipal corporations and the organs of the revolutionary democracy, acting in concert with the Provisional Government." [79]

Kerensky at first threatened to resign. A delegation headed by the Menshevik Dan called on the premier to plead for quick action in the spirit of the resolution. According to Dan's account,

[We told him] that we had a definite and concrete proposal to make to the Provisional Government: that resolutions on the question of peace, land, and the Constituent Assembly should be passed at once and made known to the population by means of telegraph and by posting bills [in the city]. We insisted that this must be done that very night in order that every soldier and every worker might know of the decisions of the Provisional Government by the next morning. . .

We pleaded . . . with Kerensky that even from a purely military point of view the struggle against the Bolsheviks would have a chance of success only if the peasant-soldiers knew that they were defending peace and land against the Bolsheviks. . .

Our conversation did not last very long. Kerensky gave the impression of a man completely enervated and worn out. To every argument he replied with irritation, saying finally with disdain that the government did not need any of our advice, that this was not the time to talk but to act. [80]

The Seizure of Power

Meanwhile, Lenin, still in hiding, had also decided that the moment had come for action. Burning with impatience, he sped a last letter to the comrades of the Central Committee on November 6: "We must not wait! We may lose everything! . . . History will not forgive delay by revolutionists who could be victorious today (and will surely be victorious today), while they risk losing much tomorrow, they risk losing all." Then, addressing himself to those who urged delay until the meeting of the Second All-Russian Congress of Soviets on the evening of the seventh, Lenin continued:

If we seize power today, we seize it not against the Soviets but for them. . . The government is tottering. We must *deal it the death blow* at any cost. To delay action is the same as death. [81]

On the same day, the Bolshevik Central Committee assembled to make the last dispositions for the uprising. Sverdlov was assigned to keep watch on the Provisional Government, Bubnov was allotted railway communications, Dzerzhinsky posts and telegraphs, and Milyutin the organization of food supplies. Kamenev and Berzin were instructed to negotiate with the Left SR's to insure their support for the insurrection. Lomov and

Nogin were dispatched to Moscow to coördinate the activities of the Bolsheviks there.[82] With events rushing toward a denouement, Trotsky took time out on the evening of the sixth to address a meeting of the Petrograd Soviet. In reporting on the measures already taken to checkmate the Provisional Government, he referred to it "as nothing more than a pitiful, helpless, half-government, which waits the motion of a historical broom to sweep it off. . . But if the government wishes to make use of the hours — 24, 48, or 72 — which it still has to live, and comes out against us, then we will meet it with a counterattack, blow for blow, steel for iron." [83]

During the night of the sixth and the early morning of the seventh, the Bolshevik forces moved quickly to seize the strong points of the capital city. Resistance was virtually nominal, and the seizures were accomplished with almost no bloodshed. The military support on which the Provisional Government counted simply melted away. A pathetic effort was made to hold the Winter Palace with the help of the Ural Cossacks, Junkers, officers, and the Women's Battalion who were stationed there. But as the Bolsheviks moved up their forces, the Cossacks and part of the Junkers and officers slipped away, and the Women's Battalion was disarmed after sallying forth in counterattack. Shortly after midnight of the seventh, the attacking forces captured the last stronghold of the Provisional Government and arrested the ministers who remained in the Palace.

The collapse of resistance in Petrograd was complete. The proclamation of the Military Revolutionary Committee summed up the day's happenings:

All railroad stations and the telephone, post, and telegraph offices are occupied. The telephones of the Winter Palace and the Staff Headquarters are disconnected. The State Bank is in our hands. The Winter Palace and the Staff have surrendered. The shock troops are dispersed, the cadets paralyzed. The armored cars have sided with the Revolutionary Committee. The Cossacks refused to obey the government. The Provisional Government is deposed. Power is in the hands of the Revolutionary Committee of the Petrograd Soviet of Workers' and Soldiers' Deputies.[84]

At eleven o'clock on the evening of November 7, the Second All-Russian Congress of Soviets assembled for its opening session. Of the approximately 650 delegates in attendance, the Bolsheviks claimed 390 and with the help of the Left SR's quickly asserted control over the proceedings.[85] Confronted with a *fait accompli*, the Mensheviks and SR's of the Right and Center abandoned the Congress. Martov, the Menshevik Internationalist whom Trotsky described contemptuously as the "inventive statesman of eternal waverings," [86] attempted to patch up a truce by proposing "to end the crisis in a peaceful manner, by forming a government composed of representatives of all the democratic elements." [87] Trotsky's reply was drenched in vitriol:

What do they offer us? . . . To give up our victory, to compromise, and to negotiate — with whom? With whom shall we negotiate? With those miserable cliques which have left the Congress or with those who still remain? But we saw how strong those cliques were! There is no one left in Russia to follow them. And millions of workers and peasants are asked to negotiate with them on equal terms. No, an agreement will not do now. To those who have left us and to those proposing negotiations we must say: You are a mere handful, miserable, bankrupt; your rôle is finished, and you may go where you belong — to the garbage heap of history.[88]

The Congress concluded its first day's business by issuing a proclamation announcing its assumption of supreme power, transferring all local authority to the Soviets, and appealing to the country to defeat all efforts of Kerensky and other "Kornilovists" to return to power. With a sure revolutionary instinct for the issues that would attract maximum support for the Bolsheviks, the proclamation promised:

The Soviet authority will at once propose a democratic peace to all nations and an immediate armistice on all fronts. It will safeguard the transfer without compensation of all land . . . to the peasant committees; it will defend the soldiers' rights, introducing a complete democratization of the army, it will establish workers' control over industry, it will insure the convocation of the Constituent Assembly on the date set; it will supply the cities with bread and the villages with articles of first necessity, and it will secure to all nationalities inhabiting Russia the right of self-determination.[89]

The next day Lenin made his first appearance at the Congress and was received with a tumultuous ovation. After the applause had died down, he quickly assumed the reins of leadership with nine fateful words, "We shall now proceed to construct the socialist order." [90] With Lenin presenting the main reports, the Congress approved the important decrees on peace and on land [91] and then concluded its work by entrusting the power of government to the newly created Council of People's Commissars.[92] The Sovnarkom, as it quickly became known, was exclusively Bolshevik in composition; its membership included Lenin as Chairman, Trotsky as Commissar of Foreign Affairs, Rykov as Commissar of the Interior, Lunacharsky as Commissar of Education, and Stalin as Chairman for Nationalities. The hour of triumph had finally come. Lenin rarely indulged in introspection or backward glances, but at that moment he paused in wonder and confided to Trotsky, "You know . . . from persecution and a life underground, to come so suddenly into power . . . *Es schwindelt.*" [93]

If Lenin found victory intoxicating and slightly unbelievable, in the eyes of his opponents the Bolshevik march to power had a nightmarish quality of incredible unreality. In the brief period of eight months, a tiny band of underground revolutionaries, numbering less than 25,000 on the eve of the March Revolution, had catapulted themselves into a governing authority of nearly 150,000,000 people. It is easier to discern in retrospect the significant factors which contributed to the Bolshevik conquest than it was at the time. If the Provisional Government had been able to withdraw from the war and carry through a land settlement satisfactory to the peasantry, it is highly doubtful that the Bolsheviks could have gathered enough support to stage a successful *coup d'état*. Yet to state this alternative, so plausibly reinforced by hindsight, is to miss the tragic imperatives of 1917.

Each of the parties which maneuvered for ascendancy in the months between March and November was the prisoner of its own illusions, its own interests, and its own vision of the future. To a Kadet leader like Milyukov it was inconceivable that Russia could betray her allies and her own national interests by suing for a separate peace; consequently, it was all too easy to attribute his own sense of patriotic exaltation and dedication to soldiers, workers, and peasants who had lost their taste for war. To SR's of the Right like Kerensky, who in a measure shared Milyukov's illusions, the successful prosecution of the war was paramount, with the agenda of economic reforms to be postponed until properly constituted legal bodies could be assembled to deal with them. To SR's of the Center and Left, who were much closer to the aspirations and expectations of the villages, land reform brooked no delay. Frustrated by the procrastinations of the Provisional Government, the Left SR's were thrown into the arms of the Bolsheviks. For Mensheviks of all shades, still loyal to the orthodox Marxian two-stage panorama of capitalist development, the socialist revolution had to be postponed until the bourgeois-democratic revolution was completed. The Mensheviks demonstrated real insight in emphasizing the difficulties of building socialism in a backward country. Their theoretical acumen was less well attuned to the political dynamism and revolutionary *élan* which the downfall of Tsardom released. For the Bolsheviks, economic backwardness was the springboard to power; for the Mensheviks, it pointed a path toward legal opposition in a consolidating bourgeois order. This was hardly a prospect for which the wretched and disinherited could develop more than qualified enthusiasm. As the Revolution deepened, the Mensheviks found themselves out-promised and out-maneuvered, with their strength sharply receding in the urban industrial centers on which they counted heavily.

Until the arrival of Lenin from exile, the Bolsheviks, too, were prisoners of ancient formulas. They oriented their policies on a perspective not very different from that of Menshevism. Lenin reversed this course and set the party on the road to the conquest of power. With an unswerving faith in his goal and a readiness to take any measures whatever to realize it, Lenin, frequently over bitter opposition, managed to transform the party into an obedient instrument of his will. His remarkable talent as a revolutionary strategist was based on an unerring sense for the deeply

felt dissatisfactions of the masses and the genius for finding the slogans
to catalyze grievances into revolutionary energy. Except for his insistence
on striking at the right moment, Lenin had relatively little to do with the
actual mechanics of the insurrection. His great contribution was to set
the stage for insurrection by identifying Bolshevism with the major forces
of mass discontent in Russian society. Lenin did not create the war-weariness which permeated the army and the nation: the material was at hand;
his task was to exploit it. With one word — peace — Lenin and the Bolsheviks fused it into a revolutionary amalgam. The land-hunger of the
peasants was an ancient grievance of which all parties were aware. The
SR's built their ascendancy in the villages on the promise to satisfy it,
but while they temporized, Lenin stole their program from under their
noses. When accused of the theft, Lenin replied, "Whether it be according
to our ideas or in the direction of the SR program does not matter. The
essential point is to give the peasantry a firm conviction that there are no
more *pomeshchiks* [landlords] in the villages, and that it is now for the
peasants themselves to solve all questions and to build their own life." [94]
With one word — land — Lenin insured the neutrality of the villages.

Factory workers constituted the strongest phalanx of Bolshevik support. Lenin bought their support by promising them a government which
"takes surplus products from the parasites and gives them to the hungry, that . . . forcibly moves the homeless into the dwellings of the rich,
that . . . forces the rich to pay for milk, but does not give them a drop
of it until the children of *all* the poor families have received adequate supplies." [95] With two slogans — bread and workers' control — Lenin captured the allegiance of substantial sections of the industrial workers from
the Mensheviks.

The Bolshevik Revolution was not a majoritarian movement. The last
free elections in Russia, the elections to the Constituent Assembly which
took place toward the end of 1917, clearly demonstrated that the Bolshevik voting strength in the country at large was not more than 25 per cent.[96]
But, as Lenin subsequently observed, the Bolsheviks did have "an overwhelming preponderance of force at the decisive moment in the decisive
points." [97] In the areas and units strategically important to the success of
the insurrection — Petrograd, Moscow, the Baltic fleet, and the garrisons
around Petrograd — Bolshevik ascendancy turned the scale. The enemies
of Bolshevism were numerous, but they were also weak, poorly organized,
divided, and apathetic. The strategy of Lenin was calculated to emphasize
their divisions, neutralize their opposition, and capitalize on their apathy.
In 1902 in *What Is to Be Done?* Lenin had written, "Give us an organization of revolutionaries, and we shall overturn the whole of Russia!" [98] On
November 7, 1917, the wish was fulfilled and the deed accomplished.

Chapter 4

The Dynamics of Power

"*The question of power,*" observed Lenin in 1921, "is the fundamental question of every revolution." [1] To understand the turnings and twistings of Soviet policy, the advances and the retreats, the continuities and the reversals, it is essential to comprehend the preoccupation with power which has motivated the responsible Bolshevik leadership at every crucial stage in the development and consolidation of the Soviet political system.

This is not to imply that the men who made the October Revolution were inspired solely by an infatuation with power for power's sake. They shared a sense of historical mission, a fanatic belief in their own destiny as agents chosen to carry forward a program of profound social reconstruction, and they sought to impose their vision on the obdurate material which history had placed at their disposal. They fashioned their instruments of power to make their dream of the future come alive, and the strategy and tactics which they improvised were designed to bring them nearer the Promised Land. Like many revolutionaries before them, they found themselves involved in a complex struggle to master the recalcitrant realities of their environment. They pressed forward where they could, and they gave way where they had to. The tragedy of unintended consequences overtook them. As they sought to come to terms with the pressures which impinged on them, visions of the future had to be modified or abandoned. Instruments became ends; the retention and consolidation of power dwarfed all other objectives. The party of revolution was transformed into the party of order.

The history of this transformation is the record of an intricate interplay among Bolshevik goals, strategy and tactics, instruments of power, and the problems posed by the environment in which they were compelled to function. When the Bolsheviks seized power on November 7, 1917, their blueprint of the future represented an ambivalent juxtaposition of long-term utopian objectives and short-term realistic expedients. In the realm of agricultural policy, their ultimate goal was the organization of large-scale socialist cultivation. They proposed to move gradually toward that goal by urging *"the village proletarians and semi-proletarians to try to transform each private estate into a sufficiently large model farm, to be conducted, at the expense of the community, by the local Soviet of agricultural workers under the direction of trained agriculturists, with the use of the best technical appliances."* [2]

Since this prospect was hardly likely to kindle the enthusiasm of a land-hungry peasantry, it was, in practice, subordinated. The land decrees enacted by the Bolsheviks on the morrow of the Revolution gave their blessing to the peasant division of the landlords' estates. In order to entrench themselves in power, the Bolsheviks adopted the peasants' own program. The long-range goal of large-scale socialist cultivation was relegated to the distant future. The Bolsheviks found themselves in the paradoxical position of presiding over an agricultural revolution which created as its first fruit a powerful stratum of petty-bourgeois peasant proprietors.

The Bolshevik program for industry faced a different set of contradictions. In an important article, "Will the Bolsheviks Retain State Power?" written in October 1917, Lenin outlined the measures which the Bolsheviks hoped to institute after the seizure of power.[3] He called specifically for the nationalization of the banks and the large syndicates such as iron, coal, oil, and sugar; the "compulsory trustification (*i.e.*, compulsory amalgamation) of industrialists, merchants, and proprietors generally"; consumer rationing; a grain monopoly; and universal labor service.[4] He pronounced himself "in favor of centralism and of a 'plan.'" "The proletariat, when victorious," Lenin stated, "will act thus: it will set the economists, engineers, agricultural experts and so on to work out a 'plan' *under the control* of the workers' organizations, to test it, to seek means of saving labor by means of centralism, and of securing the most simple, cheap, convenient, and general control." [5]

Once the dictatorship of the proletariat was established, Lenin anticipated no particular difficulty in enforcing workers' control. "Capitalism," he declared, "has simplified the functions of accounting and control, and has reduced them to such comparatively simple processes as to be within the reach of any literate person." Capitalists and higher state employees who resisted the establishment of workers' control would be treated "with severity," [6] but he anticipated little difficulty in breaking such resistance and putting all but the "incapable ones" and the "incorrigible 'resisters' *to new state service.*" [7] "As for the organizational form of the work," Lenin continued, "we do not invent it, we take it ready-made from capitalism: banks, syndicates, the best factories, experimental stations, academies, etc.; we need adopt only the best models furnished by the experience of the most advanced countries." [8]

The laboring masses, he professed to believe, could be quickly educated to take over the responsibilities of state administration. Mistakes would be made, but workers would learn by experience. "The most important thing," Lenin declared, "is to instil in the oppressed and laboring masses confidence in their own power." [9]

The chastening responsibilities of power introduced a new perspective. On April 28, 1918, Lenin addressed himself to the theme of "The Immediate Tasks of the Soviet Government." [10] Gone was the earlier faith in a smooth transition from capitalism to socialism, in the easy capitulation of the capitalists and the bourgeois specialists, in the ready adaptability of the proletariat to the tasks of state administration, in the self-disciplined productive *élan* of the working masses. It was far easier, Lenin admitted, to expropriate and nationalize industry than to manage it. "Our work of organizing proletarian accounting and control has obviously . . . *lagged behind* the work of directly 'expropriating the expropriators.'" "The art of administration," he proclaimed, "is not an art that one is born to, it is acquired by experience . . . Without the guidance of specialists in the various fields of knowledge, technology and experience, the transition to socialism will be impossible." [11] Because of the indispensability of the specialists, Lenin continued,

we have had to resort to the old bourgeois method and to agree to pay a very high price for the "services" of the biggest bourgeois specialists . . . Clearly, such a measure is a compromise, a departure from the principles of the Paris Commune . . . *a step backward* on the part of our Socialist Soviet state power, which from the very outset proclaimed and pursued the policy of reducing high salaries to the level of the wages of the average worker.[12]

Lenin justified the measure as a necessary "tribute" which the Soviet state was compelled to pay to compensate for the backwardness of the masses. "The sooner we workers and peasants learn to acquire the most efficient labor discipline and the most modern techniques of labor, using the bourgeois specialists for this purpose, the sooner shall we liberate ourselves from having to pay any 'tribute' to these specialists." [13]

Lenin's sober words reflected a new appreciation of the difficulties that the Soviet state confronted in breaking "with the accursed past." [14] The appeal for labor discipline was combined with an ominous rationalization of the necessities of coercion. The dictatorship of the proletariat, Lenin made clear, might have to be exercised not only to destroy capitalism but to impose discipline on the working masses. He proclaimed that "large-scale machine industry calls for absolute and strict unity of will, which directs the joint labors of hundreds, thousands and tens of thousands of people . . . today the . . . revolution demands, in the interest of socialism, that the masses *unquestioningly obey the single will of the leaders of the labor process.*" [15] Within less than six months after the seizure of power, the Bolsheviks were already embarked on a course which foreshadowed increasing reliance on repression.

The vision of the "commune state" yielded to the pressing contingencies of expediency. At all costs, the Leninist leadership of the Party was determined to hold onto power, and it encountered no difficulty in identifying its own ascendancy with the fulfillment of the sacred mission of realizing socialism. Persuaded of its own ultimately beneficent purposes as the surrogate of the working masses, it was prepared to destroy ruthlessly all who stood in its way, to make temporary concessions to the forces which it could not master, and to utilize those willing and unwilling allies who could be induced to march the same highway into the uncertain future.

Lenin's decisions were shaped by the conviction that the first duty of revolutionaries was to stabilize their authority. Faced with a German advance which threatened to destroy the new Soviet republic, Lenin carried the day for an onerous Tilsit peace at Brest-Litovsk which surrendered space in order to gain time and won the Bolsheviks a respite to consolidate their control of the territory which remained under their rule. Accused of betraying the world revolution and strengthening the forces of reaction in Germany, Lenin replied, "Yes, we shall see the international world revolution, but for the time being it is a . . . fairy tale — I quite understand children liking beautiful fairy tales. But I ask: is it seemly for a serious revolutionary to believe fairy tales?" [16] Repudiating revolutionary romanticism, Lenin called on his critics "to set to work to create self-discipline . . . by that you will help the German revolution, the international revolution." The preservation of the Soviet fatherland was the first duty of all revolutionaries. A disgraceful peace which preserved the Communist power to maneuver was infinitely preferable to "dying in a beautiful pose, sword in hand." [17]

The Civil War and War Communism

Faced with the onslaughts of the White generals, the Allied Intervention armies, the Poles, and rebellious anti-Bolshevik nationalist movements in the borderlands, the new Bolshevik regime recruited thousands of former Tsarist officers to supply needed military skills for the Red Army and used every variety of opportunistic appeal to disarm opposition and mobilize support for its cause. During the so-called Civil War, the Communists fought at least three different kinds of war. In one aspect — the struggle against the Whites — the Civil War was portrayed as a war to prevent the restoration of the old regime. In another aspect, in the battles to repel the Allied Interventionists and to win back the borderlands, the Civil War was presented as a patriotic war, a war to cast out the foreign invader and to reclaim the national patrimony. In a third aspect, it was a war to consolidate Bolshevik power, to eliminate every competitor from the scene, and to establish the Communist Party as the dominant and unchallenged master of the new Soviet state.

The first two aspects of the Civil War had more popular appeal than the third. By assuming the role of leader in the struggle against reaction and by purporting to serve as the custodian of the national interest, the Bolsheviks were able to tap reservoirs of sympathy and assistance which their persistent drive for exclusive power could never win. The peasant might harbor no love for Communism, but as long as the Bolsheviks stood as the only barrier which prevented the landlords from reclaiming their estates, many peasants were prepared to give the Bolsheviks grudging, or at least passive, support. Left-wing intellectuals who were at odds with the Bolsheviks found themselves drawn to the Soviet cause because the policies espoused by the Whites were even more repugnant to them. Patriotic Tsarist army officers to whom the Communist program was anathema enrolled, nevertheless, in the Soviet ranks because they saw the new Soviet state as the residuary legatee of historic national interests. Meanwhile, the Bolshevik leadership gathered its allies where it could, utilized the forces which circumstances had placed at its disposal, and drove to solidify its power.

From the beginning, the Bolsheviks concentrated all their efforts on building firm instruments of power. The Civil War period was a drawing board stage in the development of latter-day totalitarianism, but the outlines of the future edifice were already clearly apparent. Although the Party leadership still played a cat-and-mouse game with its left-wing SR and Menshevik opponents, granting them limited toleration when their support appeared essential in the struggle against the Whites and withdrawing such toleration when their activities threatened to be "harmful," the dominating position of the Communist Party was definitely established. After the break with the Left SR's in March 1918, the Bolsheviks held exclusive possession of the Council of People's Commissars and mobilized an overwhelming majority in the central Soviet organs. They occupied the commanding positions in state administration, controlled the army and the Cheka (secret police), and exercised a paramount influence in the field of mass communications and propaganda.

Nevertheless, the machinery of control fell far short of the tightly centralized bureaucratic structure into which the Soviet regime later developed. Under the impact of the Civil War, the trend toward centralism in Party management was strongly reinforced, but the Party remained a battleground of competing factions, and the mass influx of new members brought with it a miscellaneous array of discordant and not readily disciplined personalities and views. While trusted Bolsheviks held the strategic positions at the top of the administrative pyramid, the lower levels of the bureaucracy were still composed predominantly of old-regime carry-overs whose knowledge made them indispensable and whose skills frequently enabled them to determine the policies of the institutions with which they were connected. As Lenin was later to observe in his political report to the Eleventh Party Congress in March 1922,

> Suppose we take Moscow with its 4,700 responsible Communists, and sup-pose we take that huge bureaucratic machine, that huge pile — who is directing whom? I doubt very much whether it can truthfully be said that the Com-munists are directing this pile. To tell the truth, they are not doing the direct-ing, they are being directed.[18]

What was true of Moscow was infinitely more true of the periphery. Localism flourished, and the effectiveness of Communist controls de-creased in direct relationship to the distance from the great urban centers. Even the Red Army was far from being the monolithic machine which Trotsky sought to make it. The top command encountered the greatest difficulty in enforcing its authority on the armies in the field. Guerrilla units loosely attached to the army fought their own war in their own way. The former Tsarist officers whom the Bolsheviks enrolled as military specialists often met defiance from the Communist commanders and rank-and-file, and not even the word of Trotsky himself was proof against the suspicion which the old officers generated. The Cheka was a law unto itself. While it served the purposes of the Party leadership by striking terror into the hearts of the class enemy, it also became the refuge of all sorts of adventurers and scoundrels who used their untrammeled power to commit acts of pilfering and pillage for their own personal advantage.

Despite the most strenuous efforts of the Bolshevik leadership to impose central direction on the course of events, the first years of Soviet power were uniquely a period when the spontaneous and anarchic forces of the Revolution had their way. The flood of decrees from the center bore little relationship to the actual sequence of developments in the localities. The breakdown of supply and communications, the shifting lines of battle, and the initial inexperience of the new regime combined to create a situation in which authority was dispersed and broken into fragments. The capacity to lead was tested by the ability to extemporize an effective response to the crisis of the moment. *Ad hoc* improvisation became the order of the day.

For the Bolsheviks during the Civil War, there was only one determin-ing priority — survival. And survival involved mobilizing the men and the material to defeat the enemy. Every other consideration gave way before this overriding compulsion. The policy of War Communism was the rule of the besieged fortress. Efforts to put utopian dreams into practice were reluctantly adjusted to the compelling necessities of the siege.

Policy toward the peasants was a by-product of the problem of supplying the Red Army and the workers who provisioned it. The Soviet regime faced the task of extracting grain from the peasants without being able to provide them with consumer goods in exchange. It met the problem by forcible requisitions. "The essence of this peculiar 'War Communism,'" Lenin later admitted, "was that we actually took from the peasant all the surplus grain and sometimes even not only surplus grain, but part of the grain the peasant required for food, for the purpose of meeting the requirements of the army and of sustaining the workers." [19] The peasants retaliated in typical peasant fashion. They hid what they could and refused to sow more crops than were necessary to meet their own needs. While the danger of the landowners' return still loomed, the peasants refrained from more extreme measures.

With the final defeat of the Whites in 1920, the Bolsheviks were left face to face with the peasantry. As peasant disorders began to mount, the leaders had to assay the consequences of a continued catastrophic decline in agricultural production. They came to the reluctant conclusion that the food shortage could not be relieved unless inducements were held out to the peasant to increase his production. The decision to abandon the policy of forced requisitions marked the conclusion of the period of War Communism.

The industrial policy of the Bolsheviks during the Civil War reflected an overriding concern with immediate military considerations. During the first months of the Revolution, Lenin tried to confine nationalization to the commanding industrial heights and to smooth the transition from the old order to the new by utilizing the managerial skills of former capitalists and bourgeois specialists. These efforts quickly revealed themselves as abortive. Capitalists and managers abandoned their plants in large numbers, and many others were driven out by workers intent on revenging past grievances.

In the first surge of revolutionary spontaneity, the working classes displayed marked syndicalist proclivities. Assuming that the factories now belonged to them, they sought to operate them for their own account and in their own interest. The results were usually disastrous. Lacking managerial talent and technical skill and unable to impose discipline on their own members, the factory committees frequently brought their enterprises to a standstill. Their problems were, of course, greatly accentuated by the chaos and disorganization of war and revolution. Failures of communications and transport, as well as shortages of raw material, led to work stoppages, and industrial breakdowns were contagious and cumulative. The entire industrial life of Russia threatened to grind to a halt.

Under pressure of the Civil War, the Bolshevik leadership exerted every effort to revive production, to restore labor discipline, and to organize industry to serve military needs. A Supreme Council of National Economy with local branches was established to provide the framework for central direction of the economy. On June 28, 1918, virtually every important branch of industrial life was nationalized, though Lenin still sought to preserve a distinction between those enterprises to be run by state administrators and others to continue operation under their former owners for state account. Spurred on by Lenin, the Central Council of Trade Unions issued a regulation on April 3, 1918, which empowered trade-union commissions to fix productivity norms, approved the use of piece rates and bonuses to raise the productivity of labor, and invoked the sanction of expulsion from the union for violators of labor discipline.[20] After the nationalization decree, the "workers'" state, in theory at least, became the main employer. In January 1920 the Council of People's Commissars drew what it conceived to be the logical inference by introducing universal labor service and transforming military units into labor armies.[21]

As the Civil War pursued its difficult course, Lenin turned again and again to his favorite recipes for raising productive efficiency — centralized control, one-man management, and the employment of bourgeois specialists to provide technical and managerial advice. Each of these measures met strong resistance from elements in the Party, but Lenin continued to urge their adoption, and his views won increasing acceptance. The Supreme Council of National Economy gradually expanded its authority and began to master the syndicalist and localist tendencies which prevailed in industrial management. It imposed central priorities to insure supplies for the army and closed down poorly run factories in order to concentrate production in the most efficient enterprises. At Lenin's insistence, large numbers of bourgeois specialists and technicians were incorporated into the industrial bureaucracy. Their employment was defended by Lenin as a transitional necessity until the working class could produce its own specialists. In pressing the case for one-man management, Lenin met particularly strong resistance from the trade unions, for whom any retreat from collegiality implied an abandonment of the principle of workers' control. While the issue of collegial versus one-man management was never unequivocally resolved during the Civil War period, Lenin's views were approved in principle by the Ninth Party Congress in March 1920,[22] and a considerable extension of the scope of one-man management was actually achieved.

Despite Lenin's strenuous efforts to improve the administrative efficiency of the nationalized enterprises, industrial disorganization was endemic. The ravages of world war, revolution, and civil war could not be overcome by mere administrative expedients. The cities suffered from cold and hunger; the workers abandoned the factories in large numbers. Supplies were cut off; industrial production declined catastrophically. In practice, the army and the industrial labor force were supplied by a process of desperate improvisation. The output of those factories that continued to operate was reserved almost entirely for the Red Army. Any existing supplies that might be useful to the army were simply requisitioned. Such food and consumer goods as remained were available, theoretically, for distribution to the town populations at fixed prices under a system of differential rationing which favored workers performing assignments of vital urgency to the war effort.

In practice, shortages became so extreme as to render price and rationing controls meaningless. Money lost all value. Workers had to be paid in kind, and a rapidly expanding black market largely displaced the official channels of trade. Except for privileged groups in the army and the government and "bagmen" and black marketeers who flourished on the proceeds of illicit trade, want and hunger were general. The egalitarian aspirations of the Revolution were made real by the egalitarianism of universal sacrifice.

For those who identified themselves with the Bolshevik Revolution, the epoch of Civil War and War Communism was nevertheless a period of great exaltation and dedication. The revolutionary ardor of the dedicated Communists in the Red Army and elsewhere was inspired by a vision of a new social order that imparted the will to victory. For those who believed in the Communist cause, the October Revolution marked a great release of social energy. It appeared as a liberating act which brought the toiling masses to the forefront of world history. It aroused hopes and dreams of a world to be remade in the image of brotherhood, equality, and justice. Thus the totalitarian face of the Revolution, with its reliance on terror and bureaucratic controls, was slow to reveal itself to the ideologically committed and the idealistically consecrated. For them, what loomed large was the break with the past and the intoxicating freedom of a new epoch in which old taboos and institutional restraints were cast aside while new bridles and halters had still to be securely fastened.

The Civil War period, in one of its aspects, was a stage in which the power instruments of totalitarianism were being forged. In another aspect, it was also an era of considerable social experimentation during which the new regime was feeling its way into the future. The overthrow of the old regime was accompanied by a rebellion against the family and traditional moral values, by a loosening of marital ties and a new emphasis on the emancipation of women and the authority of youth, by educational innovations, and a relatively unfettered ferment of literary and artistic productivity. For many, the revolt against the old order overshadowed the consolidation of the new. Amidst the grimness of the ruins of War Communism, the rebels against the old society luxuriated in their new freedom, lived exciting lives of romantic adventure, tasted the heady wine of power, and found it good.

It is not easy to draw a balance sheet for the period of Revolution and Civil War. The Party's monopoly of legal power, the domination of the Party by its central organs, the creation of a centralized bureaucratic edifice, the rise of the secret police, the permeation of the army by Party and police controls, the tightening of labor discipline, the subordination of the trade unions to the Party — all owe their development to practices which congealed and hardened under the pressures of War Communism. Yet it was also a period when the egalitarian aspirations of the Revolution received powerful expression, when voices could be raised on behalf of "workers' control," when Party discussions were lively and uninhibited, and criticism of the leadership was not equated with treason. Utopian dreams of the rule of the masses still tempered the realities of dictatorship.

The peasant during this period was caught up in cross currents. In one sense he came into his own. The land settlement adopted and reluctantly blessed by the Bolsheviks was actually deeply repugnant to them, since it introduced the Trojan horse of private property into the very midst of the Communist citadel and raised ultimate dangers of counter-revolution. Thus it could be defended only as a tactical maneuver to facilitate the Bolshevik rise to power — and as such it was brilliantly successful. The policy of compulsory requisitions to feed the army and the towns, however, was less happy in its consequences. Although it probably saved the Soviet regime from defeat, it also alienated the countryside and caused such a sharp decline in agricultural production that repressive controls on the peasantry had to be temporarily abandoned. In the first trial of strength, the peasantry was able to extract substantial concessions despite the fact that the Communists retained their hold on the strategic instruments of power.

The lessons learned in the Civil War discredited the utopian strain in Communist ideology. As Lenin pointed out on the fourth anniversary of the October Revolution,

Borne along on the crest of the wave of enthusiasm . . . we reckoned . . . on being able to organize the state production and the state distribution of products on communist lines in a small-peasant country by order of the proletarian state. Experience has proved that we were wrong. It transpires that a number of transitional stages are necessary — state capitalism and socialism — in order to *prepare* by many years of effort for the transition to communism. . . We must first set to work in this small-peasant country to build solid little gangways to socialism by way of state capitalism. Otherwise we shall never get to communism; we shall never bring these scores of millions of people to communism. That is what experience, what the objective course of development of the revolution has taught us.[23]

The legacy of War Communism was a new appreciation of the complexities of industrial management and administration, a new sensitivity to the values of technical skill and professional competence, a newly discovered understanding of the importance of production incentives, and a fresh realization of the indispensability of labor discipline. The lessons were underlined at the end of the Civil War by famine in the countryside and hunger in the cities, by the almost complete disappearance of consumer goods, by factories standing idle and land that was not tilled. The moral was pointed even more sharply by a swelling tide of sporadic peasant risings, by strikes of factory workers, and the revolt of the Kronstadt garrison in March 1921, with its call for a third revolution to throw off the yoke of the Communists. Although the Kronstadt revolt and other risings were bloodily suppressed, their meaning was not lost on the Communist high command.[24]

The reaction of the Bolsheviks to these events illustrated a strategy to which they were to resort again and again in moments of extreme crisis. On the one hand, dissident elements who vocalized the existing discontent and who were prepared to give it organized leadership were subjected to harsh attack. On the other hand, steps were also taken to ameliorate the dissatisfaction of the mass of peasants and workers. The campaign of repression was directed in the first instance at the Menshevik and SR remnants who were held responsible for the events of the spring of 1921.[25] At the same time, Lenin also ordered a purge of the Party "from top to bottom." [26] One of the primary objects of the purge was to eliminate Party members who reflected the mood of worker restiveness and who sought to take advantage of it to oppose the Party leadership.

The New Economic Policy

Simultaneously, the Party moved to placate mass unrest by a series of measures which collectively became known as the New Economic Policy (NEP). The most important reversal of policy was the abandonment of forced requisitions in favor of a tax in kind which left the peasants free to dispose of such surpluses as remained after the tax assessment had been met. The "peasant Brest-Litovsk," as David Ryazanov called it, sought to guarantee the Party a new breathing space. As Lenin said at the Tenth Party Congress, "only an agreement with the peasantry can save the socialist revolution in Russia until the revolution has occurred in other countries." [27]

The tax in kind represented a determined, if temporary, effort to win

back the favor of the peasantry. In order to persuade the peasants to part
with their surpluses, incentives had to be provided in the form of increased
supplies of consumer goods. This made a revival of industrial production
imperative. The NEP industrial policy put initial emphasis on the
development of small industries, whether in the form of private enterprise or in the form of industrial coöperatives, in the hope that they would
most readily increase the flow of consumer goods. New enterprises were
promised freedom from nationalization. Small enterprises which had
been nationalized were leased to their former owners or industrial *artels*
(producers' coöperatives) for fixed terms with the provision that rentals
were to be paid in the form of a definite proportion of the output of the
enterprise.

The so-called "commanding heights" of large-scale industry remained
under state administration, though even these enterprises, organized in
the form of trusts, were to be operated on commercial principles with
precise economic accounting (*khozraschët*), with substantial freedom
to buy and sell on the open market, and with the obligation to operate on
a basis of profitability. Private trade was restored, and a new generation
of so-called Nepmen arose to carry on the functions of buying and selling,
sometimes through private trading concerns of their own, sometimes
concealed as coöperatives, and not infrequently as official agents of the
state trading organizations themselves. The Soviet leadership sought to
attract foreign capital by offering "concessions" to capitalist entrepreneurs,
but the bait proved unalluring, and in all but a few cases negotiations
collapsed.

The NEP marked a profound change in the political climate of the
new Soviet regime. After the romantic heroics of the Civil War period
and the tense expectation that all problems would be resolved by the
imminent triumph of the world revolution, the Party found itself thrown
back on its own resources, faced with the humdrum task of building the
conditions of survival out of the ruins which it inherited from War Communism. Many Party members found it all but impossible to adjust to
Lenin's injunction, "Learn to trade." As Lenin declared in his political
report to the Eleventh Party Congress in 1922:

> The whole point is that responsible Communists — even the best of them,
> who are unquestionably honest and loyal, who in the old days suffered penal
> servitude and did not fear death — cannot trade, because they are not business-
> men, they have not learned to trade, do not want to learn and do not understand
> that they must start from the ABC. What! Communists, revolutionaries who
> have made the greatest revolution in the world . . . must they learn from ordi-
> nary salesmen? But these ordinary salesmen have had ten years' warehouse
> experience and know the business, whereas the responsible Communists and
> devoted revolutionaries do not know the business, and do not even realize that
> they do not know it.[28]

The effect of the NEP was to bring the Party organizers to the fore; the revolutionary agitators and Civil War heroes began to fall by the way. A powerful impulse was given to the transformation of the party of revolution into the party of order.

The Party compensated for its concessions to the peasantry and the private trader by utilizing the interval of the NEP to tighten its hold on the political instruments of power. After 1922 any form of Menshevik, SR, or other anti-Communist political activity was treated as counter-revolutionary and ruthlessly extirpated. While the battle for the succession which set in even before Lenin's death produced a major Party crisis, the outcome of the struggle was a strengthening of the power of the central apparatus and the emergence of Stalin as the undisputed ruler of the Party's destinies. The Party leadership maintained a firm grip on the army, the secret police, and the administrative and trade-union apparatus. While the Party continued to be weakly represented in the countryside, it greatly expanded its membership in the major urban areas. No organized force appeared to challenge its dominating position on the Soviet political scene.

The initial recuperative effects of NEP policies fortified the position of the Party leadership. With the introduction of the tax in kind, peasant disorders died down; and after the disastrous harvest of 1921, a steady improvement in agricultural production was evident. A marked revival of light industry took place, and consumer goods became more plentiful. Although there was a lag in heavy industry accompanied by considerable unemployment and worker dissatisfaction, a modicum of relief was provided by unemployment benefits and the perceptible improvement in economic conditions generally.

The new Soviet state, nevertheless, faced a dilemma for which there was no easy resolution. However firmly it controlled the instruments of state power, it remained essentially an army of occupation in an over-whelmingly peasant country. It might conceivably have transformed itself into a peasant government by shaping its policy around peasant demands, but the socialist and industrial orientation of Communism well-nigh precluded such a transformation. Both the logic of long-term survival and the dogmas of inherited ideology dictated a program of industrialization. As Lenin put it in his report to the Fourth Congress of the Communist International, in November 1922:

> The salvation of Russia lies not only in a good harvest on the peasant farms — that is not enough; and not only in the good condition of light industry, which provides the peasantry with consumers' goods — this too is not enough; we also need *heavy* industry. . .
> . . . Unless we save heavy industry, unless we restore it, we shall not be able to build up any industry; and without heavy industry we shall be doomed as an independent country. . .

Heavy industry needs state subsidies. If we cannot provide them, then we are doomed as a civilized state — let alone as a socialist state.[29]

Given the situation in which the Soviet regime found itself in the twenties, the only important source from which an industrialization fund could be accumulated was the peasantry. Long-term foreign loans, the historical instrument of industrial development in backward countries, were not available. The concessions policy of the Soviet regime met almost complete frustration. The only remaining alternative was aptly described by V. M. Smirnov and E. A. Preobrazhensky as "primitive socialist accumulation," the diversion of the output of the peasantry and the private sector of the economy to finance investment in socialized heavy industry.

The NEP provided no ready expedients for securing a large-scale diversion of peasant production to subsidize industrialization. The introduction of the tax in kind stimulated a considerable increase in agricultural output; but it was also accompanied by a substantial reduction in agricultural exports as compared with pre-World War I days when the surpluses extracted from the peasants were used to finance a considerable inflow of foreign capital goods and luxury items. Under NEP, the peasant, after paying his tax in kind, could dispose of his remaining output in any way that pleased him. Since the terms of trade with the towns after 1922 were increasingly unfavorable to the peasantry (the so-called "scissors crisis"), the small peasant's propensity to consume his own output, which had been spurred by the agricultural revolution, was given an additional fillip. The kulaks, or well-to-do farmers, produced a far larger share of their output for the market, but when price relationships were unfavorable, they were also prepared to withhold their grain in order to drive a hard bargain to safeguard their interests. As the NEP developed, social differentiation in the countryside intensified; the less efficient peasant landowners fell back into the status of poor peasants and hired laborers, and the position of the kulaks was strengthened.

Broadly speaking, the Party leadership confronted two polar extremes among the alternatives which were available for dealing with the problem of the peasant and industrialization.[30] One position, which is commonly associated with the program of Bukharin and the Right Opposition of 1928–29, counseled avoidance of repressive measures in dealing with the peasantry. The Bukharin group was prepared to offer price concessions to the peasantry in order to encourage production for market. As long as the Party maintained its control of the instruments of power, the Right Wing believed that the road to socialism was safeguarded. It saw no danger in tolerating and even encouraging the emergence of strong peasant holdings which would direct larger proportions of their output to the market. While it was prepared to squeeze the kulak through increased taxation, it also recognized that in order to obtain large grain deliveries, more and cheaper consumer goods would have to be made available to the rural population. The implications of this position were twofold: (1) a substantial part of the burden of industrialization would be shifted to the urban population, and (2) industrialization would have to proceed at a relatively slow pace.

The opposing position, ultimately incorporated by Stalin in the First Five Year Plan, started from the assumption that a program of rapid industrialization was imperative and that nothing short of a wholesale reconstruction of Soviet agriculture could guarantee the grain reserves to carry it forward. The Stalinist plan, which was borrowed in many of its aspects from the proposals of the Left Opposition which he had earlier repudiated, involved the preliminary application of "emergency measures" against the kulaks in order to expropriate the surpluses which they were allegedly hoarding and the subsequent liquidation of the kulaks as class enemies. In order to increase the productivity of agriculture, mechanized grain factories or state farms were to be extended, and the poor and middle peasants were to be enrolled in collective farms which would be served by machine-tractor stations equipped with modern agricultural implements. This grandiose scheme also carried its hidden implications as later events were to disclose. The main burden of accumulating an industrialization fund was to be transferred to the countryside.

Fundamentally, the Stalinist program meant a revival of the Civil War policy of forced requisitions under conditions giving the state much more powerful instruments to enforce its demands. By herding the agricultural population into state and collective farms, the regime would be able to operate through a relatively limited number of controlled collective units instead of dealing individually with millions of peasant households. While the advocates of this plan professed to believe that rapid industrialization could be combined with an increase in consumption as the result of the application of modern technical methods to agriculture, in practice this hope was soon shown to be illusory. Mechanization could only be introduced slowly, and meanwhile the state faced the problem of extracting the grain from the collective and state farms to pay for the industrial base on which the production of tractors and other agricultural implements depended. Stripped of its propaganda verbiage, the Stalinist program foreshadowed a profound extension of the scope of totalitarian power. The peasantry was to be brought to heel and tied to state ends. The surpluses extracted from the peasantry were to provide the wherewithal to create a powerful industrial structure which would render the Soviet citadel impregnable.

The Era of Five Year Plans

As Stalin consolidated his position in the Party, he pressed forward with the realization of his program. The NEP was liquidated, and the era of Five Year Plans began. The new phase in the development of the Soviet system marked a Third Revolution, far more important in its long-term consequences than the February and October Revolutions of 1917 which were its entr'actes. It represented a determined effort to destroy the petty-bourgeois peasant revolution which had been achieved in 1917 and to seize the positions which the peasantry had occupied during the NEP. It launched the Soviet Union on a course of industrialization which transformed it into a first-class military power. It was also accompanied by the emergence and consolidation of a full-blown totalitarian regime which ruthlessly crushed any trace of political dissent and subordinated every form of social organization to its own purposes.

When the Third Revolution was launched in 1928 with its program of collectivization and mechanization in the countryside and rapid industrialization in urban areas, great stress was placed on its welfare objectives. The proponents of the First Five Year Plan proclaimed that it would both double the fixed capital of the economy and produce a marked increase in per capita consumption. The assumption proved highly unrealistic: the expansion of heavy industry was accompanied by a marked decline in living standards. Convinced that its own survival and future as a great power depended on a high tempo of industrialization, the regime showed itself adamant in pushing forward its program of investment in heavy industry.

Power took precedence over welfare. Stalin, in his speech to the First All-Union Conference of Managers of Socialist Industry on February 4, 1931, was insistent: "It is sometimes asked whether it is not possible to slow down the tempo a bit, to put a check on the movement. No, comrades, it is not possible! The tempo must not be reduced!" [31] Returning to the same theme at a joint plenum of the Central Committee and the Central Control Commission of the Party on January 7, 1933, Stalin explained that one of the primary purposes of the First Five Year Plan "was to create . . . all the necessary technical and economic prerequisites for increasing to the utmost the defensive capacity of the country," and frankly conceded that the production of consumer goods had been relegated "to the background." "The Party," he continued, "whipped up the country and spurred it onward . . . so as not to lose time, so as to make the utmost use of the respite to create in the U.S.S.R. the basis of industrialization, which is the foundation of her power. The Party could not afford to wait and manoeuvre; it had to pursue the policy of accelerating development to the utmost." [32]

In mobilizing support for the Five Year Plan, the Party leadership resorted to a variety of appeals. The sacrifices of today were justified in terms of the Promised Land of plenty toward which they were directed. The boldness and constructive vision of the Plan were contrasted with the pessimism and demoralization which spread through the West in the wake of the Great Depression of 1929. As Stalin strengthened his hold on the Party by eliminating his left- and right-wing competitors, he also sought to stimulate unity by unleashing a powerful resurgence of revolutionary zeal. After the lassitude and grey dullness of the NEP, the Plan opened up an exhilarating period of struggle and combat, a leap forward into the New Jerusalem. The last remnants of private capitalism appeared to be headed for extinction. The immensity of the planned enterprises, their call for sacrifice, and their promises for the future exercised a particularly powerful attraction for Communist youth. Many of the activists and idealists who had previously been drawn to Trotsky and the left-wing banner now rallied behind Stalin.

The first years of the Five Year Plan marked a return to the militant traditions of the Civil War period and War Communism. The air was electric with positions to be stormed, class enemies to be destroyed, and fortresses to be built. At least within Party and Komsomol or Young Communist circles, the outpouring of enthusiasm was genuine and impressive. It was accompanied by a temporary reaffirmation of proletarian orthodoxies. Strenuous efforts were made to increase the proportion of Party members from the bench. Egalitarianism was given a brief stimulus. Anti-religious campaigns took on new life. Komsomol fervor manifested itself in the reëstablishment of communes, in participation in the collectivization drive, and in the assumption of all sorts of disagreeable assignments. As the Plan gathered momentum, it left no aspect of Soviet life untouched. Literature and the arts became subject to its command. The schools were drawn into its service. The Soviet scene became a battlefield in which class lines were sharpened and the Party moved to the attack.

As always, when difficulties developed and hardships mounted, scapegoats were provided as a lightning rod for mass discontent. The liquidation of the kulaks was accompanied by a campaign against the old intelligentsia who were charged with economic sabotage and conspiracy with foreign powers to overthrow the Soviet regime. A whole series of proceedings — the Shakhty prosecutions of 1927–28, the trial of the Industrial Party in December 1930, the arraignment of the Menshevik professors in March 1931, the trial of the Metro-Vickers engineers in January 1933 — offered a dramatic procession of "saboteurs" and "enemy agents" who were alleged to be the source of all difficulties and who played their part in diverting dissatisfaction from the regime.

The Imperatives of Industrialization

Meanwhile, industrialization imposed its own imperatives. Construction and production became the prime problems. Revolutionary zeal alone could not produce steel, dig coal, or manufacture tractors. Mass meetings were exciting, but oratory was no substitute for locomotives. After the first burst of grandiose intoxication had exhausted itself, it became evident that industrialization presented the challenge of a new discipline which had to be patiently mastered. Efficient factory managers had to be developed and trained and engineers and technicians provided in large numbers. Illiterate or half-literate peasants had to be transformed into a modern industrial labor force, taught necessary skills, and domesticated to the demands of the assembly line. Incentives had to be provided to stimulate production and habits of order and precision instilled to assure quality production. The educational system had to be remodeled to indoctrinate students in the values of efficiency and conscious discipline and to produce the officers as well as the soldiers and "noncoms" of the new labor army. Sanctions had to be invoked to keep workers on their jobs and to prevent absence, tardiness, or "labor-flitting." The large-scale organizational requirements of industrialization appeared to call for the reinforcement of authority, the focusing of responsibility, a hierarchical structure that capitalized the values of specialization and division of labor, accounting regulations that ensured precise control, and a system of income distribution that provided incentives for increased production and efficiency. One of the most pressing needs was a vast expansion of managerial, engineering, and technical personnel. The Party leadership sought to meet this need by utilizing the remnants of the old intelligentsia, by importing foreign specialists, and by setting in motion a vast training program to produce a new Soviet-bred technical intelligentsia which might ultimately take over the management of the economy. The utilization of the old intelligentsia presented real problems since the group had only recently been assigned the role of scapegoat for the early difficulties attendant upon industrialization. Now it appeared that the technical skills of the intelligentsia were indispensable, and Stalin boldly announced a change of front. In June 1931, he proclaimed:

We must change our policy towards the old technical intelligentsia. . . . Whereas during the height of the wrecking activities our attitude towards the old technical intelligentsia was mainly expressed by the policy of routing them, now. . . our attitude towards them must be expressed mainly in the policy of enlisting them and solicitude for them. It would be wrong and undialectical to continue our former policy under the new, changed conditions. It would be stupid and unwise to regard practically every expert and engineer of the old school as an undetected criminal and wrecker. We have always regarded and still regard "expert-baiting" as a harmful and disgraceful phenomenon.[33]

Both the employment of the old intelligentsia and the hiring of foreign specialists were viewed as stopgap expedients; the major long-term task was the education of a new Soviet-trained intelligentsia. Over the next years, many new technical institutes were established, and the most ambitious elements in the younger generation crowded into them to become the engineers and industrial managers of the future.

The program of rapid industrialization lifted the new managerial and technical intelligentsia to positions of power and influence in Soviet society. The industrial revolution, like the October Revolution before it, involved a tremendous release of energy and swift upward mobility for those with the gifts and inclination to take advantage of the situation in which they found themselves. The expansion of industry opened up many new opportunities for quick promotion to commanding responsibilities. The graduates of the technical institutes entered a career arena in which there was an almost insatiable demand for qualified technical personnel. At the same time, the curricula of the technical institutes and the taxing character of the assignments which awaited their graduates enforced increasingly rigorous standards of aptitude and knowledge. Komsomol and Party membership and favorable class origins facilitated admission into the technical institutes, and even subsequent promotion, but they no longer operated as the sole guaranty of a successful career. The ability to master complex technical data became a basic and inescapable requirement for survival in important positions in Soviet industry. Leading posts were still reserved for qualified Party members. But trusted non-Party engineers were also thrust forward into positions of considerable responsibility requiring high technical qualifications, and class origin became a subordinate requirement for admission to the higher educational institutions.

As the Party leadership found itself more and more preoccupied with the complex problems of managing a society in process of rapid industrialization, it also became increasingly dependent on the technical skills of its new managerial class. During the middle and late thirties, the Party placed increasing emphasis on the recruitment of the new technical intelligentsia. At the Eighteenth Party Congress in 1939, the last barriers were razed when the Party Rules were modified to facilitate the admission of managerial and technical personnel. The reception of the technical intelligentsia into the Party constituted an important step in the direction of merging Party and state administration. The proletarian base of the Party was submerged, and its social composition registered the rising ascendancy of the new administrative and managerial elite.

As the new industrial elite emerged and crystallized, it sought to strengthen both its authority and its privileges. The Party leadership allotted it high material rewards and perquisites in order to consolidate its loyalty to the regime. Managerial prerogatives were reinforced, and one-man management became the prevailing practice in industry. The powers of the trade unions were curbed, and the activities of local Party organizations were redirected toward broad control rather than detailed interference in the minutiae of managerial decision-making. Factory directors were vested with considerable discretion to maneuver with the means at their disposal as long as the goals assigned to them were fulfilled.

At the same time, the leaders of the regime took measures to ensure that the powers of the new elite would be kept within bounds. Police and Party controls were used as instruments of surveillance to guarantee that the demands of the top leadership were fulfilled. Failure of performance or the slightest evidence of disloyalty was subject to drastic punishment. Despite its privileges and new-found authority, management functioned in a milieu of insecurity and institutionalized suspicion. The industrial elite as a class was indispensable; its individual members were expendable. Given the pressures under which it operated, the new industrial elite remained a circulating rather than a stabilized elite. Privileges attached to function; they disappeared when the function was no longer performed.

While rapid industrialization brought new prerogatives as well as responsibilities to the technical intelligentsia, its primary impact on labor was a tightening of discipline. Planned industrialization was accompanied by increasing resort to compulsion. After the defeat of the Right Opposition in 1928–29, the trade unions were stripped of such wage-bargaining functions as they still retained. Their role was limited to settling minor grievances, exhorting the workers to increase production, and administering social insurance and welfare programs.

Labor recruitment took the form of large-scale transfers of the surplus rural population to the new industrial centers. Although voluntary in form and sanctified by contracts entered into between industrial firms and collective farms, the transfers were in fact mandatory, and collective farms had no choice except to deliver the quotas assigned to them. In 1940, with the establishment of the State Labor Reserves, the recruitment of youth for service in industry was placed, in effect, on a conscription basis. As presently organized, the State Labor Reserves draft more than a million youths each year for assignment in industry, mining, transport, and specialized agricultural work. Two-year courses are provided to train skilled workers; short-term training is provided for less skilled workers. At the end of the courses, the draftees are assigned to specific enterprises where they are ordinarily required to work for at least four years. Criminal penalties may be imposed in the event that they leave school or job without official permission.

As industrialization gathered momentum, the severity of job discipline was greatly intensified. The First Five Year Plan was marked by tremendous labor turnover and absenteeism as workers rushed from factory to factory in search of better working conditions. Exhortation to workers to stay on the job proved ineffective. In October 1930 the Party leadership turned to penalties. "Deserters" and "absentees" were threatened with the loss of industrial employment for six months. This, too, proved unworkable since labor was scarce and factory managers hired any worker who offered himself. In 1932 a system of internal passports was introduced. In order to check labor-flitting, the regime next decreed that "deserters" and "absentees" be deprived of ration cards and living quarters. Even these drastic penalties were frequently evaded by enterprises desperate for labor.

Beginning in 1938, even stricter rules of discipline were instituted. In December 1938 all wage earners were provided with "labor books" containing a full record of their employment. No worker could be hired except upon presentation of his book, which remained with the enterprise as long as he was employed by it. Infractions of labor discipline could be punished by dismissal from the job, which also involved loss of living quarters and a reduction of social insurance benefits. Managers who failed to enforce these penalties were themselves subject to penal prosecutions. A decree issued in June 1940 made employees who were more than twenty minutes late for work without a valid medical excuse subject to a penalty of compulsory labor at their usual place of work with a deduction of up to 25 per cent of their wages, and repetition of the offense carried more drastic penalties. Cases of petty larceny and acts of hooliganism committed at the place of employment were punishable by imprisonment for one year. In June 1940 all workers were frozen on their jobs. Changes of employment required the express permission of management, and departures from employment without such authorization were punishable by imprisonment. In the case of defense industries or industries connected with defense, unauthorized abandonment of work was triable by court martial and punishable by sentences of from five to eight years of forced labor.[34]

Since exclusive reliance on compulsion offered a poor stimulus to increased labor productivity, the regime turned early to more positive incentives. In the first surge of enthusiasm aroused by the Five Year Plan, considerable emphasis was placed on socialist competition. The *udarnik*, or shock worker, who broke production records was featured as the new hero of Soviet society and awarded special privileges in the form of better living quarters and better supplies of food and consumer goods. This departure from the egalitarianism for which the trade unions had pressed during the NEP soon received the authoritative blessing of Stalin himself.

In an address to a conference of Soviet business executives in June 1931, Stalin denounced "the Leftist practice of wage equalization" and called for a readjustment of the wage structure which would check labor turnover and provide incentives to workers to improve their skills and raise their productivity.[35]

The effect of his speech was soon felt in a major overhauling of the system of wage payments. Wage differentials were developed to attract workers to heavy industry and to encourage their migration to the Urals and the eastern regions. Piece rates were rapidly extended in order to tailor wage payments to productivity. Output in excess of fixed norms was paid at progressively increasing rates, and the performances of Stakhanovites, or outstanding workers, were rewarded by impressive bonuses, special privileges, publicity, and honorifics. The achievements of the Stakhanovites, which were frequently managed with the unnoted assistance of supplementary helpers, led to a general raising of the average norms of output and involved increased pressure on so-called "backward" workers who did not enjoy Stakhanovite advantages. Wage differentials widened sharply, and the profile of the working class reflected a strange combination of a select labor aristocracy and a large mass of poorly paid "sweated" workers who enjoyed few, if any, amenities. The industrialization drive exacted its price in the cities as well as the countryside. Its burdens fell heavily on the mass of unskilled and semiskilled workers in the factories.

The Third Revolution, with its stress on rapid industrialization and the building of military strength, had a profound effect on the development of the Soviet system. Egalitarianism was repudiated in the search for a system of wage payments and income distribution that would maximize efficiency and stimulate production; mass welfare gave way to capital expansion and the accumulation of armaments. While the self-interest of the regime dictated the maintenance of the labor force at a level which would sustain its efficiency and command its support, the continued emphasis on construction of heavy industry and large military expenditures made the fulfillment of this objective difficult. When pressure threatened to become unbearable, as it did toward the end of the First Five Year Plan, the regime temporarily relaxed its demands. The improvement in the standard of living in the mid-thirties was designed to revive hope and to provide a foretaste of the better life to come, but the acceleration of military preparations on the eve of World War II and the bitter experience of the war itself subjected the Soviet populace to another period of great hardships. In the immediate postwar period, the standard of living rose markedly compared with the low point during the war, but the resumption of the industrialization drive at the end of the war and the new armament race ushered in by the cold war augured another phase of downward pressure on further improvement of living conditions.

Stalin's Totalitarian Formula

The organization of the economy and society to maximize industrial and military strength involved a strengthening of the totalitarian features of the regime. "The revolution from above" which was imposed on the peasantry and the cuts in consumption which "primitive socialist accumulation" demanded could not be achieved without increasing resort to compulsion. The consolidation of Stalin's absolute power, the ruthless purge of party dissidents, the strengthening of the bureaucratic and hierarchical features of the regime, the expansion in the role of the secret police, and the rise of forced labor advanced hand in hand with forced-draft industrialization and militarization.

The formula of totalitarian rule as it took shape under Stalin's ministrations was a complex one. It represented, in one aspect, a drive to safeguard his own security by obliterating all actual or potential competing centers of power. Positively, it tried to saturate and paralyze the minds of the Soviet populace with a monolithic stream of agitation and propaganda stressing the superiority of the Soviet system and the virtues of its leaders. Negatively, it sought to deny the people access to any alternative by cutting them off from the outside world and from each other. Through the secret police, it attempted to create a milieu of pervasive insecurity founded on ever-present fear of the informer and the labor camp. The Party and the secret police guarded the loyalty of army and administration and, in turn, watched each other. In this system of institutionalized mutual suspicion, the competing hierarchies of Party, police, army, and administration were kept in purposeful conflict and provided with no point of final resolution short of Stalin and his trusted henchmen in the Politburo. The concentration of power in Stalin's hands rested on the dispersal of power among his subordinates.

In another of its aspects, the Stalinist formula sought to come to terms with the demands of industrialization. It enlisted the new Soviet intelligentsia in its service and rewarded the elite among them with high material privileges and elevated social status. It created a labor aristocracy of honored Stakhanovites to serve as the bellwether of the working class. It arranged its incentive system to reward the more productive workers and to penalize the backward and the inefficient. It risked the alienation of the mass of unskilled and semiskilled workers by paying them poorly and supplying them inadequately, but it maintained its control over them by subjecting them to the most rigorous discipline.

In order to consolidate his position as the leader of the party of order in Soviet society, Stalin also endeavored to identify totalitarian rule with the forces of tradition and respectability in Russian life. This search for stability and legitimacy took him along some strange and devious paths. It led to a drastic reorganization of the educational system, the abandonment of its early experimental and progressive features, and its transformation into an authoritarian instrument to instill devotion to the regime and to prepare youth for their appointed roles in the Soviet hierarchical structure. It manifested itself in a restoration of the authority of the family, in restrictions on abortions, in encouragement of child-bearing, and in tightening marriage bonds. It produced an uneasy *de facto* "concordat" with the church in which the political loyalty of the clergy and their communicants was exchanged for a precarious toleration of religious practices. It expressed itself in a striking rehabilitation of patriotism as the cohesive force of Soviet society and sought increasingly to present the Soviet regime as the legitimate heir of the best in the Russian past. It induced a new emphasis on law as an instrument to enforce the responsibility of the subject to the state and to introduce rationality and order in the relations among state enterprises and individuals.

The drive to stabilize the regime's authority was accompanied by a profound reorientation in Soviet ideology directed toward the exaltation of statism. The theory of the withering away of the state was all but repudiated. The primacy of base over superstructure, one of the hallowed Marxist orthodoxies, was in effect reversed and the determining influence of environment minimized. The state superstructure was glorified and magnified as the creative source of all initiative and direction in Soviet society. The role of the individual was redefined in terms of conscious, disciplined subordination to state purposes.[36]

This remarkable development has its parallels in the natural history of other revolutions. Every revolutionary movement undertakes to consolidate its authority after it has won power and exhausted the dynamic momentum of its program. Even the most authoritarian of regimes cannot evade the problem of coming to terms with its environment. The price of survival involves the abandonment of utopian goals which cannot be realized, the repudiation of orthodoxies which were previously sacrosanct, and the adoption of expedients which offend the most treasured dogmas of the original revolutionary program. The most ironical chapters of revolutionary history are its unintended consequences.

The complex of influences and circumstances which contributed to the Soviet restoration of traditional symbols of authority is not easily unraveled. Industrialization was an important shaping force. In the realm of education, for example, industrial discipline appeared to call for a school system which would liquidate illiteracy; teach the elements of reading, writing, and arithmetic to all; instill habits of order, obedience, and precision; and provide an adequate foundation in mathematics and scientific subjects for those students who would go on to higher technical institutes and eventual employment in technical, engineering, and managerial capacities. The child-centered Soviet school of the twenties did not fulfill these objectives: discipline was lax; the authority of teachers was minimized; traditional subjects were not taught; experimentalism ran riot; and curricula were in process of constant revision. The educational reforms of the early thirties with their emphasis on the restoration of discipline, the reinforcement of the authority of the teacher, and the teaching of fundamentals represented a first adjustment of the educational system to the needs of the industrial order.[37] The encouragement of authoritarian family relationships and the tightening of divorce requirements find at least partial explanation in the same pattern of response: the habits of order and obedience nurtured in the well-disciplined family circle were expected to carry over to the assembly line.

The legal reforms of the thirties were also partly a consequence of the industrialization drive.[38] During the twenties law tended to be regarded as an outworn survival of bourgeois society which would soon wither away. Its transitional utility was limited to service as a proletarian weapon to suppress class enemies. Members of the working class who committed "socially dangerous" acts tended to be treated more leniently than members of the former ruling classes. The dominant legal philosophy of the period was based upon a deterministic and mechanistic version of Marxism. Criminals were looked upon as victims of their environment to be rehabilitated rather than individuals who had to be made to suffer for their faults. As Soviet society moved in the direction of Communism, crime was expected to disappear.

The large-scale social disorganization and crime waves which accompanied industrialization and collectivization made such views appear increasingly anachronistic. An industrial society called for order and discipline, and the Soviet leadership demanded that the legal system fulfill these requirements. In 1930 Stalin pronounced:

> We are for the withering away of the state. But at the same time we stand for strengthening of the proletarian dictatorship, which constitutes the most powerful, the mightiest of all governing powers that have ever existed. The highest development of governmental power for the purpose of preparing the conditions for the withering away of governmental power, this is the Marxian formula. Is this "contradictory"? Yes, it is "contradictory." But this contradiction is life, and it reflects completely the Marxian dialectic.[39]

The revisions in the legal codes which followed were marked by a substantial extension of the repressive machinery of the state and by the emergence of a new voluntaristic concept of crime in which the individual was held to strict accountability for his shortcomings and failures in meeting the demands of the regime. Blame could no longer be shifted to the environment; for, Stalin proclaimed, "There are no fortresses which Bolsheviks cannot storm." [40] The prestige of legal institutions was reëstablished; Stalin declared in 1936, "We need the stability of laws more than ever." [41] The new functions of law were to enforce the ruthless pace of industrialization, to instill the habits of self-discipline and voluntary subordination which it required, to lay the legal foundations for a rationalized industrial order, and to stabilize the position of the ruling group by providing a system of regularized sanctions and controls which would reinforce its authority.

Industrialization was important but by no means exclusive among the interacting forces that nourished the cultural and social transformation of the thirties. Behind industrialization lay the determination to create an impregnable, self-sufficient citadel which would be safe from outside attack and which could itself develop into a springboard for the expansion of Soviet power into the outside world. Dimming hopes of world revolution during the twenties threw the Soviet leadership back on its own resources. After the defeat of Trotsky and the Left Opposition, Stalin's doctrine of "Socialism in One Country" was enshrined as official dogma. Inevitably, it took on strong nationalistic overtones. In theory, the Soviet Union remained a beacon for the oppressed masses of the world. In practice, the Comintern was transformed into an instrument for the pursuit of Soviet state interests, and the leaders of the Soviet regime became increasingly absorbed in extending and consolidating their power in the only arena which was then effectively open to them.

During the early years of the industrialization drive, the nationalist orientation which it embodied was obscured by the atmosphere of class struggle which it generated. The first surge of enthusiasm was marked by a revival of orthodox Marxism and a tightening of ideological lines. This was the period of the temporary dictatorship of RAPP (Russian Association of Proletarian Writers), when writers were being mobilized as "shock workers of the Plan," when violent attacks were launched against "class enemies on the history front," and when nationalist historians such as Tarle and Platonov were accused of "bourgeois objectivism" and exiled. History as taught by the then leading historian M. N. Pokrovsky was a dance of Marxian categories; it was "politics projected into the past," with the Tsarist epoch portrayed as a period of unrelieved oppression for the masses.

As industrialization and collectivization generated their tensions and discontents and as the rise of Hitler transformed the fear of capitalist encirclement from a slogan into a real danger, the Stalinist leadership turned to nationalistic and patriotic sentiments to provide an ideological cement for its people which orthodox Marxism was powerless to give. *Pravda* on June 9, 1934, sounded the new appeal: "For the Fatherland!"

"That cry," *Pravda* declared, "kindles the flame of heroism, the flame of creative initiative in all fields in all the realms of our rich, our many-sided life. . . . The defense of the fatherland is the supreme law. . . . For the fatherland, for its honor, glory, might, and prosperity!" [42]

The new cry was to swell into a mighty chorus during the next few years. In 1934 the dead Pokrovsky was denounced as a "vulgarizer" of Marxism, and under the guidance of Stalin, Kirov, and Zhdanov, the writers of history texts received instructions which resulted in a complete revision of attitude toward the Russian past.[43] The nationalist historians were recalled and restored to their posts. The new history sought to establish the Soviet regime as the custodian of national interests. It celebrated Tsarist military victories and territorial expansion, taught pride in Russia's achievements and the accomplishments of her great men. It addressed itself particularly to those critical moments when the nation fought for its existence and repelled the invader from Russian soil. The heroic deeds of Tsarist generals such as Suvorov and Kutuzov were toasted in historical novels and plays. Peter the Great and eventually even Ivan the Terrible were refurbished as Soviet heroes and presented as farsighted patriots and great statesmen whose despotic measures were justified by the constructive ends they served.

The rewriting of history also extended into the Soviet period. Stalin was portrayed as a hero of legendary proportions; the Old Bolsheviks whom he purged were completely denigrated. The new patriotism and the cult of Stalin went hand in hand. They were propagated with particular intensity in the army, but no sector of Soviet society was neglected. As *Krasnaya Zvezda*, the army newspaper, put it in 1940, "History knows many instances when large nations and splendid armies fell to pieces, only because they were not supported by national unity, the unity of the country." [44]

The patriotic sentiments so assiduously revived in the prewar years were cultivated with redoubled vigor during World War II. They were fed by hatred of the Nazi invaders, and they contributed to bringing regime and people nearer together. The war became the Great Patriotic War, the Great Fatherland War, and a National War of Liberation. The regime sought both to stimulate and capitalize the genuine nationalist upsurge which the Nazi invasion evoked. Marxist slogans were temporarily subdued, the Patriarchate was restored, a new national anthem replaced the "International," the army was glorified, and patriotism stressed at every turn.

With the approach of victory, there was increasing evidence of a tightening of ideological lines. Beginning with the turn of the tide at Stalingrad and intensifying during 1944 and 1945, theoretical training of both Party and non-Party personnel in Marxist-Leninist doctrine, which had been neglected during the early phases of the war, once more was stressed. Special attention was devoted to the proper indoctrination of the population of the districts that had been liberated from the Germans. *Pravda*, in its issue of October 17, 1944, pronounced:

> During the occupation, the German invaders tried by every method to poison the consciousness of Soviet men and women and to confuse them. . .
>
> It is the duty of Party organizations to stimulate tirelessly the political activity of the workers. . . Particular attention must be paid to the question of implanting in the population a socialist attitude toward labor and public property, strengthening state discipline, and overcoming the private-property, anti-collective-farm, and anti-state tendencies planted by the German occupants.[45]

The mood and temper of the Soviet populace at the end of the war posed serious difficulties for the regime. After the bitter sacrifices of the war, many yearned for peace and quiet, for a relaxation of tempo, and for an opportunity to enjoy the good things of life. Soldiers who served in the West caught a glimpse of capitalist comforts and luxuries which were unavailable in the Soviet Union and transmitted disquieting doubts about the perfection of the Soviet paradise. Party propagandists and agitators encountered considerable mass apathy when they lectured on political themes. Some members of the intelligentsia displayed disturbing apolitical tendencies. Their openly expressed admiration for Western ideas and artistic models, which was partly tolerated during the honeymoon period of the war alliance, became a dangerous infection as the cold war intensified.

A series of authoritative pronouncements by Party leaders at the end of the war served as a reminder that the historical perspective of Marxism-Leninism had not been cast into the discard. Stalin's election speech of February 9, 1946, opened with an affirmation of the basic Communist postulates on the nature and causes of capitalist wars and called for a powerful industrial upsurge emphasizing heavy industry and designed to guarantee the "homeland . . . against all possible accidents."[46] The increasingly strong Western resistance to Soviet expansion, expressed in the Truman Doctrine and the Marshall Plan, was accompanied by a rapid deterioration in Soviet-Western relations. Zhdanov's blunt speech at the organizing conference of the Cominform in September 1947 left no doubts about the Soviet position. The world, Zhdanov announced, was divided into two camps, the "imperialist" camp led by the United States and the "anti-imperialist" camp led by the Soviet Union. Foreign Communists were summoned to lead the battle against the "imperialist aggressors." The Communist Party of the Soviet Union was called upon to make the Soviet population aware of the perils they faced and to discipline the masses for new sacrifices.[47]

The emphasis on the dangers of a new capitalist encirclement has been added to the specifically Russian nationalism of the war period to create a new synthesis which is propagated under the slogan of "Soviet patriotism." Soviet patriotism in its current manifestation represents a many-sided effort to mobilize support for the regime and to assert state control over every phase of Soviet life. It relies in part on pure love of country, with particular accent on the leading position of the Great Russian people in the Soviet family of nations.[48] This pro-Russian orientation now takes the form of emphasizing the positive civilizing mission of Tsarist imperialism, in contrast with the previous custom of defending it as a "lesser evil" and the still earlier practice of denouncing in unmitigated terms Tsarist oppression of national minorities. In another aspect, the new patriotism stresses the superiority of the Soviet social and political order over capitalism and accentuates the achievements of Soviet science and learning, industry and agriculture, literature and art. It also marks a return to the conception of the besieged fortress. The "capitalistic warmongers" of the West are portrayed as ready to spring upon the Soviet Union at the first opportunity. The symbol of capitalist encirclement is combined with primitive nationalism to discourage war-weariness and retreat from the tasks ahead and to arouse the energies of the nation to the urgencies of a vast new industrial and military program.

In still another aspect, Soviet patriotism seeks to ignite a xenophobic hatred for the outside, capitalist world. Beginning with the Zhdanov anticosmopolitan decrees which sought to destroy any Soviet remnants of adulation of the West and subservience to foreign thought and foreign literary schools and forms, the campaign mounted to a shrill crescendo in which Americans and their fellow-travelers in the "imperialist camp" were denounced as barbaric savages who out-Nazi the Nazis. By parading dangers, fanciful rather than real, by sealing off the Soviet populace from virtually all contact with the outside world, by appealing to the most primal instincts of obscurantist nationalism, and by saturating the consciousness of its people with a sense of the superiority of the Soviet order, the regime seeks to stimulate whole-souled devotion to Party and state interests as proclaimed by the leadership.

Soviet patriotism thus operates as an ideological tool to weld the people to the regime. Through Soviet patriotism the Party leadership proposes to create the Soviet man of the postwar world — politically conscious, proud of his society, aware of the dangers of "capitalist encirclement," and prepared to make his contribution to the consolidation and expansion of Soviet power.

In the tangled web of interacting influences which contributed to the "traditionalist" restoration that began in the thirties, probably the most basic was the leadership's drive to stabilize its position and to extend its

power in both the Soviet and world arenas. Rapid industrialization and
the revival of traditional nationalism were both directed toward this
larger purpose. Most of the significant "conservative" innovations which
accompanied them were introduced because of the same dominating preoccupation. The educational reforms of the thirties, intended first to serve
the needs of a society in process of rapid industrialization, also created
a channel through which future Soviet citizens were indoctrinated in a
conception of state service and total dedication to its demands. The revolution in jurisprudence during the mid-thirties provided the legal foundations for an industrial society, but in an even more fundamental sense,
represented an affirmation of the power of the state to control every
aspect of the life of its subjects. The new policy toward the family had
clear state purposes: prohibition of nontherapeutic abortions, rigid restrictions on divorces, the establishment of child subsidies, and the rewards held out to "heroine-mothers" of large families appeared unmistakably designed to breed fodder for army and industry. The *modus
vivendi* with the Orthodox Church was also calculated to strengthen the
position of the regime. Though the concessions made to the church were
no doubt offensive to zealous Party members, they helped during the war
to cement the loyalty of the clergy and the mass of believers to the Soviet
cause and insured the continued political subservience of the church
hierarchy in the postwar period.[49]

After the end of the war, the Party leadership pursued an unremitting
campaign to tighten its totalitarian grip on every facet of Soviet life. The
primary purpose was the ideological rearmament of the Soviet peoples,
and the prime victims were the intellectuals. Literature, drama, music,
art, and every branch of learning were purged of every trace of "bourgeois objectivism" and apoliticalness. *Partiinost'* (Party consciousness and
Party spirit) became the new watchword. Partiinost' in practice meant
total dedication to the commands of the leadership. The bureaucratic
model of Stalinism left no room for autonomy except where, as in the
limited freedom accorded to the Orthodox Church, it continued to serve
state interests.

The emergence of Stalinism in the conservative garb of the party of
tradition and order was once described as a "Great Retreat." [50] It gave
this surface appearance, yet the phrase was delusive. In utilizing such
traditional pillars of authority as nationalism, family, and the church,
Stalin did not surrender power. He consolidated it. By tapping the wellsprings of national sentiment, he broadened the base of his own influence,
tightened his control of his own dominion, and increased the leverage
which he could exert in the world theater of power.

The great tour de force of Stalinism was the construction of a totalitarian edifice which bestrides the revolutionary and authoritarian heritage

of Leninism, the dynamic nationalism of Tsarism, the stabilizing equilibrium of conservative social institutions, and the rigid bureaucratic hierarchy of a full-blown police state. The death of Stalin on March 5, 1953, left that structure temporarily intact but still to be tested in the crucible of new leadership and incalculable events. Those who inherited the mantle of Stalin's authority pledged themselves to preserve his legacy and to carry forward with his plans for strengthening Soviet industrial and armed might. Like other epigones before them, they faced the problem of containing the forces which he had set in motion and of making his revolution the last revolution. They had still to ponder what E. I. Zamyatin (one of the talented writers whom the Soviet regime muzzled) once observed, "There is no such thing as the last revolution; the number of revolutions is infinite." [51]

PART TWO

The Role of the Party

Chapter 5

The Dictatorship of the Party in Theory and Practice

The *coup d'état* of November 7, 1917, transformed the Bolsheviks at one stroke from a revolutionary to a governing party. In assuming the responsibilities of governance, the Bolsheviks faced the problem of defining their relationships to other parties and to the organs of state power which they inherited or hoped to create. The Marxist intellectual armory on which Lenin drew offered little in the way of precise guidance for revolutionaries come to power. Lenin's pamphlet, *The State and Revolution*, written while he was still in hiding in August and September 1917, assembled most of the brief quotations from Marx and Engels which bore on the subject; but as a vade mecum for the construction of the socialist state, they left much to be desired.

The Leninist exegesis of Marxism represented an effort to reassert its revolutionary content. Disregarding the occasional passages in which Marx and Engels envisaged the possibility of a peaceful, democratic road to socialism,[1] Lenin seized on the conception of the dictatorship of the proletariat as summing up the essence of Marxist doctrine on the character of state power in the transitional period between capitalism and Communism. Following Marx and Engels, he turned to the experience of the Paris Commune to illustrate the nature of the dictatorship of the proletariat in action.[2] For Lenin, the Commune demonstrated that "the working class cannot simply seize the available ready machinery of the state and set it going for its own ends"; it must "shatter the bureaucratic and military machine." He heralded measures of the Commune — the abolition of the old army and the old police, the payment of workers' wages to officials, the organization of the Commune into "a working corporation, legislative and executive at the same time," the election of delegates, the filling of all administrative and judicial posts on the basis of universal suffrage and recall — as foreshadowing the practices which the Bolsheviks would adopt on coming to power. The "commune state" would represent the incarnation of the interests of the proletariat. The power of the state would be used to crush the bourgeoisie and prepare the way for the eventual emergence of a classless communist society in which class repression would be replaced by voluntary coöperation.[3]

For socialists who visualized their victory as the culmination of a long process of industrialization in the course of which the working class became the preponderant element in society, the dictatorship of the proletariat implied majority rule. This "democratic" refuge was denied to Lenin and the Bolsheviks. The Russian industrial proletariat was a small minority in an overwhelmingly agrarian country. To exercise power in the name of the proletariat was to impose the rule of the few on the many; the dictatorship of the Russian proletariat was by definition a minority dictatorship. To make the problem more complex, the industrial working class was itself divided in its political loyalties. Some followed the leadership of the Bolsheviks; others gave their allegiance to the Mensheviks and even to the Socialist-Revolutionaries, whose main strength was with the peasantry.

One-Party Rule Versus Coalition Government

After their seizure of power, the Bolsheviks confronted a difficult choice. To govern alone was to bear the stigma of a minority dictatorship and to cement the strength of the opposition. To share power with other parties and to await the judgment of a constituent assembly based on popular elections was to risk losing the fruits of the insurrection. The path of dictatorship led irrevocably in the direction of civil war, the suppression of the opposition, and the invocation of terror. The path of coalition and constitutionalism meant compromise, concession, and the abdication of supreme power.

Within the bosom of Bolshevism, two conflicting patterns of thought struggled for ascendancy. The majority group, led by Lenin and Trotsky, pronounced in principle in favor of a Party dictatorship, though they expressed a reluctant willingness to admit representatives of other socialist parties into the government, provided the hegemony of the Bolsheviks was safeguarded. The minority, led by Kamenev and Zinoviev, advocated a coalition of Soviet parties, an agreement to share power with the Mensheviks and SR's in order to broaden the base of support for the new regime.

The position of the Leninist majority was sharply expressed in the inter-Party negotiations on the composition of the new government after the uprising of November 7. Under Lenin's leadership, the Party Central

Committee instructed its negotiators to insist on "a majority in the Central Executive Committee [TsIK], a majority in the government, and [the acceptance of] our [Bolshevik] program." Trotsky went even further and at a meeting of the Central Committee on November 14, 1917, cried out, "We should have 75 per cent." [4] Lenin's deep-rooted skepticism toward coalition came out even more sharply at a session of the Petrograd Committee of the Party held on the same day: "As for conciliation," he said, "I cannot even speak about that seriously . . . Our present slogan is: No compromise, *i.e.*, for a homogeneous Bolshevik Government." [5]

Meanwhile, the minority led by Kamenev and Zinoviev sought to escape the grim logic of one-party dictatorship. Frustrated in the Central Committee, they insisted on airing their views outside. Despite Lenin's effort to silence them by invoking the threat of Party discipline, the minority persisted in demanding a coalition. On November 17, 1917, they took the unprecedented step of using the forum of the Central Executive Committee of the Congress of Soviets to move the repeal of the press decree of November 9, utilized by the Bolshevik Sovnarkom to suppress hostile newspapers. When this motion was defeated, the minority representatives resigned from the Sovnarkom and the Central Committee of the Party. Five of the fourteen members of the Sovnarkom joined in the following statement which was read to the Central Executive Committee on November 17:

We take the stand that it is necessary to form a socialist government of all parties in the Soviet. We believe that only the formation of such a government can preserve the fruits of the heroic war won by the working class and the revolutionary army in the October-November days.

We deem the alternative to be a purely Bolshevik government which can maintain itself only by means of political terror. It is this last-named alternative which the Soviet of People's Commissars has chosen. We cannot and will not accept it. We can see that it will alienate the proletarian masses and cause their withdrawal from political leadership; it will lead to the establishment of an irresponsible regime and to the ruin of the revolution and the country. We cannot assume responsibility for such a policy, and, therefore, we give up the name of People's Commissars. [6]

At the same time, five members of the Central Committee — Kamenev, Zinoviev, Rykov, Milyutin, and Nogin — issued a declaration announcing their resignation. They charged that "the leading group of the Central Committee . . . is determined not to permit the formation of a government of the parties in the Soviet and to insist on a purely Bolshevik government . . . regardless of the sacrifices to the workers and soldiers." The statement continued:

We cannot assume responsibility for this ruinous policy of the Central Committee, carried out against the will of a large part of the proletariat and soldiers,

who are most eager for an early cessation of blood-shedding by the different
wings of the democracy.

We resign therefore from membership in the Central Committee so that we
may be free to express our opinion openly to the masses of workers and soldiers
and to ask them to support our slogan: Long live the government of the parties
in the Soviet! For an immediate understanding on these terms.[7]

Although all the signers of this statement subsequently recanted and
reassumed positions of responsibility in the Party and government, the
views which they expressed at this juncture revealed a significant crisis
of conscience in Bolshevik ranks. "We have become very fond of war,"
said Lunacharsky, "as if we were not a workers' party but a party of the
soldiery, a party of war. It is necessary to create, but we are doing nothing. We continue to polemicize in the party, and we'll keep on polemi-
cizing, until only one man remains — a dictator." [8]

The Consolidation of Single-Party Dictatorship

The determination of the Leninist majority to insure Bolshevik hegemony pushed inexorably in the direction of the consolidation of a single-
party dictatorship. Except for the brief period between December 22,
1917, and March 15, 1918, when three Left SR's held portfolios in the
Sovnarkom, the cabinet remained exclusively Bolshevik in composition.
Faced with the problem of justifying one-party rule, Lenin resorted increasingly to dialectical casuistry. In order to demonstrate that Bolshevik
power was securely founded on popular consent, he pointed to the Bolshevik majority in the Congress of Soviets. When the elections to the
Constituent Assembly disclosed an SR majority in the country, Lenin dismissed the electoral results as without significance. Replying to criticism
of the dissolution of the Assembly, Lenin said:

Those who remind us of the time when we also stood for the Constituent
Assembly and rebuke us for now "dispersing" it don't have a grain of sense
in their minds, only pompous and empty phrases. For as compared with Tsarism
and the Kerensky republic the Constituent Assembly at one time seemed to us
better than their notorious organs of power; but with their establishment the
Soviets, being revolutionary organizations of all the people, naturally became
immeasurably superior to any parliament in the world . . . All power to the
Soviets we said then, and for this we are fighting . . . The Constituent Assembly, which failed to recognize the power of the people, is now dispersed by
the will of the Soviet power . . . All power to the Soviets! And we shall crush
the saboteurs.[9]

Leninist ingenuity thus embodied the will of the people in the Soviets
and the will of the Soviets in the party of the Bolsheviks. When some of
his own followers encountered difficulty in following the argument, Lenin
warned:

Every attempt, direct, or indirect, to consider the question of the Constituent Assembly from a formal, legal aspect, within the framework of ordinary bourgeois democracy, ignoring the class struggle and civil war, would be a betrayal of the cause of the proletariat, and the adoption of the bourgeois standpoint. It is the bounden duty of revolutionary Social Democracy to warn all and sundry against this error, into which a few Bolshevik leaders, who have been unable to appreciate the significance of the October uprising and the tasks of the dictatorship of the proletariat, have fallen.[10]

With the dissolution of the Constituent Assembly on January 22, 1918, the Bolshevik break with the bourgeois legal order was complete. As Sverdlov announced in his opening speech to the Third Congress of Soviets the next day: "The Central Executive Committee and the Council of People's Commissars have definitely taken the stand for a dictatorship of the toiling elements." [11] Lenin in his speech to the Congress was even more explicit, "Every time I speak on this subject of proletarian government someone . . . shouts 'dictator' . . . You cannot expect . . . that socialism will be delivered on a silver platter . . . Not a single question pertaining to the class struggle has ever been settled except by violence. Violence when committed by the toiling and exploited masses against the exploiters is the kind of violence of which we approve." [12]

Lenin still found it inexpedient to say bluntly that the Party deemed itself the exclusive custodian of the interests of "the toiling and exploited masses" and that it proposed to assume exclusive direction of the instruments of class violence. Events were to prove more eloquent than words. The suppression of opposition parties, however, did not take place at once but proceeded by slow stages. The attack began with a Sovnarkom proclamation on December 11, 1917, declaring the Kadet Party "an organization of counterrevolutionary conspirators" and an "enemy of the people." [13] The same day an order was issued to arrest leading members of the Kadet Party and to hand them over to the revolutionary tribunal. "We have made a modest beginning," commented Trotsky.[14]

At first, the Bolsheviks moved cautiously in dealing with their socialist rivals. Opposition newspapers continued to appear, but they were subjected to harassment in the form of suspensions and the cutting-off of newsprint. On December 31, 1917, the Cheka ordered the arrest of a number of important Right SR and Menshevik leaders,[15] but meanwhile both parties continued to be nominally represented in the Central Executive Committee (VTsIK) of the Congress of Soviets. This inconsistency was eliminated on June 14, 1918, when VTsIK issued a decree excluding both parties from its ranks on the ground that they were engaged in alleged counterrevolutionary and anti-Soviet activities.

This meant that the Left SR's were the only major group remaining in VTsIK aside from the dominant Bolshevik majority. By this time, relations between the Bolsheviks and the Left SR's had reached a stage of extreme tension as the result of the opposition of the Left SR's to the Brest-Litovsk Treaty and to the confiscatory grain requisitions enforced on the country-side. On July 6, 1918, two Left SR's assassinated the German ambassador Mirbach in the hope of forcing a breach with the Germans. The abortive Left SR uprising which followed prepared the way for the elimination of this last vestige of effective opposition to Bolshevik one-party rule. Most of the Left SR delegates to the Fifth All-Russian Congress of Soviets were arrested, and thirteen were shot. In reprisal, the Left SR's turned the weapon of political terror against the Bolsheviks. On August 30, 1918, Uritsky, the head of the Petrograd Cheka, was assassinated, and Lenin was seriously wounded. The Cheka replied in kind, and the Red Terror assumed a mass character.

By the autumn of 1918, all non-Communist political organizations had been rendered practically impotent though some continued to exist in a precarious limbo of quasi-legality. Under the press of the Civil War, the Bolshevik leadership made an effort to distinguish between "loyal" Men-sheviks and SR's, who supported the Soviet government in its struggle against the Whites, and "disloyal" elements, who gave their support to the counterrevolution. On November 30, 1918, the "loyal" Mensheviks were readmitted to VTsIK, and this action was followed on February 25, 1919, by the reinstatement of SR's who were prepared to repudiate "external and internal counterrevolution." But Bolshevik toleration was based solely on expediency and the good behavior of the "captive" representatives of the minority parties. Lenin contemptuously said of them at the Eighth Party Congress, "We say to it: 'You are not a serious enemy. Our enemy is the bourgeoisie. But if you march with it, then we shall have to apply to you too the measures of the proletarian dictatorship.' " [16]

During the next few years, the position of the minority parties became more and more unenviable. Though Menshevik and SR party conferences took place occasionally and their newspapers and manifestos made sporadic appearances, these activities were subjected to constant harassment and interference. Despite Cheka arrests and persecutions, the Mensheviks as late as 1920 continued to elect delegates to local Soviets, to control important trade unions, and to participate, though without voting rights, in the All-Russian Congress of Soviets.

With the end of the Civil War and the inauguration of the New Economic Policy in 1921, the policy of contingent toleration of opposition groups was abandoned. No formal decree was issued dissolving the minority parties, but the signal for extinction was given by Lenin himself in May 1921, when he proclaimed: "We shall keep the Mensheviks and SR's, whether open or disguised as 'non-party,' in prison." [17] After the Kronstadt revolt, this condition came close to total realization. The fiction of a legal opposition was completely abandoned. Kadets, Mensheviks, and SR's were arrested in large numbers and exiled to the Far North, Siberia, and Central Asia. Some avoided arrest and won temporary absolution by writing statements to Bolshevik papers renouncing connections with the outlawed political groupings. By 1921–22, almost all opposition political activity had been driven underground, and the consolidation of the one-party dictatorship was virtually complete. The Communist Party dominated the political life of the country. With the liquidation of its competitors, there was no effective organizational voice left inside Russia to challenge the Party's claim that it constituted "the authentic spokesman of the will of the masses." [18]

How was this claim to be validated? Since the masses were no longer offered a free choice among competing political alternatives and the Communist Party commanded a monopoly of force as well as of legality, the Communists' effort to demonstrate that their regime rested on consent involved the development of a surrogate theory of representation.

Stalin has provided the most authoritative Communist exposition of this representational mystique. In his writings on the role of the Party, he began by stressing its elite character: "The Party must be, first of all, the *vanguard* of the working class." In representational terms, it must function as a priestly guardian of the highest interests of the working class.

The Party cannot be a real party if it limits itself to registering what the masses of the working class feel and think . . . if it is unable to rise above the momentary interests of the proletariat, if it is unable to elevate the masses to the level of the class interests of the proletariat. The Party must stand at the head of the working class; it must see farther than the working class; it must lead the proletariat, and not follow in the tail of the spontaneous movement. [19]

At the same time, Stalin insisted upon the Party's maintaining its connections with the working class; it must be "closely bound up with it by all the fibres of its being." It must function as a school for the training of leaders of the working class; it must transform "each and every non-Party organization of the working class into an auxiliary body and transmission belt linking the Party with the class." [20] The leadership of the Party must be asserted in trade unions, coöperatives, Soviets, and every other form of mass organization. "The highest expression of the leading role of the Party, here, in the Soviet Union . . ." Stalin proudly proclaimed, "is the fact that not a single important political or organizational question is decided by our Soviet and other mass organizations without guiding directions from the Party." "*In this sense*," he continued, "it could be said that the dictatorship of the proletariat is *in essence* the 'dictatorship' of its vanguard, the 'dictatorship' of its Party." [21]

Implicit in the Stalinist analysis of the role of the Party are two contradictory and unresolved strains. The major thrust of the theory is clearly elitist and manipulative. The Party stands above class and mass. It insists on a monopoly of leadership. It guides and directs the entire machinery of state. It does not test its policies in a forum of free elections; it mobilizes and enforces consent. At the same time, the elitist presuppositions of the Stalinist theory are tempered by what might be described as a pseudo-democratic strain.

Stalin expressed this "populist" facet of Party ideology when he observed, "Contacts with the masses, the strengthening of these contacts, readiness to listen to the voice of the masses — in these lie the strength and impregnability of Bolshevik leadership." In the same speech, he cited the legend of Antaeus — the hero who was invincible as long as he touched the earth, his mother — and then concluded, "It may be taken as a rule that so long as Bolsheviks keep contacts with the broad masses of the people, they will be invincible. And, contrariwise, it is sufficient for Bolsheviks to break away from the masses and lose contact with them, to become covered with bureaucratic rash . . . to lose all their strength and become converted into nonentities." [22]

When Stalin referred to "contact" with the masses, he did not mean control of the Party by the masses. The "solution" which he envisaged ran in terms of the Party's capacity for leadership, its ability to divine mass aspirations and to convince the masses of the correctness of the Party's slogans. Authority derives from above rather than from below. The masses are given periodic opportunities to register their approval of the Party leadership; there is no effective way in which they may register their disapproval since no alternatives are presented to them. The Bolshevik theory of Party leadership is rich in sanctions to enforce centralized control; it is characterized by an almost total absence of sanctions to insure the responsibility of the Party leadership to the masses. As a result, the "populist" strain in Bolshevik ideology is robbed of much of its potential significance.

Authority based on anointment and investment from above does not usually breed responsiveness to the forces below. All the compulsions of dictatorship drive toward the manufacture of synthetic unanimity rather than the recognition of genuine differences. The search for a "popular" basis of the dictatorship is, as Stalin rightly insisted, a necessary condition of its survival. But it is not a search for which dictatorships ordinarily come well-equipped. When restraints on arbitrary authority are self-imposed and the will of the dictator becomes the supreme law, the temptation to resort to the short cuts of compulsion becomes well-nigh irresistible. "You know yourselves," Peter the Great once observed, "that anything that is new, even though it is good and needful, will not be done by our folk without compulsion." [23] It is a sentiment that the Bolshevik practice of leadership amply documents.

The consolidation of one-party dictatorship in the USSR has been accompanied by an increasing tendency on the part of Communist ideologues to rationalize it as the highest form of democracy. To the Western ear, the rationale rings strangely.

As to freedom for various political parties [Stalin proclaimed in 1936], we adhere to somewhat different views. A party is a part of a class, its most advanced part. Several parties, and, consequently, freedom for parties, can exist only in a society in which there are antagonistic classes whose interests are mutually hostile and irreconcilable — in which there are, say, capitalists and workers, landlords and peasants, kulaks and poor peasants, etc. But in the U.S.S.R. there are no longer such classes as the capitalists, the landlords, the kulaks, etc. In the U.S.S.R. there are only two classes, workers and peasants, whose interests — far from being mutually hostile — are, on the contrary, friendly. Hence there is no ground in the U.S.S.R. for the existence of several parties, and, consequently, for freedom for these parties . . . In the U.S.S.R. only one party can exist, the Communist Party, which courageously defends the interests of the workers and peasants to the very end . . .

They talk of democracy. But what is democracy? Democracy in capitalist countries . . . is, in the last analysis, democracy for the strong, democracy for the propertied minority. In the U.S.S.R., on the contrary, democracy is democracy for the working people, *i.e.*, democracy for all.[24]

Embedded in Stalin's bland semantic jugglery is the usual dictatorial *coup de main,* the assertion that the nation is an organic unity whose true interests only the Party dictatorship can adequately express. In the Communist lexicon, class solidarity in the USSR needs no demonstration; it is simply assumed to exist. When Communist ideologists describe a single-party dictatorship as the most "democratic" form of government in the world, it is presumably because they identify the policies of the Party leadership with the welfare of the masses. If, as the Communist ideologues claim, the masses are conscious of the beatitudes which have been conferred on them by single-party rule, it might also be assumed that Communists would have no objection to testing their hold on the masses in free elections in which other parties participated. The unwillingness of Communists to submit to such tests may suggest that the Party leadership has no great confidence that the masses would in fact validate their claims. Indeed, the Communist attitude toward opposition betrays a degree of insecurity bordering on the hypochondriac. "It would be wild," says an official commentator on the 1936 Constitution,

to grant freedom of assembly, meetings, street processions, for instance to monarchists of any sort; incongruous in our streets would be people bearing Tsarist flags and singing in the Soviet land "God Save our Tsar." It would be wild to imagine that Mensheviks and Socialist-Revolutionaries should appear in our halls with an appeal to turn back from socialism to capitalism . . . And he who would attempt to call for the overthrow of the socialist system . . . or attempt to weaken the system will appear before the peoples of the Union as a criminal, having no right to enjoy the liberties envisaged by the Constitution . . .

> . . . There can be no meetings of lunatics, just as there can be no meetings of criminals — monarchists, Mensheviks, SR's, etc.[25]

The fear that the masses will be corrupted by the slightest exposure to alien doctrine runs side by side with the Party claim that it commands the monolithic confidence of the masses. Both strands, incongruous as they may seem, form part of the Communist pattern of belief. The first derives from a basic distrust of the masses which demands their protection from error by stern guardians of their true interests, and the second rests on the faith that a Party elite in possession of the true doctrine can spread its influence among the masses by devoted application and organization. Thus, indoctrination is fused with repression, and opposition to the Party leadership in any form becomes a heresy which defenders of the true creed have an obligation to stamp out.

In Marxism-Leninism, Communists profess to believe that they have a scientific method which unlocks the secrets of the universe and which equips them alone to apprehend reality and change the world in accordance with general laws of social development. This does not mean, as Stalin pointed out, that Marxism recognizes "immutable conclusions and formulas obligatory for all epochs and periods," or that a conning of Marxist texts will yield precise solutions for all varieties of practical problems. Stalin expressed his scorn of "the exegites and Talmudists [who] . . . think that if they learn these conclusions and formulas by heart and begin to quote them here and there, then they will be able to solve any questions whatsoever, figuring that the memorized conclusions and formulas suit them for all times and countries, for all of life's contingencies." [26] In the eyes of Communists, such "abuses" do not impair the validity of the substance of Marxism-Leninism itself. Indeed, they make it the more necessary to have authoritative pronouncements from the Party leadership to protect the essence of the doctrine against distortions of application.

Since Marxism-Leninism as doctrine provides no ready-made answers for the multitudinous decisions which confront a governing Party as it adapts itself to new situations, the possibility of differences of view within the Party must constantly be envisaged. Serious differences if pressed to their logical conclusion mean a split in the Party; the suppression of differences deprives Party membership of much of its potential creative significance. The official doctrine of the Party purports to avoid both extremes. According to Stalin's authoritative pronouncement:

The achievement and maintenance of the dictatorship of the proletariat is impossible without a party which is strong by reason of its solidarity and iron discipline. But iron discipline in the Party is inconceivable without unity of will, without complete and absolute unity of action on the part of all members of the Party. This does not mean, of course, that the possibility of contests of opinion within the Party is thereby precluded. On the contrary, iron discipline does not preclude but presupposes criticism and contest of opinion within the Party. Least of all does it mean that discipline must be "blind." On the contrary, iron discipline does not preclude but presupposes conscious and voluntary submission, for only conscious discipline can be truly iron discipline. But after a contest of opinion has been closed, after criticism has been exhausted and a decision has been arrived at, unity of will and unity of action of all Party members are the necessary conditions without which neither Party unity nor iron discipline in the Party is conceivable. . . from this it follows that the existence of factions is incompatible either with the Party's unity or with its iron discipline. It need hardly be proved that the existence of factions leads to the existence of a number of centres, and the existence of a number of centres connotes the absence of one common centre in the Party, the breaking up of the unity of will, the weakening and disintegration of discipline, the weakening and disintegration of the dictatorship.[27]

Lenin and the Opposition

The problem of combining unity and diversity has plagued the Party since its inception. While Lenin lived, the scope of intra-Party democracy was being progressively narrowed, but, compared with what was to develop later, discussion within the Party remained relatively free and uninhibited. Lenin's Party opponents could still propagate their views with comparative impunity, and although Lenin frequently denounced them in unbridled terms, his bark was fiercer than his bite. Thus, when Zinoviev and Kamenev broke Party discipline and agitated in the non-Party press against the October insurrection, Lenin, after the victory, was ready to forgive. In a speech before the Petrograd Committee of the Party on November 14, he is reported to have said, "I should not like [now] to assume a severe attitude toward them." [28] When Zinoviev and Kamenev, along with others, again opposed Lenin on the issue of a coalition government, he threatened them with expulsion from the Party; but when the sinners repented, they were again welcomed back into the fold.

The debate on the Brest-Litovsk Treaty shook the Party from top to bottom, but differences were freely aired. At one point the Central Committee was split into three factions: Lenin's followers advocated acceptance of the German ultimatum; Bukharin's group of Left Communists called for a revolutionary war; and Trotsky and his supporters offered the formula of "no peace no war." The motion to notify the Germans of readiness to accept peace terms carried in the Central Committee by the narrow vote of seven to six,[29] and the motion to accept the terms was won by a plurality of seven to four, with four members abstaining.[30] The issue of ratification was widely discussed in local Party organizations and finally submitted to the Seventh Party Congress, which assembled in Petrograd March 6–8, 1918. On the day before the opening of the Congress, the Left Communists appeared with an opposition newspaper — *Kommunist* — which sharply attacked the policies of Lenin. After a bitter debate, the Congress ratified the treaty by a vote of thirty to twelve.[31] In the interim, the Left Opposition captured control of the Moscow Party organization and the following month issued several numbers of another opposition journal, also called *Kommunist*.

No sanctions were invoked against members of the opposition. With the Brest issue out of the way, the Left Opposition swung over to criticism of Lenin's alleged opportunistic capitulation before the petty bourgeoisie and pressed for the extension of proletarian control in industry and administration. Lenin responded with a smashing critique of the utopianism of the Left Communists in his article, "On Left Infantilism and the Petty-Bourgeois Spirit," [32] but he took no disciplinary measures to prevent the Left from expressing its views. Meanwhile, the intensification of the Civil War and the Left SR uprising of mid-1918 brought the two factions together and restored Party unity in the face of the common menace.

The effect of the Civil War was not only to solidify the Party but to reinforce earlier tendencies to concentrate power in the hands of the top leadership. At the Eighth Party Congress, held in March 1919, Osinsky and Sapronov, former Left Communists who were soon to organize another opposition group called the Democratic Centralists, raised their voices against excessive centralization and bureaucratic control and led a wholly unsuccessful movement to expand the power of the local Party organizations.[33]

More serious was the challenge offered by the so-called Military Opposition led by V. Smirnov, also a former Left Communist. The Military Opposition was sharply critical of the policy of employing former Tsarist officers as military specialists in the Red Army and of organizing the army on a basis of professional military discipline; it called, instead, for primary reliance on partisan detachments. In a test vote at the Party Congress, Smirnov's resolution mobilized 95 votes to 174 for the majority. Again, no effort was made to invoke Party discipline against the opposition. The issue was submitted to a conciliation commission on which both majority and minority were represented, and the resulting resolution, which made some slight concessions to the Military Opposition, was unanimously affirmed by the Congress.[34]

At the Ninth Congress, in March 1920, the Democratic Centralists appeared as a full-fledged opposition group. Sapronov described the Leninist Central Committee as a "small handful of party oligarchs." Other members of the opposition complained that the Central Committee "was banning those who hold deviant views." Yakovlev was even more specific. "The Ukraine," he charged, "is being transformed into a place of exile. Those comrades who for any reason are not agreeable to Moscow are exiled there." Yurenev accused the Central Committee of "playing with men" and spoke of the dispatching of oppositionists to far places as a "system of exile." [35] Lenin's reply was evasive. It was the task of the Central Committee to distribute the forces of the Party. "Of course," he conceded, "if the Central Committee had banned the opposition before the Congress, this would be an inadmissible matter." "Perhaps," he admitted, "mistakes have been made." But, he concluded, "whatever Central Committee you choose to elect, it cannot desist from distributing forces." [36] At the Ninth Congress, Lenin was apparently still on the defensive against charges of repressing the opposition. The disciplining of oppositionists took the relatively mild form of transfer of work assignments from the center to the periphery, and even such actions were not openly acknowledged.

During the summer and autumn of 1920, growing unrest among the Party rank-and-file crystallized in the form of the so-called Workers' Opposition. The program of the Workers' Opposition called for trade-union administration of industry, democratic management of the Party, and reliance on the industrial proletariat to direct state affairs. The movement was aimed largely against the tendency of the Party leadership to arrogate all important decision-making to itself. In pressing for more autonomy and more workers' control, the Workers' Opposition registered a growing disillusionment with the failure to realize the utopian, egalitarian slogans under which the Party had marched to power. Under the leadership of Madame Kollontai and Alexander Shlyapnikov, a former metal-worker and the first People's Commissar for Labor, the Workers' Opposition gathered considerable rank-and-file support, particularly in the trade unions, but it found itself greatly handicapped in its bid for power by its failure to attract any of the first-rank leaders of the Party.

In the trade-union discussion which raged in the Party prior to and during the Tenth Party Congress, which met in March 1921, three platforms vied for supremacy. The Workers' Opposition called for trade-union control and management of industry; Trotsky and Bukharin pressed for the "statification" of the trade unions; Lenin and nine other members of the Central Committee offered an intermediate program designed to preserve a degree of autonomy for the trade unions without entrusting them with direct responsibility for economic administration. In the crucial vote at the Congress, Lenin's platform carried by an overwhelming majority. Although the Workers' Opposition was able to mobilize but 18 votes, compared with 50 for Trotsky's motion and 336 for Lenin's,[37] the vote was far from reflecting the real strength of the Workers' Opposition among the Party rank-and-file. Lenin was genuinely alarmed by the dissension, and his anxiety was deepened by the Kronstadt mutiny which broke out on the eve of the Congress.

This time Lenin was ready to invoke stern measures. In a pamphlet called *The Party Crisis*, he first rebuked Trotsky for factionalism and then turned his main fire against the Workers' Opposition. He denounced its program as out of bounds: "Of course it is permissible (especially before a Congress) for different groups to organize in blocs (and so is it to canvass for votes). But it must be done within the limits of Communism (and not Syndicalism)." [38]

In discussions at the Congress, the Workers' Opposition showed no disposition to give ground. In the eyes of Shlyapnikov, the platforms of Lenin and Trotsky were equally reprehensible; both were "economic militarizers." In the event of defeat at the Congress, the leaders of the Workers' Opposition proclaimed that there would be no retreat; they would remain within the Party, fight for their point of view, "save the Party and correct its line." To Lenin, this was the last straw.

All these arguments about freedom of speech and freedom of criticism, which appear in variegated form throughout this entire pamphlet and all the speeches of the "Workers' Opposition" constitute nine-tenths of the sense of speeches, which have no particular sense — all these are words of this order. Comrades, it is necessary to talk not only about words, but about their content as well. You cannot trick us with words like "freedom of criticism." When we said that the Party showed symptoms of disease, we meant that this indication deserves three-fold attention; undoubtedly, the disease is there: Help us to heal this disease. Tell us how you can heal it. We have spent a great deal of time in discussion, and I must say that now it is a great deal better to "discuss with rifles" than with the theses offered by the opposition. We need no opposition now, comrades, it is not the time! Either on this side, or on that, with a rifle, but not with the opposition . . . And I think that the Party Congress will have to draw that conclusion too . . . that the time has come to put an end to the opposition, to put a lid on it; we have had enough of opposition now! [39]

This outburst was a prelude to more drastic action. The resolution which the Tenth Party Congress adopted "On the Syndicalist and Anarchist Deviation in Our Party" condemned the ideas of the Workers' Opposition as "a complete rupture with Marxism and Communism," called for "an unswerving and systematic ideological struggle against these ideas," and declared "the propaganda of these ideas as being incompatible with membership in the Russian Communist Party." [40] Lenin, however, still expressed a hope that the oppositionists could be salvaged for the Party. "A deviation," he explained to the Congress, "is not a fully formed movement. A deviation is something that can be corrected. People have strayed a little from the path or are beginning to stray, but it is still possible to correct it." [41] When members of the Workers' Opposition who had been reëlected to the Central Committee offered to resign, the resignations were not accepted. Instead, they were called upon to submit to Party discipline.

Nonetheless, the Resolution on the Workers' Opposition and the even more important Resolution on Party Unity adopted by the Tenth Congress mark an important dividing line in the history of the Party. They greatly consolidated the power of the central Party leadership and set a master precedent, on the basis of which any opposition to the dominant Party machine was eventually to become identified with treason. "All class-conscious workers must clearly realize," said the Resolution on Party Unity, "the perniciousness and impermissibility of fractionalism of any kind, for no matter how the representatives of individual groups may desire to safeguard Party unity, in practice fractionalism inevitably leads to the weakening of team work and to intensified and repeated attempts by the enemies of the Party, who have fastened themselves onto it because it is the governing Party, to widen the cleavage and to use it for counter-revolutionary purposes." The resolution continued:

In the practical struggle against fractionalism, every organization of the Party must take strict measures to prevent any fractional actions whatsoever . . . Every analysis of the general line of the Party, estimate of its practical experience, verification of the fulfillment of its decisions, study of methods of rectifying errors, etc., must under no circumstances be submitted for preliminary discussion to groups formed on the basis of any sort of "platform," etc., but must be exclusively submitted for discussion directly to all members of the Party . . .

The Congress therefore hereby declares dissolved and orders the immediate dissolution of all groups without exception that have been formed on the basis of one platform or another (such as the Workers' Opposition group, the Democratic Centralism group, etc.). Nonobservance of this decision of the Congress shall entail absolute and immediate expulsion from the Party.[42]

These statements were followed by the famous Point Seven which remained unpublished until, on the motion of Stalin, it was released for general circulation at the Thirteenth Party Conference in January 1924, just before Lenin's death. The Tenth Congress' decision to keep Point Seven secret revealed an understandable reluctance to document the growing power of the central Party machine. Point Seven provided:

In order to ensure strict discipline within the Party and in all Soviet work and to secure the maximum unanimity in removing all fractionalism, the Congress authorizes the Central Committee, in cases of breach of discipline or of a revival or toleration of fractionalism, to apply all Party penalties, including expulsion, and in regard to members of the Central Committee to reduce them to the status of alternate members and even, as an extreme measure, to expel them from the Party. A necessary condition for the application of such an extreme measure to members of the Central Committee, alternate members of the Central Committee and members of the Control Commission is the convocation of a plenum of the Central Committee, to which all alternate members of the Central Committee and all members of the Control Commission shall be invited. If such a general assembly of the most responsible leaders of the Party, by a two-thirds majority, deems it necessary to reduce a member of the Central Committee to the status of alternate member, or to expel him from the Party, this measure shall be put into effect immediately.[43]

The resolutions of the Tenth Congress foreshadowed the Party purge of 1921–22 and the tightening of restrictions on all brands of oppositionist activity. Lenin set the tone for the purge when he called for the expulsion of all "rascals, bureaucrats, dishonest or wavering Communists, and of Mensheviks who have repainted their 'façade' but who have remained Mensheviks at heart." [44] The Party historian Yaroslavsky later estimated that approximately a third of the Party membership was either expelled or left the Party at this time.[45]

Despite the ban on factionalism, leaders of the Workers' Opposition continued their agitation against the line of the Central Committee. On August 9, 1921, Lenin, in accordance with Point Seven, convened a meeting of the plenum of the Central Committee to consider the expulsion of Shlyapnikov from the committee and the Party. The motion failed by one vote to secure the necessary two-thirds majority, and Shlyapnikov escaped with a stern censure and a threat that the matter would be reopened if he continued to violate Party discipline.[46] Just before the Eleventh Party Congress met in March 1922, the opposition made a desperate and pathetic bid for the support of foreign Communists by filing an appeal with the Enlarged Plenum of the Executive Committee of the Comintern (IKKI). "The Declaration of the Twenty-two." as this document came to be known, echoed the familiar grievances of the Workers' Opposition. It was submitted without the consent of the Party Central Committee or the Russian delegation to IKKI. The Comintern, not unexpectedly, replied with a resolution affirming its faith in the Russian Party leadership. The problem of dealing with the dissenters was shifted back to the Eleventh Congress of the Party, which appointed a commission [47] consisting of Dzerzhinsky, Zinoviev, and Stalin to recommend the appropriate penalties.

At the Eleventh Congress, a rapidly thinning but still determined band of Workers' Oppositionists returned to the fray. Shlyapnikov complained that "since the time the 10th Party Congress sent me into the Central Committee as whip of the workers' opposition, that committee has often sat in judgment upon me." He declared that "Comrade Frunze brought up the possibility of convincing me with machine guns that he was in the right,[48] and he designated both Lenin and Frunze as machine gunners. V. Kossior averred:

The administrative system of our Party has remained as authoritarian and to a certain degree militaristic as it was in the war period. If anyone had the courage or deemed it necessary to criticize or point out a certain deficiency which exists in the area of Soviet and Party work, he was immediately counted among the opposition, the appropriate places learned of it, and the comrade in question was relieved of his office. Let us take the Ural region as an example. Comrades Sapronov, V. Kossior, Mrachkovsky and a whole array of our Ural comrades were removed from their work in the Ural area under entirely irrelevant pretenses.[49]

Kossior characterized the Party regime as the regime of the "mailed fist." Madame Kollontai accused the Party leadership of suppressing thought and of inadequate attention to the welfare of the workers.[50]

Lenin's reply was to insist on the continued necessity of iron Party discipline. The NEP, he pointed out, was a period of retreat:

During a retreat . . . discipline must be more conscious and a hundred times more necessary . . . under such circumstances a few panic-stricken voices are enough to cause a stampede. The danger is enormous. When a real army is in retreat, machine guns are set up; and when an orderly retreat degenerates into a disorderly one, the command is given: "Fire!" And quite right.

If, during an incredibly difficult retreat, when everything depends on preserving good order, anyone spreads panic — even for the best of motives — the slightest breach of discipline must be punished severely, sternly, ruthlessly.[51]

The veiled threat of "machine guns" was explained away by Lenin in his concluding speech as directed against Mensheviks, SR's, and their ilk; oppositionists, he made clear, would be dealt with through "Party measures of discipline." [52] The commission appointed to adjudicate the affair of the Twenty-two brought in a recommendation that Kollontai, Shlyapnikov, Medvedev, Mitin, and Kuznetsov be expelled from the Party. The Congress concurred in the expulsion of the last two, who were relative newcomers to the Party, but it could not steel itself to expel such Old Bolsheviks and prominent Party workers as Kollontai, Shlyapnikov, and Medvedev. It contented itself with a stern warning to them that the Central Committee would resort to expulsion in the event of further anti-Party activities on their part.[53]

The Eleventh Congress was the last in which Lenin participated. As long as he remained active, his influence was clearly exerted in the strengthening of Party discipline and consolidation of the hold of the central machine on the Party. The Party faction was anathema to him, and in the Resolution on Party Unity, which he had drafted for the Tenth Congress, he did everything in his power to destroy the embryonic development of a two- or multi-faction system within the framework of the single-party dictatorship. He could find a place for criticism in his organizational scheme only if it presented no political challenge to the Party leadership and if it was "practical" criticism which served to improve the efficiency of the Party machine.

At the same time, his intolerance of opposition in principle was tempered by a practical realization that differences of view within the Party were unavoidable and that the function of a Party leader was to persuade first and to invoke sanctions only as a last resort. Thus he cajoled, argued, and even pleaded with his Party opponents before he confronted the necessity of declaring open war on them. Despite violent threats and tirades, the most drastic penalty which he imposed on dissenters was expulsion from the Party, and even this penalty was rarely utilized against Party members of any prominence who had rendered distinguished services in the past. If on occasion Lenin seemed to equate dissent with treason, he still shrank from drawing the practical consequences, at least so far as intra-Party struggles were concerned.

Yet the body of precedents which he created steered a course toward the outlawing of all opposition. However much practice meliorated theory with Lenin, he was responsible for the germinating conception on the basis of which all intra-Party opposition came to be extinguished. As the Party encompassed the political life of the nation and imposed a monolithic pattern on it, the Party leadership became the exclusive sanctuary of power and orthodoxy. The Party was transformed into a rigid, hierarchical, military formation in which the duty of the lower ranks was to obey and the obligation of the leadership was to command. The Supreme Leader Stalin became vested with a godlike infallibility. His pronouncements were treated as the incarnation of divine wisdom; his decisions brooked no dispute. The political monopoly of the Party was transformed into the personal supremacy of the Iron Dictator.

Stalin and the Monolithic Party

The consolidation of Stalin's power proceeded by slow steps. In the first phase of the struggle for the succession, while Lenin lay dying, Stalin, Zinoviev, and Kamenev joined in a triumvirate within the Politburo to prevent Trotsky from taking over the leadership. While Stalin was consolidating his hold on the Party machine from the strategic vantage point of the General Secretaryship, he gave the appearance of being yielding and conciliatory both in his relationships with his fellow triumvirs and with Trotsky. When Trotsky launched his first public attack on the triumvirate, December 5, 1923, with his open letter to the Communists of *Krasnaya Presnya* in which he called for a revival of criticism within the Party and an end to the regime of machine repression,[54] it was Zinoviev who demanded Trotsky's immediate arrest and Stalin who counseled caution. It was "inconceivable," Stalin said in an article in *Pravda*, to eliminate Trotsky from the leadership of the Party.[55] In view of later developments, the warning Stalin addressed to his colleagues at this time has more than piquant interest. "We did not agree with Zinoviev and Kamenev," he revealed to the Fourteenth Party Congress, "because we knew that a policy of chopping off [heads] is fraught with great dangers for the Party, that the method of chopping off and blood-letting — and they did demand blood — is dangerous, infectious: today you chop off one [head], tomorrow another, the day after a third — what in the end will be left of the Party?" [56]

While appearing as the apostle of moderation and restraint, Stalin did not hesitate to press home the charge that Trotsky and his supporters were guilty of the crime of factionalism. In his attack on Trotsky at the Thirteenth Party Conference in January 1924 Stalin wrapped himself in the mantle of Leninism and, as the loyal pupil of Lenin, accused Trotsky and his associates of violating the Resolution on Party Unity which Lenin himself had drafted. Trotsky, he insisted, sought to place himself above the Party and its Central Committee; the factional freedom which he claimed could only lead to the destruction of the Party.[57] "The opposition," Stalin declared, "expresses the temper, moods, and aspirations of the non-proletarian elements in and outside the Party. The opposition, itself unconscious of it, unlooses a petty-bourgeois element. The fractional work of the opposition is water on the mill of the enemies of our Party, on the mill of those who wish to weaken and overthrow the dictatorship of the proletariat. I said that yesterday, and today I reaffirm it." [58] The resolution adopted by the Conference called upon the Party to wage "a systematic and energetic battle" against Trotskyism as a "petty-bourgeois deviation in the Party." [59] Meanwhile, the secretariat took steps to remove or transfer the supporters of Trotsky from strategic Party and governmental posts; they were replaced by trusted followers of the General Secretary.

At the Thirteenth Congress, which assembled in May 1924, after the death of Lenin, Zinoviev led the assault on Trotsky and demanded that he confess his errors. Trotsky's reply mirrored the tragic dilemma which habitually disarmed the opposition when it faced a conflict between loyalty to conscience or to Party:

The Party in the last analysis is always right because the Party is the single historic instrument given to the proletariat for the solution of its fundamental problems. I have already said that in front of one's own party nothing could be easier than to say: all my criticisms, my statements, my warnings, my protests — the whole thing was a mere mistake. I, however, comrades, cannot say that, because I do not think it. I know that one must not be right against the Party. One can be right only with the Party, and through the Party, for history has created no other road for the realization of what is right.[60]

For the moment, Stalin was unwilling to press as far as Zinoviev. He demanded only the cessation of oppositional activity. Indeed, his organizational report to the Congress ended with a vague conciliatory gesture, "We are for friendly collaboration with the opposition . . . Whether unity will come about, I do not know, since unity in the future depends entirely on the opposition . . . The majority wishes unity . . . Whether the minority sincerely wishes it, I do not know. That depends entirely on the Comrades of the opposition." [61]

Unity on Stalin's terms meant the dissolution of the opposition and its complete subordination to the dominant group in the Politburo. This the comrades of the opposition were unwilling to accept. At the January 1925 plenum of the Central Committee and Central Control Commission, three categories of resolutions were offered for the consideration of those bodies. One proposed the exclusion of Trotsky from the Party; the second demanded his removal from both the Politburo and the War Commissariat; the third limited itself to requesting his departure from his military post.[62] On Stalin's initiative, the mildest of these variants was adopted.

With Trotsky disarmed, the rivalry which had been brewing below the surface among the triumvirs broke into the open. Stalin, now well-entrenched in the Party machine, abandoned his former colleagues and joined with the so-called Right Wing of the Politburo, Bukharin, Rykov, and Tomsky, to form a new majority. Trotsky stood aloof. The issue between the new Stalinist majority and Zinoviev and Kamenev was joined at the Fourteenth Congress in December 1925. It was preceded by a series of bitter preliminary skirmishes in the course of which Zinoviev maintained his hold on the Leningrad Party organization while the Stalinist Party machine was victorious everywhere else. On the eve of the Congress, Stalin offered Zinoviev and Kamenev some slight concessions on condition that they abstain from attack at the Congress, but the offer was unacceptable, and the Leningrad delegation entered the Congress as a solid bloc opposed to Stalin's leadership.[63]

The position of Zinoviev and Kamenev was unenviable. While both were given a full opportunity to develop their differences with Stalin at the Congress, they now found themselves in much the same position as Trotsky at the Thirteenth Congress. As the chief executioners of Trotsky at that Congress, they had led the call for Party unity and the suppression of factionalism. Now, like Trotsky, they found themselves in the position of appearing to challenge the very slogans which they had earlier defended. "When there is a majority for Zinoviev," Mikoyan remarked at the Fourteenth Congress, "he is for iron discipline, for subordination. When he has no majority . . . he is against it." [64] Zinoviev and Kamenev pleaded in vain that they had a right to appeal to the Congress as the highest tribunal in the Party to settle disputed questions. Krupskaya, the widow of Lenin, aligned herself with the opposition and made a poignant appeal against steam-roller suppression of the voice of the minority:

> For us Marxists, truth is that which corresponds to reality. Vladimir Il'ich [Lenin] said: the teachings of Marx are invincible because they are true. And our Congress should concern itself with searching for and finding the correct line. Herein lies its task. It is wrong to reassure ourselves with the fact that the majority is always right. In the history of our Party there were congresses where the majority was not right . . . The majority should not gloat in the fact that it is the majority, but should disinterestedly seek for a true decision. If it will be true . . . it will put our Party on the right path.[65]

For the assembled stalwarts of the Party machine who dominated the Congress, the distinction was too subtle. The truth to which they were committed consisted in the directions they received from their leader Stalin. The point was dramatically brought home when Kamenev climaxed a long speech with a personal attack on Stalin and the whole theory of vesting supreme power in a *vozhd'* or leader. The Congress dissolved into a noisy uproar with Stalin's supporters shouting "Stalin! Stalin!" while the Leningrad delegation shouted back, "Long live the Central Committee of our Party! . . . The Party Above All!"[66] With that demonstration, less than two years after Lenin's death, the Stalin cult was launched. Stalin for the moment was too shrewd to associate himself publicly with its development. In his final remarks to the Congress, he modestly stated, "To lead the Party except collegially is impossible. It would be stupid to dream about it after Il'ich (applause), stupid to speak about it. Collegial work, collegial leadership, unity in the Party, unity in the organs of the Central Committee under the condition of the subordination of the minority to the majority — that is what is necessary for us now."[67]

Stalin's overwhelming triumph at the Fourteenth Congress was followed by a determined and successful effort to purge the Leningrad Party organization of Zinoviev's followers. With this base of power gone, Zinoviev and Kamenev had little left except their prestige and oratory to sustain them. At this low point in their fortunes, they joined forces with Trotsky in the hope of staging a recovery. The decision came too late.

Securely entrenched in the Party organization, Stalin now moved firmly and ruthlessly to destroy the opposition. In a speech delivered to the active workers of the Leningrad organization on April 13, 1926, he announced that the time had come to put an end to the idea that the Party was a "discussion club."[68] When the discovery was made soon afterwards that Lashevich, a close friend of Zinoviev, was using his position as Deputy Commissar of War to organize an opposition faction in the army, Lashevich was promptly dismissed from his post and expelled from the Central Committee; Zinoviev was removed from the Politburo.

The opposition, nevertheless, persisted in organizing meetings, sending speakers to address local Party cells, and seeking to mobilize mass support for the impending Party conference. These activities did not go unnoticed. In the words of Trotsky, "The apparatus counter-attacked with fury . . . The opposition was obliged to beat a retreat." [69]

On October 4, 1926, Trotsky and five other prominent leaders of the opposition addressed a submissive declaration to the Central Committee in which they, in effect, sued for peace. On October 11, Stalin in a speech to the Politburo stated the terms: unconditional subordination to the decisions of the Party organs, public acknowledgment that the factional work of the opposition had been mistaken and harmful to the Party, and an agreement to desist from factional battle within the Comintern. If these conditions were accepted, Stalin agreed to moderate the tone of the attack on the opposition and to recognize the right of the oppositionists to present their views at Party congresses.[70] The opposition bowed to the ultimatum, in words, at least. On October 16, it issued a public statement renouncing factional activities which might lead to a Party split but reiterating its criticisms of Stalin and Bukharin and indicating its intention to express its views within the framework of Party discipline. Meanwhile, in late October, Trotsky was dropped from the Politburo, Kamenev lost his position as an alternate member of the Politburo, and Zinoviev was removed from the leadership of the Comintern. All, however, remained members of the Central Committee. At the Fifteenth Party Conference, which met from October 26 to November 3, 1926, the opposition was denounced as a "Social-Democratic" deviation in the Party and was warned that any effort on its part to initiate a general discussion of its platform would not be tolerated.[71]

The opposition refused to capitulate. After a temporary lull which lasted through the spring of 1927, oppositionist hopes and activities flared up again in response to the Comintern defeat in China, the breakdown of the Anglo-Soviet trade-union agreement, and the tension created by the British decision to suspend diplomatic relations with the Soviet Union. In the midst of these events, the leaders of the Trotsky-Zinoviev opposition issued the so-called "Platform of the Eighty-three" in which they blamed Stalin for all the recent failures of foreign and domestic policy and charged that the Soviet Union was in the grip of a Thermidorian reaction. In the event of war, Trotsky declared, his policy would be like that of Clemenceau; he would fight to displace the present ineffective leadership with a government capable of waging the war victoriously. Meanwhile, the opposition continued its efforts to build its own apparatus, spread its literature, and organize its mass support.

At the joint plenum of the Central Committee and Central Control Commission which met from July 29 to August 9, 1927, the Stalinist forces were again in complete control. Stalin did not mince words. Addressing himself to the charge of "degeneration" in the Party, he pointed to the opposition as the source of the danger and ominously concluded, "That danger must be liquidated." [72] Again Trotsky and Zinoviev beat a retreat, promised to submit to majority discipline, and thus temporarily saved themselves from expulsion from the Central Committee.

The new truce was broken even before it was concluded. This time Stalin was in no mood to be indulgent. Rank-and-file oppositionists who had engaged in clandestine activity were arrested in large numbers and ousted from the Party. Still others were offered the alternative of recantation or expulsion, and a parade of penitents began. The opposition leaders refused to be intimidated and persevered in their course, holding secret meetings, establishing an illegal printing press, and engaging in open demonstrations in the streets. On October 23, 1927, Trotsky and Zinoviev were expelled from the Central Committee after insinuations were raised on the basis of GPU documents that the opposition was entangled with White Guardists in a military conspiracy against the regime. Trotsky struck back hard in his speech on the motion to expel him from the Central Committee. He dismissed the charge that the opposition was engaged in counterrevolution as a crude fabrication of the GPU. "The regime of party repression," he claimed,

flows inevitably from the whole policy of the leadership . . .
The immediate task that Stalin has set for himself is to split the party, to cut off the Opposition, to accustom the party to the method of physical destruction. Fascist gangs of whistlers, fist work, throwing of books and stones, the prison bars — here for a moment the Stalin régime has paused in its course. But the road is predestined . . . The goal: to cut off the Opposition and physically destroy it. Voices are already to be heard: "We will expel a thousand, and shoot a hundred, and have peace in the party." [73]

Events now moved to their inevitable climax. On November 7, the tenth anniversary of the Revolution, Trotsky reported,

The oppositionists decided to take part in the general procession, carrying their own placards, with their slogans . . . the placards of the opposition were snatched from their hands and torn to pieces, while their bearers were mauled by specially organized units . . . A policeman, pretending to be giving a warning, shot openly at my automobile . . . A drunken official of the fire-brigade, shouting imprecations, jumped on the running-board of my automobile and smashed the glass . . .
A similar demonstration took place in Leningrad. Zinoviev and Radek, who had gone there, were laid hold of by a special detachment, and under the pretense of protection from the crowd, were shut up in one of the buildings for the duration of the demonstration. [74]

On November 14, one week later, Trotsky and Zinoviev were expelled from the Party. Two days later, Joffe, one of Trotsky's closest friends, committed suicide. On January 17, 1928, Trotsky started on the first leg of a long journey which was to take him first to exile in Alma Ata, then to deportation to Prinkipo, and finally to death by an assassin's hatchet in Mexico. The journey, which began under GPU direction, was to end under the same auspices.

The Fifteenth Congress, which met in December 1927, witnessed the final crushing of the opposition. Only a handful of oppositionists dared to appear on the platform. Rakovsky, Evdokimov, Muralov, and Bakaev were all shouted down and drowned out by a constant roar of uninterrupted heckling; Kamenev alone received a half-respectful hearing. In a dignified speech, reminiscent of Trotsky's statement at the Thirteenth Congress, Kamenev said,

> I come to this tribune with only one aim, to find a path of reconciliation between the opposition and the Party (Voices: "A lie, you're late") . . . The battle in the Party . . . for the last two years has attained such a state of bitterness as to place before all of us a choice between two roads. One of these roads is that of a second party. That road under the conditions of the dictatorship of the proletariat would be fatal for the revolution . . . That road is closed to us, forbidden and excluded by the whole system of our ideas, by all the teachings of Lenin on the dictatorship of the proletariat . . .
>
> There remains, consequently, the second road . . . This road . . . means that we submit entirely and completely to the Party. We choose that road, for we are deeply convinced that a correct, Leninist policy can be victorious only inside the Party and only through it, and not outside the Party and against it. To take that road means that we submit to all the decisions of the Congress . . .
>
> But if in addition we are to renounce our point of view, that would not be Bolshevik. This demand, comrades, for the renunciation of one's opinions has never before been posed in our Party . . . If I were to come here and declare: I renounce views that I printed two weeks ago in my theses, you would not believe me; it would be hypocrisy on my side, and such hypocrisy is unnecessary.[75]

The Congress found the declaration unsatisfactory. The Stalinist leadership demanded more than organizational capitulation. It insisted, as Stalin made clear in his political report to the Congress, on a complete repudiation of the platform which the opposition had sponsored.[76] On December 18, the Congress voted to expel seventy-five leading members of the Trotskyite opposition as well as twenty-three members of the Sapronov group. The next day Zinoviev, Kamenev, and twenty-one of their followers offered their unconditional surrender.

> Harsh as the demands of us by the Congress may be, we are obligated to bow our will and our views to the will and views of the Party . . . the sole supreme judge of what is useful or harmful to the victorious surge forward of the revolution . . .
>
> We beg the Congress to return us to the Party and to give us the opportunity of participating in its practical daily work.[77]

Even this did not suffice. The Congress voted "to instruct the Central Committee and the Central Control Commission to accept applications from active leaders of the former opposition only on an individual basis and not to make decisions on such applications until at least six months after their submission." [78] Taking advantage of these provisions, Zinoviev, Kamenev, and a substantial group of their supporters managed during the following years to gain readmission into the Party. With their surrender and degradation and the exile and imprisonment of the Trotskyites who refused to capitulate, Stalin's triumph over the Left Opposition was complete.

In the development of the struggle with the Left Opposition, the Stalinist ideology of Party leadership unfolded and crystallized. In this ideology opposition had no place. The Party was indeed not a discussion club; it was an instrument of action. The Party line as proclaimed by the leadership was sacrosanct and unchallengeable. To oppose the leadership was to weaken the Party and aid the enemies of Soviet power. Opposition thus became tantamount to treason.

The Party critic of Stalin's policies faced a number of unpalatable alternatives. The safest was to keep silent. Should the critic insist on speaking out, he risked expulsion from the Party or even worse. Since an open appeal to the Party rank-and-file was no longer tolerated by the leadership, oppositionists were necessarily pushed in the direction of conspiratorial organization. As long as the Party apparatus remained subservient to Stalin, any effort to storm the ramparts of power from within the Party was a quixotic adventure foredoomed to defeat.

The state of siege within the Party imposed its commanding imperatives on Stalin as well as upon the oppositionists. From Stalin's point of view any opposition came to represent a potential challenge to his power which had to be stamped out. In this frame of reference, the oppositionist who recanted and was silent was merely biding his time and had to be watched. A display of independent views on policy matters was a signal of opposition in process of organization. Any adventitious gathering of the disaffected became a conspiracy in being. With each new outcropping of opposition, the margin of permissible dissent narrowed and eventually disappeared. The compulsive logic of the siege marched inexorably from the arrests and imprisonment of Trotskyites in the twenties to the extermination of the Old Bolsheviks in the Great Purge of the mid-thirties.

As always with Stalin, the design unfolded by stages. Having settled accounts with the Left Opposition, he now moved against Bukharin, Tomsky, and Rykov on the Right. Disagreements over policy toward the peasantry and the pace of industrialization set the stage for the conflict. "To each new situation," Trotsky once pointed out, "the Party adapted itself only by way of an inner crisis." [79] The right-wing allies whom Stalin had mobilized to destroy the Left became restive as Stalin borrowed the program of the Left and moved toward collectivization and intensive industrialization.

With a full awareness of the danger, Stalin moved ruthlessly and expeditiously to cut down his opponents one by one. Commanding a majority in the Politburo, he first silenced his opponents in that body by insisting that all decisions be recorded as unanimous and forbidding the opposition leaders to air their differences publicly. Speaking to leaders of the Moscow organization on October 19, 1928, he announced, "In the Politburo there are neither Right nor 'Left' deviations, nor individuals conciliatory toward these deviations. This must be said quite categorically. It is time to put a stop to the gossip spread by the enemies of the Party and by the oppositionists of all kinds to the effect that there is a Right deviation, or a conciliatory attitude toward it in the Politburo of our Central Committee." [80] The same assurance was repeated, with no evidence of any embarrassment, in a speech before a plenum of the Central Committee a month later, when news of the conflict was already common knowledge among all high-ranking leaders of the Party.[81]

Events now unwound toward a familiar denouement. In a speech before a joint session of the Politburo and the presidium of the Central Control Commission at the end of January 1929, Stalin announced the "discovery" of a factional right-wing group led by Bukharin, Tomsky, and Rykov. Bukharin, he pointed out, had engaged in negotiations with Kamenev to establish a bloc with the former Left Opposition. Bukharin's article, "Notes of an Economist," was a veiled attack on the Politburo line. Stalin warned that factionalism would not be tolerated.[82] At the April plenum of the Central Committee and the Control Commission, Stalin launched a full-scale offensive against Bukharin and his colleagues. He revealed that Bukharin had rejected his "compromise" offer of February 7, 1929, by which Bukharin would be allowed to remain at his post in exchange for a complete repudiation of his views.[83] He continued:

> Bukharin spoke here of the "civil execution" of three members of the Politburo, who in his words, "were being picked to pieces" by the organizations of our Party. He said that the Party had subjected three members of the Politburo . . . to "civil execution" by criticizing their errors in the press and at meetings, while they, the three . . . were "compelled" to keep silent.
>
> All this is nonsense, comrades. These are the false words of a Communist gone liberal who is trying to weaken the Party in its fight against the Right deviation. According to Bukharin, even though he and his friends have become entangled in Right deviationist mistakes, the Party has no right to expose these mistakes, the Party must stop fighting the Right deviation and wait until it will please Bukharin and his friends to abandon their mistakes.
>
> Is not Bukharin asking too much of us? Is he not under the impression that the Party exists for him and not he for the Party? Who is compelling him to keep silent, to remain in a state of inaction when the whole Party is mobilized

against the Right deviation and is conducting determined attacks against difficulties? Why should not he, Bukharin, and his close friends come forward now and engage in a determined fight against the Right deviation and the conciliationist tendency? Can anyone doubt that the Party would welcome Bukharin and his close friends if they decided to take this, after all not so difficult, step? Why do they not decide to take this step, which, after all is their duty? Is it not because they place the interests of their group above the interests of the Party and its general line? [84]

Stalin then pronounced the verdict of the plenum: to condemn the views of Bukharin and his group and to remove Bukharin and Tomsky from their official posts with a warning that they would be expelled from the Politburo in the event of any future insubordination. Measures would also be taken, Stalin promised, to prevent any member or candidate member of the Politburo or any Party journals from giving expression to any views departing from the Party line.[85] On April 23, 1929, Bukharin was removed from the leadership of the Comintern. On June 2, Tomsky lost his position as head of the trade unions. On November 17, the plenum of the Central Committee approved the expulsion of Bukharin from the Politburo. On November 25, the Right Opposition capitulated. *Pravda* on the next day carried the following declaration signed by Bukharin, Tomsky, and Rykov:

In the course of the last year and a half there were disagreements between us and the majority of the Central Committee on a number of political and tactical questions. We stated our views in a series of documents and submissions at the Plenums and other meetings of the Central Committee and Central Control Commission.

We consider it our duty to say that in this dispute the Party and its Central Committee were right. Our views, developed in well-known documents, showed themselves to be mistaken. Recognizing our mistakes, we on our side will apply all our strength, together with the whole Party, to conduct a determined battle against all deviations from the general line of the Party and, above all, against the right deviation and conciliation with it, in order to overcome all difficulties and to guarantee the most complete and speedy triumph of socialist construction.[86]

Even this self-abasement did not suffice. At the Sixteenth Party Congress (June 26 to July 13, 1930), Tomsky was dropped from the Politburo. Toward the end of December, Rykov was also removed from that body, as well as from his position as Chairman of the Council of People's Commissars.[87] The rout of the Right Opposition was complete. Addressing the Seventeenth Congress in January 1934, Stalin could boast:

The present Congress is taking place under the flag of the complete victory of Leninism; under the flag of the liquidation of the remnants of the anti-Leninist groups.

The anti-Leninist Trotskyite group has been defeated and scattered. Its organizers are now to be found in the backyards of the bourgeois parties abroad.

The anti-Leninist group of the Right deviationists have been defeated and scattered. Its organizers have long since renounced their views and are now trying in various ways to expiate the sins they committed against the Party.

The national deviationist groups have been defeated and scattered. Their organizers have either completely merged with the interventionist émigrés, or else recanted . . .

It must be admitted that the Party today is united as it has never been before.[88]

The delegates at the Congress vied with each other in proclaiming their fealty to Stalin. Not a single note of jarring criticism disturbed the monolithic serenity of the Congress.

On December 1, 1934, a young Communist called Nikolayev assassinated Sergei Kirov, member of the Politburo, head of the Leningrad Party organization, and one of Stalin's most dependable henchmen. The circumstances surrounding the Kirov assassination remain obscure; in the official version, the assassin was alleged to be a member of an "underground counter-revolutionary terrorist group . . . consisting of former members of the Zinoviev opposition." [89] The shot fired by Nikolayev signaled the inauguration of an unparalleled campaign of repression and vengeance against former oppositionists.

The saturnalia of blood and violence within the Party over the next four years claimed victims in the hundreds of thousands. The generation of Old Bolsheviks was virtually decimated. Tomsky committed suicide. Zinoviev, Kamenev, Bukharin, Rykov, and most of the leaders of the former Left and Right oppositions were shot. Marshal Tukhachevsky, the chief of staff, and other leading Red Army generals shared their fate. The ravages of the Purge extended through the entire Party and governmental apparatus; the list of the "eliminated" was a Who's Who of Soviet celebrities.[90] The macabre spectacle had to be justified, and a series of show trials were staged in order to demonstrate, in the words of the official Party history,

that the Trotsky-Bukharin fiends, in obedience to the wishes of their masters — the espionage services of foreign states — had set out to destroy the Party and the Soviet state, to undermine the defensive power of the country, to assist foreign military intervention, to prepare the way for the defeat of the Red Army, to bring about the dismemberment of the U.S.S.R., to hand over the Soviet Maritime Region to the Japanese, Soviet Byelorussia to the Poles, and the Soviet Ukraine to the Germans, to destroy the gains of the workers and collective farmers, and to restore capitalist slavery in the U.S.S.R.[91]

Implausible as the accusations were, they were trumpeted through the length and breadth of the Soviet Union. To the Soviet citizen, whether inside or outside the Party, they were clear warning that any form of opposition to Stalin's policies could now be construed as treason. The rank-and-file Party cadres and the highest Party officials were equally suspect and equally vulnerable. "The foul murder of Comrade Kirov," Stalin declared, "was the first serious warning showing that the enemies of the people will practice duplicity and, in doing so, will disguise themselves as Bolsheviks, as Party members, so as to worm their way into our confidence and open a path for themselves into our organizations." [92] "Is it not clear," he asked, "that as long as capitalist encirclement exists there will be wreckers, spies, diversionists and murderers in our country, sent behind our lines by the agents of foreign states?" [93] "An indispensable quality of every Bolshevik in the present conditions," he went on to point out, "must be the ability to recognize the enemy of the Party no matter how well he be masked." [94]

Stalin's call for "the conversion of the Party into an impregnable fortress into which not a single double-dealer could penetrate" [95] ignited a fire of denunciations which threatened to consume the Party in the blaze of its own suspicion. When a halt was finally called to the process of self-destruction in 1938, it was revealed that thousands of innocents had been sacrificed along with the allegedly guilty. The abuses in turn were attributed to "enemies of the people" who had "wormed their way" into local Party organizations; [96] thus the legend of Stalin's infallibility was preserved. The eerie quiet of the graveyard and the prison descended on the Party. The Eighteenth Party Congress, which took place in 1939, recorded not a single dissenting vote.

With the consolidation of Stalin's power in the Party, the operative theory of the role of Party leadership underwent profound changes. While lip service continued to be given the doctrine of democratic centralism, with its provision for "the election of all leading Party bodies from the highest to the lowest," practice so far diverged from theory as to make the provision meaningless. The characteristic mode of selecting Party officials became designation from above rather than election from below. Even where elections continued to be held, they represented procedures for mobilizing and recording assent rather than forums of free choice. The Party was transformed into a disciplined military phalanx. Opposition was mutiny. The function of the command was to issue orders; the duty of the Party functionary was to carry them out.

In Lenin's day, Party leadership was still visualized as collegial. Lenin, to be sure, was recognized as *primus inter pares* within the Politburo, but his authority derived from his stature rather than his position in the Bolshevik hierarchy. Though the climate of decision was one of tightening discipline, discussion and debate were still active and vigorous in the leading Party organs, and the tradition of collective consultation and leadership was maintained. Under Stalin, the fiction of collegiality continued to be affirmed, even after the elimination of his competitors for the succession robbed it of any substantive content. In contrast with the

Leninist period, however, a new symbolism was fostered and developed by which the leadership role of the impersonal Party and its Central Committee became personalized and embodied in the stern figure of the all-wise, godlike Stalin.

The process began with the virtual deification of Lenin after his death. The initiation of a Leninist hagiolatry prepared the way for the admission of Stalin into the company of Communist saints. The modest niche which Stalin first carved out for himself was that of the faithful pupil of Lenin, the conservator of the Leninist heritage. The shouts of "Hail Stalin!" with which his faithful supporters greeted his triumph over Zinoviev and Kamenev at the Fourteenth Party Congress in 1925 marked the first stage of the ascension to the pedestal hitherto reserved for Lenin alone. As Stalin emerged undisputed master of the Party, the names Lenin and Stalin became interlocked and hyphenated. In the new mythology, they made the Revolution together; together they laid the foundations of the Soviet state. The Party was now referred to as a Leninist-Stalinist Party. Stalin became "the Lenin of today." His fiftieth birthday in 1929, the year which witnessed the expulsion of Trotsky from the Soviet Union and the crushing of the Right Opposition, was the occasion for a national celebration. Party propagandists vied with one another in tributes to his greatness. Poster portraits, statues, and busts of Stalin appeared everywhere. The cult of Stalinism was given a powerful impetus, and it gathered increasing momentum during the next decades.

As an accompaniment of the overtowering ascendancy of Stalin, the figure of the infallible Dictator emerged as the operative theory of Bolshevik leadership. His colleagues in the Politburo functioned as administrative henchmen and assistants on a high level; the Central Committee went into a shadowy eclipse; Party congresses became rallies of the faithful; and the Party apparatus served as the institutionalized projection of his will. Where Lenin had struggled, not always successfully, to hold the disparate elements in the Party together, for Stalin the suppression of disagreement and the crushing of opposition became the key to survival. The Party ceased to be a creative association which shaped policy and was transformed instead into a bureaucratic extension of the personality and dynamism of the Dictator, a privileged chorus of sycophants who sang his praises and enforced his will.

The death of Stalin left the further development of the theory and practice of Party dictatorship to be spelled out anew. While Malenkov's quick assumption of Stalin's titular designations as Chairman of the Council of Ministers and Chairman of the Party Presidium clearly marked him out as the strongest of Stalin's former lieutenants, it remained for future events to demonstrate whether he could attain Stalin's position of unquestioned ascendancy. The transformation of Stalin the man, into

Stalin the mythological Hero, required years to achieve, and the consolidation of his power was attended by a protracted ordeal of bloody purges. It appeared unlikely that the elevation of Malenkov into the company of the Communist "immortals" could be accomplished more easily.

Chapter 6

The Growth of the Party Apparatus

One of the striking characteristics of modern totalitarian dictatorship is its dependence on bureaucratic organization to make its control effective. The bureaucratization of the dictator's power is an inevitable outgrowth of the magnitude of his responsibilities. Trusted lieutenants and a party machine are indispensable concomitants of his domination. In the process of utilizing them, his authority may be both intensified and diluted. It is intensified to the degree that he succeeds in fashioning an administrative mechanism which is a reflection of his will. It is diluted to the extent that he is compelled to cede power to his subordinates and the party machine acquires a momentum and direction of its own. Every dictatorship faces the problem of institutionalizing its own authority. The power of the Leader depends on his ability to keep the essence of control in his own hands or in the hands of reliable subordinates while transforming the party machine into an obedient instrument ready to execute his slightest command.

The development of the Communist Party apparatus as an extension of the long arm of the dictator constitutes one of the most impressive and formidable organizational achievements of modern totalitarianism. To an extent unmatched by its now defunct Fascist and Nazi rivals, the Communist dictatorship has succeeded in uprooting and destroying every organized form of resistance to its demands. It has managed to survive at least one major change of leadership, a series of bitter intra-Party struggles, a profound industrial and agricultural revolution, a bloody purge in which the older generation of Bolsheviks was consumed, and a world war of unparalleled destructiveness. Through all these travails, the Party apparatus has played a central role in sustaining the power of the regime. A network of Party secretaries unites center and periphery, permeates every corner of Soviet life, and imposes the discipline of the apparatus on the society around it. Through the Party machine, loyalty is enforced, opposition eliminated, the Party line executed, new cadres developed, and continuity insured. Individual secretaries parade into prominence or obscurity, but the machine itself persists as an indispensable adjunct of dictatorship. Behind the monolithic façade, clique rivalries and struggles for power probably continue to rage even though they are rarely publicly ventilated. Reality falls short of totalitarian aspiration. Yet the machine remains the tractable creature of its director, a sounding board on which his praises are sung, and the instrument through which his policies are fulfilled.

The Origins of the Apparatus

The origins of the Communist Party apparatus reach back into the pre-Revolutionary period. Bolshevism from the beginning was characterized by an emphasis on organizational solidarity and discipline as a necessary basis for successful revolutionary action. In the long struggle to outwit the Tsarist secret police, the Bolsheviks developed an underground organization of local committees which formed the basis of Lenin's revolutionary machine. The committeemen of the underground — the *komitetchiki* (of whom Stalin was one) — were the first prototypes of the men of the apparatus — the *apparatchiki* — out of whom Stalin's Party machine was later to be constructed. When the time came for Stalin to weld his own machine together, he drew heavily on the "practical" workers of the underground who had survived the revolutionary struggle in Russia rather than on the more flamboyant cosmopolitan intellectuals who had spent the pre-Revolutionary years in *émigré* disputations abroad.

During the march to power in 1917 when the Party was flooded with new members, the Party organization itself remained in the hands of the *komitetchiki*. These seasoned workers of the underground maintained a firm grip on the rapidly expanding local Party organizations.* At the Sixth Congress of the Party — the only one held during the revolutionary year 1917 — an overwhelming preponderance of the voting delegates consisted of underground veterans who had joined the Party in 1914 or earlier.[1] The persisting strength of the underground in the Party apparatus is indicated by the fact that, as late as 1930, 69 per cent of the secretaries of the central committees of the national republics and of the regional (*oblast* and *krai*) committees were still Old Bolsheviks of pre-Revolutionary vintage.[2]

With the Party's seizure of power in November 1917 and the assump-

---

* See Chapter 3, pp. 68–69.

tion of governing responsibilities, a significant differentiation became evident in the roles played by various groups among the Old Bolsheviks. The intellectuals of the emigration tended to assume the political leadership, but their natural aptitudes and interests drove them into posts where they were preoccupied with broad problems of domestic and foreign policy rather than Party organization. The committeemen of the underground, on the other hand, tended to gravitate into the apparatus, to become local and regional Party secretaries, and to concern themselves with problems of interior Party management.

From early 1917 until early 1919, central responsibility for Party organization was concentrated largely in the hands of Sverdlov, veteran committeeman of pre-Revolutionary days, whose rich and varied experience in the underground gave him a wide acquaintance among the committeemen. Through his good offices, many of the old underground workers were assigned to the regional and local apparatus of the Party. Sverdlov was an extremely energetic and capable organizer, but he functioned largely without staff, and the only complete record of his transactions was in his head. When he suddenly died on the eve of the Eighth Congress in March 1919, the Party found itself in the embarrassing position of mourning the loss of its record office and central secretarial apparatus as well as the departure of a respected member of the Central Committee.

Sverdlov's death posed the problem of regularizing and rationalizing the central machinery of the Party. The Eighth Congress addressed itself to this task. In order to provide for the direction of the Party's wideranging activities, the Central Committee was instructed to create three new organs: (1) a Political Bureau (Politburo), to be composed of five members of the Central Committee; (2) an Organizational Bureau (Orgburo), also to be composed of five Central Committee members; and (3) a Secretariat, to consist of one responsible Secretary, who was required to be a member of the Orgburo, and five technical secretaries to be chosen from experienced Party workers.

The Politburo was charged with the responsibility of deciding all questions requiring immediate action; from the outset it became the top policy-determining organ of the Party. Lenin, Trotsky, Stalin, Kamenev, and Krestinsky were its first members. During the debates at the Eighth Congress, the objection was raised that the creation of the Politburo involved the demotion of the rest of the Central Committee into secondclass Party leaders. In order to blunt the force of this charge, the Politburo was required to deliver regular reports on its actions to the Central Committee, and members of the Central Committee who were not members of the Politburo were given the right to attend and participate in Politburo sessions with a consultative, though not a deciding, vote.

The Orgburo was authorized "to direct all the organizational work of the Party."[3] It was to meet at least three times a week, and like the Politburo, was required to render bi-weekly reports to the Central Committee. Two members of the Politburo, Krestinsky and Stalin, were also named to work in the Orgburo. The assignment of Stalin to the Orgburo was to have momentous significance. As an old committeeman of the Sverdlov stripe, his capacities were adapted to questions of interior Party management. Unlike some of his more intellectually scintillating associates in the Politburo who spurned organizational details, he was quick to realize the crucial importance of the Party apparatus in deciding the issue of supremacy within the Party. The Orgburo became his first base of operations in building his own machine.

The authority of the Secretariat was not defined by the Eighth Congress. Its powers evolved in practice. The first responsible Secretary, Krestinsky, was a lawyer-journalist who had joined the Party in 1903 and who had served in 1917 as chairman of the Ekaterinburg and Ural regional Party committees. His interests were political rather than organizational, and he made no effort to construct an independent power base of his own. Under Krestinsky, the Secretariat remained subservient to the Politburo and the Orgburo. Lenin, in his report to the Ninth Party Congress on March 29, 1920, described the interlocking responsibilities of the three organs as follows:

> During the year under review the current daily work of the Central Committee was conducted by the two bodies elected at the Plenum of the Central Committee: the Organization Bureau . . . and the Political Bureau . . . In order to achieve coördination and consistency in the decisions of these two bodies, the Secretary acted as a member of both. The practice arrived at was that it became the main and proper function of the Orgburo to distribute the forces of the Party, while the function of the Political Bureau was to deal with political questions. It goes without saying that this distinction is to a certain extent artificial; it is obvious that no policy can be carried out in practice without finding expression in appointments and transfers. Consequently, every organizational question assumes a political significance; and the practice was established that the request of a single member of the Central Committee was sufficient to have any question for any reason whatsoever examined as a political question. To have attempted to divide the functions of the Central Committee in any other way would hardly have been expedient and in practice would hardly have achieved its purpose.
>
> This method of conducting business was productive of extremely good results: no difficulties have arisen between the two bureaus on any occasion. The work of these bodies has on the whole proceeded harmoniously, and practical fulfillment was facilitated by the presence of the Secretary . . . It must be emphasized from the very outset, so as to remove all misunderstanding, that only the corporate decisions of the Central Committee adopted in the Orgburo or the Politburo, or in the Plenum of the Central Committee — exclusively such matters were carried out by the Secretary of the Central Committee of the Party.[4]

Despite this roseate report and Lenin's emphatic insistence that the Secretary had not arrogated any powers which were not delegated to him, it can be surmised that the operative efficiency of the Secretariat left much to be desired. At the Ninth Congress, a resolution was carried to "strengthen" the Secretariat by adding to it three members of the Central Committee who would devote all their time to its work. At the same time, an effort was made to demarcate the respective responsibilities of the Orgburo and Secretariat by reserving the general direction of organizational work to the Orgburo while entrusting current questions of an administrative and executive character to the Secretariat.[5] Krestinsky, Preobrazhensky, and Serebryakov were named as the new secretaries. All three aligned themselves with Trotsky against Lenin in the bitter trade-union discussion of 1920–21, and their secretarial careers were quickly terminated. At the Tenth Congress in 1921, Krestinsky was dropped from his important posts in the Politburo, the Orgburo, and the Central Committee; the others lost their positions on the Orgburo and the Central Committee. They were replaced as secretaries by Molotov, Yaroslavsky, and V. Mikhailov, of whom the first two in particular were among the staunchest supporters of Stalin in his rise to supremacy in the Party.

As a result of the secretarial overturn after the Tenth Congress, Stalin emerged as the dominant organizational spokesman and specialist in the Party. He was the only member of the Politburo who also served on the Orgburo and, as such, became its unquestioned leader. Through his ascendancy in the Orgburo, he began in effect to direct the work of the Secretariat. The announcement on April 4, 1922, of his appointment to the post of General Secretary registered a *de facto* authority which had already been achieved. Molotov and Kuibyshev were also designated as secretaries, but their position was clearly that of subordinates rather than co-equals. From the vantage point of the General Secretaryship, Stalin was to make his successful bid for supreme power.

The Bureaucratization of the Party

As the Party expanded in size, as its governing responsibilities multiplied, and as it sought to consolidate its hold over every facet of Soviet life, the role of the Party apparatus increased greatly in importance. By 1922 approximately one out of every twenty-five Party members was engaged in full-time Party work. In the first two years of the existence of the Secretariat of the Central Committee, its staff increased from 30 to 602, plus an additional contingent of 140 guards and messengers.[6] Its functions expanded to include the mobilization and allocation of Party personnel, the supervision of regional and local Party organizations through a corps of responsible instructors, and the guidance of propaganda and agitation activities. In addition, special sections were established to direct Party work in the villages, among women, and among national minorities. A list of the Party officialdom submitted to the Twelfth Party Conference in August 1922 numbered 15,325 responsible workers.[7]

The bureaucratization of Party life had its inevitable consequences. The weight of the apparatus became determinative in Party affairs. The Party official engaged exclusively on Party business was at an obvious advantage compared with the rank-and-file Party member who had a full-time job in a factory or in a government office. The sheer force of professional preoccupation with Party management rendered the officialdom the center of initiative, direction, and control. At every level of the Party hierarchy, a transfer of authority and influence became visible, first from the congresses or conferences to the committees which they nominally elected, and then from the committees to the Party secretaries who ostensibly executed their will. As long as the secretaries were still locally selected and responsible to the organizations which they served, the structure of the Party remained quasi-federative, and the forces of autonomy and dissidence continued to assert their claims. As the network of local secretaries was absorbed into the central apparatus and became dependent on it for assignments and promotions, the secretarial hierarchy emerged as a distinct group with vested interests of its own. The drive to stabilize its own position and to extend its authority became an end in itself. Its solidarity and *esprit de corps* were promoted by common concerns and intensified by attacks on its prerogatives. The rising influence of the General Secretary symbolized its own aspirations; every effort to delimit his influence was construed as an effort to undermine the power of the apparatus itself. The identification of the Party officialdom with the cause of the General Secretary ensured his eventual triumph as the unchallenged leader of the Party.

The welding of the Party apparatus into a homogeneous, disciplined, and tightly-controlled machine was achieved through two implements of central authority: (1) the Secretariat of the Central Committee operating in conjunction with the Orgburo and (2) the control commissions, central and local, which were first established in 1920 to hear "complaints" against the Party apparatus but which were rapidly transformed into instruments through which the apparatus enforced Party discipline and silenced its critics.

The key role of the Central Committee Secretariat developed out of its personnel responsibilities and its supervisory authority over the operations of local Party organizations. In 1920 a special section of the Secretariat — *Uchraspred*, the Account and Assignment Section — was established to control the "mobilizations, transfers and appointments of members of the Party."[8] During the Civil War and immediately afterwards, the central apparatus had concerned itself almost exclusively with so-called "mass" mobilizations. When Party workers were needed in quantity for particular assignments, quotas were assessed on local Party organizations which they were obligated to fill. The principle was early established that Party workers were at the complete disposition of the central command. They could be summoned when needed and assigned wherever their services were required.

Shortly after the end of the Civil War, mass mobilizations were abandoned. A report of the Central Committee for the period March 1922 to April 1923 stated: "The period of broad mobilizations, upon which main attention was focused two to four years ago, has now been succeeded by the epoch of all-around accounting of Party forces, the training and promotion of new cadres of [Party] workers, and intensified direction by the Party in all matters of assigning Party workers." [9] In making individual assignments, Uchraspred concentrated first on filling Party posts. Appointments to the highest Party positions came under the jurisdiction of the Orgburo; in such cases, the Secretariat made recommendations rather than assignments. At lower levels, the authority of the Secretariat was more extensive. The legal fiction of "elections" was still maintained, but in fact the "recommendations" of the Secretariat were mandatory.

Uchraspred rapidly extended its control down through the *guberniya* or provincial level.[10] By the beginning of 1923, its controls reached the secretarial personnel at the *uezd* or county level. The report of Uchraspred to the Twelfth Party Congress in April 1923 indicated that more than ten thousand assignments had been made in the preceding year. Approximately half of these actions involved so-called "responsible" officials.[11] Stalin, in his organizational report to the Congress, made no effort to conceal the range of Uchraspred's activities; indeed, he revealed that it was expanding its jurisdiction into the state apparatus and controlling appointments to important administrative and economic posts.[12]

By 1923 the grip of the General Secretary on the Party organization was causing his rivals for leadership the most serious concern. As Trotsky complained in a letter to the Central Committee on October 8, 1923:

In the fiercest moment of War Communism, the system of appointment within the party did not have one-tenth of the extent that it has now. Appointment of the secretaries of provincial committees is now the rule. That creates for the secretary a position essentially independent of the local organization . . .

. . . The bureaucratization of the Party apparatus has developed to unheard-of proportions by means of the method of secretarial selection. There has been created a very broad stratum of party workers, entering into the apparatus of the government of the party, who completely renounce their own party opinion, at least the open expression of it, as though assuming that the secretarial hierarchy is the apparatus which creates party opinion and party decisions. Beneath this stratum . . . there lies the broad mass of the party, before whom every decision stands in the form of a summons or a command."[13]

The Organization-Instruction Section of the Central Committee Secretariat operated as another powerful lever of control over local Party organizations. Lazar Kaganovich, the head of this section in 1922 and 1923, was one of Stalin's most faithful disciples and was eventually rewarded with a place in the Politburo for his devotion to the cause of the General Secretary.[14] In enforcing its controls over local Party organizations, the Organization-Instruction Section used a corps of "responsible instructors" who regularly visited their assigned areas, attended meetings of provincial Party conferences and committees, conveyed instructions from the center, and carried back reports on the status of Party work in the organizations which they advised and supervised. In the rare cases where local organizations showed themselves recalcitrant and refused to obey central directives, "plenipotentiaries" were sent out by order of the Central Committee "with the right to veto those decisions of the local organizations which interfered with the proper conditions of Party and soviet work." Liaison with local Party functionaries was also maintained by occasional conferences of Party secretaries in Moscow, a regular flow of written reports from the localities, and arrangements by which provincial secretaries and heads of local organization-instruction departments were summoned to Moscow to render an oral accounting of their activities.[15]

In order to strengthen control over the more distantly located provinces, so-called "regional bureaus" were established in the Secretariat in 1920 as an intermediate layer of supervision between the center and the *guberniyas*. The regional bureaus played a highly important role in buttressing Stalin's hold on the Party machinery. Stalwart supporters of Stalin were assigned to the more important bureaus.[16] The problem of bringing the peripheral Party organizations to heel presented real difficulties.[17] Distance frequently intensified the spirit of independence. Under the whiplash of purge and pressure, the impediments were mastered, and the outlying *guberniyas* under the jurisdiction of the regional bureaus became one of the firmest strongholds of the Stalin machine.

The network of control commissions, which expanded greatly after 1920, also served as an important centralizing instrument in enforcing the power of the Party apparatus. By a curious paradox, the original impetus which led to the creation of the control commissions came from members of the Workers' Opposition and Democratic Centralists who were searching for a device to prevent the Party from being dominated by its bureaucratic element. As originally conceived in 1920, the Control

Commission attached to the Central Committee was to consist in its majority of representatives of the more important local Party organizations who would be elected at *guberniya* Party conferences. The control commissions attached to the *guberniya* Party committees in turn were to be locally elected and free from domination by the central Party organs.[18] The oppositionists hoped that the control commissions would thus become independent centers through which bureaucratic malpractices could be exposed.

This hope miscarried. From the beginning, the control commissions met sabotage and opposition from the centrally-appointed Party secretaries in the localities. The personnel assigned to work in the control commissions lacked the status and prestige to enforce their somewhat ambiguous authority, and before very long they were converted into instrumentalities of the Party's secretarial apparatus. At the Tenth Party Congress in 1921, the mission of the control commissions was reformulated. Their main responsibility became that of "strengthening the unity and authority of the Party,"[19] and their energies were concentrated on stamping out opposition in the Party, although they also served as courts of appeal for Party members who were charged with all manner of violations of the Party statutes. At the Eleventh Party Congress in 1922, the authority of the Central Control Commission was broadened to include supervision and direction of the work of all local control commissions.[20] The effect of this action was to bring the local commissions within the ambit of central control and to prevent them from becoming islands of dissidence in the Party organization. Through domination of the Central Control Commission, the General Secretary could be certain that the entire control machinery of the Party was in his hands.

The Stalin Machine

The command of the Party apparatus operated as the master force in Stalin's rise to supreme power. From the vantage point of the Orgburo and the General Secretaryship, Stalin succeeded in constructing a Party machine of *apparatchiki* who came to exercise a decisive weight in Party affairs. The machine in its inception was far from being the monolithic juggernaut which it later became. Compared, however, with what was available to his rivals for supremacy, it was more than adequate to accomplish the purpose for which it was designed. Through the secretarial hierarchy, Stalin was able to extend his dominion over the local organizations of the Party and to insure the election of "loyal" slates of delegates to the Party congresses and conferences. Through his alliance with Zinoviev and Kamenev in the Politburo, he succeeded in isolating Trotsky and in neutralizing, at least temporarily, his fellow triumvirs.

Stalin's strength was concentrated in the Party apparatus. The power centers least amenable to his control in the early stages of the struggle were the policy-making organs of the Party, the Central Committee, and the Politburo. His problem, therefore, was to transmute his influence in the lower reaches of the Party's organizational structure into domination of its top policy posts. The task was not an easy one. Stalin sought to solve it by pressing for the enlargement of the Central Committee on the ground that it was desirable to introduce fresh talent into the upper councils of the Party and to promote outstanding Party workers from the localities to the center. His fellow triumvirs were not insensitive to the possible consequences of packing the committee with Stalin's henchmen, but because they feared Trotsky far more than Stalin and possibly because they shared an excessive confidence in their ability to outmaneuver their partner of convenience, they grudgingly yielded. The Central Committee was expanded from twenty-five members and fifteen candidates at the Tenth Congress in 1921 to forty members and seventeen candidates at the Twelfth Congress in 1923. Of the eight former candidates who were promoted to full membership in 1923, seven were close supporters of Stalin; the eighth, Pyatakov, was a follower of Trotsky. Of the eight new members elected without previous service as candidates,[21] four identified themselves with Stalin's machine and four became supporters of Zinoviev and Kamenev. Nearly all of the fourteen new candidate members were Party functionaries who were being rewarded for loyal service to Stalin. As a result of this stratagem, made possible by the voting strength of the apparatus on the floor of the Congress, the Stalinist caucus in the Central Committee was greatly strengthened.

Stalin's next step was to play off the Central Committee against the Politburo. The organizational resolution adopted by the Twelfth Congress admonished the Politburo for its failure to take the Central Committee into its confidence and called on the Politburo to submit all "fundamental questions" for discussion by a plenum of the Central Committee.[22] As the defender of the prerogatives of the enlarged Central Committee against the "caste of priests" who had hitherto dominated the Party leadership, Stalin even won applause from the small remnant of leftist defenders of inner-Party democracy who were still represented at the Congress.[23]

While Stalin maneuvered for power in the Central Committee, he did not neglect other sources of authority and influence. The only change in the composition of the Politburo after the Twelfth Congress was the addition of Rudzutak as a candidate for membership — and Rudzutak was a firm supporter of Stalin. The membership of the Central Control Commission was enlarged from seven to fifty members at the Twelfth Congress; its presidium of nine members was given the right to participate in meetings of the Central Committee, while three representatives of the presidium were authorized to attend sessions of the Politburo. Kuibyshev, who was named chairman of the Central Control Commission, was one of Stalin's closest associates. In addition, the presidium included such Stalinist stalwarts as Yaroslavsky, Soltz, and Shkiryatov.

Thus, even before the death of Lenin, Stalin had entrenched himself firmly in all the strategic power structures of the Party. Zinoviev's organizational strength was confined largely to Leningrad and the Comintern. Kamenev exercised considerable influence in the Moscow Party organization. Trotsky had a coterie of influential followers in the army and state administration. His prestige as a revolutionary leader was second only to that of Lenin, but he commanded little support among the Party *apparatchiki*. Their allegiance and ambitions were embodied in Stalin, and collectively they represented the only nation-wide Party machine in existence.

Out of fear of Trotsky, the troika of Zinoviev, Kamenev, and Stalin maintained an uneasy partnership in the Politburo. By the summer of 1923, however, the triumvirate was already showing signs of strain. Zinoviev, in particular, was alarmed by Stalin's growing influence. As he later revealed at the Fourteenth Party Congress, he wavered between two plans to limit Stalin's power.[24] One involved transforming the Secretariat into a technical service apparatus without appointive powers. The other involved politicizing the Secretariat by making it responsible to three members of the Politburo — Stalin, Trotsky, and a third member who might be either Kamenev, Bukharin, or himself. Zinoviev, in true conspiratorial fashion, presented his views to Bukharin, Voroshilov, Ordjonikidze, Lashevich, and Evdokimov at a conference in a cave near Kislovodsk in September 1923. At the end of the conference he drafted a proposal which was entrusted to Ordjonikidze for delivery to Stalin. According to Zinoviev's later testimony,

> Comrade Stalin . . . replied with a telegram in a coarse but friendly tone . . . Some time later he arrived . . . and we had several discussions. Finally it was decided that we would not touch the Secretariat, but in order to coördinate organizational and political work, we would introduce three members of the Politburo into the Orgburo. This . . . not very practical suggestion was made by Comrade Stalin, and we agreed to it. We introduced three members of the Politburo into the Orgburo: Comrades Trotsky, Bukharin, and myself. I attended the sessions of the Orgburo, I think, once or twice, Comrades Bukharin and Trotsky, it seems, did not come even once. Nothing came of it all.[25]

Since neither Trotsky nor Bukharin was prepared at this point to join forces with Zinoviev, Stalin was left in undisturbed control of the Party apparatus. Trotsky's decision toward the end of 1923 to launch a full-scale public attack on the triumvirate forced its members to draw together in mutual protection. By this time, however, it was clear that Stalin was the senior partner and Zinoviev and Kamenev were dependent allies. Faced with Stalin's control of the Party machine, Trotsky could score only rhetorical and literary successes, and even the latter were limited by the embargo which the apparatus placed on the circulation of his brochure on the *New Course*.[26]

Trotsky's eloquent strictures against the oligarchy of appointed secretaries and his call for a "renovation of the Party apparatus" from below won him considerable support outside the apparatus, particularly among student Communists who comprised approximately 25 per cent of the membership of the Moscow Party organization. Yet even in Moscow, where Trotsky mobilized his greatest strength, the power of the Stalinist machine proved irresistible.[27]

At the Thirteenth Congress, which assembled in May 1924, soon after Lenin's death, Stalin consolidated his hold over the Party machinery. The enlargement of the Central Committee to fifty-three members and thirty-four candidates gave Stalin an opportunity to reward an additional group of loyal Party functionaries with high office.[28] The Central Control Commission was tripled in size from 50 to 151 members. Again, meritorious service in the apparatus was recognized in making the new appointments, while Kuibyshev remained as chairman of the Commission to insure Stalin's control of its proceedings.[29] The vacancy in the Politburo created by Lenin's death was filled by the promotion of Bukharin from candidate to full membership. Stalin's position in the Politburo was now secure. While Trotsky was in opposition, Zinoviev and Kamenev were still allies, and Rykov, Tomsky, and Bukharin could be counted on to follow Stalin's lead. Kalinin, Molotov, and Rudzutak, all firm supporters of Stalin, held on as candidates. Of the three new candidates added at this time, Dzerzhinsky and Frunze were followers of Stalin, and Sokolnikov associated himself with Zinoviev.

Although signs of strain were evident in the relations between Stalin and his fellow triumvirs after the Thirteenth Congress, their hostility to Trotsky continued to hold them together in a precarious truce. In October 1924 Trotsky returned to the attack with the publication of the *Lessons of October*. This pamphlet was designed to destroy the authority of Zinoviev and Kamenev as Party leaders by reminding the Party of their sorry role in the 1917 Revolution. It was provoked by Trotsky's bitter resentment of the attacks which Zinoviev and Kamenev had leveled against him. As a political maneuver to increase Trotsky's influence, its effect was disastrous. While it accomplished its purpose of discrediting Zinoviev and Kamenev, by the same token it made them more than ever dependent on Stalin. It exacerbated their determination to revenge themselves on Trotsky, and it left Stalin's strength untouched. Stalin defended his colleagues against Trotsky's strictures but with overtones of coolness and reservation which were not lost on his supporters. He resisted the insistent demands of Zinoviev and Kamenev that Trotsky be dropped from the Politburo and Central Committee and even be excluded from the Party, but he availed himself of their support in relieving Trotsky of his duties as Commissar of War.[30]

As the prestige of Zinoviev and Kamenev fell, Stalin's rose. In a disingenuous effort to regain lost ground, Kamenev advanced Stalin's candidacy for the vacancy in the War Commissariat with the hope of dislodging him from the General Secretaryship.[31] Stalin declined the honor and appointed Frunze instead. When Frunze died shortly afterwards, he was succeeded by Voroshilov, one of Stalin's closest associates. Within the Politburo itself, Zinoviev and Kamenev now found themselves thrust aside and isolated, while Stalin leaned on Bukharin, Tomsky, and Rykov to carry his majority. The secretarial hierarchy remained firmly in Stalin's hands. Zinoviev and Kamenev were left with the alternative of resigning themselves to second-class rank or fighting to regain their status.

They determined to fight. The prospects were not very encouraging. Zinoviev and Kamenev were in a minority in the Politburo and had only a handful of supporters in the Central Committee and the Central Control Commission. Trotsky was still alienated from them and stood aside. The assets on which they counted were Zinoviev's firm grip on the Leningrad Party organization and the hope that they would also be able to carry the Moscow organization with them. Kamenev and Zinoviev had taken the initiative in arranging the transfer of Uglanov as Party secretary from Nizhni-Novgorod to Moscow, and they apparently calculated on his help in swinging the support of the Moscow organization to their side. Uglanov proved to be a frail reed and espoused Stalin's cause.[32] As a result, Zinoviev and Kamenev entered the Fourteenth Congress (December 1925) with a solid bloc of delegates from Leningrad but with hardly any voting strength elsewhere. The resolution to approve Stalin's report on behalf of the Central Committee carried by an overwhelming majority of 559 to 65.[33] The Stalinist apparatus demonstrated itself in complete control of the proceedings.

At the Fourteenth Congress, the size of the Central Committee was again greatly increased, this time to sixty-three members and forty-three candidates. The new positions were once more used to reward faithful members of the secretarial hierarchy. The new Politburo elected after the Fourteenth Congress was enlarged from seven to nine members. Stalin, Trotsky, Zinoviev, Bukharin, Tomsky, and Rykov remained as members. Molotov, Kalinin, and Voroshilov, all part of the Stalinist entourage, were advanced to full membership for the first time. Kamenev, who had delivered one of the sharpest attacks on Stalin at the Congress, was demoted from full member to candidate. The other candidates — Rudzutak, Dzerzhinsky, Petrovsky, and Uglanov — were regarded as henchmen of Stalin. The promotion of Uglanov appeared to be a recognition of the service which he performed in holding the Moscow Party organization in line for Stalin.[34]

By the beginning of 1926, the Stalinist machine was so solidly entrenched in all the key positions in the Party apparatus as to be virtually impervious to attack. The belated decision of Trotsky, Kamenev, and Zinoviev in the spring of that year to unite their forces for a last desperate onslaught rapidly revealed itself as an act of quixotic martyrdom.[35] "It is enough," said Kamenev to Trotsky, "for you and Zinoviev to appear on the same platform, and the party will find its true Central Committee." [36] This remark, which Trotsky attributes to Kamenev, laid bare a confidence in messianic oratory and an insensitivity to the power of the Party's bureaucratic phalanx which were to prove the opposition's undoing. The opposition could muster a brilliant coterie of generals, but they were generals whose forces were scattered, disorganized, and improvised, and they confronted an enemy who securely controlled both the local organizations and leading organs of the Party.

In the unequal struggle which ensued, all the power of the state and the disciplined battalions of the apparatus were on Stalin's side. The opposition was torn to pieces, limb by limb.* With the annihilation of the Left Opposition, Stalin was free to turn his energies against the Right. The Politburo which was elected after the Fifteenth Congress was soon to divide into two factions. Molotov, Rudzutak, Kuibyshev, Voroshilov, and Kalinin followed Stalin; Rykov, Tomsky, and Bukharin emerged as a right-wing opposition to challenge the pace and direction of Stalin's industrial and agrarian program. The Right Opposition proved as powerless as the Left when it confronted the Stalin machine.

The Right Wing's dream of winning supreme power was based on a complex set of calculations. First, it expected to attract the support of Voroshilov and Kalinin and thus achieve a majority of five to four in the Politburo. The hope proved illusory. "Stalin has some special hold on them that I do not know of," [37] Bukharin was reported later to have said. Second, the Right Wing counted on the solid support of the Moscow Party organization, and it expected to accumulate considerable support in the provinces as the result of dissatisfaction in Stalin's apparatus with the collectivization program. These expectations, too, were disappointed. Uglanov, the head of the Moscow Party organization, supported the Right Wing, but he proved unable to control his own subordinates. Stalin intervened in a dramatic personal appeal to a plenum of the Moscow committee and control commission which proved decisive.[38] On November 28, 1928, Uglanov and his associate Kotov were removed as secretaries of

* See Chapter 5, pp. 141–145.

the Moscow committee and replaced by Molotov and Baumann. The lesson was not lost on the rest of the apparatus, and the anticipated revolt in the provinces failed to develop. Third, the Right Wing also counted on considerable support outside the Party apparatus. Through Tomsky, the head of the trade unions, it expected to mobilize the support of the trade-union functionaries; through Bukharin, the leader of the Communist International, it anticipated help from the Comintern apparatus; through Rykov, the Chairman of the Council of People's Commissars, it looked for assistance in the top administrative hierarchy. According to Boris Souvarine, it also had the sympathy of Yagoda, the Deputy Chief of the GPU, but if Yagoda's attitude was benevolent, it displayed itself in covert rather than in open assistance to the Right.[39]

As always, Stalin moved resolutely to cut off his enemies' lines of power at the source. In April 1929 Uglanov was removed from his posts as candidate member of the Politburo and secretary of the Central Committee. Bukharin was relieved of his duties in the Comintern. In June, Tomsky lost his position of leadership in the trade unions. In November, Bukharin was dropped from the Politburo. At the Sixteenth Party Congress (June 26–July 13, 1930), Tomsky was ejected from the Politburo. In December, Rykov was dismissed as Chairman of the Council of People's Commissars and also expelled from the Politburo.

The purge of the Right Wing leaders left Stalin in undisputed control. The Politburo as reconstructed after the departure of Rykov consisted of Stalin, Voroshilov, L. M. Kaganovich, Kalinin, Kirov, S. Kossior, Kuibyshev, Rudzutak, and Ordjonikidze. The triumph of the *apparatchiki* was complete.

The Organization of the Central Committee Secretariat

As Stalin consolidated his hold on the Party and state machinery, the organization of the Central Committee Secretariat underwent substantial changes. Its basic structure from 1924 to 1930 is outlined in Chart I. By 1925, at least 25,000 Party members, one out of every forty, were full-time employees in the Party apparatus.[40] The Central Committee Secretariat alone included 767 full-time workers.[41] The arrangement of the work of the Secretariat mirrored the preoccupation of the Stalinist leadership with the selection of trusted personnel for important Party and governmental posts. The key section in the Central Committee Secretariat was the Organization-Assignment Section (*Orgraspred*). It was created in 1924 by a merger of Uchraspred and the old Organization-Instruction Section. Orgraspred functioned as the cadre office of the Stalinist Party machine. Its responsibilities were wide-ranging. It made recommendations for appointments, promotions, and transfers not only to Party offices but also to important positions in the commissariats, the trade-union bureaucracy, industry, and the coöperative network. It maintained dossiers on leading Party workers and controlled their assignments. It prepared directives on all questions relating to Party structure and organization. Through a corps of responsible instructors, it supervised the activities of local Party organizations directly, received and analyzed their reports, participated in their meetings, arranged conferences of secretaries and other Party functionaries, transmitted advice and instructions to them, and, where necessary, arranged for changes in leadership.[42] In addition, the Central Committee

CHART I
Organization of the Central Committee Secretariat, 1924–1930

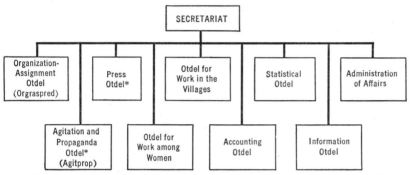

° The Press Otdel was placed under the Agitation and Propaganda Otdel in 1928.

Secretariat included an Information Section, an *Agitprop* or Agitation and Propaganda Section, a Press Section, a Women's Section, a Village Section, and other activities of lesser importance. The organization of the Central Committee Secretariat served as a model for similar secretariats at lower levels of the Party hierarchy.

The structural pattern outlined above remained in effect until 1930. During this period, the powers and responsibilities of the Secretariat steadily mounted. Between the Fourteenth and Fifteenth Congresses, Orgraspred handled the placement of 8,761 Party workers.[43] At the Fifteenth Congress, Kursky, the Chairman of the Central Auditing Commission of the Party, warned that Orgraspred was trying to do too much. He pointed out that only 1,222 of the 8,761 Party members whom Orgraspred had placed in the preceding two years were leading Party workers. He suggested that it delegate the appointment of less responsible Party workers to lower Party organs while reserving to itself the more extensive study and placement of leading Party cadres.[44] Despite Kursky's criticism, Orgraspred was not disposed to narrow its jurisdiction. At the Sixteenth Congress in 1930, L. Kaganovich announced that Orgraspred had arranged the assignments of approximately eleven thousand Party workers in the preceding two years.[45]

As the First Five Year Plan gathered momentum, the clamor for new cadres in industry and agriculture mounted in volume. Orgraspred found itself swamped by the demands which descended on it. As Kaganovich made clear in a frank speech to the Orgburo, Orgraspred became a serious bottleneck which impeded the rapid procurement and placement

CHART II

Reorganization of the Central Committee Secretariat, 1930

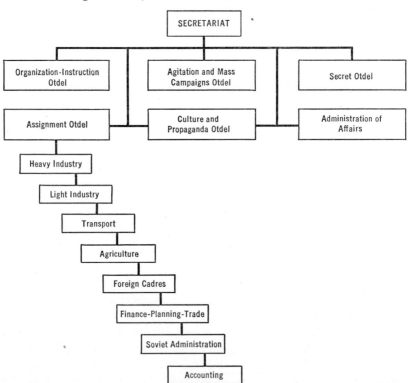

of needed Party workers.[46] This was the main driving force behind the reorganization of the Secretariat in 1930. (See Chart II.)

The essence of the reorganization was a decentralization of cadre responsibilities within the Secretariat. Orgraspred was broken up into two new sections: an Organization-Instruction Section and an Assignment Section. The Organization-Instruction Section concerned itself only with the placement of personnel in the Party apparatus and the supervision of local Party organizations. The Assignment Section was established to serve the personnel needs of the administrative and economic apparatus and was itself divided into a number of subsections: Heavy Industry,

Light Industry, Transport, Agriculture, Foreign Cadres, Financial-Planning-Trade, Soviet Administration, and Accounting. Each subsection exercised specialized personnel responsibilities within its area of jurisdiction.

The old Agitation and Propaganda Section was also divided into two new sections: an Agitation and Mass Campaigns Section and a Culture and Propaganda Section. The new Section for Agitation and Mass Campaigns was designed to whip up mass enthusiasm for industrialization and collectivization. Agitation in the villages and special work among women were included in its work program, and the separate sections formerly devoted to these activities were abolished. The Culture and Propaganda Section absorbed the old Press Section and was also given supervisory authority over education, science, literature, and the propaganda of Marxism-Leninism. Both the Culture and Propaganda Section and the Agitation and Mass Campaigns Section were entrusted with appointment and personnel powers within their respective areas of operation.

The decentralization of placement responsibilities within the Central Committee Secretariat was one response to the cadre crisis which the Party faced with the inauguration of the First Five Year Plan. Another took the form of seeking to economize on cadres by eliminating a link in the Party and governmental hierarchy. The decision of the Sixteenth Party Congress (1930) to abolish the *okrugs* (circuits) made approximately thirty thousand Party workers available for placement elsewhere. Of the actual disposition of these cadres there is no record, although Kaganovich indicated in his organizational report to the Sixteenth Party Congress that a substantial proportion would be utilized to strengthen the *raion* or district organizations of the Party.[47]

While the 1930 reorganization of the Secretariat enabled it to deal more expeditiously with its placement responsibilities, the structure of the Secretariat was poorly adapted to enforce unified Party control over the various branches of the economy and of government. There were no sections in the Secretariat where responsibility for all of the activities of a particular sector of industry or administration could be centered. Under the prevailing functional scheme of organization, the subsections of the Assignment Section had jurisdiction over personnel problems, the Organization-Instruction Section verified the fulfillment of decrees, and the Agitation and Mass Campaigns Section controlled activities in its area. In a period when industry was rapidly expanding and agriculture was undergoing fundamental change, this division of responsibility yielded increasingly unsatisfactory results. At the Seventeenth Party Congress in 1934, the decision was made to abandon the functional system and to replace it by a "production-branch" approach, by which concentrated responsibility could be achieved.

The 1934 reorganization (see Chart III) represented an effort to adapt the structure of the Secretariat to the pressing tasks of economic control. The Central Committee Secretariat was divided into the following main sections: Agriculture, Industry, Transport, Planning-Finance-Trade, Political-Administrative, Leading Party Organs, Culture and Propaganda of Leninism, and the Special Section.[48]

Each of the first five of these sections was constructed on the same pattern. Each had its subsections corresponding to more specialized branches of industry and administration. Each exercised the full range of Party

CHART III
Reorganization of the Central Committee Secretariat, 1934

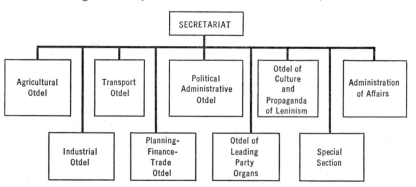

control over the particular sector of Soviet life which was entrusted to it. Within this sector it was responsible for cadres, Party organizational work, mass agitation, and checking on the fulfillment of Party and governmental decrees. The objective was not only to assure more effective direction of the burgeoning economic development of the mid-thirties but to sharpen the accountability of the Party apparatus itself.

The Section of Leading Party Organs limited its area of supervision to the Party apparatus itself. Its functions were confined exclusively to furnishing cadres for Party work and supervising leading Party organs at the *oblast, krai,* and republic levels. The new Section on Culture and Propaganda of Leninism (*Kul'tprop*) continued the work performed previously by the Culture and Propaganda Section. During the next year, it was itself dissolved into five new sections — Party Propaganda and Agitation, Press and Publishing, Schools, Cultural-Instruction Work, and Science.[49] The Special Section, the functions of which were left undescribed in the reports of the Party congress, provided a link between the Central Committee and the NKVD or police apparatus. Another facet of the 1934 reorganization involved the substitution of the Party Control Commission for the old Central Control Committee.[50] Its mission was outlined as the strengthening of control over the fulfillment of decisions of the Party and Central Committee, the enforcement of Party discipline, and punishment of violations of Party ethics.[51]

The 1934 reorganization represented an attempt to cope with the increasingly complex problem of imposing effective Party controls on an economy which was rapidly developing and diversifying. The effort to keep pace with the new industrial and agrarian developments, to guide and direct them, forced a reconstruction of the Party apparatus around the principle of industrial specialization. Every new branch of industry had to have its parallel agency of specialized Party control; by the same token, every sector of Soviet life was subordinated to its corresponding supervisory Party organ.

By 1934 Stalin's *apparatchiki* appeared to be in complete command of every strategic position in the Party and governmental hierarchy. The Seventeenth Party Congress which met in that year was described by Kirov as "the congress of victors." The parade of Party secretaries who reported at the Congress outdid each other in fulsome flattery of Stalin. In a gesture which mingled reconciliation and humiliation, such former leaders of the opposition as Bukharin, Rykov, Kamenev, and Zinoviev were also permitted to address the Congress. They paid for the privilege by joining in the chorus of adulation and again confessing their sins. "At this Congress . . ." Stalin rejoiced, "there is nothing more to prove and, it seems, no one to fight." [52]

The Apparatus and the Great Purge

The assassination of Politburo member Kirov by the Communist Nikolayev on December 1, 1934, transformed complacency into panic. Behind Nikolayev's desperate act (the motives of which remain shrouded in mystery), Stalin professed to discover a large-scale conspiratorial plot of former oppositionists and other enemies of the regime who planned to murder the top Party leadership and seize power for themselves. The mass purges of the mid-thirties, which gathered momentum after Kirov's assassination, were not confined to the extermination of former oppositionists. A substantial proportion of Stalin's own *apparatchiki* disappeared in the fury of the holocaust. Perhaps the most dramatic indication of the destructive effect of the Purge on the top Party leadership is provided by noting the fate of the Central Committee elected at the Seventeenth Congress in 1934. Of the seventy-one members, fifty-five, or 77.5 per cent, failed to appear on the Central Committee slate approved by the Eighteenth Congress in 1939. Of the sixty-eight candidate members in 1934, sixty, or 88.2 per cent, disappeared.[53]

The tremendous turnover which took place in the Party apparatus as the result of the Purge can be verified from figures quoted by Zhdanov to the Eighteenth Congress. In 1938, according to Zhdanov, "35 per cent of the members of committees of primary Party organizations, 41 per cent of the members of district committees, 46 per cent of the members of city committees, and 60 per cent of the members of regional committees, territorial committees and Central Committees of the Communist Parties of the national republics were elected for the first time." [54] By 1939 the top echelon of regional, territorial, and republic committee secretaries consisted predominantly of younger Communists who had joined the Party after the death of Lenin. Of a total of 333 secretaries of republic, *oblast*, and *krai* committees, 303, or 91 per cent, were under forty years of age, and 268, or 80.5 per cent, were reported as having joined the Party after 1924. At lower levels of the secretarial hierarchy, these youthful characteristics were even more striking. Of the 10,902 secretaries of district, city, and area committees who held office in 1939, 10,020, or 92 per cent, were under forty years of age and 10,193, or 93.5 per cent, had joined the Party since 1924. [55] The decimation of the Old Bolsheviks and the damage inflicted by mass arrests and expulsions created vast gaps in the Party apparatus into which the younger generation of the Party flowed. By 1939 the leading functionaries of the Party apparatus largely represented a generation which had been drawn into Party activity in the period after Lenin's death. A new post-Revolutionary elite emerged as the anchor of Stalin's power. By enlisting its energies and appealing to its ambitions, by promoting it rapidly to leading Party posts, and by rewarding it with the symbols of power and privilege, Stalin consolidated a fresh core of leadership and reconstructed his Party apparatus around it.

Reorganization of the Secretariat

The rejuvenation of the Party apparatus was followed in 1939 by a reorganization of its structure. One of the legacies of the Great Purge was a crisis of cadres; the recruitment of new leaders was perhaps the most serious problem which the Party confronted. Under the system put into effect in 1934, responsibility for the selection of cadres had been divided up among numerous industrial-branch departments of the Secretariat. Because of the scarcity of trained personnel, this arrangement created difficulties. "These departments," said Zhdanov, "fight and contend among themselves for people. This militates against the proper study, selection and promotion of cadres." [56] The resolution of the Eighteenth Congress on Zhdanov's report put the problem succinctly, "The division of the work of selecting cadres . . . has tended to reduce the scope of organizational work, has hampered necessary transfers of people from one branch to another, their promotion, and their efficient utilization in those sectors which at the given moment are most important to the Party." [57] "Our task now," proclaimed Stalin, "is to concentrate the work of selecting cadres, from top to bottom, in the hands of one body and to raise it to a proper, scientific, Bolshevik level . . . This body should be the Cadres Administration of the Central Committee of the C.P.S.U.(B.) and a corresponding cadres department in each of the republican, territorial, and regional Party organizations." [58]

At the 1939 Congress, Zhdanov also called for the almost complete elimination of the industrial-branch departments, the merits of which Kaganovich had propounded so vigorously in 1934. "Today," said Zhdanov, "the industrial-branch departments do not know what their functions are, properly speaking; they encroach on the functions of the business

CHART IV

Reorganization of the Central Committee Secretariat, 1939

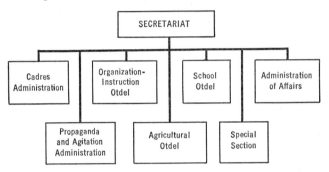

organizations, compete with them, and this gives rise to a vagueness as to who is responsible for a job, or kills responsibility altogether." Two exceptions were to be allowed, an Agricultural Department, "in view of the particular importance of controlling and supervising the activities of the Soviet and Party organizations in the sphere of agriculture," and a School Department, "in view of the fact that we have no People's Commissariat of Education for the U.S.S.R., and in view of the necessity of controlling the work of public education in all the republics, territories, and regions." [59]

The reorganization put into effect in 1939 was almost a complete return to the functional scheme which prevailed prior to 1934 (see Chart IV). The Central Committee Secretariat was divided into the following units: (1) Cadres Administration, (2) Propaganda and Agitation Administration, (3) Organization and Instruction Department, (4) Agricultural Department, and (5) School Department. At the republic, territorial, regional, and area level, the School Department dropped out, and instead a Military Department was added. At the city and district level, both Agricultural and School Departments were omitted, but the Military Department remained. The function of the latter was "to assist the military authorities in organizing the registration of persons liable to military service, in the calling up of recruits, in mobilization in the event of war, in the organization of air defense, etc." [60] The Cadres Administration exercised exclusive jurisdiction over the selection of all key personnel. The Organization and Instruction Department supervised the operation of lower Party organizations. The Propaganda and Agitation Administration, as its name implied, had a general responsibility for mass agitation and Party propaganda. The Agricultural and School Departments had the more specific mandates of checking on the fulfillment of Party and Soviet decrees within their respective areas of jurisdiction. The Party Control Commission was made subject to election and direction by the Party Central Committee and thus in effect became a part of the Central Committee apparatus. Its assigned duties were to "a) Keep a check on the fulfillment of the directions of the Central Committee . . . by Soviet organs, business organs, and Party organizations; b) Exercise supervision over the activities of the local Party organizations; c) Call to account persons guilty of violating the Program and Rules . . . or Party discipline." [61]

The abolition of the industrial-branch departments in the 1939 reorganization created a new set of problems. Responsibility for industrial performance was now dispersed throughout the entire Party apparatus, and no points of focus existed at which a total view of a particular industry could be obtained. The result, according to Malenkov's report at the Eighteenth Party Conference in 1941, was that the local Party organizations began to ignore industrial and transport problems on the ground that they had no authority or responsibility in these areas.[62] The Conference condemned this view as utterly without justification. To emphasize the continuing obligations of the Party in the economic sphere, it ordered all republic, territorial, regional, and city committees to appoint several secretaries who would be exclusively concerned with the industrial problems of the area and also, where necessary, to designate a secretary for railroad transport and another for water transport.[63] The creation of these new secretaries represented an important step away from functionalism, though as long as Zhdanov's influence remained strong within the Secretariat, the functional pattern of organization retained its vitality.

The death of Zhdanov on August 31, 1948, and the assumption of operational command of the Secretariat by G. M. Malenkov coincided with another major reorganization of the apparatus, this time marking an almost complete return to the principles espoused by Kaganovich in 1934 when the Party machinery was designed to parallel govermental and economic organization (see Chart V). While no detailed, systematic description of the new structure of the Party apparatus has been made available by Soviet authorities, it is possible to reconstruct its main outlines on the basis of fragmentary material appearing in Soviet publications.[64] The emphasis of the reform was on the decentralization of personnel work and the creation of new specialized industrial-branch departments to supervise Party work in their areas. As the *Moskovskii Bol'shevik* (Moscow Bolshevik) stated on February 2, 1949:

> The basic goal of the reorganization consisted in improvement of work regarding the selection of cadres and the implementation of the decisions of the Party and government. If previously the question of the selection, assignment, and education of cadres was studied solely by the cadres sections, now the entire apparatus . . . studies this question. The reorganization of the Party apparatus will assist in the improvement of the Party organizations, in raising their leading role and strengthening control over the activity of governmental, economic, and public organizations.[65]

CHART V

Reorganization of the Central Committee Secretariat, 1948

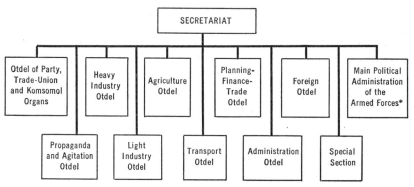

* Functions as Military Otdel of Central Committee Secretariat.

The old Cadres Department has apparently been abolished, and its functions have been redistributed within the Secretariat. The Organization-Instruction Department was replaced toward the end of 1946 by the Administration for Checking Party Organs, which has in turn had its duties absorbed by a new unit called the Department for Party, Trade-Union and Komsomol Organs. The new department, as its name implies, supervises lower Party organization, the Komsomol apparatus, and trade-union functionaries. Its functions include the placement of cadres, organizational activities, and checking on the fulfillment of Party decrees.

The most striking aspect of the reorganization is the re-creation of a series of industrial-branch departments — Heavy Industry, Light Industry, Agriculture, Transport, Planning-Finance-Trade, Administration, and perhaps others. Each of these is now vested with personnel functions as well as responsibility for increasing the effectiveness of Party control in its area.[66] The functions of the Agitation and Propaganda Department continue largely unchanged, though presumably it also controls the assignment of key personnel in all major agencies within its field of supervision. Its present range of activities embraces Party propaganda, agitation, lectures, the press, schools, the arts, literature, science, publishing, cultural enlightenment agencies, and all Party educational and research institutions. In addition, the Secretariat includes a Foreign Section (INO) which concerns itself with the choice of personnel for service abroad, relations with foreign Communist parties, and the assembly of material for decisions of the Party high command in the foreign policy field. There is also a Special Section, which is presumed to exercise jurisdiction over the secret police. The Main Political Administration of the Armed Forces (MPA), although it is located within the Ministry of Defense, may also be treated as a part of the Central Committee apparatus since it reports to and receives its instructions directly from organs of the Central Committee.

Despite the numerous structural reorganizations to which the Party's secretarial apparatus has been exposed over the years, a substantial continuity in its work is manifest. In one form or another, it has remained responsible for recommendations of candidates for leading Party and governmental posts, and it has exercised a considerable degree of autonomy in filling positions of lesser significance. As the eyes and ears of the Politburo and its successor, the Presidium, it has always borne a special responsibility for supervising the work of lower Party organizations, and it has been the avenue through which the control of the high command has been enforced on the rank-and-file. It has checked on the fulfillment of Party and governmental decrees by both Party and governmental organs. It has sustained the major burden of preparing and executing the propaganda line of the Party. It has also served as a funnel through which information has been channeled to the Soviet rulers. As the Party staff of the members of the leadership group, the Secretariat has brought problems to their attention, prepared materials for their deliberations, and embodied their decisions in the form of Party resolutions and decrees.

The search for an effective structure to realize these wide-ranging responsibilities has involved the apparatus in a whole series of abrupt reorganizations of which the latest is not necessarily the last. The waves of reform have oscillated between a functional and an industry-branch emphasis.

Each pattern of organization revealed its characteristic advantages and disadvantages. The functional scheme, by concentrating responsibilities for cadres in one center, facilitated the flexible disposition and interchange of personnel. By abolishing or minimizing Party organs which paralleled government departments, it economized on personnel, eliminated friction, strengthened the authority of the administrator, and made him solely accountable for his performance. From the point of view of Party control of the economy, however, the functional principle had obvious weaknesses. The advantages of specialization in the choice of cadres and the enforcement of Party decrees were lost.

Organization around branches of industry, too, had its strengths and defects. It offered an effective method of adjusting Party control to an increasingly complex and differentiated economy, and it created a favorable milieu for the growth of expertness both in the choice of personnel and the character of supervision. But it also involved duplication of machinery, the possibility of friction between Party and administrative organs, the disappearance of any central responsibility for personnel policy, and the danger that each industry-branch would become a miniature secretariat in itself.

The history of the Secretariat would appear to indicate that the choice of one or the other of these principles of organization at particular periods has been determined largely by the controlling urgencies of the moment. In the early days of the Secretariat, the emphasis was on the consolidation of the Party machine and the projection of its influence throughout the Soviet structure. A unified cadre apparatus played a central role in achieving this objective. As industrialization and collectivization generated an insatiable demand for new trained personnel, a dispersal of cadre functions began to occur, and in 1934, the organization of the apparatus was largely shifted over to an industrial-branch basis. The large-scale destruction of cadres during the Great Purge of the mid-thirties and the necessity of rebuilding the Party machine introduced a new functional imperative, and under Zhdanov's aegis, in 1939 a unified cadres administration was reintroduced. As problems of industrial development reasserted their importance, the Zhdanov reforms were first whittled away in 1941 and then completely reversed in 1948–49 with a return to the industrial-branch emphasis.

The size of the present-day Party apparatus, in the sense of full-time paid Party workers, remains a well-guarded secret. Estimates must necessarily be more or less plausible guesses. If the report of the Central Auditing Commission at the Nineteenth Party Congress is to be given credence, the number of full-time Party functionaries in 1952 was approximately the same as in 1939, despite the fact that Party membership more than doubled in the intervening period.[67] In 1937, when the membership of the Party was approximately two million, or a half million below the level attained in 1939, Stalin had occasion in the course of a speech to a Central Committee plenum to calculate "the leading forces of our Party."

In our Party, if we have in mind its leading strata, there are about 3,000 to 4,000 first rank leaders whom I would call our Party's corps of generals.

Then there are about 30,000 to 40,000 middle rank leaders who are our Party corps of officers.

Then there are about 100,000 to 150,000 of the lower rank Party command staff who are, so to speak, our Party's non-commissioned officers.[68]

If the upper range of these figures is accepted as a rough index of the size of the apparatus in October 1952, the calculation yields a total of 194,000 functionaries serving a Party membership of 6,882,145, or approximately one full-time Party official for every thirty-five members and candidates. This proportion is slightly higher than the one to forty ratio which Molotov announced at the Fourteenth Party Congress as prevailing in 1925.[69] Estimates ventured by some ex-Party members who have fled the Soviet Union run as high as one paid Party worker to ten members and candidates, or a total Party officialdom of over 600,000. In the absence of official statistics, these estimates can only be recorded as indicative of the range of speculation.

Whatever the precise size of the Party apparatus, it represents the hard core of the Party. From the point of view of the Party leadership, it provides a continuous circulatory system by which new elites are lifted to positions of responsibility and the demands of the leadership are transmitted to the Party rank-and-file. Over the years its character has undergone substantial change. Except in the highest circles, the underground workers of pre-Revolutionary days have practically disappeared. For most of the present apparatus, the Revolution of 1917 is either a page in the history books or something that happened so far back in childhood that its spirit and mood have to be consciously re-created in order to be a meaningful part of experience. The lives of the generation that has risen to power within the Party have revolved around the great tasks of the post-Revolutionary period — industrialization and collectivization and, more recently, the war against the Nazi enemy and the postwar reconstruction. The new generation of *apparatchiki* is increasingly technical-minded, involved intimately in problems of production, of organization, and of administration, and it is educated with these responsibilities in mind.

It has also been strongly indoctrinated in the mold of Stalinist authoritarianism. It grew up in a period when the opposition to Stalin was being broken up and a Stalin cult was being systematically developed. It was deeply indebted to Stalin and his entourage for its position in Soviet society. Unlike the old revolutionary generation, it has had very little contact with the outside world, and, except for unavoidable relations during World War II, it has been deliberately insulated from such contact. As a result, its outlook has tended to be insular, and its energies have been almost wholly absorbed in building the foundations of Soviet power. Like its old mentor Stalin, it believes in strength, toughness, authority, and control.

The life of the *apparatchik* remains hazardous. Though there have been no blood baths on the scale of the Great Purge since the mid-thirties, shakeups in the apparatus are frequent, and punishment for serious missteps is severe. Even the most powerful may fall from the heights to the lowest depths with dizzying swiftness. Yet the apparatus continues to attract the movers and shakers of Soviet society, the organization-minded men who identify themselves with the views of the top leadership and who achieve their ambitions as wielders of power rather than as architects of policy. Those who adapt themselves skillfully to the conditions of survival advance rapidly in the Party hierarchy and may even dream of attaining a place in the highest organ of Party power, the Presidium itself. The great majority must content themselves with aspirations toward lesser glory, perhaps the prize of a regional or district committee secretaryship or a less conspicuous but still influential position in the Party hierarchy.

While the individual members of the apparatus remain expendable and serve as readily available scapegoats when difficulties develop, the apparatus in the mass has become indispensable. It provides the organizational cement which holds the Party together. Out of the evanescent magic of personal despotism, a new design of government has been forged. The personal dictatorship of the Leader has embodied itself in the Party dictatorship of the apparatus. Like Frankenstein's monster, the apparatus has acquired a momentum of its own, a vested interest in its own survival which promises to outlive its creator and to perpetuate his system of rule long after the forces which shaped it have been forgotten.

Chapter 7

Party Organization, Activities, and Problems

An analysis of Communist Party organization must carefully distinguish between professed principles and operative practices. The organizational principles which Communism avows radiate a democratic aura. Democratic centralism, inner-Party democracy, and the stress on criticism and self-criticism carry overtones for Western ears which conjure up libertarian visions of free discussion and the interplay of competing ideas. In borrowing the phraseology of liberal democracy, Communism pays its opponents the semantic compliment of recognizing the continuing strength of the tradition which they embody. The verbal masquerade which Communism adopts, however, should not be permitted to obscure the dictatorial essence of its organizational philosophy.

Democratic Centralism in Theory and Practice

"Democratic centralism" is advanced as "the guiding principle of the organizational structure of the Party." It is defined in the Party Rules as follows:

a) the election of all leading Party bodies, from the lowest to the highest;
b) periodic reports of the Party bodies to their Party organizations;
c) strict Party discipline and subordination of the minority to the majority;
d) the absolutely binding character of the decisions of higher bodies upon lower bodies.[1]

Taken at face value and read through uncritical Western eyes, these tenets seem to have an obvious democratic character. The power of the Party leadership seems to rest on elections and to derive from the majority will of the Party membership. The Party leadership purports to be responsible to the rank-and-file, and presumably it can be replaced when it no longer satisfies the aspirations of the Party majority.

The hard realities are in striking contrast. In the slogan "democratic centralism," centralism has primary significance. Some authority must, of course, be delegated to lower Party organs, but its exercise must be consistent with the wishes of the high command. The position of the top Party leadership is sacrosanct; it cannot be subjected to challenge or criticism. The characteristic mode of selecting Party leaders is by coöption and designation from above rather than by elections from below. Where Party elections are preserved, they represent formal devices for registering assent rather than forums of free choice. Reports are rendered by Party leaders to the mass membership, but no report which incorporates policy decisions of the leadership can be rejected or criticized; it can only be enforced.

The attempt to define "democratic centralism" in terms of the "subordination of the minority to the majority" is meaningless. In the full-blown development of Soviet totalitarianism, Party factions are prohibited, and competing centers of power are outlawed. The Party leadership tolerates no competitors. Its voice is the voice of the entire Party. Its claims are total, and it demands a total outpouring of loyalty from its subordinates. The essence of "democratic centralism" is contained in article *d* of its formal definition: "The absolutely binding character of the decisions of higher bodies upon lower bodies." The organizational pattern of the Communist Party is that of a military hierarchy in which policy directives come from the central command and the obligation of the subordinate is to carry them out.

The Communist claim that the organizational practices of the Party are based on inner-Party democracy cannot sustain serious scrutiny. The Party Rules contain a number of references to "inner-Party democracy." While this phrase is never explicitly defined, the Rules declare that

the free and business-like discussion of questions of Party policy in individual organizations or in the Party as a whole is the inalienable right of every Party member and logically follows from inner-Party democracy. Only on the basis of inner-Party democracy is it possible to develop Bolshevik self-criticism and to strengthen Party discipline, which must be conscious and not mechanical . . . But wide discussion . . . of questions of Party policy must be so organized as to prevent its leading to attempts by an insignificant minority to impose its will upon the majority of the Party, or to attempts to form factional groupings which break the unity of the Party, attempts at splits which may shake the strength and firmness of the socialist system.[2]

As this somewhat enigmatic statement makes clear, any discussion which takes the form of an organized challenge of the policy of the Party leadership will not be tolerated. The pronouncements of the Party command are beyond criticism.

What then is the scope of permissible discussion? Its content in practice is subject to definition by the Party rulers. The leadership may open up certain limited areas for discussion and invite suggestions from lower Party organs as it did in connection with the revision of the Party Rules in 1939 and 1952. It may permit a "free and business-like discussion" so long as the discussion is addressed to the question of how the policies of the top command can be most effectively and efficiently carried out and involves no encroachment on the decision-making power of the leadership itself. "Inner-Party democracy" in the Soviet system is largely a creature of dictatorial pleasure; its frail structure lacks any other base of support. It can function only as long as it takes place within a framework of total submission to the dictates of the Party leadership; no means are provided by which the Party membership may repudiate its leaders or record its preference for policy alternatives which the high command does not approve.

Communist insistence on the existence of "inner-Party democracy" is frequently buttressed by citing the wide array of criticism and self-criticism (*samokritika*) which fills the Party press and is expressed at Party conclaves and public gatherings. Less frequently stressed are the carefully defined limits within which such criticism is tolerated or encouraged. Criticism cannot be directed at the regime, its top leadership, or the policies which they espouse. It cannot be organized criticism in the sense of representing the platform of a dissident Party faction. It must be "constructive" criticism — that is to say, criticism which is acceptable to the Party command, which serves a useful purpose in supporting its authority, and which contributes to the operational efficiency of the system over which the directing elite of the Party presides.

Typically, criticism and self-criticism are directed at levels of the Party and governmental hierarchy below the top ruling group and take the form of revelations of bureaucratic inefficiency or venality, of neglect of Party duties or administrative responsibilities, of deviation from strict Party orthodoxy, and of failure to make flexible adjustment to a changing Party line. Frequently they assume the character of a campaign which gives every evidence of being centrally directed and which is designed to concentrate public attention on the elimination of an abuse or of a shift in policy which the Party leadership is particularly concerned to emphasize at a given moment.

From the point of view of the Party command, the institution of criticism and self-criticism serves a number of useful purposes. It operates as an actual or potential prod to the inefficient, venal, or irresponsible Party or governmental administrator. Controlled criticism may be used periodically to discipline or replace local Party leaders who are ineffective, who demonstrate independence of views, or who are excessively ambitious. Criticism in such circumstances discharges an important function in ensuring an energetic and loyal Party apparatus. To the extent that denunciations and exposures are encouraged by the regime and complaints are freely volunteered, the leadership is also provided with a barometer of mass discontent. By opening up at least one channel for the ventilation of grievances, the Party leadership provides an officially approved outlet through which the vexations and tensions which accumulate in Soviet society can find partial, even if greatly restricted, expression. At the same time, the leadership protects its own infallibility by providing victims in the lower ranks of the Party and governmental hierarchy on whom popular anger and frustration can be vented. By diffusing the targets against which complaints can be directed, it dissipates the expression of resentment and prevents criticism from becoming an organized challenge to the regime itself. The regulated procedures of criticism and self-criticism are the Communist substitute for free discussion. They constitute a form of mass manipulation rather than spontaneous and creative acts of mass participation.

The operative organizational principles of Communist Party life are saturated in elitism. The directing Party center is immune from rank-and-file control. It exercises a monopoly of Party leadership, replenishing its own ranks by coöption. In the eyes of the leadership, the rank-and-file member is essentially an agent or a tool rather than an independent source of authority in his own right.

The prototype of the ideal Bolshevik which the Party leadership seeks to fashion and create is essentially that of a dedicated subordinate who identifies himself with the ruling group as the incarnation of the organizational wisdom of the Party. The stern demands which the Party requires its members to meet are made dramatically manifest in the new Party Rules adopted at the Nineteenth Party Congress in October 1952. "It is the duty of a Party member," state the rules,

a) To guard the unity of the Party in every way, as the prime condition of the Party's strength and might;

b) to be an active fighter for the fulfillment of Party decisions . . .

c) to be an example at work, to master the technique of his own job, constantly to increase his working skills, and in every way to guard and strengthen public Socialist property, as the sacred and inviolable basis of the Soviet order;

d) constantly to strengthen contact with the masses, to respond promptly to the desires and needs of the working people, and to explain to the non-Party masses the meaning of Party policy and decisions, remembering that the strength and invincibility of our Party lies in its close, inseparable ties with the people;

e) to work at increasing his own political awareness, at mastering the principles of Marxism-Leninism;

f) to observe Party and state discipline, obligatory for all Party members alike . . .

g) to develop self-criticism and criticism from below, to expose and to seek to eliminate inadequacies in work and to struggle against ostentatious self-satisfaction and complacency in work . . .

h) to report to leading Party bodies, right up to the Party Central Committee, on shortcomings in work, regardless of the persons involved . . .

i) to be truthful and honest before the Party and never permit concealment or distortion of truth . . .

j) to keep Party and State secrets and to display political vigilance, remembering that the vigilance of Communists is necessary on every sector and in all circumstances . . .

k) at any post entrusted to him by the Party, to carry out without fail the Party directives on the correct selection of cadres on the basis of their political and working qualifications. Violating these directives, selecting workers on the basis of friendship, personal loyalties, local ties, or kinship is incompatible with Party membership.[8]

What is striking about this vision of the dedicated Bolshevik — this positive hero who is endlessly propagated in Soviet literature — is its predominantly instrumental character. In theory, the model Bolshevik is expected to be a responsible individual who freely follows the Party line because he knows that it embodies the "truth." In practice, his "freedom" consists in unquestioning identification with the goals proclaimed by the Party leadership and complete subordination to its directives. While the motivational patterns which determine Party affiliation are complex and represent varying blends of careerism and idealistic dedication, successful adaptation to Party life and advancement in the hierarchy are likely to be facilitated for those who feel themselves fully integrated with the views of the Party leadership, whose personality structures do not require expression of independent political views, and whose satisfactions are obtained and ambitions realized as cogs in an organization whose ultimate purposes are beyond question. The operational philosophy of Communism is designed to breed willing robots whose "freedom" is exercised in ingenious and energetic efforts to discharge the tasks which the Party leadership assigns to them.

The Functions of the Party Organization

From the point of view of the leaders of the regime, the Party organization operates essentially as a disciplined phalanx to carry out their will. The Party has its units in every major organization and establishment in Soviet society. The Party leadership holds its local representatives responsible for the fulfillment of plans in all areas and organizations to which they are assigned. To be sure, day-to-day operating responsibilities are vested in the governmental hierarchy of managers and administrators. But every level of the governmental hierarchy is both interpenetrated with, and subject to check by, the corresponding level of the Party hierarchy. Since the Party leadership is the incarnation of supreme power in the Soviet state, its local emissaries serve not only as the eyes and ears but also as the voice of the Kremlin. As a matter of accepted practice, they are expected to keep in touch with all the enterprises and activities within their jurisdiction, to be alert to any failure of performance, to report constantly to their own higher authorities on the state of plan-fulfillment, and to take such measures, in collaboration with local administrators, as will ensure the realization of the goals and tasks which the Party high command has set.

Through the Party organization, the leadership seeks to consolidate its dominion over the key positions in Soviet society. It incorporates and assimilates the governing elite into the Party's ranks. The road to power and preferment in the Soviet system lies through affiliation with the Party; important posts in the Soviet control apparatus are reserved for trusted Party members. By absorbing the power-seekers in Soviet society and making access to authority dependent on enrollment in the Party, the Party leadership endeavors to construct a dependable governing machine which will be responsive to its commands. At the same time, it attempts to prevent the emergence of any competing power center which might challenge its monopoly of political direction. While the ruling group is primarily concerned with the selection of cadres for governing responsibilities, it also tries to preserve its link with the masses by recruiting leading workers and collective farmers as Party members. The mass membership of the Party serves the double purpose of widening its popular support and of facilitating the acceptance and execution of policies determined by the top command.

A constant objective of the Party leadership is to transform the Party organization into a completely trustworthy instrument of the ruling group. The Bolshevik steeling of the Party is accomplished primarily by indoctrination. Through an elaborate network of Party educational institutions, the Party leadership seeks to instill *partiinost* (devotion to the Party) in every Party member. While conformity is enforced by stringent discipline, the leadership demands more than mere conformity. It strives to convert every member into a responsible agent who is deeply persuaded that the ruling group possesses the keys which will unlock the secrets of the universe. The leadership endeavors in this fashion to breed a conscious acceptance of the necessity of subordination. It seeks to build a disciplined army solidified by a unifying faith.

The Party organization also utilizes its members to expand the influence of the Party among non-Party Soviet citizens. A significant feature of modern totalitarian dictatorship is the careful attention devoted to the manipulation of mass sentiment for the purpose of enrolling support for the regime. The Communist dictatorship, in part because of its own historical rise to power on a tide of exploitation of mass grievances, has always taken this function of mobilizing mass support with high seriousness. Through a complex network of agitational, educational, and propaganda activities, which are largely manned by Party specialists, and through control of the media of mass communication, the Party leadership assiduously pursues its objective of winning doctrinal ascendancy over the mind of Soviet man. Party agitation insinuates itself into every crevice of the Soviet social structure, and no competitors are tolerated. As missionary to the heathen, the Party member communicates the goals and demands of the ruling group into the farthest reaches of Soviet society.

The Central Organs of the Party

The structure of the Party is designed to provide a skeletal framework to accomplish these multiform purposes. Under the new rules ratified by the Nineteenth Party Congress (1952), the Presidium stands at the peak of the Party pyramid and replaces the old Politburo and Orgburo, both of which were abolished by the Congress. As originally established, the Presidium consisted of twenty-five members and eleven alternates. After Stalin's death, it was reduced to ten members and four alternates. According to the official announcement, the change was made "in order to ensure more operative leadership." The same communique revealed that an inner Bureau existed to guide the work of the old Presidium. Presumably, it is this Bureau which has emerged as the nucleus of the new Presidium. Headed by Malenkov and dominated by eight members who have been carried over from the old Politburo, the Presidium commands a position of unquestioned ascendancy in the Party. Formally it is chosen by the Central Committee of the Party; in fact, if past practice in connection with the Politburo and Orgburo is followed, new members are likely to be coöpted, and the role of the Central Committee of the Party will be limited to ratifying the choices which Stalin's successors approve.

According to the Party Rules, the "supreme organ" of the Party is the Party Congress which is to be convened "not less often than once every four years." Under the old Party Rules, the Congress was supposed to meet at least once every three years. Actually, a period of four years elapsed between the meeting of the Sixteenth Party Congress in 1930 and the assembly of the Seventeenth Congress in 1934. The Eighteenth Congress did not meet until 1939, some five years later, and the Nineteenth did not take place until 1952, after an interval of more than thirteen years. Since the rout of the left- and right-wing oppositions in the late twenties and the consolidation of Stalin's power, the Congresses have lost whatever creative significance they once possessed. All decisions are taken unanimously, and the discussions give every outward evidence of being carefully organized in advance to reach a foreordained result. Essentially, the Congresses have become a rally of Party and state functionaries who assemble to applaud and ratify the policies proclaimed by the ruling group. From the point of view of the leadership, the Congresses are chiefly significant as a convenient platform from which new goals and objectives may be launched, revisions in the Party line announced, changes in the Party Rules proclaimed, and shifts in the top Party command formally approved.

The Party Rules require the Congress to elect a Central Committee and a Central Auditing Commission. The latter body is of minor importance. According to the Rules, it "inspects (a) the speed and correctness of the conduct of affairs in central bodies of the Party and the organizational condition of the apparatus of the Secretariat of the Central Committee; (b) the treasury and the enterprises of the Party Central Committee." [4] The chairman of the Auditing Commission renders a brief report to the Congress in which attention is ordinarily called to instances of lax financial discipline in the affairs of Party organizations and the size and efficiency of the Party apparatus are critically appraised.

The Central Committee is, in theory at least, a far more important institution. According to the Party Rules, "in the intervals between Congresses, [it] directs the whole work of the Party; represents the Party in its relations with other parties, organizations, and institutions; organizes various Party institutions and directs their activity; appoints editorial boards of central organs of the press functioning under its control and confirms the editorial boards of Party publications of large local organizations; organizes and directs undertakings of social significance; directs the manpower and resources of the Party, and administers the central fund." It also "guides the work of the central Soviet and public organizations through the Party groups within them" and "has the right to set up political sections and assign Party organizers . . . to individual sectors of Socialist construction which may assume a special importance for the national economy in the country as a whole . . ." The Central Committee is required to hold "not less than one plenary meeting every six months." [5]

The Central Committee elected at the Nineteenth Congress comprised 125 members and 111 candidates for membership. An analysis of its composition reveals that it consisted predominantly of Party secretaries from the center, the republics, and the more important regions, as well as a substantial number of the leading members of the USSR Council of Ministers and the chairmen of the Council of Ministers of the union republics. In addition, there was a sprinkling of representation from the top military command, the police, leading officials in the Ministry of Foreign Affairs, and outstanding Party ideologists and intellectuals. The great majority of its members occupied positions in the Party and governmental hierarchy which were calculated to engage the major part of their energy. For most of them, designation to the Central Committee would appear to be a mark of prestige and status rather than an onerous additional responsibility.

In recent years, the Central Committee has been consigned to the shadowy limbo of mysterious Soviet institutions whose meetings and activities go largely unreported. The large size of the committee, the character of its membership, and the fact that the Party Rules provide for relatively infrequent meetings suggest that its significance is largely honorific. A host of decrees continues to be issued in the name of the Central Committee, but their frequency and character indicate that they derive from the Secretariat of the Central Committee rather than the committee itself. While paucity of information counsels caution in coming to firm conclusions, the available evidence points to a considerable eclipse in the role of the Central Committee as compared with the situation in the twenties.

In addition to the Presidium, the major central organs of the Party are the Secretariat and the Party Control Committee under the Central Committee. The 1952 Party Rules vest the Presidium with the power "to direct the work of the Central Committee between plenary sessions" and provide that the Secretariat shall "direct current work, chiefly as concerns verification of the fulfillment of Party decisions and selection of cadres." In accordance with the new rules, the Party Control Committee

a) verifies the observance of Party discipline by Party members and candidates; calls to account Communists guilty of violating the Party program and rules or of breaches of Party and state discipline, as well as violators of Party ethics . . .
b) examines appeals against decisions of the central committees of the Communist Parties of Union republics and of territorial and regional Party committees concerning expulsions from the Party and Party censures;
c) has its representatives, independent of local Party bodies, in the republics, territories, and regions.⁶

At the Nineteenth Party Congress, it was revealed that A. A. Andreyev, a former member of the Politburo, had been removed from his post as chairman of the Party Control Committee and replaced by M. F. Shkiryatov, an Old Bolshevik who had joined the Party in 1906 and who was closely associated with Stalin in his protracted struggle with the opposition during the twenties.⁷

The central responsibility for directing the work of the Party apparatus falls on the Party secretaries. As General Secretary of the Party, Stalin occupied a position of unquestioned ascendancy. Prior to the Nineteenth Party Congress, he was assisted by four other secretaries: G. M. Malenkov, who exercised an influence on Party organization second only to that of Stalin; N. S. Khrushchëv, who headed the Moscow Party organization and formerly played a similar role in the Ukraine; M. A. Suslov, one-time head of the Propaganda and Agitation Department of the Central Committee Secretariat; and P. K. Ponomarenko, formerly first secretary of the Belorussian Party who also held the post of Minister of Procurements. After the Nineteenth Party Congress, five new secretaries were added: A. B. Aristov, first secretary of the Chelyabinsk Party organization; N. A. Mikhailov, former head of the Komsomols; N. G. Ignatov, former Party chief of the Krasnodar region; L. I. Brezhnev, one-time head of the Moldavian Party organization; and N. M. Pegov, formerly head of the Light Industry Section of the Central Committee Secretariat.

In the reshuffle of responsibilities after Stalin's death, the number of Party secretaries was again reduced from ten to five. Malenkov gave up his position as Party secretary but retained the key posts of Chairman of the Party Presidium and Chairman of the USSR Council of Ministers. Ponomarenko, Pegov, Brezhnev, Ignatov, Aristov, and Mikhailov were shifted to other duties. The new Secretariat elected by the Central Committee on March 14, 1953, consisted of Khrushchëv, Suslov, P. N. Pospelov, N. N. Shatalin, and S. D. Ignatiev. Khrushchëv yielded his post as first secretary of the Moscow Party organization to Mikhailov and assumed the strategic office of first secretary of the Central Committee. Suslov carried over from the old Secretariat. The three new secretarial appointments were Pospelov, former head of the Marx-Engels-Lenin Institute and editor of *Pravda*, Shatalin, earlier a member of the Orgburo and a high Party functionary in the Cadres Section of the Central Committee Secretariat, and Ignatiev, a one-time representative of the Central Committee in Uzbekistan, who subsequently became Minister of State Security. Ignatiev's career was short-lived. On April 6, 1953, *Pravda* referred to him as the "former" Minister of State Security who had displayed "political blindness and gullibility" in permitting his subordinates to concoct a false case against the Kremlin doctors accused of plotting the death of Soviet leaders. The next day *Pravda* announced that Ignatiev had been released from his duties as Central Committee secretary. No announcement of a replacement was immediately forthcoming.

The Lower Party Organs

The central organs of the Party are the repository of supreme power in the Party hierarchy. Their orders and directives control the activities of all local Party agencies; the practice of "democratic centralism" involves complete subordination of all lower Party organs to the ruling group. Like all armies and bureaucratic organizations, the Party operates under a system of graded responsibilities. It has its generals, its senior and junior officers, and its noncommissioned personnel. Its pattern of organization reflects and parallels the governmental structure of the Soviet Union. At least four and sometimes five layers of administration can be distinguished. Below the all-union level, in all republics except the RSFSR, there are republican Party organizations. The republics in turn are ordinarily broken down into *oblasts* or regional Party units. In the RSFSR, there are eight territorial or *krai* Party organizations, which embrace autonomous *oblasts* as well as *okrugs* or circuit Party organizations. Most *oblasts* are divided into city and *raion* or district Party organizations. The larger city organizations in turn have their subunits in the form of urban *raions* or district Party agencies. The lowest level of the pyramid consists of the primary Party organizations in factories, offices, collective farms, state farms, machine-tractor stations, villages, military units, educational institutions, and other establishments where there are not less than three Party members. As of October 1952 the network of Party organizations below the all-union level was constituted as follows: union republic, 15; *krai*, 8; *oblast*, 167; *okrug*, 36; city, 544; *raion*, 4,886; primary, 350,304.[8] The average membership of each primary Party organization was slightly less than twenty.

The RSFSR, largest of the union republics, does not possess its own republican Party organization. The territorial and regional units into which it is subdivided report directly to the central Party organs, which function in effect both as an all-union and Russian coördinating center. According to the Party Rules, the "highest organ" of the union republic Party organization is its congress. While union republic Party congresses have met with considerable frequency in the post-World War II years, they, like the All-Union Congress, serve largely as a rally of Party functionaries who assemble to ratify decisions which have already been reached and to echo the criticisms which their superiors in the Party hierarchy pronounce.

Theoretically, the congress of each union republic elects a central committee which in turn elects "an executive body [bureau] consisting of not more than eleven members, including three secretaries whose election is confirmed by the Party Central Committee." In practice, real initiative tends to be concentrated in the secretarial apparatus of the Party and more particularly in the hands of the first secretary, who is invariably a central appointee. The bureau also plays a role of considerable influence since its membership ordinarily reflects the configuration of power in the union republic and includes such important personalities as the Party secretaries, the chairman of the Council of Ministers, the chairman of the Supreme Soviet, the Minister of Internal Affairs, and the first secretaries of the more important regional Party organizations.

The secretarial apparatus of the union republics is organized on the model of the Central Committee Secretariat in Moscow. A representative of the All-Union Central Committee is attached to the Party organization of each republic to supervise its work. In addition, each republic possesses its Party Collegium (*Partkollegiya*), whose chain of command runs to the Party Control Committee in Moscow and whose members are charged with enforcing Party discipline, observing the morality of Party members, and supervising purges and expulsions from the Party.

The first obligation of the Party apparatus of the republics is to carry out and enforce the directives and decrees which the central Party leadership transmits to it. The secretariat in each union republic performs important operational and supervisory duties. It is responsible for the selection and placement of key Party, Komsomol, trade-union, and administrative personnel in all job categories which the central apparatus assigns to its *nomenklatura* or jurisdiction; appointments to so-called "leading state and Party posts" are reserved for all-union action. Through its staff of inspectors, the republic secretariat studies and reports on the operations and deficiencies of lower Party and governmental organs and seeks to remove such shortcomings as are revealed in the course of its investigations. Its responsibilities in the propaganda and agitation field embrace the publication of Party newspapers and agitators' handbooks, the operation of courses and schools for the political training of Party and governmental personnel, the organization of Party lectures and the preparation of propagandists, and the supervision of the cultural life of the republic to ensure ideological orthodoxy and to guard against nationalist deviations. As a result of the reorganization of the secretarial apparatus of the Party in 1948, which established economic sections paralleling the various branches of the economy and administration, increasing emphasis has recently been placed on Party control of economic life. Party functionaries have been enjoined to take leadership in solving economic problems instead of confining themselves to a passive reporting role of merely signaling difficulties to their superiors.[9]

Below the level of the republics is the territorial (*krai*) and regional (*oblast*) stratum of Party administration. The equivalent of the Party Congress at this level is the Party conference, which elects a committee (*obkom* or *kraikom*), which in turn is supposed to choose a bureau and three secretaries to guide its work. The appointment of the first secretary of a *kraikom* or *obkom*, as well as of other leading Party officials of the region, is within the *nomenklatura* of the central Party apparatus, and its "recommendations" are accepted as a matter of course. The bureau of the regional Party organization ordinarily embraces its most powerful figures, the three Party secretaries, the chairman of the *oblast* executive committee (*obispolkom*), the *oblast* chief of the MVD, perhaps the editor of the *oblast* newspaper, and other important *oblast* Party and governmental functionaries. While the *obkom* secretariat is organized on the general pattern of the central secretariat, its structure and the distribution of its personnel reflect the specific economic interests of the region.

The *obkom* first secretary is an important personage in Communist Party administration. Particularly in areas far removed from Moscow's immediate supervision, he operates with considerable independence and viceregal authority. One Soviet *émigré* has described such a secretary as "on a small scale God and Tsar in the *oblast*." This pattern, however, is one which the top Party leadership seeks to discourage. Its system of controls is designed to emphasize the insecurity of local satraps and to transform them into pliant tools of the central authority. Nevertheless, the vastness of the problem of government and the necessity of adapting general directives to fit local conditions inevitably require the *obkom* secretary to exercise a considerable measure of executive initiative and vest him with important residual powers. Despite the high degree of centralization which characterizes Soviet administration, there remain large areas in which the top ruling group must depend on the discretion of local administrators. The selection and placement of personnel to occupy local Party and governmental posts furnish a striking example. As Professor Louis Nemzer has recently pointed out, "Some Party organs on the provincial [*oblast*] level are responsible for personnel in as many as 2,600 types of positions, while others on the lower district or county [*raion*] level are concerned with some 700 job-categories, which would mean that each places thousands of men in these posts." [10]

These cadre activities form only a small part of the duties of the regional Party secretariat. It bears a primary responsibility for the efficient functioning of all city and *raion* Party and Komsomol organizations in its jurisdiction, and it operates a staff of inspectors or instructors to keep its subordinate Party agencies under supervision. It is held accountable for plan-fulfillment by all the economic enterprises of its region, and it consequently must keep in touch with the entire economic life of its area and exert constant pressure on factories and collective farms to achieve and surpass the goals that have been set for them. It is also required to carry on a constant barrage of agitation and propaganda in order to raise the political consciousness of its membership and to extend the influence of Party ideology among the non-Party masses. The multiple demands which the Party leadership makes on republic and regional Party organizations are not easily resolved, and the high attrition rate among Party secretaries reflects the difficulty of the assignment.

One level below the regional Party organizations are the city Party units and the *raions* or districts. The Party Rules state that city and district conferences must be convened at least once a year, but in this instance there is no pretense that the conference is "the highest organ" of the area. The rules provide for city committees (*gorkoms*) and district committees (*raikoms*) which are required to elect a bureau consisting of from seven to nine members and three secretaries. The rules further declare that "secretaries of city and district committees must be confirmed by the regional committee, territorial committee or central committee of the Communist Party of the union republic."

According to a Soviet *émigré* who served as a *raikom* secretary and a member of an *obkom*, appointments to the post of first secretary of city and district committees must also have the approval of the Central Committee of the All-Union Party, and membership in the bureau of *gorkoms* and *raikoms* requires *obkom* approval. This same informant reports that the regional secretary plays "a leading, but behind-the-scenes role" in selecting candidates for important posts in the city and district Party organizations and usually contrives an approved slate of such candidates for election to the city and district committees.

The bureau of the *gorkom* or *raikom* is ordinarily composed of the three secretaries of the city or district, the chairman of the executive committee of the government (*gorispolkom* or *raiispolkom*), the local representative of the MVD, and other leading Party personages of the area. If there is a *raion* newspaper, its responsible editor is either a candidate or member of the bureau. If the *raion* is agricultural, the chief of the *raion* agricultural administration is likely to be on the bureau. If the district contains an important factory, its director may also be designated as a bureau member.

The city or district Party apparatus represents a miniature replica of the apparatus of higher Party organizations. Its organization reflects the character of the area. In the larger cities, the staff of professional Party functionaries may be as extensive as that of some regional and even republic Party organizations, and the *gorkom* or city committee may itself exercise supervision over a number of urban *raions*. In the rural *raions*, the staff may be relatively small and be primarily concerned with the agricultural activities of the district.

The activities of the city and district Party organizations mirror the work of the regional and republic organizations on a smaller stage. The selection and approval of personnel for local Party assignments play a major role. The election of all secretaries of primary Party organizations must be ratified by the bureau of the *raikom* or *gorkom* in whose jurisdiction the primary Party unit falls.[11] The *raikom* secretary and the bureau will also take the initiative in filling important positions in local government, the chairmanship of collective farms, and trade-union and Komsomol posts in the *raion*. Ordinarily their influence will be exercised indirectly, and the forms of local elections will be observed. If, for example, the office of chairman of the *raiispolkom* (the executive committee of the *raion* soviet), is empty, the bureau of the *raikom* will designate a candidate who will be nominated at a meeting of the *raion* soviet. The nominator will declare that the Party group in the soviet and the *raikom* recommend the candidate. Usually no other candidates are presented, and the nominee is elected unanimously. Similar procedures will be employed in filling collective farm chairmanships and other elective posts.

One of the continuing concerns of city and district Party organizations is the supervision of activities of primary Party organizations. In discharging this responsibility, the city and district Party secretaries operate through a staff of instructors, each of whom is a full-time Party functionary who is assigned to oversee the work of a group of primary Party units. Each instructor is required to familiarize himself with the protocols or minutes of all meetings of the organizations for which he is responsible and to spend at least two-thirds of his time in grass-roots contacts with members of such organizations. It is his job to identify the more promising Party activists who can be counted on to provide leadership, to know the moods and needs of the membership, to criticize inadequacies in the operations of the units, and to supply concrete guidance in remedying defects.[12]

The district and city organizations are also charged with controlling admissions and expulsions from the Party. No new member can be admitted into the Party without the formal approval of the bureau of the district or city organization. Proposals for the admission of new members are presented to the bureau by the secretary of the primary Party unit; if the bureau rejects the recommendation of the secretary, it is required to give reasons for its refusal.[13] On their own initiative and without previous consultation with the primary Party units, district and city committees may also censure and exclude Party members, though decisions to expel members require the endorsement of higher Party authorities. The district and city committees also serve as courts of appeal for aggrieved members who wish to protest disciplinary action to which they have been subjected by primary Party organizations. No Party reprimand can be entered in the record cards of individual Communists without formal approval by the district committee of the Party.[14]

The district and city committees function as the basic record offices of the Party. They are obligated to maintain record cards for all members and candidates in their area. The record cards, each of which bears the same number as the membership or candidate's card carried by a holder, provide complete and up-to-date documentation on all Communists, including changes in employment, education, awards, penalties, etc. Transfers of Party members from district to district are carefully regulated by Party instructions. Secretaries of district and city committees are obliged to interview Communists personally when they put them on the rolls or remove them from the records.[15] This requirement, however, is not always observed in practice. A recent article in *Bol'shevik* pointed out, "People are taken on the rolls or removed from them by letter in a number of cases, without being summoned to the district or city Party committee. Certain secretaries of district committees entrust the entering of new arrivals on the rolls to clerical workers, do not talk personally with new arrivals or check on their Party documents or collate their Party membership cards with their record cards." [16] Despite the rigor of the rules, startling cases are occasionally cited where persons having no connection with the Party acquire membership "by crooked means" and persons expelled from the Party in one district reappear as full-fledged members in another.

While the city and district Party organizations exercise general supervision over the economic, administrative, and cultural life of the geographical units in which they operate, their jurisdiction is not all-inclusive. They do not control the operational work of the MVD in their area; indeed, the reverse is ordinarily the case, and the surveillance of the MVD embraces the local Party organizations as well as non-Party personnel. Party work in military units which happen to be located in the district are also exempt from *raikom* or *gorkom* supervison; the Party organizations in the armed forces have their own independent channels of command. Party work in large factories or enterprises of so-called "all-union significance" is also outside the jurisdiction of the city and district committees. In such key enterprises, Party activities are headed by Party organizers of the Central Committee of the All-Union Party, who function as a part of the apparatus of the Central Committee and are responsible to it. Their task is to see that the factories fulfill their goals and that the Party organizations in the factories are mobilized to attain their objectives.

The Party officialdom at district and city levels has long been characterized by a high rate of turnover. It is at this point in the Party hierarchy that the personnel resources of the Party encounter their greatest strain. The lower-level members of the Party apparatus occupy a particularly vulnerable and exposed position. The official doctrine makes them an approved target for criticism, and many are sacrificed as scapegoats for difficulties which are inherent in the position in which they find themselves. While the rate of dismissal varies in different periods, replacements constantly take place. In the eighteen-month period after the end of World War II, for example, 90 per cent of all the first secretaries of *raikoms* in the Belorussian Republic were removed,[17] and in the Ukraine the attrition rate approached 50 per cent. In the eyes of the Party leadership, the lower Party apparatus is a testing ground for the steeled Bolshevik *apparatchiki.* Those who survive move rapidly upward, but even a cursory reading of the Party press indicates that a substantial number fall by the wayside.

The Primary Party Organizations

Below the level of the district and city Party organizations are the approximately 350,000 primary Party units which form the base of the Party pyramid. A primary Party unit may be established in any enterprise or institution where there are not less than three Party members. Its organization requires the approval of the district or city committee of the Party. Where there are less than three Party members, a joint member-candidate or a Party-Komsomol group may be established under the direction of a Party organizer appointed by the district or city committee. In Party organizations having less than fifteen members, no bureau is formed, and a secretary approved by the district or city committee is elected by the Party membership. Larger primary organizations form bureaus which in no case may exceed eleven members.* In primary organizations with not more than one hundred Party members, the Party secretary and the members of the bureau are ordinarily not exempted from their regular jobs and receive no compensation for performing their Party duties. In the larger primary organizations, the Party secretaries and sometimes others devote themselves exclusively to Party work, are classified as paid Party functionaries, and are usually assigned to their duties by the district or city committee of the Party.

The tasks of primary Party units are outlined by the Party Rules as follows:

a) to conduct agitational and organizational work among the masses for the carrying out of Party appeals and decisions, with the support of the leadership of the primary press (house organs, wall newspapers, etc.);

b) to recruit new members for the Party and to organize their political training;

c) to organize the political education of Party members and candidates and to see that they acquire a certain minimum knowledge of Marxism-Leninism;

d) to assist the *raikom, gorkom,* or political department in all its practical work;

* In large factories and offices where there are over three hundred members and candidates, a Party committee may be formed with the sanction of the All-Union Central Committee; in such establishments, the Party organizations in the individual shops are granted the rights of primary Party organizations. In establishments with over one hundred members and candidates, shop organizations may be established as subunits of the primary organizations; such shop organizations may elect their own Party bureaus. Within shop organizations and within primary Party units of less than one hundred members, smaller Party groups may also be constituted.

e) to mobilize the efforts of the masses in the factories, state farms, collective farms, etc., for the fulfillment of the production plan, for the strengthening of labor discipline and for the development of socialist competition;

f) to combat laxity and mismanagement in factories, state farms and collective farms, and to show a daily concern for the improvement of the cultural and living conditions of the workers, employees, and collective farmers;

g) to develop criticism and self-criticism and to inculcate Communists in the spirit of an uncompromising attitude toward shortcomings;

h) to take an active part in the economic and political life of the country.[18]

The work of primary units is directed by the secretary and the Party bureau. The secretary's role is central. He is not permitted to delegate such functions as the collection of Party dues, the supervision of work with Komsomols, and the leadership of the agitators' collective. The agitators' collective is composed of Party and Komsomol activists who undertake to whip up enthusiasm for Party slogans and goals by vocal agitation among their fellow workers. One of the secretary's primary responsibilities is to recruit agitators, to provide them with material, to help train them, and to regulate their assignments.[19] In the larger primary units where the secretary has the assistance of a Party bureau, it is also his duty to allocate responsibilities among various members of the bureau: one member of the bureau, for example, may be charged with the organization of political study circles, lectures, and conferences; another may occupy himself with the stimulation of paramilitary training in the enterprise; a third may edit the factory wall newspaper; and so on. The secretary and the bureau are required to make periodic reports to meetings of the membership of the primary Party unit; these meetings furnish the occasion for a review of the unit's work and an evaluation of its leadership.[20]

One of the most important functions of the primary units is the admission of new members. The procedure connected with applications for admission is designed to achieve a searching scrutiny of the candidate's qualifications. The applicant must file a declaration of his desire to enter the Party, fill out a detailed questionnaire which includes a complete life history, and submit recommendations from three Party members of not less than three-years' standing who have known and worked with the applicant for not less than one year. These recommendations must be verified by the secretary of the primary unit, and the applicant must serve a probationary period as a Party candidate for at least a year. In Party organizations where bureaus exist, applications for membership are first subject to examination by the bureau, which then makes its recommendation through the secretary to a general membership meeting of the unit. If the meeting approves the applicant, his application is forwarded to the bureau of the district or city committee for ratification. In each case, the secretary of the primary Party unit must appear personally before the bureau to defend the recommendation.[21] Applicants for admission to the Party must be at least eighteen years old. Young people up to twenty-one can join the Party only after affiliation with the Komsomol or Young Communist League. The recommendation of the district committee of the Komsomol organization is counted as the equivalent of the recommendation of one Party member.

Since the end of World War II, recruitment of new members has been carefully regulated by the Party.[22] The "chase after numerical growth" has been discouraged, and local Party units have been imperatively warned to limit admissions to "the very best sons and daughters of the Soviet people." In practice, this has meant that particular emphasis has been placed on recruitment of members of the technical and administrative intelligentsia and so-called "leading workers," chairmen and brigadiers on collective farms, Stakhanovites, shop chiefs and foremen, and others. A particularly strenuous effort is made to assimilate talented and ambitious youth into the Party in order to replenish the Party's vigor and to assist it in discharging its increasingly complex managerial and governing responsibilities.

The control functions of the primary Party organizations are described by the Party Rules as follows: "In order to enhance the role of the primary Party organizations in production and trade enterprises, including state farms, collective farms, and machine-tractor stations, and their responsibility for the state of work in these establishments, these organizations are given the right to supervise management." This apparently unequivocal statement conceals a considerable measure of ambiguity. The primary units have no right to change the goals of the enterprise, for these are established by higher authority; nor can they interfere with any orders issued by the director of the enterprise. Indeed, their major responsibility is to struggle for the fulfillment of goals and to aid management in carrying out all orders and decrees designed to achieve this objective. The administration of the enterprise is required, however, to report periodically to the Party organization and to keep it informed of problems and developments. The Party organization in turn is obligated to search for inadequacies in the work of the enterprise, to recommend measures to the management which will eliminate deficiencies, and to inform its superiors in the Party hierarchy about the state of affairs in the enterprise.[23] By bringing its authority to bear in this fashion, the Party leadership seeks to assure its control over the execution as well as the formulation of economic plans and programs.

Party work in the state apparatus takes a somewhat different form. In the words of the Party Rules, "Party organizations of ministries, which by virtue of the special conditions of work in Soviet establishments, cannot exercise supervisory functions, are obliged to signal defects in the work of the establishment, record shortcomings in the work of the Ministry and its individual workers, and submit its data and views to the Central Committee and to the heads of the ministries." [24] A recent editorial in *Bol'shevik* emphasized, "In Soviet institutions Party organizations cannot make use of the functions of control . . . Those Party units which, violating the Party Rules, appropriate for themselves the rights of a higher Party body, demand reports from the directors of institutions and even try sometimes 'to direct' peripheral institutions, commit a mistake." But, the same editorial continued:

In individual institutions there are still executives who place narrow departmental "interests" above state interests. In places there are, in particular, such intolerable instances as the heads of departments, when plans are not fulfilled by the enterprises, padding output reports, and, on the contrary, when plans are overfulfilled, concealing part of the manufactured products in order to apply them to cover up a possible breakdown in the production program in the future.
. . . Such instances became possible to a considerable extent because the Party committee . . . had not educated the personnel of these agencies sufficiently in the spirit of observance of state interests, in the spirit of Bolshevik irreconcilability to violators of state discipline.[25]

Party organizations in ministries are called upon to reveal such violations of state discipline, to give warning to their superiors, and to indoctrinate their membership in the necessity of sacrificing a narrow departmental approach in favor of broader state and Party interests. The injunction is more easily given than heeded, and the Party employee in the state apparatus finds himself frequently caught in the cross-pressures of departmental and Party interests. One of the primary purposes of the systematic political agitation and propaganda to which he is exposed is to condition him to treat the demands of the Party leadership as transcendent and to inculcate a sense that he is most effectively fulfilling his own destiny when he subordinates himself to the Party line.

The life of the Party member is ordinarily a busy and demanding one. As a member of an elite group, he is privileged, but he is also duty-bound. At work he is expected to set an example of devotion; his so-called leisure hours are filled with extra-curricular Party duties and assignments. A recent Soviet *émigré* who had formerly been a Party member said: "You have to attend meetings, pay dues, go to the Party School, study the short course of the history of the Party, study the works of Marx, Lenin, and Stalin, read the Party newspapers, explain the decisions of the Party to non-Party people, take part in putting up wall newspapers, at the time of election you have to be an agitator, . . . I had to be very disciplined and behave well, I could not be a drinking man or engage in hooliganism, or I

could not have unbecoming behavior . . . Party discipline wrapped people in a wall, and the members of the Party did not behave naturally . . ."
The Party member who distinguishes himself in discharging the obligations which are heaped upon him reaps substantial advantages. His upward mobility in the Soviet system is facilitated. Promotion brings new privileges and perquisites, but it also means added responsibilities and the hazards that go with them. The pressures which exert themselves on the upwardly mobile Communist make him a driver of those below him while he is at the same time driven from above. The laws of survival in the totalitarian party favor the tough and the adaptive; the tender-hearted and the independent-minded tend to fall by the way and disappear.

There is danger, however, in uncritical acceptance of the stereotype of the Bolshevik as an iron-disciplined, dedicated, and completely integrated instrument of the Party. This conception represents an ideal type which the Party leadership seeks to foster rather than a picture of the very diverse human material which the Party actually contains. The criticism and self-criticism appearing in the Party press make clear that some join the Party for purely "careerist" reasons, that others neglect their Party obligations or go through the motions of fulfilling them in a "passive, formalistic" spirit, and that still others have only the most cursory notion of Party ideology or doctrine. The average rank-and-file Party member falls far short of the ideal type.

Informal Party Organization

The "monolithic" Party is a façade which conceals a variety of expectations, tensions, and rivalries which in turn provide a distorted reflection of the very diverse interests which Soviet society seeks to contain. Given the character of Soviet totalitarianism, such interests can rarely express themselves openly, but it is perhaps not too wildly venturesome to suggest that they exist below the outwardly placid surface of Party uniformity and that they manifest themselves in devious maneuvers, in struggles for power, and even in conflicting conceptions of proper strategy and tactics. The informal organization of the Party probably approximates a constellation of power centers, some of greater and some of lesser magnitude and each with its accompanying entourage of satellites with fields of influence extending through the Party, the police, the administrative and military hierarchies.

The secrecy with which the Party functions and the absence of adequate documentation make it impossible to "prove" such hypotheses. Their applicability can only be inferred from the past history of inner-Party controversies and on the basis of meager hints which can be gleaned from the Party press in more recent times. In a speech to the plenum of the All-Union Central Committee on March 3, 1937, Stalin made a frank and critical reference to the phenomenon of the personal entourage and the family group.

Most frequently workers are selected not according to objective criteria, but according to accidental, subjective, narrow and provincial criteria. Most frequently so-called acquaintances are chosen, personal friends, fellow townsmen, people who have shown personal devotion, masters of eulogies to their patrons, irrespective of whether they are suitable from a political and a business-like standpoint.

Naturally, instead of a leading group of responsible workers, a family group, a company, is formed, the members of which try to live peacefully, not to offend each other, not to wash their dirty linen in public, to eulogize each other and from time to time to send inane and nauseating reports to the center about successes . . .

Take, for example, Comrades Mirzoyan and Vainov. The former is secretary of the regional Party organization in Kazakstan; the latter is secretary of the Yaroslav regional Party organization. These people are not the most backward workers in our midst. And how do they select workers?

The former dragged along with him from Azerbaijan and the Urals, where he formerly worked, into Kazakstan thirty or forty of his "own" people, and placed them in responsible positions in Kazakstan.

The latter dragged along with him from the Donbas, where he formerly worked, to Yaroslav a dozen or so of his "own" people also, and also placed them in responsible positions. Consequently, Comrade Mirzoyan has his own crew. Comrade Vainov also has his.

. . . These comrades evidently have wanted to create for themselves conditions which give them a certain independence both of the local people and of the Central Committee of the Party.[26]

There is reason to suspect that the practices of which Stalin complained in 1937 continue to form an essential ingredient in the informal organizational life of the Party. As Malenkov reported to the Nineteenth Party Congress,

"The main shortcoming is that in selecting cadres some executives are guided not by their political and professional qualifications, but by considerations of kinship, friendship, and cronyism . . . Such distortions of the Party line in selecting and promoting cadres have given rise in some organizations to the formation of a closed circle of people who shield one another and who place the interests of their group above those of the Party and state.[27]

The testimony of Soviet *émigrés* provides abundant indication that Soviet careers are still made by clinging to the coattails of the great lords of Communism and that cliques rise and fall in the Soviet hierarchy depending on the fortunes of their patrons. The recent fate of the Zhdanov entourage furnishes a dramatic example.* The settling of accounts with Zhdanov's henchmen was accompanied by the reëmergence of Malenkov as one of the major fulcrums of power in the Politburo.

* See Chapter 10, p. 276.

Absence of information makes it all but impossible to trace the real lines of power and personal influence within the Party apparatus. The existence of so-called "family circles" at lower levels of the Party and governmental hierarchy is incontrovertible; the Soviet press itself provides more than adequate documentation. The establishment and persistence of these "family circles" are attributable to a yearning for security and stability on the part of the lower Party and governmental apparatus. Faced with demands from the Party leadership which are difficult if not impossible to fulfill and confronted with the constant possibility of a crossfire of criticism from many directions, Party as well as governmental functionaries are tempted to seek a degree of independence from control by organizing mutual protection associations in which they agree informally to refrain from mutual criticism and to cover up for each other's mistakes and deficiencies. These arrangements may embrace the vertical relationships between a regional Party secretary and his subordinate district secretaries, the horizontal relationships between a Party secretary and the governmental or economic institutions which he theoretically controls, or both. In some instances they are cemented by a species of "local patriotism." Insensibly, even in a "monolithic" Party, local officials reflect the pressures of the environment in which they work and are transformed, to some degree at least, into spokesmen for local interests.

For the ruling group, the "family circles" and mutual protection associations represent evils which must be destroyed. The Party leadership seeks a rationalized impersonal hierarchy which will respond sensitively to its every wish. The "family circle" creates a nodule of autonomous power which eludes control and frustrates the execution of central policy. A variety of countermeasures have been developed to discourage the formation of mutual protection associations. District and City Party secretaries are rarely recruited from the areas in which they serve. Secretaries are frequently rotated from district to district to keep them from sinking roots into the locality. The political police of the MVD are organized as an independent hierarchy to facilitate local control. High Party organs are instructed to keep careful watch over their subordinates in the Party hierarchy. When "family circles" are revealed, they are vigorously condemned and broken up. Denunciations and criticism are specifically encouraged under the new rules adopted by the Nineteenth Congress. Despite the most drastic disciplinary measures, "family circles" and mutual protection associations persist in reappearing even after they have been theoretically extirpated. Their continuing vitality is a reminder of the difficulties which the totalitarian Party confronts in seeking to fulfill its own totalitarian aspirations.

Operations and Problems of the Party Apparatus

The operations of the Party apparatus are the object of constant criticism in the Party press. The flow of criticism reflects the viewpoint of the top Party leadership; as elsewhere in Soviet life, it tends to run in terms of slogans and campaigns which vary with the subjects of uppermost concern to the ruling group at the given moment. Some themes, however, persistently reappear.

One of the most frequently reiterated is the complaint of inefficiency in carrying out orders from above, which is usually attributed to bureaucratic attitudes toward Party work. Party officials are accused of restricting their activities to paper work, of spending all their time in compiling and demanding reports, or in receiving and forwarding mimeographed instructions of a general character. These immemorial habits of bureaucracy came in for a frank airing in an interchange between Kaganovich and Stalin at the Seventeenth Party Congress in 1934:

Kaganovich: . . . Formal paper measures are useless; you receive a report, scribble an order, and [are] finished. Sometimes an order from above is received, it is slightly paraphrased and sent down to the next link, and they send it down still lower. And so the red tape is spun out.
Stalin: And then the document is put in the files.
Kaganovich: Quite right, and then the document is put in the files.[28]

A common complaint, closely tied to this addiction to paper work, is the absence of personal contact between leaders and led. Lower Party organs grumble that their superiors are quick to rebuke them for failures but are rarely on the spot to help them with suggestions which would have averted their errors. The grievances of the lower Party organs are suggested by the following examples of typical criticism appearing in the Party press: "It is a commonly accepted custom that members of the *obkom* visit the *raions* only when there arises an inevitable necessity to collect some negative facts . . . They never find any sense in meeting the local activists and discussing local affairs with them. They never know what is going on in the *raions.* They never try to find out what the local reasons are for failing to carry out many decisions . . ." "Our *raion* is considered backward . . . but not once during the last four years has the *obkom* listened to our reports or examined the situation on the spot." [29]

One of the greatest defects in the work of the lower organs is their failure to check the execution of plans and decrees. M. D. Bagirov, the first secretary of the Azerbaidjan Party, made a characteristic acknowledgment of this besetting sin at the Eighteenth Congress of the Azerbaidjan Party in May 1951:

Checkup on fulfillment of the decisions of higher Party bodies and of one's own Party unit is a weak spot in our work. Often, in adopting a good decision, we fail to organize the work of practical accomplishment of the resolution and do not make timely check upon the accomplishment of measures that have been projected.

Frequently we begin to check on fulfillment of a decision only when it is already evident that its fulfillment has essentially fallen through.[30]

Party control of economic agencies also presents its serious problems. Some Party officials are accused of indifference to their economic responsibilities. In the words of *Bol'shevik,*

Certain Party officials mistakenly suppose that the demand to improve Party organizational and Party political work in every possible way means that Party organizations can in some way or other diminish the attention paid to the economy, avoid the decision of economic questions and occupy themselves with Party work alone. This, of course, is a delusion.[31]

At the other extreme, Party functionaries are criticized for invading the prerogatives of management, taking on responsibilities which properly belong to state and economic agencies, and issuing a stream of detailed directives in areas which fall within the discretion of the agencies themselves. M. D. Bagirov also observed at the Eighteenth Congress of the Azerbaidjan Party,

A serious shortcoming in the work of our Party units in industrial enterprises is the fact that they often undertake functions that do not belong to them, and substitute for managers; they become absorbed in business trivia, to the detriment of Party political work.

This substitution for business managers goes so far that management personnel lose all sense of responsibility and blame Party officials for the breakdown of production programs.

At the Baku Worker Factory Comrade Kozlov, assistant business manager, attributed nonfulfillment of the plan to the fact that Comrade Karapetyan, secretary of the Party unit, had not, if you please, obtained welding oxygen in time. Truly, that is the limit.

Comrades, we must put an end to such things; we must learn to combine Party political work with economic work . . .[32]

The problem of steering a mean between indifference and excessive interference is not easily resolved. Many Party functionaries become impaled on one or the other horn of the dilemma. Their effectiveness is judged by the indices of economic achievement in their area. This responsibility drives them to assume operational supervision over the economy. If they press their directing role too far, they risk the charge that they are usurping the authority of state and economic agencies. If they deflect their attention from the immediate decision of economic problems, they run the equally grave risk that plans will not be fulfilled and production will lag. Both Party officials and managerial personnel share a responsibility for actual economic results which neither can altogether evade. Their mutual dependency sometimes leads them, as has already been noted, into "friendly relationships" in which they agree to cover up for each other and not "wash their dirty linen in public." As long as economic targets are generally fulfilled, no untoward results may follow from this armistice on mutual criticism. On the other hand, the disclosure that production breakdowns have been concealed and that economic objectives have not been attained may lead to a debacle in which the whole "family" of involved Party and managerial officials is severely disciplined.

Other sources of difficulty in the economic sphere are illustrated by the charges of bribe-taking, theft, and embezzlement which the Soviet press occasionally hurls at Party functionaries. A not uncommon situation is that of the Party functionary who uses his position of authority and trust to extract favors or receive bribes from the economic organizations and administrative agencies which he is charged with supervising. G. M. Malenkov, in the course of his report to the Nineteenth Party Congress, referred frankly to the prevalance of such practices:

> Some workers in Party, Soviet and agricultural bodies, instead of guarding the interests of the collective farms' common enterprise, themselves engage in pilfering collective farm property, flagrantly violate Soviet law, engage in arbitrary practices and commit lawless acts in relation to collective farms. These workers take advantage of their official position to occupy collective farm land, make collective farm boards and chairmen supply them with grain, meat, milk and other commodities free of charge or at low price . . . and so on. All these anti-collective farm, anti-state actions inflict serious harm on the collective farm peasantry, impede the further organizational and economic consolidation of the collective farms and undermine the prestige of the Party and Soviet state.[33]

Frequently, local Party organizations are charged with hushing up instances of venality and peculation. A random example from *Pravda* illustrates the pattern.

> Ts. Vartevanyan held the position of assistant manager of a textile mill for a long time. He was no good in his job and was severely criticized several times. When it became quite obvious that he could no longer remain in that job, the city committee recommended him for the post of director of a sewing factory.
> Soon after this appointment, Vartevanyan, having bungled the work of the factory, began all kinds of malpractices and even embezzled state property.
> The factory workers repeatedly wrote about these abuses to the city Party committee, which pretended to react. Special commissions were set up to check on Ts. Vartevanyan's activities . . . Vartevanyan was finally exposed only by investigatory agencies.
> . . . The city committee did everything it could to protect him, and he was finally dismissed thanks only to the interference of the Armenian Party Central Committee.[34]

Those involved in such incidents are not always limited to Party small fry. The recent disclosure of a major wave of embezzlements and peculation in Soviet Georgia was accompanied by the purge of three of the five secretaries of the Central Committee of the Georgian Party including the first secretary, the head of the Georgian Young Communist League, the chairman of the Supreme Court, the Minister of Justice, and a number of lesser figures in the Georgian ministries.[35] While accepting bribes and thievery can be documented in the flow of criticism appearing in the Party press, no quantitative estimate of their magnitude is possible on the basis of the available data. The periodic campaigns against theft and embezzlement, with their references to concrete cases involving Party officials and their injunctions to the Party to heighten its vigilance, suggest that the examples cited above are not isolated occurrences.

Another major line of criticism to which the Party apparatus is periodically exposed is the charge of inadequate attention to political indoctrination of both its own membership and the non-Party masses. The mass influx of new members during World War II was accompanied by the admission of many front-line soldiers who were deficient in political knowledge. At the organizing conference of the Cominform in September 1947 Malenkov reported: "A considerable number of Communists, especially those who have entered the Party in recent years, have not yet succeeded in receiving the necessary political training." [36] Since the end of the war and particularly since 1947, emphasis on political education and propaganda has been intensified. As frequently happens when the Party line shifts, not all Party functionaries were equally adept at making a quick adjustment. Some found it difficult to abandon their earlier almost exclusive absorption in problems of economic control. Illustrative was the response of the secretary of the Party *obkom* of Penza to a proposal of a *raikom* to conduct a seminar for its propagandists. Since this involved diverting them from their job assignments, he protested, "We can do without it!" [37] The reaction of *Pravda* was sharply critical: "Such *obkoms* and *raikoms* are spending too much time and attention on the solution of a variety of economic-organizational matters and are ignoring the most important questions of party-organizational and ideological work." [38]

The stream of criticism in the Party press suggests that many Party officials encounter considerable difficulty in finding a proper balance between political and economic work. Faced with a steady bombardment of multiple instructions from above, they try to develop a feel for the ruling priority of the moment and make a pragmatic adjustment to its urgency. As Stalin long ago noted, the Soviet system functions by campaigns. "At the turning points of the revolutionary movement," Stalin declared, "some basic slogan is always advanced as the key slogan in order, by catching on to it, to draw in the whole chain." [39] If the emphasis of the current campaign is on agitation and propaganda, local Party organizations break out in a rash of agitators' study circles, propagandist seminars, Party schools, and meetings of Party *aktivs*. If primary attention is being devoted to economic work, questions of labor productivity, Stakhanovite achievements, socialist competition, and plan fulfillment become the order of the day. The alternating current which charges the Party line regulates the tempo of the apparatus. The adaptive Party functionary who survives and advances in the Party hierarchy develops a keen sensitivity to its radiations and learns to respond to the "key slogans" of the movement. The unadaptive supply the grist for the mill of criticism and discipline and are ground up in its remorseless turnings.

Communist Party organizational practice emphasizes conformity in the lower ranks and extreme centralization of power in the hands of the ruling group. Both have their grave operating disadvantages. The lower and middle ranks of the Party and governmental hierarchy tend, wherever possible, to avoid the burden of decision-making except at the level of execution of approved policies. If responsibilities are thrust upon them, they seek to share them with their superiors. A cartoon in *Krokodil* dramatizes an endemic disease in Soviet administration. The administrator says to his subordinate: "Don't bother me with trifling details. Settle them yourself!" The subordinate replies: ". . . but this requires your signature." "My signature?" answers the administrator, "Oh, in that case I'd better consult the Minister!" [40]

The congestion and overburden at the center which such working habits produce lead to a plaintively reiterated demand on the part of the top ruling group for the display of greater initiative below. But the environment of centralization and conformity is antipathetic to local initiative. Thus Malenkov complained at the Nineteenth Party Congress that "Party, soviet and agricultural leaders not infrequently disregard local, concrete conditions and issue the same instructions for all districts . . . such instructions, correct and necessary for certain districts and farms, are often useless, and, at times even harmful for other districts and farms." [41] Most local administrators are conditioned to act within a framework of approved instructions.

The Party, as well as the governmental hierarchy, operates under the challenge of a set of expectations and goals which strain the capacity of the officials who are charged with their realization. The pressure from the center is incessant and unyielding. The struggle to meet the arduous objectives imposed by the high command elicits a variety of responses from the local leadership. Sometimes it produces bold and ingenious efforts to attain a crude index of over-all success even at the cost of illegal transactions and manipulation of existing instructions. Sometimes it results in efforts to cover up local failures of performance in the hope that such failures can be successfully concealed from the top Party leadership.

At other times, it may involve a desperate appeal to higher authority for assistance on the ground that the resources available to the local authorities make the attainment of the planned goal difficult if not impossible.

The Party leadership holds the local functionaries responsible for results, but it is not prepared to delegate any powers to them which will lead to loss of control. Violations of minor regulations may be tolerated and forgiven, provided they contribute to promote the objectives of the ruling group. But any display of local independence which raises the implicit threat of a competing power center will be subject to summary discipline. The leaders of the regime guard their monopoly of power jealously. To safeguard it, they are willing to forego the advantages of a single, clearly defined administrative hierarchy, and they blur lines of authority by multiplying controls at every point in the government structure. Their system of power is built on the institutionalization of mutual suspicion, and the Party apparatus is both controller and controlled. The fragmentation of authority at the periphery serves as a guarantee that the Kremlin's manipulatory monopoly will remain undisturbed. It continues to anchor its power on a formula in which responsibility is universalized and command remains the prerogative of a narrow ruling group.

Chapter 8

The Composition and Social Structure of the Party

===

The Communist Party of the Soviet Union has undergone profound social changes since the early days of its incubation as the Bolshevik wing of the Russian Social-Democratic Labor Party.* From a tiny circle of less than 8,500 outlawed professional revolutionaries at the beginning of 1905, it has expanded into a ruling party of 6,882,145 members and candidates (October 1, 1952) with a major responsibility for the destiny of a third of the world's population.[1] The transformation from revolutionary to governing party has left its impact on rulers as well as ruled. The leading cadres of the Party constitute a new elite which has risen from the lower reaches of the Tsarist social system to occupy all the peaks of authority in the Soviet state.

Membership Problems of the Party

The Party's monopoly of political power has exerted an increasingly compelling influence in regulating its membership and social composition. As a closed elite Party, the Communist Party of the Soviet Union has never placed a premium on mere numbers. Its primary concern has been to preserve its character as a ruling party. Its first imperative is to staff

* An analysis of the composition and social structure of the Communist Party must draw heavily on the data which the Party has chosen to release. During the twenties, the Party issued a heavy volume of statistical material, but its reliability left much to be desired. Definitions of social categories such as workers, peasants, and employees changed over the years and made comparisons difficult. The unsatisfactory state of local Party records was notorious. In some instances, the concealment of social origins by Party members introduced an additional element of distortion. Since the twenties, the publication of Party statistics has dropped off markedly. Despite the dubious quality of the available data, broad trends can be discerned even when they cannot be precisely measured.

the important power positions in Soviet society with qualified members
who are loyal and devoted to the Party leadership. As the tasks of government become more complex and demanding, increasing weight is attached to technical competence and training. The talents of the new technical intelligentsia are not only in great demand; the Party leadership
finds it expedient also to assimilate its leading members into the Party
inner circle. The control apparatus of the Party demands subalterns as
well as chieftains. The lower ranks of the new Soviet-trained intelligentsia
provide a recruiting ground from which such needs are replenished.

To the extent that the Party puts exclusive emphasis on its responsibilities as a ruling elite, it runs the risk of isolation from the masses. The
pressure to absorb the governing elements of Soviet society into the
Party tends to divorce the Party from the lower strata of Soviet life —
the worker at the bench and the rank-and-file collective farmer. The
logic of elitism runs counter to the inherited symbolism of the Party as
a detachment of the working class. The membership policy of the Party
faces the constant strain of mediating between the indispensable requirement of a Party-dominated directing apparatus on the one hand, and on
the other, the desirability of enlisting support among the mass of ordinary
workers and farmers. The periodic efforts to widen the base of the Party
by drawing the most active and ambitious factory workers and collective
farmers into its ranks represent a search for a point of equilibrium between elitist compulsions and the need to maintain living links with the
Soviet population.

The numerical strength and the social composition of the Party depend on a series of conscious and deliberate decisions on the part of the
Party leadership. The factors which it must take into account are complex. The desiderata which it sets itself have to be reconciled with the
possibility of their attainment at a given time and place. The nature of
the choices which the Party confronts can be suggested by a series of
questions. Is there an optimum size beyond which the Party ought not
to be permitted to grow? Should the Party aim at a cross section of the
Soviet population, or should it deliberately favor particular categories or
groups? In recruiting new members, what weight should be given to
social origin, occupation, educational level, previous identification with
the Komsomols, or other evidence of effort on behalf of Party goals?
Should the Party anchor itself in the younger age groups or should it
reserve the privileges of Party membership for the older generation?
Should it make a strenuous effort to attract women into its ranks? What
balance should it strive for between urban and rural areas? Should its
membership mirror the nationality composition of the population? If not,
which nationalities should it favor and which should it ignore? The answers which evolved to these questions have reflected the Party's doc-

trinal predilections, the changing responsibilities which it has assumed, the need to fuse the Party into a trustworthy and efficient governing elite, and the pressure to strengthen its hold on those strata of Soviet society which were likely to yield it maximum support. The balance that the Party has struck among these factors has varied in different periods of its development. To understand their interplay, the history of Party membership must be reviewed.

During the Bolshevik march to power in 1917, the conditions of admission into the Party were the same for all social categories. The Party Rules approved by the Sixth Party Congress in August 1917 provided only that new members recognizing the Party program, participating in one of its organizations, subordinating themselves to all Party decrees, and paying dues would be received into the Party on the recommendation of two Party members, subject to the approval of a general assembly of the members of the local organization with which they affiliated.[2] These simple rules were designed to facilitate entry during the period of revolutionary upsurge, and with their aid, Party membership more than quadrupled from 23,600 on January 1, 1917, to 115,000 on January 1, 1918. While the Party leadership during this period came almost exclusively from the intelligentsia, the rank-and-file members were predominantly recruited from the urban proletariat of Petrograd, Moscow, and a few other industrial centers. The vast peasant population of Russia was virtually unrepresented within Bolshevik ranks. At the beginning of 1917, only 7.6 per cent of the total membership of the Party was classified as of peasant origin. By January 1, 1918, this proportion had increased to 14.5 per cent, still an insignificant element in the total peasant population. On the same date, workers accounted for 56.9 per cent, and employees and others claimed 28.6 per cent of the total strength of the Party.

The Civil War years witnessed a tremendous growth in the size of the Party (see Table 1). By January 1, 1921, the Party membership totaled 576,000, a fivefold increase in three years. During this period, the conditions of admission were somewhat tightened, but entrance remained relatively easy, and no distinctions were made between workers and peasants. The new Party Rules proclaimed by the Eighth Party Conference in December 1919 introduced a preliminary stage of Party candidacy. Candidates for membership required the recommendation of two Party members with a Party standing of at least six months. Workers and peasants were to remain candidates not less than two months; others were required to spend at least six months as candidates. In exceptional cases, new members could be admitted without passing through the stage of candidacy, provided that they were recommended by two Party members who had entered the Party before October 1917.[3]

The influx of new Party members during the Civil War period was attended by substantial shifts in the social composition of the Party. As the data in Table 2 indicate, the percentage of members of worker origin declined sharply from 56.9 per cent at the beginning of 1918 to 41 per cent at the beginning of 1921. During the same period, the peasant element in the Party rose from 14.5 per cent to 28.2 per cent and the proportion of employees and others increased from 28.6 per cent to 30.8 per cent. The rise in peasant representation was largely explained by the Party's recruitment of Red Army personnel of peasant origin; the absorption of peasant contingents into the Party represented a conscious

TABLE 1

PARTY MEMBERSHIP, 1917–1952

January 1	Members	Candidates	Total
1917	23,600		23,600
1918	115,000		115,000
1919	251,000		251,000
1920	431,400		431,400
1921	576,000		576,000
1922	410,430	117,924	528,354
1923	381,400	117,700	499,100
1924	350,000	122,000	472,000
1925	440,365	361,439	801,804
1926	639,652	440,162	1,079,814
1927	786,288	426,217	1,212,505
1928	914,307	391,547	1,305,854
1929	1,090,508	444,854	1,535,362
1930	1,184,651	493,259	1,677,910
1931	1,369,406	842,819	2,212,225
1932	1,769,773	1,347,477	3,117,250
1933	2,203,951	1,351,387	3,555,338
1934	1,826,756	874,252	2,701,008
1935	1,659,104	699,610	2,358,714
1936	1,489,907	586,935	2,076,842
1937	1,453,828	527,869	1,981,697
1938	1,405,879	514,123	1,920,002
1939	1,514,181	792,792	2,306,973
1940	1,982,743	1,417,232	3,399,975
1941 (Feb.)	2,515,481	1,361,404	3,876,885
1945	3,965,530	1,794,839	5,760,369
1947 (Sept.)	—	—	6,300,000
1952 (Oct. 1)	6,013,259	868,886	6,882,145

Source: Adapted from "Voprosv Chlenstva v VKP(b), po Dokumentam i Tsifram za 30 Let" (Questions of Membership in VKP[b]), *Partiinaya Zhizn'*, no. 20 (October 1947), pp. 73–83, and *Pravda*, October 6, 1952, p. 6. The figures for 1917–1920 are derived from Bubnov, "VKP(b)" in *Bol'shaya Sovetskaya Entsiklopediya* (1930 ed.), XI, 533; those for 1941 from *Partiinoye Stroitel'stvo*. No. 4–5 (February–March 1941), p. 143; those for 1947 from Malenkov, *Informatsionnyi Doklad o Deyatel'nosti Tsentral'nogo Komiteta Vsesoyuznoi Kommunisticheskoi Partii (bol'shevikov)* (Informational Report on the Activities of the Central Committee of the All-Union Communist Party [Bolshevik]; Moscow, 1947), p. 26.

effort of the Party to widen its influence in rural districts during the crucial Civil War period. At the same time, as the tide of battle moved in favor of the Bolsheviks, the attraction of Party membership increased for those who had previously held aloof, and the Party began to absorb more than its usual share of careerists and power-seekers.

The Character of the Party during the Twenties

With the turn to the NEP, the Party leadership grew alarmed at the declining percentage of proletarian strength. The purge of 1921, in the course of which approximately 175,000 members were expelled from the Party, was aimed, in Lenin's words, at ridding the Party "of rascals, bu-

TABLE 2

SOCIAL COMPOSITION OF THE PARTY, 1905–1929

Year	Workers		Peasants		Employees and Others	
	Number	Per cent	Number	Per cent	Number	Per cent
1905		61.7		4.7		33.6
1917		60.2		7.6		32.2
1918		56.9		14.5		28.6
1919		47.8		21.8		30.4
1920		43.8		25.1		31.1
1921		41.0		28.2		30.8
1922	171,625	44.4	102,997	26.7	111,691	28.9
1923	154,920	44.9	88,673	25.7	101,441	29.4
1924	196,339	44.0	128,358	28.8	121,392	27.2
1925	453,141	56.7	211,700	26.5	133,961	16.8
1926	612,202	56.8	278,706	25.9	185,906	17.3
1927	637,768	55.7	217,411	19.0	288,874	25.3
1928	740,731	56.8	299,091	22.9	264,649	20.3
1929	940,136	.61.4	333,287	21.7	258,924	16.9

Source: Bol'shaya Sovetskaya Entsiklopediya (1930 ed.), XI, 534.

reaucrats, dishonest or wavering Communists, and of Mensheviks who have repainted their 'facade' but who have remained Mensheviks at heart." [4] Faced with the necessity of retreat and concessions to the peasantry and the private trader, the Party sought to purify its ranks and root itself in the support of its proletarian formations.

At the Twelfth Party Conference in August 1922 the Party Rules were revised to discourage the admission of non-proletarian cadres.[5] During the twenties, the Party waged a vigorous campaign to increase its proletarian component. Lenin's death provided the signal for a series of recruitment drives which were deliberately designed to attract workers to the Party. As Table 3 demonstrates, of the 212,330 persons admitted to Party candidacy during the "First Lenin Call" in the first half of the year 1924, 92.4 per cent were classified as workers, 5.8 per cent as peasants, and only 1.8 per cent as office employees or others. The "Second Lenin Call" in 1925 was less successful in achieving overwhelming proletarian predominance, but beginning with the "October Call" in 1927, the stress on worker ascendancy was resumed. In that year, 70.2 per cent of the Party candidates were classified as workers. By 1929, the corresponding figure reached 81.2 per cent, while candidates of peasant origin provided only 17.1 per cent of the total, and office workers and other categories accounted for only 1.7 per cent.

The impact of these recruitment drives was registered in the changed social composition of the Party. The worker element in the Party increased from 41 per cent in 1921 to 61.4 per cent in 1929, while the

TABLE 3

NUMBER OF CANDIDATES ACCEPTED
AND THEIR SOCIAL ORIGINS, 1924–1929

Period	Number Accepted	Workers (per cent)	Peasants (per cent)	Employees and Others (per cent)
1924				
Jan.–June	212,330	92.4	5.8	1.8
July–Dec.	103,878	64.5	22.2	13.3
Total	316,208	83.3	11.1	5.6
1925	321,862	54.8	29.5	15.7
1926	167,184	48.4	38.8	12.3
1927	176,180	70.2	23.9	5.9
1928	262,043	73.4	21.9	4.7
1929	297,630	81.2	17.1	1.7

Source: *Bol'shaya Sovetskaya Entsiklopediya* (1930 ed.), XI, 534.

peasant proportion declined from 28.2 per cent to 21.7 per cent and the category of office employees and others fell even more sharply from 30.8 per cent to 16.9 per cent. The emphasis on worker recruitment continued to manifest itself through the year 1932. On July 1 of that year 65.2 per cent of the Party's membership was listed in the worker category. Between 1929 and 1932 however, the peasant element in the Party also increased from 21.7 per cent to 26.9 per cent, while the classification of employees and others showed a further steep decline from 16.9 per cent to 7.9 per cent.[6]

The high proportion of so-called "worker" Communists who were enrolled in the Party during this period is open to misinterpretation. The statistics on the social composition of the Party classify members by social origin rather than by occupation. A different picture emerges when occupational classifications are examined. Thus, on July 1, 1932, when 65.2 per cent of the Party membership were classified as workers, only 43.5

per cent were actually workers by occupation. While 26.9 per cent were classified as peasants, only 18.3 per cent were employed in agriculture. In terms of actual work performed, 38.2 per cent of the Party members were engaged in administrative or other forms of nonmanual labor.[7] While strenuous efforts were made during the late twenties to increase the proportion of production workers in the Party, these efforts were only partially successful.

The November 1928 plenum of the Central Committee set a goal of 50 per cent which was to be attained by 1930. The goal was never reached, though it was closely approached on July 1, 1930, when 48.8 per cent

TABLE 4

COMPARISON OF URBAN-RURAL DISTRIBUTION OF POPULATION
AND OF COMMUNIST PARTY MEMBERSHIP, 1920–1927

Residence	Population Census	Party Census	Number of Communists per 10,000 population
	August 28, 1920	July 1, 1922	
In cities	20,239,500	313,780	155.0
In villages	109,152,200	200,749	18.4
Total	129,391,700	514,529	39.8
	December 17, 1926	January 10, 1927	
In cities	26,297,300	839,617	319.3
In villages	120,716,300	307,457	25.5
Total	147,013.600	1,147,074	78.0

Source: Statisticheskii Otdel TsK VKP(b) (Statistical Department of the CC A-UCP[b]), compiler, *Sotsial'nyi i Natsional'nyi Sostav VKP(b), Itogi Vsesoyuznoi Partiinoi Perepisi 1927 goda* (Social and National Composition of the A-UCP[b], Results of the All-Union Party Census for 1927; Moscow-Leningrad, 1928), p. 18.

of the Party consisted of workers from the bench. From that point on, the proportion of production workers began to decline sharply, and by July 1, 1932, it had fallen to 43.5 per cent. One reason was the promotion of worker Communists to Soviet, Party, economic, and other administrative responsibilities. Substantial groups of Communist workers were sent to rural areas to spark the collectivization drive, and others were dispatched to schools to be trained for the technical and managerial responsibilities which industrialization thrust upon the Party. The insistent needs of the Party for trusted personnel to discharge its governing responsibilities led to a steady transfer of its best worker cadres into administration. The pressure was all the more compelling because the Party Rules as well as Party sentiment raised a barrier to recruitment from the old intelligentsia, and a new Soviet-trained intelligentsia was still in an embryonic stage. The Party thus operated as a funnel through which the upward social mobility of the most ambitious worker Communists was accelerated.

While these changes were taking place within the Party, the total size of the Party registered a striking growth after an initial period of contraction in the early twenties. Following the purge of 1921, Party strength declined from 576,000 members on January 1, 1921, to 472,000 members and candidates on January 1, 1924. From that low point, it increased by January 1, 1933, to 3,555,338 members and candidates, the highest level reached in the pre-World War II period.

Though the Party expanded tremendously from the mid-twenties to the early thirties, it remained essentially an urban outpost in a predominantly rural nation. As Table 4 reveals, even as late as 1927, the number of village Communists totaled only slightly more than 300,000 in a rural population of more than 120,000,000, a ratio of one Party member to every 400 peasants. M. Khataevich, writing in *Bol'shevik* in February 1925, described the great bulk of the village Communists as functionaries whose tie with the land was tenuous and whose rate of political illiteracy was high.[8] The Red Army was frequently the school which initiated the village Communist into the Party. A careful investigation of Communist peasants in the Belorussian villages in 1929 disclosed that more than three-fifths of those surveyed had received their Party indoctrination in the army.[9] The layer of indoctrination, however, was thin. In the 1929 purge more than 15 per cent of the village Communists were expelled from the Party.[10]

The weakness of the Party in the villages greatly hampered the collectivization drive. Although the Party leadership took the drastic step in 1930 of dispatching 25,000 worker-activists from the industrial centers to the countryside in order to strengthen the village cadres, its rural forces remained inadequate. With the intensification of the pace of collectivization, energetic efforts were made to enlist the new *kolkhozniks* in local Party organizations. These efforts enjoyed only moderate success. By mid-1932, the total number of Communists in village organizations had mounted to 800,000, a ratio of approximately one Communist to every 150 rural inhabitants. A large proportion of these village Communists, however, represented new recruits of uncertain loyalty and dubious quality.[11]

The real strength of the Party was concentrated on the industrial front. The 1927 Party census revealed that Communists formed 11.6 per cent of the total industrial labor force. This average, however, concealed sharp variations in different branches of industry. In the oil industry, the proportion was 18 per cent, in the polygraphic industry 17.9 per cent, in the leather industry 16.9 per cent. At the other extreme were the textile industry with only 7.3 per cent, the ore-mining industries with 8.9 per cent, and the coal industry with 9.2 per cent. In between were the important metal-fabricating industries with 13.8 per cent and the food industries with 14.6 per cent.[12] While no comparable breakdowns are available for the early thirties, the Party stratum among all industrial workers on January 1, 1932, was reported to be 13.3 per cent.[13] The greatest lags were noted on the new large construction projects where the proportion of Party members ran from 2.2 per cent to 7 per cent.[14] The constant inflow of fresh workers from the countryside served to dilute the Party nuclei on the new projects. Party representation in the industrial labor force as a whole, nevertheless, remained substantial and impressive.

Though the composition of the Party remained predominantly masculine in this period, the roster of women in the Party showed a steady growth from 8.2 per cent of the Party membership on January 1, 1924, to 15.9 per cent on July 1, 1932. In absolute terms, the increase was far more impressive. On July 1, 1932, the number of women Communists totaled slightly less than 500,000 compared with 38,500 on January 1, 1924. In terms of social origin and occupation, women Communists revealed some substantial divergences from the pattern of the Party as a whole. In 1926, for example, when 25.4 per cent of the Party membership consisted of members who were peasants in origin, the corresponding percentage among Communist women was only 14.9 per cent. Women in the category of employees and others totaled 27.3 per cent compared with only 17.4 per cent for the Party at large. These same relationships carried over to occupational categories. Women Communists were very weakly represented in peasant employment and much more strongly entrenched in nonmanual occupations. During the late twenties, these disparities became less evident as a result of the Party drive to recruit women in rural areas. By 1930, the occupational classification of women Communists closely mirrored the picture for the Party as a whole. In terms of social origins, however, the 1926 divergences continued to manifest themselves, though in lesser degree.

The nationality complexion of women Communists revealed a striking predominance of Great Russians in terms of sheer numbers and a particularly strong representation among Jewish, Finnish, Lettish, Esthonian, and Polish women (see Table 5). The high proportion of Communists in these groups is probably explained by a combination of educational advantages and the progress of the emancipation movement in the western borderlands. As Table 5 makes clear, the Party encountered its greatest difficulty in recruiting women Communists in areas where old religious and social customs retained their hold despite the Revolution. The tradition of treating women as an inferior group carried over into Party life.

The nationality composition of the Party as a whole during the twenties showed a strong Great Russian coloration. As Table 6 demonstrates, the Great Russian Communists accounted for 72 per cent of the Party membership in 1922. Despite strenuous efforts to broaden the nationality base of the Party, they still claimed 65 per cent of the Party membership in 1927, while the Great Russian component in the total population was

TABLE 5

COMMUNIST WOMEN IN VARIOUS ETHNIC PARTY GROUPS
BASED ON PARTY CENSUS DATA FOR 1922 AND 1927

Ethnic Group	1922			1927		
	Total number	Percentage of all Communists of Ethnic Group	Rank by per cent	Total number	Percentage of all Communists of Ethnic Group	Rank by per cent
Jewish	4,717	24.1	1	8,684	23.0	1
Finnish	185	19.8	2	271	17.6	3
Lettish	1,775	18.7	3	2,119	18.1	2
Esthonian	285	14.5	4	476	15.2	4
Polish	641	11.3	5	1,245	13.3	5
Cherkessi	4	11.1	6	9	7.0	11
German	230	10.4	7	414	10.8	7
Lithuanian	126	8.6	8	232	10.0	8
Russian	19,558	7.2	9	58,283	11.3	6
Armenian	219	5.7	10	542	4.4	20
Buriat	5	4.9	11	39	8.2	9
Ukrainian	1,041	4.7	12	5,580	6.7	13
Komi	31	3.4	13	76	7.5	10
Belorussian	183	3.3	14	1,247	5.0	17
Kalmyk	5	3.2	15	17	4.6	19
Turko-Tatar-Kumic	174	2.7	16 (Tatar)	425	4.7	18
Mordvian	43	2.6	17	88	3.8	—
Georgian	178	2.5	18	376	3.7	—
Bashkir	11	2.3	19	34	2.5	—
Chuvash	23	2.2	20	85	4.4	—
Votiak	7	2.1	—	29	6.9	12
Mariat	3	0.9	—	30	5.9	14
Avars	—	—	—	17	5.4	15
Karelian	5	2.1	—	22	5.1	16

Source: *Sotsial'nyi i Natsional'nyi Sostav VKP(b)*, p. 139.

less than 53 per cent. An analysis of the 1927 Party census also reveals that the Jewish, Latvian, Esthonian, Polish, Armenian, and Georgian Communists recorded a substantially higher percentage of Party strength than did their compatriots in the total population. On the other hand, the Party representation of Ukrainians, Kazakhs, Uzbeks, Tatars, and other minorities was notably less than their proportion in the total Soviet population.

While comparable data have not been released for succeeding years, an analysis of the nationality affiliations of the delegates to the Sixteenth Party Congress in 1930 gives some indication of prevailing trends. The Great Russian group at the Congress accounted for 57.4 per cent of the delegates compared with 62 per cent at the Fifteenth Congress in 1927. The Jewish delegation increased from 7.4 per cent in 1927 to 10.6 per

TABLE 6

COMPARISON OF NATIONAL ETHNIC GROUPS IN THE TOTAL
POPULATION AND IN THE PARTY

National Ethnic Group	Percentage of Total Population 17 Dec. 1926	Rank	Percentage of National Ethnic Group to Total Number of Communists			
			1922 Party Census		1927 Party Census	
			Members only	Rank	Members and candidates	Rank
Russian	52.91	1	72.00	1	65.00	1
Ukrainian	21.22	2	5.88	2	11.72	2
Belorussian	3.22	3	1.47	7	3.18	4
Kazakh	2.70	4	—	—	1.05	11
Uzbek	2.65	5	0.54	13	1.19	8
Tatar	2.02	6	1.05	9	1.37	7
Jewish	1.82	7	5.20	3	4.34	3
Georgian	1.24	8	1.96	5	1.49	6
Turkic	1.16	9	0.65	11	0.98	12
Armenian	1.07	10	1.02	10	1.66	5
Mordvian	0.91	11	0.43	16	0.34	16
German	0.84	12	0.59	12	0.49	13
Chuvash	0.76	13	0.28	18	0.33	17
Polish	0.53	14	1.50	6	1.06	10
Kirghiz	0.53	15	1.32	8	0.24	19
Bashkir	0.49	16	0.13	21	0.21	20
Osetian	0.19	17	0.45	15	0.40	14
Karelian	0.17	18	0.06	27	0.07	31
Esthonian	0.10	19	0.53	14	0.35	15
Latvian	0.09	20	2.53	4	1.17	9

Source: For Population, Frank Lorimer, *The Population of the Soviet Union: History and Prospects* (Geneva, 1946), pp. 55–61. For Party, "On the Question of the National Composition of the RKP," *Izvestiya TsK,* no. 7–8 (55–56) (August–September, 1923), p. 61; *Sotsial'nyi i Natsional'nyi Sostav VKP(b),* p. 114.

cent in 1930. The Ukrainians declined from 9.8 per cent to 8.6 per cent; the Letts from 4.7 per cent to 4.3 per cent; and the Belorussians from 2.9 per cent to 2.8 per cent.[15] Both the Armenian and Georgian delegations at the Sixteenth Congress were substantially stronger than their ratio of the general population, while the Uzbeks, Kazakhs, Turkmens, and other minority delegations were notably weaker.

The efforts of the Party to expand its strength among the minority nationalities enjoyed only moderate success. While the membership in thirty-four national Party organizations grew from 762,000 on January 1, 1931, to 1,087,000 on April 1, 1932, the percentage of indigenous nationals in these organizations increased only from 50.9 per cent to 53.8 per cent.[16] These averages, moreover, concealed wide variations in individual performance. The data available for 1930 make this clear. As of July 1, 1930, for example, the Armenian Party organization was 89 per cent Armenian, while only 17.8 per cent of the Bashkir Party organization were native Bashkirs. Other national organizations in which Communists of the indigenous nationality were particularly weak included the Karelian organization with 25.3 per cent, the Buriat-Mongol with 31.6 per cent, the Tatar with 36.3 per cent, the Azerbaidjan with 39.5 per cent, the Kirghiz with 42.8 per cent, the Turkmen with 43.2 per cent, the Kazakh with 45.2 per cent, the Tadjik with 47.9 per cent, and the Uzbek with 48.5 per cent.[17] Such national Party organizations tended in fact to be dominated by Great Russians or other representatives of dominant nationalities in the Party who were stationed in the area. The Party press of the period is replete with references to the backwardness of the local minority cadres in these regions. As late as 1932, 36.7 per cent of the Tadjik and 24.9 per cent of the Uzbek Party organizations were officially classified by the Party Central Committee as illiterate.[18]

One of the striking aspects of the Party in this period was its youthful character. According to the Party census of 1927, 25.3 per cent of the members were under twenty-five years of age, 53.8 per cent under thirty, 85.8 per cent under forty, and 97.2 per cent under fifty. The extreme youth of the Party rank-and-file was matched by the relative youth of its top command. Of the 121 members and candidates elected to the Central Committee at the Fifteenth Party Congress in 1927, 56, or 46.3 per cent, were under forty years of age; 90, or 74.4 per cent, were under forty-five; and 105, or 86.8 per cent, were under fifty.[19] The data available clearly reveal that the face of the Party was turned toward youth and that the Party leadership found its firmest support in the younger age spans.

The educational level of the Party membership during the twenties was low. As Table 7 indicates, some over-all progress was registered between 1922 and 1927 in increasing the Party stratum with a higher or middle education. Illiteracy decreased. At the same time, the emphasis on the recruitment of production workers resulted in a substantial dropping off of Party members with a formal lower-school education.

The low educational qualifications of the factory workers who were welcomed into the Party during this period set a barrier against their utilization in managerial and administrative posts. The dilemma which the Party leadership faced was mirrored in the comments of the Party press. Party organizations were scolded for tolerating illiteracy and for neglecting political schooling. The more ambitious Communist workers were encouraged to enroll in *tekhnikums* in order to raise their qualifications, and great emphasis was placed on home study as well as on factory schools which were designed to prepare cadres of skilled workers. As the industrialization and collectivization programs generated a growing demand for engineers, technicians, agronomists, scientific workers, and managerial personnel, hints were thrown out that the Party would welcome into its ranks members of the technical intelligentsia and that the Party Rules might have to be modified to facilitate their entry.[20] No immediate action was taken, but the great change which ultimately took place in 1939 was already foreshadowed.

TABLE 7

COMPARISON OF EDUCATIONAL LEVEL OF PARTY MEMBERS IN 1922 AND 1927 DISTRIBUTED BY SOCIAL CLASSIFICATION

(In per cent)

Social Origin	Higher		Middle		Lower		Home and Self		Illiterate		Not Indicated 1922 only
	1922	1927	1922	1927	1922	1927	1922	1927	1922	1927	
Workers	—	0.1	1.0	3.9	80.5	63.9	15.4	30.3	2.7	1.8	0.4
Peasants	—	0.1	0.6	3.6	70.3	60.9	17.1	28.5	11.3	6.9	0.7
Employees	2.2	3.0	19.8	20.9	72.8	62.8	4.7	12.8	0.3	0.5	0.2
Others	1.8	1.6	19.6	12.7	65.4	51.9	7.9	30.5	4.5	3.3	0.8
Total	0.6	0.8	6.3	7.9	75.1	62.8	13.0	26.1	4.6	2.4	0.4

Source: For 1922, *Izvestiya TsK*, no. 1 (49), (January 1923), p. 45. For 1927, *Izvestiya TsK*, no. 47–48 (220–21), (December 31, 1927), p. 18.

The difficulty which the Party leadership was encountering in recruiting qualified Party cadres for managerial positions was revealed in an analysis of the educational backgrounds of directors of state enterprises as of January 1, 1928. Of the directors studied, 89.3 per cent belonged to the Party, and 10.7 per cent were non-Party. Of the Party directors, only 2.8 per cent had a higher education, compared with 58 per cent of the non-Party directors. Of the Party directors, 78.6 per cent had only a lower-school education compared with 14.8 per cent for the non-Party directors. More than 70 per cent of the Party directors consisted of workers who were promoted to managerial posts.[21] The problem of training Party cadres for high technical and managerial responsibilities was still unsolved.

Within the Party organization itself, the leading posts were still monopolized by Old Bolsheviks. Of the 121 members and candidates elected to the Party Central Committee at the Fifteenth Congress in 1927, all but ten had joined the Party before 1917. Most of them were former professional revolutionaries and underground workers who had won their spurs in the struggle to overthrow Tsarism. At lower levels in the Party organization, the Old Bolsheviks were much less strongly represented. In 1927 they accounted for only 22.6 per cent of the central committees of the national republics; 58.2 per cent of the members of these committees entered the Party in the period from 1917 to 1920. The *oblast* or regional committees had an Old Bolshevik contingent of 12.1 per cent. Civil War veterans of the 1917–1920 period accounted for 63.9 per cent. In the *guberniya* or provincial committees, the percentage of Old Bolsheviks declined to 11.9 per cent and in the *okrug* or circle committees to 5.2 per cent. In both cases, the committees were dominated by the 1917–1920 generation.

A different pattern emerges when the more than thirty-one thousand secretaries of primary cells are analyzed. In 1927, less than one per cent were pre-1917 veterans. The majority, 50.9 per cent, joined the Party in 1924 or later.[22] At the base of the Party apparatus, the secretarial hierarchy already represented a new post-Revolutionary generation around which Stalin was to consolidate his power.

The characteristics of the Party at the end of the twenties and the beginning of the thirties can be briefly summarized. In terms of social origin, its membership was predominantly working class. In terms of occupation, workers at the bench only slightly exceeded those performing administrative or other nonmanual work. The Party was overwhelmingly urban in composition; its rural representation was woefully weak. The primary strength of the Party was concentrated in the industrial centers and in large-scale enterprises in heavy industry. Although the number of women was increasing, in 1932 they constituted less than one-sixth of the Party membership, and of this by far the greater part was embraced in the Great Russian, Jewish, and western border nationalities. The nationality weight of the Party was concentrated among the Great Russian, Jewish, Latvian, Esthonian, Polish, Armenian, and Georgian Communists. The Ukrainians, the Central Asiatic groups, and the other minor nationalities of European Russia were still very inadequately represented in the Party. The age levels of Party members and leaders revealed a strikingly youthful profile, though the leading posts in the Party were still reserved for veterans of the pre-Revolutionary struggle. The educational level of the Party was low, and one of its consequences was a serious deficiency in trained Party personnel capable of discharging the large managerial tasks which industrialization and collectivization imposed on the Party leadership.

Party Membership in the Thirties

The peak numerical strength of the Party during the thirties was reached in 1933 when the number of members and candidates exceeded three and a half million. The mass enrollment and tremendous expansion of the early thirties created serious problems of assimilation. The quality of the new members who were recruited in the factories and collective farms left a great deal to be desired; their ideological level was extremely low. On December 10, 1932, the Party Central Committee announced the suspension of further admissions and ordered a purge of all members and candidates. The determination to restrict entry was reinforced by a drastic change in the Party Rules enacted by the Seventeenth Party Congress in early 1934. In regulating admissions, four categories were established: (1) industrial workers with a production record of not less than five years; (2) industrial workers with a production record of less than five years, agricultural workers, Red Army men from among workers or collective farmers, and engineers and technicians working directly in shops or sectors; (3) collective farmers, members of handicraft or artisan artels, and elementary school teachers; (4) other employees. Persons in the first category were required to submit three recommendations from Party members of five-years' standing and were to remain candidates for one year. The period of candidacy for all other categories was fixed at two years. Persons in the second category had to obtain five recommendations from Party members of five-years' standing; persons in the third category, five recommendations from Party members of five-years' standing plus the recommendation of the representative of the political department of the machine-tractor station (MTS) or of the district Party committee; and persons in the fourth category, five recommendations from Party members of ten-years' standing.[23] While the 1934 revision of the Party Rules registered a substantial improvement in the relative position of engineering and technical personnel (an adjustment which represented a response to the urgencies of industrialization), the severity of the new entrance requirements raised a barrier which even the most favored group found difficult to surmount.

Beginning in 1933, the Party underwent a series of purges which resulted in a reduction of membership from 2,203,951 on January 1, 1933, to 1,405,879 on January 1, 1938. In the same period, the number of candidates shrank from 1,351,387 to 514,123. The impact of the 1933 purge was particularly severe, reducing the total number of members and candidates from more than 3,500,000 on January 1, 1933, to slightly more than 2,700,000 on January 1, 1934. The incidence of the 1933 purge was especially great among collective farmers and the new industrial workers of peasant origin who had flocked into the Party during the First Five

Year Plan. The older industrial centers such as Moscow and Leningrad were less hard hit than the newly developed areas in the Urals and Eastern Siberia.[24]

The 1933 purge was limited to ten of the leading *krai* and *oblast* organizations. During 1934, the purge was extended to the rest of the Party. By January 1, 1935, the total number of members and candidates had declined to 2,358,714, a loss of over 340,000 within the period of a year. The assassination of Kirov in December 1934 gave the purge a new urgency, and its sharpest edge was turned against former members of the opposition.

In the course of the 1933–34 purge, the Party leadership discovered that Party records were in a chaotic state and that no effective control was exercised over Party cards and other documents. On May 13, 1935, the Party Central Committee demanded that all Party documents be screened in order "to bring Bolshevistic order into our own Party house." On December 25, 1935, it issued another order demanding the completion of the screening operation by February 1, 1936, at which time local Party organizations were to begin exchanging new Party cards for old ones. In its decree of December 25, 1935, the Central Committee also ordered the termination of the purge, but in practice the screening of Party documents and the provisions for the exchange of Party cards operated to prolong the purge.[25] Local Party organizations were enjoined to use these opportunities to unmask "enemies" who had infiltrated into the Party and to eliminate passive elements "who do not deserve the high name of party members." By January 1, 1937, the total number of members and candidates had declined to slightly less than 2,000,000, a loss of over 350,000 in two years.

The resumption of recruitment, which had originally been set by the decree of December 25, 1935, for June 1, 1936, was subsequently postponed until November 1, 1936. The year 1937 marked the height of the Great Purge, the *Yezhovshchina*, and the Party was caught up in a wild fury of denunciations and mass expulsions. By January 1, 1938, despite new admissions, Party strength had declined to 1,920,002, the lowest level reached during the thirties. The signal for the end of the *Yezhovshchina* was given in January 1938 by the Party Central Committee in its decree "On the Mistakes of Party Organizations in Excluding Communists from the Party, On Formal Bureaucratic Attitudes toward the Appeals of Excluded Members of the VKP(b), and On Measures to Eliminate These Deficiencies." [26] The blame for past excesses was placed on so-called "careerist-Communists" who had sought to advance in the Party by bringing irresponsible accusations and denunciations against those who stood in their way. The immediate result of the decree was a purge of so-called careerists. It was followed in due course by the reinstatement of some Party members who had been "unjustly" expelled and by a sharp increase in admissions.

By January 1, 1939, the number of members and candidates reached 2,306,973 and by January 1, 1940, the total Party strength was listed at 3,399,975. More than 40 per cent of this total represented new members and candidates who had joined in the preceding two-year period. This vast increase was greatly facilitated by a revision of the Party Rules at the Eighteenth Congress in 1939. Under the new rules, all differentials among workers, peasants, and intellectuals were eliminated. A uniform candidacy period of one year was established, and all applicants for membership were required to submit recommendations from three Party members of three-years' standing who knew the applicants from having worked with them for not less than a year.

The Enlistment of the Intelligentsia

The social structure of the Party underwent substantial modifications during the late thirties. Although comprehensive data on Party membership were no longer released after 1932, the trend of development can readily be deduced from scattered material appearing in the Party press. The most significant change was the reception of the new Soviet-trained intelligentsia into the Party. The Five Year Plans bred a new social stratum of plant managers, engineers, technicians, and scientific personnel who played an increasingly important role in running and directing the economy. As long as this social element was penalized by discriminatory admission requirements barring it from Party membership, the Party leadership faced the danger that the bureaucratic-managerial group on which it had to rely would develop into an antagonistic force that would be isolated from Party influence. To avert this danger, the managerial and technical group had to be assimilated into the Party, and the Party had to overcome its traditional attachment to the notion that the proletariat was the leading class in Soviet society.

The Party's shift in attitude was authoritatively foreshadowed by Stalin in a speech delivered to a conference of business executives on June 23, 1931. He declared, "No ruling class has managed without its own intelligentsia." "Our policy," he proclaimed, "is by no means to transform the Party into an exclusive caste," and he called on the working class to *create its own industrial and technical intelligentsia.*" [27] In his speech "On the Draft Constitution of the U.S.S.R.," delivered to the Extraordinary Eighth Congress of Soviets on November 25, 1936, he carried his theme one step further. "Our Soviet intelligentsia," he now pronounced, "is an entirely new intelligentsia, bound up by its very roots with the working class and the peasantry . . . 80 to 90 per cent of the Soviet intelligentsia are people who have come from the working class, from the peasantry, or from other strata of the working population . . . Formerly it had to serve the wealthy classes . . . Today it must serve the people . . . And that is precisely why it is now an equal member of Soviet society, in which, side by side with the workers and peasants . . . it is engaged in building the new, classless, Socialist society." [28]

When the Party resumed large-scale recruitment in 1938, the technical intelligentsia was eagerly welcomed into the ranks. The enlistment of the intelligentsia assumed the character of a campaign. The reports of local Party organizations gave primacy to the number of engineering-technical personnel that they had succeeded in recruiting for the Party.[29] This profound shift in the social base of the Party created its strains. As Stalin remarked at the Eighteenth Party Congress:

> In spite of the fact that the position of the Party on the question of the Soviet intelligentsia is perfectly clear, there are still current in our Party views hostile to the Soviet intelligentsia and incompatible with the Party position. As you know, those who hold these false views practise a disdainful and contemptuous attitude to the Soviet intelligentsia and regard it as an alien force . . . hostile to the working class and the peasantry . . .

> This theory is now out-of-date and does not fit our new, Soviet intelligentsia. Our new intelligentsia demands a new theory, a theory teaching the necessity for a cordial attitude towards it, solicitude and respect for it, and cooperation with it in the interests of the working class and the peasantry.[30]

The abolition of differential entrance requirements by the Eighteenth Party Congress in 1939 gave formal recognition to a change of policy which was already far advanced. Zhdanov, in proposing the new policy of uniform admission for all categories, made the objective of the new rules crystal clear.

> Our best Stakhanovites, once they have become foremen or directors, that is, have been promoted to executive posts because of their abilities and services, find themselves, when applying to join the Party, in the position of second rate people.

> These antiquated requirements are clung to by retrograde people who are not anxious for the advancement of new and young forces.
> . . . They furnish a pretext for the cultivation of an attitude of disdain towards advanced people who because of their education or services have been promoted to leading posts.[31]

During the next years, the Party continued its efforts to absorb the new intelligentsia into its ranks. While no data are available for the Soviet Union as a whole, figures on local Party organizations bear witness to the trend. In Chelyabinsk province, for example, during 1941 and the first two months of 1942, the new Party candidates consisted of 660 workers, 289 collective farmers, and 2,025 white-collar workers. Members admitted in the same period numbered 903 workers, 399 collective farmers, and 3,515 white-collar workers.[32] More than 70 per cent of the new candidates and members could be broadly classified as belonging to the new intelligentsia.

This striking change in the social structure of the Party was part of a process of adaptation to the insistent demands of industrialization and collectivization. The problem of the relationship of the new Soviet intelligentsia to the Party was "solved" by facilitating its absorption into the Party. After the elimination of the Old Bolsheviks in the Great Purge of 1936–1938, the Party was replenished and reinvigorated by the admission of younger cadres of bureaucrats, engineers, plant directors, collective farm chairmen, foremen, and Stakhanovites. In the process, a considerable step was taken, at least at the level of personnel, toward a fusion of Party and administration.

The dominant weight of the Party remained strongly urban. In the early thirties, a determined effort was made to strengthen the rural Party organizations. As Kaganovich pointed out at the Seventeenth Party Congress, between 1930 and 1934 about 50,000 urban workers were sent into the rural districts on Party assignments. Over 18,000 of these workers were dispatched to political departments of machine-tractor stations and state farms.[33] Between the Sixteenth Party Congress in 1930 and the Seventeenth Congress in 1934, the rural membership of the Party increased from 400,000 to over 800,000, or approximately 30 per cent of the total membership. Despite this impressive growth, about 50 per cent of the *kolkhozes* or collective farms remained without Communists.[34]

The impact of the purge of the mid-thirties was particularly severe in rural areas. On January 1, 1933, the Party claimed 36,196 *kolkhoz* Party organizations. By November 1, 1934, their number had declined to 24,333 and by January 1, 1935, had shrunk further to 18,313. Between November 1, 1934, and January 1, 1935, the number of territorial organizations in rural areas dropped from 11,193 to 8,696. This decrease left many collective farms and rural areas either with no Party members or with "single Communists" whose isolation from the Party became a matter of serious concern.[35]

During the next years, the situation continued to deteriorate. At the Eighteenth Party Congress in 1939, Andreyev referred "to the unsatisfactory number of primary organizations and Communist Party members on the collective farms." "In the past year," he declared, "we have had a certain increase in the number of Party members on the collective farms, but we cannot consider it a normal state of affairs when on 243,000 collective farms there are only 12,000 primary Party organizations with a total membership of 153,000, including candidate members."[36] A substantial majority of the rural Communists, moreover, consisted of administrative and managerial personnel — chairmen of rural soviets and rural coöperatives, teachers and agricultural experts, *kolkhoz* chairmen, book-keepers, and brigadiers, and state farm and machine-tractor station employees. Rank-and-file collective farmers were sparsely represented. The rural membership of the Party largely represented a projection of the bureaucratic state apparatus into the countryside.

Though the Party remained overwhelmingly urban in composition, its strength among actual workers declined substantially during the thirties. The emphasis on recruitment of the technical intelligentsia consigned workers at the bench to a secondary role. In recruiting new working-class cadres, the Party turned increasingly toward so-called "leading" workers — shop chiefs, foremen, and Stakhanovite workers — who represented the aristocracy of industrial labor. Statistical tabulations on the number of Party members directly engaged in production disappear after the early thirties; the Party press showed no disposition to document the receding influence of the ordinary worker in the Party. Trends can, nevertheless, be deduced from the extremely fragmentary material that was made available. At the Seventeenth Party Congress in 1934, Kaganovich cited data to demonstrate the high proportion of Communists engaged in industry. Out of 700,000 workers in eighty-five of the largest enterprises, 94,000, or slightly under 14 per cent, were members of the Party.[37] Later material indicated a substantial drop in the proportion of worker Communists. In 1937, for example, the Party organization in the Leningrad Metal Plant numbered 1,076 out of a total working force of 10,000. Of this group, 170 had a higher education, and 277 had a secondary education, from which the inference can be drawn that the proportion of Party members actually engaged in production probably did not exceed 6 or 7 per cent.[38] While the profile of the Party remained preponderantly urban, its center of gravity was shifting perceptibly from production workers to the new managerial and technical intelligentsia.

The data on the role of women in the Party during the thirties indicate a tendency toward stagnation and arrested development. As of July 1932 women composed about 16 per cent of the total Party membership compared with 8 per cent on January 1, 1924. By January 1, 1941, however, the proportion of women in the Party had declined to 14.9 per cent.[39] At the lowest levels of the Party hierarchy, women occupied approximately one-sixth of the offices.[40] Women encountered much greater difficulty in penetrating the higher Party hierarchy, though here some progress was registered. At the 1934 Party Congress, women comprised 7.2 per cent of the voting delegates. In the 1939 Congress, the figure rose to 9.1 per cent.[41] In general, the influence of women in the Party lagged behind their increasingly significant role in the social, economic, and educational life of the Soviet Union. The top leadership of the Party was reserved for its male element.

The withholding of data by the Party press makes it virtually impossible to establish the precise national-ethnic composition of the Party during the thirties. Some general conclusions can be inferred from the Eighteenth Congress data summarized in Table 8. As this table indicates, the strength of such regional Party organizations as Moscow, Leningrad, Ivanovo, and Yaroslavl testified to the continuing power of the Great Russians in the Party. Outside the Great Russian heartland, the Party was particularly strong in the Transcaucasus area of Armenia, Georgia, and Azerbaidjan. The Ukrainian Party organization was somewhat under-

TABLE 8

COMPARISON OF PARTY STRENGTH AND POPULATION RATIOS IN
SELECTED REGIONS AND NATIONAL REPUBLICS
OF THE USSR, 1939

	Percentage of Voting Delegates, 18th Party Congress	Percentage of Total Population
Moscow *oblast*	13.3	5.2
Leningrad *oblast*	9.1	3.8
Ivanovo *oblast*	2.4	1.6
Yaroslavl *oblast*	1.7	1.3
Armenia	1.23	.74
Georgia	2.36	2.08
Azerbaidjan	2.8	1.88
Ukraine	17.3	18.2
Belorussia	2.36	3.27
Uzbekistan	1.40	3.68
Tadjikistan	.25	.91
Turkmenistan	.31	.73
Kazakhstan	2.42	3.6

Source: Report of the Mandate Commission to the Eighteenth Party Congress in *XVIII S"ezd VKP(b) Stenograficheskii Otchët*, pp. 146–147, and Frank Lorimer, *The Population of the Soviet Union: History and Prospects*, pp. 241–243.

represented in relation to the population of the Ukraine. The weaknesses of the national Party organizations were most strikingly evident in Belorussia and the Central Asian republics of Uzbekistan, Tadjikistan, Turkmenistan, and Kazakhstan.

It should be noted that the statistical data contained in Table 8 tend to obscure the extent of Great Russian ascendancy in the Party. In the Central Asian republics, for example, Great Russians and other outside nationalities were strongly represented in the local Party organizations and tended to dominate the top levels of the Party hierarchy. The indigenous nationalities were, however, registering gains compared with earlier periods. In 1935 native Uzbeks accounted for 65 per cent of the membership of the republic Party organization compared with 48.5 per cent in 1930, the Tadjiks for 50 per cent compared with 47.9 per cent in 1930, and the Turkmens for 50 per cent compared with 43.2 per cent in 1930.[42] Comparable data are unavailable for other groups. The Jewish Communists seem to have lost strength in the wake of the Great Purge of the late thirties. A study of the composition of the supreme soviets of the national republics in 1938 revealed that only 2.5 per cent of those elected were Jews.[43] Eight years earlier, they had accounted for more than 10 per cent of the delegates to the Sixteenth Party Congress. By the end of the thirties, the Great Russian and Transcaucasian Communists appear to have emerged as the most solidly entrenched ethnic groups in the Party.

While the Party retained its dominantly youthful character during this decade, a marked increase in average age level was noticeable by the mid-thirties. The purge of 1933–34 wreaked its greatest havoc among recent Party recruits, who were predominantly in the younger age range.[44] Although no comprehensive material on the age distribution of the whole Party is available for this period, a report on the composition of the Tula Party organization in 1935 gives some indication of the trend.[45] Three per cent of the Tula members were less than twenty-five years old compared with 25.3 per cent for the Party at large in 1927; 27 per cent were under thirty years, compared with 53.8 per cent for the Party as a whole in 1927.

The Great Purge of 1936–1938 reversed this trend. The decimation of the Old Bolsheviks and the destruction wrought among the Civil War generation opened the way for the recruitment of younger cadres and the rejuvenation of the Party. At the 1939 Party Congress, Malenkov reported that 70 per cent of the Party members dated their membership from 1929 or later; only 8.3 per cent of the membership had joined the Party before 1920. At the 1934 Party Congress 80 per cent of the delegates had a pre-1920 Party standing; the corresponding percentage at the 1939 Party Congress was only 19.4. The delegates at the 1939 Congress were a remarkably youthful group: 49.5 per cent were under thirty-five, 81.5 per cent were under forty, and 97 per cent were under fifty.[46] The secretarial hierarchy of the Party revealed an even greater accent on youth.* The available statistics emphasize the youth of both Party rank-and-file and officialdom; particularly significant is the fact that leading Party functionaries had been drawn into Party activity largely in the period after Lenin's death. The Party was on the way to being dominated by a new post-Revolutionary generation consolidated around the power and leadership of Stalin.

The period of the thirties witnessed a substantial improvement in the educational qualifications of Party members. The reception of the tech-

* See Chapter 6, p. 172.

nical intelligentsia into the Party was accompanied by a striking rise in the proportion of Party members with a higher or secondary school education. The number of Communists with a higher education increased from approximately 9,000 in 1928 to 127,000 in 1939; the number with a secondary education rose from 110,000 to 335,000 over the same time span.[47] This advance was particularly noteworthy among the leading cadres of the Party. At the Seventeenth Congress in 1934, about 10 per cent of the delegates had a higher education. At the Eighteenth Congress, in 1939, the comparable figure was 26.5 per cent.[48] In 1939, 28.6 per cent of the secretaries of regional, territorial, and republic Party committees had a complete university education, and 30 per cent had either a complete secondary school education or an incomplete university education. Nearly 5 per cent of the secretaries of district, city, and area committees were university graduates, while 23.5 per cent had either an incomplete university education or had been through secondary schools.[49] At the Eighteenth Congress, Andreyev claimed impressive gains in the educational qualifications of Soviet administrative and economic personnel: "The proportion of university graduates among the People's Commissars of the U.S.S.R. and the R.S.F.S.R. is 53 per cent, among the Assistant People's Commissars 68 per cent, among the directors of the chief boards and syndicates of the People's Commissariats 60 per cent and among the directors of economic establishments 27.6 per cent." [50] Comparable gains were reported at lower levels of the economic and administrative hierarchy. These developments represented a response to the overriding need for qualified personnel in responsible positions. The assimilation of the new Soviet intelligentsia into the Party was followed by its rapid elevation to leading positions.

The changes in the character of the Party during the thirties can be briefly summarized. After a period of rapid expansion in the early thirties, the Party suffered a series of purges which reduced its membership by almost one-half. In 1938 growth began again, and by the beginning of 1940 the Party had almost reached the peak membership registered in 1933. The most significant social change was the reception of the new Soviet-trained intelligentsia into the Party. The industrial worker lost his preferred position, and after 1934 peasant strength also shrank substantially. Although the Party remained predominantly urban in composition, the newly favored categories both in town and country were the administrators, the technicians, and the "leading workers." The role of women declined slightly; their influence was more marked in the lower reaches of the Party hierarchy than in the male-dominated higher echelons. The Great Russian and Transcaucasian Communists maintained their strong position, while the Jewish Party membership declined in importance, and Ukrainians and Belorussians continued to be under-represented. Communist weight in the Central Asian republics remained weak although some progress was registered in comparison with the twenties. The Party retained its youthful character. After an increase in the average age of Party members in the first half of the thirties, the trend was reversed by the elimination of most of the Old Bolsheviks in the Great Purge. The rejuvenation of the Party was accompanied by a considerable improvement in the educational backgrounds of Party members, with the most impressive gains at higher levels of the economic, administrative, and political apparatus.

War and Postwar Expansion

With the end of the Great Purge, the Party entered a phase of rapid expansion. In the three years from the beginning of 1938 to early 1941, the Party doubled in size; at the Eighteenth Party Conference, which met in February 1941, a total of 3,876,885 members and candidates were represented. During the war years, the membership of the Party soared to a new peak. Early in the war, the Party relaxed its standards of admission in order to encourage members of the armed forces and particularly front-line fighters to apply for entrance.[51] According to one Soviet authority, during the year 1942 alone 1,340,000 new members were inducted.[52] Many of the new members were recruited without particular attention to their ideological equipment or political sophistication. The Party's first concern was to strengthen its mass base in the crucial military formations. By January 1, 1945, the size of the Party attained the unprecedented figure of 5,760,369. By September 1947 it had mounted to 6,300,000. Almost half of this number was accounted for by those who had joined the Party during the war and postwar period.[53] After 1947 expansion continued at a much slower rate. Data released at the Nineteenth Party Congress indicate that the total membership of the Party on October 1, 1952, was 6,882,145, of whom 6,013,259 were full members and 868,886 candidates.[54]

After the war, admission of new Party members was much more carefully regulated. The Party concentrated on weeding out recent recruits who were found deficient in political knowledge or who proved inefficient, untrustworthy, or venal in discharging Party assignments or administrative tasks. While no official figures were released on the total number of postwar Party expulsions, at least one indication of the extent of recent Party turnover is available. In the Azerbaidjan Party organization, which had a total membership of 108,737 on April 1, 1951, 12,685, or more than 10 per cent, lost their status as Party members between January 1949 and April 1951. In the same period, 10,249 new members were added.[55] While it cannot be automatically assumed that these figures are typical of the Party as a whole, they do point to a continuing turnover of substantial proportions in Party membership.

Changes in Social Composition

The tremendous expansion in the size of the Party during the war years was accompanied by changes in its social composition. The prewar emphasis on recruitment of the technical intelligentsia was temporarily interrupted. The mass admissions of rank-and-file Red Army soldiers during the war had the effect of strengthening both the worker and peasant components of the Party. During the war years, workers constituted 32.1 per cent of those accepted as candidates of the Party, compared with 24.4 per cent in a comparable period before the war.[56] While similar figures are unavailable for collective farmers, it appears very likely that the Red Army enticed a higher proportion of peasants into the Party than did the *kolkhozes* from which they came. It is also probable that the postwar purge had a particularly severe impact on worker and peasant Communists, since their deficiencies in political knowledge made them peculiarly vulnerable to expulsion.

After the war, the drive to recruit the new Soviet intelligentsia and to identify the Party with the administrative, managerial, and technical elite was resumed and intensified. The proportion of workers accepted as candidates for Party membership decreased substantially. From Minsk in 1949 it was reported that only 11.6 per cent of the postwar Party recruits were workers. In Kirghizia the corresponding figure was 15.9 per cent. In December 1951 a writer in *Bol'shevik* pointed out that workers constituted only 22.7 per cent of those admitted into the Party in Yaroslavl province in the preceding eighteen months.[57] At the Congress of the Kazakhstan Party in December 1951, the proportion of workers was reported as 26 per cent, compared with 46 per cent in the employee category.[58] The pattern which emerges from these fragmentary reports testifies to a consolidation of the dominant position of the new Soviet intelligentsia in the Party.

The Party retained its predominantly urban character in the war and postwar years. Its strength in rural areas, however, appeared to be increasing. By 1947 the number of rural Communists totaled 1,714,000, or approximately 27 per cent of the Party membership.[59] Of this total, however, a substantial number probably consisted of rural administrative and technical personnel and the bureaucracies of the *kolkhozes*, state farms, and machine-tractor stations. The significant absence of statistics on the number of Communist collective farmers would seem to indicate that the Party continues to be thinly represented in this stratum. On the rare occa-

TABLE 9

PARTY MEMBERSHIP IN SELECTED OBLASTS, KRAIS, AND NATIONAL REPUBLICS AND RATIO OF PARTY MEMBERSHIP TO POPULATION, 1952

	Voting Delegates, 19th Party Congress (1 delegate per 5000 members)	Party Members (candidates excluded)	Estimated Population (1950)	Ratio of Party Members per 1000 Population
USSR	1,192	6,013,259	201,300,000	29.91
Moscow	129	646,000	9,450,000	68.36
Leningrad	60	300,000	4,800,000	62.50
Gorki	25	125,000	3,600,000	34.72
Sverdlovsk	23	115,000	3,000,000	38.33
Rostov	18	90,000	2,550,000	35.29
Saratov	18	90,000	2,400,000	37.50
Khabarovsk	18	90,000	1,250,000	72.00
Krasnodarsk	17	85,000	3,000,000	28.33
Voronezh	17	85,000	3,450,000	24.64
Primorye	17	85,000	1,475,000	57.63
Chelyabinsk	16	80,000	2,100,000	38.09
Kuibyshev	16	80,000	1,950,000	41.02
Bashkiria	15	75,000	3,000,000	25.00
Tatar	15	75,000	2,850,000	26.31
Molotov	14	70,000	2,250,000	31.11
Kemerovo	14	70,000	1,950,000	35.89
Altai	14	70,000	2,400,000	29.17
Ukraine	153	765,000	40,500,000	18.88
Kiev	20	100,000	3,500,000	28.57
Kharkov	16	80,000	2,500,000	32.00
Stalinsk	15	75,000	3,000,000	25.00
Dnepropetrovsk	12	60,000	2,200,000	27.27
Kazakhstan	42	210,000	6,000,000	35.00
Georgia	32	160,000	3,555,000	45.00
Belorussia	28	140,000	7,220,000	19.39
Uzbekistan	25	125,000	6,000,000	20.83
Azerbaidjan	23	115,000	3,100,000	37.09
Armenia	—	61,440(1949)	1,345,000	45.69
Latvia	—	50,000	1,800,000	27.78
Lithuania	—	36,000	2,700,000	13.33
Esthonia	—	31,000	1,000,000	31.00
Moldavia	—	22,266(1949)	2,660,000	8.00

sions when concrete data are cited, presumably to present the most favorable picture, this weakness becomes apparent. At the Azerbaidjan Party Congress in May 1951, M. D. Bagirov boasted that of 672 rural candidates for Party membership admitted into the Azerbaidjan Party organization from January 1949 to April 1951, 226 or 36 per cent were collective farmers.[60] In 1948, according to Khrushchëv, then secretary of the Ukrainian Party, only 11,895 of the 28,207 collective farms in the Ukraine had Party organizations.[61] One of the factors contributing to the decision in 1950 to merge collective farms into larger units was the sparseness of Party representation in many of the old *kolkhozes*. In reducing the number of *kolkhozes* from 254,000 on January 1, 1950, to approximately 97,000 in October 1952,[62] it became possible to establish Party units on the great majority of the collective farms and to strengthen direct Party controls appreciably. Although the rural Party organizations still remain the weakest link in the Party apparatus, their strategic leverage in the countryside appears to have been substantially increased by the amalgamation movement.

The Role of Women

One of the striking by-products of the war years was the enhanced role of women in the Party. The proportion of women increased from 14.9 per cent on January 1, 1941, to 17 per cent on January 1, 1945, and 20.7 per

---

NOTE TO TABLE 9

Source: Voting delegate or membership figures derived from Report of the Mandate Commission of the Nineteenth Party Congress, *Pravda*, October 9, 1952, p. 6; population estimates derived from Theodore Shabad, *Geography of the USSR* (New York: Columbia University Press, 1951).

Note: The membership figures in this table are approximations derived by multiplying the number of voting delegates assigned to a particular Party organization by 5,000. The rules of the Congress specified that each voting delegate would represent 5,000 Party members. In cases where exact membership figures are available, they do not always correspond with the data listed above. As of September 1, 1952, the exact membership of the Georgian Party was 160,045, compared with the 160,000 in the table. The Azerbaidjan membership was 103,517 instead of 115,000; the Kazakhstan figure was 201,687 instead of 210,000; and the Ukrainian Party organization had only 676,190 members rather than the 765,000 indicated in the table. (See *Current Digest of the Soviet Press*, IV, no. 41 [November 22, 1952], 7, 16, 24, 29.) These discrepancies are probably explained by the fact that the Congress delegations include representatives from the military and MGB-MVD units stationed in the area and that the latter are not ordinarily included in the membership reported at regional or republic Party congresses. This supposition is supported by the size of the delegations from Khabarovsk and Primorye (the Maritime Province) which almost certainly reflects the concentration of units of the Soviet Far Eastern Army and MGB-MVD security troops in the area.

cent on July 1, 1950.[63] During the war the burden of sustaining the home front fell heavily on Soviet women, and many were rapidly advanced to positions formerly reserved for men. Among those admitted to territorial (nonmilitary) Party organizations during the war, 41.3 per cent were women.[64] This trend perpetuated itself in the postwar period and was also reflected in the increasing utilization of women for Party administrative work. On January 1, 1945, 40,370 women functioned as secretaries of primary Party units. By January 1, 1950, their number had increased to 47,106. On January 1, 1945, there were 951 women serving as secretaries of district, city, region, provincial, territorial, and republic committees; by January 1, 1950, 1,386 women held such posts.[65] At the Nineteenth Party Congress in October 1952 women accounted for 12.3 per cent of the total number of voting delegates, compared with 9.1 per cent at the Eighteenth Party Congress in 1939. The directing agencies of the Party, however, remained masculine preserves. No woman was named to the new Presidium. Of the 125 full members of the Central Committee chosen by the Nineteenth Party Congress, two were women; of the 111 alternate members, four were women. In certain regions, moreover, women played a markedly subordinate role.[66] The Party journal *Bol'shevik*, in its issue of January 1, 1951, noted that in the newly acquired areas such as Lithuania, Latvia, Esthonia, and the western provinces of the Ukraine and Belorussia, as well as in the Soviet republics of Central Asia, "the women's *aktiv* is still small . . . the training of cadres of women of the nationalities still lags behind." [67]

The data released by the Party since the beginning of World War II yield no specific information on the national-ethnic composition of the Party. Ethnic trends can only be inferred from the over-all figures on Party membership in the various national republics and the Great Russian regions. Table 9 summarizes the available material, drawn from the Report of the Mandate Commission of the Nineteenth Party Congress in October 1952. It should be stressed that the figures listed for various regions and national republics are totals and provide no breakdown between the local indigenous nationality and members of other nationalities who happen to hold membership in the Party organization.

As Table 9 makes clear, the Great Russian *oblasts* and *krais* were generally characterized by high rates of Party membership. This was particularly evident in the capital region of Moscow with its concentration of officialdom, but it was also true of Leningrad and other industrial areas. Party representation, however, fell off substantially in rural *oblasts*. Voronezh *oblast* in the central Black Earth area, for example, had only 24.64 Party members per thousand population, a ratio well below the national average of 29.91 per thousand.

The Transcaucasian Communist Party organizations retained the strong position which they had won in an earlier period. The Armenian Party with a representation of 45.69 Communists per thousand population, the Georgian Party with 45 per thousand, and the Azerbaidjan organization with 37.09 per thousand were all considerably in excess of the national average. Table 9 also reveals the Kazakhstan Party as surprisingly strong, with a ratio of 35 members per thousand. It is possible that this ratio is inflated because of an inadequate allowance for the substantial increase in the population of Kazakhstan in recent years.

The Ukraine, with an over-all average of 18.88 Party members per thousand population, remained one of the weaker Party bases. Party strength in the capital region of Kiev and in industrial *oblasts* such as Kharkov, Stalinsk, and Dnepropetrovsk was much closer to the national average. The low Party representation in the Ukraine was primarily a reflection of the thinness of Party membership in rural areas. Other areas in which Party membership fell substantially behind the national average included Moldavia with 8 members per thousand, Lithuania with 13.33 per thousand, Bolorussia with 19.39 per thousand, and the Central Asian Uzbek republic with 20.83 per thousand. All these represented areas of previous weakness. The Latvian and Esthonian parties, which had also been numbered among the weaker organizations in the immediate postwar period, registered sharp gains in membership after 1949. By 1952 Party penetration in these republics approximated the national average. Though information on Jewish Party membership in recent years is unavailable, the postwar campaign against "rootless cosmopolitans," with its marked anti-Semitic overtones, would suggest that the eclipse of the Jewish element in the Party which set in during the thirties has probably been accentuated.

During the war years the Party maintained its position as the party of youth. Indeed the mass Party recruitment of Red Army soldiers substantially lowered the average age of Party members. By 1946, 18.3 per cent of all members were under twenty-five; the corresponding figure before the war was 8.9 per cent. In 1946, 63.6 per cent of the membership was under thirty-five years.[68] While the Party rank-and-file retained its youthful character, the top leadership of the Party was perceptibly aging. At the Eighteenth Congress in 1939, 49.5 per cent of the voting delegates were under thirty-five. At the Nineteenth Congress in 1952, only 5.9 per cent of the delegates were in this age group. In 1939, 32 per cent of the delegates were in the thirty-six to forty age group; in 1952, only 17.7 per cent were in this age range. In 1952, 61.1 per cent of the delegates were between forty and fifty years of age; in 1939, only 15.5 per cent of the delegates had been in this age span. The over-fifty group claimed 15.3 per cent of the delegates in 1952 compared with a mere 3 per cent in 1939.[69]

Educational qualifications of Party members continued to show improvement. By 1947 the Party claimed more than 400,000 Communists with higher education.[70] This represented 6.32 per cent of the total Party membership as compared with 5.08 per cent in 1939. Nearly 1,300,000 Communists, or 20.54 per cent of the Party, were listed in 1947 as having completed secondary schools.[71] This compared with 14.2 per cent of the Party membership in 1939. The improvement in the upper sector of the Party apparatus was even more impressive. At the Eighteenth Party Congress in 1939, only 26.5 per cent of the delegates had a higher education.[72] At the Nineteenth Congress 709, or more than 58 per cent of the 1,192 voting delegates, had equivalent educational backgrounds. Of the 709 delegates with a higher education, 282 were engineers.[73] The absorption of the new Soviet technical cadres into the inner circles of the Party was strikingly manifest.[74]

In consolidating its position as a governing elite, the Party leadership has tended to anchor its power on the support of the new Soviet technical and administrative intelligentsia. Its recruitment policy reflects this emphasis. It seeks to incorporate the rising stratum in Soviet society — the engineers and technicians, the plant managers, the Party and governmental bureaucrats, and the "leading workers."

The membership of the Party mirrors its weaknesses as well as its strength. In enlisting the new Soviet intelligentsia as its primary cadre, the Party's position among rank-and-file workers has tended to weaken, and it risks increasing isolation from the production line. Its representation in rural areas is thin and consists in large part of administrative and directing personnel in rural centers, *kolkhozes*, state farms, and machine-tractor stations. The ordinary collective farmer, even more than the ordinary factory worker, falls outside the circle of the Party elite. While the Party has strengthened its position among women, their role remains limited, and in outlying areas such as the Central Asian republics they continue largely inactive in Party affairs. The nationality weaknesses of the Party are the obverse of its Great Russian strength. The Ukraine, Belorussia, Moldavia, and Lithuania remain retrograde areas in terms of Communist penetration. While the Party has expanded its membership in the Central Asian republics over the years, these regions, too, represent relatively weak Communist outposts. Party controls become increasingly attenuated as one moves from the great industrial centers into the peripheral areas of the border nationalities and the agricultural hinterland.

The composition of the Party reflects an increasing crystallization of elitist tendencies. All the functional imperatives of industrialization drive in this direction. If these tendencies continue unarrested, the Party faces the prospect of increasing alienation from the mass of workers and peasants who remain outside its ranks. To obviate this danger, the Party may periodically broaden its membership. At the same time, it can discharge its governing responsibilities effectively only by assimilating the most highly trained and educated representatives of the oncoming generations. The ability of the Party to survive as a functional elite may well depend on its continuing skill in balancing these diverse pressures.

Chapter 9

The Komsomol—
Youth under Dictatorship

One of the most striking characteristics of modern totalitarianism is the conscious attention which it devotes to the organization and indoctrination of youth. The Soviet dictatorship from its earliest days has carried on such activity at a level of intensity unmatched by its now defunct Fascist and Nazi rivals. Through the Young Communist League, or Komsomol, and its junior affiliate, the Pioneers, the leaders of the regime undertake to harness the energy of youth and to prepare its most active and loyal members for Party responsibilities. The membership of the Communist Party today is overwhelmingly composed of individuals who served their apprenticeship in the Young Pioneers and the Komsomol, and waiting at the threshold of power is a new generation of approximately sixteen million Komsomols and nineteen million Pioneers from whose ranks the Communist elite of the future is to be recruited.[1]

What has been the history of this effort to assimilate and discipline the younger generation? What manner of training do the young people receive? What are the values that the present leadership seeks to implant in them? What motives induce them to join the Komsomol? How is the Komsomol organized? What are the activities of its membership? How are the oncoming waves of Soviet youth relating themselves to the society which has produced them? To what extent are they deeply loyal to the present regime? Is there evidence of disaffection among them, and if so, does this disaffection present any important threat to the stability of the regime itself?

To put these questions is not to suggest that anything resembling conclusive answers can be deduced from the available data. Interpretations of the moods and attitudes of Soviet youth run a spectacular gamut. The official view of the Party leadership is that the younger generation is fanatically and passionately devoted to Communism. The counterclaim of some former Soviet citizens is that the whole body of Soviet youth is ready to rise up in revolt against the regime at the first opportunity. Neither of these extreme views can stand serious scrutiny. Even a cursory reading of the literature of self-criticism in the Soviet press yields sufficient denunciations of political passivity in Komsomol circles to cast grave doubt on the official picture of Soviet youth as a monolithic embodiment of zealous orthodoxy. On the other hand, interviews with Soviet defectors and non-returners, many of whom themselves passed through the Komsomol school, indicate the continued presence, though in diminished degree, of a hard core of fanaticism among Komsomols. Such testimony from individuals who bitterly hate the Soviet regime makes it impossible to describe the younger generation as entirely lost to the Communist cause.[2]

The Growth and Development of the Komsomol

The problem of the generations in Soviet society can only be understood in terms of the historical perspective in which it has evolved. Every generation bears the unmistakable imprint of the formative experiences to which it has been exposed. The history of Soviet youth, and indeed of Soviet society, has been a unique tale of turmoil in a turbulent age. The Revolution, the Civil War and War Communism, the NEP, the Five-Year Plans, collectivization, the Great Purge of 1936–1938, World War II, and the years of strain which followed have all left their marks on succeeding generations of youth. Over most of the period, life has been lived in an atmosphere attuned to crisis, of dangers real and fancied, of superhuman demands on youth, of endless emergencies, and of constant strife and tension. The casualties have been high. The Revolution has consumed its children as well as its makers. Like most revolutionaries who attempt a sharp break with the past, the Communist leadership has placed its primary reliance on youth to generate the momentum of innovation. It was Lenin who wrote, long before the Revolution, "We mean to leave the collection of weary thirty-year-old ancients, revolutionaries 'come to their senses,' and Social Democratic renegades to people like the Constitutional Democrats. We always mean to remain the Party for the youth of that class to which the future belongs."[3]

Before the Revolution, the Bolsheviks maintained no separate organization for the younger generation. The reason was an obvious one. The cadres of the Party were themselves recruited largely from the youth. Through these cadres the Party sought to penetrate and exercise influence on the circles of young students and workers which sprang up sporadically in the period of the 1905 revolution and the years thereafter.[4] Indeed, a resolution calling for such action among students, introduced by Lenin at the Second Congress of the Russian Social-Democratic Labor Party in 1903 (when the Bolsheviks and the Mensheviks were still organizationally united), represents the first recorded party action in this area.[5] But until 1917, aspirations reached far beyond achievement, and the Bolsheviks remained a small sectarian group with little in the way of mass influence either among the youth or their elders.

Even after the outbreak of the March Revolution, the Bolsheviks were slow to assume the initiative in organizing an affiliated youth movement. In Petrograd, the storm center of revolutionary activity, the leadership in youth organization was taken by an idealistic young student, P. Shevtsov, who attempted to turn the energies of youth in a cultural and nonpolitical direction. Under his auspices, a number of young workers in the Petrograd factories were banded together in a league called "Work and Light" which repudiated the class struggle and called upon youth "to join no party, but to work together ourselves according to the precepts of brotherly feeling." [6] The program of the league urged a great expansion of schools, the foundation of a university for working-class youth, the establishment of clubs and theaters, youth hostels, and excursions into the woods to share the joys of nature.

The vagueness of this program, removed as it was from the immediate realities of political and economic struggle, provided the Bolsheviks with their opportunity to make a vigorous counterappeal to working-class youth. They sent their representatives into the Work and Light league with the objective of attacking its program, discrediting Shevtsov, and winning support for their cause. Under the leadership of a twenty-one-year-old Bolshevik, V. Alekseyev, a Socialist Association of Young Workers was organized. It called for an intensification of the class struggle and immediate measures to improve the working conditions of juvenile labor. Faced with a vigorous challenge from this group, Shevtsov began to lose his grip over his own league, and in August 1917 Work and Light was disbanded by a vote of its members. Meanwhile, the Socialist Association of Young Workers expanded into a city-wide organization of working-class youth with a program copied largely from the Bolshevik model. By December 1917 it had attained a membership of approximately 15,000.[7] In the large industrial centers, the Bolsheviks sought to increase their appeal to youth by stressing such popular reforms as the outlaw of child labor, the six-hour day for young workers, the establishment of minimum wages, social insurance benefits, compulsory free education for those under the age of sixteen, and the right to vote at the age of eighteen. By identifying themselves with the specific economic grievances of young workers, the Bolsheviks mobilized an additional increment of support in their successful bid for power in November 1917.

The organization of a Communist youth affiliate on an all-Russian scale was delayed until almost a year after the November Revolution. The 176 delegates who foregathered for the First Congress of the Komsomol, or Communist Association of Youth, in Moscow from October 29 to November 4, 1918, represented an initial membership of only 22,100.[8] They were, as was to be expected, overwhelmingly Communist in their political sympathies, but also present was a scattering of non-Party youth as well as a few delegates from other left-wing groups still collaborating with the Communists. The major struggle at the Congress took place over the designation of the organization as Communist. Some expressed concern that this appellation would frighten youth away from affiliation, but their anxiety was swept aside by the majority. The Congress, although proclaiming itself an "independent" organization, declared its solidarity with the Party and adopted the Communist tag by an overwhelming majority. At the Second Congress, meeting in October 1919, with 96,000 members represented, the Party bond was tightened. The Congress expressed its complete adherence to the program and tactics of the Party and recognized its own Central Committee as immediately subordinate to the Party Central Committee.

During the Civil War period, all of the energies of the Komsomol were concentrated on the struggle against the Whites. In successive mobilizations the Komsomols were rushed to the front, where they functioned as agitators, commissars, and shock troops to provide leadership and inspiration for less dependable conscripts. But through the end of 1919, they remained a relatively small band, and it was not until the prospects of victory brightened during 1920 that they began to take on the character of a mass organization. By the time the Third Congress met in October 1920, their membership had climbed to approximately 480,000.

The rapid growth in membership brought forth new problems. The Komsomol was not then as tightly controlled as it was later to become. It began to spawn deviations.[9] Even before the Second Congress, a group led by Dunayevsky had been pressing for the organization of special youth sections in the trade unions. This was denounced by the Party as an effort to pit the interests of young workers against those of their elders and as a syndicalist deviation detracting from the authority of the Komsomol organization itself. Dunayevsky and others continued to urge wider mass participation in determining Komsomol policies, but their claims were decisively rejected, and disciplinary measures were taken against the deviators. Restiveness under the central controls which were already emerging within the Komsomol found its expression in renewed demands for more organizational democracy and local autonomy. This position was strongly espoused by the so-called "Ukrainian opposition," which also insisted on the exclusion of intellectuals from the association.

These oppositionist tendencies, which had their analogue in the Workers' Opposition within the Party itself, were sharply attacked and repudiated at the Third Komsomol Congress.

The Third Congress marked the beginning of the turn from war to peace. In addressing the Congress, Lenin sounded a new call. "The task before the elder generation of revolutionaries," he declared, "was comparatively simple. For them it was a matter of doing away with the bourgeoisie, of inspiring hatred for it among the masses, of awakening class-consciousness in the workers. The task before your generation is infinitely more complicated: the erection of the Communist society." [10] Lenin's injunction to the Congress to "learn, learn, learn,"to master the knowledge that the despised capitalist society had accumulated, to practice discipline, and to seek proficiency in the prosaic tasks of school and workshop came as something of a shock. The shock was accentuated by the adoption of the New Economic Policy in the spring of 1921.

After the heroics of Civil War battlefields and War Communism, adjustment to the NEP did not come easily. To many, the NEP seemed a retreat from socialism, a surrender after victory. Opposition to it was lively and violent in Komsomol circles. A few of the more fanatic committed suicide in protest. Still others were unable to make the transition from military to civilian life and sank into despair as unhappy victims of the Revolution they had helped to create. Grumbling among young workers mounted as working conditions failed to register hoped-for improvements and as unemployment increased. Enthusiasm gave way to disillusionment, and the Komsomol organization itself underwent a crisis. By October 1922, at the meeting of the Fifth Congress, membership had plummeted to 247,000, and Party leaders were seriously alarmed.[11]

From 1922 on, strenuous efforts were made to recapture and consolidate the loyalty of Soviet youth. One of the resolutions passed by the Fifth Congress provided for the organization of the Pioneer association to attract the pre-Komsomol generation and to condition and prepare it for Komsomol membership. Measures were taken to improve working conditions for young factory workers and to give them some degree of protection against unemployment by imposing a minimum quota of juveniles on every industrial undertaking.[12] The system of factory schools (FSU) was extended, thus making available a modicum of education to young workers in the factories. Efforts were also made to compensate for the weakness of the organization in the countryside by sending Komsomol activists to rural centers to recruit members and build up local organizations. Greater stress was placed on political indoctrination within the Red Army, where peasant youths called up for military service were more amenable to Komsomol blandishments than they were in the villages where counterinfluences were still powerful.

As a result of these measures, the tide was reversed. By January 1, 1924, the membership of the Komsomol again exceeded 400,000.[13] By January 1, 1925, after the "Lenin Levy" when the Party appealed to youth to commemorate Lenin's death by closing ranks, membership rose to a million. The second million was reached in 1927 on the eve of the Five Year Plan.[14]

While the Komsomol registered substantial gains in membership during the later phases of the NEP, the period was not without its problems. The level of political literacy among Komsomols was low, particularly in rural areas. Among the more politically alert, the grey dullness of the NEP dampened enthusiasm. The strong response which Trotsky and the Left Opposition received among the more educated and politically conscious Komsomols becomes explicable against this background. Trotsky's call for world revolution evoked stirring memories of the first days of the Revolution and drew on a tradition of militant activism which the NEP had the effect of thwarting. The purge of the Left Opposition within the Party left its scar on the Komsomol, though as events turned out, the wound healed quickly.

The initiation of the Five Year Plan in 1928 aroused an outburst of zeal and fervor among the Komsomols for which only the period of Revolution and Civil War furnished a parallel.[15] Here was an enterprise which in its immensity, its call for sacrifice, and its promise for the future was peculiarly appealing to youthful idealism. Komsomols were mobilized in the thousands to construct such industrial giants as the Stalingrad tractor factory, the Dnepropetrovsk electric station, and the new factories in the Urals and Siberia. They were drafted to work in the Don Basin when coal production lagged. They built a new industrial center on the Amur River in the Far East named Komsomolsk in their honor. They were sent by the thousands to participate in collectivization, to liquidate the kulaks, to help establish *kolkhozes*, and to staff the new machine-tractor stations. They set the pace as *udarniks*, or shock brigadiers, and as leaders in socialist competition. They took upon themselves the task of stamping out illiteracy and conducting anti-religious propaganda among the backward masses. They crowded the newly-established technical institutes to prepare themselves to become the engineers and industrial managers of the morrow.

The outpouring of energy was impressive, yet the almost superhuman demands which the Plan imposed on youth also exacted their toll. The initial delirium of dedication and enthusiasm was succeeded by more prosaic daily irritations compounded of poor food, crowded housing, and the constant spur to make bricks out of straw. The more tenderhearted among the Komsomols were broken by the harsh realities of dekulakization and famine in the villages. "These years are very difficult for our young people," wrote the Soviet novelist Gladkov. "They burn out quickly, over-work themselves, and suffer from nervous troubles; at the age of eighteen or nineteen many are either stunted or dried up and old in spirit. No fewer than one-third of the patients in the sanitarium are Komsomolites, and they are all like aged, used-up people, who have gone through a great deal already." [16]

It was the hard and the tough who survived. The sensitive and the weak dropped out as casualties of forced-draft industrialization and collectivization. Their places were taken by representatives of the oncoming generation recruited from the Pioneers. The size of the Komsomol organization continued to expand. By the time of the Ninth Congress of the Komsomols in 1931, membership reached the three million mark. At the Tenth Congress in April 1936 the membership approximated four million.[17]

The mid-thirties marked an important turn in the membership policies and program of the Komsomol. Until that period, the Komsomol had been regarded as a relatively exclusive class organization. The rules of the Komsomol described it as "a mass organization, proletarian in its essence, uniting in its ranks the broad strata of the foremost class-conscious and politically literate youth." [18] Membership was mainly re-cruited from proletarian elements in the cities and from the poorer peas-antry in the villages. At the 1936 Congress, the rules were modified to liberalize the conditions of admission. Henceforth, the Komsomol was to be "a mass non-party organization, affiliated with the VKP(b) [the Party], which unites in its ranks the broad stratum of the progressive, politically literate, toiling youth of the town and village." Social origins were no longer decisive in determining eligibility for membership. The new rules stressed instead the broader criterion of loyalty to the Soviet regime.[19]

This deliberate decision to widen the base of the Komsomol was ac-companied by a marked shift of program. In the stress on emergency economic activity during the First Five Year Plan, the Communist educa-tion of the youth was neglected. "Some of our regional committees," re-ported A. V. Kosarëv, first secretary of the Komsomol, "had become, so to say, some sort of small, sickly economic Narkomats [ministries] . . . We have to remember that our basic task is the organization and Communist education of the youth and children." [20] Under the banner of Stalin's new watchword "Cadres decides everything," the main task of the Komsomol was reformulated as the Communist indoctrination of youth. The Kom-somol leadership was also called upon to emphasize "cultural" as well as political work, to organize athletic competitions, ski excursions, musicales, dramatics, dances, and evening literary discussions in order to minister to the many-sided interests of youth and to attract its support. Under the impetus of these measures, membership grew sharply. By October 1939 it had climbed to nine million.[21]

The late thirties brought trials and tribulations as well as successes. The Great Purge had its maximum impact on the Party, but it also struck the Komsomols hard. The central apparatus of the Komsomol was decimated. A. V. Kosarëv, the first secretary, was removed, and many of the top functionaries of the organization disappeared with him.[22] At the height of the Yezhovshchina, a veritable reign of terror was unleashed among Komsomols as well as Party members. Denunciations were rife in all the local organizations. Expulsions took place in the hundreds and thousands as the NKVD relentlessly pursued the so-called "Trotskyite-Bukharinist-German-Japanese-Fascist spies, diversionists, murderers, double-dealers, hostile elements, and enemies of the people" who were alleged to have infiltrated the Komsomol as well as the Party.[23] By the spring of 1938, the Party leadership was prepared to admit that many mistakes had been committed in the course of the wholesale expulsions. Efforts were made to repair the damage by punishing "slanderers responsible . . . for unjust accusations" and restoring some of the victims to their former status in the Komsomol organization.[24] But the heritage of bitterness left by the Purge persisted, and its continuing effects were visible as one of the motivations which inspired Soviet defection during and after World War II.

Not all of the consequences of the Purge, however, were negative. The havoc wrought by the Purge among the older generation was much greater than among the youth. In the process, many responsible posts in both the Party and governmental hierarchies were vacated, presenting the Komsomol activists who survived the Purge with magnificent opportunities for rapid promotion to positions of influence and large responsibilities. Those Komsomols who were catapulted to power over the graves of their elders were welded to the regime and incorporated in its leadership group.

Other developments in the prewar years served to generate discontent among some members of the Komsomol rank-and-file. On October 2, 1940, the government instituted a system of tuition fees for the last three years of secondary education and higher schools.[25] It also established a State Labor Reserve scheme whereby each year up to a million youths between the ages of fourteen and seventeen were to be drafted for training as industrial workers.[26] The introduction of tuition fees meant that those students who could not qualify for scholarships or were unable to draw on family resources to support them had to abandon their hopes of higher education. The advantages conferred on the financially better-situated left a reservoir of bitterness among those who were forced to withdraw from the higher schools as a result of the decree. At the same time, the restrictions on freedom of occupational choice as a result of the labor draft also induced frustration and discontent. While it is difficult to appraise the significance of the dissatisfaction produced by these measures, the testimony of young Soviet defectors and non-returners is virtually unanimous in stressing the growth of a mood of disenchantment in that segment of Soviet youth which was most adversely affected.

The success of the Soviet army in surviving the Nazi onslaught and pressing on to victory may suggest that the mood was a passing one or that in any case it did not go deep enough to affect the will to fight. Yet the problem of the loyalty of Soviet youth to the regime cannot be disposed of with a mere reference to the pragmatic fact of Soviet victory. The mass surrenders of the early days of the war point to a serious problem of morale as well as difficulties of matériel and generalship. All of the evidence available through interviews indicates that the mass atrocities committed by the Nazis in the course of their Russian campaign and the contempt with which they treated the Slav *Untermenschen* had much to do with stiffening resistance. Hatred of the Nazis unleashed a genuine and widespread national upsurge of feeling which the Party leadership was shrewd enough both to stimulate and exploit. Communist slogans were muted, and the wellsprings of national sentiment were tapped to the full. The bars of admission to Party and Komsomol were lowered for members of the armed forces; the millions who enrolled during the war responded primarily to patriotic appeals. By October 1945 the claimed membership of the Komsomol was fifteen million, approximately half of the population in the eligible age group.[27]

After the war there was a sharp drop in Komsomol membership. The data released on the occasion of the Eleventh Congress of the Komsomol in March 1949 showed a membership roll of 9,283,289, a figure roughly equivalent to the 1939 membership.[28] No official explanations of this decline were vouchsafed, though reports in the Komsomol press indicated considerable concern over the large number of automatic exclusions as "a result of non-payment of dues, failure to attend meetings, and unwillingness to discharge the social and political obligations that go with membership." [29] At the Congress, the Komsomol by-laws were amended to lower the age of admission from fifteen to fourteen, and the candidacy stage was abolished.

After the Eleventh Congress, an intensive campaign was waged to increase Komsomol membership. By August 1952 more than sixteen million youths were enrolled in its ranks.[30] According to N. Mikhailov, then Komsomol first secretary, the organization enlisted nearly 75 per cent of all university students, 61 per cent of those attending industrial schools, and about 65 per cent of the students in the seven- and ten-year schools who were eligible for membership.[31] The Komsomol appeared well on the way to becoming an all-embracing mass organization of Soviet youth rather than an elite category second only to the Party.

The history of the Komsomol is a record of persistent and strenuous efforts by the Party leadership to base itself on the support of the on-coming Soviet generations. Despite these efforts, the daily experiences of life under the Soviet regime erode loyalties among the youth as well as among their elders and make necessary the widespread use of repressive and disciplinary measures. Terror and secret police surveillance are integral features of the Soviet system. This does not mean, however, that the role of indoctrination as it expresses itself through the Komsomol or other channels can be dismissed as without significance. Each new generation as it grows to maturity offers the Party leadership a fresh opportunity to implant its stamp upon the future. The capacity of a totalitarian regime to mold the minds of the young while they are still malleable is a formidable weapon. Its power should not be underrated.

Training the Komsomols

The process starts in the kindergarten where children's play, singing, and storytelling are used, as a recent Soviet textbook put it, "to instill love of the Soviet fatherland, its people, its leaders, and the Soviet Army." [32] The child is first enrolled in the "Little Octobrists" where his political indoctrination begins. At the age of nine, he joins the Young Pioneers. [33] Membership in the Young Pioneers, which now approximates nineteen million, is virtually universal in the eligible age group of nine to fifteen. Indeed, the drive to affiliate is so great in the early impressionable years that the threat of exclusion is frequently a sufficient sanction to discipline the most unruly. Entrance into the Pioneers is the occasion for an impressive initiation ceremony replete with symbolism and emblems calculated to appeal to the very young. [34]

Once enrolled in the Pioneers, the new member becomes part of a "link" of eight to twelve youngsters who elect their own leader. The "links" are united in a "brigade" with about forty members in the same or adjoining classes. Each brigade chooses its council of five to represent it and carries on its activities under the direction of a Komsomol leader. Their activities vary with the age level of the Pioneers. In the younger classes, meetings provide the occasion for tales of the childhood of Lenin or Stalin or stories of heroism on the part of young Pioneers in the war against the Nazis. With older children, political instruction becomes more pointed. The biographies of Lenin and Stalin are studied more carefully, with emphasis on their revolutionary activities. The heroic exploits of the Soviet army are celebrated; there are lectures on the Constitution, and national and international events are reviewed from the Party standpoint.

Political instruction in the narrow sense forms only one part of the

Pioneer program. There is also a variety of organized activities such as excursions for nature study; trips to museums and places of historical interest; athletic competitions; literary, dramatic, and musical evenings; and opportunities to pursue hobbies at school or at the so-called Houses of Pioneers which are set aside as centers of extracurricular activity. There is the requirement to engage in socially useful work, which may embrace such diverse activities as helping to edit a wall newspaper for Pioneers, gathering scrap, working in the school garden or on a neighboring *kolkhoz*, or even helping combat "religious prejudices" in the home. The interference with school programs which such assignments breed has led to periodic protests by Soviet school authorities against overburdening the child with outside tasks. The present tendency is to integrate Pioneer activities as closely as possible with the school, to emphasize classroom obligations as the first responsibility of the Pioneer, to stress the authority of the teacher, and to arrange the Pioneer program so that it supports, rather than conflicts with, the school curriculum.

The Pioneers are designed to take care of children between the ages of nine and fifteen. At the age of fourteen, however, the child becomes eligible for membership in the Komsomols, provided, of course, that he can satisfy the conditions for admission.[35] These conditions include recommendation by one member of the Communist Party or by two persons who have been Komsomol members for at least a year. Recommendation by the council of a Pioneer brigade is equivalent to one recommendation by a Komsomol member. The candidate for admission must be approved both by the local Komsomol organization which he seeks to enter and by the district or town committee which exercises jurisdiction over that local organization.

Enrollment in the Komsomols is thus a much more selective process than joining the Pioneers. The Komsomol is the reservoir from which Party members will be recruited, and in the eyes of the Party leadership at least, this is the period of tutelage when qualifications can be sifted and political ardor tested. The rules of the organization require each member to study Marxism-Leninism, to engage in constant efforts to raise his political literacy, to expound the political line of the Party and the Komsomol organization, to participate actively in the political life of the country, to provide an example of socialist attitudes toward work and study, to protect socialist property, and to struggle decisively against all breaches of socialist legality and order. The Komsomol is also supposed to demonstrate political vigilance by guarding military and state secrets; to master the cultural, scientific, and technical knowledge which will enable him to perfect his qualifications; to study the art of war; to be always ready to give his strength and if necessary his life for the defense of his socialist fatherland; to seek to stamp out drunkenness, hooliganism, the remains of backward religious prejudices, and uncomradely attitudes toward women; to participate actively in the work of his Komsomol organization; to attend all meetings; and to fulfill all commands swiftly and accurately.[36]

These requirements represent a Party ideal rather than a realistic description of the behavior of a rank-and-file Komsomol initiate. There are Komsomol activists who seek to approximate the ideal and who demonstrate all the hallmarks of ideological devotion and dedication. But if the testimony of ex-Komsomol defectors is to be credited, this group constitutes a small minority, perhaps no greater than 10 to 20 per cent of the membership. The motives that inspire others to affiliate tend to be both more earthy and more complex. For many, careerism apparently plays a major role. The knowledge that Komsomol and Party membership opens the way to power and preferment in the Soviet system is a strong inducement for the ambitious to affiliate even when ideological fervor burns low. Sometimes the attraction of membership is predominantly social. Young women among the Soviet non-returners point especially to Komsomol-sponsored discussion clubs, excursions, dances, and musicales as contributing greatly to the attractions of membership. Some ex-Komsomols among the defectors emphasize the pride which they felt in being singled out as of leadership caliber. Others report that they were so molded and formed by previous indoctrination that they simply accepted Komsomol membership as a natural expression of the role which they were expected to play in life. This attitude of uncritical acknowledgment of the existing structure of authority appears to be widespread, at least until it is challenged by unhappy experiences in Soviet society, exposure to the West, or other corrosive influences.

Organization of the Komsomols

The organization of the Komsomols is closely modeled on the hierarchical pattern of its big brother, the Communist Party.[37] At the bottom of the pyramid are the primary organizations in factories, collective farms, state farms, educational and other state institutions. Each primary organization must have at least three members and is established with the consent of the district or town committee which exercises supervision over it. When a primary organization consists of more than a hundred members, it may be broken down into sub-groups in shops of a factory, different faculties of a university, and so on. When a group has less than ten members, a secretary is selected to provide leadership. In larger groups, a committee or bureau as well as a secretary serve as the directing nucleus. Both perform their Komsomol duties in addition to their regular employment. Full-time Komsomol secretaries are ordinarily assigned by the central apparatus only to important enterprises or institutions where there is a substantial membership and a work program requiring their exclusive attention. In most cases, the primary Komsomol organizations operate under the control of the district or town Komsomol committees and their secretaries, but in the armed forces and in other institutions where special political sections have been established, the line of responsibility is directly to the head of the political section or to his assistant in charge of Komsomol activity. In units of the armed forces, the Komsomol organizations function under the immediate direction of the Assistant Commander for Political Affairs and in close collaboration with the Party organization in the unit. The chain of command in such cases runs through the armed forces' political hierarchy rather than to the apparatus of district and regional Komsomol committees.*

At the district or town level, supervisory power is concentrated in a committee which in turn elects a bureau and a number of secretaries. The testimony of ex-Komsomols indicates that "election" is a euphemism as far as the secretaries are concerned. They report that the secretaries are full-time Komsomol functionaries who are assigned by higher echelons in the organization and are automatically confirmed in their responsibilities by the committees. The rules of the Komsomol require that district or town secretaries be members or candidates for membership in the Party with two years of experience in Komsomol work. The key figure in the organization is the first secretary. The importance of the role is attested by the fact that 99 per cent of all first secretaries in towns and 95.2 per cent of all first secretaries in districts in 1949 were Party members.[38] The first secretary exercises general supervision over all Komsomol work. More specific responsibilities — such as the direction of Pioneers; activities in schools, factories, or collective farms; work with young women; physical culture and sports; military training; and organization and agitation — are assigned to members of the district or town Komsomol apparatus.

The next higher levels in the Komsomol hierarchy are the regional and republic organizations. Here the basic pattern of organization is essentially the same as below. There is the regional or central committee of the republic, a smaller bureau within it, and a full complement of secretaries with assigned responsibilities for different aspects of Komsomol activity. Secretaries are required to be Party members with at least three years of experience in Komsomol work. Operating under them are substantial staffs of full-time Komsomol functionaries with specific responsibilities running the gamut of the organization's activities.

The central administrative organization of the Komsomol consisted in 1949 of a Central Committee of 103 members and 47 candidates, a control commission of 31 members, a bureau of 11 members, 5 secretaries,

---

* See Chapter 14, p. 411.

and a large secretariat, all of whom operated under the general direction of the first secretary, N. A. Mikhailov.[39] In November 1952 N. A. Shelepin replaced Mikhailov. Theoretically, the highest organ in the Komsomol is the All-Union Congress, which according to the rules is to meet at least once every three years. Until the Tenth Congress in 1936 meetings were held with reasonable regularity. There ensued a thirteen year break before the Eleventh Congress finally assembled in 1949. The report of the Mandate Commission of the Eleventh Congress is revealing.[40] Of the 1362 delegates who participated, 548 were leading functionaries in the Komsomol apparatus. Only 126 delegates were classified as workers and 126 as collective farmers. Of the delegates, 953 were either Party members or candidates. Despite the fact that Komsomol membership ordinarily expires at the age of twenty-six, 669 delegates were twenty-six or older. Of these, 195 delegates were over thirty. While forty-four nationalities were supposed to be represented in the Congress, 850 delegates, or over 60 per cent, were Great Russians. The impression which is unmistakably conveyed is of an assembly of Party members and *apparatchiki* disguised as over-aged Komsomols and with a marked Great Russian coloration. As in the case of the Party Congress, the Komsomol Congress appears to have developed into a rally of functionaries called together to ratify and applaud the decisions of the leadership.

According to the rules, the Central Committee exercises policy direction between Congresses while the Control Commission watches over budget, personnel, and the execution of decisions. While both these bodies meet with reasonable frequency and in fact play a much more important role than the Congress, they in turn operate under the direction of the first secretary.

Activities of the Komsomols

Although the responsibilities of the Komsomol organization embrace a wide range of diversified activities, the emphasis in contrast with the Pioneers is very much on the political. Komsomol activities include (1) political instruction of Komsomol members; (2) political instruction and leadership supplied by the Komsomols to the Pioneers, to nonaffiliated youth, and to other groups; (3) military and para-military training and physical culture and sports; (4) leadership and assistance in carrying out governmental and Party programs; (5) social and cultural activity.

The political indoctrination of all Komsomol members is a central concern of the Party. As has been observed, it begins seriously with the Pioneers and increases in scope and intensity as children grow older. No aspect of the school curriculum is without some political content, though in the upper grades, instruction in history and the Soviet Constitution is used as the primary vehicle for instilling Party consciousness and loyalty. Ordinarily, instructors in these subjects are Party members or candidates. In the advanced institutes and universities, there are also extensive programs of instruction in Ist-Mat (Historical Materialism) or Dia-Mat (Dialectical Materialism) as well as in allied political topics. Such instruction is invariably entrusted to Party members. In addition, the Komsomol organization carries on an extensive program of political education under its own auspices. In 1949 there were said to be 237,125 political circles and schools in which more than four million Komsomols were studying aspects of Marxism-Leninism.[41] This activity was directed by a corps of more than 200,000 propagandists, of whom over 45 per cent were Party members. In addition, many Komsomols were reported to be engaged in self-study programs devoted to the official history of the Party, the works of Lenin and Stalin, and other political topics.

A specialized press served as a vehicle of Komsomol and Pioneer indoctrination. *Komsomolskaya Pravda*, the central Komsomol journal, had a circulation of seven hundred thousand, and *Pionerskaya Pravda*, the central Pioneer journal, was issued in editions of one million copies. A total of thirty-seven Komsomol and seventeen Pioneer newspapers were published as well as eight Komsomol and fifteen children's magazines with a total circulation of around four million.[42]

The members of the Komsomol are not only indoctrinated, they are also required to indoctrinate. The Komsomols have a special responsibility for the Young Pioneers. The Komsomol leaders of the Pioneer brigades not only supervise play and social activity but are supposed to instill Communist consciousness in their charges. Komsomol activists also serve as counselors in Pioneer summer camps. They take the lead at school assemblies in delivering reports and speeches on current political themes. They serve as agitators to explain Party policy to the "backward" masses. They participate actively in preëlection campaigns, loan drives, and collections for a variety of revolutionary causes.

Komsomols are also expected to provide leadership in the area of physical culture, sports, and military training. The first obligation of the Komsomol, according to a recent Soviet text, is to ready himself for service in the Soviet Army. "The Komsomol member must be a leading physical culturist." [43] Preparatory to their own military service, they are required to take an active role in DOSAAF, the para-military civilian defense agency which serves the various branches of the armed services.[44] In this capacity, they engage in shooting practice, air raid drills, first aid, long marches, parachute and glider training, and political meetings at which the necessity for military preparedness is constantly reiterated.

The Komsomol is also expected to serve as a model and example for the youth of the country by assisting his Party and government in every way. He is supposed to volunteer for the most strenuous and disagreeable tasks, to help with the harvest, to enlist for the new construction job, to work in the mines, or to go wherever his organization sends him. Whether he be in the factory or the school, he is expected to be an outstanding worker, a paragon of discipline, a stimulus to his associates, and a constant help to his superiors in carrying out their responsibilities. He is adjured to be constantly on guard against "enemies of the people"; ex-Komsomols testify that the more zealous members of the organization are frequently enrolled by the secret police as *seksoty*, or informers, to report on their comrades and associates both inside and outside the Komsomol.[45]

Finally, the Komsomol is expected to cultivate many-sided interests in order to make himself a "whole" man. This is an aspect of Komsomol work which the less fervid members find most attractive because of its relative removal from the political realm. The literary, dramatic, dancing, and singing groups sponsored by the Komsomol provide some relief from the incessant and concentrated political bombardment to which youth is exposed, but even these forms of social-cultural activity are far from being apolitical. Thus, Komsomols participating in a series of evenings devoted to Pushkin discuss papers on such themes as "Pushkin and the Decembrists," "Pushkin on Capitalism," "Pushkin-Patriot," "Pushkin and the Present," and "Pushkin's Criticism of America." [46] The dramatic groups read and produce plays from the contemporary Soviet repertoire which are heavily saturated with doctrinal content. Even the dancing and singing are partly organized around political themes. In the Soviet state there is no real escape from the long arm of ideological control.

Problems of Loyalty and Disaffection

What manner of man does the Komsomol seek to create, and what values does the top Party leadership seek to implant in the minds of youth? A recent Soviet monograph entitled *Young Communists in the USSR*, which describes the demands made on Komsomols, furnishes a vivid and illuminating insight into Party goals and purposes. "The most important task of the Komsomol organization," says the monograph, "is to maintain in all the youth Soviet patriotism, Soviet national pride, the aspiration to make our Socialist state ever stronger." [47] "Whatever the Komsomol may do, with whatever works or studies he may occupy himself, he must always be prepared to enter the ranks of the Soviet Army at the first call of the Party and the Soviet government." [48] In civil as well as military life, he must provide a shining example of self-sacrifice and discipline. The Komsomol is told that he lives in the greatest and most progressive country in the world and that what gives his country its strength is the leadership of the Communist Party guided by the teachings of Marx, Engels, Lenin, and Stalin. Every Komsomol is obligated to carry out the policies of the Party steadily and consistently. "All his life must be subordinated to the great aim — the struggle for Communism." [49]

This image of the ideal Komsomol with its stress on the virtues of disciplined obedience to Party dictates embodies the ultimate values which the Party leadership seeks to inculcate. But the energies of youth, even under dictatorship, elude such tight constraints. In the words of the anonymous author of *Young Communists in the USSR*, "The survivals of the old way of life have still not been finally overcome. . . . The baneful influence of bourgeois ideology sometimes penetrates into the midst of our youth." [50]

It is no easy matter to come to any reliable judgments on the extent of disaffection among the Soviet younger generation. In the absence of free access to people in the Soviet Union itself, judgments must necessarily be reached on the basis of self-criticism appearing in Soviet publications and on interviews with ex-Komsomols and other former Soviet citizens who have had extensive contacts with Soviet young people. The data derived from these sources do not lend themselves to sweeping conclusions or exact statistical formulations; at best, when cautiously utilized, they point to the existence of certain stresses and weaknesses in the ability of the regime to command the support of youth.

It is possible on the basis of interviews with defectors to identify categories of youth whose loyalty to the regime can be considered doubtful. Children of parents who have been persecuted by the Soviet regime constitute such a group, though not all of them can be automatically classified as disloyal. They include such diverse elements as the descendants of the "former people" of Tsarist times, the offspring of the kulaks who were dispossessed in the course of collectivization, and the children of victims of the purges and of inmates of the forced labor camps. Because they belong to suspect groups, their career expectancies may be limited, and their tendency to become covert opponents of the regime may be reinforced by frustration and resentment. Even those who manage to transcend the handicaps of their social background, to enter the Komsomol, and to embark on promising careers in Soviety society, live with the constant fear that their pasts will rise up to plague them. Public affirmations of loyalty conceal inner torments and tensions.

The peasant youth in the villages and collective farms appears to be another category in which Communist indoctrination is at a relatively low level. Komsomol enrollment in rural areas has always been significantly lower than in the urban industrial centers, and despite constant efforts to improve the ratio, the villages remain a weak link in the chain.[51] It is in the countryside that cross-loyalties exert their most significant influence. The persistence among the older generation of antipathy to col-

lectivization, memories of past suffering and resentment of present hardships, and deeply ingrained religious attitudes leave an impress on the
younger generation which Communist propaganda in the schools cannot
wholly counteract or eradicate. Indeed, the relative weakness of the
Communist apparatus in the villages contributes to the persisting strength
of countervailing family influences. As the young are drained away from
the villages for military service or industrial work, they are, of course,
removed from family pressures and are subjected to more intensive Communist indoctrination. In the process, new converts are won for the Komsomol and the Party, but how genuinely and profoundly fundamental
attitudes shift is by no means clear.

Other youths whose loyalty can be regarded as at least suspect are
those who were repatriated from Germany and Austria at the end of
the war, or who participated in the Red Army advance through Eastern
and Central Europe, or who had duty later with the occupation forces
or administration. While some who shared this experience were able to
rationalize and assimilate it in terms of the propaganda stereotypes in
which they had been indoctrinated, for others the exposure to the West,
with its opportunity to see how ordinary workers and farmers live abroad,
offered such a blatant contradiction to official Party propaganda as inevitably to plant doubts and generate discontent. One of the problems of
the Soviet regime in the postwar years has been to isolate and neutralize
these centers of infection. Repatriates who have since escaped from the
Soviet Union report that they were treated by the Soviet secret police
with the utmost suspicion, that many repatriates were arrested and presumably shipped to forced labor camps, and that relatively few were
permitted to resettle in their former homes. The demobilized soldiers and
officers who related their discoveries in the West to friends and neighbors
at the end of the war are also reported to have encountered serious difficulties. The sharp drop in Komsomol enrollment after 1945 may be interpreted in part at least as an index of attrition of loyalties among returning
veterans. N. Mikhailov, in an article in *Bol'shevik* at the end of 1946,
acknowledged the mood of "demobilization" which had spread among
Soviet youth.[52] Similar problems have arisen in connection with the morale
of occupation forces, despite the most strenuous efforts by the regime to
assign only the most politically reliable troops to occupation duty. Defectors report that such troops are subjected to the most intensive indoctrination and that their contacts with the local population are limited
to an indispensable minimum. While these measures have been markedly
effective recently in checking defection, they cannot altogether prevent
the gathering of impressions whose cumulative effect may be ideologically
corrupting.

Disaffection may also be a product of individual as well as group experiences. The youth who finds himself consigned to the State Labor Reserves when he would greatly prefer to continue his education, the student who is forced to give up his studies because he cannot afford to pay the necessary tuition fees, the young worker who cannot adjust to the tight labor discipline of the Soviet system with its severe penalties for absence and tardiness, the independent-minded young intellectual who is forced to suppress his views lest it cost him his career, the victims of denunciation and purges, the politically "backward" young people who find the constantly reiterated propaganda a bore and long for "bourgeois" comforts and gayety — these are only samples of Soviet life-situations which breed irritation and frustration, though they are ordinarily well hidden under a surface show of compliance and affirmation.

Some corroboration of the existence of such attitudes among Soviet youth is available in official Soviet sources. The monograph *Young Communists in the USSR* is loud in its denunciations of "bourgeois survivals among some of the youth." [53] "It is necessary to unmask, to ridicule commonplace bourgeois tastes . . . unworthy of Soviet youth, by some youths and girls of rotten bourgeois 'culture.'" [54] "Such backward people are willing to declare: 'One's personal life is nobody's business; how I live concerns only myself and no one else' . . . Such a point of view is profoundly incorrect and pernicious." [55] "The remnants of the past find their expression also in various superstitions and prejudices which permeate youth." [56] These religious inclinations are referred to as a "delusion which poisons the hearts of young people" and which must be combated by "thoughtful and patient anti-religious propaganda." [57] The Komsomol is called upon to fight "against servility before the bourgeois West, and rotten apoliticalness." [58] Mikhailov in his keynote speech to the Eleventh Congress of the Komsomol was particularly critical of what he called the "formalism" of political work in the universities, and he sharply attacked apolitical and cosmopolitan influences in "several" Leningrad universities.[59] At the December 1949 plenum of the Central Committee which followed the Eleventh Congress, considerable concern was also expressed over the failure of several leading Komsomol organizations to recruit new members and the tendency of some of the existing membership to lose interest and drop out. The lag in rural recruitment was singled out as particularly unsatisfactory.[60]

Both Soviet reports and the information supplied by ex-Soviet citizens indicate some degree of disaffection among Soviet youth. But they sharply disagree on the quantitative distribution of such attitudes. In the official view, Soviet youth is overwhelmingly devoted and loyal, and it is only a small minority who are backward, indifferent, or hostile. The impression derived from interviews with ex-Komsomols among the Soviet defectors is quite different. They agree that there is a firm nucleus of Komsomol activists who are genuine ideological converts. This group rarely loses faith and indeed may even become more fanatic as it grows older. It is from this element that the Party and the secret police recruit their most devoted cadres. Around this nucleus, in the view of defector informants, there is a much larger circle of youth who join the Komsomol for reasons which may be described as largely careerist in character. Overtly, they are pro-regime; they take an active part in political life and go through the motions of conformity in order to make their way in Soviet society. But they lack the fanaticism of the first group. Their inner "real" political affiliation may embrace such widely different attitudes as passive acceptance of the regime, apathy, cynicism, or even bitterly suppressed resentment of the life-situations in which they find themselves. Such apt terms as "the outer cover" (*vneshnyaya obolochka*) and "the reddish scale" (*krasnovataya okalina*) have been coined to describe these careerists with the implication that you don't have to scratch very deep to find the real animal. Yet so far as surface behavior goes, they give every evidence of being not only loyal but active Soviet citizens who support the regime's purposes.

Around this group stretches the outer circle of Soviet young people who never affiliate with the Komsomol and who, in purely numerical terms, run into the millions. This circle includes such diverse elements as the majority of young collective farmers, a substantial number of young workers in industry, and many young intellectuals who evade membership even when the opportunity to affiliate is presented, sometimes at considerable risk to their future careers. It is not easy to generalize on the political attitudes of the non-Komsomols, but if defector evidence is to be trusted, they harbor the powers of inertia and apathy in Soviet society; they include much latent hostility to the regime; and they represent that sector in Soviet society where political indoctrination meets its most passive response.

The testimony of defectors, both young and old, is virtually unanimous in emphasizing a decline in the ideological *élan* of youth as compared with the idealism of Civil War days or the great outpouring of energy and dedication which accompanied the first phase of the Five Year Plans. As Soviet society has crystallized into a militarized, authoritarian, and hierarchical pattern, the apocalyptic vision of the free, classless Communist utopia becomes an increasingly tarnished dream, with little power to stir the imagination or devotion of any except the very immature. Instead, reliance is placed primarily on Soviet patriotism to provide the ideological cement which holds Soviet society together and on such practical goals as the rapid development of heavy industry and the building up of military strength as the means of expansion of Soviet power. The problem of the regime is to harness the energies of youth to achieve these goals. In attempting to solve this problem, ideology is only one of many weapons and not necessarily the most important.

Perhaps the most potent is the power of the regime to control the career expectancies of youth, to reward achievement which fits in with the goals of the leadership and to punish deviant conduct with the most severe penalties. The system of incentives offers the highest prizes to those who manage to incorporate themselves into the leadership of Party, secret police, army, and administration; it provides attractive emoluments for the intellectuals who are willing to sing the tunes of the regime; and it gives special bonuses to the managers, the engineers, and the shock brigadiers who distinguish themselves in production. It buttresses financial awards with a system of honorifics designed to be particularly attractive to the less sophisticated.

The obverse side of the medal is the use of fear and terror as political weapons. For the workers who lag in production there is the discipline of a wage system that consigns the laggard to a minimum level of subsistence. For all who deviate from the straight and narrow path of conformity to the leadership's demands, there is the omnipresent danger of arrest by the secret police and confinement in a forced labor camp. Whip and carrot combine to extirpate the slightest overt demonstration of opposition to the regime.

At the same time, the regime is shrewd enough to understand that this system of rewards and punishments must be given ideological justification if it is to possess the minds as well as enlist the energies of youth. The appeal of the ultimate utopian goal is not wholly abandoned even if it is less stressed and less effective. But blame for the postponement of its realization is placed on the continued existence of the cunning capitalist enemy without; the Soviet Union must be an armed fortress and live in a state of siege if it is to survive and triumph over the capitalist encirclement. At the same time, Communist victories in Europe and Asia are used to support the promise that the ultimate world triumph will not be too long delayed, that the voice of the future is the voice of Communism, and that present sacrifices prepare the way for the Promised Land of plenty which is to come.

Meanwhile, youth is told it must work, obey, and learn to fight. The main enemy this time is the United States instead of the Nazis. Every propaganda organ builds an image of the aggressive American imperialist as a barbaric replica of the Nazi out to dominate the world. The objective of this compaign is to channel all the genuine hatred which the Nazis provoked and all the frustration and aggression which accumulate within Soviet society against this new external-enemy symbol of America. Soviet young people are warned that they must be prepared to make the sternest sacrifices to defend their homes, their families, and their fatherland.

Soviet achievements, they are taught to believe, are a symbol of hope and liberation for the oppressed masses in capitalist-dominated countries.

This in its basic outlines is the indoctrination to which Soviet youth is being currently exposed. It is reiterated in every mass media, in vocal agitation, and in every nook and cranny of the Soviet educational and propaganda system. Its power to persuade those who caught a glimpse of the West may be questioned. There is abundant indication, both in the reports of defectors and in the series of postwar ideological purges and campaigns which have been directed against cosmopolitanism and adulation of the West, that it meets with some resistance in intellectual and, perhaps, other circles. But the rising generation of youth is now almost totally sealed off from the West and insulated against outside contacts. Its emotions and energies are subject to exclusive manipulation by the Party leadership. The power of the Kremlin to mold the children who have come of age since World War II should not be underestimated. In the years since the Revolution, the attrition of loyalties in the middle-aged and the elderly has been counterbalanced by the capacity of the regime, through the Komsomol and the Young Pioneers, to indoctrinate a part of each new generation with its own values. Whether or not this indoctrination survives the trials and tribulations of later life, it has played and may continue to play a role of crucial significance in replenishing the life energies of the regime.

Chapter 10

The Party Command—
Politburo and Presidium

The Presidium of the Communist Party occupies the most exalted position in Soviet society. Established in October 1952 at the Nineteenth Party Congress as a successor agency to the Politburo and the Orgburo, it stands at the pinnacle of the Party and governmental hierarchies, supplying the goals and policies which determine the direction of Soviet development and representing the highest level of decision-making in the Communist world. Its manifest importance as the center of initiative for Soviet and world Communism makes the closest study of its composition, its actions, and its outlook a matter of imperative concern. Yet few ventures in scholarly inquiry face such baffling and frustrating obstacles. Since the consolidation of Stalin's power in the late twenties, the internal operations of the Soviet high command have been shrouded in mystery and secrecy. No records of its deliberations are accessible, and its working processes are among the best-kept secrets of Soviet life. Some clues concerning the role which the Presidium may be expected to play can be obtained by examining the history of its main predecessor, the Politburo, which long occupied the leading place in Soviet life.

Origins and Development of the Politburo

The first reference to the organization of a Political Bureau occurs in the minutes of the Central Committee meeting of October 23, 1917. On the motion of Dzerzhinsky, a Politburo was established to provide "political leadership in the uprising." Its membership consisted of Lenin, Zinoviev, Kamenev, Trotsky, Stalin, Sokolnikov, and Bubnov.[1] With the success of the insurrection, its purpose was achieved, and the Politburo as originally constituted passed out of existence. At the Eighth Party Congress in March 1919 the Politburo was reëstablished as a permanent organ of Party leadership.*

From the beginning, the Politburo played a dominating role in Party affairs. The urgencies of Civil War and Allied Intervention contributed to centralization of power. Under the impact of crises, the meetings of the Central Committee took place less frequently, and the actual initiative in directing the course of policy and administration was largely transferred to the Politburo.

The habits of War Communism carried over into the NEP period. Even issues of trivial significance could not be resolved without reference to the Politburo. In his political report to the Eleventh Congress in March 1922, Lenin cited the classic case of the effort of the Moscow Consumers' Coöperative Society to arrange for the purchase of a small quantity of canned goods from a French businessman who had a cargo available in Libau and was willing to accept Soviet currency in payment.[2] The transaction could not be consummated until the Politburo had enacted a proper authorizing resolution, and the Commissar of Foreign Trade Krassin had discussed the proposal with Kamenev, a member of the Politburo. "I have given you one example," reported Lenin, "to show that concrete minor matters are dragged before the Political Bureau . . . everything that comes up at the Council of People's Commissars is dragged before the Politburo." "I hope," he continued, "that the Congress will . . . endorse the resolution that the Political Bureau and the Central Committee be relieved of minor matters, and that the responsible officials should take greater responsibilities upon themselves."[3]

Despite Lenin's protest, the tendency to overburden the Politburo with detail persisted after his death. As late as 1927, when such information was still being released, Kursky, the chairman of the Central Auditing Commission, reported to the Fifteenth Party Congress that during the preceding year, each member of the Politburo was deluged with 6,682 pages of material which he was required to read in order to deal adequately with the Politburo agenda.[4] The Politburo's work plans, which were published for the years 1926 and 1928, represent a formidable conspectus of the entire range of Soviet life. The subjects covered by the 1926 plan include the five-year perspective plan, the plan for electrification, the control figures for the year 1926–27, the condition of war industry, a report on the metal industries, the state budget, credit and finance, a report on exports and imports, the procurement of grain, the condition of the trading network, a report on concessions, trade-union activities, wage payments, labor discipline, the revision of the territorial-administrative structure, elections to the Soviets, the condition of the Red Army, artels, consumers' coöperatives, state farms and collective

* See Chapter 6, p. 154.

farms, reports by the Ukrainian, Moscow, and Northern Caucasus Party
organizations on their activities, a report by the Orgburo on the Party
apparatus and its links with the state apparatus, and so forth.[5] Missing
from the list are all references to foreign affairs. The omission did not
imply any lack of attention to that important area of Politburo responsibilities. Indeed, there were few fields in which the Politburo was more
constantly engaged. As Lenin observed in 1923, "Have we not in the
Political Bureau discussed from the Party point of view many questions,
both minor and important, concerning the 'moves' we should make in
reply to the 'moves' of foreign powers in order to forestall their, say,

TABLE 10

POLITBURO MEMBERS, 1919-1952

Lenin, V. I.	1919–1924	*Kaganovich, L. M.	1930–1952
Stalin, J. V.	1919–1952	Kirov, S. M.	1930–1934
Trotsky, L. D.	1919–1926	Kossior, S. V.	1930–1938
Kamenev, L. B.	1919–1925	Ordjonikidze, G. K.	1930–1937
Krestinsky, N. N.	1919–1921	Andreyev, A. A.	1932–1952
Zinoviev, G. E.	1921–1926	Chubar, V. Ia.	1935–1938
Rykov, A. I.	1922–1930	*Mikoyan, A. I.	1935–1952
Tomsky, M. P.	1922–1930	Zhdanov, A. A.	1939–1948
Bukharin, N. I.	1924–1929	*Khrushchëv, N. S.	1939–1952
*Molotov, V. M.	1925–1952	*Beria, L. P.	1946–1952
*Voroshilov, K. E.	1925–1952	*Malenkov, G. M.	1946–1952
Kalinin, M. I.	1925–1946	Voznesensky, N. A.	1947–1949
Rudzutak, Ia. E.	1926–1932	*Bulganin, N. A.	1948–1952
Kuibyshev, V. V.	1927–1935	Kosygin, A. N.	1949–1952

* Members of the Presidium, March 6, 1953.

cunning, if we are not to use a less respectable term? Is not this flexible
amalgamation of a Soviet institution with a Party institution a source of
great strength in our politics?"[6]

As the 1926 work plan reveals, the typical procedure of the Politburo
involved discussion and action based on a report by the agency charged
with initial responsibility in the given field. When the report was delivered by one of the governmental departments or commissariats, a co-
report by the Central Control Commission and the Commissariat of
Workers' and Peasants' Inspection was customary. When the subject matter fell outside the jurisdiction of the commissariats or was purely Party
in scope, the Politburo acted on the basis of reports by its own subcommittees, special commissions of the Central Committee, recommendations
of the Orgburo, and statements of republic and regional Party organizations. Sometimes the matter was carried over for further discussion by
the plenum of the Central Committee; in most instances, however, the
Politburo made the final decision.

The excerpt from the 1928 work plan which is available follows the pattern of the 1926 plan, though it is briefer and less informative.[7] Again, the work plan demonstrates the extraordinary range of the Politburo's interests; the subjects listed range from crop deliveries and the industrial and financial plan for 1928–29 to the program of the Communist International, universal obligatory primary education, and measures to improve radio and cinema programs.

Even for the relatively well-reported period of the twenties, the accessible official documentation on the internal deliberations of the Politburo is sparse and unrevealing. The scattered excerpts from Politburo minutes contained in the Trotsky Archives in the Harvard College Library are curiously lifeless documents which represent little more than a log of those in attendance, proposals made, and actions taken. There is no summary of the flow of the discussion and no report of the surging debates which shook the Politburo to its foundations in those restless years. If a relatively rich record of the main outlines of the struggle for power within the Politburo is now available, it is largely because the conflict spilled over the walls of the Politburo, involved the Central Committee and other leading Party organs, was ventilated in Party congresses and conferences, and was chronicled in the Party press and opposition literature. With the elimination of the Left and Right oppositions in the late twenties and the consolidation of Stalin's power, a curtain of darkness descended on the inner deliberations of the Politburo. The legend of a monolithic Politburo was propagated to buttress the ideal of the monolithic Party. As the Stalin cult gathered momentum and lifted him to a position of undisputed supremacy, his Politburo lieutenants seemed to shrink into a secondary orbit of pale stars who shone in his radiance and emphasized his eminence by the sycophantic character of their public genuflexions.

The men whom Stalin gathered round him as he consolidated his hold on the Politburo were profoundly different in background and outlook from those who had fallen by the wayside in the bitter struggles of the twenties. The group of the shelved and the defeated included Krestinsky, Trotsky, Zinoviev, Kamenev, Bukharin, Tomsky, and Rykov. With the exception of Tomsky, all were intellectuals of cosmopolitan interests and experience derived from years spent in emigration. Even Tomsky, who began his career as a lithographic worker and quickly became a Bolshevik trade-union organizer, attended the London Congress as a delegate in 1907 and participated in the Paris conference of the editors of *Proletarii* in 1909. As a group, they were articulate, argumentative, and independent; all of them, including Tomsky, had opposed Lenin at one time or another in the course of their Party careers. During the period of revolutionary preparation, they had functioned primarily as agitators, propagandists, and journalists; they were men of the word and the pen whose original interests ran to oratorical and literary pursuits.

After the Bolshevik conquest of power, they moved quickly into positions of prominence in public life. Trotsky, Kamenev, Rykov, and Tomsky all displayed great organizing talents, but as a group they found themselves attracted to policy posts in state administration and foreign affairs and tended to avoid the drabber responsibilities of internal Party management. Krestinsky served for a brief period (1919–1921) as secretary of the Central Committee, but the experiment was unsuccessful, and the bulk of his career was spent as Ambassador to Germany and Vice-Commissar for Foreign Affairs. Trotsky was briefly Commissar for Foreign Affairs and then served with outstanding distinction as Commissar of War. Zinoviev made his primary contribution as chairman of the Communist International. Kamenev occupied a variety of important administrative posts, including the chairmanship of the Moscow Soviet, the vice-chairmanship of the Council of People's Commissars, the chairmanship of the Council of Labor and Defense, and the directorship of the Supreme Council of National Economy. He also served briefly (1926–27) as Ambassador to Italy. Bukharin's assignments included the editorship of *Pravda* (1917–1929), responsibility for the Communist International after Zinoviev's downfall, and the editorship of *Izvestiya* after his own decline in power. Tomsky concentrated almost exclusively on trade-union affairs; as chairman of the All-Russian Central Council of Trade Unions, he played a central role in shaping trade-union policy until his dismissal from that post. As chairman of the Council of People's Commissars of both the USSR and the RSFSR, Rykov's energies were almost exclusively engaged in directing and coördinating the governmental apparatus. Perhaps the most striking common characteristic of the group (and an important cause of their failure) consisted in the fact that after 1921 not a single one of them was concerned in an important way with the management of the Party organization and its Central Committee Secretariat.

Stalin's own sympathies were with the "practical" workers of the Party apparatus. In a very revealing letter to the German Communist leader Maslow in 1925 (and not included in his collected works), he wrote, "With us in Russia, 'old leaders' from among the literati wither away continuously. This process increased during periods of revolutionary crisis and slowed down during periods of crystallization of forces, but it took place continuously . . . That is a process necessary for the renovation of the leading cadres of a living and developing party." [8] Stalin's distaste for the literati was notorious. He found himself much more at ease with the *apparatchiki* who, like himself, were frequently of lowly origins, had had limited opportunities for education and foreign travel, had little interest in theoretical disputations, and who served their apprenticeship in the Party organization.

Stalin's Lieutenants

An analysis of the Politburo lieutenants whom Stalin included in his circle as he eliminated his left- and right-wing opponents makes this crystal clear. Of the ten members of the 1931 Politburo, only three — Kuibyshev, Ordjonikidze, and Molotov — can be positively identified as of middle- or upper-class origin.[9] All three, however, shared Stalin's predilection for the details of Party management. The career profiles of the 1931 Politburo reveal that loyal, disciplined service in the apparatus served as the highroad to admission into Stalin's inner circle. Except for Voroshilov and Kalinin, whose later reputations were made outside the secretarial hierarchy, this is the common tie which binds the lives of the lieutenants.

Molotov from the beginning showed the traits of the perfect *apparatchik*. His gifts and interests were organizational, and he devoted himself to his secretarial labors with assiduous application. In 1916 he was assigned to the Russian Bureau of the Central Committee of the Party. After short periods of service as chairman of the Council for National Economy in 1918 and chairman of the Executive Committee of the Novgorod region, he became secretary of the Ukrainian Communist Party in 1920 and secretary to the Central Committee of the Party in 1921. When Stalin was made General Secretary of the Party in 1922, Molotov remained as a co-secretary and faithful subordinate. His election to the Politburo in 1925 came as a reward for meritorious service in the Party apparatus and undeviating loyalty to the General Secretary.

L. M. Kaganovich, after serving as chairman of the Nizhni-Novgorod *guberniya* committee in 1919 and head of the Tashkent government in 1920, became the director of the Organization-Instruction Department of the Central Committee Secretariat and a member of the Turkestan Bureau of the Central Committee in 1922. In 1924 he was named one of the secretaries of the Central Committee. The following year he became general secretary of the Ukrainian Party organization. In 1928 he returned to Moscow as secretary of the Central Committee and was made a member of the Orgburo. In 1930 he became head of the Moscow Party organization and was also elected to full membership in the Politburo.

Kirov's rise to power conformed to the same pattern. After long pre-Revolutionary experience as an underground Party worker, he was appointed secretary of the Azerbaidjan Party organization in 1921 and secretary of the Northwest Bureau of the Central Committee in 1926. In the latter year, he was transferred to Leningrad as first secretary and from this vantage point was elevated to the Politburo in 1930.

S. V. Kossior's career followed a parallel course. After serving as a local Party secretary and member of the Party central committee in the Ukraine, he was named secretary of the Siberian Bureau of the Central Committee in 1922. In 1925 he became one of the secretaries of the Central Committee; in 1928 he was designated as the first secretary of the Ukrainian Party organization; and in 1930 he was raised to membership in the Politburo.

Kuibyshev achieved prominence as one of the secretaries of the Party Central Committee in 1922–23. He became chairman of the Party Central Control Commission and Commissar for Workers' and Peasants' Inspection in 1923, from which point he found his way into the Politburo in 1927.

Ordjonikidze's rise was almost identical. After occupying the position of secretary of the Transcaucasian Party organization, he followed Kuibyshev in 1926 as chairman of the Central Control Commission and People's Commissar for Workers' and Peasants' Inspection. In 1930 he was made a member of the Politburo.

Rudzutak served as chairman of the Central Asian Bureau of the Party from 1921 to 1924. In 1923–24 he moved into the limelight as one of the secretaries of the Party Central Committee. In 1924 he became vice-chairman of the Council of People's Commissars and the Council of Labor and Defense, while he also occupied the post of Commissar for Transport. In 1927 he was raised to Politburo membership.

The careers of Voroshilov and Kalinin fall into a somewhat different pattern. Although Voroshilov served an apprenticeship in the apparatus as a member of the Southeastern Bureau of the Central Committee between 1921 and 1924, his advancement was achieved primarily along military lines. As an outstanding guerrilla leader during the Civil War, he was closely associated with Stalin in the defense of Tsaritsyn. After the Civil War and until 1924, he commanded the North Caucasus Military District, was then transferred to the Moscow Military District, and succeeded Frunze as War Commissar in 1925. The next year he became a member of the Politburo.

Kalinin, the only member of the group of peasant background, began his career as a Party organizer and underground worker. Chosen in 1919 to replace Sverdlov as chairman of the All-Russian Central Executive Committee, he continued to perform the same functions in the Central Executive Committee of the USSR after 1924 and was named to the Politburo in 1926. From the beginning, his role was more ceremonial than influential. As the symbol of the *muzhik* come to power, he provided a link with the countryside that Stalin was quick to appreciate and exploit.

The history of the Politburo during the thirties is still wrapped in darkness and obscurity. Of Stalin's nine faithful disciples in 1931, one,

Kirov, was assassinated in 1934; two others, Kuibyshev and Ordjonikidze, died in 1935 and 1937 respectively. If the highly suspect version circulated by Vyshinsky at the 1938 Moscow trial is to be believed, both the assassination of Kirov and the alleged medical murder of Kuibyshev were organized by Yagoda, the head of the NKVD, and his fellow conspirators. The death of Ordjonikidze in 1937 at the height of the Purge gave rise in turn to rumors of conflict with Stalin and intimations of foul play, though evidence to buttress such charges is lacking. Two other members of the Politburo, Rudzutak and Kossior, disappeared in the Great Purge around 1938. Chubar, who was added to the Politburo in 1935, apparently was also liquidated. In addition, four candidate members of the Politburo, Postyshev, Eikhe, Petrovsky, and Yezhov, vanished. Yezhov, who succeeded Yagoda as head of the NKVD, became the scapegoat for the excesses of the Purge. The somewhat ludicrous charge of "Ukrainian bourgeois nationalism" was directed against Postyshev, a Russian, and Kossior, a Pole, both of whom served in the Ukraine.[10] The elimination of the other purged members of the Politburo circle went unheralded and unexplained. None figured in the great Moscow trials of 1937 and 1938. The system of insecurity on which Stalin's power was founded ended by enveloping and devouring members of his own inner circle in the Politburo itself.

The four new persons added to the Politburo during the thirties who managed to survive the Purge were Andreyev, admitted in 1932; Mikoyan, admitted in 1935; and Zhdanov and Khrushchëv, both admitted in 1939. The careers of these members of the Politburo followed the traditional course of upward mobility through the apparatus. Andreyev, who began as a specialist in trade-union affairs and was chairman of the Railroad Workers' Union between 1920 and 1928, also drew important Party assignments. In 1924–25, he served as one of the secretaries of the Central Committee. In 1928–29, he was assigned to the secretaryship of the North Caucasus Party organization. In 1930–31, he became chairman of the Central Control Commission, from which post he was promoted to the Politburo.

Mikoyan, a veteran of the Baku Bolshevik Committee in 1917, was deeply involved in revolutionary activity in the Caucasus until 1920. From 1920 to 1922 he occupied the post of secretary of the Nizhni-Novgorod *guberniya* Party committee; from 1922 to 1926 he served as secretary of the North Caucasus Party organization. In 1926 he became People's Commissar for Trade; in 1931, Commissar for Supplies; and in 1935, Commissar for the Food Industry. At that point he was also elevated to membership in the Politburo.

Zhdanov's first important Party assignment was the secretaryship of the Nizhni-Novgorod Party organization, which he filled for the twelve-year period between 1922 and 1934. After the assassination of Kirov in 1934, he was transferred to Leningrad as Party secretary, was made a Politburo candidate the next year, and in 1939 was promoted to full membership.

Khrushchëv was the harbinger of a new Politburo generation. He was the first member to be admitted to the inner circle who had entered the Party after the Revolution. A coal miner and the son of a coal miner, without education, he joined the Party in 1918 and enrolled in a Rab-Fak or Workers' Faculty, which provided elementary schooling for adult workers. After graduation, he was assigned to Party work in Stalino and Kiev as a "promoted worker." In 1929 he was sent to the Industrial Academy for training as a future industrial executive. At the same time, he served as head of the Party organization in the academy. When he completed his course, he was retained for Party work, and in 1934, Kaganovich, the head of the Moscow Party organization, chose him as his second secretary. He succeeded Kaganovich as first secretary the following year. In 1938 he was shifted to the Ukraine as first secretary, and the next year became a full member of the Politburo.

During the forties, five new members were added to the Politburo: Beria and Malenkov in 1946, Voznesensky in 1947, Bulganin in 1948, and Kosygin in 1949. Of the five, only Malenkov and Beria fall more or less clearly into the pattern of *apparatchiki* who rise to power through the secretarial hierarchy. In the case of Beria, however, a long period of service in the secret police both preceded and succeeded his tour of duty as a Party secretary. The three others, Bulganin, Kosygin, and Voznesensky, were primarily state administrators rather than Party managers. The stress on experience in state administration and economic management which these promotions signified represented a marked break with the earlier practice of reserving Politburo membership for successful *apparatchiki*. As a response to the complex urgencies which the Soviet high command faced in managing a society in process of rapid industrialization, this new departure was not without considerable long-range significance.

Notable also in these promotions was an absence of emphasis on lowly economic origins. Although Beria has been described in Soviet sources as the son of a poor peasant, an element of doubt is introduced by the fact that he received a higher education at the Baku Polytechnic Institute, a rare feat in that period for children of poor peasants. Malenkov's social origins are obscure, but the fact that he attended a gymnasium in Orenberg between 1912 and 1917 points to the existence of some family means. Voznesensky and Bulganin have both been listed as sons of white-collar workers; the official records omit all mention of Kosygin's social origin.

The background of technical training which characterized the group also deserves emphasis. Beria's attendance at a Polytechnic Institute has already been noted. Malenkov spent three years at an engineering institute in Moscow between 1922 and 1925. Kosygin was also trained as an engineer. Voznesensky completed a postgraduate course in economics at the Institute of Red Professors in Moscow and became an economic planner. Bulganin's educational background is unknown, but his reputation as a competent industrial manager was made between 1922 and 1931 when he became, first, head of the construction department, and later, manager of the important Soviet electrical equipment plant Elektrozavod in Moscow. "In these years," one of his official biographies reports, "Bulganin completed his education 'on the run' from the technical experts under him." [11]

Another characteristic shared by the group is the fact that not a single one of the five can be classed as an Old Bolshevik. Beria and Bulganin joined the Party in 1917, Voznesensky in 1919, Malenkov in 1920, and Kosygin, the youngest of the group, in 1927. Beria, Bulganin, and Malenkov underwent their baptism of fire in the Civil War period, though none of them played an outstandingly significant role in the stormy events of that period. Voznesensky's Civil War role is obscure; his official biography indicates only that he was sent to the Sverdlovsk Party University in 1921 for a higher education. Kosygin, who was a mere boy of twelve when the Bolsheviks seized power in 1917, is completely a product of the Soviet era.

The career lines of the five reveal quite divergent patterns. Malenkov represents the quintessence of the Party *apparatchik*. During the Civil War, he served as a political commissar on the Eastern and Turkestan fronts and became head of the Political Department of the Turkestan Army. Between 1922 and 1925 he attended the Higher Technical School in Moscow and also occupied the post of secretary of the school's Party organization. In 1925 he joined the apparatus of the Party Central Committee and became a member of Stalin's personal secretariat. Between 1930 and 1934 he headed the Organization-Instruction Department of the Moscow Party organization, and from 1934 to 1939 he directed the Department of Leading Party Organs in the Central Committee Secretariat; here his responsibilities included the placement of Party cadres and the supervision of local Party organizations. In 1939 he became one of the secretaries of the Central Committee, in which position he continued to direct the cadre activities of the Party. In 1941 he was made a candidate member of the Politburo. During the war, he played a crucial role as a member of the State Committee for Defense, which functioned as an inner war cabinet. His major assignments during and after the war included responsibility for the production of aircraft and the chairmanship of the Committee for the Economic Rehabilitation of Liberated

Areas. In 1946 he became a vice-chairman of the Council of Ministers and a full member of the Politburo.

Beria's career exemplifies the combination of the successful Chekist and Party secretary. In 1921 he entered the service of the Cheka. During the next ten years, he rose rapidly in the secret-police hierarchy, finally becoming the head of both the Georgian and the Transcaucasian GPU organizations. He was transferred to Party work in 1931, and during the next seven years, served as secretary of the Georgian and Transcaucasian Party organizations. In 1938 he replaced Yezhov as head of the NKVD and the next year was made a candidate member of the Politburo. During the war, he continued as head of the secret police, served as a member of the State Committee for Defense, and was entrusted with the special assignment of raising the output of armaments and munitions. In 1946 he was rewarded by promotion to full membership in the Politburo.

The case of Voznesensky provides a marked variant from the typical tale of rapid upward mobility through service in the Party hierarchy. Although Voznesensky served as a Party official in the Donets mining area after graduation from the Sverdlovsk Party University in 1924, his advancement to the Politburo was essentially a reward for specialized competence in the field of economic planning. After he was graduated from the Institute of Red Professors, he became a professor there and in 1934, at the age of thirty-one, was made its president. The next year, at the invitation of Zhdanov, the secretary of the Leningrad Party organization, he was named chairman of the planning commission in that area. As a protégé of Zhdanov and a beneficiary of the Great Purge, his promotion was rapid. In 1938 he became chairman of the State Planning Commission of the USSR (Gosplan) and in 1941 was made a candidate member of the Politburo. In 1941 he was named to the newly created post of Vice-Premier for Economic Affairs, and the next year he was also appointed to the State Committee for Defense. He became a full member of the Politburo in 1947. In 1949, without any explanation, he suddenly disappeared from public life. A successor was designated as Gosplan chairman, and Voznesensky's name ceased to appear among the Politburo elect. Close observers of the Soviet scene tended to link his fall from grace with the dispersal of the Zhdanov entourage which followed the latter's death in 1948. Voznesensky's fate remains a mystery; like other victims of the silent purge, his record and achievements have simply been erased from Soviet history.*

* In a *Pravda* article of December 24, 1952, M. Suslov described Voznesensky's volume on the economy of the USSR during World War II as an "anti-Marxist" book which propagated "false subjectivist views in the field of the Political Economy of Socialism." Suslov also released the text of the Central Committee decree of July 13,

For Bulganin and Kosygin the road to supreme power appeared to represent recognition of superior administrative rather than Party achievements. Although Bulganin began his career as an officer in the Cheka, he transferred to economic work in 1922 and made his reputation in the next decade as a talented industrial administrator. From 1931 to 1937 he served as chairman of the Moscow Soviet. In 1938 he became chairman of the State Bank. During the war, he served as political commissar of the Moscow Front; the military rank of lieutenant general was conferred on him in 1942 in recognition of his part in the successful defense of Moscow. In 1944 he became a full general and also replaced Voroshilov as a member of the State Committee for Defense. Two years later he was named Minister of the Armed Forces and a candidate member of the Politburo. His promotion to full membership followed in 1948.

Kosygin's rapid advance began in 1938, during the purge period, when he was named Commissar of the Textile Industry. In 1940 he became vice-chairman of the Council of People's Commissars with special responsibility for all consumer-goods industries. A year later he was named Premier of the Russian Soviet Federated Socialist Republic and continued in this position during the war. In 1946 he became a candidate member of the Politburo as well as vice-chairman of the Council of Ministers. In 1948 he served temporarily as Minister of Finance. In 1949 he was shifted to the Ministry of Light Industry while retaining his position as vice-chairman of the Council of Ministers. During the same year, he also became a full member of the Politburo. For reasons which were undisclosed, Kosygin was demoted to an alternate membership on the new Presidium in October 1952 and was removed altogether from that body when it was reorganized after Stalin's death.

Division of Responsibilities in the Politburo

Before it was dissolved at the Nineteenth Party Congress in October 1952, the Politburo consisted of eleven full members and one candidate. The members, in the order of their seniority, were Stalin, Molotov, Voroshilov, Kaganovich, Andreyev, Mikoyan, Khrushchëv, Beria, Malenkov, Bulganin, and Kosygin. The candidate member, Shvernik, had been frozen in that status since 1939. Stalin's position was one of unique authority. As General Secretary of the Party and chairman of the Council of Ministers, his was the power of ultimate decision over the whole range of Party and state concerns. The other members of the Politburo, with the exception of Khrushchëv, held the titles of vice-chairmen of the Council of Ministers.

Molotov was commonly regarded as Stalin's first deputy for state ad-

1949, in which the editors of *Bol'shevik* were denounced for "servile glorification" of Voznesensky's book.

ministration with a special responsibility in the area of foreign affairs. In the decade preceding World War II he had served as chairman of the Council of People's Commissars, and between 1939 and 1949 he also held the portfolio of Commissar (later Minister) of Foreign Affairs. His retirement from that post was part of a general policy of divesting Politburo members of specific ministerial duties in order to reserve their energies for policy-making, coördination, and supervision.

Voroshilov's role was that of a senior military adviser. Until June 1940 he served as Defense Commissar. After the debacle of the first phase of the Finnish war, he was replaced by Timoshenko. During the war, he remained a member of the State Committee for Defense until 1944 when he was succeeded by Bulganin and dispatched to the Far East to help prepare the Soviet attack on Japan. Voroshilov, who was born in 1881, was the oldest member of the Politburo group, next to Stalin. While he probably continued to exercise an important influence on military decisions, his responsibilities in this area were increasingly shared with Bulganin.

Kaganovich had the reputation of being the troubleshooter of the Politburo. His career was a long record of being rushed from breach to breach to repair breakdowns and introduce order where chaos had prevailed. As first secretary of the Ukrainian Communist Party between 1925 and 1928, he attracted nation-wide attention for his energetic leadership in the construction of Dneprostroi. As secretary of the Moscow Party organization between 1930 and 1935, his most dramatic achievement was the building of the Moscow subway. In 1933 he was temporarily shifted to the critical agricultural front and was largely responsible for organizing the political sections of the machine-tractor stations through which the disintegrating collective-farm structure was salvaged and restored. In 1935 he became Commissar of Railroads and applied similar techniques to improve the efficiency of the Soviet Union's overloaded and poorly functioning transportation network. When Ordjonikidze died in 1937, Kaganovich succeeded him as Commissar of Heavy Industry. When oil production began to lag in the prewar years, he was given the assignment of putting the oil industry on its feet. In 1938 he returned to the railroads and during the war, as a member of the State Committee for Defense, was responsible for all wartime transportation. After the war, he was put in charge of a newly created Ministry of Building Materials. When the 1946 drought created an emergency in the Ukraine, Kaganovich was dispatched there to replace Khrushchëv as first secretary and to lead the work of reconstruction. In December 1947 he returned to Moscow, where as one of the vice-chairmen of the Council of Ministers, it was assumed that he continued to exercise major supervisory authority over the group of ministries concerned with transportation and heavy industry. Kaganovich's talents as an executive and administrator made him an important figure in the Politburo, but during the postwar period he no longer occupied the outstanding position which he attained in the early thirties when he was frequently referred to as a favorite disciple of Stalin.

Andreyev's duties in the Politburo were twofold. As chairman of the Party Control Commission, he had a continuing responsibility for enforcing Party discipline. As vice-chairman of the Council of Ministers and chairman of the Council on Kolkhoz Affairs, he operated as one of the top agricultural experts of the Politburo. Andreyev's original assignment was trade-union affairs, and he remained active in that area until 1928. In the trade-union discussion of 1920–21, Andreyev followed the lead of Trotsky and Bukharin. Although he quickly disassociated himself from these mentors and threw in his lot with Stalin, he remained the only member of the Politburo with a record of past association with oppositionists. He was also the only member to whom a public rebuke was administered by name in the postwar years. On February 19, 1950, an unsigned article appeared in *Pravda* severely criticizing Andreyev for championing the use of the *zveno* or link system of organizing work on collective farms in preference to reliance on the larger unit of the brigade.* On February 28, a little more than a week later, *Pravda* published a letter from Andreyev "confessing" his errors. The *Pravda* attack obviously echoed an earlier Politburo debate and decision. The use of Andreyev as a public scapegoat to signal a change in policy was followed by more drastic measures. At the Nineteenth Party Congress, he was removed from the chairmanship of the Party Control Committee and not included as a member or candidate member of the new Presidium. Although he remained a member of the Party Central Committee, the decline in his status apparently marked the end of his career as a major political figure.

Mikoyan functioned as the Politburo specialist on foreign and domestic trade. For ten years prior to 1949, he headed the Ministry (formerly Commissariat) of Foreign Trade. Still earlier, he served variously as People's Commissar for Trade, for Supplies, and for the Food Industry. As vice-chairman of the Council of Ministers, he continued to supervise the Soviet domestic and foreign trade network.

Khrushchëv devoted himself mainly to Party affairs. For many years, he was known as the Politburo's Ukrainian expert. He served as first secretary of the Ukrainian Party organization from 1938 to 1949, except for the year 1946–47 when he was temporarily replaced by Kaganovich. In December 1949 Khrushchëv was shifted to the Moscow Party organization as first secretary and was also designated as one of the Central Committee secretaries. In addition, Khrushchëv became a Politburo

---

* For a discussion of this dispute, see Chapter 16, p. 456.

spokesman on agricultural policy. His election speech of March 7, 1950, initiated a far-reaching collective-farm merger campaign.[12] Like Andreyev earlier, Khrushchëv soon found himself in troubled waters. Whereas Andreyev had been publicly rebuked for his conservatism in clinging to the *zveno* or link system of organizing agricultural production, Khrushchëv suffered a rebuff because of the radical and overambitious character of his proposals for the resettlement of the rural population in large *agrogorods* or rural towns.* But Khrushchëv's status remained unaffected by the indirect attack launched against the views he had espoused. Unlike Andreyev, he became a member of the new Presidium and played a leading role at the Nineteenth Party Congress as the Party spokesman on the revised rules which were approved by the Congress.

Beria was the Politburo specialist on the police and terror apparatus of the regime. Although he abandoned his ministerial post in 1946, both the Ministry of Interior (MVD) and that of State Security (MGB) continued to function under his direction. Because of the security aspects involved, it was also widely assumed that the Soviet atomic energy developments were subject to Beria's general supervision. He also maintained a special interest in the Georgian Party organization.

Malenkov's primary area of jurisdiction was the Party apparatus. During the immediate postwar years, his prestige suffered a temporary eclipse, and in 1946 he ceased to be listed as a Party secretary. Meanwhile, Zhdanov occupied the limelight as the ideological spokesman of the Party. On July 21, 1948, *Pravda* revealed that Malenkov had been restored to his secretarial authority. The death of Zhdanov on August 31, 1948, was followed by a ruthless purge of his dependents in the apparatus. Voznesensky was dropped from the Politburo. A. A. Kuznetsov and G. M. Popov were removed as Central Committee secretaries, and Popov also lost his post as head of the Moscow Party organization. P. S. Popkov was dislodged as secretary of the Leningrad Party organization. M. I. Rodionov was ousted from the chairmanship of the Council of Ministers of the RSFSR. Colonel-General I. V. Shikin was demoted from the position of head of the Main Political Administration of the Army and replaced by F. F. Kuznetsov, a Malenkov protégé. The elimination of the Zhdanov entourage gave every surface evidence of being Malenkov-inspired. By installing his own henchmen in these key vacancies, Malenkov consolidated his control of the Party apparatus and emerged as the most powerful of Stalin's lieutenants.

Bulganin's activities were concentrated in the area of national defense, where he shared responsibility with Voroshilov in advising the Politburo on military affairs. In 1949 Bulganin relinquished his duties as Minister of Armed Forces to Marshal Vasilevsky, but as vice-chairman of the Coun-

* For a discussion of this episode, see Chapter 16, pp. 457–458.

cil of Ministers, he continued to play a major role in supervising and co-ordinating defense administration on behalf of the Politburo.

Kosygin's area of responsibility was light industry. As Minister of Light Industry, he was the only Politburo member to retain a ministerial portfolio. As vice-chairman of the Council of Ministers, his jurisdiction probably extended as well to the group of ministries most closely related to his major specialty.

Shvernik, the only candidate member of the Politburo, was for many years the Party specialist on trade-union affairs. In 1930 he succeeded Tomsky as chairman of the All-Union Central Council of Trade Unions and held that post for fifteen years. When Kalinin resigned as titular head of the Soviet state shortly before his death in 1946, Shvernik replaced him. As chairman of the Presidium of the Supreme Soviet, he performed the heavy burden of ceremonial duties connected with that office.

As this enumeration indicates, each of Stalin's lieutenants in the Politburo was vested with specific responsibilities which he discharged while also participating in the collective deliberations of that body. Malenkov and, to a lesser degree, Khrushchëv provided the link with the Party secretarial apparatus, Beria with the police, Bulganin and Voroshilov with the armed forces, while Molotov and the remaining members of the Politburo assumed jurisdiction over other aspects of administration and economic policy. The division of functions within the Politiburo served to reinforce Stalin's over-all control of the strategic levers of power in Soviet society.

The Presidium

At the Nineteenth Party Congress, the Politburo and Orgburo were abolished and replaced by a greatly enlarged Presidium. No satisfactory explanation of this startling move was provided. Khrushchëv's theses on changes in the Party Rules merely proclaimed, "It is expedient to transform the Politburo into a Presidium of the Party Central Committee, organized to direct the work of the Central Committee between plenary sessions, since the title Presidium better accords with the functions which the Politburo actually performs at the present time. As regards the current organizational work of the Central Committee, as practice has shown, it is expedient to concentrate this work in one body, the Secretariat, in which connection there is to be no Orgburo of the Central Committee in the future." [13]

An analysis of the composition of the Presidium selected at the Nineteenth Congress may throw some light on the objectives of the reorganization. On its face, the new Presidium greatly broadened the character of the Soviet high command.[14] Its members and alternates included all ten of the Central Committee secretaries and all thirteen of the vice-chairmen

of the USSR Council of Ministers. In addition to merging the commanding heights of Party and state administration, the Presidium included the
head of the trade unions and the former first secretary of the Komsomols,
two representatives from the Ukraine, the first secretary of the Belorussian Party, a sprinkling of regional Party leaders, two high-ranking
Party ideologists, an old Comintern specialist, and some of the Soviet
Union's outstanding economic administrators.* The appointments to the
Presidium could be and were interpreted as an effort to consolidate and
stabilize the peak structure of authority in Soviet society around its most
powerful Party and governmental leaders.

The promotions to the Presidium also appeared to register a further
step in the shift of authority to the Soviet post-Revolutionary generation.

* The following were named to the Presidium as full members: J. V. Stalin, General Secretary of the Party Central Committee and Chairman of the USSR Council
of Ministers; V. M. Andrianov, First Secretary of the Leningrad *obkom*; A. B. Aristov,
Secretary of the Party Central Committee and First Secretary of the Chelyabinsk
obkom; L. P. Beria, Vice-Chairman of the USSR Council of Ministers; N. A. Bulganin,
Vice-Chairman of the USSR Council of Ministers; K. E. Voroshilov, Vice-Chairman
of the USSR Council of Ministers; S. D. Ignatiev, Minister of State Security and
representative of the Central Committee in Uzbekistan; L. M. Kaganovich, Vice-
Chairman of the USSR Council of Ministers; D. S. Korotchenko, Chairman of the
Ukrainian Council of Ministers; V. V. Kuznetsov, head of the Soviet trade unions;
O. V. Kuusinen, Chairman of the Presidium of the Karelo-Finnish Supreme Soviet
and veteran Comintern functionary; G. M. Malenkov, Secretary of the Party Central
Committee and Vice-Chairman of the USSR Council of Ministers; V. A. Malyshev,
Vice-Chairman of the USSR Council of Ministers and Minister of Shipbuilding; L. G.
Melnikov, First Secretary of the Ukrainian Party; A. I. Mikoyan, Vice-Chairman of
the USSR Council of Ministers; N. A. Mikhailov, former First Secretary of the Kom-
somol and Secretary of the Party Central Committee; V. M. Molotov, Vice-Chairman
of the USSR Council of Ministers; M. G. Pervukhin, Vice-Chairman of the USSR
Council of Ministers; P. K. Ponomarenko, Secretary of the Party Central Committee
and Minister of Procurement; M. Z. Saburov, Vice-Chairman of the USSR Council
of Ministers and Chairman of the State Planning Committee (Gosplan); M. A. Suslov,
Secretary of the Party Central Committee; N. S. Khrushchëv, Secretary of the Party
Central Committee and First Secretary of the Moscow *obkom;* D. I. Chesnokov, chief
editor of *Questions of Philosophy* and co-director of *Kommunist* (formerly known as
Bol'shevik); N. M. Shvernik, Chairman of the Presidium of the USSR Supreme Soviet;
M. F. Shkiryatov, Chairman of the Party Control Committee of the Central Com-
mittee.

The following were named to the Presidium as alternate members: L. I. Brezhnev,
Secretary of the Party Central Committee and former First Secretary of the Moldavian
Party organization; A. Ya. Vyshinsky, Minister of Foreign Affairs; A. G. Zverev, Min-
ister of Finance; N. G. Ignatov, Secretary of the Party Central Committee and First
Secretary of the Krasnodar *kraikom*; I. G. Kabanov, Chairman of Gossnab (State
Committee for Material-Technical Supply of the National Economy); A. N. Kosygin,
Vice-Chairman of the USSR Council of Ministers and Minister of Light Industry;
N. S. Patolichev, First Secretary of the Belorussian Party organization; N. M. Pegov,
Secretary of the Party Central Committee and former head of the Light Industry Sec-
tion of the Central Committee Secretariat; A. M. Puzanov, former First Secretary of
the Kuibyshev *obkom* and Chairman of the RSFSR Council of Ministers; I. F.
Tevosyan, Vice-Chairman of the USSR Council of Ministers and Minister of the
Metallurgical Industry; P. F. Yudin, high-ranking Party ideologist and active in Com-
inform affairs.

The new members of the inner circle included only two Old Bolsheviks — Kuusinen, who joined the Party in 1905, and Shkiryatov, who entered the next year. Five others — Korotchenko, Pervukhin, Suslov, Vyshinsky, and Zverev — joined the Party during the Civil War years. The remaining eighteen became members in 1924 or later. Of these, eight were still so obscure in 1939 that they were not chosen as delegates to the Eighteenth Party Congress. The elevation of this group seemed to introduce a new generation of leadership into the Party high command.

The membership of the enlarged Presidium provided a clear indication of Malenkov's strengthened position in the Soviet hierarchy. The predominance of the *apparatchiki*, who were widely considered to be protégés and supporters of Malenkov, combined with the central role assigned to him at the Nineteenth Party Congress, presumably with Stalin's blessing, suggested that Malenkov had registered a considerable gain in power and influence as the result of the realignment of the Party leadership. The old Politburo accounted for ten of the twenty-five full members of the Presidium. Of the remaining fifteen, ten could be classified as Party functionaries, four were primarily state administrators and one, S. D. Ignatiev, became Minister of State Security after a long period of service in the Party apparatus. Of the eleven alternates, five were Party workers, five state officials, and one, Puzanov, was a Party functionary who had recently been shifted to government service as chairman of the RSFSR Council of Ministers. Aside from S. D. Ignatiev, the newly promoted leaders included no delegates from the armed forces and the police ministries (MGB and MVD). The weight of numbers in the new Presidium was clearly on the side of the Party apparatus, although the state administrators constituted a strong secondary group.

The sudden death of Stalin on March 5, 1953, precipitated a new reorganization of the top structure of Party and government authority. Under the leadership of Malenkov, the old Politburo members in the Presidium rallied to present a united front to the nation and to the world. Within twenty-four hours after the release of the news of Stalin's death, a whole series of arrangements and dispositions of offices was announced as a "decision" of a joint meeting of the Party Central Committee, the USSR Council of Ministers, and the Presidium of the USSR Supreme Soviet. The Party Presidium was reduced in size to ten members and four alternates. Their assignments are listed in Table 11.

As Table 11 makes clear, Malenkov emerged as the leading figure in the reconstructed Presidium. His firm grip on the Party apparatus cleared the way for his assumption of leadership. Control of the police gave Beria a position second only to that of Malenkov. His elevation to the number two place in the Party hierarchy dramatized the crucial role of the police formations in the Soviet power structure. Molotov suffered a demotion. Deprived of the support of Stalin, he lacked a power base from which to stake out his claim to supreme authority. Despite his prestige as an Old Bolshevik and his long experience in administration, he found himself consigned to a secondary role as Minister of Foreign Affairs and as a member of the Presidium of five which was established to guide the work of the Council of Ministers. Stalin's old comrade-in-arms Voroshilov was assigned the largely honorific dignity of head of state, a position formerly occupied by Kalinin and Shvernik. Khrushchëv became First Secre-

TABLE 11

MEMBERSHIP OF THE PRESIDIUM OF THE CENTRAL COMMITTEE OF THE COMMUNIST PARTY, MARCH 6, 1953 *

	Members
G. M. Malenkov	Chairman of the Council of Ministers
L. P. Beria	Minister of Internal Affairs and First Deputy Minister of the Council of Ministers
V. M. Molotov	Minister of Foreign Affairs and First Deputy Minister of the Council of Ministers
K. E. Voroshilov	Chairman of the Presidium of the USSR Supreme Soviet
N. S. Khrushchëv	First Secretary of the Central Committee of the Party
N. A. Bulganin	Minister of Defense and First Deputy Minister of the Council of Ministers
L. M. Kaganovich	First Deputy Minister of the Council of Ministers
A. I. Mikoyan	Minister of Internal and External Trade and Deputy Minister of the Council of Ministers
M. Z. Saburov	Minister of Machine Building
M. G. Pervukhin	Minister of Electric Power Stations and Electrical Industry
	Alternates
N. M. Shvernik	Chairman of the All-Union Central Council of Trade Unions
P. K. Ponomarenko	Minister of Culture
L. G. Melnikov	First Secretary of the Ukrainian Party organization
M. D. Bagirov	First Secretary of the Azerbaidjan Party organization

* Members and alternates are listed in the rank order of the official announcement.

tary of the Central Committee but was relieved of his duties as head of the Moscow Party organization. Bulganin resumed the important post of Defense Minister and, together with Malenkov, Beria, Molotov, and Kaganovich, became a member of the Presidium of the Council of Ministers. Kaganovich's duties as one of the first deputy ministers were not disclosed, although it was widely assumed that his area of jurisdiction would probably embrace transportation and sectors of heavy industry. Mikoyan became Minister of Internal and External Trade, areas of Soviet life which had long been subject to his supervision. The two remaining members of the Presidium — Saburov and Pervukhin — were successful economic administrators in the field of heavy industry.* Their inclusion in the inner group testified to the importance which the new leadership attached to achievement in this significant sphere.

The designation of Shvernik to head the Soviet trade-union apparatus returned him to a post which he had occupied from 1930 to 1946, when he replaced Kalinin as titular head of state. Ponomarenko was relieved of his duties as Central Committee secretary and transferred from his former position as Minister of Procurements to head the new Ministry of Culture. Melnikov served as the link with the Ukrainian Party apparatus. M. D. Bagirov, who headed the Soviet secret police in Azerbaidjan from 1921 to 1930 and held the post of first secretary of the Azerbaidjan Party organization after 1933, was the first Communist of Turkic and Moslem origin to be included in the leadership group.

The stability and effectiveness of these governing relationships remained to be tested. The successful resolution of the immediate crisis did not necessarily guarantee that a bitter struggle for Stalin's mantle would not ensue. Still to be determined was whether Malenkov would be able to mobilize sufficient power to dominate his colleagues or whether he would find himself compelled to function as part of a collegial executive. As long as Malenkov and Beria maintained an *entente cordiale*, no effective challenge to their authority appeared probable. If rivalry intensified between them and one or another surrendered to the temptation to rid himself of his colleague, a purge of major proportions appeared predictable. Meanwhile, the new Presidium, like the Politburo in its earlier Stalinist incarnation, endeavored to convey an impression of monolithic unity. Such internal differences and alignments as existed among the leadership remained a closely-guarded family secret.

Information on the internal organization of the Presidium is unavailable and is hardly likely to become plentiful in the near future. If the Presidium follows the working practices of the Politburo, it will probably organize itself around a system of subcommittees and specialists to deal

---

* M. Z. Saburov first came to public notice as deputy chairman of Gosplan in 1938. During World War II, he played an important role in Gosplan and as chairman of the Economic Council for Defense Industry. In the early postwar period, he served as deputy chief of the Soviet Military Administration in Germany. In 1946, he resumed his duties as deputy chairman of Gosplan. In 1949, he was promoted to the position of chairman, in succession to Voznesensky, and was also named a vice-chairman of the Council of Ministers.

M. G. Pervukhin also began to attract attention in 1938 when he was named Deputy Commissar for Heavy Industry. The next year he was elected a member of the Central Committee of the Party and also designated People's Commissar for Electric Power Stations and the Electrical Industry. During World War II, he served as one of the vice-chairmen of the USSR Council of People's Commissars. From 1940 to 1943, he chaired the USSR Council for Electricity and Fuel. From 1943 to 1950, he was Commissar and Minister for the Chemical Industry. In 1950, he became a vice-chairman of the Council of Ministers.

with groups of related problems. The testimony of the few former Soviet high officials who have fled to the West and whose duties brought them into contact with the Politburo circle indicates that this pattern prevailed in the pre-World War II period.

According to one highly placed informant familiar with the Commissariat of Foreign Affairs under Litvinov in the late thirties, the Politburo exercised a particularly taut control in that area. When Stalin chose to intervene, his views were invariably decisive. Molotov, the informant reports, played an important role because of his position as chairman of the Politburo subcommittee on foreign affairs. The other members of the subcommittee at that time were Mikoyan, who took the lead on questions of foreign trade, and Zhdanov, who before his death exercised a special responsibility for Comintern (and later Cominform) affairs. The Commissariat of Foreign Affairs, according to this informant, moved along on its own momentum as long as existing Politburo directives covered the contingencies with which it was confronted. If a policy issue arose which could not be disposed of on the basis of past instructions, the Commissar of Foreign Affairs referred the matter to Molotov as chairman of the Politburo subcommittee on foreign affairs. Usually, matters of lesser importance were resolved at this level or in consultation with the full subcommittee. If, in the view of Molotov, the issue was one of major importance, the matter would go on the agenda of the Politburo or would be settled directly in consultation with Stalin. When a full-dress meeting of the Politburo was convoked, the Commissar of Foreign Affairs would report directly to that body with his recommendations. The Politburo would also be supplied with background memoranda prepared by the Foreign Section of the Central Committee Secretariat, which had at its disposal sources of intelligence that were not necessarily available to the Foreign Affairs Commissariat. The Politburo decision, once reached, would be communicated to the Commissariat in the form of a binding directive which the Commissariat would then utilize as a basis for action.

In other areas, the Politburo functioned in similar fashion, though not necessarily with such close and immediate attention to detail. Each specialist member of the Politburo acted as a court of first instance on matters under his jurisdiction and presumably disposed of many issues of lesser magnitude without consulting his colleagues. Informants claim that a substantial part of the agenda of the Politburo concerned urgent issues referred to it through the ministries. This did not mean that the Politburo functioned only in response to ministerial pressure or that it was at the mercy of the data and recommendations supplied by the ministries. Through the secretarial apparatus of the Central Committee, it mobilized the separate informational resources of the Party hierarchy, which operated as a control on the ministries and brought problems to the attention of the Politburo which the ministries sometimes preferred to conceal. The secret police provided still another powerful instrument of verification and investigation for the ruling group. Since the Politburo presided at the crossroads where all these lines of control converged, it obviously had information at its disposal which was available nowhere else in such concentrated form. Informants who claim to speak with authority report that the Politburo was regularly serviced by a series of secret information bulletins prepared and collated by various branches of the Central Committee Secretariat and bearing such titles as: The Internal Situation in the USSR, The Economy of the USSR, The International Situation of the USSR, The Economy of the Capitalist Countries, Press Bulletin of the Central Committee of the USSR, Foreign Politics, The Situation in the Party.

Is the Soviet high command kept accurately informed of developments at home and abroad? Are there flaws in the data supplied to it? Is it insulated from reality by the character of its own information-gathering facilities or by the climate of expectations in which it moves? Important as these questions are, they cannot be definitively answered with the facts at hand.

There is authoritative evidence indicating that Soviet news services abroad transmit comprehensive and detailed coverage of the world press to Moscow. But the mountains of material have to be reduced to manageable proportions before they are brought to the attention of the leadership. What the rulers read reflects the selection and emphasis of an editorial staff which may be guided by its own preconditioning as well as its sensitivity to the anticipated reactions of its readers. The tendency to embrace data that confirm established predilections while rejecting the unpalatable facts that offend one's preconceptions is a weakness from which no one is wholly free. Totalitarian societies appear to be particularly susceptible to such manipulation. Every dictatorship has a tendency to breed sycophancy and to discourage independence in its bureaucratic hierarchy. When the pronouncements of the dictator are sacred and unchallengeable, the words which subordinates throw back at him tend to flatter his whims rather than to challenge his analyses. No dictatorial regime can entirely escape the distortion of this echo effect. The ideological screen through which facts are received, filtered, and appraised contributes an additional possibility of misrepresentation. The danger in the case of the Soviet Union is accentuated by the rigid doctrinal stereotypes about the outside world imposed by the acceptance of Communist ideology. Not even the most pragmatically-oriented member of the ruling group can wholly liberate himself from the frame of responses that represent the residue of a lifetime immersion in Communist thought patterns.

It is also clear, however, that the Soviet high command has developed its own methods of safeguarding the integrity of its sources of information. By pitting the competitive hierarchies of administration, Party, and secret police against each other at lower levels of the governmental structure, it frees itself from exclusive dependence on any single channel of fact-gathering and encourages rivalries among the various agencies to correct distortion and prevent concealment. In this fashion it mobilizes the cumulative resources which competition sometimes generates. The same technique is applied in the foreign field where a variety of intelligence agencies function side by side with no point of final coördination short of the Kremlin itself.[15] It would be a profound mistake to identify the version of the news circulated by the press to the Soviet public with the full range of facts and data on the basis of which the leadership acts. The Soviet press, in the Communist view, is primarily a channel for the propagation of policies which have already been decided upon rather than a news-gathering instrument on the basis of which decisions are reached. If a conclusion may be drawn from very fragmentary data, it would be to suggest that the climate of decision-making in top Party circles is more deeply affected by the mental screen through which facts are interpreted than by any profound lacunae in the facts themselves. The values with which the leaders confront reality represent the distortions from which they cannot escape.

Perhaps the greatest single source of distortion derives from the enemy image which is deeply imbedded in Marxist-Leninist patterns of thought. The politics of Communism is built around the concept of the implacable adversary who has to be overwhelmed and destroyed lest he in turn annihilate Communism. The dialectics of Leninism which the leadership has been trained to apply are essentially a vision of progress and triumph through conflict and struggle. Such a *Weltanschauung* reduces any accommodation to a negative virtue. Compromise becomes at best a disagreeable necessity rather than a creative achievement. Retreat can be defended only "as a legitimate form of struggle"; as Stalin once put it, "under certain unfavorable circumstances the retreat is as appropriate a form of strife as the advance." [16] The essence of politics remains the clash with the enemy. In the authoritative words of Stalin, "Capitalist encirclement — that is no empty phrase; that is a very real and unpleasant feature . . . there are many countries, bourgeois countries, which continue to carry on a capitalist mode of life and which surround the Soviet Union, waiting for an opportunity to attack it, break it, or at any rate to undermine its power and weaken it." [17]

Since leaders outside the Communist fold are credited with hostile intentions against the Soviet Union and even the temporary ally of today represents a political enemy tomorrow, the information that filters through to the ruling group tends to be perceived, arranged, and analyzed in categories which take such hostility for granted. Expressions of antagonism to the Soviet Union constitute verification of the profundity of the Communist perception of reality; professions of friendship tend to be discounted as wily or naïve stratagems designed to lull the vigilance of the Soviet leadership. The basic premises from which the Kremlin operates breed their polar reactions and induced confirmations. Hostility generates counterhostility, and the theory of the enemy contributes to the creation of the very circumstances that it was devised to explain.

The Goals of the Soviet Leadership

How do the Soviet rulers visualize their objectives? What is their outlook on the world? The classic formulation, which Stalin chose to repeat in his letter to Ivanov in 1938,[18] was pronounced by Lenin: "We live not only in a state, but *in a system of states,* and the existence of the Soviet Republic next to a number of imperialist states for a long time is unthinkable. In the end either the one or the other must triumph. Until that end comes, a series of most terrible conflicts between the Soviet Republic and the bourgeois states is inevitable. This means that the ruling class, the proletariat, if only it wants to and will rule, must prove this also by its military organization." [19]

The Soviet leadership is dedicated to the proposition that the survival and expansion of its power depend on strength, and it sees the secret of its future in the continued rapid industrialization and militarization of the Soviet Union. Stalin stated in 1931:

> To slacken the tempo [of industrialization] would mean falling behind. And those who fall behind get beaten . . . No, we refuse to be beaten! One feature of the history of old Russia was the continual beatings she suffered for falling behind, for her backwardness . . . Do you want our Socialist fatherland to be beaten and to lose its independence? If you do not want this you must put an end to its backwardness in the shortest possible time . . . There is no other way. That is why Lenin said during the October Revolution: "Either perish, or overtake and outstrip the advanced capitalist countries."
>
> We are fifty or a hundred years behind the advanced countries. We must make good the distance in ten years. Either we do it, or they crush us.[20]

Early in 1946, Malenkov returned to the same theme:

> Our friends respect us because we are strong . . . and will only respect us as long as we are strong. The weak are not respected . . . If we are respected it means that they will hesitate to hinder us in our great task of construction . . . we are a mighty force already today . . . and this should be remembered by those who think that our people shed their blood, made tremendous sacrifices, and won victory in order to let others enjoy its fruits.[21]

A continued emphasis on swift industrialization forms the heart of Soviet postwar planning. In Kremlin thinking, military power is intimately intertwined with economic power. The impregnability of the Soviet citadel depends on its military-economic potential. As Soviet strength mounts, its capacity to exert pressure on the non-Soviet world increases accordingly. That, at least, is the Kremlin pattern of analysis.

The outward projection and expansion of Soviet power constitute a primary goal. As Stalin once reminded us, the Soviet rulers operate on the doctrine of Karl von Clausewitz "that war is the continuation of politics by violent means." [22] In this struggle, political and military weapons are treated as interchangeable. The choice of weapon depends on time, place, and circumstance. If military force promises to be decisive, there is no inhibition against its employment. The only operative limits which the Soviet leadership recognizes are the capabilities at its disposal and its own estimate of the risks involved in each act of expansion.

One of the very rare inside glimpses of Kremlin motivations is provided by the correspondence with Tito on the occasion of his break with the Cominform. In a letter of May 4, 1948, dealing, among other things, with Yugoslav dissatisfaction with the failure of the Soviet Union to take military action to seize Trieste, the Central Committee of the Communist Party of the Soviet Union wrote, "Since all other means were exhausted, the Soviet Union had only one other method left for gaining Trieste for Yugoslavia — to start war with the Anglo-Americans over Trieste and take it by force. The Yugoslav comrades could not fail to realize that after such a hard war the USSR could not enter another." [23] This letter (which was not intended for publication) strongly suggests that the primary check on Soviet aggressive designs was its feeling of weakness rather than any scruples about the use of force if force promised to be effective. Indeed, the reliance on Soviet military power to install "friendly" regimes in the satellite states of Eastern Europe is symptomatic of the enlarged role which is reserved for Soviet bayonets as an instrument of Communist persuasion. In rebuking the Yugoslav Communist Party for its alleged arrogance and boastfulness, the Central Committee of the Communist Party of the Soviet Union wrote:

> Even though the French and Italian CPs have so far achieved less success than the CPY, this is not due to any special qualities of the CPY, but mainly because after the destruction of the Yugoslav Partisan Headquarters by German paratroopers, at a moment when the people's liberation movement in Yugoslavia was passing through a serious crisis, the Soviet army came to the aid of the Yugoslav people, crushed the German invader, liberated Belgrade and in this way created the conditions which were necessary for the CPY to achieve power. Unfortunately the Soviet army did not and could not render such assistance to the French and Italian CPs. [24]

But Kremlin dreams of world power are not based on military force alone. It is an article of faith among Communist ideologues that economic crises and the rivalries of imperialist states will ultimately lead to the collapse of capitalism and the triumph of world Communism. In the short run, however, Communist theoreticians have confronted the Soviet leadership with two alternative views. One is the possibility that the so-called "camp of capitalism" will temporarily stabilize and consolidate itself. Should this be achieved, the Soviet bloc would face a grand coalition of its antagonists ready to resist Soviet expansion and even to roll back Soviet power. The other possibility is that the "camp of capitalism" will prove unstable, that "contradictions" among the so-called "imperialist states" will lead to another round of capitalist wars, and that the resulting chaos and disintegration will prepare the way for a world Communist victory.

Stalin, in his article on "Economic Problems of Socialism in the USSR," published on the eve of the Nineteenth Party Congress, decisively rejected the first possibility. He revealed, however, that the view which he repudiated had found some support among his Party colleagues:

Some comrades affirm that, in consequence of the development of new international conditions after the second world war, wars among capitalist countries have ceased to be inevitable. They consider that the contradictions between the camp of socialism and the camp of capitalism are greater than the contradictions among capitalist countries, that the United States of America has made other capitalist countries sufficiently subservient to itself to prevent them from going to war with one another and weakening one another, that forward-looking people of capitalism have learned enough from the experience of two world wars which inflicted serious damage on the whole capitalist world not to permit themselves again to draw the capitalist countries into war among themselves, that in view of all this, wars among capitalist countries have ceased to be inevitable.[25]

"These comrades," Stalin continued, "are mistaken . . . The inevitability of wars among the capitalist countries remains."[26] Malenkov, in his report to the Nineteenth Congress, was less categorical. He confined himself to the observation that "the contradictions which today rend the imperialist camp *may* lead to war between one capitalist state and another."[27] Despite this difference of emphasis, both agreed on the necessity of mobilizing every resource of Soviet foreign policy to accentuate the cleavages among capitalist states and to weaken the strength of the anti-Soviet coalition.

The discussions at the Nineteenth Congress and the first official pronouncements after Stalin's death suggest that the Party leadership still appraises the hazards of total war as too dangerous to its own survival. Instead, the Kremlin seeks alternative means to advance its objectives. It husbands and builds up its own military and economic power for a possible future trial of arms under more propitious circumstances. It uses the interval of truce to consolidate its control and cement its relations with its own satellites and allies. It tries to lull the fears of its potential enemies by proclaiming itself the exponent of peaceful coexistence between capitalist and socialist states. It exploits the rivalries of non-Communist states and offers the lure of trade advantages and nonaggression pacts to attach them to the Soviet orbit. It utilizes its Communist outposts throughout the world to build "national" and "peace" fronts which are intended to weaken Western unity. It holds itself ready to promote the elements of civil war in vulnerable areas by supporting the efforts of local Communists to stir up unrest and win power.

In this grand design, the "peace" campaign currently being waged by the Kremlin plays a multiple role. It represents in part an effort to persuade the Russian people that Soviet military preparations are purely defensive and that the real threat of aggression comes from without. In part, it is designed to impose checks on the rearmament of the West by planting doubts about its necessity in the face of peaceful Soviet intentions. Its purpose is also to confuse and divide non-Communist sentiment by painting American policy-makers as warmongers and imperialists who seek to impose their way of life on the rest of the world. Another aim is to win new converts to the Communist cause by identifying the Soviet Union as the apostle of peace. It further seeks to prepare the way for an ultimate Communist seizure of power. As Stalin cautiously hinted in his "Economic Problems of Socialism in the USSR": "Under a certain confluence of circumstances, the struggle for peace may possibly develop in one place or another into a struggle for socialism." [28]

Whether these tactics will be effective remains to be seen. If they are not successful, they will undoubtedly be modified. The Communist faith in ultimate victory makes room for periods of retreat as well as advance, for the ebb and flow of the revolutionary tide, for oscillating phases of relative quiescence and strong offensive. Whenever the Kremlin faces opponents whose power is appraised as appreciably greater than that of the Soviet bloc, a period of defensive consolidation is indicated. Whether the pause will be prolonged or become the springboard for a new outburst of Soviet expansion will depend on developments during the interval. If the Kremlin succeeds in attaining a predominant power position, it can be expected to translate its strength into new gains to be achieved peacefully if possible, by war if necessary. If its relative position becomes weaker over the years and the dynamic momentum of its forward drive is decisively checked, it will become possible to envisage a future in which the Soviet leadership gradually loses its evangelical fervor and sense of imperial destiny and resigns itself to function within a framework of limited objectives and circumscribed ends.

PART THREE
Instruments of Rule

Chapter 11

Constitutional Myths and Political Realities

In Western eyes, constitutions exist to impose limits on the governments which they create. Whether embodied in formal documents or in customary usage, they attempt to confine each branch of government to its prescribed role, to safeguard citizens against abuse of power by officialdom, and to enforce the continuing responsibility of the governing authorities to the electorate. In more positive terms, they seek to liberate political energies by creating a forum in which competing political forces find free expression, in which the government of the day is subject to a constant flow of criticism from its opponents, and in which changes of government and shifts in public policy may be achieved by registering the shifting preferences of the voting constituency. Where constitutionalism is incorporated in the living texture of society, it generates respect for the dignity of the individual. Men walk in freedom and dare to dissent from the views of their rulers.

This conception of constitutionalism is alien to the Soviet Union. Its ruling group is self-perpetuating, and it cannot be dislodged save by revolution. Its powers are all-embracing and without limit. So-called "constitutional" arrangements derive such force as they possess from its sanction; the whole apparatus of government and administration is subject to its dictates. The leaders of the regime enforce a standard of orthodoxy from which there can be no dissent. Opposition is outlawed and invested with the stamp of treason. Citizens have duties and obligations; such rights as they exercise depend on the precarious beneficence of the ruling group. Freedom is equated with obedience. Individual values must conform to the system of values prescribed by the top leadership. Men walk in subservience and bow to a power which they dare not defy.

From the point of view of the Soviet rulers, the constitutional documents of the USSR and the union republics perform several useful functions. In the first place, they make the formal governmental structure explicit. No dictatorship can escape the problem of devising a system of central and local authorities which will be responsive to its will. By incorporating these arrangements in pseudo-constitutional form, the ruling group gives them an air of legitimacy and stability which no series of administrative ukases can ever communicate. In the second place, the constitutions play an important propaganda role both at home and abroad. The emphasis in the constitutions on mass mobilization of the electorate and mass participation in the proceedings of the Soviets is designed to evoke an illusion of monolithic support for the dictatorship. The manipulated unanimity of "plebiscitory democracy" is intended to demonstrate that opposition to the regime has ceased to exist and that the ruling group is the living incarnation of its people's aspirations. From this platform the regime's spokesmen go on to claim that their constitution is the most democratic in the world, that Western constitutions serve as mere camouflage for the dictatorship of monopoly capital, and that only the Soviet Constitution guarantees the advancement of mass welfare. The utilization of the Constitution as an instrument of propaganda is not limited to domestic audiences. The Constitution of the USSR has been carefully drafted to feature the economic security which the Soviet system is alleged to provide, to leave the impression that ultimate power resides in the hands of the toilers rather than in a narrow ruling clique, and to implant a vision of an idyllic society in which all conflicts have been resolved and all problems can be solved. It seeks to rally support for the Soviet cause in non-Soviet lands by appealing to the dissatisfied, the frustrated, and the gullible whose perceptions of the inadequacies of the societies in which they live can readily be transformed into an idealization of the virtues of a social system which they have not experienced.

The Dissolution of the Constituent Assembly

The constitutional history of the Soviet state is the record of a widening gap between claim and reality. The course of institutional development has been in the direction of increasing concentration of power at the center, the strengthening of the repressive machinery of the regime, the suppression of opposition both inside and outside the Party, the virtual deification of the Supreme Leader, the abandonment of early trends towards egalitarianism in favor of inequality of rewards, the crystallization of a rigidly organized, hierarchical society, and the replacement of the initial multinational policy by a new type of Soviet patriotism in which Great Russian chauvinism plays an important though not exclusive role. For the most part, these changes have received no formal constitutional recognition. Yet in a larger sense, they represent the usages which embody the operative constitutional practice of the Soviet Union. Their consolidation in Soviet life gives the formal constitutional documents a quality of increasing unreality.

The early history of Soviet constitutional development is a reminder that Bolshevism has never been greatly concerned with constitutional niceties. When the Bolsheviks seized power on November 7, 1917, one of their first acts was to utilize the All-Russian Congress of Soviets to decree the establishment of "a temporary workers and peasant government" to "bear the name of the Council of People's Commissars" and to rule "until the convocation of the Constituent Assembly." [1] In the days before the seizure of power, the Bolsheviks had launched bitter attacks against the Kerensky government for its delay in calling a Constituent Assembly. As a result of pressure from the Bolsheviks and other parties, the Kerensky government fixed November 25, 1917, as the day for holding elections to the Constituent Assembly. Once the Bolsheviks were in power, they faced the question of whether elections should be held and, if held, whether the Constituent Assembly should be permitted to assemble and complete its work. The Bolsheviks found themselves in a curious dilemma. They had attacked the Provisional Government so sharply for its dilatory tactics that it did not appear politically expedient to cancel or even delay the elections. They had, however, no intention of depositing their newly won power in a hostile Constituent Assembly. Lenin advocated postponement of the elections, but after a very warm intra-Party discussion, other counsel prevailed. The decision to proceed with the elections was approved, recognizing, as one Bolshevik put it, that if the Constituent Assembly turned out to be refractory, "we may have to dissolve it with bayonets."

The elections were held in an atmosphere of relative freedom. The Bolsheviks received approximately 25 per cent of the total vote. Sixty-two per cent went to the moderate socialists of various hues, with the Socialist-Revolutionaries receiving a predominant majority. The remaining 13 per cent was distributed among the Kadets and other middle-class and conservative parties.[2] The Bolshevik vote was concentrated largely in Moscow, Petrograd, and other industrial centers. The big SR vote was rolled up in the rural districts where the Bolsheviks had yet to penetrate and consolidate their authority.

On January 18, 1918, the first and only meeting of the Constituent Assembly took place at the Tauride Palace in Petrograd. The palace was heavily guarded and surrounded by trustworthy Bolshevik sailors and Red Guards. The Bolshevik bloc failed to gain control of the proceedings. With the aid of their allies the Left SR's, the Bolsheviks were able to muster only 136 votes while the Right SR's commanded 237 votes on the crucial motion to make their program the order of the day.[3] The Bolsheviks and Left SR's then withdrew from the Assembly, leaving the rest of the delegates to continue their talk until far into the night. At five in the morning, a sailor who headed the guard of the palace approached Chernov, the chairman of the Assembly, and requested the delegates to leave the hall "because the guard is tired." [4] The delegates dispersed, presumably to meet again the next day. The next session was never held.

On January 19, 1918, the Central Executive Committee of the Soviets, which was dominated by the Bolsheviks, issued a decree dissolving the Constituent Assembly on the ground that it served as a cover for "the bourgeois counter-revolution in its efforts to crush the power of the Soviets." [5] The delegates who sought to reassemble on the nineteenth were not allowed to enter the palace. This marked the end of the first post-1917 experiment in constitution-making.

On January 23, 1918, the Third Congress of Soviets, which was controlled by the Bolsheviks and Left SR's, met to endorse the dissolution of the Constituent Assembly. Sverdlov, the Bolshevik chairman of the Congress, declared,

> The dissolution of the Constituent Assembly must be counterbalanced by the Third All-Russian Congress of Soviets — the sole sovereign organ which represents truly the interests of the workers and peasants . . .
> The Central Executive Committee and the Council of People's Commissars have definitely taken the stand for a dictatorship of the toiling elements . . . We are of the opinion that during the period of socialist construction there should be a dictatorship . . . to insure the victory of socialism.[6]

The logic of this position led inexorably toward the consolidation of a one-party dictatorship. Having overthrown both the Provisional Government and the Constituent Assembly and having established complete control of the Congress of Soviets and the machinery of government, the Bolsheviks faced the problem of giving these profound changes some form of pseudo-constitutional expression. The outline of the new "constitutional" order soon began to take shape. The dissolution of the Constituent Assembly was followed by formal assumption of supreme governing authority by the Third All-Russian Congress of Soviets. At the closing session of the Congress on January 31, the assembled delegates unanimously approved a proposal to abandon the designation of "Provisional Workers' and Peasants' Government" and to refer to the supreme power henceforth as the "Workers' and Peasants' Government of the Russian Soviet Republic." [7]

The Constitution of 1918

On January 28, 1918, the Congress of Soviets initiated action to embody these changes in constitutional form. By resolution, the Russian

Socialist Soviet Republic was declared to be "a federation of Soviet republics founded on the principle of a free union of the peoples of Russia." Its supreme organ was defined as the All-Russian Congress of Soviets. The Congress of Soviets was to choose a Central Executive Committee which was to be vested with supreme power between sessions of the Congress of Soviets. The Council of People's Commissars was to be "elected or dismissed in whole or in part" by either the Congress of Soviets or the Central Executive Committee. "All local matters" were to be settled exclusively by the local soviets, but higher soviets reserved the right "to regulate affairs between the local soviets and to settle differences that may arise between them." [8]

The Central Executive Committee was charged with the task of drafting a constitution in accordance with these principles for submission to the next Congress of Soviets. On April 1, 1918, it designated a committee of fifteen, headed by Sverdlov and including two Left SR's and one Maximalist, to prepare the final document.[9] The presence of the non-Bolsheviks on the committee and the relative looseness of Party discipline in this period assured a wide airing of views, and the debates revealed substantial differences of outlook. The basic conflicts were between those who pressed for a strengthening of central power and others who wished to safeguard the autonomy of the local soviets; between some who favored a concentration of legislative and executive powers in the supreme organs of government and others who sought their separation and delimitation; between some who urged a syndicalist solution based on autonomous trade-union federations and those who rejected syndicalism in favor of political centralization; between those who supported a form of federalism built on nationality-territorial divisions and others who advocated the establishment of federal republics organized around economic-territorial interests; and between some who pressed for equal representation of the peasantry and industrial workers and those who sought to safeguard the hegemony of the industrial proletariat by guaranteeing it a preferred electoral position. Under the influence of Sverdlov and Stalin, who played a major role in the deliberations of the committee, the luxuriant debate was brought under control, and the basic lines of Bolshevik policy were impressed on the constitutional draft. They involved subordinating the local soviets to centralized authority, safeguarding the concentration of legislative and executive power in the supreme governmental organs, repudiating the syndicalist deviation, organizing the federal republic on nationality-territorial lines, and recognizing the industrial working class as the principal supporting pillar of the regime.

The Constitution of the Russian Socialist Federated Soviet Republic (RSFSR) as finally approved by the Fifth All-Russian Congress of Soviets on July 10, 1918, consisted of two parts. The first, the Declaration of the

Rights of Toiling and Exploited People, stated the policies of the new regime and ratified specific actions which it had taken. The remaining chapters elaborated the general principles of the new Constitution and spelled out the forms of the new governmental structure. The primary objective, in Steklov's words, was to establish "a dictatorship of the proletariat, a powerful centralized government." [10] Members of the so-called "exploiting" classes — businessmen, monks and priests of all denominations, police agents of the old regime, and other similar categories — were disfranchised and denied the right to hold public office. All central and local authority was vested in the laboring masses and their plenipotentiary representatives in the soviets.

The Bill of Rights was restated in class terms. Freedom of speech, of press, of association, of assembly, and of access to education was to be reserved to the working class. Liberty of conscience was guaranteed "for the workers" by separating church from state and school from church; freedom of religious and anti-religious propaganda was to be assured to every citizen. Discrimination against national minorities was outlawed; "Soviets of regions with special usages and national characteristics" were to be permitted to unite in "autonomous" regional unions which would enter the RSFSR on a federal basis. The Constitution specified duties as well as privileges. Universal military service was established, and "the honor of bearing arms in defense of the revolution" was reserved for the working class. The duty to work was proclaimed; "he who does not work," the Constitution stated, "shall not eat."

The structure of government outlined by the Constitution represented essentially a codification of institutions which had already emerged. Supreme authority was vested in the All-Russian Congress of Soviets. This Congress was to be composed of representatives of urban soviets on the basis of one deputy per 25,000 *voters* and representatives of provincial Congresses of Soviets on the basis of one deputy for every 125,000 *inhabitants*. The ratio in favor of urban workers and the system of indirect elections for rural deputies were designed to neutralize the numerical preponderance of the peasantry and to prevent it from swamping the Soviet machinery.

In the intervals between sessions of the All-Russian Congress, supreme power was deposited in a Central Executive Committee (VTsIK) consisting of not more than two hundred members chosen by the Congress. VTsIK was authorized to appoint a Council of People's Commissars to direct the various branches of government and administration. Each of the eighteen Commissariats was to be headed by a People's Commissar and a collegium attached to the Commissariat. The right to make decisions was reserved to the People's Commissar; in the event that the collegium disagreed, it could appeal to the Council of People's Commissars or to the presidium of VTsIK. The competence of the All-Russian Congress of Soviets and VTsIK was all-embracing. Their enumerated powers were supplemented by a provision that they could "decide on any other matter which they deem within their jurisdiction."

Below the level of the All-Russian central institutions, the Constitution provided for a hierarchical arrangement of local soviets which extended downward from the regional (*oblast*) level to the provincial (*guberniya*), county (*uezd*), rural district (*volost*), and village soviets. The larger urban soviets were represented directly in the *oblast* or *guberniya* Congress of Soviets; the urban soviets of towns of less than ten thousand population sent their delegates to the county soviets. Each level of local government down to the rural district had its own congress of soviets and its own executive committee. Town and village soviets also designated their own executive committees.

The responsibilities of local authorities were stated with intentional vagueness. While they were required to adopt "all appropriate measures for developing the cultural and economic life of their territory" and to solve "all questions of purely local importance," they were also subject to the control of superior organs in the Soviet hierarchy and were required to execute "all instructions issued by the appropriate higher organs of Soviet authority." Since the authority of the supreme Soviet organs was subject to their own determination, the centralist thrust of the Constitution was patent. The system of local soviets was visualized essentially as machinery of local administration. In the first turbulent phase of the Revolution, the slogan "All Power to the Local Soviets" had infected elements in the Party itself. The Constitution sought to tame these dispersive and autonomous tendencies. Its budgetary provisions made this clear. A national budget was authorized, and the authority to distribute revenue between central and local authorities was reserved to the All-Russian Congress of Soviets and VTsIK. Although local soviets were authorized to impose taxes for "purely local needs," their budgetary estimates had to be approved by higher Soviet authorities, and the estimates of all town, provincial, and regional soviets had to be ratified by VTsIK and the Council of People's Commissars. In this context, the reference to the new Soviet Constitution as "federal" appears to be largely verbal jugglery. All of its important operative provisions fit the pattern of a highly centralized unitary state.

In presenting the Constitution to the Fifth All-Russian Congress of Soviets for ratification, Steklov described it as "not a finished product." [11] The most glaring example of its incompleteness was its failure to contain a single reference to the Party of the Bolsheviks, the chief architect of the Constitution and the real source of authority in the Soviet state. The 1918 Constitution resembled a play with its most important character missing or at least lurking in the wings. Behind the façade of the soviets and the toiling masses was the Party caucus, arrogating to itself the right both to determine the composition of the soviets and to speak as the sole voice of the masses. While other socialist parties still maintained a precarious existence during this period, the Bolshevik monopoly of legality was rapidly being consolidated, and its control of the formal machinery of government was already far advanced.

The Struggle to Reclaim the Tsarist Patrimony

The circumstances of Civil War and Allied Intervention contributed to the Constitution's tentative and transitional character. The writ of Bolshevik authority was largely confined to the Great Russian interior; the task of reclaiming the Tsarist patrimony had still to be achieved. The new Bolshevik regime was engaged in a desperate struggle for survival. Faced with insurrection and counterrevolution on a whole circle of fluid fronts, the limits of its effective authority shifted with the changing fortunes of war and the strength which its opponents could muster. Confronted with opposing force, the Bolsheviks imposed their rule when the means were available and granted independence when no alternative solution was feasible.* After the Bolsheviks had recognized the independence of Finland on December 31, 1917, Soviet military forces combined with Finnish Red Guards to capture Helsinki and establish a Finnish Socialist Workers' Government on January 28, 1918. A treaty of friendship was concluded by the new Soviet regime with that government on March 1, 1918, but the attempt to seize power encountered unanticipated resistance. The Bolsheviks were driven out, and the independence of Finland was finally confirmed by a peace treaty in 1920.

The experience in the Baltic states was broadly parallel. At the time of the Bolshevik Revolution, Lithuania was under German occupation. Soviet regimes were established in Latvia and Esthonia but were dissolved by the advancing German armies. After the German collapse in November 1918, anti-Soviet national governments emerged, but Soviet armies quickly rushed in to fill the vacuum created by the German retreat and proclaimed Soviet republics in all the Baltic states which were immediately recognized by the RSFSR. As with Finland, the fate of the Baltic states was decided on the battlefield. Local military forces enjoying British and Allied aid succeeded in driving the Soviet armies beyond the frontier, and in 1920 treaties were concluded recognizing the independence of Latvia, Esthonia, and Lithuania.[12]

In Belorussia and the Ukraine, the Bolshevik forces succeeded in establishing and consolidating their ascendancy. Toward the end of Decem-

---

* For a more extended and thorough discussion, see the forthcoming book by Richard Pipes, *The Formation of the Soviet Union*, Harvard University Press.

ber 1917, the anti-Bolshevik Belorussian Rada was overthrown by the Bolsheviks and replaced by a Soviet government. This government in turn was swept away in February 1918 by the advancing German armies which installed a Belorussian Rada of their own. After the armistice in November 1918, Soviet troops occupied Belorussia, expelled the Rada, and proclaimed a provisional Belorussian Socialist Soviet Republic on January 1, 1919. The new Belorussian SSR was a purely Bolshevik creation. It was established on the authority of the Sixth Northwestern Regional Conference of the Russian Communist Party which, acting on the instructions of the Party Central Committee, quickly transformed itself into the First Congress of the Communist Party of Belorussia and voted to establish the Belorussian SSR.

Developments in the Ukraine were more complicated. The Central Rada was originally established in the spring of 1917 as a broadly representative alignment of Ukrainian political groups supporting autonomy within a federated republic of Russian states. Its representative character was certified by Stalin himself when he referred to the Rada as "organized on the principle of a sharing of power between the bourgeoisie, on the one side, and the proletariat and the peasantry, on the other." [13] Since the Rada was not a Soviet organ and resisted Bolshevik domination, the Bolshevik leaders quickly decided that its authority had to be undermined. Building on the soviets which had sporadically erupted in various parts of the Ukraine in the course of 1917, the Bolsheviks sought to weld them together into a political force capable of displacing the Rada as the governing power in the Ukraine. On December 6, 1917, Stalin dispatched the following instruction to the Kiev Soviet: "The power in the country, as in other parts of the state, must belong to the workers', soldiers', and peasants' deputies . . . Convene at once the regional congress of workers', soldiers', and peasants' deputies of the Ukraine . . . On the issue of Soviet power . . . there can be no concessions whatever." [14] On December 24, 1917, a so-called All-Ukrainian Congress of Soviets, dominated by the Bolsheviks, assembled at Kharkov and announced that it had assumed full power in the Ukraine. Since actual authority still reposed in the Rada, which refused to yield to the soviets, the Bolsheviks determined to establish a Soviet regime by force. With the Red Army advancing on Kiev, the Rada on January 22, 1918, proclaimed the independence of the Ukraine. On February 8, 1918, the Soviet army occupied Kiev and installed its own Soviet government there.

The Rada then appealed for help to the Germans, who quickly swept out the new Ukrainian Soviet government and, dismissing the Rada itself, soon installed their own puppet government in the form of the *hetman* Skoropadsky. After the German military collapse, elements of the old Rada proclaimed a Ukrainian Directorate in Kiev, while Soviet armies once more advanced into the Ukraine and occupied Kharkov and Kiev. On March 5, 1919, the Third All-Ukrainian Congress of Soviets assembled in Kharkov and approved a constitution for the Ukrainian SSR which was substantially a replica of the Constitution of the RSFSR.

During the next two years the Ukraine became a no man's land through which rival armies marched and countermarched, and Reds, Whites, and peasant Greens were locked in combat of indescribable confusion. In July 1919 Denikin's White armies seized Kiev and advanced northward. In December, after Denikin had been defeated, the Red Armies recaptured Kiev. The next year, Petlura, the "dictator" of the Directorate, joined with the Poles in a fresh invasion of the Ukraine and occupied Kiev in May–June 1920. With the repulse of the Polish invasion, a peace of sorts settled on the Ukraine, though partisan activity against the Soviet regime continued through much of the next year. By mid-1921 Soviet power in the Ukraine was more or less firmly established.

Developments in the Transcaucasus followed a somewhat analogous pattern. At the time of the October Revolution, the Bolsheviks constituted a weak force in the Transcaucasian provinces. Their chief stronghold was Baku, where, for a period, they established a local Bolshevik government; elsewhere, they formed small minority groups which could not aspire to power without outside aid. The leading party in Georgia was the Menshevik, in Armenia the Dashnak, in Azerbaidjan the Musawat or Equality Party. All were anti-Bolshevik. After an abortive effort to establish a Transcaucasian Federal Republic, the three constituent units, Georgia, Armenia, and Azerbaidjan, each proclaimed their independence and sought to go their separate ways. But the viability of the new republics was short-lived. In mid-1918 Turkish forces occupied the greater part of Armenia and Azerbaidjan, and a German garrison, on the invitation of the Georgians, took over Georgia to prevent its falling into Turkish hands. The retreat of the German and Turkish armies after the armistice left a vacuum which the British temporarily filled. With the withdrawal of the British forces toward the end of 1919, the independent Transcaucasian republics were left face to face with Soviet Russian power.

The Bolshevik leadership wasted no time in pouncing on the helpless victims. The first casualty was Azerbaidjan. In the spring of 1920, a Communist rising in Baku challenged the power of the Azerbaidjan government. The Military Revolutionary Committee in charge of the rising addressed an urgent appeal to Lenin: "Being unable to repulse the attacks of the united bands of the internal and foreign counterrevolution by our own forces, the Military Revolutionary Committee offers the government of the Russian Soviet Republic a fraternal alliance for the common struggle against world imperialism. We request . . . aid." [15]

Aid was quickly forthcoming. The Red Army overran Azerbaidjan and established the Azerbaidjan Socialist Soviet Republic.

Armenia came next. In late November of 1920 another Communist rising was contrived on the border between Azerbaidjan and Armenia, and again the Military Revolutionary Committee in charge invoked the aid of the "heroic" Red Army. On December 2, 1920, the new Armenian Soviet Republic was recognized by Moscow; it was badly shaken by a revolt in mid-February 1921, in the course of which the anti-Bolshevik rebels seized Erivan and a number of principal towns, but the Red Army again came to the rescue and saved the new Soviet regime.

It was now Georgia's turn. The seizure of Georgia was made awkward by the terms of the peace treaty which the Soviet government had concluded with Georgia on May 7, 1920, in a period when the Polish war was going badly. Article I of the treaty stipulated that "Russia recognizes unconditionally the existence and independence of the Georgian state, and voluntarily renounces all sovereign rights which belonged to Russia with respect to the Georgian people and territory." In Article II, Russia agreed "to refrain from any kind of interference in the internal affairs of Georgia." [16] Despite the treaty, an armed Communist insurrection broke out in February 1921. Again Soviet aid was requested, and on February 21, 1921, Soviet forces crossed the frontier, seized Tiflis four days later, and immediately proclaimed the Georgian Socialist Soviet Republic.

The next step in the consolidation of Communist power in the area was the establishment in 1922 of the Transcaucasian Federated Socialist Republic. This measure met strong resistance from a group of Georgian Communists led by Budu Mdivani, as well as scattered resistance in Armenia and Azerbaidjan. Mdivani and his followers were dismissed from their Party posts and purged because, as Stalin put it, "they not only disobeyed, but struggled against the decision of the Party." [17] Thus local patriotism, even when wrapped in a Party guise, was compelled to bow to the centralizing tendencies of the Party leadership.

The extension of Soviet power to other areas was largely determined by Bolshevik military success during the Civil War period. As the Allies withdrew their military contingents and the White Armies were dispersed and defeated, the Bolsheviks encountered little difficulty in disposing of such organized centers of local resistance as remained. The devices used to incorporate the newly regained territory varied with the local situations. In the course of 1920, VTsIK issued decrees creating the Bashkir, Tatar, and Kazakh Autonomous SSR's as well as the Chuvash and Kalmyk Autonomous Regions. All were included within the framework of the RSFSR. As Soviet authority penetrated the North Caucasus, two new autonomous SSR's were established in January 1921 as part of the

RSFSR — Daghestan and the Republic of the Mountaineers. The latter was subsequently subdivided into several autonomous regions. In October 1921, after the subjugation of the turbulent Tatars in the Crimea, that area was constituted the Crimean Autonomous SSR within the RSFSR.

The establishment of Soviet ascendancy in Central Asia had to await the arrival of Red Army contingents in 1920. With their aid, the independent principality of Khiva was dissolved and replaced by the Soviet Republic of Khorezm which soon signed a treaty yielding military and political control to the RSFSR. Meanwhile, the Bolshevik forces also invaded Bokhara, drove out the emir, proclaimed a Soviet Bokhara, and transferred effective power to an embryonic and none too reliable Bokharan Communist Party led by Faizulla Khodjayev. Soviet Bokhara followed the example of Soviet Khorezm and subordinated its military and economic policy to that of the RSFSR by a treaty of alliance signed on March 4, 1921, which nominally guaranteed the complete "independence" of the new republic. The new structure of government in Soviet Central Asia was completed in April 1921, when a decree of VTsIK created an autonomous Turkestan SSR, with headquarters at Tashkent, as a unit of the RSFSR.[18] Despite the presence of the Red Army, disorders continued and erupted in the form of a serious anti-Soviet rebellion led by Enver Pasha and the Basmachi. After considerable fighting, the revolt was quashed, and on August 4, 1922, Enver himself was killed. By the fall of 1922 Soviet authority was substantially established in most of the Central Asiatic region, though minor missions of Red Army pacification continued to be necessary over the next years.

The projection of Soviet power into Siberia faced a series of obstacles in the form of the Czech legions, local authorities of anti-Bolshevik complexion, the Kolchak armies, the forces of Semenov, the *ataman* of the Siberian Cossacks, and the Japanese military forces entrenched in the Maritime Province. The withdrawal of the Czech legions and the disintegration of the Kolchak armies toward the end of 1919 opened the way for the assertion of Bolshevik power in Western Siberia. Meanwhile, the Far Eastern Republic, a so-called buffer state between the Japanese and Soviet armies, established its authority in the Trans-Baikal territory of Eastern Siberia. Although ostensibly independent and recognized as such by the Soviet government on May 14, 1920, the Far Eastern Republic was soon transformed into a puppet regime of the Bolsheviks and was eventually annexed to the RSFSR by a VTsIK decree of November 15, 1922. The Japanese and their henchman Semenov remained in control in Vladivostok and the Maritime Province until the end of October 1922, when the Japanese troops were withdrawn, and the Soviet occupation of Siberia was completed.

In reclaiming the Tsarist patrimony, the Bolsheviks depended heavily on the strength of the Red Army. But force was not their only weapon. The presence of foreign interventionist armies on Russian soil aroused patriotic sentiments which the Bolsheviks were able to capitalize for their own purposes. The reactionary character of the policies espoused by the White generals antagonized many who bore no love for the Bolsheviks but reluctantly embraced their cause because the alternative of a restorationist regime appeared even more unpalatable. To some of the poorer peasants and to the submerged groups among the national minorities, the Bolsheviks frequently appeared in the guise of liberators. The promises that they made held out a hope of escape from old oppressions which the White generals symbolized.

Soviet Nationality Policy

Soviet nationality policy was designed to fuse the scattered fragments of the empire which the Red Army was welding together. The Russian Constitution of 1918 proclaimed "the equality of all citizens, regardless of race or nationality" and declared it "contrary to the fundamental laws of the Republic . . . to repress national minorities, or to limit their rights in any way." Regions "with distinctive customs and national characteristics" were to be permitted to unite into "autonomous regional unions" which could enter the RSFSR "on a federal basis." But autonomy as defined by Stalin, the Commissar of Nationalities, was a divisive as well as a unifying concept. Stalin stated the official view in May 1918 with unvarnished clarity: "Autonomy is a form. The whole question is what class content is contained in that form. The Soviet Power is not against autonomy — it is for autonomy, but only for an autonomy where all power rests in the hands of workers and peasants, where the bourgeoisie of all nationalities are not only deprived of power, but also of participation in the elections of the governing organs." [19] In creating autonomous soviet socialist republics or regions within the RSFSR, the obligation was to dislodge the national bourgeoisie from power and to deposit authority in the hands of the representatives of the toiling masses, the Communist Party itself. Any departure from this principle could be justified only on grounds of expediency. In Central Asia, for example, substantial concessions were made to local merchants and clergy in the early days of Soviet rule in order to facilitate the acceptance of Soviet power; as Communist control was consolidated, the concessions were abrogated.[20]

At the same time, as the Bolsheviks entrenched themselves in power and faced the complex problem of governing the diverse nationalities of the new Soviet empire, divided counsel was manifest. At one extreme were the abstract internationalists among the Bolsheviks for whom any manifestation of national consciousness was outdated. This group took as its point of departure Lenin's maxim of 1913, "The proletariat not only does not undertake to fight for the national development of every nation, but . . . warns the masses against such illusions." [21] The supporters of this point of view were sometimes Great Russians but also frequently Russified non-Russians who had fallen under the spell of the Luxemburg "heresy" and who considered any efforts to stimulate national feeling among the backward peoples as dangerous and reactionary. Since they opposed any concessions to the demands of the national minorities for autonomy, their practical program gave unwitting support to Great Russian chauvinism and coincided with the real interests of the state bureaucracy, which was still in large part a carry-over from the old regime and predominantly Great Russian in composition. The assumption of Great Russian superiority penetrated the highest Party circles. Even Zinoviev, speaking before the Petrograd Soviet on September 17, 1920, gave vent to a Soviet version of the "white man's burden" when he declared, "We cannot do without the petroleum of Azerbaijan or the cotton of Turkestan. We take these products which are necessary for us, not as the former exploiters, but as older brothers bearing the torch of civilization." [22] Lenin had in mind such deeply ingrained attitudes when he declared at the Eighth Party Congress in 1919, "Scratch many a Communist and you will find a Great Russian chauvinist." [23]

At the other extreme were the Communists of the national republics, such as Skrypnik in the Ukraine and Mdivani in Georgia, who not only sought to minister to the cultural and economic aspirations of the minority nationalities but also pressed for real autonomy at the periphery. Carried to the extreme, these views yielded the heresy of local nationalism. It was perhaps no mere coincidence that Mdivani was soon to be purged and Skrypnik was to end his days by suicide.

The dominant view as embodied in Party resolutions during this period sought to avoid both the extremes of Great Russian chauvinism and excessive concessions to local nationalism.

The task of the Party [a resolution of the Tenth Party Congress stated] is to assist the toiling masses of the non-Great Russian peoples in catching up with Central Russia . . . and to help them:

a. To develop and consolidate their own Soviet state system in forms consistent with these people's national way of life;

b. To develop and consolidate their own courts, administrative agencies, economic bodies, and government organs, using the native tongue and staffed by local people familiar with the customs and psychological characteristics of the local population;

c. To set up a press, schools, theaters, community centers, and cultural and educational institutions generally, using the native tongue;

d. To organize and develop a comprehensive system of instruction and schools (with first attention to the Kirghiz, Bashkir, Turkmen, Uzbeks, Tadjiks, Azerbaidjanians, Tatars, and Daghestanians), for the purpose both of general education and vocational and technical training, and conducted in the native tongue, in order more speedily to train indigenous personnel as skilled workers and as Soviet and Party staff members in all spheres of administration, and above all in the sphere of education.[24]

As this resolution made clear, the Party leadership was prepared to encourage the use of the native tongue among the minority nationalities and to exert its influence to raise their educational standards. In doing so, however, its primary purpose was to utilize the native language, culture, and educational system as a vehicle for the Sovietization of the minority peoples. In order to win the support of non-Russian nationalities, it was necessary, as Stalin pointed out, that "all Soviet organs in the border territories — the courts, the administration, the economic organs, the organs of direct government (as well as the organs of the Party) be composed, as far as possible, of local people who know the way of life, the manners, customs, and language of the local population." [25] This policy of *korenizatsia* (from *koren'* or root) which involved utilizing persons of the native or "rooted" populations, was easier to announce than to apply. Insofar as it was applied, however, it helped strengthen the hold of the new Soviet regime on the minority nationalities.

In fostering the cultural development of the backward minorities, Soviet nationality policy endeavored to draw a sharp distinction between form and content. As Stalin said in an address at the Communist University of the Toilers of the East on May 18, 1925:

How are we to make the building of a national culture, the development of schools and courses in the native tongue, and the training of personnel from among the ranks of local people, compatible with the building of socialism, with the building of a proletarian culture? Is this not an unresolvable contradiction? Of course not! We are building a proletarian culture. That is absolutely true. But it is also true that proletarian culture, which is socialist in content, assumes different forms and modes of expression among the various peoples that have been drawn into the work of socialist construction, depending on differences of language, way of life, and so forth. Proletarian in content and national in form — such is the universal human culture toward which socialism is marching.[26]

As this quotation makes clear, Stalin envisaged a multinational state which remained in essence a Communist monolith. The monopoly of direction from the Communist center was to remain undisturbed.

While the Party leadership was prepared to recognize the necessity of adjusting its mode of government to the specific features of different national cultures, it was not prepared to abandon the principle of centralism on which the Party organization itself was constructed. In the early struggles against the Bund and other national groups who sought to organize the Party on federalist and nationality lines, both Lenin and Stalin had decisively rejected organizational federalism as concealing within itself "the elements of disintegration and separatism." [27] Faced with the responsibilities of power, they continued to insist upon "a single, indivisible proletarian collective body, a single party, for the proletarians of all the nationalities in a given state." [28] As the Bolsheviks expanded their control of the borderlands, nominally separate Communist Parties were organized, such as the Communist Party of Bolsheviks of the Ukraine and the Communist Party of Belorussia. But such Parties functioned in all essential respects as administrative subunits of the Russian Communist Party. They sent delegates to its Congresses and were expected to subordinate themselves to the directives of the Central Committee and other leading bodies of the Russian Party. As Andreyev declared at the Fourteenth Party Congress: "Our Party . . . is a centralized party. All the national Parties which exist among us — the Ukrainian, Transcaucasian, Central Asiatic — all exist with the legal right of regional or provincial committees; the Party remains centralized, a unity from top to bottom." [29] Leaders of the local Parties who manifested restiveness under central discipline or who defied the central Party authorities did not remain leaders long. The supreme Party organs brooked no challenge. The national Party groups remained incorporated in the Russian Party until the Fourteenth Party Congress in 1925, when the name of the Party was changed from the Russian Communist Party of Bolsheviks — RKP(b) — to the All-Union Communist Party of Bolsheviks — VKP(b). The change of name marked no substantial change in relationships between center and periphery. It merely registered the response of the Party to the formal creation of the Union of Soviet Socialist Republics and represented a semantic adjustment to the new constitutional entity.

As the new Soviet state emerged from the chaos of Civil War and Intervention and regained a substantial part of the Tsarist patrimony, it faced the problem of devising a unified governmental structure for the reclaimed areas and embodying this settlement in constitutional form. The solutions arrived at in the heat of conflict were essentially improvisations. Some of the reconquered territories were simply incorporated in the RSFSR as autonomous republics or regions. In other cases, as in the Ukraine, Belorussia, and the Transcaucasus, nominally independent SSR's were established with which the RSFSR concluded treaties of alliance that, in effect, subordinated these republics to the RSFSR. The treaty with the Ukrainian SSR, signed on December 28, 1920, provided essentially for a military and economic union.[30] The Russian and Ukrainian Republics merged their Commissariats of War and Navy, People's Economy, Foreign Trade, Finance, Labor, Transport, and Posts and Telegraphs. This model was followed in Belorussia and the Transcaucasus with only minor variations. The status of the Bokhara and Khorezm

Soviet Republics in Central Asia involved a greater degree of autonomy. There were no unified commissariats; instead, the treaties concluded with them provided for a military alliance and a preferred economic position for the RSFSR. The "independence" of Bokhara and Khorezm did not last long. In October 1923 Bokhara was transformed into a socialist state, and in 1924 Khorezm followed. In that year, the Turkestan ASSR was abolished, and Soviet Central Asia was divided into two new union republics, the Uzbek and the Turkmen. Bokhara was absorbed into the Uzbek SSR, and Khorezm was broken up and allotted to the Uzbek republic and the Kazakh ASSR.

The Establishment of the USSR and the Constitution of 1924

The signal for formal unification of the new Soviet empire was first given in the resolution on the national question which was enacted by the Tenth Party Congress in 1921. The resolution called for a "union of the several Soviet republics as the only path of salvation from the imperialist yoke and national oppression." [31] At the Ninth All-Russian Congress of Soviets, in December 1921, delegates appeared from the ostensibly separate republics of Ukraine, Belorussia, Azerbaidjan, Georgia, and Armenia, and no objections were registered. Their representatives were included in the VTsIK of the Russian Congress, and the decrees of that body were treated as binding in the territories of the allied republics.[32] Meanwhile, the stage was set to have the demand for unification come from the national republics themselves.[33] On December 13, 1922, the first Transcaucasian Congress of Soviets, which had itself only recently been organized over the strenuous objection of Mdivani and other leading Georgian Communists, passed a resolution urging the formation of a Union of Soviet Socialist Republics. The same day, the Ukrainian Congress of Soviets enacted a similar resolution, and the next day the Belorussian Congress of Soviets joined the chorus. On December 26 the Tenth All-Russian Congress of Soviets, on a motion by Stalin, added its approval. Four days later the delegates of the four republics, who were in fact already represented in the All-Russian Congress of Soviets, reconstituted themselves as the First Congress of the Soviets of the USSR. In that capacity, they ratified a solemn declaration approving the formation of the USSR and a draft treaty which was to become the basis of the Constitution of the new Union. The guiding role of the Party was evidenced from the outset. Of the delegates to the First Congress, 94.8 per cent were Party members.

The First Congress selected a new VTsIK or Central Executive Committee, and its presidium designated a commission to draft the final version of the new Constitution. Important differences of view among members of the drafting commission soon became evident. A running battle ensued which extended to the Twelfth Party Congress and the Central Committee and was finally resolved only by the Politburo itself. The debate revealed at least three different conceptions of the shape which the new Union should possess. At one extreme were the opponents of federalism, who, according to the Twelfth Party Congress resolution on the national question, regarded the union of republics "not as a union of equal state entities with a mandate to guarantee the free development of the national republics, but as a step toward the liquidation of the republics, as a beginning of the organization of the so-called 'one and indivisible' republic." [34] This group opposed the creation of a second chamber in which the nationalities would have separate representation; they sought to weld the Soviet empire into a tightly organized unitary state. At the Twelfth Party Congress, Stalin denounced them as "Great Power chauvinists"; without identifying the culprits, he referred to speeches which were delivered at the February 1923 plenum of the Central Committee which "had no resemblance to Communism, speeches which had nothing in common with internationalism." [35]

At the other extreme were the Ukrainian Party leaders, Rakovsky and Skrypnik, and representatives of the other minority nationalities, who pressed for a form of union which would guarantee the non-Russian republics a measure of real autonomy. This group favored a second chamber composed of representatives of the four union republics. To prevent the RSFSR from dominating this chamber, Rakovsky proposed that no single republic could have more than two-fifths of the total votes. The Ukrainian delegates also suggested that the Union Soviet and the Soviet of Nationalities should each have its own presidium. Loath to give up the perquisites which they had previously enjoyed in the foreign field, they also urged that the Commissariats for Foreign Affairs and Foreign Trade should be made union-republican rather than all-union or unified commissariats, as the official draft proposed. Stalin, in the course of a speech on June 12, 1923, to a gathering of responsible workers from the national republics and *oblasts*, made frank reference to the difficulties which the Ukrainians were causing.

I must say that the Politburo is in some disagreement with the Ukrainian comrades . . . It is not true that the question of confederation versus federation is a trivial issue. Was it an accident that the Ukrainian comrades . . . omitted from the Constitution the sentence that the republics "join in one union state"? . . . Was it an accident that the Ukrainian comrades in their counterproposal proposed not to unite the People's Commissariat for Foreign Trade and Foreign Affairs, but to transfer them into the category of directed commissariats? Where would the one union state be if each republic retained its own NKID and NKVT? . . . I perceive from the insistence of several Ukrainian comrades their desire to define the Union as something between a confederation and federation, with the preponderant weight on the side of confederation . . . We are constructing, not a confederation, but a federal republic, one union state, uniting military and foreign affairs, foreign trade, and other matters.[36]

The Constitution of the USSR as it was finally approved by VTsIK on July 6, 1923, and ratified by the second All-Union Congress of Soviets on January 31, 1924, embodied the views of Stalin and the Politburo. Its opening section was an ideological manifesto that described the world as divided into the rival camps of capitalism and socialism, declared the need for a united front of Soviet republics in the face of the capitalist encirclement, and boldly proclaimed the organization of the USSR as "a new decisive step towards the union of workers of all countries in a World Socialist Soviet Republic." Part Two of the Constitution contained the treaty by which the partners to the Union — the Russian, Ukrainian, Belorussian, and Transcaucasian Republics — declared their agreement to unite "in one union state." The powers of the supreme organs of the USSR were outlined in an all-embracing list which included foreign affairs and foreign trade, questions of war and peace, direction of the national economy, fiscal policy, the state budget, control of the armed forces, and other matters of lesser importance.

The jurisdiction of the union republics was stated in residual form; the republics were authorized to exercise such powers as were not vested in the government of the USSR. Since the authority of the central government embraced education, public health, courts of justice, and other matters ordinarily conceived of as of local significance, the initiative of the union republics was confined within relatively narrow limitations. The boundaries of the union republics, however, could not be changed without their consent, and the Constitution also solemnly proclaimed that each union republic retained the right "freely" to secede from the union. The real meaning of this "right" was elucidated by Stalin in an article in *Pravda* on October 10, 1920. "Of course," he commented, "the border regions of Russia, the nations and tribes, which inhabit these regions . . . possess the inalienable right to secede from Russia," but "the demand for secession . . . at the present stage of the revolution [has become] a profoundly counterrevolutionary one." [37]

The Constitution established the Congress of Soviets as the supreme organ of authority in the USSR. Following the pattern of the 1918 Russian Constitution, its membership consisted of representatives of city and town soviets on the basis of one deputy for each 25,000 voters and of representatives of provincial and district congresses of soviets on the basis of one deputy for every 125,000 inhabitants. The Congress of Soviets elected a Central Executive Committee (VTsIK) composed of two chambers, a Council of the Union, selected on the basis of population, and a Council of Nationalities, made up of five delegates from each union and autonomous republic and one delegate from each autonomous region. The two chambers shared the powers reposing in VTsIK, which functioned as the supreme authority of the USSR between sessions of the Congress of Soviets. The concurrence of both chambers was required for all decrees and regulations promulgated in the name of VTsIK. In the intervals between sessions of VTsIK, its presidium, which included representatives of both chambers, exercised the authority vested in VTsIK.

The Constitution provided for three categories of People's Commissars. The first category of all-union commissariats, which existed only in the Sovnarkom or Council of People's Commissars of the USSR, included Foreign Affairs, Military and Naval Affairs, Foreign Trade, Ways of Communication, and Posts and Telegraphs. The second category of union-republic or unified commissariats existed both in the government of the USSR and the union republics, with the latter responsible for executing the decisions taken at the center. This group included the Supreme Council of National Economy and the Commissariats of Food, Labor, Finance, and Workmen's and Peasants' Inspection. The OGPU or Unified State Political Administration, which was also provided for in the Constitution, was attached to the Sovnarkom of the USSR but functioned locally through representatives "attached to the Sovnarkoms of the union republics." The third category of so-called republic commissariats existed only in the republics and had no counterparts in the government of the USSR. These commissariats included Internal Affairs, Justice, Education, Health and Social Welfare. The government of the USSR, however, retained authority to issue basic regulations in all these fields. While these arrangements provided varying degrees of decentralized administration for different types of governmental functions, policy control remained highly centralized. Behind the façade of the federal structure loomed the discipline of a unified Party hierarchy. Neither its monopoly of political power nor even its existence was acknowledged by the Constitution.

Unlike the 1918 Constitution, the Constitution of the USSR made provision for a Supreme Court and a Procurator attached to the Central Executive Committee of the USSR. The jurisdiction of the Supreme Court included giving opinions on questions of Union legislation to the Supreme Courts of the union republics, examining decisions of the lower courts to discover infractions of Union law, rendering decisions on the constitutionality of laws passed by the union republics, and settling disputes among them. The Supreme Court, however, had no power to pass on the constitutionality of Union legislation or to declare any act of its organs *ultra vires*. In the event that the Procurator disagreed with any decisions of the Supreme Court, he had the right to protest before the presidium of the USSR Central Executive Committee. The Supreme Court was thus strictly subordinate to VTsIK, which retained supreme judicial as well as legislative and executive power.

The USSR Constitution of 1924, like the earlier Russian Constitution before it, radiated a sense of legerdemain and make-believe. It outlined the formal governmental structure of the new Union, but the springs of power in the Soviet system were hidden. The dominating role of the Party was concealed behind an elaborate array of pseudo-representative institutions which functioned as transmission belts to register the will of the Party leadership.

This is not to imply that the employment of constitutional forms served no useful purpose for the Soviet ruling group. Dictatorships ordinarily prefer not to reveal themselves in all their stark nakedness. By assuming a constitutional disguise, they clothe the realities of arbitrary power in the protective garb of tradition and legitimacy. They pay constitutionalism the ultimate compliment of borrowing its façade to conceal the authoritarian character of their governing formula.

Nor were the debates in Party circles which accompanied the drafting of the Constitution without significance. They revealed that the Party still mirrored the tensions which accompanied the creation of the Union. The efforts of the Ukrainian and other non-Russian Communists to retain a measure of autonomy expressed deep-rooted aspirations which continue to plague the Soviet empire. At the same time, the decision of Stalin and his associates in the Politburo to reject an undisguised unitary solution and to find a place in their constitutional scheme for a Council of Nationalities and a federation of union republics demonstrated political acumen. Though the Constitution actually circumscribed national autonomy within narrow bounds, the preservation of the forms of nationality representation was calculated both to placate national feeling and to become a platform for mobilizing support among the submerged nationalities of the East.

The admission of new union republics into the USSR in succeeding years illustrated the continuing value of the device. Turkmenistan and Uzbekistan joined the ranks of Soviet Socialist Republics in 1925. Tadjikistan was elevated to the status of a union republic in 1929. At the same time, new autonomous republics and regions were created to give formal recognition to minority nationality aspirations.

Soviet nationality policy during the twenties and early thirties represented an ingenious endeavor to combine central control with the forms of local autonomy. Particularly during the twenties, a genuine, if not always successful, effort was made to broaden the use of the local language in the national republics and regions, to recruit native personnel into the Party, and to employ them in public administration, sometimes even in posts involving considerable responsibility. At the same time, the central Party authorities were quick to stamp out any display of independence or local chauvinism by the new native leadership. A frank letter from Stalin to Kaganovich and other members of the Central Committee of the Communist Party of the Ukraine, written on April 26, 1926, but published in full for the first time in 1948, reveals the real thrust of Soviet nationality policy in this period.[38] Though Stalin declared himself in favor of the gradual Ukrainization of the Party and governmental apparatus, he made clear that he was opposed to forcible Ukrainization and particularly opposed to any Ukrainian movement which assumed "the character of a struggle for the alienation of Ukrainian culture and Ukrainian social life from general Soviet culture and social life." [39] He bitterly attacked the Ukrainian Communist novelist Mykola Khvylovy, who had advanced the slogan "Away from Moscow" as a guide to Ukrainian intellectuals, and he warned that such an "un-Marxist" motto could lead only to "a struggle against 'Moscow' in general, against Russians in general, against Russian culture and its supreme achievement — Leninism." [40] Khvylovy's patron, Shumsky, the Ukrainian Commissar of Education, was soon removed from his post. A campaign inaugurated against Ukrainian chauvinism led to the arrest in 1929 of many prominent intellectuals who had opposed the Bolsheviks during the Civil War and who were alleged to hold membership in a conspiratorial Union for the Liberation of the Ukraine (SVU). Skrypnik, Shumsky's successor as Ukrainian Commissar of Education, committed suicide in 1933 when he too came under attack as a Ukrainian chauvinist.

During the late twenties, a concerted effort was also made to eradicate centers of local chauvinism in other national republics. In Belorussia, a large number of officials and intellectuals were arrested in 1929 because of their supposed membership in the National Democratic Party, an underground organization opposed to Communist rule. The purge of "nationalists" extended to Armenia, the Crimea, Turkestan, and other areas and included Party members as well as non-Party intellectuals. The consolidation of Stalin's control over the Party and governmental apparatus was accompanied by increasingly rigorous supervision of the national republics from Moscow.

The industrialization program inaugurated in the late twenties also contributed to reinforce the tendencies toward centralization. The new industrial commissariats which were charged with the administration of the program were created on an all-union or unified basis. Only small-scale local industry remained subject to the exclusive jurisdiction of the union republics. By the mid-thirties, Soviet federalism was revealing itself as an increasingly transparent fiction.

The USSR Constitution of 1936

At this time a new chapter in the constitutional history of the USSR was suddenly unfolded. On February 1, 1935, the plenum of the Central Committee of the Party instructed Molotov to appear before the Seventh All-Union Congress of Soviets and to suggest changes in the Constitution directed toward:

(*a*) Further democratization of the elective system — in the sense of substituting equal elections for elections not fully equal; direct elections for elections having multiple stages; and secret elections for elections which were open; and (*b*) making more precise the social-economic bases of the Constitution — in the sense of bringing the Constitution into conformity with the present correlation of class forces in the USSR (the creation of new socialist industry, the liquidation of the kulaks, the confirmation of socialist property as the basis of Soviet society, etc.).

The Congress of Soviets unanimously approved Molotov's proposal, and its Central Executive Committee designated a Constitutional Commission headed by Stalin to draft the text of the new Constitution. Among the members of the Commission were Bukharin and Radek who were shortly to discover the real value of the constitutional "safeguards" which they were elaborating.

On June 1, 1936, Stalin submitted a draft of the new Constitution to a plenum of the Central Committee of the Party. The plenum approved and ordered the convocation of an Extraordinary All-Union Congress of Soviets to ratify the Constitution. Meanwhile, some unusual steps were taken. On June 12, 1936, the draft of the Constitution was published, and the citizenry of the Soviet Union was invited to engage in a nationwide discussion of its contents. Proposals for amendment were invited. In the words of Vyshinsky, "The draft was read with delight and discussed in all the industrial and transport enterprises, in sovkhozes and kolkhozes, and in government offices . . . The Soviet people greeted the appearance of the draft of the new USSR Constitution with enormous enthusiasm and approved it with one accord." [41] It was evident that Stalin was anxious to have the world note that a discussion was proceeding and that the people of the Soviet Union "approved" the work of their leaders. On November 25, 1936, the Extraordinary Eighth All-Union Congress of Soviets assembled, and Stalin appeared personally before it to present a final draft of the Constitution which incorporated some of the suggestions which had emerged in the course of the discussion. On December 5, 1936, the final text of the Constitution was unanimously approved by the Congress.

Stalin's speech before the Congress provided at least a partial clue to the motives which inspired the revision of the Constitution and the large-scale mass discussion that accompanied it. Stalin began his address by pointing out that a new Constitution was necessary in order to bring the fundamental law into conformity with the social and economic changes that had taken place in the Soviet Union since 1924. The developments which he stressed were the socialization of industry under the Five Year Plans after the mixed economy of the NEP, the collectivization of agriculture, the liquidation of the kulaks, and the emergence of the collective farm system. As a result of these changes, he claimed, the class structure of the Soviet Union had been transformed. Landlords, kulaks, capitalists, and merchants had been eliminated. There remained only workers, peasants, and the intelligentsia, all joined together in a harmonious pattern of common interest. "The new Constitution . . ." Stalin stated, "proceeds from the fact that there are no longer any antagonistic classes in society; that society consists of two friendly classes, of workers and peasants; that it is these classes, the labouring classes, that are in power." [42] Hence, argued Stalin, it was possible to introduce universal suffrage without any restrictions and without any disfranchised classes. Hence, it was also possible to abolish inequality between workers and peasants, to eliminate indirect elections and the system of weighting the votes of urban workers more heavily than the votes of the rural peasantry. Hence, it became possible to have secret elections because all classes were solid in their loyalty to the regime. He paused briefly to deflate the arguments of critics that the draft Constitution changed nothing since it left the monopoly of the Communist Party unimpaired. "I must admit," he declared, "that the draft of the new Constitution . . . preserves unchanged the present leading position of the Communist Party of the U.S.S.R. . . . In the U.S.S.R. only one party can exist, the Communist Party, which courageously defends the interests of the workers and peasants to the very end." The Party, he argued, was the custodian of the interests of the working masses; it provided "democracy for the working people, *i.e.*, democracy for all . . . That is why I think that the Constitution of the U.S.S.R. is the only thoroughly democratic Constitution in the world." [43]

The real significance of this exercise in casuistry became evident toward the end of Stalin's speech when he dealt with the value of the new Constitution as a weapon of Soviet foreign policy.

The international significance of the new Constitution . . . can hardly be exaggerated.
Today, when the turbid wave of fascism is bespattering the Socialist movement of the working class and besmirching the democratic strivings of the best people in the civilized world, the new Constitution of the U.S.S.R. will be an indictment against fascism, declaring that Socialism and democracy are invincible. The new Constitution of the U.S.S.R. will give moral assistance and real support to all those who are today fighting fascist barbarism. [44]

This was the period of popular fronts when the Soviet Union was seeking to pacify liberal opinion in the so-called capitalist democracies, when it was preaching collective security and trying to organize a system of pacts and alliances against Hitler and his allies. The Soviet Constitution of 1936 and the large-scale discussion which attended its adoption were designed to persuade the Western democracies that the Soviet Union was a true democracy or that it was at least moving in a democratic direction and that it enjoyed the full support of the Soviet peoples. In the larger context of Soviet foreign policy, one of the major objectives of the 1936 essay in Soviet constitution-making appears to have been the desire to forge a common bond with the Western powers in resisting Nazi, Fascist, and Japanese aggression. The Great Purge which followed hard on the heels of the adoption of the Constitution destroyed much of its effect, and the alliance which it sought to cement did not come until the Nazi attack on the Soviet Union.

The Constitution of 1936, although amended in detail over the years, remains in effect today. Its plan can be briefly summarized. Chapter One, entitled the Organization of Society, proclaims the USSR as a "socialist state of workers and peasants" and outlines the role of state, collective farm, and private property. Particularly notable in terms of its intended appeal to the West is the declaration in Article 10 that "the right of citizens to personal ownership of their incomes from work and of their savings, of their dwelling houses and subsidiary household economy, their household furniture and utensils and articles of personal use and convenience, as well as the right of inheritance of personal property of citizens, is protected by law." [45]

The next eight chapters of the Constitution lay down the political structure of the state. After reiterating that the USSR is a federal state and that each union republic reserves the "right freely to secede," the powers of the central governmental organs are specified in such all-embracing scope as largely to negate the federal pattern on which the government is allegedly constructed. The highest organ of state authority is declared to be the Supreme Soviet of the USSR. The Supreme Soviet is divided into two chambers: the Soviet of the Union, which is directly elected on the basis of one deputy for every three hundred thousand inhabitants, and the Soviet of Nationalities, which is also directly elected on the basis of twenty-five deputies from each union republic, eleven deputies from each autonomous republic, five deputies from each autonomous region, and one deputy from each national area. Both chambers serve for a term of four years and have equal rights in initiating and enacting legislation. In case they disagree and their disagreements cannot be reconciled (an eventuality that is hardly likely to occur under a system of one-party rule), the Presidium of the Supreme

Soviet has the authority to dissolve the Supreme Soviet and order new elections.

The Presidium is elected at a joint session of both chambers. As originally established in 1936, it consisted of a chairman, eleven vice-chairmen, a secretary, and twenty-four members. Its membership has since been reorganized to provide for a chairman, sixteen vice-chairmen, a secretary, and fifteen members. The Presidium functions as a collegial presidency. It performs the ornamental functions of head of state, convenes and dissolves sessions of the Supreme Soviet, and appoints and relieves cabinet ministers on the recommendation of the Council of Ministers and subject to subsequent confirmation by the Supreme Soviet. It has the power to annul decisions of the Council of Ministers (before 1946 called Council of People's Commissars) in case they do not conform to law. It interprets laws of the USSR, issues decrees, exercises the right of pardon, ratifies and denounces treaties, proclaims martial law, issues mobilization orders, is authorized to declare war in the intervals between sessions of the Supreme Soviet, and performs a number of other functions of lesser significance.

Executive and administrative authority is vested in a Council of Ministers whose appointment requires the confirmation of the Supreme Soviet. Theoretically the Council of Ministers is responsible to the Supreme Soviet and its Presidium; members of the Supreme Soviet may address questions to the ministers who are required to "give a verbal or written reply in the respective chamber within a period not exceeding three days." The stenographic reports of the sessions of the Supreme Soviet give no indication that this "right of interpellation" is exercised.

The 1936 Constitution, like its predecessor, provides for three types of ministries: all-union, union-republic, and republic. Since 1936, there has been a considerable expansion in the number of all-union and union-republic ministries with heavy industry largely reserved for all-union jurisdiction while light industry, agriculture, and trade are entrusted to the union-republic ministries. The decentralization of operative functions in the latter case is combined with continued centralization of planning and direction. Decisions and orders of the Council of Ministers of the USSR are binding on all lower organs.

The government of the union republics consists of a Supreme Soviet of one chamber, its Presidium, and a Council of Ministers composed of union-republic and republic ministries. The union-republic ministries are subordinated to the council of ministers of the union republic and its supreme soviet as well as to their counterpart ministries at the center. The republic ministries are directly subordinate to the union republic's council of ministers and its supreme soviet. Autonomous republics also possess their own supreme soviets, presidiums, and councils of ministers.

The local organs of state authority (territories, regions, districts, cities, rural localities, etc.) include soviets elected for a two-year term and the executive committees or *ispolkoms* which are formally responsible to the soviets and selected by them.

The Constitution also provides for a judicial system consisting of a Supreme Court of the USSR, supreme courts of the union republics, territorial and regional courts, courts of the autonomous republics and autonomous regions, area courts, special courts of the USSR established by the Supreme Soviet, and people's courts. People's courts are popularly elected for three-year terms; the members of other courts are selected by their corresponding soviets for five-year terms. Cases are heard in public "unless otherwise provided by law." The accused "is guaranteed the right to be defended by counsel," a right which many survivors of the Great Purge testify was suspended in their cases despite the explicit phraseology of the Constitution. According to Article 112 of the Constitution, "judges are independent and subject only to the law." A recent commentary by a Soviet jurist, N. N. Polyansky, sheds light on the meaning of this formula.

The independence of the judges referred to in Article 112 of the Stalin Constitution does not and cannot signify their independence of politics. The judges are subject only to the law — this provision expresses the subordination of the judges to the policy of the Soviet regime, which finds its expression in the law.

The demand that the work of the judge be subject to the law and the demand that it be subject to the policy of the Communist Party cannot be in contradiction in our country.[46]

The Constitution creates a Procurator-General who is appointed by the Supreme Soviet of the USSR. The procurators in lower jurisdictions operate under his direction and exercise "supervisory power over the strict execution of law by all ministries and institutions subordinated to them, as well as by public servants and citizens of the USSR." The Constitution also provides (Article 127) that "no person may be placed under arrest except by decision of a court or with the sanction of a procurator." The testimony of many Soviet *émigrés* who fell into the hands of the Soviet secret police indicates that this requirement is ordinarily a formality which has no practical significance in restraining arbitrary arrests. The extensive powers of the Procuracy are elaborated in statutory rather than in constitutional form. They include the right to protest decisions of the USSR Supreme Court to the Presidium of the Supreme Soviet, to appear in criminal cases in support of the state's indictment, and to intervene in civil cases where state interests are involved.

Chapter Ten of the Constitution contains a statement of the Fundamental Rights and Duties of Citizens. The list of rights includes the right to work, the right to rest and leisure, the right to maintenance in old age and in case of sickness or loss of capacity to work, the right to education, sex equality, absence of discrimination on account of race or nationality, freedom of conscience, freedom of speech, freedom of press, freedom of assembly, freedom of street processions and demonstrations, freedom to unite in public organizations, the inviolability of the person and the homes of citizens, and privacy of correspondence.

This impressive list of "rights" needs to be interpreted against the background of Soviet actualities. The right to work is not a right to choose one's work freely but a duty to work in disciplined subordination to state purposes. It means working at the post to which one is assigned, at wages and under conditions which are determined by higher authorities over whom one has no control. There is no right to strike, and violations of labor discipline are subject to drastic penalties. For at least several million Soviet citizens, it means forced labor in concentration camps with little or no hope of eventual liberation.

The "right" to rest and leisure depends in the Soviet Union, as in other parts of the world, on the availability of means to enjoy rest and leisure. Only a minority of the Soviet labor force commands sufficient resources to finance a visit to a vacation resort or the influence necessary to obtain entrance into a rest home. The tendency in recent years to cut down on holidays, to lengthen the working day, to emphasize work discipline, and to increase work quotas indicates that rest and leisure are low in the scale of values which the Soviet regime is currently fostering. Social insurance benefits also fall far short of the ideal proclaimed in the Constitution. While free medical care is available, its quality leaves much to be desired. Certifications of temporary or permanent work disability are extremely difficult to obtain, and, except for "leading" workers, the financial aid forthcoming is frequently inadequate. Old age pensions for ordinary workers are often pitifully small.

The "right" to education is also a qualified one. Although there has been an impressive expansion of educational facilities under the Soviet regime, the commitment of the state to provide free education for all is limited to the first seven classes. Outstanding students receive state stipends or scholarships to continue their education beyond that point. Other students attending the higher schools are required to pay fees, and their ability to do so frequently depends on parental resources. The effect of recent developments in Soviet educational policy is to screen out the vast majority of Soviet youth for training and service in lower industrial ranks while reserving opportunities for higher education to the specially qualified and the financially well endowed.

The constitutional provision which accords equal rights to women (Article 122) registers the fact that women have become an integral part of the Soviet industrial and agricultural labor force and that the regime has made a determined effort to mobilize their skills and productive capacities for state purposes. Although the proportion of women in high Party and governmental offices is still small, there has been a notable increase in the number of women occupying professional and administrative posts of lesser responsibility. The effect of the new attitude toward women has been particularly revolutionary in the Soviet East, where women had long been relegated to a servile and secluded role.

The constitutional inhibition against racial or national discrimination (Article 123) needs to be read against the recent tendency to accord priority to the Great Russian nation and to regard any display of local patriotism among the non-Great Russian nationalities as a threat to the unity of the Soviet empire. The emergence of Great Russian chauvinism under the cover of Soviet patriotism, which began prior to World War II, has been accompanied since 1947 by a campaign against "rootless cosmopolitans" with clear anti-Semitic as well as anti-Zionist overtones.* While official policy remains ostensibly opposed to anti-Semitism, anti-Semitic cartoons and articles have appeared in the Soviet press, and evidence of discrimination against Jews in Soviet public life has accumulated in the postwar years.[47]

The constitutional guarantee of freedom of conscience (Article 124) must also be classified as a qualified right. Religious organizations in the Soviet Union operate under the tutelage of the State Council on Church Affairs. They are forbidden to undertake any functions other than the practice of religious rites. Strenuous pressure has been exerted to transform them into adjuncts of the regime. At the same time, the official policy of the Party leadership remains hostile to religion in any form, and the whole weight of the educational system has been thrown on the side of discouraging religious belief. Members of the Party and Communist youth organizations are forbidden to participate in religious ceremonies; anti-religious propaganda forms an essential element in Communist indoctrination. The ultimate objective, in Vyshinsky's words, is the eradication of religion "by socialist reëducation of the toiling masses, by anti-religious propaganda, by implanting scientific knowledge, and by expanding education." [48]

The clauses in the Constitution (Article 125) safeguarding freedom of speech, freedom of the press, freedom of assembly, and freedom of street processions and demonstrations are prefaced by the significant proviso

---

* In announcing the release of the arrested Jewish doctors who were charged with plotting "terroristic" activities against Soviet leaders, *Pravda*, in an editorial of April 6, 1953, blamed officials of the Ministry of State Security for attempting "to inflame . . . feelings of national antagonism which are profoundly alien to socialist ideology." Whether this pronouncement marks the end of the anti-Semitic campaign remains to be seen.

that these rights are to be exercised "in conformity with the interests of the working class, and in order to strengthen the socialist system." Put more bluntly, they cannot be utilized to criticize or challenge the ascendancy of the Party leadership. As innumerable commentaries on the Constitution make clear, these "liberties" are reserved for adherents and denied to opponents of the regime. Freedom, in the Soviet constitutional lexicon, is the duty to ratify the policies of the ruling group and not the right to criticize them. "The right to unite in public organizations" (Article 126) is subject to the same qualification. It is the right to join organizations which the regime has established and which it approves.

The constitutional articles providing for inviolability of the person (Article 127) and the inviolability of the homes of citizens and privacy of correspondence (Article 128) have no operative content. They were transformed into a hollow mockery by the ravages of the Great Purge, which reached the peak of its intensity in the first year of the life of the new Constitution. As the Yezhovshchina gathered force, constitutional niceties were forgotten, and the will of the NKVD terror apparatus became the embodiment of supreme law. Due process in the Soviet sense is not a matter of constitutional definition but largely a product of dictatorial indulgence.

Other provisions of Chapter Ten of the Constitution define the responsibilities of Soviet citizens. These include the duty to abide by the Constitution, to observe the laws, to maintain labor discipline (Article 130), to safeguard and strengthen public socialist property (Article 131), and the "sacred" duty to defend the Fatherland (Article 133). Article 132 proclaims universal military service as part of the fundamental law of the land. Unlike the proclamation of rights, this statement of duties carries its sanctions in the form of a substantial body of legislation designed to ensure enforcement.

The remaining substantive chapters of the Constitution are concerned with the electoral system and the procedure for amending the Constitution. The chapter on the electoral system provides for universal, direct, and equal suffrage and the secret ballot (Article 134). It establishes the minimum age for voting as eighteen and guarantees the right to vote to all except "insane persons and persons who have been convicted by a court of law and whose sentences include deprivation of electoral rights" (Article 135). "The right to nominate candidates," according to Article 141, "is secured to public organizations and societies of the working people: Communist Party organizations, trade unions, coöperatives, youth organizations and cultural societies." This equivocal statement, which merely lists the Party as one of a number of public organizations which submit nominations, is apparently designed to obscure the fact that Soviet voters are presented with a single slate of candidates chosen by the Party in advance of the election. The Constitution also provides (Article 142) that deputies are liable to recall "upon decision of a majority of the electors"; in fact such action depends on Party initiative. Constitutional amendments require a majority of two-thirds of the votes cast in each chamber of the Supreme Soviet (Article 146). Since Party discipline ensures unanimous votes, the leaders of the regime have encountered no difficulty in securing the enactment of any amendments which they deemed desirable. Indeed, no negative vote has ever been registered against a constitutional amendment.

The Constitution of 1936 marks an important advance over earlier constitutional efforts in at least one important respect. For the first time, the existence of the Party is acknowledged in a constitutional document. The Party is mentioned in two places. Article 141, as has already been noted, lists the Party as one of the organizations which has the right to nominate candidates for public office. Article 126 specifies that "the most active and most politically conscious citizens in the ranks of the working class and other sections of the working people unite in the Communist Party of the Soviet Union (Bolsheviks), which is the vanguard of the working people in their struggle to strengthen and develop the socialist system and is the leading core of all organizations of the working people, both public and state." The description of the Party as "the leading core of all organizations . . . both public and state" represents the first frank constitutional recognition of its position, even though other provisions of the Constitution appear deliberately drafted to minimize or even conceal its real role. The emergence of the Party into constitutional visibility provides a marked contrast with earlier ventures in Soviet constitution-making.

Prior to the drafting of the 1936 Constitution, the USSR consisted of seven union republics — the Russian, Ukrainian, Belorussian, Transcaucasian, Turkmen, Uzbek, and Tadjik SSR's. In 1936 the Transcaucasian Federated Soviet Republic was dissolved, and its constituent units — Azerbaidjan, Georgia, and Armenia — were admitted to the USSR as union republics. At the same time, two new union republics — the Kazakh and Kirghiz SSR's — were also added to the USSR, making a total of eleven union republics. The next burst of expansion, which brought the Soviet Union to its present level of sixteen union republics, took place in 1940. As an aftermath of the Russo-Finnish War, the Karelian Autonomous Republic, which had been part of the RSFSR, was reorganized as the Karelo-Finnish SSR. In June 1940 Rumania ceded Bessarabia and Northern Bukovina to the Soviet Union, and on August 2, 1940, the Moldavian Autonomous Republic, which had previously been part of the Ukrainian SSR, absorbed the newly organized territory and became a union republic. In August 1940 the three Baltic states — Latvia, Lithuania, and

Esthonia — were also incorporated into the Soviet Union as separate union republics.

In the years since 1936 the Constitution of the USSR has undergone a host of minor amendments, but none has significantly changed the basic structure of the Constitution or altered the political configuration of the regime. Most of the amendments have merely registered the admission of new union republics, shifts in political subunits, and rearrangements of commissariats or ministries. Perhaps the most startling development took place in February 1944 when amendments were enacted providing that "each Union Republic has the right to enter into direct relations with foreign states and to conclude agreements and exchange representatives with them" (Article 18a) and also providing that "each Union has its own Republican military formations" (Article 18b). At the same time, the Commissariats of Defense and Foreign Affairs were transformed into union-republic instead of all-union commissariats. In presenting the amendments for adoption by the Supreme Soviet, Molotov hailed them as signifying "a great broadening in the range of activity of the union republics, which had become possible as a result of their political, economic and cultural growth." [49]

The "broadening" of activity which Molotov saluted in 1944 failed to develop. The Ukraine and Belorussia are represented in the United Nations where they provide two additional votes for the USSR, but none of the sixteen republics has been permitted to exchange diplomatic representatives with foreign states or enter into agreements with them. A British proposal to establish diplomatic relations with the Ukraine, which was made in August 1947, met a frigid rebuff. In retrospect, it seems clear that the 1944 amendments represented an effort to equip the union republics with the external appurtenances of statehood in the hope that all sixteen could gain admission into the United Nations as separate entities. When this hope was defeated, the amendments lost most of their meaning though they remain on the books as a vestigial reminder of a diplomatic maneuver.

Equally curious, though perhaps less significant, was the amendment of March 15, 1946, which changed the name of the Council of People's Commissars to the Council of Ministers.[50] This reversion to Tsarist and bourgeois terminology was variously hailed as a manifestation of the pull of traditionalism, as a symbol of the Soviet search for respectability, and as another Machiavellian maneuver to quiet the fears of the West. Whatever the underlying pattern of motivation, the old wine continued to ferment in the new bottles.

The Soviet experiments in constitution-making and the elaborate paraphernalia of elections and meetings of soviets which they have produced raise interesting questions concerning the role of these institutions in a one-party dictatorship. To the observer who approaches Soviet elections from the viewpoint of Western parliamentarianism, they seem a meaningless show in which the Soviet voter is presented with no alternative except to endorse a slate of candidates designated by the Party leadership. Why does the regime go to great expense to hold elections, and why does it exert tremendous pressure to drive its people to the polls to ratify foreordained choices? Are not elections a superfluous and dispensable luxury in a totalitarian system?

The leaders of the Soviet regime do not think so. In their view, to quote Vyshinsky, "The Soviet election system is a mighty instrument for further educating and organizing the masses politically, for further strengthening the bond between the state mechanism and the masses, and for improving the state mechanism and grubbing out the remnants of bureaucratism." The elections show "that the entire population of the land of the Soviets are completely united in spirit." [51]

These statements hint at the real functions of Soviet elections. They offer a dramatic occasion for a campaign of agitation and propaganda on behalf of the Soviet system. In the words of *Kul'tura i Zhizn'* (Culture and Life), the journal of the Department of Agitation and Propaganda of the Central Committee of the Party:

The tasks of Party organizations in preparing for the elections is to strengthen further the ties between Party and people, to ensure a new and mighty increase in the political activity and labor of the working people and to direct this activity toward fulfillment of the post-war Stalin Five Year Plan ahead of schedule.

By concrete fact and example, Party organizations must show the advantages of the Soviet social and state system over the capitalist system and the superiority of Soviet democracy over bourgeois democracy. They must explain the great principles of the USSR Constitution and the significance of the mighty motive forces of the Soviet system — Soviet patriotism, moral-political unity in Soviet society, the friendship of peoples in the USSR. [52]

Soviet elections serve as a form of national mobilization. Like the plebiscites under Napoleon and Hitler, they are intended to demonstrate, both to the world outside and the enemy within, that the people of the Soviet Union are solidly aligned with the regime. The announcement, for example, of the results of the 1950 elections to the USSR Supreme Soviet solemnly proclaimed that 99.98 per cent of all eligible voters cast ballots in the elections and that 99.73 per cent voted for "candidates of the Communist and non-party bloc" to the Council of the Union and 99.72 per cent provided the same endorsement for candidates to the Council of Nationalities. [53] Not surprisingly, the statistical triumph was widely heralded in the Soviet press as a "majestic demonstration of the unity of the Soviet people." [54] By manipulated unanimity, totalitarian regimes strive to create an impression of monolithic support and unshakeable strength. Effectively managed elections contribute to this end.

Soviet elections are also designed to create an illusion of representation and participation in public affairs. Candidates meet with groups of voters, address them, and receive "instructions" from them which are ordinarily aimed at the elimination of bureaucratic shortcomings or at obtaining some improvement in local services and facilities such as a new school or hospital or a better water and electric-power supply. Even though these instructions are confined within narrowly prescribed limits and can never be utilized to air any disagreement with the policies of the regime, they provide a channel through which localities may file their petitions of grievances. In this sense, they approximate a form of limited local representation. Since deputies are sometimes influential persons in their own right, they may intercede with the ministries to obtain some redress of grievances for the localities they represent.[55] Such intervention has its boundaries. As one former deputy, P. K. Ignatov, noted philosophically in his memoirs, "One must accustom oneself to take a broad, government view of things and not to regard everything from Armavir's narrow view." [56] Since locality interests must defer to projects with higher priorities which are centrally determined, the role of the deputy as a spokesman for local interests has its defined limits. His first obligation is to follow the Party directive and execute the commands of the Party leadership. In the final analysis, the leaders of the regime visualize themselves as the ultimate custodians of the interests of the Soviet electorate.

The utilization of the soviets as an instrument of governance has its own supporting rationalization. In the authoritative words of Stalin, the Soviets are a "transmission belt" linking the Party with the masses, "organizations which rally the labouring masses . . . under the leadership of the Party." [57] They are also, according to Stalin, *the most democratic and therefore the most authoritative organizations of the masses, which facilitate to the utmost their participation in the work of building up the new state and its administration, and which bring into full play the revolutionary energy, initiative and creative abilities of the masses in the struggle for the destruction of the old order, in the struggle for the new, proletarian order.*" [58]

Stripped of their rhetorical flourishes, these statements point to the important role the soviets play in the Communist system of political controls. The soviets themselves are Party-dominated. Responsibility for selection of the membership of the soviets and for direction of their activity remains with the Party. In each soviet, the inner board of control is invariably the Communist fraction. At the same time, the Party leadership seeks to utilize the mechanism of the soviets to broaden its influence with the masses, to enlist sympathetic non-Party elements in the tasks of administration and government, and to reward outstanding achievement by designating the deserving for membership in the Soviets.

At lower levels of the governmental hierarchy, the soviets discharge an important function in ensuring large-scale participation in community activities. In the winter elections of 1947–48, approximately 1,600,000 deputies were chosen to serve in local soviets.[59] In addition, many soviets follow the practice of organizing groups of *aktivs* who are available to assist the soviet members in carrying out their responsibilities. While actual administrative assignments are reserved for the *ispolkoms* or executive committees of the soviets rather than ordinary soviet deputies or members of the *aktiv*, the latter are drawn into a consideration of communal plans and activities, even if it be only in the form of passive attendance at meetings at which reports are rendered by the chairman and members of the *ispolkom*. Ordinarily, however, both deputies and members of the *aktiv* are expected to take the lead in checking the execution of work assignments by soviet officials, in mobilizing voluntary labor for civic improvements, and in serving as agitators among the masses to spread devotion to soviet goals. Since a substantial part of the work plans of local soviets is concerned with the maintenance and expansion of communal services and involves such everyday needs of the electorate as housing, sanitation, transportation, and recreation, interest in the activities of local soviets is not too difficult to arouse. Party-directed participation at this level of government builds on a genuine concern with common requirements.

By contrast, the role of the Supreme Soviet appears largely ornamental and decorative. The matters which engage its attention are of transcendent importance. They embrace such weighty problems as the Five Year Plans, the enactment of the annual budget, and the organization of the government of the USSR. But the proceedings of the Supreme Soviet convey the impression of a well-rehearsed theatrical spectacle from which almost all elements of conflict have been eliminated. The slight budget modifications which are initiated by the Supreme Soviet and the occasional criticisms of the performance of lagging ministries give every evidence of being part of a prepared script. Like the elections, the meetings of the Supreme Soviet symbolize national unity. The proposals of the government are unanimously hailed and unanimously ratified.

The composition of the Supreme Soviet reflects its character as a rally of the faithful. The deputies consist predominantly of members of the Party and governmental apparatus. Only a small minority are ordinary workers and collective farmers, and most of these are usually Stakhanovites who are being specially honored for their productive achievements. The Supreme Soviet is a mobilization of leading figures of Soviet society, but the forum in which they operate lacks creative significance. All important decisions come ready-made from the Party leadership. The task of the Supreme Soviet is not to question but to execute, to clothe the Party thesis in the garb of constitutional legality. The result is necessarily to minimize the authority of the whole apparatus of soviets. As long as the top Party command remains the real seat of power in Soviet society, the soviets and the constitutional structure built around them remain imposing façades rather than sovereign organs.

The Soviet regime has demonstrated great skill in using the trappings of mass democracy to mask the entrenched position of the dictatorial elite which dominates Soviet society. Constitutional myths and symbols have been ingeniously adapted to contribute to the illusion of mass participation and mass control. But the actual configurations of power in the Soviet system are difficult to conceal. The political realities of Soviet life speak the unmistakable language of a one-party dictatorship in which ultimate power is deposited in a narrow ruling group in the Kremlin.

Chapter 12

The Control of the Bureaucracy—
Public Administration
in the Soviet Union

One of the salient outgrowths of modern totalitarianism is the bureaucratization of its power structure. The Leader who bestrides the
peak of the totalitarian edifice is the victim of his own limitations. He
cannot decide everything, and even when he exercises his power to decide, he must depend on bureaucratic instruments to project his will.
Authority becomes institutionalized, and its fragments are distributed
among the manifold sub-bureaucracies which collectively contribute to
the illusion of totalitarian omniscience.

The ways of bureaucracy elude totalitarian and nontotalitarian labels.
Bureaucracies everywhere generate their own special interests and aspirations. They guard the expert knowledge which is the source of their
power and resist the encroachment of interlopers who seek to invade their
jurisdiction. They display what Soviet critics have termed "a narrowly
departmental approach" and build their loyalties and hopes around the
complex of concerns that have been entrusted to their care. They develop
their own routines and working habits and are not easily persuaded to
abandon them once they have become established. The Soviet bureaucracy
manifests many of the traits characteristic of bureaucratic behavior generally.

At the same time, Soviet totalitarianism also imposes its own peculiar
requirements on the bureaucracy. Soviet public administration exhibits
attributes which sharply differentiate it from the administrative systems
prevailing in Western constitutional democracies. Its scope is all-embracing. It seeks to organize the total experience of man in Soviet society.

Every branch of the economy and every form of social expression, from art, music, and letters to sports and the circus, are subject to administrative regulation and direction. The totalitarian imperative drives to transform the nation into a hierarchy of public servants operating within a framework of disciplined subordination to state purposes.

Soviet public administration is one-party administration. The conception of the politically neutral civil servant who serves his successive political masters "with equal fidelity and with equal contempt" is utterly foreign to the Soviet scene. Soviet public administration is suffused with political content. Every field of administration, however technical, is regarded as a channel for the propagation of the Party line and the directives of the top leadership. As Stalin once put it, "not a single important political or organizational question is decided by our Soviet and other mass organizations without guiding directions from the Party." [1] The Party itself is a creature of its high command. Functioning in this capacity, it permeates Soviet society, occupies the strategic positions of power in state administration, issues policy instructions which guide administrative activity, checks on their execution, and attempts to serve as an organ of continuous discipline and control.

In practice, this picture of monolithic unity is only imperfectly realized. Behind the totalitarian façade, the struggle of the elite formations of Soviet society for power and influence continues to find expression. The Party apparatus, the police, the army, and the administrative bureaucracy vie with one another for preferment, and the local and departmental interests of different sections of the bureaucracy exercise their counterinfluence on the Party. The public affirmations of unanimity on which all totalitarian regimes insist serve to obscure the diversity of interests which they can neither eliminate nor dare openly acknowledge. Although Soviet totalitarian controls drive some of the most vital interests in the society into a subterranean zone of illegality, other equally important concerns find partial and distorted articulation through the frequently camouflaged processes of bureaucratic representation and manipulation. The play of these pressures continues to operate within the limits imposed by the ruling priorities of the Party leadership. The monolithic control of the Party high command largely takes the form of enforcing its priorities and resolving the conflict which their execution generates. The pressure from above is ruthless and unremitting, and evasion from below is resourceful and not unavailing.

Soviet public administration gives little weight to the rights of the individual. It is oriented toward a conception of state interests which every branch of government is dedicated to promote. The problem of erecting safeguards against the abuse of administrative power is therefore conceived differently from its counterpart in Anglo-American constitutional systems with their heritage of devotion to personal liberty. The safeguards that Soviet jurists stress are the state controls designed to insure efficient performance of official function. When Soviet lawyers speak of administrative responsibility, they have in mind a conception of state service which is embodied in the law, not a set of limitations to protect the individual from the administration.[2] When state interests and individual interests clash, the duty of the Soviet administrator is always toward state interests. Soviet administrative law is built around the interests of the collectivity as interpreted by the Party leadership.

Soviet public administration replaces Western constitutional restraints on administration by a formidable proliferation of central controls of a variety and on a scale without parallel in the West. Despite efforts to strengthen executive authority in recent years, the typical Soviet administrator functions in an environment in which his every decision is subject to the possibility of check, recheck, and countercheck. The plan under which he operates must be approved by the State Planning Committee. His staff arrangements are controlled by standards established by the State Civil Service Commission. His financial transactions are subject to the scrutiny of the Ministry of Finance. The Minister of State Control maintains a check on his efficiency, enforces strict control over the expenditure of funds, and makes certain that he is fulfilling all government orders and decrees. The Procurator General watches the legality of his actions. The secret police of the Ministry of Internal Affairs (MVD) keeps him under constant observation to ensure his political reliability. The whole range of his activity, as well as that of the control organs, is always under careful surveillance by representatives of the Party. It is not too far-fetched to describe this complex network of controls as a system of power founded on cross-espionage and the institutionalization of mutual suspicion.

The insecurity developed by these arrangements engenders its own antidotes. In order to escape the unbearable burden of suspicion and distrust which the system imposes on those who are involved in it, both controlled and controllers sometimes form "mutual protection associations" and cover up for each other's sins and omissions in discharging the tasks for which they are held jointly responsible. The urge to find a peaceful sanctuary is deep-seated among Soviet administrators, and it comes into sharp conflict with the Hobbesian war of all against all upon which the ruling group relies in order to maintain its own security. The literature of Soviet administration is filled with criticism of administrators who enter into so-called "family relations" with the control organs that surround them. Despite the virulence of the denunciations, the phenomenon is recurrent, and it apparently registers a strongly felt need to erect barricades against the intrusive checks used by the regime to maintain the pressure of its power. The interstices of every totalitarian regime contain concealed pockets of effective bureaucratic resistance. The Soviet rulers engage in a ceaseless effort to stamp out this resistance and forge the bureaucracy into a pliable instrument of their will.

The Background of Soviet Public Administration

The history of Soviet public administration is the record of a search for a formula to guarantee both the loyalty and the efficiency of the administrative apparatus. After the seizure of power, the Soviet regime was plagued by an absence of trained administrators in whom the leadership could have confidence. The pre-Revolutionary bureaucracy was a repository of established governmental routines and procedures, but its skills were not readily adaptable to the new order, and in any event, many of its members regarded their new overlords with enmity. The Party itself attracted few members trained in the arts of civil administration. The problem of transforming a revolutionary party into a governing party presented real problems. The qualities which made for success in agitation and propaganda were not easily transferable to industrial management or other administrative responsibilities. Five years after the Revolution, Lenin commented,

> We now have a vast army of governmental employees, but we lack sufficiently educated forces to exercise real control over them. Actually, it often happens that at the top, where we exercise political power, the machine functions somehow; but down below, where these state officials are in control, they often function in such a way as to counteract our measures. At the top, we have I don't know how many, but in any event, I think several thousand, at the outside several tens of thousands, of our own people. Down below, however, there are hundreds of thousands of old officials who came over to us from the Tsar and from bourgeois society and who, sometimes consciously and sometimes unconsciously, work against us. Nothing can be done here in a short space of time, that is clear. Many years of hard work will be required to improve the machine, to reform it, and to enlist new forces.[3]

The Party leadership resorted to a variety of expedients in order to cope with the problem of its inadequate administrative resources. Since it could not dispense with the old-regime specialists and bureaucrats, it enlisted them in its service and surrounded them with Party and police controls in order to ensure their loyalty. Party members who displayed a talent for administration were sent to special "industrial academies" for intensive training and assigned to responsible administrative posts. The major long-term effort was concentrated on educating the oncoming generation for technical and administrative responsibilities.

To a remarkable degree, the goals of industrialization and collectivization, which were incorporated in the First Five Year Plan, imposed their own administrative imperatives. The execution of a program involving rapid industrialization and the collectivization and mechanization of agriculture placed a great premium on technical and managerial competence. Technical education took important strides forward, and a new Soviet-trained intelligentsia began to pour out of the higher educational institutions established to serve the needs of industry and administration. Though the level of technical education frequently fell far short of the best Western standards, a considerable improvement was registered in comparison with past Soviet performance, and significant additions to the pool of managerial and technical personnel were achieved.

The importance of management found increasingly strong recognition. This took various forms. Old-regime technicians and specialists, who had been utilized as scapegoats for the early difficulties which attended the industrialization drive, began to be treated with unaccustomed consideration. The vista opened up to the new generation of managers and engineers was one of rapidly expanding opportunities and hopes of speedy promotion. Managerial salaries and bonuses were greatly increased, and efforts were made to strengthen the operating authority of the managerial class.

During the early thirties there was an increasing tendency to turn from collegial to one-man management. Authority which had been dispersed among many specialists along functional lines was now concentrated in a single executive. He was held accountable for the over-all operations of a particular enterprise or factory or the administrative activities of a commissariat in a defined territory, and his approval was required for all orders issued in the name of the organization for which he was responsible. In resolving the competing claims of hierarchy and specialty, the balance was tilted in favor of hierarchy. The day-to-day operating authority of the line administrator was reinforced, even though the results of his labors were still subject to constant surveillance and control.

The rewards and responsibilities heaped upon the administrator were not without their countervailing hazards. Representatives of the Party and the secret police watched him carefully, and a fall from grace might involve a sentence to a forced labor camp or an even worse fate. The Great Purge did not spare the ranks of industrial and administrative management. Yet its effect was to emphasize the indispensability of the managerial and technical group, and it was followed in 1939 by a revision of the Party Rules expressly designed to facilitate the assimilation of the administrative and managerial class into the Party. Indeed, the calculated effort in the late thirties to recruit new Party members from this group did much to transform the Party into an administrative and managerial elite and to unite Party and state administration.

By the late 1930's, the Soviet Union had gone far toward consolidating a tightly disciplined bureaucratic hierarchy. Increasing attention was given to administrative, technical, and managerial competence, and growing emphasis was placed on inequality of reward as a method of recognizing status, rewarding achievement, and penalizing incompetence. Whatever dissatisfactions the system generated received little opportunity for overt expression. Doctrinal unity was rigidly enforced. Through a series of purges culminating in the Great Purge of 1936–38, the remnants of old and new oppositions were liquidated. Stalin and his entourage emerged as infallible spokesmen of the new orthodoxy and undisputed masters of Party and state.

Prewar and War Developments

With the rise of the Hitler menace, economic and administrative resources were increasingly turned toward the armament industries and military preparations. The prewar period was marked by considerable progress in rationalizing the administrative structure. A host of new commissariats were created, particularly in the heavy industry field. Old industrial commissariats were broken up and divided into smaller and more manageable units. Efforts were made to eliminate unnecessary intermediate layers of supervision between the basic production units and the central commissariats in Moscow and the republics. The so-called two or three link system was adopted as a model scalar pattern for the organization of a commissariat. Under this system, the factory or enterprise in the field reported either directly to the commissariat or through not more than one, or at the most two, intermediate links. Active measures were instituted to reduce bloated administrative staffs, to install systems of job description and classification, and to transfer central office personnel into the field. Yet practice lagged far behind aspiration, and the speech of Malenkov at the Eighteenth Party Conference in February 1941 furnished numerous examples of wasteful utilization of manpower in many branches of industry and transport.[4]

During the war and the immediate postwar period, the multiplication of new industrial commissariats continued. The basic motivation for their creation appeared to be the same as in the prewar period — the drive for more readily manageable units. Yet the very expansion in their number created a serious problem of coördination. The problem was recognized with the outbreak of war. On June 30, 1941, the State Committee of Defense was constituted as an inner or super cabinet.[5] It was composed exclusively of members of the Politburo circle.* Until its dissolution on September 4, 1945, it functioned as a supreme war cabinet. Specific super-

---

* Originally it consisted of Stalin as chairman, Molotov as vice-chairman, and Voroshilov, Beria, and Malenkov. On February 3, 1942, Mikoyan and Voznesensky were added to its membership. On February 20 of the same year, Kaganovich joined the committee. On November 22, 1944, Voroshilov was relieved of membership and Bulganin filled his place.

visory powers over related groups of commissariats were allocated to various members of the committee, and the committee as a group undertook to give coördinated direction to the war effort. For the most part, the committee functioned through established agencies of government. In specified areas near the front, however, it had its own field representatives in the form of local committees of defense.[6] These local committees were composed of the secretary of the regional or city Party committee as chairman, the local military commander, a representative of the Commissariat of Internal Affairs, and the chairman of the regional or city soviet — a significant quadrumvirate of Party, army, police, and administration which illuminates the basic structure of power in the Soviet Union. In the areas in which these committees were established, they exercised supreme governing authority for the duration of the war. At the end of the war, both they and the State Committee of Defense were dissolved, and the previously existing system of governmental controls was reinstated.

Postwar Administrative Developments

With the end of hostilities, the Soviet Union faced serious problems of demobilization, reconversion, and reconstruction. The pattern of industrial location had been substantially shifted to the east during the war, and administrative readjustments had to be made to take account of these new developments. In the war-ravaged areas, enormous tasks of rehabilitation presented themselves. As early as 1943, a special committee attached to the Council of Commissars was designated to direct work on the restoration of the economy in regions liberated from the German occupation. Early in 1946, the first of the postwar Five Year Plans was announced. Its proclaimed objective was not only to restore but to surpass the prewar level in industry and agriculture. Long-range plans were sketched to triple the prewar level of industrial production.

The announcement of these ambitious economic goals was followed by few spectacular changes in administrative structure. The commissariats were rechristened ministries by a constitutional amendment of March 15, 1946, but this reversion to traditional nomenclature involved no redefinition of functions.[7] More significant was the movement which was inaugurated in 1948 to reduce the number of ministries. The following table makes this tendency clear.[8]

	1924	1936	1947	Early 1949	1952	March 15, 1953
All-Union ministries	5	8	36	28	30	12
Union-Republic ministries	5	10	23	20	21	13
Total	10	18	59	48	51	25

The reduction from fifty-nine ministries in 1947 to forty-eight in early 1949 was largely brought about by consolidating or abolishing various industrial ministries which had grown in such profusion after 1936. It registered a conviction that the process of ministerial atomization had gone too far, that scarce manpower was being wasted in unnecessary administrative overhead, and that more of the burden of coördination had to be shifted to the ministerial level. Between 1949 and 1952 several new ministries were created, though the total still fell far short of the 1947 peak. After the death of Stalin in March 1953, the process of ministerial consolidation was given a sharp impetus, and the total number of ministries was reduced to twenty-five.*

As the following table makes clear, the recent fluctuations in the size of the Soviet Council of Ministers are primarily a reflection of organizational changes in the economic or industrial field. The ministries (all-union and union-republic) are tabulated by subject matter.

Ministries	1924	1936	1947	Early 1949	1952	March 15, 1953
Administrative-political	4	5	6	7	8	7
Social-cultural	0	1	3	3	3	2
Economic	6	12	50	38	40	16
Total	10	18	59	48	51	25

While the administrative-political and social-cultural ministries have remained more or less stable, the number of economic ministries registered a sharp drop from fifty in 1947 to sixteen in 1953. Of the sixteen economic ministries in existence on March 15, 1953, eleven were all-union or centralized ministries and only five were union-republic or federated ministries. The all-union economic ministries were almost exclusively concerned with one or another branch of heavy industry; the five union-republic ministries operated in such areas as agriculture, food, fishing, lumber, building materials, and light industry.

Despite the recent shrinkage in the number of ministries, the Council of Ministers of the USSR remains a large body. Prior to Stalin's death, internal cohesion and coördination were provided by an inner cabinet com-

* As a result of the drastic reorganization put into effect after Stalin's death and ratified by the Supreme Soviet on March 15, 1953, the following ministries made up the new Council of Ministers: (1) Foreign Affairs, (2) Internal Affairs, (3) Defense, (4) Internal and Foreign Trade, (5) Agriculture, (6) Culture, (7) Light and Food Industry, (8) Metallurgy, (9) Machine Building, (10) Transport and Heavy Machine Building, (11) Electric Power Stations and the Electrical Industry, (12) Coal, (13), Oil, (14) Chemicals, (15) Defense Industry, (16) Building Materials Industry, (17) Timber and Paper, (18) Construction of Heavy Industry and Machine-Building Plants, (19) Transport, (20) Communications, (21) Sea and River Transport, (22) Health, (23) Justice, (24) Finance, (25) State Control.

posed of Stalin as chairman, and thirteen vice-chairmen. After Stalin's death, the coördinating and directing function was deposited in a newly created Presidium, which consisted of Malenkov, the chairman of the Council of Ministers, and four first deputy chairmen — Beria, Minister of Internal Affairs; Molotov, Minister of Foreign Affairs; Bulganin, Defense Minister; and Kaganovich, who was assigned no specific ministerial portfolio.

The Structure of Soviet Administration

The structure of Soviet administration can be briefly sketched. At the apex of the pyramid stands the Presidium of the Council of Ministers, exercising supreme policy-making and coördinating responsibilities. At the next lower level, there are twenty-five all-union and union-republic ministries which make up the Council of Ministers, and in addition, a substantial number of other chief administrations, committees, commissions, councils, and agencies which are attached to the Council of Ministers.[9]

The scheme of ministerial organization necessarily varies with subject matter, but it is possible to detect and describe a fairly uniform pattern.[10]

Of the twenty-five ministries represented in the Council of Ministers, twelve are all-union or centralized ministries. Typically, the all-union ministry covers one or another branch of heavy industry, and it is not without significance that this area of highest priority in Soviet planning is also the most tightly centralized and controlled. The all-union ministry operates with a field organization which is directly responsible to it. The enterprises in the field may be grouped territorially, around a production complex, or on a combined territorial-production basis. Whatever the principle of field organization adopted, the lines of control run directly to the central ministry.

At the head of the ministry is the minister and a number of deputy or assistant ministers with supervisory responsibilities divided among them. There is also a small collegium composed of high officials of the ministry with whom the minister meets periodically for advice. Members of the collegium cannot interfere with the minister's power to make decisions, although they may appeal to the Council of Ministers in the event that they disagree with any decision announced by him. In addition to the collegia, many ministries have established advisory councils, which ordinarily consist of from forty to seventy members. Approximately one-half of the membership is made up of administrators of enterprises in the field. The councils are intended to promote an exchange of experience between field and center and to facilitate closer relationship between them.

The line organization of the ministry is built around the so-called production-territorial principle. In accordance with this principle, similar enterprises located in a particular region are grouped for purposes of supervision and made responsible to one of the production-territorial divisions of the central ministry. All orders and communications of the ministry with respect to enterprises in the field originate in the production-territorial divisions. In addition to these line or operating divisions, there are a number of staff or functional units bearing such titles as Economic Planning Section, Financial Section, Capital Construction Section, Personnel Section, Accounting Section, Juridical Section, the Secretariat, the Administrative Office, and not to be forgotten, the Special Section which is staffed by and responsible to the Ministry of Internal Affairs. With the exception of the last, which represents a security control over the ministry rather than a subordinate part of its apparatus, the staff sections do not have the power to issue orders on their own responsibility. They may prepare plans and technical instructions, but these plans and instructions are communicated to the field through the appropriate production-territorial division in the name of the minister, who retains the ultimate authority to veto or ratify them.

The central structure of the union-republic ministries does not differ markedly from that of the all-union ministries. There is the same use of collegia and councils, the same type of apportionment of duties among line and staff agencies, the same tendency to turn away from the functional dispersion of power and to concentrate executive authority in line divisions organized on the territorial-production principle.

There are two important distinctions between the all-union and union-republic ministries. In the first place, the pattern of organization in the union-republic ministries is less centralized. Where the all-union ministries operate with a field organization immediately and directly responsible to Moscow, the union-republic ministries work in the field through counterpart ministries in each of the sixteen republics which compose the USSR. These counterpart ministries supervise all of the enterprises or administrative subdivisions of the ministry which are located in that republic. In this fashion a substantial part of the burden of operative control is shifted from Moscow to the capitals of the various republics.[11] The second distinction between the all-union and union-republic ministries involves the agencies to which the two types of ministries answer. The all-union ministry is responsible only to the central government. The counterpart ministries in the republics, on the other hand, are responsible to the Council of Ministers and legislative organs of the republic as well as to their own union-republic ministry at the center. In the unlikely event of a conflict of view between central and republican authorities, it is a reasonably safe presumption that the views of the center prevail.

Each republic of the USSR has its own council of ministers. This council is also made up of two types of ministries — the union-republic ministries already noted and so-called republican ministries, which vary in number from republic to republic but which ordinarily include at least Education, Social Insurance, Local Industry, and Communal Economy. The republican ministries have no counterparts in the all-union Council of Ministers. Their lines of responsibility head up in the councils of ministers and legislative organs of the individual republics.

Below the level of the republic, there are usually at least three subordinate layers of administration — the autonomous republics, *oblasts*, or *krais*, which may be treated as regional administrative units; the *raions* or district units; and the towns, villages, and hamlets, which may be described as local units. The urban areas operate under a separate regime. The largest cities are directly subordinate to the republic and are themselves broken up into *raions* or districts. The cities of moderate size report to the *oblasts* or *krais*, while the smaller towns are subordinate to the *raion* governments.

At each level of this hierarchy, there are various administrative departments which are responsible both to the executive committee of the soviet elected at that level and to the administrators exercising corresponding functions at the next higher level. In the event of conflict arising out of such double supervision, the higher soviet organs are vested with the right to resolve the dispute. As might be expected, the administrative structure diminishes in complexity as it descends from region to locality. There are regional administrative departments of Finance, Trade, Health, Education, Local Industry, Communal Economy, Social Insurance, Roads, Cultural-Educational Institutions, and Art Affairs. There are also administrations representing Justice, Agriculture, the Building Material Industry, the Local Fuel Industry, Transport, Light and Food Industry, Architectural Affairs, the Planning Committee, and a Personnel Section attached to the chairman of the executive committee of the soviet. In addition, every region has its representatives of the Ministry of Internal Affairs.

The *raion* or district government also has its full complement of administrative services, though on a less comprehensive scale than the region. The administrative sections of the *raion* include Agriculture, Education, Finance, Trade, Health, Social Insurance, Cultural-Educational Institutions, Roads, Communal Economy, Local Industry, the Planning Committee, a Personnel Section attached to the chairman of the executive committee of the *raion* soviet, and representatives of the Ministry of Internal Affairs. Although there are urban as well as rural *raions*, the *raion* is of primary importance as an agency of rural government. The agricultural sections in the rural *raions* are of key significance and play a particularly important role in overseeing the machine-tractor stations and collective farms in the district.

Administrative organization in cities, towns, and villages is largely a function of the size of the community and the complexity of the services which have to be performed. In the larger cities which are directly subordinate to the republic or region, the range of administrative activity and the number of administrative sections are at least equal to, and sometimes considerably greater than, those of the *raion* governments. Communal services and local industry necessarily play a central role. Indeed, they occupy the same strategic position in the urban complex of administrative services as agricultural administration does in the rural *raions*. In the smaller towns which are subordinate to the *raions*, the scope of administrative activity is substantially narrower, and there are rarely more than two to four administrative sections. In the villages and hamlets there are none. Such administrative duties as are required are performed by the chairman and secretary of the executive committee of the village soviet.

As this sketch indicates, the structure of Soviet public administration is built around differential treatment of various types of administrative functions and activities. In the case of the all-union heavy industry ministries, the pattern is one of extreme centralization, with the field organization responsible directly to Moscow. In the union-republic ministries, policy control is centralized, but some administrative decentralization is achieved by utilizing the republic and its subordinate layers of government as instruments of supervision. Where administrative activities are of diversified local significance, the point of policy control is the republic, with operational responsibilities lodged at the regional, district, and local levels. At each level of government, administrative action is theoretically subject to check by soviets which are popularly elected at that level. Such checks are described by Soviet jurists as infusing elements of mass participation and control into the administrative process. In fact, they are far from representing spontaneous popular action. Although local soviets do serve as forums at which critical shafts are hurled at the bureaucracy, such criticism usually gives evidence of having been carefully organized in advance, and its public expression is unthinkable without prior clearance with the Party authorities who direct proceedings in the soviets. If the soviets do little more now than provide the trappings and symbolism of mass participation, they do represent a potential instrument of control which may conceivably be activated under different auspices and circumstances. At present, the Soviet administrative apparatus turns for its significant controls in other directions.

These controls include (1) the Party, (2) the secret police, (3) the plan, (4) financial controls, (5) the Ministry of State Control, (6) legal controls, and (7) personnel controls. The functions performed by Party and secret-police controls are treated elsewhere;* the discussion below will be devoted to an analysis of other controls exerted on Soviet administration.

Planning Controls

The plan plays a central role in Soviet life. Its discipline regulates the tempo and activity of every Soviet administrator. Each branch of state administration has specified goals which it must meet over defined time intervals. Success in attaining and surpassing these goals means rewards, prestige, and the promise of rapid rise in the Soviet administrative hierarchy. Continued failure in meeting planned goals carries the threat of disciplinary action, a blighted career, and swift and brutal descent to the lower depths of Soviet life.

Prior to 1948, the over-all responsibility for preparing and checking the execution of the national plan was concentrated in the State Planning Commission (*Gosplan*). On January 9, 1948, by decree of the Presidium of the Supreme Soviet, the central planning structure was reorganized.[12] The State Planning Commission was renamed the State Planning Committee, and one of its major functions, that of working out material balances for the economy and distributing scarce materials to industry, was removed from its jurisdiction and assigned to the newly created State Committee for Material-Technical Supply of the National Economy, which quickly became known as *Gossnab*. By the same decree, a third organization, *Gostech* or the State Committee for the Introduction of Advanced Technique into the National Economy, was also created. This last committee, however, had only a short life. It was abolished by decree of the Presidium of the Supreme Soviet on February 17, 1951.[13] After the death of Stalin, the central planning machinery was again reorganized, and the planning functions of Gossnab were reabsorbed by Gosplan.

Before this reorganization, Gossnab served as the central materials planning and allocation body, while Gosplan was apparently confined to planning output, production, and other aspects of Soviet life.[14] Requests for materials had to be submitted to Gossnab, which was required to confirm norms of materials utilization for all consuming agencies, to make allocations to them, and to plan material balances for the whole economy. Gossnab plans required the approval of the Council of Ministers. The intimate relationship between materials planning and output and production planning pointed to the necessity of the closest liaison between Gossnab and Gosplan, and it was presumably this consideration which led to the decision to reunite both functions in Gosplan.

Information on the internal organization of Gosplan dates back to

* See Chapters 6, 7, 13, 15, and 16.

1941.[15] At that time, Gosplan was organized on the model of a union-republic ministry but with a higher degree of centralized control than was usually customary in that type of ministry. The central organization of Gosplan was a miniature replica of the whole range of governmental functions. It embraced a series of sections paralleling the various commissariats and branches of governmental activity, a second series broken down on a regional basis, and a third series of functional sections organized around the task of balancing and synthesizing the interrelationships between ministerial and regional planning. Each of the union republics also has its separate Gosplan organization operating under the supervision of the central planning body. Indeed, Gosplan pervades the entire governmental structure. There are planning committees in all the regions, districts, and important towns and cities, and planning organs in every ministry and all agencies and enterprises responsible to it.

The process of drafting the national plan begins with the assembly of data on the existing state of plan fulfillment, the determination of the main targets for the next planning period, and the working out of preliminary balance sheets which will make it possible to realize these targets. Basic guide lines and policies are established by the Party command, but the more refined elaboration of objectives and interrelationships is made by Gosplan in the light of specific plans submitted by ministries, enterprises, and the various republics, territories, and regions. These plans are interlinked, and, when necessary, modified to meet the demands of the Party leadership and to conform with available resources. Frequently, concrete targets for the various ministries, branches of the economy, and regions are established only after strenuous and protracted negotiations between Gosplan and the affected agencies, in the course of which the agencies seek to extract maximum advantages from Gosplan, while Gosplan, under pressure from its superiors, seeks in turn to impose maximum sacrifices on them. The national economic plan worked out by Gosplan requires the approval of the Council of Ministers. After such approval is given, it is issued as a directive which is binding on all subordinate agencies and which forms the basis of the more detailed plans worked out by them. At every level of the bureaucratic hierarchy, lower and higher organs continue the struggle for preferential advantage until the enterprises and agencies at the base of the planning pyramid end up with a set of defined tasks which theoretically regulates their performance for the period specified in the plan.

The original emphasis of Gosplan was on the drawing-up of plans. Recently, more attention has been devoted to checking on execution, with increasing use of report devices and field inspection to ascertain progress and detect evasions. Soviet plant managers and bureaucrats have developed remarkable ingenuity in manipulating the criteria of plan fulfillment to create an illusion of over-all successful performance. Soviet official sources constantly refer to the necessity of combating this type of abuse. "It is necessary," says A. Kursky in his volume on Soviet planning,

ruthlessly to expose such anti-state practices as deliberately drafting output plans for enterprises below their capacity, setting crop targets below capacity, and fulfilling plans quantitatively at the expense of quality. Some business executives are prone to fulfill the plan for gross output by producing articles that require the expenditure of less labour, while failing to produce the planned assortment of articles, or else fail to reach the target for reduction of cost of production, or turn out inferior-quality goods.

It is the function of the planning bodies to expose such cases in good time and to secure the fulfillment of the state plan in respect of all its indices.[16]

In 1949 the Minister of State Control, L. Mekhlis, commented:

The heads of some enterprises, and not only of some, quite frequently conceal productive capacities, act craftily in drawing up the plan so as to be able to fulfill and overfulfill it without particular effort and to be in good standing. It is a matter of honor for the state controllers to uncover such machinations. Unfortunately, we are far behind in this.[17]

At the Nineteenth Party Congress in October 1952 Malenkov documented the continued existence of these and other "abuses."

The Central Committee and the government have brought to light instances of some functionaries who, placing narrow departmental and local interests above the interests of the state, and concealing from the government, on the pretext of looking after the enterprises in their charge, material resources at their disposal, took the path of violating Party and state laws. Facts are also known of business executives, with the connivance of Party organizations, submitting obviously inflated lists of required raw materials and supplies, and of doctoring output reports to conceal nonfulfillment of production programs . . .[18]

Earlier in his speech, Malenkov stated:

Some establishments, in an effort to fulfill the gross output plan, resort to a practice that is inimical to the interests of the state, producing articles of secondary importance above the plan, while failing to meet state plan assignments in respect to major items.

Some industries violate state discipline in relation to quality of goods . . . Light industry enterprises still turn out large quantities of inferior quality goods . . .

One of the chief reasons for the failure to fulfill state plans is the uneven flow of output at enterprises during the month . . . many establishments operate by fits and starts, producing nearly half of the month's output in the last ten days, which leads to undercapacity operation, overtime, more waste, and upsets the work of allied enterprises . . . Such shortcomings in the work of industry cannot be tolerated.[19]

Despite the danger of such abuses, there has been persistent pressure to escape the burdens of overcentralized planning. One response has been the tendency to decentralize planning for small plants producing handicrafts or other consumer goods out of locally available material for local consumption. In numerous cases, larger plants which have acquired a high degree of production experience have been permitted considerable initiative in working out their own programs, subject always to possible correction from above in the event that plant managers set low goals in order to facilitate plan-fulfillment. Under the new rules of March 1947 for drafting the national economic plan, quarterly and monthly plans are no longer submitted to the USSR Council of Ministers for approval; instead, the annual plan is divided into quarterly indices.[20] The existence of the plan, however, constitutes a control from which no Soviet administrator can wholly escape. Between the plan as blueprinted and the plan in action, gaps can and frequently do develop, and the result is inevitably a great deal of hasty improvisation, adjustment, and manipulation all along the line. The Soviet planning process is not a clocklike mechanism that regulates the timetable of production and administration with exact precision. It registers the tensions generated by a leadership intent on rapid industrialization and a bureaucratic and managerial apparatus which is struggling to meet or temper the heavy demands made on it. The plan is a spur to intensified effort, and as such it forms one of the distinguishing features of Soviet administration in all of its related aspects.

Financial Controls

The Soviet system of financial controls provides an essential instrument for checking the execution of the plan and for supervising administrative efficiency generally. Financial powers are largely concentrated in the Ministry of Finance and its subordinate banking organs. They embrace the preparation of the budget and the exercise of control over all financial transactions, including the extension of credit by short- and long-term banks.

The role of the Ministry of Finance in budgetary administration gives it strategic leverage as a control agency.[21] The budget in the Soviet Union may be regarded as the financial expression of the plan. One of the main tasks of the ministry is to translate the physical objectives of the plan into financial terms. All budgets are prepared in accordance with instructions issued by the ministry, and every governmental unit from the smallest village to the central government is required to operate within a budgetary framework. Each level of government has its assigned objects of expenditure and its specified allocation of revenues. The central government, however, receives the overwhelming bulk of expenditures and revenues, amounting to nearly 80 per cent of the total budget in 1951.[22] This allocation provides a significant index of the extent of financial centralization in the Soviet system.

The unified budget of the USSR includes the budgets of all local as well as central institutions. After initial preparatory work by the Minister of Finance, it is first submitted to the Council of Ministers for approval. If approved, it is then presented to both houses of the Supreme Soviet and referred to their respective budget commissions. While suggestions for change may be made by these commissions, these changes are subject to veto by the Council of Ministers. After discussion in the Supreme Soviet, the budget is unanimously ratified. Similar procedures are reënacted at each of the lower levels of government.

Once the budgets have been approved and allocations made to the various ministries and units of government, the control machinery of the Ministry of Finance comes into play. One form of control is exercised by the banks supplying short- and long-term credit. Enterprises applying for credit must submit their balance sheets and supply supplementary financial information to indicate whether they are or are not operating in accordance with the plan. Periodic checks are made by the banks, and regularly scheduled reports of over-all financial operations must be rendered to the Ministry of Finance itself. In addition, the central ministry has its own control-inspection apparatus. The controller-inspectors of the ministry may descend upon an enterprise or government department at any time and conduct investigations on the spot with free access to all financial and other data. The report prepared by the controller-inspector is made available to the agency being investigated for such explanatory comment as it may wish to append. Thus supplemented, it is then forwarded to the ministry for action. If violations of law or of budgetary discipline are revealed, the report may form the basis for punitive action.

The Ministry of State Control

The control-inspection administration of the Ministry of Finance works closely with the Ministry of State Control.[23] This ministry, which was given commissariat status in 1940 as a successor agency to the Soviet Control Commission, exercises a general watchdog role over state property and administration. Like the Ministry of Finance, it is charged with strict control over expenditures of state funds, and it also has a broader mandate to check the fulfillment of all governmental decisions. Although a union-republic ministry, its administrative apparatus is highly centralized. The central ministry is organized into divisions paralleling the various branches of state administration with a chief controller in charge of each division. Its controllers are installed in all important enterprises, military districts, railroads, warehouses, and other agencies which are directly subordinate to the all-union government. The organization of the ministries of state control in the republics is patterned on the model of the central ministry. Chief controllers of these ministries are appointed by the council of ministers of the republic in agreement with the Ministry of State Control of the USSR.

The Ministry of State Control has a formidable array of sanctions at its disposal. Like the control-inspection administration of the Ministry of Finance, it has right of access to all administrative records. It may undertake documentary audits on its own responsibility or draw on the audits of the Ministry of Finance as a basis for further investigation. When the Ministry of Finance uncovers violations of budgetary discipline, the matter is ordinarily referred to the Ministry of State Control for disposition. Where the offenses are minor, the ministry may merely administer a reprimand, publish the reprimand in the press, or impose a fine on the offender up to the equivalent of three months of his salary. In more serious cases, it may order the removal of the offender from office and may submit the matter to the courts for criminal prosecution. It has the authority to issue directives to agencies which it has investigated. If the remedial measures which it orders are not put into practice, disciplinary penalties can be invoked.

The Ministry of State Control has been traditionally regarded as an important Party outpost to check the efficiency and honesty of state administration. Its controllers in the field have worked closely with local Party agencies during audits and inspections. Former Minister of State Control Mekhlis, who was retired from the post in October 1950 because of "ill health," was an important figure in the Party apparatus and also served as a member of the Orgburo of the Party.[24] The appointment of V. N. Merkulov, a former Minister of State Security, as Mekhlis's replacement may presage a closer *rapprochement* between the Ministry of State Control and the secret police.

Legal Controls

Legal controls over administration are primarily exercised through three channels: (1) the Procuracy, (2) the courts, and (3) the system of state arbitration (*Gosarbitrazh*) for settling disputes between government enterprises.

The Constitution of the USSR (Article 113) vests the Procurator General with "supreme supervisory power over the strict execution of the laws by all ministries and institutions subordinated to them, as well as by public servants and citizens of the USSR." The Procurator General is elected by the Supreme Soviet for a seven-year term; he, in turn, appoints procurators of republics, territories, and regions and approves the appointment by the republic procurators of district, area, and city procurators. The hierarchy of procurators operates independently of local authorities and of the Ministry of Justice. It is subordinate solely to the Procurator General of the USSR.

The Procuracy's supervisory powers over administration cover a wide field. It operates under a general mandate to prevent Soviet governmental bodies from exceeding their powers. Procurators may participate in the sessions of soviets in their area of jurisdiction, though they do not exercise voting rights. They may challenge the legality of ordinances issued by executive committees of soviets; such ordinances are automatically suspended in the event that the executive committees fail to reconsider them within a defined period of time. Procurators are also entitled to receive copies of all orders and decrees issued by administrative agencies. If they deem such acts illegal, they may file protests with the next higher governmental authority. Thus, protests against the acts of regional administrators will be filed with republican agencies, and charges that a minister has exceeded his authority will involve an appeal to the Council of Ministers.

The powers of the Procuracy also embrace supervision over the courts and the administration of justice. Procurators serve as public prosecutors in criminal cases. They may order the arrest of those suspected of crime, and they appoint the examiners who conduct the pre-trial investigations in criminal cases. They exercise a general supervision over all civil proceedings and may enter such cases at any time. They may appeal the decisions of lower courts in both civil and criminal cases, and appellate courts are required to hear their opinion before rendering a decision in such cases.

Although the powers of the Procuracy appear important and wide-ranging, their actual impact on administration is difficult to assess. The testimony of Soviet *émigrés* is almost unanimous in indicating that they exercised virtually no influence in controlling the arbitrary authority of the MGB and MVD. On the other hand, the numerous reports in the Soviet press of the arrest of government officials for embezzlement of government property or other violations of state discipline would seem to indicate that the procurators play an important role in attempting to stamp out some of the abuses of local administration. Occasional press reports also reveal that some procurators are themselves susceptible to bribery and corruption and that others are drawn into a network of close "family relations" with local officials which largely negates their watchdog role.[25] The effort to make the procurator impervious to local influence by subordinating him completely to the center has apparently not been entirely successful. Nevertheless, the Procuracy remains, on the whole, a guardian of state interests, and the leaders of the regime rely on it as an important instrument in restraining bureaucratic excesses and in enforcing devotion to state purposes.

The judicial system also imposes curbs on the bureaucracy. The Soviet Criminal Code provides drastic penalties for administrators who misuse their power. "Abuse of authority" by officials in state enterprises and organizations is punishable under Article 109 by deprivation of liberty for a term of not less than six months. Article 111 provides for deprivation of liberty for a term up to three years for "failure to use one's authority when there is a duty to do so, coupled with a negligent or unconscionable attitude toward the obligations imposed by one's position." [26] Under Article 128, "thriftlessness" is punishable by deprivation of liberty for a term up to two years or corrective labor tasks for a term up to one year. Under Article 128a, directors, chief engineers, and chiefs of divisions of technical supervision in industrial establishments are subject to imprisonment for a period of from five to eight years "for the release of products of poor quality or those insufficiently completed, or the release of production in violation of the established standards." By a decree of the Presidium of the Supreme Soviet, February 10, 1941, the unauthorized sale, exchange, or release of equipment and materials by administrators and managers is subject to a penalty of two to five years' imprisonment. A Presidium decree of June 4, 1947, provides a penalty of seven to ten years' confinement in a corrective labor camp for embezzlement of state property and five to eight years for embezzlement of collective farm, coöperative, or other public property. For a second offense or when the crime is committed by an organized group on a large scale, the penalty ranges from ten to twenty-five years in case of state property, and eight to twenty years for collective farm, coöperative, and other public property.[27] By a decree of June 9, 1947, the maximum penalty for disclosure of state secrets by civilian officials is fixed at twelve years of confinement in a corrective labor camp. The sentence may be increased to fifteen years if inventions, discoveries, and technical improvements constituting a state secret are transmitted abroad. In the event that such actions qualify as treason or espionage, more extreme punishment may be imposed.[28]

These drastic provisions of Soviet law are part of the framework of restraints which surround Soviet administrators. From the evidence at hand, it is difficult to determine whether the incidence of official crime has in fact decreased as the legal penalties have become more severe. The courts, like other agencies in the Soviet control apparatus, operate by campaign and example. Recent drives against corruption and embezzlement by state officials would appear to indicate that the devotion of the bureaucracy to state interests remains a major concern of the leadership.[29]

Another form of legal control over officialdom is exercised through the system of arbitration known as Gosarbitrazh. The Chief Arbitrator, who is attached to the Council of Ministers of the USSR, supervises a hierarchy of arbitrators who penetrate the major sectors of Soviet industry and reach down into the various republics, territories, and regions. Uniformity is maintained through the power of the Chief Arbitrator to remove cases from lower organs to his own jurisdiction. Disputes between enterprises within a particular ministry are decided by arbitrators appointed by the minister and may be transferred to Gosarbitrazh only if the minister consents.

The jurisdiction of Gosarbitrazh embraces "disputes concerning the execution of a contract or the quality of goods, and also other property disputes between institutions, enterprises, and organizations of the socialized sector of the national economy." [30] In effect, Gosarbitrazh functions as a commercial court. It is obligated to enforce "contractual and plan discipline," and its decisions are guided "by the laws and dispositions of the central and local organs of state power and also by the general principles of the economic policy of the USSR." [31] The cases decided by Gosarbitrazh cover the whole range of conflict points between enterprises in the USSR — disputes over failure to deliver supplies or delayed deliveries, refusals to accept delivery or pay the prices demanded, wrangles over the quality of goods supplied, and a host of other disagreements which arise in the complicated relationships between buyers and sellers. The awards of the arbitrators may invalidate some contracts, order specific performance of others, and assess penalties for violations in accordance with the damage inflicted. In the course of disputes before Gosarbitrazh, illegal acts by managers of enterprises or other responsible administrators may be disclosed. Gosarbitrazh itself has no power to take direct action against such officials. This does not mean, however, that their acts go unpunished. If the economic crime is a serious one, the procurator may order the arrest of the offending official, and criminal penalties will be invoked by the courts.

Controls on Personnel

Soviet personnel controls rely on a combination of compulsion, incentives, and exhortation to stimulate administrative efficiency and inculcate loyalty. The drive for efficiency has been accompanied by increasing emphasis on the rationalization of personnel practices.

One of the persistent problems of Soviet administration has been the marked tendency of Soviet public servants to gravitate to the central ministry rather than to the field and to seek out the white-collar rather than the work-bench assignment. The inflation of administrative overhead furnishes a recurrent theme in the Soviet literature of self-criticism. The organization of the Commissariat of Worker-Peasant Inspection in 1920 represented one of the earliest efforts to keep such bureaucratic excesses in check. Through this commissariat, a primitive system of personnel classification was introduced, and ceilings were placed on the size of staffs to be employed in the various government agencies.

In more recent times, the function of controlling personnel practices has fallen to the State Commission on the Civil Service.[32] This commission, which was created in 1935, was originally attached to the Commissariat of Finance, though its members were appointed by the Council of People's Commissars. In June 1941 it was detached from the Commissariat of Finance and made an independent body responsible to the Council of People's Commissars as a whole. Its mission is to improve administrative management throughout the government service. Among its functions are the establishment of standard systems of job classification for all government employees, the fixing of ceilings on the size of staffs, the approval of changes in organizational structure, the initiation of measures to eliminate surplus staff or unneeded administrative apparatus, and the determination of typical organizational structures and tables of organization for different kinds of governmental units. In carrying out these responsibilities, the State Commission on the Civil Service works closely with the Council of Ministers. Classification systems of major importance are submitted to the Council of Ministers for approval and may even be promulgated jointly by the Council and the Central Committee of the Party. Salary scales and staff ceilings in ministries and agencies of the central government require the affirmation of the Council of Ministers and are issued as decrees of that body. The commission also relies heavily on the inspection staff of the Ministry of Finance in enforcing its regulations. All government agencies are required to register their staffs with the Ministry of Finance; such registration is intended to ensure compliance with commission regulations.

The State Commission on the Civil Service, in contrast with the United States Civil Service Commission, is not a recruiting body. Recruitment of highly qualified administrative and technical personnel is the responsibility of the various ministries and agencies. Every sector of industry and administration has its parallel system of advanced schools and institutes which feed their graduates into the branch of public administration for which they prepare. Annual admission quotas are set for each school. Students who are accepted and who graduate with a satisfactory record are referred to an appropriate government agency or enterprise for assignment to a job. They are required to remain on this job for at least three years. Refusal to accept the assignment or withdrawal without official permission may be cause for criminal prosecution.

Before March 15, 1953, mass labor recruitment was a primary responsibility of the Ministry of Labor Reserves, which was given ministerial status in 1946 as a successor agency to the Chief Administration of Labor

Reserves. In the governmental reorganization after Stalin's death, the functions of the Ministry of Labor Reserves were assigned to the newly created Ministry of Culture. One of its important duties is to draw manpower from the farms to essential industries. In exercising its manpower mobilization functions, the ministry is obligated under a special decree of May 21, 1947, to give priority to heavy industry and transportation. It enters into contracts with ministries on its preferred list and agrees to supply them with specified contingents of labor over a defined period. Recruitment is undertaken through local offices of the ministry with the coöperation of rural soviets and collective farm chairmen. The representatives of the ministry also conclude individual contracts with workers on behalf of the industrial enterprises for which they are recruiting. Except in the case of seasonal labor, these contracts specify a minimal period of service of one year. Contracts for work in the Far East require a minimum of two years' employment, and special inducements are held out to workers who sign for longer periods.[33]

The ministry is also charged with the conscription of annual quotas of youth for industrial training and assignment. These State Labor Reserves provide a steady stream of new recruits for industry, mining, transport, and since 1948, for skilled work in agriculture. Approximately a million youths are drafted each year. Two types of training are provided: two-year courses for skilled workers, and six-month courses for less skilled labor. Boys aged fourteen through seventeen and girls of fifteen and sixteen may be assigned to the two-year courses. The age limits for the six-month courses range from sixteen through eighteen for both sexes.[34] In each case, the emphasis is on practical job training. On graduation, the draftees are required to work for a specified term, generally four years, in the enterprise to which they are assigned. Severe penalties may be imposed if they leave school or job without official permission.

Recent personnel policy in the Soviet Union has gone far to transform the public service into a disciplined military hierarchy in which the rank-and-file public servant has many obligations but relatively few rights. Titles, ranks, insignia, and uniforms, common in Tsarist days, have reappeared in various parts of the public service. First introduced in the armed forces, they have spread to a number of categories of civil servants, including diplomats, public prosecutors, and railroad employees. As one of the official texts on Administrative Law puts it, "The purpose of the introduction of ranks and uniforms for these categories of government officials is the further strengthening of service discipline and the elevation of the official authority of these workers. The rank expresses special qualifications of the worker, his service experience, his merits, and his authority as a worker in a certain branch of government." [35]

The emphasis on the hierarchical element in administration has also been accompanied by a general tightening of labor discipline. While the appearance of contractual freedom in labor relations is still maintained and the practice of concluding collective labor agreements was renewed in 1947 after a long hiatus, the trade unions in fact operate as instruments of Party and governmental policy, and their primary function is to promote labor discipline and increase labor productivity. Labor remains subject to a degree of control without parallel in Western society. Tardiness or absenteeism without justifiable reason is severely penalized. Every employee is required to have a "labor book" or passport in which a record is kept of all past employment and reasons for employment transfers. Employees are prohibited from changing their employment or resigning without the express permission of the administration of the establishment in which they are employed. Certain categories of technical and skilled labor can be transferred from one establishment to another regardless of the individual's wishes. Nor is this type of service discipline confined to lower-rank workers. Executives are exposed to a similarly severe regimen, tempered by greater material privileges but also carrying the hazards that go with large responsibilities.

Compulsion does not exhaust the complex pattern of Soviet personnel policies. Positive incentives to higher productivity are provided by differential wage payments carefully graded to reflect and stimulate increased work output on the part of individual workers. A system of supplementary incentives in the form of bonuses, prizes, orders, and medals is utilized to recognize outstanding work. Appeals are made to emulative instincts by organizing campaigns of "socialist competition" among enterprises and individual workers and rewarding the winners with a fanfare of publicity as well as more tangible recognition. Through exhortation and indoctrination, the Party leadership attempts to persuade both officials and workers to identify their interests with state interests and to reconcile themselves to sacrifices in the present for the promise of a paradise to come. Soviet personnel policy thus remains many-sided. Its unifying objective is the drive to increase output through every means and at any price.

Bureaucratic Politics in a Totalitarian System

The Soviet bureaucratic structure is commonly visualized as a tightly centralized administrative hierarchy in which all initiative and decision-making power are concentrated in the top leadership and in which the lower officials serve as mere automatons to execute the will of the ruling group. While this stereotype performs the useful function of emphasizing the high degree of centralization which characterizes the Soviet system, it also distorts reality by ignoring the fluid play of bureaucratic politics that underlies the monolithic totalitarian façade.

The Soviet bureaucracy operates under the strain of constant pressure from above to accelerate the program of rapid industrialization to which the regime is committed. This program accords top priority to military needs and the expansion of heavy industry. Scarce resources are allocated in accordance with these dominating priorities. The "key sectors" which have been chosen for intensive development enjoy a preferential position in the Soviet economy, but no part of the Soviet bureaucracy is immune from the insistent and implacable demands of the leadership for maximum output and effort.

The "success" of the bureaucracy is judged by its ability to meet the demands made on it. Since the demands are great and the resources available to meet them are ordinarily limited, each sector of the bureaucracy is driven to fight for a plan which it can carry out and for an allocation of resources which will enable it to discharge its obligations. This struggle is in essence political. While it is broadly contained within the framework of the ruling priorities of the leadership, there is still considerable room for maneuver. The planning experts, whose precise calculus is supposed to define the tasks of the bureaucracy, are not divorced from the play of bureaucratic politics. Indeed, Gosplan is a focal point around which the battle for special treatment rages. The battle is waged by negotiation, by personal influence, and by invoking the assistance of the powerful. Each bureaucratic group is constantly engaged in an effort to mobilize as much political support as it can muster, right up to the member of the Party Presidium responsible for its performance.

Bureaucratic representation in the Soviet context expresses itself in a struggle for preferential advantage. Because each part of the bureaucracy operates with an eye to the feasibility of the demands which are made on it, it becomes an unwitting spokesman for the claims of that sector of Soviet life for which it is responsible. The dictates of survival compel it to mediate between two types of pressure, the drive from above to extract the last reserves of energy from the population and the resistance from below which seeks to tailor commitments to capabilities. In the process, Soviet administrators develop a certain agility in counteracting the squeeze in which they are caught, and the more powerful or influential manage, in some degree at least, to shift the viselike grip to other sections of the bureaucracy or the economy.

This crossfire of pressures occurs at every level of the bureaucratic hierarchy. Once a plan has been determined, the same ministry which has fought for a "reasonable" plan and "favorable" allocations for itself must resist the efforts of its own subordinate enterprises to carve out protected positions for themselves which will shift the squeeze to other enterprises in the ministerial domain. The enterprises, like the ministries, struggle with every means at their disposal to obtain plan quotas that will be easy to meet and to accumulate large reserves of supplies and other resources to facilitate plan-fulfillment. The responsibility of the enterprise is limited to its own performance, while the record of the ministry is the record of all the agencies subordinate to it. Thus the ministry finds itself in the position of being both driver and driven. The enterprise is in the same position with respect to its component parts.

The tensions generated by the industrialization drive set the stage for a steady tug of war between the central leadership and the bureaucracy. The leadership faces the constant problem of ensuring that the pressure which it exerts will be transmitted to the base of the bureaucratic pyramid and not be diffused and frustrated by bureaucratic manipulation and resistance. The ruling group has developed a variety of ingenious devices to make its control operative throughout the bureaucratic structure. It appeals to the self-interest of the bureaucratic elite by an incentive system which offers attractive bonuses and other large rewards for production in excess of plan. It combines positive incentives with negative controls which impose harsh penalties for failure. It pits one bureaucracy against another and relies on the rivalry between them to enforce its demands on both. It depends heavily on the separately organized Party and police hierarchies to control administration, and it supplements this type of surveillance and pressure by planning, financial, personnel, legal, and investigatory controls which are built into the administrative structure. It endeavors to prevent the growth of "family relations" between the controlled and the controllers by frequent shifts of personnel and by periodic campaigns against officials who cover up for each other's sins. It takes advantage of the activist's desire to move ahead in the Soviet system by stimulating pledges of "over-plan" production and by encouraging denunciations of officials who evade the demands made on them. It seeks to protect the activists and careerists from retaliation by punishing "suppressors of criticism" who attempt to escape the controls which surround them by eliminating the critics in their own domain.

The essence of bureaucratic politics in the Soviet system consists in a search for a viable equilibrium between the pressures from above for maximal output and the inescapable limitations which factors of scarcity and human frailty impose. The successful Soviet administrator must be more than loyal and efficient. He must learn to manipulate the environment around him to meet the demands which are made on him. He cannot afford to be overscrupulous in obeying legal regulations if the price of conformity means failure to meet his set goals. He operates under an overriding compulsion to drive through to plan-fulfillment, and every expedient is justified which advances this transcendent purpose. In the Soviet Book of Acts, much is forgiven success, but nothing is forgiven failure.

Despite the remarkable skill with which some administrators manipulate the system for their own ends, the Soviet bureaucracy as a whole responds to the regime's inexorable demand for rapidly expanding industrial production. The pressure from above may be distributed unevenly as it is transmitted through the bureaucratic hierarchy, but it is distributed nonetheless. The administrators who fail to meet the expectations of the leadership disappear from the scene. The drivers and the manipulators survive.

The high-pressure system of Soviet administration imposes its costs. The administrators who drive are also driven, and the toll on their nervous energy and reserves of strength is great. The strain under which they operate is communicated to those below. The ultimate victims are not the administrative and managerial class, but the mass of collective farmers and unskilled and semiskilled workers who bear the major burden of the industrialization effort. The price of forced draft industrialization is the tensions and dissatisfactions which it inevitably generates.

The Party leadership attempts to protect itself against these consequences by both negative and positive measures. Its powerful instruments of surveillance and repression discourage any overt expression of disloyalty. It acts positively to build a labor aristocracy by reserving special rewards for its Stakhanovites and more productive skilled workers. It places great emphasis on attaching the loyalties of the new Soviet intelligentsia to the regime. It accords a privileged position to its bureaucratic elite and holds out the promise of rapid promotion for the most loyal and talented representatives of the younger generation. This conscious effort on the part of the regime to consolidate a subservient, but none the less privileged, layer of bureaucracy between itself and the Soviet populace represents an important aspect of its search for stability. The road which the regime has chosen to tread is that of primary reliance on a system of bureaucratic and police controls to engage the energies of the masses and to hold popular discontent in check. It builds its power on its elite formations and places its wager on their capacity to command that minimum degree of popular support which even a totalitarian dictatorship needs if it is to function effectively.

Chapter *13*

Terror as a System of Power

Terror is the linchpin of modern totalitarianism. What distinguishes twentieth-century totalitarianism from earlier patterns of more primitive dictatorship is not the use of terror and a secret police as instruments of control but rather their high development as an organized system of power. With the emergence of totalitarianism, terror has become elaborately institutionalized, has developed its own bureaucratic apparatus and specialized professionalisms, and has spread its net over the whole range of society. The large-scale organizational rationalization of the totalitarian terror machine introduces a new dimension of cold-blooded efficiency and calculated violence in comparison with which even the Jacobin terror takes on the character of a spontaneous and chaotic *Jacquerie*.

This does not mean that terror is the only method by which a totalitarian regime maintains itself in power. Loyalty and devotion must also be elicited. The skillful totalitarian dictator weaves a complex web of controls in which indoctrination and incentives have their appointed places. Agitation and propaganda may rally fanatic support, and appeals to self-interest may enlist the energies of the ambitious and bind their fortunes to the regime. When discontent accumulates, "loyalty" to the regime may be consolidated by providing scapegoats on whom frustrated aggression may exhaust itself. The shrewd totalitarian dictatorship may go further and permit ventilation of grievances of a nonpolitical and nonorganized character. It may even institutionalize such expression as the Soviet dictatorship does when it sanctions criticism of bureaucratic malpractice or inefficiency. Such criticism may play a constructive role in strengthening the regime since it accomplishes the triple function of draining off aggression on the part of its subjects, prodding the bureaucracy to improve its performance, and sustaining the illusion that the supreme leadership is genuinely concerned about popular annoyances and vexations.

Yet ultimately the totalitarian dictator must depend on terror to safeguard his monopoly of power. Behind the totalitarian façade, the instrument of terror can always be found, ready for use when needed, operative, above all, even when not visible by the mere fact that it is known to exist. Because the totalitarian regime provides no legitimate channel for the expression of political dissent, its constant concern is to prevent or eliminate its illegal existence. To accomplish this purpose, it recruits its specialists in espionage and terror and uses fear as a political weapon. The secret police becomes the core of totalitarian power, an omnipresent and pervasive force which envelops every sector of society in an ominous cloud of suspicion and insecurity. The task of the secret police is to serve as the eyes and ears of the dictatorship, as well as its sword. It must not only hear what people say; it must also be prepared to diagnose their souls and plumb their innermost thoughts. It must transform every citizen into a potential watchdog and informer to check and report on his friends and neighbors. It must sow distrust, for distrust will discourage organization and revolt.

The Defense of Terror

The practice of totalitarian terror generates its own underlying theoretical justifications. The role of terror in Communist ideology furnishes a prime example. Violence is accepted as implicit in the class struggle. As Lenin said in defending the dissolution of the Constituent Assembly, "Violence when it is committed by the toiling and exploited masses is the kind of violence of which we approve." [1] This instrumental attitude toward violence prepares the way for its sanctification when employed by the Party in the name of the working class and by the Party leadership in the name of the Party.

The rationalization of terror embraces two central propositions. The first emphasizes the safety of the Revolution as the supreme law. In the words of Lenin, "The Soviet Republic is a fortress besieged by world capital . . . From this follows our right and our duty to mobilize the whole population to a man for the war." [2] The second emphasizes the intransigence of the enemies of the Revolution, the necessity of crushing them completely if the Revolution itself is not to be destroyed. "What is the 'nutritive medium,'" asks Lenin,

which engenders counterrevolutionary enterprises, outbreaks, conspiracies, and so forth? . . . It is the medium of the bourgeoisie, of the bourgeois intelligentsia, of the kulaks in the countryside, and, everywhere, of the "non-Party" public, as well as of the Socialist-Revolutionaries and the Mensheviks. We must treble our watch over this medium, we must multiply it tenfold. We must multiply our vigilance, because counterrevolutionary attempts from this quarter are absolutely inevitable, precisely at the present moment and in the near future.[3]

In essence, Stalin's defense of terror, delivered in an interview with a visiting Foreign Workers' Delegation on November 5, 1927, covers much the same ground, though with notably less frankness.

> The GPU or Cheka is a punitive organ of the Soviet government. It is more or less analogous to the Committee of Public Safety which was formed during the Great French Revolution . . . It is something in the nature of a military-political tribunal set up for the purpose of protecting the interests of the revolution from attacks on the part of the counterrevolutionary bourgeoisie and their agents . . .
>
> People advocate a maximum of leniency; they advise the dissolution of the GPU . . . But can anyone guarantee that the capitalists of all countries will abandon the idea of organizing and financing counterrevolutionary groups of plotters, terrorists, incendiaries, and bomb-throwers after the liquidation of the GPU . . . ?
>
> . . . We are a country surrounded by capitalist states. The internal enemies of our revolution are the agents of the capitalists of all countries . . . In fighting against the enemies at home, we fight the counterrevolutionary elements of all countries . . .
>
> No, comrades, we do not wish to repeat the mistakes of the Parisian Communards. The GPU is necessary for the Revolution and will continue to exist to the terror of the enemies of the proletariat.[4]

The real significance of Stalin's theory of Soviet terror did not become fully manifest until the period of the Great Purge in the thirties. The liquidation of the Old Bolsheviks made it altogether clear that the salient role of terror in Stalinist ideology was to serve as a bulwark of defense for his own monopoly of Party leadership. Since this involved establishing a regime of terror within the Party, Stalin was faced with the problem of reconciling his innovation with the traditional notion that terror was reserved for the class enemy. The problem was neatly and ruthlessly solved by identifying any form of opposition to Stalin with counterrevolution and foreign espionage.[5] The formula of capitalist encirclement proved elastic enough to embrace the enemy inside the Party as well as the enemy outside. Stalin put it as follows:

> It should be remembered and never forgotten that as long as capitalist encirclement exists there will be wreckers, diversionists, spies, terrorists, sent behind the frontiers of the Soviet Union by the intelligence services of foreign states . . .
>
> It should be explained to our Party Comrades that the Trotskyites, who represent the active elements in the diversionist, wrecking and espionage work of the foreign intelligence services . . . have already long ceased to serve any idea compatible with the interests of the working class, that they have turned into a gang of wreckers, diversionists, spies, assassins, without principles and ideas, working for the foreign intelligence services.

It should be explained that in the struggle against contemporary Trotskyism, not the old methods, the methods of discussion, must be used, but new methods, methods for smashing and uprooting it.[6]

After the Great Purge, Stalin again faced the problem of reconciling the retention of these strong-arm methods with the claim that antagonistic classes had ceased to exist in the Soviet Union. In his report to the Eighteenth Party Congress in 1939, Stalin addressed himself to the issue, "It is sometimes asked: 'We have abolished the exploiting classes; there are no longer any hostile classes in the country; there is nobody to suppress; hence there is no more need for the state; it must die away — Why then do we not help our socialist state to die away? . . . Is it not time we relegated the state to the museum of antiquities?"[7] Again Stalin rested his case for the retention of the terror apparatus on the allegation of capitalist encirclement:

These questions not only betray an underestimation of the capitalist encirclement, but also an underestimation of the role and significance of the bourgeois states and their organs, which send spies, assassins and wreckers into our country and are waiting for a favourable opportunity to attack it by armed force. They likewise betray an underestimation of the role and significance of our socialist state and of its military, punitive and intelligence organs. which are essential for the defense of the socialist land from foreign attack.[8]

Writing in 1950, after a considerable expansion of Soviet power as a result of World War II, Stalin remained committed to "the conclusion that in the face of capitalist encirclement, when the victory of the socialist revolution has taken place in one country alone while capitalism continues to dominate in all other countries, the country where the revolution has triumphed must not weaken but must strengthen in every way its state, state organs, intelligence agencies, and army if it does not want to be destroyed by capitalist encirclement."[9] Behind these rationalizations was the crystallization of a system of government in which terror had become the essential ingredient. Defended originally as an expression of the class interests of the proletariat, its edge was first turned against all opponents of Communist ascendancy and finally against any appearance of challenge to the domination of the ruling clique.

The Creation of the Cheka

The genealogy of the Bolshevik apparatus of terror reaches back to the first weeks after the seizure of power. In pre-Revolutionary days, the Bolsheviks had occasion to acquire an intimate familiarity with the operations of the Tsarist *Okhrana* or secret police; the lessons they learned then were later to be applied and amplified. Lenin quickly decided that the Bolsheviks would have to develop their own Okhrana. In a memorandum dated December 19–20, 1917, he called on Dzerzhinsky, the commandant of Smolny, to organize the struggle against counterrevolution and sabotage.[10] On December 20, the Council of People's Commissars approved a decree establishing the Cheka or All-Russian Extraordinary Commission.[11] Dzerzhinsky was made the first chairman of the eight-member commission. One of its early acts was an appeal "to all local soviets to proceed immediately to the organization of similar commissions." Workers, soldiers, and peasants were instructed to inform the Cheka "about organizations and individual persons whose activity is harmful to the Revolution." [12] At the same time, a system of revolutionary tribunals was established to investigate and try offenses which bore the character of sabotage and counterrevolution. The judges of the revolutionary tribunals were to fix penalties in accordance with "the circumstances of the case and the dictates of the revolutionary conscience." [13]

In the confusion of the first months of the Bolshevik Revolution, terror was far from being a monopoly of the specialists in terror. The Cheka was still in its organizational phase, and its regime was singularly mild compared with what was to come. Acts of violence against the bourgeoisie were common, but they were usually committed by revolutionary mobs and undisciplined sailors and soldiers and were not ordinarily officially authorized and inspired. The early death sentences of the Cheka were imposed on bandits and criminals. As the White forces began to rally their strength, the Cheka spread its net more widely and turned to sterner measures. On February 22, 1918, the Cheka ordered all local soviets "to seek out, arrest, and shoot immediately all members . . . connected in one form or another with counterrevolutionary organizations . . . (1) enemy agents and spies, (2) counterrevolutionary agitators, (3) speculators, (4) organizers of revolt . . . against the Soviet government, (5) those going to the Don to join the . . . Kaledin-Kornilov band and the Polish counterrevolutionary legions, (6) buyers and sellers of arms to equip the counterrevolutionary bourgeoisie . . . all these are to be shot on the spot . . . when caught red-handed in the act."[14]

The terror began to gather momentum. Gorky's newspaper *Novaya Zhizn'* (New Life) reported, "Executions continue. Not a day, not a night passes without several persons being executed." [15] On the night of April 11, 1918, the Cheka staged a mass raid on anarchist centers in Moscow; several hundred were arrested and approximately thirty were killed while resisting arrest.[16] Though the curve of Cheka activity was rising, its operations still remained on a limited scale.

The terror was given a sharp impetus by the effort of the Left SR's to seize power in Moscow soon after the assassination of the German Ambassador Mirbach on July 6, 1918. Large-scale arrests of Left SR's followed, and at least thirteen were shot.[17] As the punitive actions of the Cheka increased, the SR's replied in kind. On August 30, 1918, Uritsky, the head of the Petrograd Cheka, was assassinated, and Lenin was seriously wounded. The attack on Uritsky and Lenin unleashed mass reprisals. In Petrograd alone, more than five hundred "counterrevolutionaries and White Guards" were immediately shot. The slaughter in Moscow included "many Tsarist ministers and a whole list of high personages." The President of the Provincial Soviet of Penza reported, "For the murder from ambush of one comrade, Egorov, a Petrograd worker, the Whites paid with 152 lives. In the future firmer measures will be taken against the Whites." [18] The prominent Chekist Latsis declared,

We are no longer waging war against separate individuals, we are exterminating the bourgeoisie as a class. Do not seek in the dossier of the accused for proofs as to whether or not he opposed the soviet government by word or deed. The first question that should be put is to what class he belongs, of what extraction, what education and profession. These questions should decide the fate of the accused. Herein lie the meaning and the essence of the Red Terror. [19]

The demonstrative massacres which followed the attack on Lenin were designed to strike fear into the hearts of all opponents of the Bolsheviks. The terror was mainly directed against the former nobility, the bourgeoisie, the landowners, the White Guards, and the clergy. But it was by no means confined to these groups. The SR's and Mensheviks, too, felt its sharp edge, and peasants who resisted the requisitioning of grain or who deserted from the Red Army were also among its victims. The Red Terror had its counterpart on the White side; the victims in this grim competition were numbered in the tens of thousands and perhaps hundreds of thousands.[20]

As the Cheka broadened the scope of its activities, it also jealously resisted any interference with its claimed authority. Its tendency to set itself above and beyond the law aroused concern even in Bolshevik circles. At the Second All-Russian Conference of Commissars of Justice held in Moscow July 2–6, 1918,

Comrade Lebedev . . . pointed out that granting the necessity for the existence of the Extraordinary Commissions, it was nevertheless important to delimit their sphere of activity . . . Otherwise we shall have a state within a state, with the former tending to widen its jurisdiction more and more. . .

Comrade Terastvatsaturov said that . . . in the provinces the question of the activities of the Extraordinary Commissions is a very acute one. The Commissions do everything they please . . . The president of our Cheka in Orel said: "I am responsible to no one; my powers are such that I can shoot anybody." [21]

The reply of Krestinsky, the Commissar of Justice, emphasized the difficulty of imposing restraints on the Cheka. "So long as the Cheka functions," concluded Krestinsky, "the work of justice must take a secondary place, and its sphere of activity must be considerably curtailed." [22] The Cheka was vigorous and effective in asserting its prerogatives both against local soviet authorities and the Commissariat of Justice. The Chekist Peters put it bluntly, "In its activity the Cheka is completely independent, carrying out searches, arrests, shootings, afterwards making a report to the Council of People's Commissars and the Soviet Central Executive Committee." [23]

After the end of the Civil War and the inauguration of the NEP, an effort was made to impose legal limits and restraints on Cheka operations. On the initiative of V. M. Smirnov, an Old Bolshevik of the Left Opposition, the Ninth Congress of Soviets, meeting in December 1921, adopted a resolution, which, after expressing gratitude for the "heroic work" of the Cheka "at the most acute moments of the Civil War," recommended that curbs be imposed on its powers.[24]

The GPU

On February 8, 1922, VTsIK (the All-Russian Central Executive Committee) issued a decree abolishing the Cheka and its local organs and transferring its functions to a newly created State Political Administration (GPU), which was to operate "under the personal chairmanship of the People's Commissar for Interior, or his deputy." The following tasks were assigned to it: "(a) Suppression of open counterrevolutionary outbreaks, including banditry; (b) Taking measures to prevent and combat espionage; (c) Guarding rail and water transport; (d) Political policing of the borders of the RSFSR; (e) Combating contraband and crossing of the borders of the republic without proper permission; (f) Executing special orders of the Presidium of the VTsIK or of the Sovnarkom for protecting the revolutionary order." Special army detachments were placed at the disposal of the GPU, and the field organization was made "directly subordinate" to the central GPU. Although the GPU was given full authority to undertake searches, seizures, and arrests, procedural restraints were imposed on it. Arrested prisoners were to be supplied with copies of their indictments not later than two weeks after their arrest. After holding a prisoner for two months, the GPU was required to free him or hand him over for trial, unless special permission for continued detention was received from the Presidium of VTsIK. The decree further provided that criminal cases "directed against the soviet structure or representing violations of the laws of the RSFSR" were henceforth to "be exclusively judged by the courts," and the People's Commissariat for Justice was vested with authority to supervise the execution of these provisions.[25]

After the establishment of the USSR, the GPU was transformed into the OGPU and given all-union functions. The new Constitution of the

USSR attached the OGPU directly to the Council of People's Commissars and granted its chairman an advisory vote in that body. The Constitution also gave the Procurator of the Supreme Court "supervision of the legality of the actions of the OGPU." [26] A special decree of the Presidium of the TsIK (Central Executive Committee) of the USSR dated November 15, 1923, codified these changes.[27]

The bridles imposed on the GPU-OGPU by these decrees proved verbal rather than real. Although uneasiness over the arbitrary authority exercised by the GPU was widespread even in Party circles, Lenin was persuaded that the regime could not dispense with terror. On May 17, 1922, he wrote Kursky with reference to the Criminal Code, "The Courts must not do away with terror; to promise such a thing would be either to fool ourselves or other people." [28] In the eyes of the Party leadership, the OGPU had become indispensable; its *de facto* authority to take summary action against enemies of the regime was a weapon which the regime showed no disposition to relinquish.

During the NEP period, the vigilance of the GPU was particularly directed against two categories, the "KR's or counterrevolutionists" and the "politicals." The "KR's" included one-time Kadets and supporters of the Right parties in the pre-Revolutionary period, Tsarist bureaucrats, White Guards, priests, landowners, nobility, industrialists, and other former members of the well-to-do classes. The "politicals" represented the remnants of the parties of the Left — Mensheviks, SR's, and Anarchists — who had once shared the amenities of Tsarist prisons together with the Bolsheviks. As old comrades-in-arms as well as opponents of the Bolsheviks, the "politicals" for a time enjoyed relatively favorable treatment in OGPU prisons and camps; toward the end of the NEP, their privileges were abolished, and all traces of pre-Revolutionary sentimentalism virtually disappeared.[29]

In retrospect, the NEP period appears as a comparatively peaceful and "liberal" interlude in the state of siege which the Soviet regime has maintained since 1917. Older ex-Soviet citizens who abandoned their native land during and after World War II still refer to it as the "golden age" of the Soviet period. While the OGPU was building up and consolidating its power during the mid-twenties, its direct impact on the mass of Soviet citizens who had no connections with the "former people" or with pre-Revolutionary parties of the Left was still slight. The OGPU no doubt inspired fear even among those who were not caught in its coils, but the limited character of the categories against which its punitive actions were directed created a widespread illusion of safety and security.

The operations of the OGPU during this period reflected the dominant preoccupations of the Party leadership. Particular attention was devoted to checking on church activities, persons of unfavorable social origins, and former members of opposition parties. As the struggle of the Trotsky opposition mounted in intensity, the OGPU concerned itself increasingly with nonconformity and deviation within the Party itself. Its field of supervision included the foreign embassies and foreign visitors. Through its Economic Administration, it sought to restrain malpractices and sabotage in industry; its Special Section penetrated the armed forces and kept a watchful eye on their morale, loyalty, and efficiency. Its Foreign Section conducted espionage abroad, observed the activities of Russian *émigré* colonies, and reported on personnel in all Soviet foreign missions. Its specially assigned troops were charged with guarding rail and water transport, policing the borders of the Soviet Union, and suppressing any counterrevolutionary risings which might take place.[30]

During the NEP, most prisons and so-called "corrective labor colonies" were outside the jurisdiction of the OGPU. The concentration camps directly administered by the OGPU were reserved for hardened criminals, so-called "counterrevolutionaries," and "politicals." The Northern Camps of Special Designation (SLON), of which the most notorious were located on the Solovetski Islands, formed the primary base of the OGPU detention network. According to one former inmate, in 1925 the Solovetski Monastery housed about 7,000 prisoners. "Two or three years later the prisoners totalled well over 20,000." [31] Prisoners at first worked solely to meet camp needs. The system of large-scale exploitation of prison labor in lumbering, mining, and construction of public works had its antecedents in NEP experiments, but during the middle twenties its operations were still on a limited scale.

With the abandonment of the NEP and the decision to proceed with a program of rapid industrialization and agricultural collectivization, the OGPU began to play a much more prominent role. Its energies were concentrated on three targets: the Nepmen or private traders, who had been permitted to flourish under the NEP; the old intelligentsia, who were made the scapegoats for early failures and difficulties in the industrialization drive; and the kulaks, who offered active or passive opposition to the collectivization program. As a result of the cumulative impact of these campaigns, the OGPU became the intimate caretaker of the destinies of millions instead of tens of thousands.

The roundup and repression of the Nepmen assumed intensified form as the NEP period drew to a close. At the height of the NEP in 1924, the number of privately owned shops totalled 420,366.[32] The proprietors of these shops became a special object of OGPU attention. There is no way of knowing precisely how many were incarcerated by the OGPU, how many were condemned to administrative exile, and how many succeeded in eluding the OGPU by shifting their occupations and disappearing into the anonymity of the rapidly expanding industrial labor force. Many were caught up in the drive which the OGPU spearheaded to accumulate *valuta* in order to finance the purchase of machinery abroad. Nepmen, members of the former well-to-do classes, and other persons suspected of hoarding gold or other valuables were arrested in large numbers and their property confiscated.[33]

The persecution of the old intelligentsia, which revived in intensity after the beginning of the Five Year Plan, was inspired by distrust of their loyalty to the Soviet regime. As hardships mounted and living conditions deteriorated, the Party leadership utilized the old intelligentsia as a scapegoat to divert popular discontent and frustration. Every breakdown in production tended to be treated as an act of sabotage for which some old-regime engineer was held personally responsible. The acts of "sabotage" were in turn magnified into conspiracies to overthrow Soviet power in which foreign capitalist enemies of the USSR were alleged to be deeply involved.

The OGPU was given the responsibility of preparing a series of show trials which would lend plausibility to these flimsy accusations. The production lag in the Donets Coal Basin in 1927–28 led to the widely advertised Shakhty prosecution of Russian technicians and old-regime engineers who were alleged to have conspired with the Germans to commit acts of sabotage and espionage. In the autumn of 1930 forty-eight specialists in the food industry were arrested and shot for alleged membership in a counterrevolutionary organization charged with sabotaging the workers' food supply. In December 1930 came the famous *Prompartiya* (Industrial Party) trial in which Professor Ramzin and seven other prominent Soviet engineers were accused and convicted of organizing a secret political party, committing acts of sabotage, and conspiring with France to overthrow the Soviet regime. Six of the defendants received death sentences which were subsequently reprieved; the two others were given ten-year terms of imprisonment. In March 1931 another trial was dramatically staged. Fourteen professors and officials were convicted of counterrevolutionary activity and sabotage in conspiracy with the Mensheviks abroad. One of the main culprits was Professor Groman of Gosplan, whose real sin apparently was in insisting that the targets of the First Five Year Plan were unrealistically high.

The drive against the intellectuals was not limited to show trials. As Sidney and Beatrice Webb observed in a volume notable for its generally friendly tone to Soviet achievements:

This much-discussed prosecution of Professor Ramzin and his colleagues inaugurated a veritable reign of terror against the intelligentsia. Nobody regarded himself as beyond suspicion. Men and women lived in daily dread of arrest. Thousands were sent on administrative exile to distant parts of the country. Evidence was not necessary. The title of engineer served as sufficient condemnation. The jails were filled. Factories languished from lack of technical leadership, and the chiefs of the Supreme Economic Council commenced to complain "that by its wholesale arrests of engineers the GPU . . . was interfering with industrial progress." [34]

On June 23, 1931, Stalin called a halt to the policy of specialist-baiting.* Having accomplished his purpose of frightening the intellectuals into submission, he now faced the necessity of utilizing their indispensable skills. The new line announced by Stalin was soon echoed and re-echoed by lesser dignitaries. Soltz, a member of the Central Control Committee of the Party, proclaimed, "We are not accustomed to value the human being sufficiently. To withdraw men from important posts in industry and civil service by arresting and sentencing them without adequate justification has caused the state tremendous loss." [35]

In the period immediately after Stalin's pronouncements, a substantial number of engineers were released from prison or recalled from exile. Professor Ramzin, the convicted "agent" of the French General Staff, resumed his lectures at the Institute of Thermodynamics. Other engineer "traitors" and "saboteurs" received similar treatment. Encouraged by the promise of a more liberal dispensation, the old technical intelligentsia again began to take its place in industry, to recover its courage, and to assume the "production risks" out of which so many earlier charges of wrecking had developed.

The liberal interlude was not destined to be prolonged. With the sharp deterioration of living conditions in the winter of 1932–33, scapegoats again became necessary, and a new wave of persecution engulfed the old intelligentsia. In January 1933 another show trial was staged, this time directed against six British Metro-Vickers engineers, ten Russian technicians, and a woman secretary who had been associated with them. All were charged with sabotage of power stations and the usual accompaniment of conspiracy and espionage. Two months later the OGPU announced the discovery and punishment of a large-scale conspiracy in the People's Commissariat of Agriculture and State Farming. The accused were charged with using their authority to wreck tractors and to disorganize sowing, harvesting, and threshing in order "to create a famine in the country." Thirty-five of the alleged culprits were shot; twenty-two received ten-year sentences; and eighteen were ordered confined for eight years. The victims were all alleged to be descended "from bourgeois and landowning classes." [36] The pall of terror enveloping the old intelligentsia was lifted slightly after the favorable harvest of 1933. In July 1934 Andrei Vyshinsky, then Deputy State Prosecutor, ordered local prosecutors to cease their policy of indiscriminate prosecution of engineers and directors for administrative failures.

* See Chapter 4, p. 104.

The mass incidence of OGPU arrests during the period of the First Five Year Plan was most widely felt in the countryside. The commitment to collectivize and mechanize agriculture involved a decision to liquidate the kulaks as a class, on the ground that they were inveterate enemies of Soviet power and could be counted on to sabotage collectivization. Stalin estimated in November 1928 that the kulaks constituted about 5 per cent of the rural population, or more than one million of the twenty-five million peasant families. The OGPU was assigned the task of ejecting them from their land, confiscating their property, and deporting them to the North and Siberia. Some of the more recalcitrant were shot when they resisted arrest or responded with violence to efforts to dispossess them. The great majority became wards of the OGPU and were sentenced to forced labor in lumber camps or coal mines, or on canals, railroads, and other public works which the OGPU directed. At one stroke, the OGPU became the master of the largest pool of labor in the Soviet Union. Its own enterprises expanded rapidly to absorb them; those for whom no work could be found in the OGPU industrial empire were hired out on contract to other Soviet enterprises encountering difficulty in mobilizing supplies of free labor.

The mass deportation of the kulaks meant a tremendous growth in the network of OGPU forced labor camps. At the same time, the jurisdiction of the OGPU over ordinary criminals was enlarged. All prisoners serving sentences of more than three years were transferred to OGPU care, even if the crimes were not of a political character. No official statistics were made available on the population of the camps in the early thirties, but some indication of the magnitudes involved is provided by the fact that Belomor, the canal project connecting Leningrad and the White Sea, alone utilized more than two hundred thousand prisoners.[37] By the end of the First Five Year Plan, forced labor had become a significant factor in manning the construction projects of the Soviet economy.

The NKVD and the Great Purge

The powers of the OGPU were concurrently enhanced. It was given authority to enforce the obligatory passport system introduced in large areas of the Soviet Union at the end of 1932. In July 1934 the OGPU was transformed into the People's Commissariat of Internal Affairs, or NKVD. The enlarged activities of the NKVD included responsibility for state security, all penal institutions, fire departments, police (militia), convoy troops, frontier guards, troops of internal security, highway administration, and civil registry offices (vital statistics). The reorganization of 1934–35 involved a consolidation of the repressive machinery of the Soviet state. For the first time, all institutions of detention were placed under one jurisdiction. The secret police and their supporting military formations were united with the ordinary police. A formidable structure of power was cemented.

Some contemporary commentators tended to view the reorganization as an effort to impose limits on the arbitrary authority of the secret police.[38] The bases for these hopes were twofold. In July 1933 a new office, the Procuratorship of the USSR, was established, and among its duties was "the supervision . . . of the legality and regularity of the actions of the OGPU." The statute creating the NKVD appeared to restrict its judicial powers. A special council attached to the NKVD was vested with authority "to issue orders regarding administrative deportation, exile, imprisonment in corrective labor camps for a term not exceeding five years." [39] No mention was made of any NKVD authorization to inflict the death penalty. The statute seemed clearly to imply that criminal cases not disposed of administratively by the NKVD were to be transferred to the courts for trial and that crimes such as treason and espionage, which involved the possibility of the death penalty, were to be triable by the Military Collegium of the Supreme Court or other military tribunals. Whatever may have been the intent behind these measures to restrict the NKVD, subsequent events testified to their futility. In the Great Purge touched off by the assassination of Kirov, legal forms lost all significance. The arbitrary power of the NKVD reached previously unattained heights; the "Yezhovshchina" (as the worst phase of the purge became known after its sponsor, the NKVD head Yezhov) entered the language as a symbol of lawlessness run riot.

Before 1934 the victims of the OGPU-NKVD were largely former White Guards, the bourgeoisie, political opponents of the Bolsheviks, Nepmen, members of the old intelligentsia, and kulaks. During the late twenties and early thirties, some members of the Trotsky-Zinoviev and Right oppositions were also arrested by the OGPU and condemned to administrative exile or confinement in political *isolators*; but as Anton Ciliga, who was sentenced to one of the latter, records, the political prisoners received "special treatment," had books at their disposal, held meetings and debates, published prison news sheets, and lived a relatively privileged existence compared with the wretched inhabitants of the forced labor camps. Until 1934, the Party was largely exempt from the full impact of the OGPU-NKVD terror; the relatively few oppositionists who were confined in OGPU prisons were still treated with comparative humanity.[40]

In December 1934, when Kirov was assassinated by Nikolayev, allegedly a former member of the Zinoviev opposition, a new era in NKVD history opened. The "liberal" regime which the imprisoned "oppositionists" enjoyed came to an abrupt end. The concentrated power of the NKVD was now directed toward uprooting all actual or potential opposition in the Party. For the first time, the Party felt the full brunt of the terror.

The murder of Kirov was followed by drastic reprisals. Nikolayev and a group of his alleged confederates were charged with having formed a so-called Leningrad Center to organize the assassination and were condemned to death. More than a hundred persons who had been arrested prior to Kirov's death as "counterrevolutionaries" were promptly handed over to military commissions of the Supreme Court of the USSR for trial, were found guilty of preparing and carrying out terrorist acts, and were instantly shot. This demonstrative massacre was accompanied by the arrest and imprisonment, on charges of negligence, of twelve high NKVD officials in Leningrad. In the spring of 1935, thousands and perhaps tens of thousands of Leningrad inhabitants who were suspected of harboring opposition sentiments were arrested and deported to Siberia. In the sardonic nomenclature of exile and concentration camp, they came to be referred to collectively as "Kirov's assassins."

Zinoviev, Kamenev, and all the principal leaders of the Zinoviev group were also arrested and transferred to the political *isolator* at Verkhne-Uralsk. During the summer of 1935, Zinoviev, Kamenev, and an assortment of lesser figures were secretly tried for plotting against the life of Stalin. According to Ciliga, "Two of the prisoners were shot: one collaborator of the G.P.U. and one officer of the Kremlin Guard. The others escaped with sentences ranging between five and ten years." [41] Stalin, in addressing the graduates of the Red Army Academies at the Kremlin on May 4, 1935, observed,

These comrades did not always confine themselves to criticism and passive resistance. They threatened to raise a revolt in the Party against the Central Committee. More, they threatened some of us with bullets. Evidently, they reckoned on frightening us and compelling us to turn from the Leninist road . . . We were obliged to handle some of these comrades roughly. But that cannot be helped. I must confess that I too had a hand in this.[42]

During 1935 the purge gathered momentum, but its proportions were still relatively restricted. The dissolution of the Society of Old Bolsheviks on May 25, 1935, was an ominous portent of things to come.[43] On May 13, some two weeks earlier, the Party Central Committee had ordered a screening of all Party documents in order to "cleanse" the Party of all opposition elements.[44] As Zhdanov stated in a report at the plenum of the Saratov *kraikom*, "Recent events, particularly the treacherous murder of Comrade Kirov, show clearly how dangerous it is for the Party to lose its vigilance . . . I have to remind you that the murderer of Comrade Kirov, Nikolayev, committed his crime by using his Party card." [45] By December 1, 1935, 81.1 per cent of all Party members had been subjected to screening, and 9.1 per cent of these were reported as expelled.[46]

On December 25 the Central Committee of the Party, dissatisfied with the modest results of the verification of Party documents, ordered a new purge. Beginning February 1, 1936, all old Party cards were to be exchanged for new cards; the issuance of new Party documents was to serve as the occasion for a rigorous unmasking of enemies who had survived the earlier screening.[47] The bite of the first phase of the purge is indicated by the striking decline of Party membership from 2,807,786 in January 1934 to 2,044,412 in April 1936.[48] In a little over two years, more than one out of every four members and candidates disappeared from the Party rolls. Their fate can be inferred from the diatribes which the Soviet press of the period directed against "wreckers, spies, diversionists and murderers sheltering behind the Party card and disguised as Bolsheviks." [49]

The Great Purge reached its climax in the period 1936–1938. Its most dramatic external manifestation was the series of show trials in the course of which every trace of Old Bolshevik opposition leadership was officially discredited and exterminated. The first of the great public trials took place in August, 1936.[50] Zinoviev, Kamenev, Ivan Smirnov, and thirteen associates were charged with organizing a clandestine terrorist center under instructions from Trotsky, with accomplishing the murder of Kirov, and with preparing similar attempts against the lives of other Party leaders. All sixteen were executed. In the course of the trial, the testimony of the accused compromised many other members of the Bolshevik Old Guard. A wave of new arrests followed. On August 23, 1936, Tomsky, hounded by a sense of impending doom, committed suicide.

In January 1937 came the Trial of the Seventeen, the so-called Anti-Soviet Trotskyite Center, which included such prominent figures as Pyatakov, Radek, Sokolnikov, Serebryakov, and Muralov. This time the accused were charged with plotting the forcible overthrow of the Soviet government with the aid of Germany and Japan, with planning the restoration of capitalism in the USSR, and with carrying on espionage, wrecking, diversive, and terrorist activities on behalf of foreign states. Again, the trial was arranged to demonstrate that Trotsky was the *éminence grise* who inspired, organized, and directed all these activities. The prisoners in the dock fought for their lives by playing their assigned role in a drama designed to destroy Trotsky's reputation. Radek and Sokolnikov were rewarded with ten-year prison sentences. Two minor figures were also sentenced to long prison terms. The remaining thirteen were shot.

On June 12, 1937, *Pravda* carried the announcement of the execution of Marshal Tukhachevsky and seven other prominent generals of the Red Army "for espionage and treason to the Fatherland." This time no public trial was held. The Party press merely declared that the executed generals had conspired to overthrow the Soviet government and to reëstablish "the yoke of the landowners and industrialists." [51] The conspirators were alleged to be in the service of the military intelligence of "a foreign government," to which they were supposed to have indicated their readiness to surrender the Soviet Ukraine in exchange for assistance in bringing about the downfall of the Soviet government. Besides Tukhachevsky, the Deputy People's Commissar of Defense, the list of the executed included General Yakir, Commander of the Leningrad Military District; General Uborevich, Commander of the Western Military District; General Kork, Commander of the War College in Moscow; General Primakov, Budënny's Deputy Commander of Cavalry; Feldman, head of the Administration of Commanding Personnel in the Defense Commissariat; Putna, the former Soviet military attaché in Great Britain; and Eideman, President of the Central Council of *Osoaviakhim*, the civilian defense agency. Gamarnik, who served as the Party's watchdog over the army in his capacity as head of the Political Administration of the Red Army (PUR), committed suicide to avoid arrest. The execution of Tukhachevsky and his associates was the prelude to a mass purge of the Soviet armed forces in the course of which the top commanding personnel was particularly hard hit.

The slaughter of the Old Guard continued with the Trial of the Twenty-one, the so-called Anti-Soviet Bloc of Rights and Trotskyites, in March 1938. Among the prisoners in the dock were Bukharin, Rykov, and Krestinsky, all former members of the Politburo; Yagoda, the former head of the NKVD; Rakovsky, the former chairman of the Council of People's Commissars in the Ukraine and Soviet ambassador to England and France; Rosengoltz, the former People's Commissar of Foreign Trade; Grinko, the former People's Commissar of Finance; and Khodjayev, the former chairman of the Council of People's Commissars of Uzbekistan. The indictment against them embraced the usual combination of treason, espionage, diversion, terrorism, and wrecking. The bloc headed by Bukharin and Rykov was alleged to have spied for foreign powers from the earliest days of the Revolution, to have entered into secret agreements with the Nazis and the Japanese to dismember the Soviet Union, to have planned the assassination of Stalin and the rest of the Politburo, and to have organized innumerable acts of sabotage and diversion in order to wreck the economic and political power of the Soviet Union. If the testimony of Yagoda is to be believed, he not only murdered his predecessor in office, Menzhinsky, but also tried to murder his successor, Yezhov; he facilitated the assassination of Kirov, was responsible for the murder of Gorky, Gorky's son, and Kuibyshev; he admitted foreign spies into his organization and protected their operations; he planned a palace coup in the Kremlin and the assassination of the Politburo.

If these lurid tales strain the credulity of the reader, they nevertheless represent the version of oppositionist activity which Stalin and his faithful lieutenants found it expedient to propagate. Without access to the archives of the Kremlin and the NKVD, it is doubtful whether the web of fact and fancy behind the show trials will ever be authoritatively disentangled. The hatred of the former leaders of the opposition for Stalin can be taken for granted. That their hatred carried them to the point of conspiring together to overthrow him is not unlikely, though the evidence adduced at the trials to support the charge is lame and unconvincing. What appears singularly implausible are the allegations that Old Bolsheviks who had given their lives to the Communist cause would plot with the Nazis to restore capitalism in the Soviet Union, would function as their puppets and espionage agents, and arrange to hand over large portions of the Soviet Union to them as compensation for dethroning Stalin.

How then explain the confessions of guilt in open court? It is important to recall that the great majority of the executed, including all the military leaders, were tried *in camera*; presumably, despite the pressure to which they were exposed, they could not be persuaded to confess publicly to the crimes with which they were charged. The prisoners who appeared in the show trials represented a small handful of the accused, though they included a number of the leading figures of the Leninist epoch of the Party. What inspired them to pour out their guilt and to confess to deeds of which they were patently incapable? Why did only one of them, Krestinsky, use the opportunity of the public trial to repudiate the admissions of guilt which he had made in his preliminary examination, and why did he return the next day to repudiate his repudiation? Were Krestinsky and the rest shattered by the continuous interrogations and tortures of the NKVD examiners? Did they perform the roles assigned to them in the show trials in the desperate hope of winning clemency for themselves or their families? Were they inspired by a twisted sense of Party loyalty in which the ritual acknowledgment of crimes they had not committed and recantation of sins they were not guilty of served as an act of atonement for earlier breaches of Party unity? Was their attachment to the Communist dream so strong that their own capitulation and debasement appeared as a minor perversion in the glories and achievements of Soviet construction? Did they genuinely believe, as Bukharin claimed in his final plea, that "everything positive that glistens in the Soviet Union acquires new dimensions in a man's mind. This in the end disarmed me completely and led me to bend my knees before the Party and the country"? [52]

The answers to these questions are buried with the dead. From Stalin's point of view, the motivations of the repentant sinners at the show trials were irrelevant. What counted was the creation of a legend which stamped the oppositionists irrevocably as spies and traitors to the Soviet cause. To liquidate the whole generation of Old Bolsheviks without pretext or explanation would have represented too naked an exposure of the mechanics of a regime in which any form of dissidence had become a sufficient ground for extermination or imprisonment. The role of the show trials was to demonstrate to the Soviet public and to the world that the Bolshevik Old Guard had become a fifth column which was desperately seeking to undermine and dismember the Soviet state and that the Great Purge had its ultimate justification in considerations of national security and defense. Behind the camouflage of this myth, Stalin proceeded with ruthless determination to consolidate his own power by eliminating every actual or potential rallying point for an alternative government.

The history of the Great Purge is still obscure. Despite a flood of memoir literature in recent years which does much to illuminate the experiences of the victims, the role played by Stalin and his Kremlin intimates remains in the shadows. The development of the purge can be conveniently divided into three periods. The first dates from the assassination of Kirov to the removal of Yagoda as head of the NKVD in late September 1936. During this period, the purge was gathering momentum, but its sharpest edge was reserved for the remnants of the Trotsky-Zinoviev group and other left-wing oppositionists inside and outside the Party. The symbol of this phase of the purge was the Zinoviev-Kamenev trial in August 1936. In this period, Stalin appeared to be settling accounts with the Left, and while the victims were by no means confined to Old Bolsheviks who were suspected of harboring sympathies for Trotsky or Zinoviev, they constituted a primary target. The public signal for the widening of the purge was given at the Zinoviev-Kamenev trial; the prearranged testimony implicated the Right as well as the Left in the "plot" to wipe out Stalin. The whole Bolshevik Old Guard appeared compromised. The climax of this phase was reached with the removal of Yagoda as head of the NKVD and the purge of his leading associates in the secret police apparatus. The mystery of Yagoda's demotion was later "clarified" by the official revelation that he was one of the prime movers in the conspiracy. The actual cause of Yagoda's fall from grace remains an enigma. Plausible hypotheses stress his alleged sympathy for the Right Opposition in 1928–29, the danger which his entrenched position in the NKVD represented to Stalin, and the desirability from Stalin's point of view of eliminating an official who knew too much.

The crescendo of the Great Purge was reached in the second period, which extended from late September 1937, when Yezhov was appointed head of the NKVD, until the end of July 1938, when Lavrenti Beria was designated as Yezhov's deputy and eventual successor. The announcement of Yezhov's removal did not come until December, but meanwhile Beria assumed *de facto* command of the NKVD organization, and early in 1939 Yezhov disappeared and was probably liquidated.

The period of the Yezhovshchina involved a reign of terror without parallel in Soviet history. Among those arrested, imprisoned, and executed were a substantial proportion of the leading figures in the Party and governmental hierarchy. The Bolshevik Old Guard was destroyed. The roll of Yezhov's victims included not only former oppositionists but many of the most stalwart supporters of Stalin in his protracted struggle with the opposition. No sphere of Soviet life, however lofty, was left untouched. Among the purged Stalinists were three former members of the Politburo, Rudzutak, Chubar, and S. V. Kossior, and three candidate members, Petrovsky, Postyshev, and Eikhe. An overwhelming majority of the members and candidates of the Party Central Committee disappeared.[*] The senior officer corps of the armed forces suffered severely. According to one sober account, "two of five marshals of the Soviet Union escaped arrest, two of fifteen army commanders, twenty-eight of fifty-eight corps commanders, eighty-five of a hundred and ninety-five divisional commanders, and a hundred and ninety-five of four hundred and six regimental commanders."[53] The havoc wrought by the purge among naval commanding personnel was equally great. The removal of Yagoda from the NKVD was accompanied by the arrest of his leading collaborators, Agranov, Prokofiev, Balitsky, Messing, Pauker, Trilisser, and others. The Commissariat of Foreign Affairs and the diplomatic service were hard hit. Among the Old Guard, only Litvinov, Maisky, Troyanovsky, and a few lesser lights survived. Almost every commissariat was deeply affected.

The purge swept out in ever-widening circles and resulted in wholesale removals and arrests of leading officials in the union republics, secretaries of the Party, Komsomol, and trade-union apparatus, heads of industrial trusts and enterprises, Comintern functionaries and foreign Communists, and leading writers, scholars, engineers, and scientists. The arrest of an important figure was followed by the seizure of the entourage which surrounded him. The apprehension of members of the entourage led to the imprisonment of their friends and acquaintances. The endless chain of involvements and associations threatened to encompass entire strata of Soviet society. Fear of arrest, exhortations to vigilance, and perverted ambition unleashed new floods of denunciations, which generated their own avalanche of cumulative interrogations and detentions. Whole categories of Soviet citizens found themselves singled out for arrest because of their "objective characteristics." Old Bolsheviks, Red Partisans, foreign Communists of German, Austrian, and Polish extraction, Soviet

[*] See Chapter 6, p. 171.

citizens who had been abroad or had relations with foreign countries or foreigners, and "repressed elements" were automatically caught up in the NKVD web of wholesale imprisonment. The arrests mounted into the millions; the testimony of the survivors is unanimous regarding crowded prison cells and teeming forced labor camps. Most of the prisoners were utterly bewildered by the fate which had befallen them. The vast resources of the NKVD were concentrated on one objective — to document the existence of a huge conspiracy to undermine Soviet power. The extraction of real confessions to imaginary crimes became a major industry. Under the zealous and ruthless ministrations of NKVD examiners, millions of innocents were transformed into traitors, terrorists, and enemies of the people.

How explain the Yezhovshchina? What motives impelled Stalin to organize a blood bath of such frightening proportions? In the absence of revealing testimony from the source, one can only venture hypotheses. Stalin's desire to consolidate his own personal power appears to have been a driving force. The slaughter of the Bolshevik Old Guard may be viewed partly as a drastic reprisal for past insubordination; it was more probably intended as a preventive measure to end once and for all any possibility of resistance or challenge from this direction. The extension of the purge to the Stalinist stalwarts in the Party and governmental apparatus is much more difficult to fathom. It is possible that many fell victim to the system of denunciations in the course of which their loyalty to Stalin was put in question, that a number were still involved in official or personal relationships with former oppositionists, that some were liquidated because they displayed traces of independence in their dealings with the Supreme Leader, that others were merely suspected of harboring aspirations toward personal power, and that still others simply furnished convenient scapegoats to demonstrate the existence of a conspiracy that reached into the highest circles.

Implicit in any understanding of the Yezhovshchina is a theory of the role of terror in Stalin's formula of government. The consolidation of personal rule in a totalitarian system depends on the constant elimination of all actual or potential competitors for supreme power. The insecurity of the masses must be supplemented by the insecurity of the governing elite who surround the Supreme Dictator. The too strongly entrenched official with an independent base of power is by definition a threat to the dictator's total sway. The individuals or groups who go uncontrolled and undirected are regarded as fertile soil for the growth of conspiratorial intrigue. The function of terror thus assumes a two-fold aspect. As prophylactic and preventive, it is designed to nip any possible resistance or opposition in the bud. As an instrument for the reinforcement of the personal power of the dictator, it is directed toward ensuring perpetual

circulation in the ranks of officeholders in order to forestall the crystallization of autonomous islands of countervailing force.

The manipulation of terror as a system of power is a delicate art. A
dictator in command of modern armaments and a secret police can transform his subjects into robots and automatons, but if he succeeds too
well, he runs the risk of destroying the sources of creative initiative on
which the survival of his own regime depends. When terror runs rampant,
as it did at the height of the Yezhovshchina, unintended consequences
follow. Fear becomes contagious and paralyzing. Officials at all levels
seek to shirk responsibility. The endless belt of irresponsible denunciations begins to destroy the nation's treasury of needed skills. The terror
apparatus grows on the stuff on which it feeds and magnifies in importance until it overshadows and depresses all the constructive enterprises of the state. The dictator finds himself caught up in a whirlwind of
his own making which threatens to break completely out of control.

As the fury of the Yezhovshchina mounted, Stalin and his intimates
finally became alarmed. Evidence accumulated that the purge was over-
reaching itself and that much talent sorely needed by the regime was
being irretrievably lost. The first signal of a change of policy was given
in a resolution of the January 1938 plenum of the Party Central Committee entitled "Concerning the Mistakes of Party Organizations in Excluding Communists from the Party, Concerning Formal-Bureaucratic
Attitudes toward the Appeals of Excluding Members of the VKP(b), and
Concerning Measures to Eliminate these Deficiencies." [54] The resolution
identified a new culprit, the Communist-careerists, who sought to make
capital out of the purge by securing promotions through provocatory denunciations of their superiors. It was these careerists, the resolution
charged, who were primarily responsible for sowing suspicion and insecurity within Party ranks and for decimating the Party cadres. The resolution concluded with a ten-point program designed to put an end to mass
expulsions and to secure the rehabilitation of former members who had
been expelled as the result of slanders. The immediate effect of this resolution was to produce a new purge of so-called Communist-careerists. At
the same time, the Party press began to carry stories of the reinstatements
of honest Communists who had been the unfortunate victims of unjustified denunciations. [55]

The third and final phase of the Great Purge involved the purging of
the purgers. In late July 1938 Yezhov's sun began to set when Beria took
over as his deputy. In December, Yezhov was ousted as head of the
NKVD and appointed Commissar for Inland Water Transport, from
which post he soon disappeared unmourned but not forgotten. During the
same month came the sensational announcement of the arrest, trial, and
shooting of the head of the NKVD of Moldavia and a group of his exam-

iners for extracting false confessions from innocent prisoners. The enemies
of the people, it now appeared, had wormed their way into the NKVD
apparatus itself and had sought to stir up mass unrest and disaffection
by their brutal persecution of the guiltless.

It was now the turn of Yezhov and his collaborators to play the role
of scapegoat for the excesses of the purge. A wave of arrests spread
through the NKVD organization. The prisons began to fill with former
NKVD examiners; many prisoners who had been tortured by these same
examiners had the welcome experience of greeting their former tormen-
tors as cellmates in prisons and forced labor camps.[56] The "Great Change,"
as it was soon to become known, was marked by a substantial amelioration
in prison conditions and examining methods. According to Beck and
Godin, "Prisoners were released by the thousands, and many were restored to their old positions or even promoted." [57] A new era appeared to
have dawned.

Stalin now presented himself in the guise of the dispenser of mercy
and justice. Excesses of the purge were blamed on subordinate officials
who had exceeded their authority, saboteurs who had tried to break the
indissoluble link which bound Leader and people, and careerists and
counterrevolutionaries who had insinuated themselves into the Party
and NKVD organizations in order to subvert and undermine the Soviet
regime. At the Eighteenth Congress in 1939, Zhdanov reeled off case
after case of so-called slanderers and calumniators who had tried to advance themselves in the Party by wholesale expulsions of honest Party
members. Quoting from Stalin, he repeated, "Some of our Party leaders
suffer from a lack of concern for people, for members of the Party, for
workers . . . As a result of this heartless attitude towards people . . .
discontent and bitterness are artificially created among a section of the
Party, and the Trotskyite double-dealers artfully hook on to such embit-
tered comrades and skillfully drag them into the bog of Trotskyite wrecking." [58] Zhdanov called for a change in Party Rules to ensure "an attentive
approach and careful investigation of accusations brought against Party
members," which would "protect the rights of Party members from all
arbitrary procedure," and "abolish the resort to expulsion from the Party
. . . for trifling misdemeanours." [59]

Thus, the pressure of the purge was temporarily relaxed as Stalin
sought to enlist the energies and loyalties of the new governing elite
whom he had promoted to positions of responsibility over the graves of
their predecessors. Again, as in the collectivization crisis earlier, Stalin
demonstrated his remarkable instinct for stopping short and reversing
course at the brink of catastrophe.

The full circle of the Great Purge offers a remarkable case study in
the use of terror. Arrests ran into the millions. The gruesome and harrow-

ing experiences of the victims blackened the face of Stalinist Russia. The
havoc wrought in leading circles appeared irreparable. Yet despite the
damage and the hatred engendered, the dynamic momentum of the industrialization program was maintained. The arrests of responsible technicians and officials frequently produced serious setbacks in production,
but as their replacements acquired experience, order was restored, and
production began to climb again. While many functionaries reacted to
the purge by shunning all responsibility, others responded to the fear of
arrest by working as they had never worked before.[60] Terror functioned
as prod as well as brake. The acceleration in the circulation of the elite
brought a new generation of Soviet-trained intelligentsia into positions
of responsibility, and Stalin anchored his power on their support. Meanwhile, Stalin emerged from the purge with his own position consolidated.
The major purpose of decapitating the Bolshevik Old Guard had been
accomplished. Every rival for supreme power who was visible on the
horizon had been eliminated. The Party and the nation were thoroughly
intimidated. The purgers had been purged and the scapegoats identified.
The ancient formula of protecting the infallibility of the Leader by punishing subordinates for their excessive ardor was impressively resurrected.

The moving equilibrium on which Stalin balanced his power structure
entered a new phase. The temporary lifting of the blanket of fear was
designed to restore morale, to revive hope and initiative, and to reforge
the bonds between regime and people which the purge had dangerously
strained. But the mitigation of the terror involved no abandonment of the
system. For the totalitarian dictator, terror is an indispensable necessity,
and its invocation is a guarantee that no organized force will rise to challenge his undisputed rule. The Stalinist refinement on the use of terror
as a system of power involved oscillating phases of pressure and relaxation which varied with the dictator's conception of the dangers which he
confronted. The essence of control was never abandoned. At the same
time, when the pressure became too great, a mirage of security and stability was held out in order to enlist the energy and devotion of the oncoming generations. It is a system which devours many of its servants, but
as in games of chance, since the winners and survivors are highly rewarded and cannot be identified in advance, the ambitions of the players
are periodically renewed, and the regime bases its strength on their sacrifices.

As the Great Purge drew to a close, the major efforts of the NKVD
were concentrated against elements which might prove unreliable in the
event that the Soviet Union became involved in war. After the Soviet-
Nazi pact and the partition of Poland, the NKVD undertook wholesale
arrests in the newly occupied areas. The victims ran into the hundreds
of thousands and included whole categories of people whose "objective

characteristics" could be broadly construed as inclining them to anti-Soviet behavior. The great majority were deported to forced labor camps in the Soviet North, from which the survivors were amnestied by the terms of the Polish-Soviet pact concluded after the Nazi attack on the Soviet Union.[61] The Soviet occupation of the Baltic States in June 1940 was also followed by large-scale NKVD arrests and deportations of so-called anti-Soviet elements.[62]

After the Nazi invasion, the NKVD engaged in widespread roundups of former "repressed" people and others whose records aroused suspicion of disloyalty to the Soviet regime. The Volga-German Autonomous Republic was dissolved, and its inhabitants were dispatched to forced labor camps or exile in the far reaches of Siberia. With the turning of the tide at Stalingrad and the advance of the Soviet armies westward, the NKVD found new victims among the population of the reoccupied areas. Many were arrested on the ground of actual or alleged collaboration with the Germans, and the forced labor camps reaped a new harvest. A number of the national minorities served as a special target of NKVD retribution because of their alleged disloyalty. The Kalmyk and Chechen-Ingush Republics were dissolved. The Crimean Tatars were penalized for their "traitorous" conduct by the abolition of the Crimean Autonomous Republic. The Autonomous Republic of the Kabards and Bolkars was dismembered, leaving only the Kabardinian ASSR. Meanwhile, German war prisoners accumulated, and the NKVD took over the responsibility of running the camps in which they were confined.

After the capitulation of the Nazis, the NKVD confronted the vast new assignment of sifting the millions of Soviet citizens who found themselves in Germany and Austria at the end of the war. Most of them were war prisoners and *Ostarbeiter* who had been shipped west by the Germans as forced labor. Some, however, had retreated with the German armies in order to escape Soviet rule. Others had fought in Nazi military uniform or in separate anti-Soviet military formations such as the Vlasov Army. The latter when caught received short shrift; the great majority were executed. All of these elements on whom the NKVD could lay its hands were rounded up at assembly points and subjected to intensive interrogations by the NKVD before being shipped back to the Soviet Union. The NKVD followed a calculated policy of treating the "returners" as contaminated by their contact with the West. In order to isolate them from the Soviet populace, large numbers were dispatched to forced labor camps on suspicion of disloyalty or traitorous conduct.[63]

Much less is known about police activities inside the Soviet Union since the end of the war. Large-scale deportations have been reported from the border areas of Esthonia, Latvia, Lithuania, Karelia, and the Western Ukraine; the native population has been shifted to remote areas in Siberia and replaced by Russians, frequently war veterans, brought in from other regions.[64] From reports in the Soviet press of campaigns against collective farm abuses, of cases of venality and corruption among bureaucrats and industrial administrators, of purges of the Party apparatus and among intellectuals, it can be inferred that the secret police continues to claim its victims in widely diversified strata of Soviet society. While the available information is too sparse to justify any sweeping conclusions, there have been no indications thus far of any repetition of the mass retributions of the 1936–1938 period, except for the large-scale campaigns against so-called "untrustworthy" elements in the border regions. Elsewhere, if the testimony of escaped Soviet citizens is to be given credence, the secret police makes its presence felt by individual rather than group arrests. Its arbitrary power and pervasive organization help to sustain its reputation as the most feared weapon in the Soviet arsenal of power.

The Organization of the Terror Apparatus

Current official material concerning the organization of the police and terror apparatus of the Soviet state is virtually nonexistent. The traditional policy of the Soviet regime has been to impose a blanket of secrecy on this phase of its operations. This blanket has been substantially lifted in recent years by the revelations of Soviet escapees who have served in the secret police or whose work brought them into intimate contact with it. Much of the detailed information which has been made available in this fashion dates back to 1941 or even earlier. While some of it has undoubtedly been outdated by subsequent organizational changes, an analysis of the structure of the police apparatus as it prevailed a decade ago may well have continuing significance in indicating the range and character of police responsibilities.

In February 1941 it was announced that the NKVD would be divided into two commissariats, the NKGB or People's Commissariat of State Security and the NKVD or People's Commissariat of Internal Affairs.[65] With the outbreak of war, however, the two commissariats were reunited,[66] and the planned division did not take place until April 1943. In 1946 the commissariats were renamed ministries and became the MGB or Ministry of State Security and the MVD or Ministry of Internal Affairs.[67] The MGB inherited the secret police functions of the old NKVD; all other functions were relegated to the MVD. In 1949–50 the border guards and troops of internal security were also transferred to MGB jurisdiction.[68] After the death of Stalin in March 1953, the MGB and MVD were again reunited in a new Ministry of Internal Affairs (MVD). Beria became head of the MVD and emerged as the second ranking figure in the new constellation of leadership.

The state security apparatus of the MVD is particularly important in terms of its impact on Soviet life since its agents penetrate every crevice of the social structure. Its responsibilities include the protection of high governmental and Party officials, the enforcement of security regulations, the conduct of espionage abroad, the organization of counterintelligence activity in the Soviet Union and abroad, the censorship of correspondence within the Soviet Union and with foreign countries, the planting of agents in all Soviet organizations, and the supervision of a network of informers to detect disloyalty and to report on the attitude of the Soviet populace toward the regime.

While the MVD is a union-republic ministry, it is organized on a highly centralized pattern. The USSR ministry also serves as the ministry for the RSFSR. In the other union republics there are separate ministries, but the ministers are named centrally and approved *pro forma* by the republican authorities. The MVD has an extensive field organization which operates at the *krai, oblast,* city and *raion* levels. Its military formations are organized like the army in military districts and are ordinarily directly responsible to the ministry of the republic or, in the case of the RSFSR, to the central ministry.

While no authoritative current information is available on the internal structure of the security apparatus of the MVD, the organization of its predecessor agency in the NKVD in the period 1939–1941 has been extensively described in the reports of escapees. A number of accounts compiled by different informants agree in identifying the same basic subdivisions, usually described in Soviet terminology as Chief Administrations. The First Administration was concerned with the security of high Party and governmental leaders. The Economic Administration (EKU) was responsible for coping with wrecking, sabotage, production failures, and other "counterrevolutionary" activity in Soviet industry and agriculture. All personnel occupying responsible positions in Soviet economic life had to be investigated and cleared by EKU, which operated through special sections located in all industrial enterprises of any importance. EKU was also responsible for the collection of economic information from foreign countries. The Secret Political Administration concentrated its fire against members of the Trotsky-Zinoviev and Right oppositions, former Mensheviks, SR's, and members of other anti-Bolshevik parties, leaders of the church and religious sects, nationality deviationists, and members of the intelligentsia whose devotion to the Soviet regime was in question. The Special Section was concerned with the loyalty of the armed forces. Its representatives were assigned to all military and naval formations and constituted an elaborate special hierarchy with its own independent channel of command responsible directly to the NKVD. The Counterintelligence Administration directed its efforts toward combating foreign intelligence agents operating within the USSR. Its responsibilities included surveillance of foreign visitors and foreign embassies and consulates on Soviet soil. The Transport Administration focused its activities on the protection of goods in transit, the fulfillment of state plans for freight movements, and protection against sabotage or other damage to the transportation network. The Foreign Administration devoted its primary efforts to espionage activity outside the Soviet Union. Its responsibilities included the control of Soviet personnel stationed abroad, the penetration of Russian anti-Soviet *émigré* organizations, the collection of intelligence of value to the Soviet leadership, and the recruitment of foreign Communists, sympathizers, and others as agents in the Soviet spy network.[69]

The central administrations of the state security organization had their counterparts in the union republics, the *krais*, *oblasts*, and larger urban centers. The lowest links in the system were the *raion* or district organizations where the nature of operations was governed largely by the character of the *raion*. In the rural *raions*, the state security representatives operated through circles of informers who penetrated the collective and state farms, the machine-tractor stations, and the villages of the area. In the urban *raions*, which correspond to large wards in American cities, the headquarters staff directed a network of agents strategically placed to cover the apartment houses, factories, offices, and other communal enterprises of the district. The majority of the informers utilized by the professional staff of the security service were unpaid. They usually consisted of zealous members of the Party and Komsomol organizations, compromised individuals on whom the NKVD had a special hold, and others who were intimidated into serving the secret police because they feared unpleasant consequences if they failed to coöperate.

The meager information which is available on the recruitment and training of professional security personnel is derived largely from reports of former members of the Soviet secret police who left the service approximately a decade ago. Before the Great Purge, the higher circles of the NKVD organization were still dominated by Old Chekists who had won their spurs during the Civil War period and who had supported Stalin in his struggle with the Right and Left oppositions during the twenties. New officials of the NKVD were recruited almost exclusively from trusted Party members who were assigned to NKVD work by the cadres sections of the secretariat of the Party Central Committee and lower Party organs. The purge of Yagoda and his entourage was also accompanied by the elimination of many Old Chekists from responsible positions. Rapid promotions from the ranks became the order of the day. At the same time, the NKVD was compelled to resort to widespread mass recruiting of new personnel in order to cope with the burdens of the Yezhovshchina. Again, the selection and assignment process was handled through Party channels. Under orders transmitted through the Central Committee secretariat, quotas were imposed on local Party and Komsomol organizations, and Party members and even Komsomols who were deemed trustworthy were transferred to NKVD work. The purge of Yezhov and his followers created another personnel crisis for the NKVD. Again, upward mobility was rapid, and the vacancies were filled by the designation of Party personnel for NKVD assignments. Under Beria, more emphasis was placed on professional qualifications in recruiting NKVD personnel. The new employees were used to control sectors of Soviet life with which they were familiar. Particularly noteworthy was the use of engineers for work in the special sections of industrial enterprises.

During the Great Purge, the training of professional NKVD personnel had to give way to the urgencies of speeding new recruits into operative work. Even in this period, a network of special schools was maintained to instruct those who had been selected for NKVD duty. Courses were accelerated, and the training of lower-ranking personnel was concentrated in so-called "inter-*krai*" schools located in Moscow, Leningrad, Kharkov, Kiev, Odessa, Baku, Tiflis, and other large centers. At these schools students were exposed to a combination of political indoctrination, military training, and instruction in criminal law and procedure, investigation, intelligence and counterintelligence. NKVD officials who were slated for promotion to responsible positions in the apparatus were dispatched to the central NKVD school in Moscow where more intensive training was given in specialized aspects of NKVD work.

The NKVD encountered no difficulty in attracting recruits. The privileges which it commanded marked it out as an elite service. A major in the state security organization had the rank and perquisites of a commander of an army brigade; a colonel of state security was on the same level as the commander of an army division. In a scarcity economy, the NKVD officialdom inhabited an island of plenty. The advantages of affiliation were not lost either on the cynical careerists or the fanatics among Soviet youth. The Party leadership depended on the NKVD as one of its primary pillars of support. The rewards which were held out were designed to bulwark the edifice of NKVD loyalties.

The Methods of the Secret Police

An analysis of the methods of the Soviet secret police involves an examination of the various stages at which it operates: (1) surveillance and investigation, (2) arrest and examination, (3) sentence and imprisonment.

The apparatus of the secret police reaches directly into every organized formation in Soviet society. The head of the special section in the factory, the plenipotentiary of the secret police in the regiment, the head of the *raion* MVD office in rural areas all operate under the same mandate to keep the Soviet populace under careful supervision to ensure loyalty to the regime. This does not mean, however, that every Soviet citizen is equally exposed to police observation. Certain categories are singled out for special attention. Among them are one-time members of hostile social classes or political parties, former oppositionists, "repressed people" and others whose sentiments are regarded as particularly dubious. Certain areas of Soviet life are watched far more carefully and intensively than others. The armed forces, military plants, industries of strategic military significance, transport, the institutes and universities, and the intelligentsia generally are subjected to particularly close scrutiny.

In carrying on its surveillance, the secret police relies on a variety of techniques. A dossier is maintained on every subject in whom the secret police has an interest. In plants of strategic military importance, for example, responsible workers cannot be employed or promoted without clearance with the MVD. All such employees are required to fill out questionnaires and list detailed biographical information with the MVD for inspection and control. If checks of these documents raise any doubts on the score of political trustworthiness, the recommendations of the MVD will be decisive. In addition, the head of the special section in the plant or his analogue elsewhere will utilize a network of informers to gather compromising material concerning persons with whom they have contact. Denunciations will be encouraged, sometimes to be checked and sometimes merely to be filed in the appropriate dossier. Accidents and production failures will be investigated with a view to discovering the existence of wrecking or sabotage. If the offense is a mild one, the culprit may simply be called in by the head of the special section and dismissed with a warning; in more serious cases, arrest and imprisonment are quick to follow. On occasion, interrogation will itself be employed as a form of surveillance and intimidation. Individuals in whom the secret police are interested will be summoned for questioning. Reasons will not be disclosed. Those who have been through this experience testify that it can be thoroughly shattering and that it leaves its victims with the conviction that the shadow of imminent arrest hovers over them.

The procedure in connection with arrest is also designed to strike terror into the hearts of the accused. Theoretically, no arrest can take place without the prior approval of the Procurator; in practice, this requirement is largely a paper formality. During the Great Purge almost all arrests were made at night. Agents presented themselves at the home of the victim with an order authorizing them to make the arrest and search the premises. The search was made in the presence of a witness.

All material regarded as compromising was confiscated; at the same time, a list was made of the articles appropriated and a receipt given for their detention. Once the search was finished, the agents escorted the accused to the place of detention, where his money and any articles on his person which he could use to harm himself were expropriated. Again, receipts were punctiliously given for the money and goods expropriated. The accused was then put in a cell to await the pleasure of the examiner assigned to his case. During the Great Purge, this waiting interval sometimes stretched out to several weeks or even several months.

When the prisoner was finally called out for interrogation, usually at night, the examiner ordinarily began by trying to persuade the prisoner to make a voluntary admission of guilt. The examination was almost invariably based on the assumption of the guilt of the accused; the primary task of the examiner was therefore to extract a confession from the prisoner and to compel him to disclose the names of all accomplices with whom he was involved. If the accused proved unamenable to persuasion, the examiner resorted to intimidation, threats, or physical violence. The prisoner might be warned that failure to confess would lead to retaliation against his family; the longer the accused held out, the more severe would be the penalty. If the prisoner still proved recalcitrant, he would be subjected to the nerve-wracking ordeal of continuous interrogations which might stretch over a period of weeks. During this period "on the conveyor" as it was called, the accused would be deprived of sleep, interrogated constantly by a rotating team of examiners, made to stand at attention while the questioning was going on, and beaten or slapped into consciousness when he collapsed from exhaustion. All but the iron-willed succumbed to this incessant bombardment. At the end, a "confession" would be signed, and the accused would be ready for trial or sentencing.

In the case of most political prisoners during the Great Purge, the indictment was usually based on Article 58 of the Criminal Code of the RSFSR or similar provisions in the codes of other republics. The paragraphs of this article provided vague definitions of such crimes as high treason, armed revolt, espionage, sabotage, terror, counterrevolutionary agitation, and association with counterrevolutionary organizations. The task of the examiner was to extort a "confession" which could be brought within the ambit of one or more of these paragraphs. Once the confession had been obtained, the pronouncement of sentence would depend on the seriousness of the offense. In most cases, prisoners were sentenced *in absentia* by special boards attached to the NKVD, the so-called "troika" or committee of three in the provinces, or by a special council in Moscow. "When the Yezhov period was at its height," Beck and Godin report, "sentences of less than five years' forced labor were very rare. Normally they were for eight or ten years' forced labor, but sentences of twenty-five years' forced labor or imprisonment were not uncommon." [70] In some cases, perfunctory closed trials were held before the military tribunal of the Supreme Court. Although the accused was present, counsel was not provided, and no opportunity was given to call witnesses to prove innocence or guilt. The death sentences pronounced by the military tribunal claimed many victims among senior military officers, officials of the NKVD, and high Party personnel. A very few cases, usually covering less serious offenses, were referred to the ordinary regional courts for disposition.[71]

Forced Labor

The prisoners condemned to forced labor became charges of GULAG, the Main Administration of Camps. This agency, a subdivision of the MVD, administers the vast network of forced labor camps and also hires out forced labor to Soviet industrial enterprises. The great mass of the prisoners at the disposal of GULAG during the Great Purge were assigned to heavy, unskilled labor — cutting timber, building roads, mining coal, dredging for gold, and other similarly burdensome tasks. "Norms" were established for all varieties of labor; the degree of fulfillment determined the rations to which the prisoners were entitled. Those who met their norms received five hundred to six hundred grams of bread a day and a hot meal of inferior quality, enough to sustain life only at a very low level. While overfulfillment was rewarded with more normal rations, the work targets were set so high that such an accomplishment was extraordinarily difficult. Those who failed to attain the norms received a basic ration of three hundred grams of bread a day, a diet which was virtually a sentence to starvation. Intellectuals unused to hard physical labor often fell into this category. Some highly qualified specialists among them were given an opportunity by GULAG to work at their specialties; the great majority were utilized as unskilled laborers.

The position of the political prisoners was made even more difficult because of the persecutions to which they were subjected by the ordinary criminals. As "enemies of the people," the "politicals" represented the lowest stratum of prison society. In the organization of prison labor, foremen and overseers tended to be drawn from the ranks of the criminals. Camp authorities looked on with benevolent neutrality as the criminals stripped the "politicals" of their food and their possessions. The long arm of the secret police followed the prisoners into the prison barracks themselves. Attached to each camp was a state security section which operated an informers' network both among the prisoners and the free personnel who formed part of the camp administration. Prisoners who spoke their minds too freely ran the risk of denunciation, reduction of rations, confinement in *isolators*, or even an extension of their terms of confinement.

Estimates of the number of people confined in forced labor camps in the Soviet Union run a wide gamut, even within the same period. The Soviet government has not seen fit to release any official statistics. Most estimates represent the guesses of former prisoners who escaped from the Soviet Union and whose personal experience was ordinarily confined to one or a few camps or even sections of camps. Beck and Godin, in an account of the Great Purge which is distinguished by its sobriety and restraint, estimated the total number of prisoners "living in detention under the NKVD" during the Yezhovshchina as between seven and fourteen million.[72] Alexander Weissberg, a distinguished scientist who was imprisoned in Kharkov during the Yezhovshchina, hazarded the guess that between 5 and 6 per cent of the local population was arrested in the 1937–1939 period. By projecting this percentage to the country at large, Weissberg arrived at a total of nine million arrests, of which two million represented criminal charges and seven million were attributable to the purge.[73] After reviewing a wide variety of estimates by former inmates of forced labor camps, Dallin and Nicolaevsky, in a work devoted exclusively to forced labor, concluded that the totals ranged in different periods from seven to twelve million.[74] In the nature of things, these estimates are not susceptible to precise corroboration.

Perhaps the most revealing collection of unquestionably authentic data on the role of forced labor in the Soviet economy is contained in an official Soviet document entitled "State Plan of Development of the National Economy of the USSR for 1941." [75] This classified Soviet document, which was captured by the Nazis in the rapid advance of the first months of the war, contains a detailed statement of economic targets for 1941; it also includes a rich assortment of material on the economic activities of the NKVD. The 1941 plan lists a projected capital investment of 37,650,000,000 rubles, exclusive of capital investments of the Commissariats for Transportation, Defense, and Navy. Out of this sum, the NKVD accounted for 6,810,000,000 rubles, or about 18 per cent. In presenting the 1941 economic plan, Voznesensky, the chairman of Gosplan, reported the total capital investment planned for 1941 as 57,000,000,-000 rubles.[76] The NKVD share of this total was approximately 12 per cent. On the basis of the 1941 capital investment data, Naum Jasny reached the conclusion that the NKVD was expected to account for 17 per cent of the total 1941 construction and that the number of concentration camp inmates engaged in NKVD construction projects alone would approximate 1,172,000. The 1941 plan indicated that lumbering was the second most important industrial activity of the NKVD. The total share of the NKVD in this industry was about 12 per cent, but this percentage was substantially exceeded in the northern areas of the USSR. In Arch-angelsk *oblast*, it was 26 per cent; in the Khabarovsk *krai* and the Karelo-Finnish Republic, more than 33 per cent; in Murmansk *oblast*, more than 40 per cent; and in the Komi Autonomous Republic, more than 50 per cent.[77] Other NKVD industrial targets mentioned in the plan included 5,300,000 tons of coal out of a total 191,000,000 tons; 250,000 tons of oil out of a total 35,000,000 tons; 150,000 tons of chrome ore out of a total of 370,000; and 82,000,000 bricks to be produced in the Khabarovsk and Maritime *krais*.[78]

It should be noted that the captured version of the 1941 plan is in-complete. Data on gold production and armaments were not included and were apparently reserved for separate supplements which circulated among a very restricted group. Information from other sources indicates that gold mining was virtually an NKVD monopoly; the vast develop-ment in the Kolyma region was administered by the NKVD through its subsidiary *Dalstroi* and was largely manned by forced labor. On the basis of sober reading of the reports of former inmates of the concentration camps in the Kolyma area, it would appear that Dalstroi utilized from two hundred thousand to four hundred thousand forced laborers in the 1941 period.[79] This, it should be stressed, is a conservative figure. The estimate of Dallin and Nicolaevsky runs from one and a half to two million prisoners.[80]

The 1941 plan does not list the number of camp inmates. The data on the economic activities of the NKVD, however, make it possible to arrive at a fairly reliable estimate of approximately three and a half million.[81] This total applies only to forced labor confined in prison camps under direct NKVD jurisdiction. It does not include persons hired out to other enterprises. It does not include persons sentenced to exile in remote areas who remained under NKVD supervision even though they lived and worked under the same conditions as the rest of the population. Nor does it include the arrested who were being held for investigation and sentence in remand prisons or those serving terms of confinement in ordinary prisons. It does not include workers penalized for tardiness or absenteeism by being compelled to work at their jobs at substantially reduced pay. And it takes no account of the degree of compulsion which is ordinarily attached to job assignments and transfers of so-called "free" labor in the Soviet system. It is obvious that estimates of "forced labor" will vary widely, depending on the categories which are included.

Since 1941, no authoritative internal source comparable to the State Plan has become available. The accounts of released prisoners for sub-sequent years indicate that large contingents of new forced laborers have been steadily flowing into the camps, but estimates must be speculative to a high degree, and no attempt will be made here to undertake even a crude estimate of the present population of the forced labor camps. Reports that the MVD has been charged with the sole responsibility for the building and operation of all atomic developments and the large-scale construction projects launched under the postwar Five Year Plans point toward a continuing reliance on forced labor as an essential aspect of the Soviet system.

The role of forced labor in the Soviet economy has given rise to sharp controversy. Those who view the concentration camps as an asset to the Soviet economy argue that the MVD derives a substantial profit from the exploitation of slave labor, that the productivity of the concentration camp inmates is considerably in excess of the cost of their upkeep, and that the profits realized from the use of slave labor are "an important element of the government's industrialization fund." [82] The accelerated development of the Soviet North and other remote areas, it is contended, would have been impossible had the government been forced to rely on free labor.

Those who regard the concentration camps as a liability to the Soviet economy are usually ready to concede that the existence of large pools of forced labor has facilitated the exploitation of resources in regions where primitive conditions and hardships are barriers to the recruitment of free labor. But they also point out that the productivity of slave labor is considerably less than that of free workers and that the alleged profits involved disappear when full account is taken of the expense of maintaining the MVD apparatus, both outside and inside the camps. They also stress the high mortality rates in the camps and the great losses involved for the Soviet economy when scarce skilled workers, highly qualified engineers and other professionally trained experts, whose education has involved high costs for the state, are utilized as unskilled laborers.

The initial impetus for the establishment of concentration camps was provided by political rather than economic considerations. The arrests of hundreds of thousands or millions of Soviet citizens were not originally planned as a method of obtaining slave labor power. The large-scale economic enterprises of the NKVD-MVD were developed in order to exploit the prisoners whom the secret police had accumulated. As these enterprises were established, they acquired a momentum of their own. The manpower that they consumed had to be replaced by new contingents, and the NKVD-MVD encountered no great difficulty in finding pretexts for replenishments. A system of power in which the security of the leadership is founded on the insecurity of its subjects demands a continuous crop of fresh victims. The regime of forced labor serves to ensure that the leadership will at least derive some advantage from this process.

The Hazards of Terror

The reliance on terror as an instrument of dominion has its elements of danger. It is not easy to control. A secret police develops its own laws of growth. The more discord it discovers or develops, the more indispensable it becomes. Its tendency is always to extend its own sovereignty, to seek to emancipate itself from all external controls, to become a state within a state, and to preserve the conditions of emergency and siege on which an expansion of its own power depends. Once terror becomes an end in itself, there is no easy and natural stopping place. From the viewpoint of the leadership, there is an even greater worry, the fear that as the secret police apparatus emancipates itself from external controls, it becomes a menace to the security of the highest Party leaders themselves. It is a risk of which the Party leadership has been aware and against which it has taken precautions. Every effort is apparently made to ensure the subordination of the MVD to the central Party organization. Employees are required to be Party members. The secretaries of the Party organizations in the MVD are used as the eyes and ears of the Party Central Committee to ensure loyalty to the Party. The Special Section in the secretariat of the Central Committee is presumed to have a particularly close supervisory relationship to the secret police. Special groups of the Party Control Committee are assigned to watch over the MVD. In these and perhaps other ways, the Party leadership seeks to safeguard itself against the possibility that "the avenging sword of the Revolution" may turn against the revolutionary leadership itself.

Thus far, no head of the Soviet secret police has succeeded in using his position as a platform from which to strike out for supreme power. The first director of the Cheka and OGPU was Felix Dzerzhinsky, an Old Bolshevik of unimpeachable idealism whose whole career documented the proposition that there is no fanaticism so terrible as that of the pure idealist. Dzerzhinsky gave no evidence of Napoleonic ambitions and died in 1926 without attaining Politburo status. His successor, Menzhinsky, was a much lesser figure, and though he continued as head of the OGPU until 1934, he never moved beyond the second rank of Party leaders. Yagoda, who came next, was removed from office in 1936 and executed in 1938. His successor, Yezhov, was relieved of his duties in 1938 and disappeared in 1939, presumably a scapegoat for the excesses of the Great Purge. Neither Yagoda nor Yezhov could be counted in the front ranks of Party leaders. Beria, who succeeded Yezhov, was the first head of the NKVD to enter the Politburo, where he became an outstanding figure. His rise to power, however, gave every evidence of reflecting Stalin's tutelage rather than any independent leverage which his position as head of the NKVD afforded. Thus far, the vigilance of the ruling group has been proof against all dreams of utilizing the terror apparatus as the road to supremacy. The proposition that Beria may carve a new path has still to be tested.

Even if the Party leadership is successful in imposing its mastery on the secret police, there are other disadvantages in a regime of terror which are not so amenable to skillful manipulation. A system which relies on a large secret police as a basic core of its power is highly wasteful of manpower. The main occupation of the secret police is that of spying, investigating, examining, guarding, and controlling others. Large numbers of talented people are removed from productive work. There is always the hazard that the secret police will run amok and do serious and perhaps unintended harm to the productive and administrative machinery of the state. The atmosphere of universal suspicion which terror breeds is not ordinarily conducive to creative thinking and displays of individual initiative. If the weight of terror becomes too great and the penalty of any administrative failure or mistake is MVD detention, it becomes difficult to persuade people to take responsibility. Even those driven by fear of the secret police to work as they have never worked before begin to crack under the strain. It is no easy task to apply terror and at the same time to hold it in leash.

Perhaps the most subtle danger in a police regime of the Soviet type is its impact on the quality of political decisions at the very highest level. The MVD is one of the main pillars that sustains the regime. It is also a primary source of intelligence regarding both domestic and international developments. Since the MVD apparatus lives and grows on emergency and danger, its justification hinges upon the maintenance of a state of siege. Consequently, the intelligence that filters through the MVD to the top political leadership is apt almost unconsciously to emphasize the storms that are brewing, the plots against the regime, and sinister threats at home and abroad. The risk which the Party leadership faces is that it too will become the unconscious victim of the Frankenstein's monster which it has created. The ultimate hazard of terror as a system of power is that it ends by terrorizing the master as well as the slave.

Chapter 14

The Party and the Armed Forces

Every revolutionary movement which comes to power faces the task of building a loyal and efficient military establishment to consolidate its conquests. In order to ensure loyalty, the leaders of the revolution fill the army with their supporters. In order to secure efficiency, they find themselves compelled to professionalize their fighting force. In the aftermath of profound social upheaval, these two objectives are not easily fused. Revolutionary armies do not automatically inherit the technical military skills and professional leadership of the armies which they displace. The destruction of the old army involves the dispersal of its officer cadres. The sympathies of the officer corps are seldom enrolled on the side of the revolution. When loyalty is in question, technical qualifications are a dubious asset. Revolutionary armies thrive on the devotion which they elicit and the new talent which they bring to the fore. But they cannot dispense with discipline and professional direction.

The Creation of the Red Army

After the seizure of power in November 1917, the Bolsheviks inherited an army in process of dissolution. Its disintegration had been speeded by Bolshevik propaganda which played on the war-weariness and land-hunger of the peasant rank-and-file. With the old army scattered to the four winds, the Bolsheviks confronted the problem of creating a new army on which they could build their power. The military formations on which they could rely were a motley lot. They consisted of armed workmen recruited in the Petrograd and Moscow factories and organized into so-called Red Guards, sailors from the Baltic Fleet, and a few army units of the Petrograd garrison. With these elements at their immediate disposal, the Bolsheviks faced the task of staving off a rapid German advance and coping with the forces of counterrevolution.

The first decision of the Bolsheviks was to make peace with the Germans. This meant making peace on German terms. The terms were harsh, and many of the Bolshevik leaders were not prepared to accept them. After prolonged debate, Lenin prevailed with the argument that there was no alternative. On March 3, 1918, the Bolsheviks signed the Treaty of Brest-Litovsk by which they gave up 34 per cent of Russia's population, 32 per cent of her agricultural land, 54 per cent of her industry, and 89 per cent of her coal mines. Colossal as these losses were, they left the Bolsheviks free to concentrate their energies on the armed struggle against the Whites and the Allied Intervention. This was the school in which the Red Army was forged.

The first steps in the construction of the new army represented a curious mélange of visionary utopianism and gradually sharpening realism. The dream of an egalitarian people's army, derived from the Paris Commune, possessed the minds of the Bolshevik leadership and guided the early army decrees. The order of December 29, 1917,[1] abolishing military ranks and titles was followed by another decree of the Council of People's Commissars on January 12, 1918, proclaiming the formation of a socialist army which was to be "built up from below on the principles of election of officers and mutual comradely discipline and respect." [2]

The army was recruited on a voluntary basis. According to the decree of January 28, 1918, the new "Worker-Peasant Red Army" was to be composed "of the more class-conscious and organized elements of the toiling masses." Their loyalty to the regime was to be vouched for by the Party, trade unions, army committees, "or democratic organizations, standing on the platform of the Soviet Government." [3] Volunteers were required to enlist for a period of three months' service; they received a salary of fifty rubles a month plus keep and provision for their dependents. In the next few months, only 106,000 men joined the Red Army. The recruitment drive was a failure.

The early Red Army was a sorry organization from a professional point of view. Discipline was virtually nonexistent. Soldiers spent most of their time holding meetings, debating orders, and shaping up bargaining demands. The speech made by a soldier delegate to a conference of Red Army men in Petrograd in late March 1918 suggests the temper of the rank-and-file. "Either give us 300 rubles a month with food, clothing and lodging," he shouted, "or we will show the Council of People's Commissars that we are able to defend our interests." [4] The men attracted to the Red Army were not always drawn by idealistic motives. Trotsky put it bluntly when he reported, "Although we got a number of self-sacrificing young workmen, the majority of those who enlisted were vagabonds of the worst kind." [5]

The units of the Red Army functioned as quasi-autonomous principal-ities which were held together by common interest rather than command. Officers were ordinarily elected from the ranks. A typical letter reported, "A private . . . was elected commander of our brigade . . . The brigade is run by a committee . . . in which there is not a single officer. Things are in great confusion and every battery lives as it pleases." [6] It was this disorder which led Trotsky to conclude, "A real army cannot be run by elected committees and elected officers who may be dismissed at any moment by their subordinates." [7] The survival of the Bolshevik regime in the early months of 1918 was less a tribute to its military prowess than it was a by-product of the weaknesses and disunity of its antagonists.

The Trotsky Reforms

In March 1918 Leon Trotsky was designated People's Commissar for War and entrusted with the responsibility of reorganizing the military establishment. The series of reforms that he inaugurated laid the foundation for the professionalization of the Red Army and its transformation into an effective and loyal fighting force.

The first of Trotsky's major achievements was the creation of a central military authority. In early 1918 the control of military operations was dispersed and disintegrated. The organization of units of the Red Army was the responsibility of military departments of the local soviets. The local soviets did not limit themselves to recruitment; they assumed full control of the forces they had mobilized. "Local patriotism" took on virulent forms. "Every county," Trotsky complained, "almost every township, believes that the Soviet power can be best defended by concentrating on the territory of the given township as much as possible of aviation, matériel, radio equipment, rifles, armored cars. All try to conceal this matériel — not only in the provinces, but even in the centers, nay, even in the regional organizations of Petrograd." [8] Local army commanders insisted on retention of their own freedom of action and resented and defied the dictates of Moscow.

Trotsky addressed himself to the task of overcoming these centrifugal tendencies in the interest of coördinated operations and unified strategy. The Supreme Military Council, which was established on March 1, 1918, limited its activity to the German front. In May 1918 an Operations Department was created to direct Red Army strategy on the various Civil War fronts, but it continued to meet strong local resistance. In July the command of all the armed forces in the field was entrusted to I. I. Vatsetis, an ex-Tsarist colonel of the general staff. On September 2 a Revolutionary War Council under the chairmanship of Trotsky was set up to coördinate all operational, administrative, and supply activities relating to the Red Army. A member of the council had to countersign orders of the commander in chief; his freedom of action, however, was to be safeguarded "in all questions of a strategic-operative character." [9] On November 30, 1918, the structure of central authority was completed with the establishment of the Council of Defense. Its functions embraced "the mobilization of the forces and resources of the country in the interests of defense." [10] The strengthening of the organs of central control was an important factor in molding the Red Army into a homogeneous fighting unit.

In order to guarantee a supply of trained manpower for the army, Trotsky strongly supported the introduction of compulsory military training and conscription. By the spring of 1918 voluntary recruitment had demonstrated its complete ineffectiveness. The total size of the Red Volunteer Army on May 10 was only 306,000 men. The great majority had enlisted for short-term service, and replacements were difficult to obtain on a volunteer basis.[11] On April 22 the Soviet government instituted compulsory military training. Peasants who did not employ hired labor and all workers in the age group of eighteen to forty were required to undergo twelve hours of military training per week for a period of eight weeks. Soon afterwards, members of the bourgeoisie, who were excluded from the new army, were mobilized for hard noncombatant labor in rear areas. Trotsky told them, "Our grandfathers and fathers served your grandfathers and fathers, cleaned up dirt and filth, and we will compel you to clean up dirt." [12]

On June 12, 1918, conscription began with the mobilization of five age groups (twenty-one to twenty-five) in fifty-one counties in the Volga, Ural, and Western Siberia areas which were threatened by White invasion. This action was followed by partial mobilizations in the Moscow and Petrograd areas. The decree of June 29 made all males between the ages of eighteen and forty liable to military service. By the end of the year the size of the Red Army had increased to eight hundred thousand. By January 1, 1920, it reached a total of three million, and during 1920 it mounted to a peak of five and a half million. This impressive reservoir of manpower was one of the decisive elements in determining the outcome of the Civil War.

Trotsky also seized the initiative in pressing for the restoration of discipline in the army. In the summer of 1918 the election of officers was abolished and the authority of appointed commanders reinforced. Stern punishment was meted out to deserters, mutineers, and cowards. "At all costs, and at any price," insisted Trotsky, "it is necessary to implant discipline in the Red Army." [13] When doctrinaire word-spinners among the Bolshevik military workers began to busy themselves with elaborating new military theory to guide the operations of the Red Army, Trotsky provided an earthy reminder:

We must now devote our whole attention to improving our material and making it more efficient rather than to fantastic schemes of reorganization. Every army unit must receive its rations regularly, foodstuffs must not be allowed to rot, and meals must be cooked properly. We must teach our soldiers personal cleanliness and see that they exterminate vermin. They must learn their drill properly and perform it in the open air as much as possible. They must be taught to make their political speeches short and sensible, to clean their rifles and grease their boots. They must learn to shoot, and must help their officers to ensure strict observance of the regulations for keeping in touch with other units in the field, reconnaissance work, reports and sentry duty . . . they must learn to wind their puttees properly so as to prevent sores on their legs, and once again they must learn to grease their boots. That is our programme for next year in general and next spring in particular, and if anyone wants to take advantage of any solemn occasion to describe this practical programme as "military doctrine," he's welcome to do so.[14]

This classic deflation of the amateur Party strategists was designed to bring home the basic importance of training and discipline, virtues which too many of the Red Army warriors were ready to discard as outworn relics of the bourgeois past. The martinet qualities of Trotsky left an indelible impress on the Red Army; without his attention to the practical details of army organization — of transport, supply, training, and discipline — the Red Army might have degenerated into a loose confederation of guerrilla bands.

Perhaps the most important of Trotsky's reforms was his insistence on the necessity of building the Red Army around a corps of trained military commanders. The material out of which such a corps could be constructed consisted of the remnants of the Tsarist cadre officers who remained in Bolshevik territory, the former noncommissioned officers of the old army, professional revolutionaries and leaders of the Red Guard who had displayed an aptitude for military affairs, and outstanding Red Army men who could be quickly trained for command responsibilities. The glaring deficiency of the Red Army was the absence of trained personnel to fill the higher command and staff posts. For Trotsky, the moral was clear. The Red Army had to enlist the knowledge of the old officers and utilize them until the Red Army produced its own trusted cadres.

The decision to employ the Tsarist officers met sharp opposition within the Party on practical as well as doctrinal grounds. The critics argued that the old officer corps was hostile to the Soviet regime, could not be trusted to discharge command responsibilities, and would betray the Soviet cause at the first opportunity. Trotsky replied:

There is danger in everything. We must have teachers who know something about the science of war. We talk to these generals with complete frankness. We tell them: "There is a new master in the land — the working class. He needs instructors to teach the toilers . . . how to fight the bourgeoisie." . . . If these generals serve us honestly we shall give them our full support. . . . If they attempt . . . counterrevolution, we shall find a way to deal with them.[15]

Backed by Lenin and despite unremitting grumbling in the ranks of the Party, Trotsky proceeded to carry out the decision to employ former Tsarist officers. From June 1918 to August 1920 more than forty-eight thousand were either drafted or volunteered for service in the Red Army.[16] The list included S. Kamenev, a former Tsarist colonel of the general staff who became Commander in Chief of the Red Army in June 1919, Colonel Boris Shaposhnikov, who later became a Marshal of the Red Army and Chief of Staff, A. A. Svechin, a former major general of the imperial general staff who headed the Red Army Supreme Staff and later occupied the chair of military history at the Soviet War College, and a group of young officers including Tukhachevsky, Uborevich, Primakov, Kork, and Putna, all of whom rose rapidly to high Soviet commands in the Civil War period and held leading posts in the Red Army until they were liquidated in the Great Purge of 1937.

"A small group of officers . . . ," Trotsky reported, "have caught the spirit of the Revolution and the new age . . . They are doing everything they can to increase the military power of the Soviet Republic. They should be respected and supported." [17] But not all of the officers proved useful. Trotsky described many of them as "time-servers, men without initiative, without principles, and without even enough energy to join the Whites." [18] Stalin complained to Lenin: "The 'staff' workers know only how to 'draw schemes' and propose plans . . . they are absolutely indifferent to operational activities . . . in general, they feel themselves to be strangers, guests." [19] Trotsky frankly admitted that "many of them betrayed us and went over to the enemy." [20] Yet he continued to insist that the old officers were indispensable. "To refuse the service of military specialists because individual officers play the traitor is about as reasonable," he argued, "as to drive out all the railway engineers . . . because there are a few saboteurs among them." [21]

Stern measures were taken to ensure the "loyalty" of the old army officers who were inducted into Red Army service. A system of hostages was instituted. If officers betrayed the Red Army, Trotsky warned that their families would suffer the consequences. His notorious order of September 30, 1918, called for the immediate arrest of "the families of . . . deserters and traitors." "Let them know," Trotsky declared, "that they are at the same time betraying members of their own families: fathers, mothers, sisters, brothers, wives, and children." [22]

The installation of a system of political commissars was also designed as a safeguard against treason and sabotage. The commissar functioned as the direct representative of the Soviet regime in the army. His primary duty, as outlined in Trotsky's decree of April 6, 1918, was "to prevent army institutions from becoming nests of conspiracy or employing weapons against workmen and peasants." [23] Commissars were instructed to direct Party work in the army, to carry on political propaganda among the raw peasant and worker recruits, and to control the activity of the commanding personnel. Orders and reports were to be signed jointly by commander and commissar. Authority to issue military, operative decisions was to rest with the commanding personnel. The responsibility of the commissar in countersigning such orders was limited to a certification that the order was not dictated by counterrevolutionary considerations. Where commissars could not approve orders, they were to report their opinions to higher authorities. "A Commissar," said the decree, "may prevent the execution of a military order only when he has justifiable grounds for belief that it is inspired by counter-revolutionary motives." [24]

The juxtaposition of imperial army officer and Communist commissar was fraught with conflict, since it was impossible to draw a precise line between their powers. Mutual suspicion poisoned the relationship and made friction inevitable. Trotsky made a determined effort to drive his two horses in tandem. "A commissar who fails to prevent the desertion of a commanding officer," he warned, "will have to answer for his negligence with his own life." [25] At the same time, commissars were directed "not . . . to give orders, but to watch," to avoid quarrels and to "behave respectfully to military experts who fulfill their duties conscientiously." [26] Such instructions were easier to deliver than to translate into practice. As the commissars acquired military competence and experience, the scope of their control inevitably widened. The majority of the officers of the old army were regarded as potentially disloyal, to be used because of their professional training but to be discarded as soon as the Red Army had trained its own proletarian replacements. Many of the Tsarist officers were destined to become expendables as a new generation of Red Commanders rose from the ranks.

The new corps of commanders for the Red Army also drew heavily on the noncommissioned officers of the old army. On August 13, 1918, Trotsky pronounced: "Non-commissioned officers! . . . The Soviet government calls you to the *posts of commanding officers* . . . You are the children of the toiling people; the worker-peasant army is *your* army . . . Every non-commissioned officer serving in the Red Army . . . is hereby raised to the status of squad commander. The Soviet government gives you the opportunity . . . to rise to the very height of military art." [27] Between June 12, 1918, and August 15, 1920, the Red Army received 214,717 former Tsarist noncommissioned officers, as well as 26,766 lower medical and veterinary personnel.[28] Their number included at least three future Marshals of the Red Army, Voroshilov, Budënny, and Blücher.

Trotsky also established a number of short-term command courses to which workers who had served in the Red Guard and others who had demonstrated leadership ability in the ranks were dispatched for rapid conversion into Red Commanders. During the Civil War years, nearly forty thousand cadets were graduated from these courses.[29] Trotsky frankly admitted that the courses were "quite inadequate." "But," he continued, "considering the fact that many in the army did not even know how to handle a rifle, these four-month short-course men [stood out and] were made . . . officers." [30] The percentage of Communists among the graduates of the command courses was high. In 1918, they composed 70 per cent of the graduates; in 1919, 54 per cent; in 1920, 62 per cent; and in 1921, 65 per cent.[31] The zeal and devotion of the cadets helped to make up for their lack of military knowledge. "Everywhere," reported the Director of Soviet Military Education, "praise was given to the revolutionary firmness and self-sacrifice of the young *kraskomy* [abbreviation for Red Commander]." [32]

Trotsky relied heavily on the Party to infuse spirit and resolution into the Red Army. From a third to a half of the total Communist Party membership was sent into the Red Army during the Civil War period. According to the Soviet military historian F. Nikonov, the combat efficiency of units of the Red Army was measured in terms of the percentage of Communists in the ranks. Units with less than 4 to 5 per cent of Communists were regarded as poor; units with 6 to 8 per cent were average; and those with 12 to 15 per cent were treated as shock troops.[33] Trotsky claimed:

The conduct of Communists in the Red Army has a decisive significance for the morale and the military capability of units. It is necessary, therefore, to distribute Communists in an organized way, to guide them attentively and to keep careful check of their work . . .

. . . It is necessary that in each platoon, section and squad there should be a Communist, even if a young one — but devoted to the cause. He should observe the morale of the nearest fellow-fighters, explain to them the problems and the aims of the war, and, in case he is himself perplexed, approach the commissar of his unit or some other responsible political worker for elucidation. Without such internal, unofficial, personal, day-by-day and hour-by-hour agitation . . . under all conditions of the combat situation, the official agitation through articles and speeches will not give the required results.[34]

As the Civil War entered its later phases, an elaborate Party organization was built up within the army. Party cells and collectives were established in all military units. The Party cells functioned under the supervision of the political commissars, who were now required to be Party members and who directed all propaganda and "cultural enlightenment" work in the Red Army. The commissars operated with their own independent chain of command. The All-Russian Bureau of Military Commissars, which originally coördinated their activity, was soon replaced by the Political Department of the Revolutionary War Council, which in turn was transformed in May 1919 into the Political Administration of the Red Army and placed "under the immediate guidance of the Central Committee of the Communist Party." [35]

If the Party provided the leaven without which "the army would have fallen into dust," it was the commissars who supplied the fanatical faith and enthusiasm which inspired the Party rank-and-file to take the lead on the battlefield. "In . . . our commissars, the foremost front-fighter Communists," said Trotsky, "we have obtained a new communist order of Samurai, which — without any caste privileges — knows how to die and teaches others to die for the cause of the workers' class." [36] Lenin added his tribute at the Eighth Congress of the Party on March 23, 1919, when he observed, "If this war is waged with much greater energy and with exalted gallantry, it is only because for the first time in history an army has been created which knows what it is fighting for." [37] While this panegyric hardly applied to the great mass of the peasantry who were dragooned and conscripted into Red Army service in the course of the Civil War, it was largely true of the disciplined phalanx of indoctrinated Party members who supplied the driving power and iron will which held the Red Army together and carried it to victory.

By the spring of 1921 the Bolsheviks were undisputed masters of Russia. The White armies had been defeated, and the Allied forces were in process of withdrawal. The Civil War served as a great school of military affairs for the new Soviet state. A new crop of military leaders had emerged — Trotsky, Frunze, Budënny, Voroshilov, Timoshenko, and Stalin on the Party side and Tukhachevsky, Shaposhnikov, Egorov, and numerous others among the old Tsarist officers. The experience of Civil War and Intervention left a heritage of military-mindedness and a conviction of the necessity of being constantly prepared for war. Its effect on the Communist leadership was to reinforce a feeling of isolation and encirclement, to buttress the view that the world was divided into armed camps and that the camp of socialism would always be in danger unless there was adequate military strength to sustain and defend it. Lenin declared at the Eighth Congress of Soviets in late 1920: "We must maintain our military preparedness. We cannot deem our task ended with the blow already dealt imperialism, but we must exert our strength to the utmost to preserve our Red Army in complete military preparedness and to heighten its military preparedness. This, of course, will not interfere with the freeing of a certain part of the army and its swift demobilization." [38]

The Peacetime Military Establishment

Although a substantial demobilization took place over the next few years, the transition from war to peace was accompanied by a sharp division of opinion over the character of Soviet military policy and the nature of its future military establishment. The professional officers of the old imperial army who had risen to high positions in the Red Army were almost unanimous in favoring a large regular army. Such an army, they believed, would not only be far more efficient than a citizen army of militia; it would also provide a far more hospitable environment for the utilization of their talents. A few of them, like Tukhachevsky, who had become imbued with revolutionary zeal, supported the concept of a large regular army on other grounds. Tukhachevsky visualized a professional army composed of ardent, dedicated sons of the proletariat. Such an army, he believed, would be ideally suited to carry the revolutionary offensive to other lands. It would enlist "reinforcements . . . from the workers inhabiting the territory occupied by the Red Army." "This accession of a stream of international fighting forces," he declared, "is a characteristic feature of the Red Army methods of warfare." [39]

The Party leadership was inclined to favor a citizen army of territorial militia. In the context of the NEP "breathing spell," Tukhachevsky's militant internationalism seemed out of place. A professional army, moreover raised the specter of Bonapartism; the Party was concerned to construct an army which it could control. At the Ninth Party Congress, in April 1920, Trotsky advanced an ingenious scheme for organizing a militia system around the production process. Under his plan, militia units were to be established in all industrial centers, and commanders were to be recruited from "the best elements of the local proletariat." [40] The plan was designed to safeguard the ascendancy of the numerically weak proletariat. Its disadvantages consisted in its failure to tap the large reservoir of rural manpower and in the dubious military efficiency of militiamen whose major energies were engaged in production. Although the Ninth Party Congress approved Trotsky's project in principle, no steps were taken to carry it out.

The Kronstadt rebellion and the wave of peasant uprisings at the end of the Civil War involved a setback for the advocates of the militia system. "For the present moment," the Tenth Party Congress (1921) resolved, "the agitation of some comrades for the factual liquidation of the existing Red Army and the immediate transition to the militia is wrong and dangerous in practice." [41] After the introduction of the NEP, relations with the countryside improved, and the hazard of recruiting peasants for militia duty appeared less serious. At the same time, the lesson of the peasant risings left a permanent impress, and the Party leadership showed itself loath to base its power solely on a territorial militia.

The conflicting views with regard to the Soviet peacetime establishment were finally resolved in 1923–24 by a compromise. The army was to consist of two elements: a regular or cadre army and a territorial army based on the militia system. The size of the cadre army was fixed at

562,000 men and remained at that level until 1935. The period of service in the cadre army varied with the branch of service. Under the 1924–25 regulations, it was two years in the infantry, cavalry, and artillery, three years for the air force and coastal defense units, and four years for the navy. In addition, special military formations were separately maintained under the jurisdiction of the OGPU. These included some 100,000 frontier guards and another 150,000 troops of internal security. In the territorial army, the term of active service varied from eight to eleven months. This was usually spread over a five-year span with periods of six weeks to three months each year spent in camp or on maneuvers.[42]

Under the system of obligatory service which was put into effect in 1923–24, all eligible males were required to undergo pre-draft service training. This program included some 420 hours of political indoctrination and basic military instruction spread over a two-year period. Each year some 1,200,000 men reached military age. Of these, approximately 850,000 to 900,000 were certified as physically fit for service. Only those whose social origins were proletarian or quasi-proletarian were eligible for assignment to the army. "Non-toiling" elements and others whose social background was questionable were relegated to service detachments in which they performed menial tasks. Draftees with dependents, those performing work of state importance, or those who were adjudged unfit for service in the regular army were assigned to the territorial army. The remaining recruits were posted for service in some branch of the regular army. On completion of service with the colors, the Red Army soldier passed into the reserve, where he remained subject to recall to active duty in the event of war.[43]

As a result of this reorganization, the cadre army receded in numerical importance. "Until 1934," according to Erich Wollenberg, "74 per cent of the Red Army's divisions were territorial ones, leaving only 26 per cent for the standing army." [44] The percentages, however, are deceptive. Within each territorial unit, cadre troops numbered from one-tenth to one-sixth of the total. Technical arms such as the air force, tank and armored car detachments, the engineers, and the signal corps were manned almost exclusively by cadre units. The great bulk of the territorial units were composed of infantry.[45]

The reconstruction of the army was marked by a number of important developments. The paramount goal remained the welding of the armed forces into an efficient instrument of the Party leadership. Especial emphasis was placed on the training of new commanding personnel. The short-term command courses of Civil War days were discontinued. Regimental schools were developed for the training of "lower command personnel." A whole network of military academies was established with courses of from three to four years' duration to prepare higher commanding personnel. In regulating admission, preference was given to young Red Commanders who had risen from the ranks. Officers of worker or peasant origin who had distinguished themselves in the Civil War period were marked out for special training and advancement, while officers of the old imperial army were mustered out in large numbers. Of the more than forty-eight thousand Tsarist officers who were recruited during the Civil War, only forty-five hundred remained in the Red Army in 1930. They constituted approximately 10 per cent of the total officer personnel, compared with 76 per cent in 1918.[46] By 1927, Communists, candidates for Party membership, and Komsomols together formed more than 55 per cent of the total officer corps.[47] Over the next few years, the number of Party-affiliated commanders continued to increase. By 1931, 51 per cent of all Red Army officers were Communists. By 1934, the proportion of Party members had risen to 68.3 per cent. In the higher strata of the officer corps, Party saturation was even more impressive. By 1928, 53.6 per cent of all regimental commanders, 71.9 per cent of all divisional commanders, and 100 per cent of all corps commanders were Party members.[48]

As the Communist element in the army took possession of the command posts, the position of the political commissars became anomalous. Their situation was aggravated by the fact that many of them sided with Trotsky in the intra-Party struggle against the triumvirate of Stalin, Kamenev, and Zinoviev in 1923. The removal of Trotsky and his deputy Skliansky from the leadership of the War Commissariat was followed by a purge of the personnel of the Political Administration. Frunze, who succeeded Trotsky as War Commissar in 1924, died the next year and was replaced by Voroshilov, a staunch supporter of Stalin. The new head of the Political Administration, Bubnov, took measures to transform it into a Stalinist stronghold in the army and installed loyal followers of Stalin in all key positions.

In June 1924 the Organization Bureau of the Party issued an order which in principle provided for unity of command in the army. A Central Committee circular dated March 6, 1925, elaborated the Orgburo pronouncement.[49] Two forms of "unity of command" were declared permissible. Under one, the commander retained full control of all combat training and economic and administrative work, while the commissar was given jurisdiction over Party work and the political and moral guidance of the unit. Under the other, which was only to be put into effect when the commander was especially trustworthy, the functions of the commissar were also handed over to the commander. The general guidance of political work remained under the control of the Political Administration, which continued to operate under the supervision of the Central Committee of the Party.

While the command authority of the new officer corps was considerably strengthened by these measures, in practice "unity of command" was still subject to substantial limitations. Commissars were retained in most units and operated with complete autonomy in the area of Party and political enlightenment work. Their Party status and independent channel of command made them important factors to be reckoned with, particularly when the commander was non-Party or a Party member of very recent vintage. Promotion frequently turned on the recommendation of the political workers. Once the Stalinist leadership had transformed the Political Administration into its own creature, it found the commissar a useful balance wheel in checking the professional *esprit de corps* to which even Communist commanders fell victim as they immersed themselves in their military duties. "Unity of command" was further delimited by the organs of the OGPU in the army. The OGPU Special Sections operated independently of the military command and kept a sharp watch on the loyalty of both commanding personnel and rank-and-file.

The emphasis during the twenties on strengthening the position of the Party in the army gave the Political Administration a new role of central importance. Under its aegis, the army barracks were transformed into schools of Communism. The political workers were charged with the indoctrination of the annual contingents of largely peasant recruits who arrived for training. At least two hours of every day were devoted to classes on political and allied subjects. The steady pounding away was not without its effect. When the 1924 class was recruited, it included 24,700 Communists. When discharged two years later, Party membership had risen to 66,000. Between 1924 and 1928 the proportion of Party members, candidates, and Komsomols in the army increased from 16 per cent to 37 per cent.[50]

The predominantly peasant composition of the army nevertheless caused the Party leadership concern. The prevalence of "peasant moods" among recruits created a barrier which Party propaganda had difficulty in penetrating. The dissatisfactions of the village were carried over into the army and raised questions about the dependability of the troops in the event that they were ordered to suppress peasant disorders. While the Party pursued its indoctrination program with unremitting zeal, at the same time it took precautions to ensure a strong proletarian core in key branches of the armed service. A minimum of 50 per cent of troops of proletarian origin was assigned to armored and transportation units. The air force was allocated 40 per cent, the signal troops 30 per cent, the OGPU units 25 per cent, the cavalry 12 per cent, while the infantry was given only 8 per cent.[51] This quota system, which traced its roots to Trotsky's original proposal to build the army on a firm proletarian base, was designed to distribute proletarian strength where it was calculated to be most effective.

The period of the middle and late twenties represented an era in the history of the Red Army when primary emphasis was placed on training and Party penetration. Within the officer corps, the ascendancy of the Red Commanders was being consolidated. While the cadre army was well trained, the territorial militia was a more doubtful military asset. Both, however, were subjected to intensive Party propaganda and control. By the end of the twenties, the regime appeared to have made marked progress in transforming the army into a dependable political instrument.

Mechanization and Mobilization

The great weakness of the Red Army in this period was its inadequate utilization of modern means of technical warfare. This lag reflected Russian industrial backwardness. As far back as 1924, Frunze, the Commissar of War, warned that the Red Army, for all its vast manpower resources, was at a marked disadvantage in competing with Western armies which were solidly supported by a strong industrial base. "The war of the future," he predicted, "in a considerable measure, if not entirely, will be the war of machines." [52] Because of the slow tempo of industrialization and the primitive character of the Soviet automotive industry, the Red Army made little progress in mechanization during the NEP. The ordinary Russian soldier lacked technical training and had little opportunity to acquire it. Tukhachevsky and other top Soviet commanders during the twenties declared repeatedly that the technical backwardness of Russia had to be overcome if the Red Army was to avoid defeat in future wars.

This was one of the principal impelling forces behind the industrialization program which was embodied in the Five Year Plans. The First Five Year Plan laid the industrial base for a powerful armament industry. From the beginning, the equipment of the Red Army was given priority over all competing demands. Much technical military progress was achieved. While the size of the army remained the same, the qualitative improvement in weapons was tremendous. During the Second Five Year Plan (1933–1938), defense industries expanded about two and a half times as rapidly as industry as a whole. The Red Army acquired ultramodern weapons and was put on wheels and wings. Particular emphasis was placed on the development of artillery, tanks, and planes. The mechanization of the army involved a tremendous growth in defense appropriations. The military and naval budget rose from 1,420,700,000 rubles in 1933 to 23,200,000,000 rubles in 1938.[53] By 1940, it had mounted to 56,800,000,000 rubles.[54] The rise in defense expenditures was accompanied by great emphasis on industrial self-sufficiency. New industrial centers were erected beyond the Urals, and military factories were dispersed with the contingency of war in mind.

At the same time, increasing emphasis was placed on the psychological and technical preparation of the Soviet people for war. In 1927 a number of state-sponsored organizations which supported the activities of various branches of the armed services were merged into one agency — *Osoaviakhim*, the Society for the Furthering of Defense, Aviation, and Chemical Warfare. Osoaviakhim was organized to coördinate the defense training of civilians. By 1939, more than twelve million members were enrolled in its ranks. Osoaviakhim sponsored mass sports of a military nature; it trained air-raid wardens, drivers, parachutists, machine gunners, snipers, marksmen, and technical specialists in all fields related to military defense. In essence, it constituted a form of total mobilization for total war and was a significant factor in making the Soviet population both machine-minded and war-minded.

The technical instruction provided by Osoaviakhim was supplemented by increasing use of nationalistic appeals to provide the emotional driving power behind total mobilization. During the late thirties, all the resources of the Soviet propaganda apparatus were mobilized to inculcate patriotism. The glorious military traditions of the Russian past were revived; Tsarist generals like Suvorov and Kutuzov were exalted as popular heroes who had fought to preserve the national heritage. The new patriotism was designed to unify the nation against the imminent danger which seemed to loom from Hitler's Germany. The new oath required of soldiers in the Red Army eliminated all references to "loyalty to the international proletariat." The recruit now swore "to defend my homeland, the Union of Soviet Socialist Republics." Proletarian class-consciousness was soft-pedaled in the interest of national unity.

Meanwhile, radical changes were taking place in the Red Army. One of the most important was the great increase in the size of the standing army. In 1934 its strength was raised from 562,000 to 940,000 men. The next year, it was further expanded to 1,300,000 men. By 1939 the whole army was placed on a cadre basis. Voroshilov reported to the Eighteenth Party Congress in that year:

The territorial system . . . began to conflict with the defensive requirements of the state as soon as the principal imperialist countries started to increase their armies and to put them in a state of readiness for war even in peace-time . . .

As a consequence, it was found necessary to abolish the territorial system as the structural basis of our army and to adopt the cadre system exclusively. Today our whole army is uniformly built on the cadre principle.[55]

At the same time, all national military units in the army were dissolved, and their troops were scattered and merged in the cadre army.

The Universal Military Service Act of 1939 made service in the armed forces obligatory for all citizens of the USSR. The test of class origins was abandoned in determining eligibility to bear arms. The term of service was substantially increased. Ground troops were required to serve two years, junior commanders three years, troops and junior commanders in the air force and land frontier guard three years, coast defense forces four years, and the navy five years. The imminent threat of war and the intricacy of modern technical weapons furnished the compelling reasons for the change. At the same time, the draft age was lowered to nineteen and the age limit for reservists increased from forty to fifty.

While the army was undergoing technical renovation and greatly expanding in size, it was also subjected to a political crisis of major proportions. The announcement on June 12, 1937, of the execution of Marshal Tukhachevsky and seven other high-ranking Soviet generals "for espionage and treason to the Fatherland" and the suicide of Gamarnik, the Deputy People's Commissar for Defense who headed the Political Administration of the Army, was the prelude to a large-scale purge of the Soviet high command and the top Party apparatus in the army.

The purge of the high command was followed by a series of measures to strengthen the Party leadership's control over the army. Gamarnik was replaced as head of the Political Administration by L. Mekhlis, a staunch Stalinist, who promptly removed the remnants of the Gamarnik entourage from leading positions in the army's Party apparatus. The reconstruction of the political machinery of the army involved a heaven-sent opportunity for those in the lower ranks. Mekhlis claimed at the Eighteenth Party Congress that "many thousands of splendid Bolsheviks of the Leninist-Stalinist breed have been promoted from below to leading posts." [56] The installation of trustworthy personnel was also accompanied by a restoration of the authority of the political commissars. The decree of August 15, 1937, made the commissars coequal with the commanding personnel in military as well as political affairs. Voroshilov stated the new relationship at the Eighteenth Party Congress: "The commander and the military commissar constitute a single unit in the matter of directing the military and political training and education of their unit . . . Both the commander and the military commissar will lead their unit, their formation, into action." [57] This double-headed system of command under which all orders were to be signed jointly by the commander and by the commissar was an index of the nervousness and apprehension which the Great Purge had aroused. The decision to keep the army under the closest political supervision reflected the contemporary fears of the Party leadership.

At the same time, the Party leadership sought to mobilize the support of the younger commanders, who were rapidly promoted to the numerous leading positions vacated by victims of the purge. While many of the officers who were lifted to large responsibilities lacked the experience of high command, their mastery of the newer technical methods of warfare was frequently greater than that of the less adaptable Civil War generation whom they replaced. Their devotion to the Party was secured by the recognition which their talents had received.

In order to consolidate the loyalty of the reconstructed officer corps, their perquisites, rates of pay, and living conditions were considerably improved. As the following table demonstrates, salaries were substantially raised, though part of the increase was cancelled out by inflation.[58]

| | *Pay in rubles* | | *Percentage* |
	1934	*1939*	*increase*
Platoon Commander	260	625	240
Company Commander	285	750	263
Battalion Commander	335	850	254
Regimental Commander	400	1200	300
Division Commander	475	1600	337
Corps Commander	550	2000	364

The well-being of the commanding personnel was also assured by a special system of military coöperatives, *Voentorg*, which guaranteed the officer corps and their families a variety of food, clothing, and other supplies and services which were not available to the general population. Officers enjoyed preferential advantages in obtaining housing for their families.

Rank, gold braid, high pay, and well-tailored uniforms were only the outer symbols of the new-found prestige of the commanding personnel. Relationships between officers and men were repatterned on a rigid hierarchical basis. Discipline was tightened. Compulsory saluting of superiors became mandatory. Insubordination in the ranks was to "be punished by the most unmerciful measures."[59] As World War II approached, the authority and perquisites of the new officer corps were reinforced in every direction. The professional imperatives of a smoothly functioning fighting machine reasserted their importance.

One major problem remained — the familiar problem of balancing the competing demands of professionalism and Party control. The system of command under which authority was shared by commander and commissar had obvious military disadvantages. It undermined the authority of the commander and was fraught with possibilities of conflict. Yet the Party leadership could not abdicate its control of the army without running a risk that the officer corps would develop into an independent power center. The very privileges which the Party leadership conferred on the officer corps to ensure its loyalty accentuated the danger. Even the enrollment of most of the higher commanding personnel in the Party provided no guarantee that professional *esprit de corps* would not develop into a more decisive cohesive force than Party membership.

The setbacks suffered in the first stages of the Russo-Finnish war sharpened the dilemma. Numerous instances of friction between commander and commissar in the heat of battle documented the inefficiency of the double-headed system of command.[60] With the replacement of Voroshilov as People's Commissar of Defense by Marshal Timoshenko, the army reverted to unity of command. The decree of August 12, 1940, abolished the political commissars and replaced them with Assistant Commanders for Political Affairs (*zampolits*), whose sphere of action was limited largely to political propaganda and education. Although this order greatly strengthened the authority of the army command in purely military matters, the hierarchy of political workers in the army remained subject to the instructions of the Political Administration of the Army, which in turn functioned as part of the apparatus of the Party Central Committee. As A. I. Zaporozhets, one of its high officials, explained in a speech on December 13, 1940, "We Bolsheviks cannot separate work on political education from the business of military preparation. All Party political work, including propaganda, must be directed to lifting the military capabilities of the unit. Every political worker must occupy himself with military preparation, with administration, and with all other questions involving the life of the unit." [61] The Party leadership was not ready to interpret unity of command as meaning that the Party abandoned its supervision of the armed forces. Although military initiative and leadership were stimulated by the abrogation of the requirement that orders of the commander required the commissar's countersignature, the political workers still functioned as the Party's eyes and ears in the army. The officer corps remained conscious of their presence and of the authority which they represented.

On July 16, 1941, shortly after the Nazi invasion of the Soviet Union, the institution of political commissars was reëstablished. This action was taken apparently because of the large-scale surrenders of the early days of the war and the collapse of resistance which they seemed to portend. The restoration of the powers of the commissars was designed to stiffen the will to resist and to guard against the possibility of treachery in the officer corps. The response of the Party to crisis was to strengthen the authority of its most loyal phalanx.

When the tide of battle turned, the Party reverted to earlier arrangements. On October 9, 1942, the *zampolits* again replaced the commissars, and unity of command in military matters was restored. By this time, the loyalty of the Soviet officer corps had survived the test of battle; the Party could afford to experiment with a pattern of military-political relations in which the high command was left free to press home the assault while the political workers concentrated on building morale and inspiring the troops with patriotic ardor.

During the war, the Party continued its unremitting efforts to strengthen its position in the army. On the eve of the war, according to Voroshilov's speech at the Eighteenth Congress, more than half of the army consisted of Communists and members of the Young Communist League.[62] The proportion in the officer corps was strikingly higher. The political personnel of the army in 1939 totaled 34,000, compared with 15,000 in 1934 and only 6,389 in November 1918, at the height of the Civil War. Early in the war, when the army was undergoing vast expansion, the Party relaxed its standards of admission in order to encourage members of the armed forces, and particularly front-line fighters, to apply for entrance. During the year 1942 alone, more than 1,340,000 new members were recruited into the Party. The great majority came from the armed forces. It was evident that the Party was consciously reaching out to strengthen its mass base in the crucial military formations.

The Party leadership found it expedient during the war years to broaden its appeal both to army and nation by muting revolutionary and class ideology and stressing nationalism and patriotism as socially unifying objectives. The glorification of the army and the high command formed part of the pattern of the national rally. As the war drew to a close, however, the Party reasserted its ascendancy. The Soviet organs of mass communication put increasing emphasis on the role of the Party as the major instrument of victory, and the heroic exploits of Soviet marshals and generals were painted in subdued colors. Precautionary measures were taken to fend off the possibility of Bonapartism. When there were signs at the end of the war that Marshal Zhukov was becoming too prominent a figure, he was promptly removed from the limelight and given a much less conspicuous military command in the Ukraine.* Ideological indoctrination of the army, which had been relaxed during the war, was revived and intensified. The Party leadership tightened its grip on the army. The officer corps was not only expected to be efficient; it was required to demonstrate unswerving devotion to the regime.

Party and Police Controls in the Army

In order to ensure the loyalty of the Soviet armed forces, the Party leadership has developed a complex but highly integrated system of controls which penetrates every aspect of army life. The system is com-

---

* As part of the "national rally" after Stalin's death, Zhukov was restored to a position of prominence as one of two First Deputy Ministers of Defense of the USSR. At the same time, Bulganin, a member of the inner group in the Presidium, replaced Marshal Vasilevsky as Minister of Defense. Vasilevsky was demoted to First Deputy Minister of Defense.

posed of two parallel hierarchies which operate independently of the military command. One, which may be called political, consists of the political workers and the network of Party and Komsomol organizations in the Red Army. It performs the function of infusing the army with Party spirit by positive indoctrination and agitation. The other, which may be described as punitive, consists of security organs of the MVD, whose duties are to root out disaffection and disloyalty in the army.

The control of political work in the Soviet army is presently centered in the Main Political Administration (MPA), which functions both as a part of the USSR Ministry of Defense and as the Military Department of the Central Committee of the Party. The responsibilities of MPA embrace all propaganda and educational activities in the army, including the supervision of Party and Komsomol organizations. Its central organization prepares the programs of political instruction which are followed in the army; edits and publishes army publications of an educational or propaganda character; and supervises the army clubs, movies, educational circles, libraries, and other organized centers of army life through which the Party line is constantly propagated. Through its subordinate apparatus of political instructors and inspectors, it keeps in touch with the state of army morale and renders regular reports to the Party leadership. It also maintains a series of special schools for the training of junior political personnel and the Lenin Military Political Academy in Moscow for senior political officers. Candidates for admission to these schools are ordinarily recruited from Party members in the army who combine military knowledge with some practical experience in Party political work in army units.[63]

The organizational structure of MPA follows the army chain of command. Representatives of MPA are stationed at all levels of the army organization, down to and including the company. In the zone of the interior, MPA operates through the Political Administration of the military districts (PUOKR); in the combat forces, its organization radiates down from the Political Administration of the army group (PUARM) to the company. The heads of PUOKR and PUARM and their deputies are appointed by MPA with the sanction of the Party Central Committee; Party regulations require that they be Party members of five years' standing. At lower levels of the military hierarchy, MPA is represented by corps *zampolits*, or Assistant Commanders for Political Affairs, who head the Corps Political Departments; by divisional *zampolits*, who direct the Divisional Political Departments; by regimental (and occasionally) battalion *zampolits*; and finally by the *politruk* or political leader of the company.

The functions of the political officers vary with their position in the hierarchy and the jurisdiction of the staffs to which they are assigned.

At the level of the military district and the army group and even the corps and the division, the responsibilities of the political departments center largely on supervision and direction of the work of political officers in lower echelons. Problems of training and assignment of political officers; inspection of the quality of political instruction and the state of work in lower units; preparation of programs and materials for use in classes; the editing of newspapers, pamphlets, and other publications; and even the routing of books, magazines, movies, and speakers to military units occupy the major energies of the staff. At the level of the regiment and below, political agitation assumes an increasingly operative and face-to-face character. The *zampolit* of the regiment heads a Political Section (*politchast*) which is ordinarily composed of his secretary, a propaganda instructor, the club director, and the secretary of the regimental Party bureau. He has at his disposal the *politruks* of the companies and, in some cases, battalion *zampolits*. Instructors attached to the divisional staff are also available to provide assistance when necessary.

The regimental *zampolit* is responsible for the political health of the regiment. He is in charge of all Party political work and all cultural-educational activity. It is his task to make certain that all the soldiers and officers of the regiment are being thoroughly indoctrinated, that the Party and Komsomol organizations are flourishing, that recreational facilities are provided, and that the leisure-hour activities of the unit are being properly directed into "constructive" political channels. He is required to render weekly reports to the divisional *zampolit* on the state of regimental morale and to keep a constant check on the political reliability of the unit to which he is attached.

The *politruk* is the regimental *zampolit's* link with the company. In 1943 the post of *politruk* in the company was abolished, and the company commander was made directly responsible for political indoctrination in his unit. This innovation apparently was unsatisfactory; in 1949–50, *politruks* reappeared at the company level, and the program of political agitation in the army was intensified.

The political conditioning of the Red Army conscript begins with his first contact with army life. Even before he is called up, his political record is subject to scrutiny by the MVD and the *raivoenkomat* (district military agency). A markedly unfavorable political report may even lead to assignment in a labor battalion. After being checked, recruits are dispatched to military camps where they are divided into groups of twenty-five or thirty for purposes of political indoctrination. During this period, a political worker lives with them, examines their mail, leads political discussions, and familiarizes himself with the political attitudes of the group.

After the first intensive period of indoctrination, the political life of the soldier revolves around the company. The day starts with a talk on current events by the *politruk*, who reads extracts from the newspapers and comments on the news. Biweekly sessions lasting two hours each are devoted to systematic political instruction. The topics discussed may include the duties of service and the oath of induction, the history of the Red Army, the traditions of the unit, the USSR Constitution, the Five Year Plan, international problems, the role of the Party, the lives of Lenin and Stalin, the meaning of Soviet patriotism, the dangers of foreign espionage, and so on. Political workers also strive to fill the soldiers' free hours with political content. The movies shown at the Red Army clubs or Red Army Houses are designed to impress the current demands of the Party line upon them. The unit newspaper and the books and pamphlets in the regimental reading room or "Leninist corner" are also calculated to steep the soldiers in Party orthodoxies. The political environment in which they are placed is arranged to leave them no alternative except to demonstrate devotion to the regime.

Nor is the political indoctrination of the officer corps neglected. Special efforts are made to increase the proportion of Party membership among the officers. Systematic courses and lectures on Marxist-Leninist theory and on more important international and domestic themes are provided to heighten their political awareness. As officers of the Soviet army, they are expected to take leadership in contributing to the political preparedness of the units for which they are responsible.

In order to check on the quality of political work in the army, MPA officials periodically inspect army units, visit political classes, interrogate officers and men on political themes, and evaluate the state of political morale. Prior to such inspections tension mounts, troops are exhorted to "improve" themselves, and political instruction is intensified. Unfavorable political reports reflect on the commander as well as on the *zampolit*; the pressure to lift the level of political consciousness is incessant and unyielding.

In projecting Party influence into the army, MPA relies heavily on the network of Party and Komsomol organizations which permeates every military unit. The Party and Komsomol organizations in the army are directly responsible to MPA and the Central Committee and are independent of the territorial Party organs of the areas in which they happen to be located. The Party secretaries of military districts and army groups are nominated — that is, designated — by the Party Central Committee. Party secretaries at lower levels are "nominated" by MPA or one of its subordinate organs. Party secretaries down to and including the regiment devote all their time to Party work and are freed of any other military responsibilities. They function, in effect, as part of the apparatus of MPA. The *partorgs*, or Party secretaries of primary Party organizations in the company or battalion, perform their Party assignments in addition to their regular military duties. They are ordinarily appointed by the regimental Party secretary.[64]

The Party secretaries and *partorgs* have a specific obligation to stimulate the growth of Party organization in the army and to strengthen the loyalty and devotion of Party members to the regime. They are responsible for Party education, for the organization and conduct of Party meetings, for carrying out all Party decrees, and for the enforcement of Party discipline within the unit. It is also their duty to mobilize Party members to assist the *zampolit* or *politruk* in carrying on agitation among non-Party army personnel. Party members are expected to inspire others by their exemplary behavior, their sense of discipline, their political consciousness, and their willingness to sacrifice themselves in the interest of Party and state. They are the cornerstone on which the activity of the Political Administration of the army is based.

The activities of the Party in the army are reinforced by the organization of Communist youth. The Army Komsomols are directed by the Komsomol section of MPA; like the Party organs, they are directly responsible to the *zampolits* of the units in which they function. Secretaries of Komsomol organizations at the level of the regiment and higher are required to be Party members or candidates; their appointments must have the approval of the *zampolit*. Primary Komsomol organizations function at the company level. If the organization consists of less than twenty members, it is headed by a *komsorg*, or Komsomol organizer; if it exceeds twenty members, it is governed by a presidium of three to five members and a secretary. In either case, the secretary or *komsorg* has to be approved by representatives of the Political Administration.

The Komsomol organizations, like the Party, provide a reservoir of activists on which the Political Administration draws. Assistants to the *politruks* are recruited from Komsomol ranks, and the abler among them may be assigned to act as group leaders in study groups and discussions at the platoon level. Komsomols are enjoined to carry on cultural-educational work among their more passive colleagues, to assist in the editing of unit news sheets, to help in regimental club work, to popularize the "Leninist corners" where books and pamphlets are available, and to serve as a stimulant and example in heightening the political awareness of the army rank-and-file. By appealing to the ambitious as well as to the ideologically dedicated, the Political Administration manages to enlist a flow of energy from Komsomol ranks which helps to charge the army with Party zeal.

Party organization within the Red Army may be visualized as a series of widening concentric circles designed to bring even the least active and politically conscious elements under the spell of Party influence. At the center are the MPA apparatus and the paid Party secretaries who direct and coördinate all political activity. Around them is a much larger circle of Party members and candidates who are particularly strongly represented in the officer corps but who also make their weight felt among the noncommissioned officers and the rank-and-file soldiers. Around the Party is the far wider circle of Komsomols who are primarily recruited among the younger soldiers and noncommissioned personnel. The great outer circle consists of the unaffiliated passive elements in the army who are least responsive to Party and Komsomol influence but who are nevertheless saturated in an incessant stream of agitation and propaganda which radiates out from the MPA apparatus.

In order to strengthen its hold on the army, the Party is constantly struggling to expand its field of influence. The soldier who stands out in the ranks and shows leadership potential is drawn into the Komsomol or the Party. The army Komsomol who demonstrates activist qualities is advanced to Party membership. The ambitious officer knows that Party membership will facilitate his promotion. A bond of interest as well as of indoctrination unites Party member and Komsomol to the Party cause. The strength of the Soviet system of political controls consists in the determined effort to capture the positive loyalty of the armed forces and to incorporate their most activist elements in the ruling elite.

Affirmative appeals are supplemented by a highly developed system of security controls. The MVD organization in the armed forces parallels the military and political hierarchy and maintains its own independent chain of command. All military installations and military formations down through the battalion have their attached Special Sections, which are officered by MVD personnel especially chosen to keep an eagle eye open for the slightest sign of disaffection in the armed forces. As elsewhere in Soviet society, the MVD officialdom operates through a system of informers who are strategically placed in each military unit. Denunciations are encouraged, and incoming and outgoing mail of army personnel is periodically examined. MVD control is applied to the officer corps as well as to the rank-and-file, to Party as well as non-Party personnel. Dossiers are maintained on all members of the armed forces, and personal-history files are thoroughly checked for any evidence of past anti-Soviet activity. Promotions depend on clearance from the special sections. No aspect of army life is closed to MVD scrutiny or investigation; its arbitrary power to arrest those who attract its disfavor and to consign them to prison or forced labor generates an atmosphere of insecurity from which even the most thoroughly indoctrinated Soviet military unit is not wholly free. The power which the special sections possess is suggested by an incident narrated by Mekhlis, the head of the Political Administration, at the Eighteenth Party Congress. Mekhlis was discussing some of the abuses associated with the Great Purge.

The representative of the Special Section in a certain regiment told the Commissar, Gashinsky, that he was after the club superintendent, a *politruk* by the name of Rybnikov. Gashinsky passed this on in confidence to the Party organization and Rybnikov was expelled by the primary Party organization. It soon turned out that Rybnikov was not a bad Bolshevik and that the Special Section was after him . . . to get him to work in their department. The mistake was corrected, but only after Comrade Rybnikov had been put to a lot of mental suffering.[65]

The fear which the special sections inspire gives a peculiar tone to Soviet Army life. Officers and men are attuned to carrying on their activities under the assumption that they are under constant surveillance by security agents. The pervasive impact of MVD controls is deeply felt.

The formula by which the Party leadership imposes its will on the armed forces is a blend of many elements, of which the punitive controls of the MVD are only one. In order to instill affirmative loyalty, the leadership relies on indoctrination and skillful manipulation of incentives. Both positive and negative controls play an indispensable role in sustaining the power of the Party leadership. The ruling group is interested in maintaining an army which will not only be powerful and efficient but also loyal and subservient. To attain these objectives it knows that it cannot depend on terror alone. Neither can it dispense with terror. Under the system of parallel hierarchies which it has installed in the armed forces, the MPA operates as a check on the military command, the MVD controls both the MPA and the military command, and the MVD itself is held in leash by its Party controllers. By establishing independent and competing lines of authority and by institutionalizing their mutual suspicion, the Party leadership seeks to prevent the army from developing into an autonomous political force. The separate channels of power within the armed forces converge at no point short of the Party Presidium. The concentrated ascendancy of the ruling group over the army depends on the diffusion of power within the army. The political insecurity of the military command is a guaranty of the military security of the political command.

Tensions in the Soviet Army

The strains and tensions which this system of control generates reflect the specific characteristics of Soviet military organization. The intrusion of independent political and police hierarchies into the army chain of command produces multiple zones of conflicting authority with their by-products of friction and rivalry. The following analysis of these conflicts is based largely on the accounts of former Soviet army officers and soldiers who have escaped to the West.

The Soviet army officer finds himself at the center of a series of cross-pressures which are not easily resolved or accommodated. As a professional army officer, he has a prime responsibility for the military efficiency of his unit. Whether or not he is a member of the Party, he is also held accountable, together with his *zampolit*, for the political education of his troops. Neither military nor political preparedness can be neglected without running the risk of reprimand or a more serious penalty. If he is a Party member, he is further obligated to devote extra hours to such Party assignments as fall to his lot. He is expected to be a model of exemplary behavior, and he lives with the constant knowledge that his every word and action are subject to scrutiny by his political officer or the representative of the special section. The reconciliation of all these competing demands and pressures is not conducive to peace of mind.

Relations with the *zampolit* offer a fertile source of friction. The cadre officer, even when he is a Party member, tends to place his military duties in the forefront of his consciousness. The *zampolit* is driven by the nature of his assignment to emphasize political work among the troops. Conflicts between commander and *zampolit* may frequently develop out of the competing claims which they make on the time and energies of the military unit for which they are both responsible. The commander who is jealous of his command prerogatives encounters a formidable rival in a *zampolit* who can report to his own higher authorities that the commander is ignoring the importance of political indoctrination. The cadre officer knows that his advancement depends on political loyalty as well as on military efficiency and that one important criterion of his loyalty is the political report which his *zampolit* writes about him. As a result, the officer is placed in the frustrating situation of being in some respects subordinate to the *zampolit* whom he theoretically commands. If his attitude to the *zampolit* is too submissive, he risks undermining his own authority with his troops. If he presses the *zampolit* too hard, he invites retaliation. Some escaped Soviet officers report no great difficulty in working out a successful *modus vivendi* with their *zampolits*; the majority regard the relationship as fraught with difficulty and frustration. The ambivalent position in which the commanding officer finds himself demands the skill of the diplomat as well as the training of the professional soldier.

If dependence on the *zampolit* is a source of resentment, the relationship with the MVD Special Section inspires real fear. Most Soviet officers, like other Soviet citizens, adjust themselves to an environment in which the presence of an informer is a likely possibility, but few learn to enjoy it. One of the major reasons given by escaped officers to explain their break with Soviet society is the desire to be free of the atmosphere of suspicion and distrust which MVD surveillance generates. The activities of the MVD in the army are a constant reminder that a careless word may mark the end of a military career and provide a ticket of admission to a forced labor camp. The officer who wishes to survive and advance in the army learns to suppress any rebellious thoughts which he may entertain, to discipline his tongue, and to make the public affirmations of loyalty which will demonstrate his complete devotion to the regime. Even those who successfully control their overt behavior win no reprieve from the attention of the special sections. They live with the realization that a misstep will bring swift retribution, and they cannot escape the gnawing maggot of insecurity which the MVD implants in every Soviet subject.

The grievances of the army rank-and-file take a somewhat different form. Although they too feared the MVD special sections, soldiers who escaped from the Soviet army have indicated in interviews that the impact of MVD controls is more deeply felt among the officers than among the ordinary soldiers. The complaints of men in the ranks chiefly concern harsh discipline, the special privileges of the officer corps, and the extent to which even their leisure hours are invaded by political indoctrination.

Resentment of stringent discipline is particularly marked among the troops assigned for occupation duty in Germany and Austria. The enforced isolation from the local population and the confinement of soldiers to barracks and clubs when they are off duty lend a concentration-camp aspect to their life. Even though absence without leave is subject to the most severe penalties, soldiers of the occupation army find ways of establishing liaisons with the female contingent in the local population, and contact with the West and its "decadent" capitalist luxuries has a disintegrating effect. The MVD is constantly on the watch for the first sign of disaffection. A few of the "contaminated" Red Army men make a break for freedom and escape to the West; the majority of the transgressors are arrested and sent home.

Resentment of the privileges of the officer corps also serves as a source of disaffection. In the Red Army of the twenties, the commanders led a relatively spartan existence which was, in many respects, indistinguishable from that of the men whom they were leading. Their pay was low; in 1924, a corps commander received 150 rubles a month, roughly the amount earned by a skilled metal worker. There was no special officers' mess; officers and men shared the amenities of the Red Army clubs. The hierarchy of military life was tempered by egalitarianism; soldiers and commanders mingled freely, with no social barrier to separate them.[66]

The Soviet army today is organized on a very different basis. Officers form a privileged caste. The gap between their standard of life and that of the private in the army has substantially widened. Officers have their separate mess and their separate clubs. Relations between officers and men have become increasingly formalized and hierarchical. The deepening gulf between officers and men breeds envy and hostility among the rank-and-file. Though these feelings are suppressed while soldiers are subjected to the discipline of service, they are freely voiced by the Red Army men who have escaped to the West.

The program of political education also encounters a certain amount of passivity and indifference among the rank-and-file. Soldiers complain that agitation and meetings take up their free periods and leave them no intervals for rest and relaxation. The steady propaganda bombardment to which Red Army men are exposed creates its own immunities. One escaped soldier reported that he and his comrades learned to sleep through political speeches with their eyes open. Another stated that not more than 10 per cent of the personnel took the political discussions seriously. The remainder answered questions by political officers with a non-committal "I don't know" or gave stock answers. Interviews with escapees indicate that the veneer of indoctrination wears thin when Red Army soldiers confront realities in the West which glaringly contradict the image of the West upon which they have been fed. Few Red Army soldiers challenge the assertions of political workers; those who harbor doubts are ordinarily wise enough to conceal them. Resistance takes the form of apathy and inertia.

The strains and tensions which undoubtedly exist in the Soviet Army should not be interpreted to mean that the Party leadership stands in any imminent danger of losing its control of the armed forces. The officer corps may resent the intrusion of political workers into command responsibilities, and it may loathe the milieu of suspicion and distrust which the MVD creates, but it is ordinarily powerless to change the situation in which it finds itself. At the same time, its distaste for the negative aspects of Soviet army life is balanced by the vested interest which it has acquired in the survival of the Soviet regime. According to Marshal Vasilevsky's report to the Nineteenth Party Congress, 86.4 per cent of the Soviet officer corps are Communists or Komsomols.[67] The top command is composed exclusively of Communists. Promotion and advancement depend on identification with the system. The Soviet officer corps occupies a privileged position in the Soviet social system; its material advantages and the honors accorded it make it one of the most attractive havens in Soviet life. Subservience is sweetened by perquisites and enforced by a system of controls which makes any assertion of independence a highly hazardous adventure.

The grievances of the army rank-and-file also appear to present no serious threat to the domination of the top ruling group. Harsh discipline, the gulf between officers and men, and political and police controls induce grumbling and resentment, but their undermining effect in building a rejection of the Soviet system is counterbalanced by other factors which operate to consolidate the loyalty or obedience of the armed forces to the regime. The emphasis on Soviet patriotism and love of the Fatherland, which figures powerfully in recent Soviet army propaganda, functions as a cementing factor. The continuous indoctrination to which the armed forces are exposed leaves its residual deposits. While many Red Army soldiers remain more or less impervious or indifferent in the face of the propaganda barrage, large numbers find themselves unconsciously absorbing an image of a hostile outside world and a pride in Soviet "achievements" which contribute to solidarity with the regime. The soldier activists who join the Komsomol and Party set a tone which commands the passive acceptance of the more apathetic. Military discipline and MVD surveillance reinforce obedience. There is no channel through which the dissatisfactions of the rank-and-file can find organized expression and present an effective challenge to the regime.

As long as the political and police controls in the army remain centered in the hands of a unified Party leadership, it is improbable that the Soviet army will emerge as an independent political force. The diffusion of power within the army and the mutual suspicion which the control organs generate assure the atomization of the officer corps and the fragmentation of all possible centers of disloyalty. The appearance of a Soviet variety of Bonapartism depends on the enervation of political and police controls within the army. It is unlikely that such a development will take place short of a defeat in war which dethrones the Communist regime or of a contest for power within the ruling group in which the support of the officer corps becomes the decisive factor in determining the outcome of the struggle.

PART FOUR
Controls and Tensions

Chapter 15

Controls and Tensions
in the Soviet Factory

The organization of the Soviet factory reflects an effort to accommodate the functional imperatives of industrialization and the system of controls on which the leaders of the Soviet regime rely to maintain their power. Industrialization imposes its own discipline wherever it spreads. It requires the creation of a trained labor force which will work in subordination to the rhythm of the assembly line. The complex division of labor of the industrial order puts a special premium on skill in planning and directing a multitude of minute interdependent relationships. Since management plays a key role in providing such direction, the inevitable effect of a program of intensive industrialization is to lift the commanding staffs of factories and enterprises to positions of great importance and responsibility. The leaders of the Soviet regime have perforce been driven to adapt their structure of authority to absorb the new managerial and technical elite created by the industrial revolution. This is reflected not only in the factory but also in the rapid promotion of representatives of the new elite to leading posts in Party and state administration. The preoccupation of the top leadership with problems of production has made the technical and managerial intelligentsia an indispensable adjunct of power and given its members an increasingly significant role in the directive apparatus of the Soviet state.

The Crucial Role of Management

The dependence of the regime on the managerial and technical elite presents the Soviet ruling group with difficult problems. The leadership must be concerned both with the efficiency and loyalty of its managerial and technical cadres. It cannot dispense with efficiency since the productive potentialities of its industrial machine hinge on the quality of management. At the same time, it must also command the undivided loyalties of its managers and technicians if its own position of supreme authority is not to be gradually undermined. The effort to guarantee both efficiency and loyalty produces ambivalent and contradictory organizational pressures. The drive for efficiency leads to emphasis on one-man management and a reinforcement of the authority and perquisites of the managerial class. The anxiety about loyalty induces strenuous efforts to assimilate the technical and managerial intelligentsia into the Party and involves reliance on Party and police controls to hold the growing power of the managerial elite in check. The distribution of authority in the Soviet factory registers the effect of these cross-pressures.

A brief reference to earlier patterns of organization in the Soviet factory may bring recent developments into sharper perspective. In the first years of the Soviet regime, the Communist Party had few members who were qualified to undertake managerial assignments in industry. Many of the old-regime managers and technicians fled abroad. Although those who remained were regarded with sharp distrust, it was also recognized that their skills would have to be utilized. Faced with the task of operating the newly nationalized industries, the Party found itself compelled to resort to a variety of expedients. Usually a Communist or a trusted worker who had demonstrated some initiative but lacked technical training was put in charge of a factory as the Red Director, while an old-regime engineer was designated as his assistant to provide technical guidance. Sometimes the roles were reversed, and the engineer-expert was appointed manager, while a trusted Party member served as his deputy or controller to guard against sabotage and to make certain that the orders of superior authorities were carried out. In either case, this system of dual control functioned badly. The Red Directors or controllers commonly regarded the experts with suspicion and hostility, and the experts reciprocated with hatred and contempt. The experts were reluctant to take responsibility, and the Party representatives were equally reluctant to grant it. Friction and turmoil were the inevitable by-products.

The situation was further complicated by the existence of the so-called "triangle." Party authorities, trade-union representatives, and management divided and shared responsibility for the operations of the plant. During the first decade of the Soviet regime, various efforts were made to demarcate their respective jurisdictions, but none of these attempts enjoyed notable success. The Party secretaries in the factories regarded virtually every action of management as within their province to review and reverse, and the trade unions, at least until 1929, continued to intervene actively in all managerial decisions affecting labor.

In 1929, as the First Five Year Plan gathered momentum and emphasized the crucial role of management in determining its success, a strong effort was made to fortify managerial prerogative. The trade-union apparatus was purged, and its members were warned not to "intervene directly in the running of the plant and moreover, not [to endeavor] to replace plant management." Trade-union representatives were instructed to "help to secure one-man control" and to concentrate their efforts on enforcing labor discipline and stimulating "the productive initiative of the working masses." The same Party resolution which incorporated this injunction also cautioned Party organizations against "direct intervention . . . in the operational-productive work of the plant management." [1] The Party cells were to concern themselves with checking the execution of Party directives and were not to interfere in the hiring of personnel, the allocation of work assignments, or other "operational-economic orders" of management. While the 1929 Party resolution dealt a permanent blow to the managerial pretensions of the trade unions, it was less effective in clarifying relations between Party and management. The line between general supervision and detailed interference was not easy to draw. The intent of the resolution was clearly to buttress the authority of management, but the Party leadership had no intention of abdicating its control functions. It continued to hold its local Party functionaries responsible for the economic performance of the factories in which they were placed.

The strengthening of managerial authority was accompanied by strenuous efforts to improve the technical qualifications of old Communist managers and to train new specialists in large numbers. Veteran Communist factory directors were given leave to attend the Industrial Academy in order to fill in the gaps in their educational background. Special arrangements were made to provide private lessons and correspondence courses for directors who could not be released from their factory assignments. In the first phase of the Five Year Plans, great emphasis was also placed on the accelerated training of new specialists, who were recruited heavily from so-called "proletarian" cadres. The courses to which they were exposed were intensive and highly specialized. The system of accelerated education and narrow specialization proved seriously defective. It was replaced in the mid-thirties by a more rounded engineering curriculum, which allowed adequate time to master fundamentals and to which admission was regulated by strict entrance examinations rather than favorable social origins.

A substantial improvement in the educational qualifications of Soviet managerial and technical personnel was soon noticeable. As late as 1934, 50 per cent of the factory directors in the Soviet Union had only a primary-school education. By 1936, this percentage had been reduced to 40 per cent.[2] In the same period, the proportion of factory directors with some form of higher education increased from 26 per cent to 46 per cent, a sharp rise which reflects the attendance of many veteran Communist directors at the cram courses of the Industrial Academy as well as the infusion of new blood from the technical institutes.[3]

The Great Purge of 1936–1938 sharply altered the social and educational physiognomy of the directing personnel in Soviet industry. The Red Directors of the early twenties largely disappeared from the Soviet stage. Many of the Red Specialists, who were given accelerated training in the first stages of the Five Year Plan and who rapidly rose to positions of responsibility, also fell by the wayside. They were replaced by young engineers who had only recently graduated from the technical institutes and universities. The new generation lacked the practical experience of its predecessors, but it was far more broadly and systematically educated. The effect of the Great Purge was to lift the best of the recent graduates of the engineering schools into posts of key industrial importance. By 1939 from 86 to 87 per cent of the factory directors in defense industry and ferrous metallurgy were listed as having a higher education.[4] Most of the young engineers who rose to power in the wake of the Great Purge affiliated with the Party. Their indebtedness to the regime was reinforced by the exceptional opportunities to which they fell heir. With the assimilation of the new Soviet technical intelligentsia into the Party, the position of the manager and the engineer grew stronger. The new industrial elite exerted increasing influence in the higher councils of Party life, and a number of its members were promoted to important posts in leading Party organs.

The drive for industrial efficiency also helped strengthen managerial authority. Although the 1929 Party resolution endorsed the principle of one-man management in Soviet industry, its thoroughgoing adoption was another matter. While the interference of trade unions in production decisions was substantially eliminated and the power of local Party cells somewhat curbed, most plants continued to be managed on the so-called "functional" system. Under this regime, various managerial responsibilities were divided among "functional" departments, each enjoying the right to issue orders within its area of jurisdiction. The factory manager under this arrangement was at best a coordinator, with little real power to enforce his demands. Responsibility was dissipated among a host of independent departments each of which operated as a sovereign in its own sphere.

The Seventeenth Party Congress, which met in 1934, launched a full-scale attack on the "functional" system of management.[5] As a result, the authority of plant directors and shop chiefs was substantially fortified. The functional departments were not abolished, but the rule was established that any instructions which they prepared to guide factory operations required the approval of the director, and all factory orders were issued in his name. The factory director was made fully responsible for the operations of the plant. The shop chiefs reported directly to him and received their orders from him.

The Organization of the Soviet Factory

The existing pattern of organization in the Soviet factory is built around the all-embracing responsibility of the director. In the words of an official handbook on Soviet industrial management,

> The director of an enterprise is its full empowered manager. He has at his disposal all the material and monetary resources of the enterprise, and directly manages the drafting of workshop tasks (technical, industrial and financial plans), and of the plans for technical progress and capital construction. The director selects all the basic personnel, establishes the procedure for the work of the entire collective, verifies the results and the progress of the work of the personnel, and maintains labor, planning and financial discipline. The orders from a director of an enterprise have unconditionally obligatory force for all workers. The director bears full responsibility for the work of the enterprise as a whole, for the fulfillment of the quantitative and qualitative indices of the state planned task, for the correct and economical expenditure of resources, and for the correct organization of labor.[*]

In discharging his managerial responsibilities, the factory director is assisted by an auxiliary administrative apparatus. Its character and complexity vary with the size and nature of the plant. Chart VI outlines the pattern of organization in a typical ferrous metallurgical plant. The chief engineer of the factory functions as the first assistant to the director. As the director's deputy, his responsibility embraces the work of the entire enterprise, but his specific role is ordinarily confined to the technical direction of production. His immediate area of supervision includes the production workshops, the designing workshops, the repair shops, the experimental workshops, the electro-technical workshops, and the department for the technical safety of labor. The chief engineer is ordinarily aided by an assistant chief engineer, who has direct responsibility for working out technological processes, time norms, and new designs in preparatory production planning.

The remaining departments of the factory are immediately subordinate to the director. They embrace a wide variety of functional activities including planning, accounting and finance, sales and procurement of supplies, labor and personnel, capital construction, quality control, workers' supply and housing, and other matters of general administration.

The large factory is composed of a number of workshops, each of which is headed by a chief or superintendent who is held accountable for the total performance of the shop. His responsibilities include the drafting and execution of shop plans, the procurement of supplies for the shop, the organization of labor, the regulation of productive processes,

CHART VI

Chart of the Management of a Ferrous Metallurgical Factory

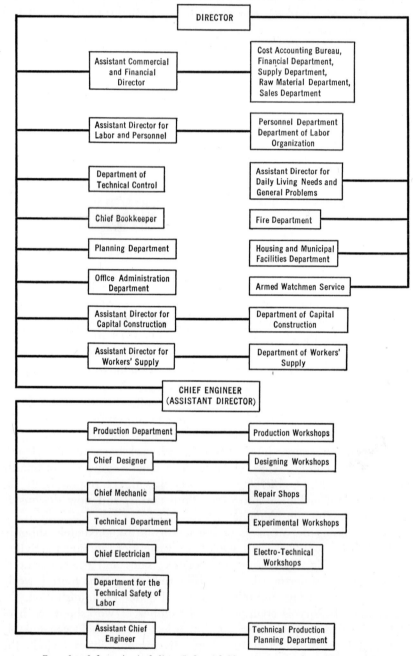

Reproduced from A. Arakelian, *Industrial Management in the USSR*, p. 128.

and the control of the quality of the finished output. The shop chief in a large workshop is provided with a staff which ordinarily includes a chief shop engineer, a shop planning and dispatching bureau, a technical bureau, a mechanic, a bookkeeper, and an office manager. In small shops the staff ordinarily is limited to a planner, a technical norm-setter, a repair foreman, and a clerk.

The shop is usually broken down into sections headed by foremen, and the sections in turn are divided into brigades directed by brigade leaders. The foreman functions as the direct link between the shop chief and the workers. He transmits operational orders to his section, allocates work, materials, and tools, provides instruction, and sees that assigned tasks are executed. The foreman also enjoys substantial rights. He can impose small fines for the violation of labor discipline. He has a bonus fund to reward the best workers, and he exerts considerable influence in establishing pay categories for workers in his section.

Officially, the foreman is the "lowest commander of production." He is released from production duties and expends his energy organizing the work of others. The brigade leaders, on the other hand, are not freed from ordinary labor. They work along with other members of their brigade. They assist the foreman by setting the pace for the other members of the brigade and helping to instruct them in their assigned tasks. The brigade leaders form a recruiting ground from which foremen are selected and Stakhanovites are rewarded. As such, this bottom link in the administration of Soviet industry performs an important role in stimulating increased productivity.

The distribution of functions which has been described above constitutes the official Soviet textbook version of the organization of the Soviet factory. It is in essence a blueprint of formal structure. Like most organization charts, it conceals more than it reveals. The picture which it conveys is that of a neatly ordered administrative hierarchy in which the factory director is ensconced at the pinnacle, each position subordinate to him is precisely delineated, and the duty of the subordinate is to yield unquestioning obedience to the commands of his superior. The actual structure of authority is neither so neat nor so simple.[7]

Within the administrative chain of command there are both common and conflicting interests. All elements in the factory share a concern with plan-fulfillment and the accompanying rewards. Their joint involvement in meeting or exceeding the plan creates the setting for a system of mutual support in maintaining the productive output of the factory. This system shows few signs of strain as long as the plant is successfully fulfilling its obligations to the state. Under such conditions, minor evasions of regulations may be ignored, and the factory staff may overlook each other's mistakes and inadequacies.

Sharp conflicts of interest arise when factory output begins to lag and plant officials are compelled to run dangerous risks in order to attain or simulate plan-fulfillment. The nature of these problems may be suggested by a series of questions: Shall the chief engineer postpone necessary repairs on the production line and risk a breakdown because continued production is essential to current plan-fulfillment? Shall the chief bookkeeper falsify his accounts to conceal illegal procurement expenditures or other financial overpayments? Shall the head of the department of technical control certify sub-quality output as meeting standards in order to show plan-fulfillment? Shall the assistant director of labor and personnel take on workers who have left other factories without permission because his own factory is in dire need of labor? Shall the head of the planning department report plan-fulfillment when parts of the plan, such as labor productivity and correct assortment of output, have not in fact been met? Members of the factory staff may find themselves under tremendous pressure from the director to take measures which are clearly illegal but which nevertheless seem necessary to meet the factory plan. The conflicting loyalties which the pressure for rapidly expanding industrial production generates are not easily contained within the symmetrical outlines of the factory organization chart. The successful Soviet factory director holds them in a precarious equilibrium, but his capacity to do so depends ultimately on his ability to meet the demands which the regime makes on him.

The Soviet factory director disposes of impressive resources in fusing his subordinates into a coöperative team. His power to hire and fire helps to ensure subservience in the administrative chain of command. It is obviously to his interest to build an entourage on whose loyalty he can count and who are ready to execute his directives without cavil or qualification. The Director's Fund, which is at the exclusive disposition of the director and which increases in size with the success of the enterprise, can be employed to reward fidelity as well as efficiency. It may be used to placate potential critics and to win consent for various quasi-legal or illegal operations which appear essential to plan-fulfillment. The favors which the director may confer and the disciplinary sanctions which he can invoke discourage insubordination. The director who enjoys the confidence and support of his superiors in the ministry and the Party is in a particularly strong position. Subordinates challenge his authority at their peril.

At the same time, this impressive structure of power can readily disintegrate and collapse when a director proves unsuccessful. In such circumstances, all the latent conflicts of interest in the factory come to the surface, and arrangements of mutual support break down. Subordinate officials seek to divest themselves of responsibility for the catastrophe, and denunciations multiply. Ultimately the crisis may be resolved by the removal of the director and the purge or transfer of those luckless subordinates who cannot escape blame for the debacle. A new director is appointed, and the struggle for plan-fulfillment resumes.

The controls which operate in the Soviet factory represent a complex balance of power. Superimposed on the factory director and his subordinates in the administrative hierarchy are two independent and separate channels of command, the Party and the secret police. In addition, there are the trade-union functionaries, though their subordination to factory management has become more and more marked with the passage of the years.

Party Controls in the Factory

Party activities in the factory have undergone substantial modification over the last two decades. There is less disposition to interfere in the details of day-to-day factory operations and much greater emphasis on the use of Party functionaries to check plan-fulfillment and to carry on agitation and propaganda to stimulate increased output. Since the late thirties, membership in the factory Party organizations has increasingly been recruited from managerial personnel, engineers, technicians, shop chiefs, foremen, brigadiers, and Stakhanovite workers. Indeed, these groups tend to dominate the membership of the factory Party organizations. The absorption of these groups into the Party is not unrelated to its newfound willingness since the thirties to build up the authority of the managerial apparatus.

The Party undertakes, however, to differentiate its role from that of management. It operates through an independent hierarchy of Party secretaries. In factories of some size, the Party secretary is a full-time Party functionary who is directly responsible to his superiors in the Party hierarchy rather than to the management of the plant. The mandate which guides his activity involves him in both collaborative and potentially antagonistic relations with factory management. Both Party secretary and factory manager share a common interest in the success of the plant, since both are held responsible for its results. But interpretations of the criteria of success may diverge sharply in response to the very different organizational pressures to which each responds. It is in the narrow interest of the factory manager to have a plan which he can realize and to confine proposed increases to modest increments which remain within the limits of feasibility. To some extent, the factory Party secretary may share the same outlook, but he is also under constant pressure from above to goad management into promising increases, to stimulate feats of Stakhanovism which will result in greatly raised worker norms, and to organize "spontaneous" pledges by management and labor to accelerate plan-fulfillment. The factory director welcomes agitation for extra effort in meeting his plan, but he can only be bitterly opposed to making promises which he knows he cannot perform.

Similar difficulties arise in connection with the control functions of the Party secretary. It is his duty to keep in touch with all parts of the enterprise, to be alert to any failure of performance, to "signal" his superiors in the Party hierarchy in the event of difficulties, and to report constantly to his own higher authorities on the state of plan-fulfillment. The Party secretary may be tempted to gloss over deficiencies in order to achieve neighborly relations with the factory director. He may allow himself to become indebted to the factory director for favors, in exchange for which he tempers his criticism or withholds unfavorable reports. But if he surrenders to such temptations, he also exposes himself to serious risks. The Party secretary who becomes involved in too intimate "family relations" with the administrator whom he is ostensibly controlling is not likely to endear himself to his superiors in the Party hierarchy.[8] The reasons are obvious. He ceases to be a dependable reporter, and the regime can no longer rely on him to keep it informed of industrial developments. He blocks one of the most important avenues of pressure on which the leadership depends to maintain its grip on the industrial manager.

The dilemma confronting the factory Party secretary is a painful one. He faces real difficulty in defining his role vis-à-vis the director and his relations with his own higher Party authorities. If the Party secretary subordinates himself completely to the director, he loses his usefulness as a control instrument and risks a serious reprimand from his superiors in the Party hierarchy. If he puts major emphasis on his control function and uses his position to bring constant pressure on the director to increase his output and to inflate future plans, he also makes trouble for himself. He is almost certain to arouse the hostility of the director and his administrative staff. He runs the grave risk that the increase in planned output which he demands may be unrealizable and that he will have to share responsibility for the resulting debacle. If he presses his control too far, he may be reprimanded for interfering with the director's prerogatives and displacing, instead of controlling, economic organs. The Party secretary must steer a wary course in order to avoid these shoals.

Fortunately for most Party secretaries, the dilemma is not necessarily an insoluble one. The relationship between Party secretary and factory director need not be one of pure antagonism. If the factory director can help make the reputation of the Party secretary by successfully mastering production problems, the Party secretary can also be of assistance to the director by contributing to the prestige of the factory as a politically alert community. Sometimes the secretary can be useful in solving more immediate production crises. The agitation activities under his direction may spur the workers to intensified efforts when plan-fulfillment threatens to lag. When supplies cannot be obtained through any other means, the resourceful Party secretary may be able to utilize Party channels to get the needed items. Collaborative assistance of this sort may do a great deal to temper the latent antagonism which is implicit in the role of the Party secretary as a guardian and controller.

Yet the Party secretary dare not abdicate his role as an independent nucleus of power in the factory. The canny secretary quickly develops a sense of the potentialities and limits of his authority. He will be prompt to expose the deficiencies which the weak factory director is powerless to remedy. He will be equally sensitive to the necessity of maintaining an *entente cordiale* with the strong factory director who produces results. His professional career as a Party functionary depends on his success in reconciling the cross-pressures to which he is exposed. The authority which he exercises is a function of the situation in which he finds himself.

Police Controls in the Factory

The representatives of the secret police also are an important controlling force in the Soviet factory. Every factory of any importance has its Special Section headed by an MVD emissary who functions independently of the factory administration and reports directly to his superiors in the MVD chain of command. The head of the Special Section has his network of factory informers who are under instructions to report any evidence of disaffection or any irregularities of behavior which come to their attention. Anonymous denunciations are encouraged, and an environment of suspicion is created in which the fear of the informer acts as a restraint on unguarded comment or on grievous violation of state and Party directives. The Special Section maintains a dossier on all key employees in the factory administration. Their biographies are carefully investigated for any indication of disloyalty to the regime, and they are kept under close surveillance to ensure their devotion to state interests. The Special Section demonstrates a particular interest in industrial breakdowns and so-called "economic crimes" which prevent plan-fulfillment. Serious accidents in the plant, the ruining of valuable machinery, and other similar disasters are invariably followed by Special Section investigations. The unfortunates whose carelessness, incompetence, or excessive zeal expose them to MVD attention often seek to win absolution by reporting their "crimes" in advance of discovery. The visit to the Special Section office is a form of insurance against denunciation.

The role of the head of the secret police unit in the factory is essentially negative. While he bears some positive responsibility along with the factory administration and the Party secretary for the production record of the plant, his own vigilance as a secret-police agent tends to be measured by the number of spies, saboteurs, and criminals whom he has discovered and exposed. The natural tendency of the secret police to magnify its indispensability may easily lead to a situation in which every accident is transformed into an act of sabotage and every error of judgment is identified as the plot of a spy or a wrecker. The secret police faces its own problem of discriminating between sabotage and unavoidable accident, of distinguishing between managerial subterfuges which facilitate plan-fulfillment and others which cover up serious failures, of making a record as a vigilant uprooter of heresy and dissent while still preserving the productive efficiency of the factory organization. An overzealous special section may wreak havoc in the factory administration, since even the most secure director will hesitate to challenge a display of MVD authority. In order to obviate this danger, there has been an increasing tendency since the late thirties to appoint personnel with engineering training to the factory special sections.

The independent position of the secret police and the privileged status which its members enjoy in the Soviet hierarchy make it difficult to assimilate them into the "family circles" which many factory directors try to build in order to stabilize their positions. Though the directors find it expedient to cultivate the heads of their special sections, "family relations" with them are not easily achieved. It is, perhaps, not without significance that managerial personnel who have fled from the Soviet Union reflect an almost universal fear of the secret police while their attitudes toward Party controls in the factory manifest traces of ambivalence. The existence of these differences may suggest that police controls in the factory function with greater independence and effectiveness than do Party controls. It may also go far to explain the disposition of the top leadership to put increasing reliance on the secret police in strengthening its hold on the basic institutions of the Soviet economy.

The Role of the Trade Unions

The role of the trade unions in the factory has undergone a remarkable transformation since the early days of "workers' control," when an abortive effort was made to realize the syndicalist dream of the factory run by and on behalf of the workers. Over the years, the trade unions have been relegated to the position of minor satellites of management in the constellation of power which makes up the Soviet factory.[9] The influence which trade-union functionaries exert in the factory is well below that exercised by the factory director, the Party secretary, and the head of the special section. Theoretically, the chairman of the factory committee is in an independent position since he is named to his post by his superiors in the hierarchy of trade-union functionaries. In practice, he usually must be acceptable to the factory director and to the Party secretary.[10] His role as a guardian of workers' welfare is subordinate to his obligation to help speed up increases in labor productivity and to enforce labor discipline. The overriding drive which regulates the tempo of the Soviet factory is the compulsion to produce, and the trade unions have had to adjust their activities to this perspective.

The Soviet trade unions have virtually nothing to do with the hiring of labor, the planning of production, the determination of wage rates, the establishment of output norms, and the fixing of hours of labor. These decisions are prerogatives of state administrators. While Soviet law neither specifically forbids nor specifically authorizes the right to strike, it can safely be assumed that any effort to exercise such a right would be treated as a grave challenge to the authority of the state and punished accordingly. The Statute of the Soviet Trade Unions adopted by the Tenth Congress in 1949 provides that every worker "is *under the obligation* . . . strictly to observe State and labor discipline"; no exceptions are made in favor of justifiable work stoppages.[11]

The Soviet collective labor agreement is a very different instrument from its Western counterpart. It is not a product of arms-length bargaining between management and labor about wages, hours, and working conditions. In the main, it represents a joint promise by management and the unions to fulfill and surpass the production plan of the government. The trade unions pledge that labor will observe labor discipline and increase its productivity. Management promises to provide the conditions which will make such an increase possible. A small area remains within which a modicum of bargaining may take place. The factory shop committee may press management to undertake housing construction and repairs, to build schools and extend medical care, and to carry out other types of welfare activity. The obligations which management assumes in this sphere are necessarily limited by the budgetary and material allocations which it can obtain from its superior authorities in the ministry and in Gosplan.

The major activities of the Soviet trade unions embrace the administration of social insurance funds; the management of sanatoria, rest homes, and similar establishments; responsibility for various auxiliary food, housing, and welfare activities attached to the factory; the enforcement of safety regulations; the stimulation of mass sports and para-military activity; the promotion of measures to increase labor productivity; and participation in a limited grievance procedure. The unions are organized around the execution of these functions. The trade union in each factory elects a *fabzavkom* or factory committee which is headed by a chairman who is theoretically elected at a general union meeting. In larger factories, the chairman is usually a professional trade-union functionary who is assigned to his task by his superiors in the union apparatus and whose designation is formally approved at an "election" in which he is the only candidate.[12]

The functions of the trade union are carried out through a number of commissions in which union members participate. In recent years, these commissions have included the following: (1) The Council on Social Insurance, which is composed of insurance delegates elected by the workers and charged with the local administration of all matters affecting workers' compensation, health insurance, invalid pensions, old age insurance, maternity leave, vacation pay, and the like. The social-insurance system is used as an instrument to stimulate labor productivity and discipline. The benefits give substantial advantages to workers who join trade unions, who stay on the same job for long periods of time, and who distinguish themselves as Stakhanovite performers. (2) The Wages Commission, which has nothing to do with the establishment of basic wage rates. It may, however, be consulted by management in connection with the application of these rates to the plant. The primary role of the Wages Commission is to facilitate the installation of progressive piece rates and to encourage "socialist emulation" among the workers. (3) The Commission for Labor Protection, which provides a reservoir of part-time voluntary workers who assist the full-time labor inspectors employed by the central trade unions. Both professional and volunteer inspectors are expected to check the observance of safety rules, vacation provisions, the length of the working day, regulations for the protection of female and child labor, and similar matters. (4) The Commission for Cultural and Educational Activities, which is responsible for workers' clubhouses, recreational facilities, the provision of passes to rest houses and sanatoria, and the organization of courses to raise the qualifications of workers and to indoctrinate them in Party and state ideology. (5) The Housing Commission, which, as its name implies, is concerned with the construction and repair of workers' housing. Since it has no funds and facilities of its own, its task is to persuade management to honor the commitments incorporated in the factory collective labor agreement. (6) The Commission for Workers' Supplies, which is the trade-union counterpart of the Workers' Supply Department of the factory administration. This department manages the auxiliary farm and garden enterprises which many factories have established to feed their workers. The Commission for Workers' Supplies checks the operations of these enterprises as well as the factory canteens and coöperative stores attached to the factory. In some instances, a separate Commission for Gardening and Auxiliary Farming has been established. (7) The Commission for Workers' Inventions and Rationalization, which has the mission of stimulating inventions and rationalization suggestions on the part of workers. It is also supposed to see that worthwhile proposals are properly rewarded and effectively utilized.

As this summary indicates, the primary appeal of Soviet trade-union activity lies in the insurance and welfare area. The exclusion of the unions from the field of production decisions and wage policy has been compensated for to some extent by putting major emphasis on trade-union membership as a source of benefits to its members. Mass involvement and participation in the administration of the welfare activities of the union take the place of independent bargaining and democratic control of industrial life.

A limited role is also allotted to the unions in the settlement of workers' grievances against management. The factory committee of the trade union participates on an equal basis with management in the work of the Norms and Conflicts Commission (RKK), which deals with certain types of complaints from workers and managers. Ordinarily, the factory director or his appointee presides over the RKK.

The jurisdiction of the RKK does not embrace all types of disputes which might conceivably arise between labor and management.[13] Issues which Soviet law clearly reserves for managerial decision cannot be adjudicated by the RKK. Essentially, the work of the RKK is confined to the application of existing law defining the rights of workers and management. Typical worker complaints dealt with by the RKK include claims for job reclassification, for overtime, vacation, and severance pay, and for reinstatement with back pay because of unjustified dismissal from employment. Management may also appeal to the RKK to enforce claims for damage done to factory property by workers or to recover fines imposed on them for violation of the rules of employment.

Ordinarily, cases are referred to the RKK only if a preliminary discussion between the factory foremen and the trade-union representative fails to produce a settlement. If the members of the RKK fail to agree, the dispute may be taken to the People's Court. In some instances, where the dispute is outside the jurisdiction of the RKK, the complaint may go directly to the People's Court. While the awards of the RKK are usually final, they are subject to revision by higher trade-union authorities. If these authorities set the award aside, the aggrieved party may take an appeal to the People's Court. Workers involved as plaintiffs in labor cases are entitled to the free legal services of a union lawyer, and courts to which appeals are taken must consider labor cases within five days after the commencement of the suit. Decisions of the People's Courts may be appealed or protested in the usual manner.

Judgments as to the efficacy of this grievance procedure vary widely. The impression conveyed by official Soviet sources and by at least one ex-Soviet lawyer who represented management in labor cases is that the RKK and the People's Courts decide a majority of labor cases in favor of worker complainants.[14] Ex-Soviet workers, on the other hand, minimize the significance of the grievance machinery by pointing out that many Soviet workers are afraid to bring their complaints to the attention of the authorities and that the fundamental grievances of the ordinary worker revolve around low wages, long working hours, and the stringency of labor discipline for which appeals to the RKK and the People's Courts provide no remedy.

The retention of a limited grievance procedure in the Soviet factory is an indication of its usefulness to the Party leadership. The well-publicized cases in which workers' complaints lead to corrective action have important propaganda significance. They help to instill faith in the sense of equity of the regime, and they provide a symbolic justification for the sacrifices that the industrialization program imposes. Even though the grievance machinery is greatly restricted in scope, it provides a partial outlet for the frustrations of Soviet factory life. The relief it affords is a positive contribution to the strength and productive efficiency of the regime.

Tensions in the Soviet Factory

The tensions prevailing in the Soviet factory are largely a product of the constant pressure from above for increased production. They are accentuated by the system of controls which the regime has developed to make this pressure effective. The tensions affect both controllers and controlled; the form in which they express themselves varies with the role which different individuals and groups in the factory are expected to discharge.

The major concern of the factory director is plan-fulfillment. His future in Soviet society is determined by his success or failure in discharging the obligations which the regime imposes on him. He is richly rewarded in prestige and material benefits as long as he is successful. But the penalties of failure are drastic, and a sustained record of plan-underfulfillment is a sure road to oblivion. The stresses under which the factory director operates are caused by the difficulties which he confronts in meeting his plan. As one moves from the high to the low priority areas of the Soviet economy, these difficulties mount. The director of a munitions plant is a much more powerful claimant on scarce resources than the director of a textile plant. The priority table of the leadership and the restrictions of a scarcity economy place directors in light and consumer-goods industries in a particularly difficult situation, since the resources which are legally made available to them are frequently inadequate to perform the tasks which they have been assigned.

The Soviet factory director is naturally interested in having a plan which he knows he can fulfill. He will bargain to the best of his ability with his superiors in the ministry and Gosplan to prevent unreasonable demands from being made on him. His search for a safety factor sometimes leads him to overstate his requirements and to try to accumulate hoards of scarce materials against the danger of future shortages. While such activity is an understandable by-product of the director's absorption with his own production record, it also involves him in danger if it is carried too far. The director may find himself in serious difficulties because he has "concealed production potentialities," hoarded commodities which are badly needed in other sectors of industry, and adopted a "narrow-minded departmental" approach toward state interests. The dilemma created by the constant need to mediate between the pressure from above for maximum production and the natural desire to limit factory plans to feasible proportions is a source of tension from which no Soviet factory director can wholly escape.

Many Soviet directors also find themselves in the unhappy predicament at one time or another of having to violate the law in order to fulfill the plan or to simulate plan-fulfillment. The subterfuges to which they feel compelled to resort are ingenious and inexhaustible.[15] Procurement irregularities are not limited to overstating requirements and hoarding short items. Practically all factories find it expedient to employ *tolkachi*, so-called "pushers" or supply agents, whose job it is to use all means, legal and illegal, to obtain the supplies which the factory needs. Theoretically, so-called "funded" or allocated commodities cannot be released unless a buyer possesses an allocation order. In practice, these restrictions are sometimes evaded. One of the functions of the *tolkachi* is to arrange deals which make such evasion possible. Sometimes scarce items are obtained by payment of black-market prices, sometimes by an exchange between factories on a *quid pro quo* basis, and sometimes by diverting resources from construction or repair to production. The *tolkachi* depend heavily on *blat*, or personal influence, to dislodge the supplies they need. They cultivate potential suppliers and may cement the relationships by lavish entertainment, favors, gifts, and even bribes. The expenditures of the *tolkachi* may be substantial, and the factory director and the chief bookkeeper must arrange some method of concealing them in the accounts of the enterprise. Practices such as these, to which the factory director may feel forced to resort in order to meet his production target, expose him to possible attack as a law violator.

The factory director who falls behind in his plan or only partially fulfills it is sometimes tempted to conceal his failure by reporting over-all plan-fulfillment in terms of ruble value of output or number of items produced. The production reported may include sub-quality output and incomplete items, or it may represent an incorrect assortment of goods. The director who encounters difficulty in completing his plan is frequently prone to concentrate on goods which are profitable, which consume small amounts of material, and which are easy to produce, while other items in the plan go unproduced or are manufactured only in small quantities. Reports of plan-fulfillment may also conceal wage and other financial overexpenditures and give a deliberately falsified view of the profit position of the plant.

The risks which factory directors who resort to these types of subterfuge run depend upon a variety of factors. If the past record of the director is good and the malingering is well camouflaged and of minor significance, no untoward consequences are likely to ensue. Both the director's superiors and his associates and subordinates share a common interest in supporting a director who produces results. If the violation of plan discipline is serious, the director may find himself in real trouble. Much depends on the current preoccupations of the leaders of the regime. If the leadership, for example, is sponsoring a campaign against sub-quality output, the director who has turned out a large quantity of *brak*, or spoiled goods, may be used as an object lesson. He may be summarily dismissed from his post and even turned over to the prosecutor as an economic criminal. Powerful political connections may save the skin of the director who finds himself in temporary difficulties, but such influence is unlikely to be exerted on behalf of a director with a long record of failure. The Soviet elite is permeated with the gospel of success. The director who cannot survive the test of output is destined to become an expendable.

The hazards which surround the Soviet factory director are formidable. He is frequently forced into a life of illegality in order to fulfill his function. Many of the most difficult problems which he must resolve are not of his making. The pressure from above for greater and greater output is unrelenting. The police and Party controls which surround him are a source of fear as well as irritation.

Yet there are also compensating satisfactions. There is the pride of achievement, the satisfaction of building and producing despite what often appear to be insurmountable obstacles. There is the prestige and power attached to office and the substantial material rewards and perquisites which go with it, at least as long as the director continues to occupy his post. And there is the hope that the director may be able to make his position secure and earn promotion in the Soviet hierarchy as he proves his indispensability. This array of satisfactions, privileges, and aspirations needs to be balanced against the tensions inherent in the director's role in the Soviet factory. It is not unlikely that the same directors who deeply resent the demands which the regime makes on them continue to derive satisfaction from the functions which they perform and the privileges which they exercise in Soviet society.

Lower supervisory personnel have their own characteristic problems and grievances. Important cleavages of training and career prospects divide the shop superintendents from the foremen and brigadiers. The shop superintendents are usually engineers with some form of higher technical education who can look forward to becoming chief engineers or factory directors in the event that they achieve outstandingly successful records. The foremen and the brigadiers, on the other hand, are typically workers with limited technical education who cannot ordinarily aspire to positions in the higher managerial cadres of industry. It is the rare foreman who rises beyond the position of chief foreman in the factory hierarchy. For most brigadiers, the position of foreman represents the highest rung in their ladder of possible achievement.

These differences in education and perspective produce differences in identification and sympathies. The shop superintendent tends to identify with the higher managerial elite. His major concern is to impress his superiors with his energy and resourcefulness. At the same time, his primary loyalty is to the shop, since he is judged on its record. Just as the factory director is driven to subordinate the interests of the ministry to that of his own factory, the shop superintendent is equally driven to subordinate the interests of the factory to that of his own shop. This centripetal obsession may generate serious friction between the shop superintendent and the factory director, particularly when the director finds it expedient or necessary to make decisions which restrict the output of the shop in the interest of factory performance as a whole. Since the shop superintendent is nearer to the workers than the central factory management, he is also more alive to the need for wage payments which will sustain their productive output. He may connive with his foremen at upgrading of workers and other types of overpayment which are designed to improve worker morale. But the pressure from above for maximum exploitation of labor resources and the resistance of workers to such exploitation are not easily reconciled. The effort to achieve a reconciliation produces its own intrinsic stresses and tensions which are inseparable from the shop superintendent's role.

The problems of the foremen and brigadiers are somewhat analogous. The regime makes a strenuous effort to command the loyalties of both groups by enlisting many of them in the Party and by offering them material advantages which rank-and-file workmen do not enjoy. The factory administration counts on them to transmit the pressure for increased effort to the workers. But because foremen and brigadiers are involved in face-to-face relations with workers and frequently share a background of common experience, they are apt to be particularly aware of the workers' real grievances and inevitably become a depository of their complaints. Within limits, they may even intervene to ease the strain for ordinary workers by certifying that norms have been fulfilled when they have not in fact been met, by helping to upgrade workers, or by facilitating other types of overpayment for work done. But the foreman who is overgenerous with the factory's resources risks detection, dismissal, and discipline. Both foremen and brigadiers are caught in a buffer role between the shop superintendents who press for higher output and reluctant workers who seek an adequate relation between pay and effort. The strain which this role induces does not make the life of the foreman or brigadier an altogether happy one, although it is compensated for in part by the privileges which attach to membership in the Soviet labor aristocracy.

The sharpest sources of stress and tension in the Soviet factory derive from the sacrifices demanded of the rank-and-file workers. A distinction must be made between the labor aristocracy of brigadiers, Stakhanovites, and highly skilled workers on the one hand, and the mass of unskilled and semi-skilled labor on the other. The labor aristocracy enjoys substantial privileges which are not shared by the ordinary worker. The monthly earnings of a Stakhanovite may be five to ten times those of an unskilled worker. The Stakhanovite receives special bonuses and perquisites; he has a first lien on new housing, and he is at the top of the workers' priority list when space is assigned in rest homes and vacation resorts. The Soviet industrial system is arranged to give maximum encouragement to the bellwethers of production.

The treatment of the rank-and-file unskilled or semi-skilled laborer who barely succeeds in meeting his norm is quite different. Earnings are fixed at a level hardly more than adequate to sustain productive efficiency. There is constant pressure to increase output norms. In reporting on their life in the Soviet Union, former Soviet workers complain of low wages, poor food, and inadequate housing. They grumble about the number of compulsory deductions from pay — the obligatory state loans, trade-union dues, and special assessments for various organizational purposes. They tend to be bitterly critical of Stakhanovite records, which they describe as arranged performances to enforce a speedup and which are usually accompanied by increases in output norms without corresponding increases in pay. Workers, they assert, have no freedom to express their real grievances. Trade unions are dismissed as creatures of the Party and of factory management. Complaints are loud about labor discipline and the excessively severe penalties for tardiness and absence from work.

Yet there are also mitigating circumstances. The demand for skilled labor is great, and the more ambitious workers have opportunities to take special courses or receive instruction which will enable them to upgrade their qualifications. The shortage of labor serves to temper labor discipline, and the laws against lateness and absenteeism are not always rigidly enforced. Some workers leave their jobs despite the decree against unauthorized departure, and their new employers, who may be in desperate need of labor, sometimes prefer not to ask too many questions. Foremen occasionally find ways of arranging supplementary compensation when the plight of the worker is desperate.

Despite such administrative loopholes, the lot of the ordinary Soviet worker is far from an attractive one. While real wages have substantially improved in recent years compared with the depths reached during World War II, they remain very low compared with the West, and they probably have yet to match the level attained in the Soviet Union itself during the NEP or even the mid-thirties. The Fifth Five Year Plan, announced at the Nineteenth Party Congress in October 1952, promises an improvement, but the emphasis which the plan places on heavy-industry construction and militarization makes any spectacular advance in living standards highly unlikely. The prospect for the rank-and-file worker during the next years is, at best, one of gradual amelioration of his sacrifices. It is not a vista calculated to enlist enthusiastic and whole-souled devotion to the regime. Nor does it produce organized mass protest. If the reports of Soviet escapees are to be trusted, the dominant attitude of ordinary Soviet laborers is one of resigned apathy. They bear what they must because there seems to be no other alternative.

The tensions in the Soviet factory reflect the pressures under which its personnel operates. Forced draft industrialization exacts its toll. The burdens which it imposes are felt in some degree at every level of the factory hierarchy. They generate substantial dissatisfaction, but there is no available medium through which cumulative grievances can find organized expression. The calculated mixture of incentives, indoctrination, and repression which the regime has installed in the factory appears adequate to hold discontent in check and to maintain the drive for increased output.

Chapter 16

Controls and Tensions
in Soviet Agriculture

The peasantry is the Achilles heel of Soviet Communism. Despite more than a third of a century of intensive effort, the Soviet regime has yet to succeed in capturing the positive allegiance of the mass of its peasant population. Although controls in the countryside have been greatly tightened since collectivization and the possibility of organized resistance to the regime's dictates has been virtually eliminated, a smoldering resentment remains. It is visible in the apathy with which the rank-and-file collective farmer performs his assignments in the *kolkhoz*, and also in the great difficulties which the regime has encountered in increasing collective-farm output. It was made dramatically manifest in the early days of the Nazi occupation, when spontaneous peasant efforts to dissolve the collective farms erupted in many places and were checked only by the decision of Nazi administrators to retain the kolkhozes because of their utility as food-collecting instrumentalities. The reports of former peasants among the Soviet non-returners reflect an almost universal hatred of the collective-farm system. The young peasant soldiers who have fled from the Red Army since the end of World War II register much the same negative attitude. Though their testimony can be discounted as not necessarily representative, the reservoir of rural discontent on which it draws gives every evidence of being genuine and widespread.

The Soviet Regime and the Peasantry

The gulf that divides the regime from the peasantry has been deepened by collectivization. The world of the peasant is bounded by his profound attachment to the land. When he is established on his own property, he obstinately resists being swept into the anonymity of the collective. When he is landless or has only dwarf holdings, his revolutionary aspirations take the form of a hunger for land. The small garden plots assigned to kolkhoz households for individual use represent a grudging concession on the part of the Soviet authorities to this deep-seated urge. Yet the very limits and restrictions within which they must be operated only feed the fires of frustration. The collective farm remains a symbol of bondage to the state rather than an independent way of life with which the average peasant can identify.

The cleavage between the regime and the mass of collective farmers has been accentuated by the failure of collectivization to bring about a marked improvement in the standard of living of the average peasant. It is conceivable that the peasantry might have reconciled itself to the destruction of many of the traditional institutions of peasant life if collectivization had opened up a vista of expanding material welfare. While collectivization has provided a modicum of benefits for a relatively narrow stratum of collective-farm chairmen, brigadiers, and other members of the kolkhoz aristocracy, these rewards have not been shared with the great majority of ordinary kolkhozniks.

In essence, collectivization has functioned as a device by which the major sacrifices of the program of rapid industrialization have been imposed on the peasantry. Through the large-scale compulsory deliveries which the collective farms make to the state at nominal prices, food has been siphoned from the countryside to feed the rapidly expanding population in the industrial centers. The residual supply remaining on the collective farms has rarely been sufficient to provide more than a minimum subsistence for the average collective farmer. Although the burdens of industrialization have not been confined to the countryside, they have weighed less heavily on the urban population. The priority accorded to supplying major industrial centers has helped to draw peasant labor into industry. It has also left a heritage of bitterness among collective farmers, who see their interests sacrificed to advance a program that offers them little in the form of immediate benefits.

Communist attitudes toward the peasantry have long represented a curious combination of dependence and hostility. The dependence has been coerced by the necessity of winning and consolidating power in an overwhelmingly peasant country. The hostility and distrust remain as an ineluctable legacy from Marx. They derive from the conviction that the petty-bourgeois aspirations of the peasantry make it a natural enemy of any form of collectivism. The peasant left to his own devices is a man of property with a stubborn devotion to his own land and a hatred of those who would take it from him. In Lenin's words, "Small-scale production gives birth to capitalism and the bourgeoisie constantly, daily, hourly, with elemental force, and in vast proportions." [1]

The strange amalgam of hostility and dependence characterizing the Communist attitude toward the peasant is reflected in Soviet agricultural policy. When the regime operates under the apparent necessity of wooing or winning peasant support, concessions to the peasantry are forthcoming. When it feels powerful enough to disregard peasant sentiment, opposition is brushed aside, and the Communist leadership ruthlessly enforces its demands on the peasantry. While the pendulum of policy has swung back and forth with the regime's changing assessment of its own position, the secular trend has been in the direction of ever-tightening agricultural controls and the mobilization of peasant resources to support the vast industrialization effort.

The Development of Soviet Agricultural Policy

The course of development of Soviet agricultural policy illustrates this tendency. The peasant revolution of 1917–18, which involved the expropriation of the landlords' estates and their division among independent peasant households, was fully sanctioned by early Soviet legislation. But this was primarily a tactical expedient. As Lenin observed in 1919, "In October 1917 we seized power *together with the peasantry as a whole.* This was a bourgeois revolution, inasmuch as the class war in the rural districts had not yet developed . . . the real proletarian revolution in the rural districts began only in the summer of 1918." [2] In carrying on this struggle, the major enemy was identified as the kulak, or rich peasant, while the major support on which the Bolsheviks relied were the so-called "Committees of Poor Peasants." The middle peasants were treated as a vacillating force whom the Bolsheviks could not afford to alienate. Lenin frequently urged his followers to refrain from coercion in dealing with them. [3]

In practice, the pressures of Civil War drove Soviet authorities to seize grain wherever they could lay hands on it. Little distinction was made among different social strata of the peasantry in carrying out the requisition policy. The response of the peasants to this type of forced confiscation was what might be expected. Peasants reduced their plantings to meet only their own consumption needs, did their utmost to conceal their reserves from the requisitioning authorities, and occasionally responded to seizures by violent attacks on the food collectors. The catastrophic decline in production caused severe food shortages in the cities as well as in many rural areas. Grumbling mounted as food became increasingly scarce, and the Bolsheviks stood in danger of completely alienating the countryside. The Kronstadt revolt in March 1921 and the peasant rising in Tambov and other provinces in the winter of 1920–21 marked the height of the crisis. Even though the Bolsheviks ruthlessly punished the participants in these disorders, they also concluded that a change of policy was imperative.

The New Economic Policy, which was introduced in 1921 and lasted until 1927–28, marked a reversion to the policy of concessions to the peasantry. A tax in kind replaced compulsory requisitioning, and peasants were free to dispose of their surpluses after satisfying their fixed obligation to the state. Although the title to land remained in state hands, the tenure of the peasant in the land was guaranteed by law. Peasants were permitted considerable freedom in leasing additional land and employing hired labor, practices which had been prohibited under War Communism. The peasant was given an incentive to produce, and a considerable revival in agricultural output soon followed. Peasant home consumption increased substantially, and a general improvement in the living standard of the countryside was visible.

If the concessions of the NEP were received with considerable satisfaction by the peasantry and contributed to its partial reconciliation to the regime, they raised more troublesome problems for the Communist leadership. While Lenin was adamant in justifying the necessity for the NEP, his defense did not extend beyond defending it as a strategic retreat which gave the Soviet regime an opportunity to consolidate its position and to prepare the way for the next leap forward toward socialism. The NEP unleashed tendencies which appeared to challenge the basic premises of Communist ideology and strategy. As Lenin himself observed when the NEP was first introduced, "We must not shut our eyes to the fact that the replacement of requisitioning by the tax means that the kulak element under this system will grow far more than hitherto. It will grow in places where it could not grow before." [4] The entrenchment of a substantial class of independent peasant proprietors could only be viewed with alarm by a Party which had been taught that the kulak was the prime enemy in the countryside and that the nationalization of the land was a prelude to the spread of large-scale socialist agriculture.

The agricultural pattern that crystallized under the NEP raised still other difficulties. As the rural population increased, the average size of peasant holdings declined. The retention of the scattered strip system of farming and the lack of draft animals and modern implements resulted in inefficient farming. The new peasant farm units placed a smaller proportion of their output on the market, both because home consumption mounted and the scarcity and high price of consumer goods offered peasants few inducements to sell their surpluses. The unfavorable terms of trade between rural and urban areas mirrored the dilemma which the regime faced in dealing with the peasantry. In order to stimulate agricultural output and to entice the peasants to part with a larger share of their production in a free market, it was necessary for the regime to make consumer goods available at relatively favorable prices. If they were not available, the peasants tended to curtail their output, to increase their consumption, and to hoard such surpluses as they accumulated.

The regime's decision to embark on a program of rapid industrialization, with major emphasis on the expansion of heavy industry, greatly sharpened this dilemma. The implication of this decision was clearly that consumer goods would be scarce and high-priced and that the regime would have little to offer the peasants in the way of incentives to increase their output or to dispose of their surpluses. At the same time, it was imperative that a large supply of grain be available at low prices, both to feed the expanding industrial population and to provide exports to pay for imports of machinery and other essential industrial items. With the regime committed to a program of accelerated, large-scale industrialization, it soon became apparent that this objective could not be realized within the framework of the NEP. The ruling group therefore determined to shatter the NEP relationships. Inevitably they were driven toward a revival of the practice of compulsory requisitions which had proved so disastrous during the period of War Communism. The policy of concessions to the peasantry was terminated, and a new era of open warfare loomed.

The first victims were the kulaks, the more prosperous peasants on whom the regime had to depend heavily during the NEP to provide surpluses for urban consumption. The efforts of the kulaks to withhold grain from the government because of their dissatisfaction with the low prices offered by the state were met with what Stalin described as "emergency measures . . . methods of public coercion." [5] In plain language, force was employed to seize the kulaks' stores. As the kulaks fought back, the regime intensified its offensive. In 1929 it launched the policy of eliminating the kulaks as a class. Under the banner of this slogan, approximately a million peasant families were deprived of their farms and property and sent into exile or forced labor.

In order to replace and expand the grain surpluses which the kulaks had produced and to avoid the difficulties which had attended compulsory requisitioning under War Communism, the regime turned confidently to collectivization and mechanization. Soviet agriculture was to be reorganized around two types of large-scale production units, the *sovkhoz*, or state farm, and the *kolkhoz*, or collective farm. Initially, great hopes were placed in the sovkhozes to provide a quick substitute for the kulak output. The sovkhozes were visualized as great grain factories which would be completely mechanized with tractors and combines, which would be operated by skilled agricultural technicians and workers, and which would serve the peasants as socialist models of large-scale farming and advanced technique. Beginning in 1928 a number of huge new state farms were organized on free land in the southeastern, eastern, and southern regions of the USSR. Difficulties quickly developed. The land allotted to the grain sovkhozes was usually semi-arid, full of weeds, and sparsely settled. Crop failures were common because of drought. The soil required intensive cultivation and weeding, but seasonal labor to perform these operations was difficult to obtain and was not particularly efficient. Combines and tractors were not effectively utilized. Skilled operators and repair facilities were lacking. Combines became clogged with weeds and were put out of commission. Tractors broke down and could not be mended. Because of the vast expanse of the sovkhozes, supervision was difficult under the best of circumstances, and inexperienced managers had great difficulty in providing the necessary skillful leadership. The grandiose expectations which were centered on the sovkhozes met bitter disappointment. At the Seventeenth Party Congress in 1934 Stalin openly acknowledged the "discrepancy" between "the enormous sums the state has invested in the state farms with the actual results they have achieved to date." [6] The decision was made to subdivide the large farms into smaller, more manageable units, and a halt was called on their expansion. Since the early thirties the state farms have accounted for a minor part of the total Soviet agricultural output, though they remain of some importance in certain highly specialized branches of agriculture.

The original plan for the establishment of kolkhozes, or collective farms, contemplated a relatively slow tempo of development. By 1932 the crop area included in collective farms was expected to embrace about 36,000,000 acres, compared with 298,000,000 acres to remain in individual holdings.[7] This relatively modest objective was apparently dictated by the shortage of mechanical power. Until tractors and combines could be provided in large numbers, there appeared to be little advantage in rushing ahead with wholesale collectivization. Meanwhile, such tractors, combines, and other farm machinery as were available were pooled in so-called MTS or machine-tractor stations, which were designed to serve the needs of a group of neighboring collective farms and to make possible maximum utilization of equipment.

The Drive for Collectivization

Toward the end of 1929 the policy of gradual collectivization was suddenly reversed. In a series of speeches and decrees, Stalin gave the signal for a rapid acceleration of the collectivization program. It was no longer necessary, he claimed, to wait until tractors and combines were produced in large quantities. "A tremendous expansion of the crop area" could be achieved simply by merging individual holdings and by tilling waste land, field boundaries, and virgin soil.[8] The land of the kulaks would be absorbed into the new collective farms, and this additional "sweetening" would serve as an extra inducement to make the poor and middle peasants wish to join.

Behind the move to intensify the rate of collectivization was the realization on the part of the Party leadership that most of the peasants were opposed to the new kolkhozes. As long as the regime relied on persuasive measures and voluntary affiliation, progress was painfully slow. By October 1929 only 4.1 per cent of the total number of peasant households had organized themselves into kolkhozes. When the signal came from the Kremlin that speed was essential, the whole machinery of Party and government was mobilized to force the peasants to join.[9]

The use of pressure tactics yielded a quick statistical triumph. The proportion of peasant households enrolled in collective farms mounted to 58.1 per cent in March 1930.[10] But as reports accumulated that the peasants were slaughtering their cattle and draft animals in order to avoid confiscation and that the new collective farms were paper organizations to which the peasants refused to contribute their labor, the leaders of the regime began to realize that they had won a Pyrrhic victory. On March 2, 1930, Stalin again reversed course with the publication of his famous article, "Dizziness from Success." [11] In this and subsequent pronouncements, he blamed misguided local Party and Soviet authorities for excesses in forcing the pace of collectivization. Stalin's article was interpreted by many peasants as a *laisser-passer* entitling them to withdraw from the kolkhozes. The mass exodus which followed reduced the percentage of peasant households in the kolkhozes from 58.1 in March to 23.6 in June 1930. In the Central Black Soil region, where 82 per cent of the peasants had been reported as collectivized in March 1930, only 18 per cent were left in May.[12]

Despite this setback, the campaign for collectivization was resumed in the fall of 1930. This time more subtle means of "persuasion" were combined with the old reliance on force and threats. Discriminatory taxation was imposed on individual peasants, while those who joined the collective farms were offered certain forms of tax alleviation as well as the advantages of sharing in the credits, machinery, seed grain, and other privileges and preferences which were promised to the kolkhozes. The regime was now adamant in insisting on entry, and efforts to avoid collectivization were increasingly hazardous and difficult. By the middle of 1931, 52.7 per cent of all peasant households had been collectivized. The proportion increased steadily over the next years, amounting to more than 90 per cent in 1936 and 96.9 per cent in 1940.[13]

The collectivization crisis of the early thirties exacted a terrible price.[14] The liquidation of the kulaks involved the uprooting and exile of millions of peasants and robbed the countryside of its most efficient and enterprising element. The slaughter of livestock and draft animals inflicted a wound on the Soviet economy from which it took nearly a decade to recover. The disorganization of work in the new collective farms contributed to the disastrous harvests of 1931 and 1932. Despite the drastic decline in crop yields, the authorities were ruthless in enforcing their demands on the countryside, and near famine conditions prevailed in many rural areas. Motivated by an overriding compulsion to feed the rapidly growing industrial centers and to provide supplies for export, the regime "contracted" with the kolkhozes to obtain grain and other items in amounts determined exclusively by the regime's needs and quite unrelated to the problem of keeping the members of the kolkhoz alive. An unknown number of peasants, variously estimated at from one to several million, died from starvation in these hungry years. The "contracts," by which obligatory deliveries to the state were enforced, were in effect a revival of the compulsory requisitions of War Communism. Although the substitution of a relatively small number of collective farms for millions of peasant households greatly facilitated the state's food collection activities, the large-scale expropriations of the early thirties offered the collective farmers little impetus to produce. The regime again found itself faced with the problem of fashioning incentives to stimulate output.

Beginning in 1933 the procurement system was revised. Fixed deliveries based on acreage planted (or supposed to be planted) were substituted for the largely arbitrary assessments which had previously been made in the guise of "contracts." The new system provided inducements to increase production. Since the obligations to the state were definite and any surplus which the kolkhoz accumulated was distributed to its members in proportion to the workdays which they earned, the self-interest of the membership was served by an expansion of output.

As this stimulus took effect and as the disorder of the early days was overcome, the performance of the kolkhozes improved substantially. The harvests of 1933, 1934, and 1935 registered yearly gains. Although there was a sharp drop in 1936 as a result of drought, the 1937 harvest yielded a bumper crop. During the next two years, production declined but still remained above the output of the NEP years.[15]

During the mid-thirties, the kolkhozes went through a process of consolidation and stabilization. After the bitter friction of the first phase of collectivization, the regime succeeded in imposing its controls, and a precarious *modus vivendi* with the peasantry was arranged. In exchange for obligatory deliveries to the state at very low prices, the collective farmers received certain minor concessions. Each peasant household was granted a small garden plot adjacent to its dwelling and was also permitted to own a few cattle, sheep, and goats, as well as an unlimited number of fowl and rabbits. Any surplus which the collective farmers achieved out of kolkhoz earnings could be sold at prices prevailing in the free market rather than at the low prices fixed for delivery to the state. The principles of remuneration embodied in the Collective Farm Charter of 1935 were designed to reward skill and productivity. The collective farmers were thus provided with individual incentives to increase their production within the framework of the burden which they collectively shouldered.

While these concessions were welcomed by most of the peasantry, they did not necessarily reconcile them to the collective farm yoke. The demands of the state were great, and the procurement plan had to be met regardless of whether the harvest was good or bad. In years of poor crops, the plight of the collective farmers bordered on desperation, and even when crops were good, the standard of living of the average collective farmer was rarely much above a minimum level of subsistence. Despite the fact that the Collective Farm Charter called for payments to collective farmers which reflected their output, egalitarian tendencies frequently prevailed in the distribution of kolkhoz income, and the incentive to work hard on the collective farm operated with only limited effectiveness. Most collective farmers preferred to pour their energies into their own garden plots. They performed their assignments on the collective farm without spirit and without enthusiasm.

Though the attitude of the peasants toward the collective farms remained largely negative, from the point of view of the regime collectivization marked a triumphant step forward. As an accompaniment of collectivization and mechanization, a substantial migration of rural labor to the new industrial centers was achieved without impairing the output of the countryside. Even more important, collectivization, after overcoming its initial difficulties, provided a greatly improved system for ensuring the urban food supply. The collective farms were an infinitely more efficient food-gathering device than the millions of small farms which they replaced. Instead of trying to collect taxes in kind from twenty-five million peasant households, each with its developed techniques of evasion, the regime could now largely limit its procurement activities to a quarter of a million collective-farm units. From the administrative point of view, this represented a vast improvement and simplification. Moreover, evasion was rendered difficult by the intimate participation of machine-tractor stations in the harvesting of crops of many collective farms. The MTS themselves functioned as procurement agencies, since they collected fees in kind for their services, while they also operated as an unparalleled local intelligence service to check on the performance records of the collective farms they served. The dimensions of state procurement steadily mounted.[16]

As the Soviet authorities consolidated their ascendancy in the countryside, they intensified their demands on the collective farmers. In 1939 a new campaign was launched to tighten control of the collective farms. Investigation revealed that more than two and a half million hectares of land had been unlawfully diverted from the collective farms to private garden plots and that many so-called collective farmers had only a nominal attachment to their kolkhozes and spent most of their time on their own gardens. The joint Party and governmental resolution of May 27, 1939, "On Measures toward Safeguarding the Collectivized Land from Being Squandered," was designed to put an end to these abuses.[17] A survey to check the size of all garden plots was ordered, so that land stolen from the collective farms could be reclaimed. Severe penalties were provided for those farmers found in unlawful possession of such land. A minimum number of workdays was prescribed for each member of the kolkhoz regardless of sex. The USSR was divided into three zones, and the minimum for each was fixed respectively at 100, 80, and 60 labor days. Nonfulfillment of these minima was to be punished by expulsion from the kolkhoz and loss of private garden plots. A joint Party and governmental resolution of April 13, 1942, subsequently raised the minima to 150, 120, and 100 labor days and provided a specific allocation of labor days which had to be worked during different seasons of the year.[18]

Meanwhile, efforts were also made to stiffen work discipline and to provide additional inducements for increased productivity. On August 1, 1940, Soviet agricultural authorities were ordered "to put an end to the intolerable practice that in some kolkhozy, MTS, and sovkhozy, kolkhozniki and the workers of the MTS and sovkhozy, instead of starting work at 5–6 o'clock, report for harvesting work at 8–9 o'clock and stop work in the field before sundown." [19] A government decree of December 31, 1940, first introduced in the Ukraine and later extended to other areas, provided a premium system to encourage output in excess of planned goals. Under this system, kolkhoz brigades exceeding their plan were to be rewarded with a certain proportion of the surplus which they produced. This was to be made available either in kind or in the form of a cash equivalent.

At the same time, the regime made further demands of the peasantry. In 1940 the basis for computing crop deliveries to the government was shifted from the actual acreage planted to the amount of tillable land in possession of the kolkhozes. This change in the method of assessing compulsory deliveries was accompanied by a substantial boost in the amounts which the collective farms were required to yield to the state. While this measure was probably influenced by the pressure to accumulate reserves against the contingency of war, its effect on the collective farmers was onerous and sharpened their resentment of the burdens which the state imposed on them.

World War II and Postwar Developments

The impact of World War II on Soviet agricultural production was critical. In the first years of the war the Nazis occupied a large part of the richest and most productive land in the Soviet Union. The regime attempted to compensate for this loss by substantially increasing the production of food stuffs in Siberia and Central Asia, but despite these efforts and the encouragement of urban workers to cultivate vegetable plots, food shortages were frequently desperate. Though the basic needs of the armed forces and essential industry were met by drawing on reserves and Lend-Lease aid, malnutrition accounted for many civilian casualties, and in besieged localities such as Leningrad there were few families whom starvation passed by.

Despite the disorganization of war, the kolkhoz remained the basic form around which Soviet agriculture was organized. In areas occupied by the Nazis, many kolkhozniks hopefully looked forward to the dissolution of the collective farm system. These expectations were disappointed when the Nazis determined to retain the great majority of the kolkhozes because of their convenience as food-gathering devices. Disappointment was succeeded by complete disillusionment as the Nazi requisitions became increasingly burdensome and many villages began to experience the full brunt of Nazi atrocities. The patriotic sentiment aroused by Nazi brutality led many of the kolkhozniks in occupied areas to identify their fate with the survival of Soviet power. While the Soviet authorities continued to be regarded as oppressors, they were, as some of the kolkhozniks are reported to have remarked, "at least ours." In nonoccupied areas, similar patriotic impulses narrowed the gap between collective farmers and the regime. As the armed forces drained the kolkhozes of manpower, the women, old men, and children who replaced them worked all the harder because they were bound to the front by the knowledge that the fate of husbands, brothers, and sons depended on them. The reservoir of patriotism on which the regime was able to draw buttressed the wartime effectiveness of the kolkhoz as a procurement mechanism.

Another effect of the war, however, was to weaken the fabric of kolkhoz controls. In areas abandoned by the Nazis, the kolkhozes usually had been stripped of their cattle and draft animals, and only the most primitive farm implements remained. Collective farmers utilized the general confusion and disorder to enlarge their garden plots at the expense of the kolkhoz. In the reoccupied areas farms usually had to be reorganized from the ground up, and the shortage of supervisory personnel, draft animals, and mechanical power heightened tendencies toward individual self-help. In nonoccupied as well as reoccupied areas, collective farmers were under a powerful incentive to pour maximum effort into their own garden plots rather than into the communal enterprises of the kolkhoz. With food scarce, prices skyrocketed on the free market. Any surpluses from the garden plots could be readily bartered at advantageous rates for the possessions of the hungry population of the towns. Collective farmers who were in a position to do so used the war emergency to accumulate stores of goods as well as substantial hoards of currency. Within the framework of the collective-farm system, a lively revival of individual enterprise found spontaneous expression. While the war still raged, little was done to curb these tendencies. Indeed, rumors were rife in the villages (and were apparently tolerated by the regime) that the end of the war would see a fundamental revision of the kolkhoz system and a new charter of freedom for the peasantry.

These sanguine expectations met a sharp rebuff. The history of Soviet agricultural policy in the post-World War II period is essentially a record of tightening control over all kolkhoz activities. The opening gun in this postwar campaign was fired on September 19, 1946, with the publication of a joint resolution of the Party Central Committee and the Council of Ministers, "On Measures for the Liquidation of Violations of the Charter of the Agricultural Artel in the Collective Farms." [20] The brunt of the resolution was directed against the "plundering" of collective-farm property which had taken place during the war as a result of illegal enlargements of house and garden plots. Other abuses were also listed. As a result of the inflation of the administrative staffs of the kolkhozes the resolution charged, "Grafters and parasites frequently hide themselves on useless, artificially invented jobs, avoiding productive work . . . and live at the expense of the labor of those collective farmers who work in the fields and tend the cattle." [21] Local Party and governmental officials were accused of squandering collective farm property "by forcing the management and the chairman of the collective farms to issue them, free of charge or at low price, property, cattle, and produce belonging to the collective farms." [22] The principles of the Collective Farm Charter were being violated by excluding collective farmers from "participation in the business of the collective farms . . . The matter has reached such a point of outrage," the resolution piously proclaimed, "that the chairmen are appointed and dismissed by the district Party and government organizations without any knowledge of the collective farmers." [23]

A special Council on Kolkhoz Affairs was established on October 8, 1946, to put an end to these abuses and to restore order on the collective farm front.[24] This council was headed by A. A. Andreyev, a member of the Politburo, and was composed of important Party officials, agricultural administrators, and heads of collective farms. Operating through its own field inspection service of controllers, the council reached down from the center through the *oblasts* (regions), from which it supervised the regular agricultural agencies charged with kolkhoz administration.

The Council on Kolkhoz Affairs was given a broad charter. It was to enforce collective farm rules, to prevent the alienation of collective-farm land or property, to strengthen discipline in the kolkhozes, to regulate the relations between the kolkhozes and the MTS, and to see that the kolkhozes fulfilled their obligations to the state. Subject to the consent of the Council of Ministers, the Council on Kolkhoz Affairs was authorized to issue directives to all governmental agencies concerned with kolkhoz life. As a result of its activity, *Pravda* asserted, some fourteen million acres of illegally appropriated land were restored to the kolkhozes.[25] Measures were also taken to reduce padded administrative staffs. In the two years following the issuance of the September 1946 decree, an official Soviet agricultural organ claimed, some 535,000 members of kolkhozes were shifted from administrative to productive work and another 213,000 were removed from kolkhoz payrolls because they had no real connections with the kolkhozes.[26] Despite this apparently substantial achievement, complaints about bloated administrative staffs continued, and on September 14, 1948, new measures were ordered to deal with this endemic disease of kolkhoz bureaucracy.

While the leaders of the regime utilized the Council on Kolkhoz Affairs to tighten administrative control of the kolkhozes, they also sought to reinvigorate Party controls in rural areas. At the February 1947 plenum of the Party Central Committee, Andreyev called for a mobilization of Party organizers to strengthen Party authority in the kolkhozes and machine-tractor stations. After the plenum, trusted Communists from urban areas were sent in substantial numbers to serve as assistant directors of political affairs in the MTS. From this vantage point, a vigorous campaign was launched to expand the network of MTS and kolkhoz Party organizations. Despite this effort, Party representation in rural areas remained thin. Although the number of kolkhoz Party units tripled between 1939 and 1949, approximately 85 per cent of the kolkhozes were still without primary Party organizations.[27] At the Seventeenth Congress of the Ukrainian Communist Party in September 1952, L. G. Melnikov, the first secretary, reported that only 138,054 members and candidates, or 17.7 per cent of the total in the republic, were engaged in agricultural pursuits.[28]

In the postwar years, determined efforts were also made to reduce the private property of kolkhozniks to a minimum and to discourage them from diverting their energies from the kolkhoz to their own private plots. The 1947 monetary reform struck a particularly heavy blow at the hoards of currency which some collective farmers had accumulated. The rate of taxation on income from sources other than the collective farm was substantially increased in 1948 and raised again in 1950 and 1951. Holders of garden plots who owned cows, sheep, and poultry had to deliver increasingly large percentages of their output of meat, milk, eggs, and other products to the state.[29]

At the same time, the system of remuneration within the collective farm was revised to penalize laggards and to reward the productive. The seven-category system of classifying and compensating labor was replaced in 1948 by a nine-category system.[30] Under the new arrangement, income differentials were substantially widened, and a number of less-skilled kolkhoz jobs which had previously been paid at relatively high rates were reclassified into less well-paid categories. Kolkhozniks who exceeded their plans were rewarded with credits of additional workdays in proportion to the percentage of overfulfillment. Failure to reach planned goals was punished by deductions of workdays. Thus, incentives and penalties were combined in order to raise the output of kolkhoz labor.

A somewhat similar scheme was adopted in 1949 in connection with the launching of a three-year plan to increase communal livestock herds on kolkhozes and state farms. Collective farms which succeeded in building up their herds to the minima prescribed by the plan were rewarded with a 10 per cent reduction in their delivery quota of animal products to the state; those kolkhozes which failed to meet the new requirements were compelled to deliver an additional 10 per cent above their normal quota.[31]

The postwar drive to reëstablish effective control over the kolkhozes was also accompanied by a campaign to replace the *zveno* (literally, link) or small team by the much larger brigade as the basic unit of agricultural production. During the early and middle thirties, the brigade had been the officially approved form of organizing kolkhoz labor. Toward the end of the thirties, there was an increasing tendency to break down the brigades into *zvenya* or teams of a dozen or so workers who concentrated on working a small plot from the sowing through the harvest. Originally, the zveno was used in connection with technical crops such as sugar beets and cotton where a great deal of hand labor was required, but in the late thirties it spread rapidly to grain farming. At the Eighteenth Congress of the Party in 1939, Andreyev, the agricultural spokesman of the Politburo, strongly endorsed the zveno system. He argued that "the collective farmers working in large brigades are not held personally responsible for the quantity and quality of their work . . . the more the work on the collective farm is individualized, that is, performed by teams or separate collective farmers, and the greater the material encouragement of their labour, the more efficient it will be as regards crop yields and stock raising." [32] During the war and immediate postwar years, the zveno system was widely heralded as the most efficient method of organizing kolkhoz labor. The loss of tractor power during the war and the consequent necessity of relying on hand labor contributed to strengthening the position of the zveno system.

Suddenly, in one of those sweeping reversals in which Soviet history is embarrassingly rich, the zveno system was repudiated. On February 19, 1950, an unsigned article in *Pravda*, entitled "Against Distortions in Collective Farm Labor Organization," explicitly condemned Andreyev for his advocacy of the zveno system, criticized the use of the zveno in grain farming as obstructing the effective use of tractors, combines, and other machinery, reasserted the importance of the brigade as the basic form of organizing kolkhoz labor, and indicated that the zveno system would be retained only temporarily for the cultivation of sugar beets, vegetables, and certain other intensive crops "inasmuch as production of these crops is not yet adequately mechanized." [33] The appearance of this authoritative pronouncement was followed on February 25 by the publication of a letter in *Pravda* by Andreyev in which he confessed his errors and promised "to rectify them in deeds." [34]

This unusual spectacle of the use of a Politburo member as a whipping boy to signal a change in policy pointed to the importance of the issues at stake in this seemingly minor conflict over methods of organizing kolkhoz labor. Behind the attack on the zveno system, as Lazar Volin has indicated, was the apprehension "that the small zveno unit might eventually supplant not only the brigade but also the kolkhoz itself." [35] As the *Pravda* article put it, "Substitution of teams for brigades would signify the splitting of a single large-scale collective unit into small cells, scattering the energies and reserves of the collective farm, and a return from advanced technology and collective forms of labor to individual, manual labor. It would mean shaking the very foundations of large-scale collective socialist agriculture." [36] The fear of the disintegrative potentialities of the zveno system was reinforced by the difficult control problem which it presented. The zveno system required a much greater number of politically reliable leaders than the brigades, and such leadership was in short supply in rural areas. From the point of view of the regime, the kolkhoz could be more effectively controlled through a few trusted brigadiers who were amenable to Party influence than through a large number of zveno leaders whose interests were identified with the rank-and-file collective farmers.

The replacement of the zveno by the brigade was closely linked with the kolkhoz merger movement which was launched almost simultaneously. On March 8, 1950, N. S. Khrushchëv, who succeeded Andreyev as the Politburo's agricultural spokesman, used the columns of *Pravda* to signal the opening of the new campaign. In calling for the amalgamation of contiguous small kolkhozes into larger units, Khrushchëv listed a number of benefits which the regime hoped to attain. The mergers, he claimed, would facilitate mechanization and the adoption of the most advanced agricultural practices. They would yield increased production and higher income for collective farmers, greater farm surpluses, and presumably, larger deliveries to the state. They would also make possible a substantial reduction in administrative expenditures and the selection of outstanding managers and agricultural specialists to direct the new kolkhozes.

One of the paramount objectives of the merger campaign — left unstated by Khrushchëv — was the regime's desire to tighten its control over the collective-farm structure. The merger of small collective farms resulted in a substantial increase in the number of kolkhozes with primary Party organizations and an intensification of Party influence. The reduction in the number of collective-farm chairmen meant that those who were retained were likely to be the most politically reliable, as well as technically proficient. The regime appeared headed toward the consolidation of a managerial corps in the kolkhozes which would be increasingly isolated from the rank-and-file farmers and which would function as an effective state instrument to extract maximum output from them.

The merger campaign inaugurated by Khrushchëv in the spring of 1950 rapidly gathered momentum. By the end of the year, Minister of Agriculture I. A. Benediktov reported that the number of kolkhozes had been reduced from 252,000 to 123,000. In October 1952 Malenkov indicated that only 97,000 were left.[37] In many cases, however, the amalgamation was "legal" rather than real, and actual unification of operations remained to be carried out. In some areas, including Leningrad *oblast*, the size of garden plots was substantially contracted, to the consternation of many kolkhozniks.[38]

As the merger campaign intensified, more grandiose aims unfolded. In a speech delivered in January 1951 and published in *Pravda* on March 4, Khrushchëv proposed the construction of collective-farm settlements or agro-cities around which the new collective farms would be organized. He also suggested that private garden plots be reduced in size, be located on the outskirts of the new settlements, and be tilled in common.[39]

This apparently authoritative pronouncement, however, was soon repudiated. The next day, March 5, *Pravda* announced that "through an oversight in the editorial office . . . an editorial note was omitted in which it was pointed out that Comrade N. S. Khrushchëv's article was published as material for discussion." [40] Soon thereafter, G. A. Arutyunov, the first secretary of the Armenian Party, stated that the proposal to relocate collective farmers in agro-cities was opposed to Party and Soviet government policy. The scheme to reduce private garden plots was also pronounced "unacceptable" and "contrary to the collective farm statutes." [41] At the Nineteenth Party Congress, Malenkov declared:

Some of our leading workers, especially in connection with the merging of the smaller collective farms, were guilty of a wrong, narrow, utilitarian approach to questions of collective-farm development. They proposed the hasty, mass resettlement of villages to form big collective-farm towns, the scrapping of all the old farm buildings and the farmers' homes and the setting up of big "collective-farm towns," "collective-farm cities," "agro-cities" on new sites, regarding this as the most important task in the organizational and economic strengthening of the collective farms. The error these comrades make is that they have forgotten the principal production tasks facing the collective farms and have put in the forefront subsidiary, narrow, utilitarian tasks, problems of amenities in the collective farms. Amenities are undoubtedly of great significance, but after all, they are subsidiary, subordinate, and not principal tasks and can be solved successfully only on the basis of developed common production.[42]

As this statement clearly implies, the first priority of the regime is to increase collective-farm output. The heightened control over the kolkhozes which the merger movement makes possible is designed to achieve that objective.

The Organization of the Kolkhoz

The formal organizational structure of the kolkhoz remains unaffected by the merger movement. Theoretically, the highest authority in the kolkhoz is the general meeting of working members over sixteen years of age. The Collective Farm Charter of 1935 authorizes the general meeting to elect a chairman, a board of managers, and an auditing commission to check kolkhoz accounts. It also provides that the general meeting shall:

Confirm the program of annual production, the estimate of revenue and expenditures, the building program, the standards of normal output, and the remuneration rates in terms of labor days;
Confirm the contract with the machine-tractor station;
Confirm the annual account of the management . . . ;
Confirm the size of various funds to be put aside and the amount of produce and money to be distributed per labor day;
Confirm the rules of internal organization governing the conduct of the business of the artel.[43]

Official Soviet publications hail these powers as an indication of the impressive extent of "kolkhoz democracy." In reality, they are largely nonexistent. Formally, the chairman is "elected" by the kolkhoz, but the general meeting has no alternative except to ratify a candidate who is designated or approved by the district Party and governmental authorities. Frequently, the chairman is an outsider who has had no previous connection with the kolkhoz which "elects" him as its leader. The board of managers which the general meeting of the kolkhoz "elects" ordinarily represents a slate designated by the kolkhoz chairman. The charter expressly provides that the members of the auditing committee must be approved by the executive committee of the district Soviet (*raiispolkom*).

The reiterated use of the verb "confirm" to describe the powers of the general meeting is deliberate. The kolkhoz cannot reject the production plan of the government; it can only "confirm" it. Similarly, deliveries to the state, arrangements with the MTS, provisions for the establishment of various kolkhoz reserve funds, and the fixing of output norms and principles of remuneration are all determined by higher authorities. The duty of the kolkhoz general meeting is not to decide these matters but simply to execute the directives which are handed down to it. With the very substantial increase in the size and membership of the new amalgamated kolkhozes, the role of the general meeting is likely to become even more innocuous. "Kolkhoz democracy" in practice is merely another variant of the technique of mobilized participation and assent which the modern totalitarian state utilizes to maintain the fiction of unanimity.

The responsibility for day-to-day management of the kolkhoz is centered in the chairman. According to the model charter, the direction of kolkhoz affairs is vested in a board of managers of from five to nine members who are elected by the general meeting for a period of two years. The chairman of the kolkhoz also serves as the chairman of the board of managers and is required to convoke a meeting of the board "not less than twice a month to discuss the current business and to make the necessary decisions." [44] On the recommendation of the chairman, the board of managers elects a vice-chairman from among its own membership to assist the chairman in discharging his managerial responsibilities. Brigadiers and managers of livestock farms are appointed by the board of managers for a period of not less than two years. An accountant may be appointed by the board of managers from among the members of the kolkhoz or hired from outside. All orders for payment must be signed jointly by the accountant and the chairman or vice-chairman of the kolkhoz.

Chart VII represents the organizational structure of a typical kolkhoz. While there are minor variations from this pattern depending on the size and character of the enterprises associated with the kolkhoz, in broad essentials most collective farms conform to it. The board of managers ordinarily consists of the chairman, vice-chairman, the leading brigadiers, and one or two Party-oriented rank-and-file collective farmers who are added to provide a flavor of "kolkhoz democracy." The actual power resides in the chairman and the leading kolkhoz administrators whom he recruits to assist him.

One of the persisting problems in kolkhoz administration is the constant tendency to inflate the managerial apparatus. Legally, expenditures on administrative and service personnel are limited to 3 per cent to 8 per cent of the annual accumulation of workdays.[45] The allowable percentage decreases as workday accumulations mount. In spite of this decree, the padding of administrative payrolls has long been a characteristic of kolkhoz life, and the repeated campaigns to check it have rarely enjoyed more than temporary success. An official 1947 study of the distribution of earnings in collective farms in six regions showed that the share of income going to administrative and service personnel increased from a range of 7 to 10 per cent in 1940 to 12 to 18 per cent in 1945.[46] Despite the claim that administrative expenditures were drastically reduced as a result of the joint Party-government resolution of September 19, 1946, two years later a new decree published on September 14, 1948, again complained of "unnecessary positions of secretaries, timekeepers, production

CHART VII
The Structure of a Typical Kolkhoz

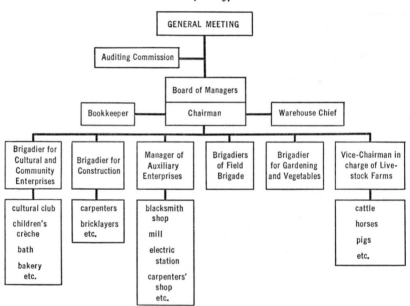

Adapted from K. P. Obolensky, *Upravlenie Delami v Peredovykh Kolkhozakh* (The Management of Affairs in Leading Kolkhozes; Moscow, 1949), p. 15.

managers, coachmen of the kolkhozy executive boards, and other workers."[47] One of the proclaimed goals of the 1950 merger movement was the reduction of administrative overhead. A year later, criticism again began to be aired in the Soviet press that administrative expenses were not decreasing as anticipated.[48] If past experience is any guide, the struggle to contract the kolkhoz bureaucracy is likely to be both protracted and of dubious effectiveness.

For many years, one of the greatest weaknesses of the collective farms has been the shortage of qualified managers. The rapid turnover in kolkhoz management, which has been frequently deplored in Soviet official publications, has reflected the seriousness of this problem. While the merger movement has substantially reduced the corps of collective-farm chairmen, it has also greatly complicated their burdens and supervisory responsibilities. The need for specialized training is far greater than ever before. Of the sixteen thousand collective farms in the Ukraine in September 1952, only three thousand were headed by agricultural specialists.[49] To repair this deficiency, special training courses for kolkhoz managers have been organized. Under a revised plan, which was put into effect in 1951, three-year agricultural courses were established to prepare new kolkhoz chairmen, and one-year courses were instituted to raise the qualifications of chairmen in office. Graduates of the three-year courses are to be awarded the title of junior agronomist, while graduates of the one-year courses are to be styled technicians and organizers of kolkhoz production. In addition, three-year courses are also available for collective farmers who wish to become brigadiers, managers of livestock farms, or otherwise improve their qualifications. Enrollment in such courses, however, involves no release from regular kolkhoz duties.[50] While it is too early to appraise the effectiveness of these measures, they appear to represent an ambitious and serious effort to raise the standards of kolkhoz management. If carried out as planned, they are likely to have pronounced influence in lifting the level of kolkhoz production.

The system of remuneration which the regime has installed in the collective farms guarantees management a privileged position in the kolkhoz hierarchy. The compensation of a collective-farm chairman is based on a complicated formula. His basic pay consists of a flat number of workday credits per month and a monthly cash payment in rubles. The number of basic workday credits which he receives depends on the size and character of the farm and on his seniority. Thus, the nature of the farm may entitle him to seventy-five to one hundred workday credits per month. After three years' service, he receives a 5 per cent increase, after four years 10 per cent, and if he remains chairman five years or longer, he is entitled to an additional payment of 15 per cent. His basic cash income rises with the annual cash income of the kolkhoz. If the cash income of the kolkhoz is between 50,000 and 100,000 rubles, the chairman is entitled to draw 125 rubles a month. As the kolkhoz income mounts, the monthly cash salary of the chairman increases correspondingly. If the kolkhoz overfulfills its plan, the chairman receives a substantial bonus which ranges from 10 to 25 per cent of his basic workday credits and 15 to 40 per cent of his cash income. Conversely, if the kolkhoz underfulfills its plan, the chairman is penalized by a deduction of 1 per cent of his workday credits for each percentage of underfulfillment. In no case, however, may the deduction exceed 25 per cent.[51] As a result of the application of this formula, the earnings of collective-farm chairmen vary widely. Since the value of the workday credit in kind and cash differs substantially from kolkhoz to kolkhoz, the variations in the income of collective-farm chairmen may in some cases be quite extreme. Even when the kolkhoz chairman is relatively poorly off in terms of official earnings, his strategic position in the kolkhoz enables him to supplement his income by extra-legal tapping of kolkhoz resources. The columns of criticism in official Soviet publications are filled with examples of collective-farm chairmen whose search for a good life has led them into extracurricular activities of this type.

The compensation of subordinate managerial personnel follows the pattern applicable to collective-farm chairmen. The vice-chairman of the kolkhoz ordinarily receives from 80 to 90 per cent of the salary of the chairman. The bookkeeper is paid at the rate of 60 to 80 per cent of the chairman's salary.[52] The basic earnings of brigadiers range from thirty to sixty workday credits per month. Supplementary workday credits are provided for plan-overfulfillment, and penalties are imposed for under-fulfillment.[53]

All workers in the kolkhoz are hierarchically graded and operate under the same system of incentives and penalties which applies to management. By a decree of the Council of Ministers of April 19, 1948, all jobs in the kolkhoz are allocated to one of nine categories. Workers in the highest skilled category receive five times as much compensation as those in the lowest category. Every job has its approved norms of daily output, and a value is assigned to the job in terms of workday credits. Workday credits should not be confused with actual days of labor performed. Thus, a skilled tractor driver may receive as much as three to five workday credits for each day of labor performed, while the kolkhoz water boy may earn only a half of a workday credit for his daily stint. Supplementary workday credits are provided for brigades which exceed their production plans, while deductions are made in the event that the plan is not fulfilled. Since these supplementary credits are divided among the members of the brigade in proportion to the annual total of workdays which each accumulates, they necessarily favor the workers in the higher categories. In addition, special bonuses may be awarded to kolkhoz Stakhanovites, and they may also be honored with the title of "Heroes of Socialist Labor" or with the Order of Lenin. Since 1947 however, the privileges which these awards formerly carried have been sharply restricted.[54]

The system of remuneration used in the kolkhozes places rank-and-file members in a markedly disadvantageous position. Except for such returns as they derive from their garden plots, they have no fixed income on which they can count. The value of the workday credits which they earn represents merely a residual claim on a share of kolkhoz income after all other prior claimants are satisfied. The kolkhoznik is last in a long line when the income of the kolkhoz is distributed.

The state exercises a first lien on kolkhoz output. The "first commandment" of Soviet agriculture demands that government requirements be met, regardless of all other considerations. Each kolkhoz must deliver to the government specified quantities of crops and animal products at low fixed prices, and these assessments cannot be evaded. The rates of delivery run 15 to 25 per cent higher for collective farms not served by machine-tractor stations. Kolkhozes that receive MTS assistance are required to make added payments in kind for services rendered. In addition, they must make special provision for the MTS tractor drivers who are ordinarily recruited from kolkhoz members. Tractor drivers are paid partly in cash by the MTS and partly in workday credits by the kolkhozes. Since their work is considered highly skilled, they ordinarily receive three to five workday credits for fulfilling their daily tasks and are entitled to liberal bonuses if they exceed them. In contrast with other members of the kolkhoz, they are also guaranteed a minimum payment in grain for each workday credit which they earn. If the tractor brigade fulfills its plan, the guaranteed grain minimum amounts to 3 kilograms or 6.6 pounds per workday credit. Otherwise, the minimum is 2 kilograms per workday.[55] Since these minima are considerably in excess of average kolkhoz earnings, the tractor drivers enjoy a protected position which is denied to the ordinary collective-farm member.

After obligations to the state are fulfilled, the kolkhoz is next required to set aside part of its output for various communal purposes. Mandatory "set-asides" include seed for the next year's sowing, feed for livestock, and emergency reserves. In addition, the kolkhoz may also reserve part of its income for construction and repair and for various educational and cultural purposes. It must also dispose of part of its output in order to obtain cash to meet its fixed ruble commitments to kolkhoz administrative personnel.

After all of these claims have been satisfied, such grain and cash as remain in the possession of the kolkhoz are available for distribution to its members. The amount which each member receives depends on the number of workday credits which he has accumulated and on the value of the workday. Thus, if 100,000 kilograms of grain and 100,000 rubles are available for distribution and 100,000 workday credits have been earned by all members of the kolkhoz in the course of the year, the value to be assigned to each workday is one kilogram of grain and one ruble in cash. The farm member who is credited with 300 workdays during the year will receive 300 kilograms of grain and 300 rubles as his share of kolkhoz income. The earnings of the kolkhoznik depend not merely on the task which he performs and on the skill with which he discharges it, but also on what remains in the kolkhoz treasury after all prior commitments have been fulfilled.

Since these commitments tend to absorb the greater part of kolkhoz income, the amounts ordinarily available for distribution to rank-and-file collective farm members are very small indeed. Soviet official sources usually confine their reports of the income of collective farmers to the experience of so-called "leading" collective farms. In such "showcase" enterprises, according to one recent account, payments ranged from 4 to 7.8 kilograms of grain and 5 to 7 rubles per workday credit.[56] Former Soviet peasants who have fled to the West claim that such earnings are quite exceptional and beyond the wildest dreams of most kolkhozniks. According to their reports, even in relatively good harvest years in the post-World War II period, the value of a workday credit ran as low as 200 to 400 grams of grain and 50 kopeks (half a ruble) and rarely exceeded one to two kilograms of grain and three to five rubles. At the Seventeenth Congress of the Ukrainian Communist Party in September 1952, L. G. Melnikov, the first secretary, cited 1951 data for two "millionaire" collective farms which corresponded with these upper limits. In one, the value of the workday credit was 2 kilograms of grain and 3.10 rubles, in the other 1 kilogram of grain and 1.60 rubles.[57] Because of the low average worth of the workday credit, the system of incentive payments exercises only a limited attractiveness for the rank-and-file kolkhoznik.

The great majority of collective farmers depend heavily on their garden allotments to eke out a subsistence income. So great is the temptation to divert energy from kolkhoz labor to intensive cultivation of the private garden that the regime has been forced to erect a series of barricades to discourage such diversion. Collective farmers who fail to accumulate the minimal workday credits which are prescribed by law are subject to expulsion from the kolkhoz and to loss of their garden allotments. The income tax on the private earnings of collective farmers has been steadily increased in recent years. Additional burdens are imposed on the private economy of collective farmers in the form of compulsory deliveries to the state. If the collective farmer possesses a cow, he is required to deliver approximately forty-five kilograms of meat and over three hundred liters of milk per year. Although the regime has thus far refrained from outright abolition of the private garden plots, it seeks to make the private economy of the collective farmers increasingly burdensome and unattractive and to force kolkhoz members to look to kolkhoz labor as their primary source of support.

The Soviet ruling group views the collective farms as merely a transitional stage of development in Soviet agriculture. Ultimately, as Stalin made clear in his "Economic Problems of Socialism in the USSR," it is anticipated that the collective farms will be "elevated" to the level of national property and will be deprived of their right to sell such surpluses as they accumulate. Instead, the output of collective farms will go directly to the state, which will undertake to provide manufactured goods in exchange. "Such a system," Stalin stated, "will facilitate the transition from socialism to communism . . . it will make it possible to include the basic property of the collective farms and their products in the over-all system of national planning." [58] While Stalin made no specific reference to private garden plots, presumably they too are headed for extinction. Stalin's article provided no timetable for the installation of the new order. While he suggested that "it should be introduced without particular haste," he also declared that "it should be introduced steadily, unwaveringly, without hesitation, step by step reducing the sphere of operation of commodity turnover and increasing the sphere of operation of product exchange." [59] Complete nationalization of the rural economy thus represents the final goal of Soviet Communism.

Controls in Soviet Agriculture

The system of controls which the regime has installed in Soviet agriculture follows a pattern which is characteristic of other sectors of Soviet life. Broadly speaking, there are three main lines of control: administrative, Party, and police. The administrative chain of command runs from the USSR Ministry of Agriculture through the republics and *oblasts* to the agricultural sections of the executive committees of the district soviets. These district agricultural sections in turn are responsible for the collective farms and MTS in their area. In addition, the Council on Kolkhoz Affairs exercises broad powers with respect to collective farming. It supervises the enforcement of kolkhoz legislation, drafts new legislation, and serves as a complaint bureau with respect to collective farm administration.

At the local level of collective-farm administration, the district procurement organization, the agricultural sections of the executive committees of the district soviets, and the machine-tractor stations play key roles. All function under the direction of the Ministry of Agriculture. The task of the district procurement agency is to make certain that all kolkhozes in the area meet their delivery quotas. The district agricultural section, which is ordinarily directed by an agronomist, is responsible for the production and work plans of the collective farms. It provides technical "advice" on crop rotation and farm practices, directs the sowing and harvesting plans of the kolkhozes, approves work quotas and remuneration rates, and exercises a general oversight over all aspects of kolkhoz management. When MTS are available in the district, detailed supervision is delegated to the machine-tractor stations, and the district agricultural section functions chiefly as a control agency and a link with higher authority.

The MTS constitute the most powerful instrument of state control in the countryside. They provide pools of tractors and other agricultural machinery to perform such kolkhoz operations as lend themselves to mechanization. Since payment for their services is made in kind, they also operate as a procurement agency. In addition, they are vested with extensive powers to plan and direct kolkhoz activities. By the very nature of their assignment, they become intimately involved in kolkhoz operations and are thus in a peculiarly strategic position to guard state interests and to prevent the evasion of obligations on the part of the kolkhozes which they supervise.

Ostensibly, relations between the MTS and the kolkhoz are regulated by a contract which is negotiated between them. In fact, the agreements follow a standard form prescribed by higher authority, and no important divergence of principle is permitted locally. The contract specifies in detail the work which the MTS will perform and the time when it will be done. It also registers the agreement of the kolkhoz to put specific farm practices into effect and to provide and pay necessary manpower for tractor brigades as well as to supply field brigades which will synchronize their work with the activities of the MTS crews. Each MTS operation is ordinarily paid for in kind at a variable rate based on the estimated crop yield per acre. If the yield exceeds the plan, the rate of payment increases. In the event that the MTS fails to fulfill its obligations to the kolkhoz, the rate of payment may be lowered. Payments in kind for MTS services are substantial, amounting in 1939 (the last year for which data are available) to 19.2 per cent of the total grain crop.[60]

The organization of the MTS reflects the nature of their activities. In principle, the rule of one-man management prevails. The director is appointed by the USSR Minister of Agriculture and legally can be dismissed only by him. The assistant director for political affairs is a Party appointee and is responsible in his Party capacity to the Party district committee. It is his duty to supervise the work of the MTS Party and Komsomol organizations, to develop propaganda and agitation activities among MTS workers and in neighboring kolkhozes, to stimulate Party and Komsomol organizations in the kolkhozes which the MTS oversees, and to assist the director in enforcing agreements with the kolkhozes and in searching out deficiencies in their operations. The senior agronomist, who also usually bears the title of assistant director, is responsible for the organization of kolkhoz production and for the preparation of instructions on crop rotation, depth of plowing, and agricultural practices. The senior engineer-mechanic, who also frequently enjoys the title of assistant director, is charged with the distribution, maintenance, and repair of tractors and other mechanical equipment. The chief bookkeeper keeps MTS accounts, certifies the completion of work assignments, and approves all withdrawals from the State Bank to meet MTS payroll or other obligations. The chief of fuel procures fuel and lubricants and regulates their consumption in accordance with planned allocations. Each of these leading members of the managerial staff heads a department concerned with his specialty.[61]

The field work of the MTS is performed by so-called tractor brigades, each of which is headed by a brigadier. The tractor brigades are manned by collective farmers who are temporarily attached to the MTS and who receive the major portion of their compensation from the kolkhozes in the form of workday credits with guaranteed grain minima for every workday accumulated. All other employees of the MTS are on the state payroll and are paid a base ruble salary in accordance with their qualifications. Premiums and bonuses are provided to reward plan-overfulfillment. In the case of the director, the annual premium may range from ten to twenty times his monthly salary.[62] The leading officials of the MTS are also entitled to free houses, garden plots, cows, and poultry.[63]

The employees of the MTS thus enjoy a sheltered position which is denied to kolkhoz members. They are protected from crop adversities and are guaranteed a fixed salary regardless of kolkhoz performance. Their interests are interlocked with the kolkhozes to the extent that their premiums depend on kolkhoz output. At the same time, their task is to exert constant pressure on the collective farms to increase their productivity and to take every measure to prevent the evasion of commitments to the state. These activities are hardly calculated to endear them to rank-and-file kolkhozniks. While most collective farmers are prepared to recognize the abstract benefits of mechanization, they see these benefits going not to themselves but to the regime and the rural aristocracy, of which the managing personnel of the MTS are leading members.

The administrative chain of command in the collective farms is paralleled by a Party chain of command. The secretary of the district Party committee (*raikom*) plays a key role in supervising the activities of all Party and Komsomol organizations in the kolkhozes and MTS of the district. He shares responsibility with the district agricultural administrators for the state of plan-fulfillment. It is his duty not only to assist them in fulfilling their tasks but to point out deficiencies in their work and to call these deficiencies to the attention of his superiors in the Party hierarchy. The secretary of the district Party committee ordinarily either recommends or approves the appointment of collective-farm chairmen and ratifies the Party members who are "elected" by the kolkhoz Party organizations to serve as secretaries. He is supposed to be in intimate contact with the affairs of all the kolkhozes under his jurisdiction, though it is apparent from accounts in the Soviet Party press that this requirement is frequently honored in the breach. A recurrent complaint against district committee secretaries, in the words of Khrushchëv, is "that they deal superficially with the collective farms, make only flying visits to the farms, do not study their economy thoroughly and substitute . . . 'pep talks' and reprimands in place of serious work with the personnel of the countryside . . . It happens not infrequently that the district committee learns belatedly and quite unexpectedly of a breakdown in the work of a collective farm." [64]

The difficulty which district committee secretaries encounter in making their control of the collective farms effective reflects the weakness of Party organization in rural areas. As late as 1949, only about 36,000 out of more than 250,000 collective farms had Party organizations.[65] While the number of kolkhoz Party units has undoubtedly increased substantially as a result of the amalgamation movement, Party membership is still spread thin in the countryside. Where Party organizations exist in the kolkhozes, they tend to be dominated by the management of the kolkhoz and usually consist of the collective-farm chairman, his deputy, the leading brigadiers, and perhaps a sprinkling of collective farmers in the higher skilled categories. In order to establish a kolkhoz Party organization, a minimum of three members is required. In the period prior to amalgamation, the average kolkhoz Party organization rarely had more than six or seven members. Where kolkhozes have less than three Party members, special Party-Komsomol groups are organized under the direction of Party organizers appointed by the district Party committee. If there are no Party members in the kolkhoz, Party work is assigned to the Komsomol organizations which exist in the great majority of kolkhozes.[66]

Party and Komsomol members in the kolkhoz are expected to take a leading role in the life of the kolkhoz. It is their responsibility "to occupy front-line positions in the battle for the harvest and for livestock productivity," to conduct agitation for increased production, to explain and defend Party and governmental decisions, to control the activities of collective-farm management, to secure rigid enforcement of the Collective Farm Charter and government decrees, and to instill devotion to the regime and its leadership.[67] These exacting requirements are sometimes only indifferently realized. To quote Khrushchëv again:

> There are serious shortcomings in the work of many Party organizations in the villages . . . Unfortunately, Party meetings are not always held regularly, and often they are poorly organized . . . on some collective farms there are, unfortunately, some Communists who work badly on the farm and spend their time making speeches and trying to lecture the collective farmers . . . Such Communists disgrace the lofty title of Bolsheviks.[68]

Because of the weaknesses and shortcomings of the kolkhoz Party organizations, the district Party secretaries rely heavily on the assistant directors for political affairs in the machine-tractor stations to make their control effective in rural communities. During the early years of the great collectivization drive, the MTS were used as a Party spearhead to penetrate the villages. Thousands of urban Party workers were colonized in the MTS. Specially selected Party organizers were designated to serve as chiefs of the MTS political departments (*politotdely*), which assumed leadership in the struggle to accelerate collectivization. These departments were originally independent of the district Party committees, and the overlap in their responsibilities generated rivalry and friction. In 1934, after the back of the resistance to collectivization was broken, the political departments were transformed into MTS primary Party organizations and brought under the direct control of the district Party committees. In 1950 the departments were revived in the western provinces of the Ukraine, Belorussia, Moldavia, and in the Lithuanian, Latvian, and Esthonian republics.[69] In these recently acquired or reacquired territories, where the Party was especially weak and the collective-farm economies still remained to be consolidated, the MTS political departments were again made independent of the district Party committees, and experienced Party organizers from the outside were brought in to head them and to intensify Party work in the kolkhozes.

In all other areas of the Soviet Union, the MTS assistant directors for political affairs remain subject to the direction of the district Party committees. From accounts in the Soviet press it would appear that the assistant directors for political affairs have been responsible for a substantial increase in the number of MTS Party organizations.[70] They have also helped strengthen the Party's hold on the kolkhozes, although the recurrent complaints of the backwardness of kolkhoz Party units suggest that the situation is still far from satisfactory to the Party leadership. Nevertheless, the assistant directors for political affairs in the 8,500 machine-tractor stations which dot the countryside constitute an imposing phalanx of Party officialdom, and together with the district and kolkhoz Party organizations, they provide an increasingly pervasive though still tenuous network of Party controls in rural areas.

Administrative and Party controls are supplemented by police controls. The Ministry of Internal Affairs (MVD) has its representatives in every district center, and the district procurator also functions as an agency of state control to enforce compliance with government regulations and to safeguard kolkhoz property. MVD surveillance is exercised through a network of informers who penetrate the collective farms, villages, and MTS of the area. Informers are expected to report criticism of the regime and all cases of misappropriation of kolkhoz or MTS property or other violations of government regulations which come to their attention. In addition, the MVD also encourages anonymous denunciations and accumulates dossiers on all important employees in the district. Where arrests appear warranted, the MVD may invoke its administrative powers to confine the offending culprit in a prison or a forced labor camp. The MVD works closely with the district procurator, who also has his own independent investigators to search out violations of government orders and decrees. The procurator may act on the basis of complaints or on his own initiative. In contrast with the MVD, the procurator prosecutes his cases in the ordinary courts. The actions of the procurator are commonly directed against unlawful extension of private plots, the stealing of kolkhoz or MTS property, the evasion of compulsory deliveries, and other forms of illegal activity. In serious cases, the penalty may extend to twenty-five years of forced labor.

Tensions in Soviet Agriculture

Despite this formidable array of administrative, Party, and police controls, the collective farm remains one of the weakest links in the Communist power structure. The word "kolkhoz" is used colloquially by Soviet citizens as a synonym of disorder, misery, and lack of initiative. With monotonous regularity, the same complaints appear again and again in the Soviet press, and they focus largely on the "backwardness" of many collective farmers and the abuse of power by collective-farm managements and agricultural authorities in the localities.

The fundamental "sin" of the kolkhoz in the eyes of the Party leadership is the survival of "individualistic psychology" among kolkhoz peasants. The collective farmers' "petty-bourgeois propensities" express themselves in a determination to utilize every available outlet to pursue personal interests in preference to the collective interests of the kolkhoz and the state. Official spokesmen on Soviet agriculture are loud in their denunciations of "idlers and slackers," "backward collective farmers" who "work at low pressure," and "work only enough to remain in the collective farm and retain the rights and privileges of the collective farmer." [71] There are constant attacks in the press against collective farmers who expend most of their energy on their private plots, who busy themselves with "private business," and pilfer collective-farm property. Despite repeated campaigns to extirpate the evil, accounts of unauthorized appropriation of collective-farm land continue. Thus, *Izvestiya* reports, "more than 20,000 instances of unauthorized appropriation of collective-farm lands were disclosed in the Altai territory in 1950. In four districts alone . . . 7,000 hectares of communal land have been misappropriated . . . Quite recently, when 99,300 collective farmers' lots were surveyed, it was found that they occupied 1,670 hectares too many." [72] Such examples are far from uncommon, and they apparently have a strange and alarming habit of reappearing after they have been theoretically eliminated. Where such phenomena persist, it would appear that collective-farm managements connive to conceal them from higher authorities or at least tolerate or remain indifferent to them. Although the evidence available is too fragmentary to justify any large-scale conclusions, it does suggest that in some instances at least collective-farm chairmen identify themselves with the interests of the farm membership and serve as a buffer against the state's demands. In such cases, it is also possible that the chairman's toleration may be purchased by bribes or even that the unauthorized expropriations may be limited to a clique within the collective farm which enjoys the chairman's favor.

The Soviet press documents numerous cases of corruption and other forms of abuse on the part of collective-farm managerial personnel and district agricultural and Party officials. These include squandering collective-farm resources on illegal bonuses, free meals, and festivities; embezzlement of communally owned cattle and other property; the illegal sale of surplus farm produce to favored individuals at below-market prices; padding administrative payrolls; and incurring and concealing excess administrative expenditures. When such practices occur on a large scale and over a protracted period, they are usually covered up by a system of mutual protection involving collective-farm managers and district Party and governmental officials.

In some instances, drastic action is invoked to check such abuses. After an investigation in the Altai territory, *Pravda* reported on April 19, 1952:

> Grigoryev and Nesterov, former secretaries of the Ust-Koksa and Sorokino District Party Committees; Gordeyev, Vice-Chairman of the Yaminskoye District Soviet Executive Committee; Suloyev, representative of the Ministry of Procurements for Sorokino district; Zinchenko, Secretary of the Ust-Kalmanka District Party Committee, and Baranov, Chairman of the Ust-Kalmanka District Soviet Executive Committee, all thrust their hands into the collective-farm pocket without the slightest prick of conscience, taking out dairy cattle and produce for a song and exchanging poor horses for pedigreed stud animals. For gross violations of the Collective Farm Statutes they have been expelled from the Party. Criminal proceedings are now being instituted against these pilferers of collective-farm property.[73]

While many such examples of pilfering can be cited from the Soviet press, Soviet sources usually imply that they represent relatively isolated instances. The testimony of former Soviet peasants, on the other hand, leaves the impression that collective-farm administration is honeycombed with bribery and corruption. Even if this impression be discounted as exaggerated, the widespread airing of cases of theft, embezzlement, and corruption in Soviet official publications and the tendency of punitive measures to increase in severity would appear to indicate that the abuses against which they are directed represent serious problems which are not easily solved.

The tensions which prevail in the Soviet countryside arise from deep-seated forces in Soviet life. The main burden of industrialization has fallen on the shoulders of the peasantry. The resentment which this inspires in the peasants merges with their traditional distrust of the city and the belief that they are being exploited by their urban masters. Many peasants feel that collectivization has largely robbed them of their independence and reduced them to a form of neo-serfdom in which the new Communist bureaucracy replaces the old landowners. The dynamic changes which the Soviet revolution has unleashed have also profoundly disturbed the equilibrium of traditional rural institutions. These strains are evident in family life, religious practices, adjustments to mechanization, and attitudes toward the Soviet regime. They receive their most dramatic expression in a gulf between peasant generations.

In analyzing the tensions which exist in the Soviet countryside, it is important to distinguish the different strata of Soviet rural society as well as to differentiate between the prosperity of the relatively few leading "model" kolkhozes and the generally low standards which are characteristic of kolkhoz life. The social gradations of the countryside are an outgrowth of the Soviet system of controls. At the peak of the Soviet rural social pyramid are the district Party and government officials — the district Party secretary, the chairman of the executive committee of the district soviet, the district procurator, the MVD representatives, the head of the district agricultural agencies, and others holding similar responsibilities. Only slightly below them in power and status are the directors and assistant directors for political affairs of the machine-tractor stations as well as the leading managerial personnel of the MTS, those occupying similar positions on state farms, and the chairmen of the collective farms of the area. The rural aristocracy may also be considered as embracing the agronomists and other specialists on the staffs of the MTS, state farms, and kolkhozes; the brigadiers and other representatives of management on the collective farms; and the village intelligentsia, consisting of soviet chairmen, Party secretaries, doctors, and school directors. Between the rural aristocracy and the mass of ordinary collective farmers at the base of the social pyramid, there are a variety of intermediate categories. These include the skilled workers who are regularly employed on the MTS staffs; the tractor and combine drivers who are supplied by the kolkhozes to the MTS; the kolkhoz Stakhanovites; and a relatively narrow stratum of skilled collective farmers whose annual accumulation of workday credits is well above the kolkhoz average.

As is perhaps to be expected, the burdens of collective-farm existence bear most heavily on the mass of rank-and-file collective farmers. It is here that grievances accumulate and maximum sacrifices are exacted. The picture of kolkhoz life which emerges from interviews with ordinary collective farmers who have fled to the West is grim and dark. Except in the "millionaire" kolkhozes, the yearly earnings of the farmers rarely provide more than a minimum subsistence, and in years of drought and bad harvests, even this minimum may not be attained. The pressure is always in the direction of increasing work norms; as the authoritative journal *Sotsialisticheskoe Zemledelie* (Socialist Agriculture) recently put it, "When work norms in force on collective farms are reviewed it is essential to raise them toward the level of productivity attained by leading workers so that lagging collective farmers may become the equals of the advanced ones." [74] Because earnings under the workday system are low, the farmers utilize every opportunity to supplement their kolkhoz earnings by work on their private garden plots. The struggle for survival is bitter, and in years of shortage there may be a high incidence of thefts of kolkhoz property and stealing of grain from the fields or the kolkhoz storehouse.

Since the end of World War II, informants report, the collective-farm villages have largely been emptied of men in the prime of life, except for returning war invalids. Women do most of the heavy work, and the elderly men who survive occupy various petty administrative posts. The younger men who were demobilized from the army after the end of the war frequently avoided returning to the villages and were absorbed by industry in the towns. A substantial proportion of those who did return sought and often found places in the collective-farm managerial stratum. The State Labor Reserve system continually drains off the youth of the villages, and those drafted for labor service ordinarily end up as industrial workers. Because of the unattractiveness of kolkhoz life, the kolkhoz chairmen face a constant problem of keeping the younger members from escaping from the villages. Theoretically, no member of the kolkhoz can travel beyond a defined area around his collective farm without a permit from the chairman, and no kolkhoz member can be accepted as a factory worker without a certificate from the collective-farm chairman that he has been released. But because of the shortage of industrial labor, these restrictions are not infrequently evaded, and the kolkhozes find themselves with a real scarcity of manpower.

The hatred of the older generation for the kolkhoz yoke is barely concealed behind an outer layer of sullen servility. For the elderly collective farmers, the period of the NEP still looms as the best period of Soviet rule. Memories of the "great hunger" of the early thirties and the exasperations generated by collective-farm controls contribute to a continuing hostility toward their Communist masters. The younger generation gives evidence of being more pliable. For some, the road to a new life lies in flight to the urban industrial centers. A few of the more ambitious utilize such channels of advancement as are open to them in the countryside and become part of the rural aristocracy or acquire skills which enable them to rise above the rank-and-file kolkhoznik. But the majority of those who remain in the kolkhoz as ordinary collective farmers are condemned to share the way of life of their elders; in greater or lesser degree, they also absorb their resentment. They continue to regard the kolkhoz as an instrument of exploitation. They watch the products of their labor disappear into state warehouses while they continue to eke out a bare, shabby existence. They see the kolkhoz run by outsiders who represent the regime rather than the kolkhoz membership. They note the visible state representatives in the kolkhoz, the MTS, and the district centers enjoying a standard of life to which they cannot aspire. Not infrequently, they also witness evidence of corruption among the officials who rule them, and such displays are hardly calculated to reconcile them to the sacrifices which these same officials require of them. They know that even the fields have ears, and that if they grumble too loudly, a trip to a forced labor camp may await them. They endure what they cannot change, but beneath the exterior of fatalistic resignation and apathy, a simmering discontent persists which may conceivably rise to plague the regime in some future crisis.

The tensions which pervade the rural aristocracy are of a different order. Unlike the rank-and-file collective farmers, its members have identified their fate with the survival of the regime or at least have enlisted for service in its control apparatus. Their grievances are not primarily economic. By ordinary Soviet standards, they live well. The privileges they enjoy mark them out from their rural neighbors. This is not to imply that the new Soviet intelligentsia embraces assignments to rural areas with enthusiasm. In a very revealing speech at a plenary session of the Moscow province Party committee, in December 1950, N. S. Khrushchëv declared,

> There are, it seems, a sort of sorry agronomists who have been graduated from the Timiryazev Agricultural Academy, agricultural institutes and technical schools, have received higher and secondary agricultural training, and work in Moscow as conductors, dispatchers, warehousemen, photographers, porters, waiters, etc. Some comrades proposed sending these people into the districts and to the collective farms and using them to advance agriculture. I think such "specialists" would be of no help at all. They are, to put it bluntly, deserters; deserters, because they completed studies at an educational institution and deceived the state, deceived the collective farmers who hoped for their help, while they prefer to set themselves up in Moscow at any work rather than go to work on the collective farms.[75]

The remarks of Khrushchëv provide an unintentional index of the low estate of the rural aristocracy and the difficulties which the regime confronts in recruiting talent to administer the kolkhozes.

For the rural administrators who accept the responsibilities which are placed upon them, the sources of tension are threefold: the pressures under which they operate, the distrust with which they are surrounded, and the instability of their position. As in all other areas of Soviet life, the rural administrator works under constant pressure from above to increase output and to fulfill and overfulfill planned goals for production and delivery to the state. Such pressure is always nerve-wracking, but it can become particularly acute in Soviet agriculture when the procurement demands of the state in years of drought and bad harvest spell serious food shortages and even semi-starvation in rural areas. The collective-farm chairmen and the local agricultural officials live in the midst of the misery which they are compelled to create. Even the most insensitive among them cannot be altogether indifferent to the suffering around them in years of short crops. Indeed, ex-kolkhozniks now in emigration report cases after the 1946 drought when collective-farm chairmen took it upon themselves to help the starving population by decreasing state deliveries and issuing grain from kolkhoz stores to those who were short of food. According to these same reports, the chairmen of the kolkhozes were arrested and sentenced to forced labor for illegally disposing of government property. The first commandment of Soviet agriculture is that state demands be fulfilled. As M. D. Bagirov, the first secretary of the Azerbaidjan Communist Party, declared at the Eighteenth Congress of that organization in May 1951, "The Party demands that an end be put to the erroneous consumer approach to problems of collective farming." [76]

The collective-farm administrators who divide their loyalty between the kolkhozes and the state and seek to mediate between them find themselves in a difficult position. From the point of view of the regime, there is only one test of the loyalty and efficiency of the rural administrator — his capacity to meet the procurement targets that the state establishes for him. The tensions generated by this pressure form an inescapable part of the environment in which the Soviet rural aristocracy functions.

Difficult strains are also created by the atmosphere of distrust which surrounds the rural administrator. Though Party and police controls are weaker in rural areas than in the cities and thin out perceptibly in remote and peripheral areas, they nevertheless exist. As elsewhere in Soviet life, they leave the administrator with a sense that he is not wholly trusted and that he is enclosed within a system of controls and surveillance. While he ordinarily adjusts to the system because he has no other alternative, there is a residue of resentment and disillusion which sometimes builds up into a feeling of alienation from the regime. Soviet administrators who flee to the West frequently point to such resentment as one of the important factors motivating their decision to escape.

The tensions of members of the rural aristocracy are accentuated by the instability of their positions. For many years, there has been a noticeably high rate of turnover among collective-farm chairmen and leading members of the district Party and governmental bureaucracy. This fluidity is explained not only by the problem which the regime confronts in recruiting able personnel for rural administrative assignments but also by the tendency of the more ambitious to escape to urban centers and by the regime's policy of utilizing its rural officialdom as scapegoats for the tribulations of the countryside. As in other sectors of Soviet life, the members of the rural official group have sought to combat this instability by entering into "family relations" with each other and forming mutual protection associations which are designed to insulate them from top control. In some instances, as has been noted above, these mutual protection associations have served as a cover for corruption and abuse of power by members of the rural aristocracy. In order to break up such groups, the regime has been forced to multiply its controls. Thus, a ceaseless tug of war takes place in which the rural officialdom seeks to stabilize its position while the leaders of the regime invoke countermeasures to make their control effective by accentuating the insecurity of the lower echelons of their own apparatus. The price of such insecurity is hidden bitterness and frustration.

Despite these sources of aggravation and despite the disaffection of individual administrators, the rural aristocracy as a group appears to identify its future with the survival and strength of the Soviet regime. Together with the privileged categories of skilled workers in the machine-tractor stations and the kolkhozes, it represents the firmest base of Soviet power in the countryside. Except in rare and isolated instances, it is not a channel for the expression of rural grievances but an instrument by which the power of the regime is projected into the rural communities. Short of a major crisis in which the authority of the ruling group is effectively challenged, it is likely to continue to buttress the prestige of the regime and to enforce its demands on the peasantry.

The discontent of the mass of collective farmers remains an important factor in Soviet life, but it is unlikely to become a vital revolutionary force except in a period of general upheaval. As long as the regime retains its firm grip on the system of agricultural controls, it is difficult to see how peasant disaffection can find an organized focus. The pulverizing force of the modern totalitarian machine cripples the will to resist and robs resistance of the hope of victory. The peasant aspirations for a new order in the countryside must await the downfall of Soviet totalitarianism.

Chapter 17

The Political Cohesiveness
of the Soviet System

A totalitarian system on the march often gives the impression of remorseless and overpowering strength. Its weaknesses become fully apparent only after its downfall. The Soviet regime has survived the arduous vicissitudes of more than a third of a century of revolution, war, and internal struggle. It has emerged from the ordeal as one of the two most powerful states in the world. Does this capacity to endure and expand signify that Soviet totalitarianism can avoid the fate of its Fascist and Nazi imitators? Have the Soviet leaders discovered a new formula of power which is likely to carry them from control of the present Soviet orbit to world domination? Or are there fatal weaknesses in the Soviet scheme of government which doom it to eventual extinction?

The political cohesiveness of the Soviet system cannot be measured with barometric precision. Strengths and weaknesses can be identified and trends and problems discerned, but the prediction of future developments remains a notoriously hazardous enterprise. The Soviet regime today is different in many respects from the political order that took shape in the first decade after the Revolution. The next decade, in turn, may bring changes which even the most prescient observer cannot now anticipate.

The pattern of the future is, nevertheless, contained in the present, even if only in embryonic form. During the period of Stalin's rule, the Soviet system of controls crystallized and hardened. It demonstrated its capacity to hold discontent in check and to enlarge and consolidate its effective monopoly of power. Does it promise long-term stability? Is it a personal instrument fated to disintegrate with the passing of its prime mover? Or does it possess an institutional cohesiveness capable of maintaining its forward momentum well beyond the life span of its creator? Any attempt to answer these questions demands an analysis of the pattern of Soviet controls, their capabilities and stresses, and the inner dynamics of Soviet society which they have sought to contain and direct.

The Soviet Control System

The system of rule which Stalin's successors inherit represents a legacy which they cannot easily renounce. He erected a structure of centralized, absolute authority in which unquestioned obedience to his dictates was a *sine qua non* of survival. He ruthlessly eliminated every known actual or potential competitor for supreme power and encouraged the development of a leadership cult in which his own god-like infallibility was an object of official worship. He developed a system of competing and overlapping bureaucratic hierarchies in which both the Party and the secret police, penetrating and watching each other, simultaneously pervaded and controlled the administration and the armed forces. He reserved his own ultimate authority to direct and coördinate the system by providing no point of final resolution for differences and conflicts among the hierarchies short of himself. He made a virtue out of the interplay of lines of authority by holding both controllers and controlled responsible for the fulfillment of plans and directives. He built a vested interest in confusion by utilizing the processes of mutual control and institutional rivalry to protect his own security.

While safeguarding his own personal domination against any possibility of challenge, Stalin was perforce compelled to give his authority institutional expression. The great bureaucratic hierarchies of the Party, the secret police, the armed forces, state administration, and industrial management respond to the directives of the Soviet ruling group, but these organizations cannot be dismissed as mere robots depending for their every movement on an impulse from above. They are power structures in their own right. Each of them represents a pool of functional competence on which the leaders of the regime must draw in order to make their purposes effective. Individual administrators may be expendable, but the apparatus as a whole is indispensable. Each of its specialized parts manifests the characteristics of bureaucracy everywhere. It seeks to transmute skill into influence and power. It views every decision from the vantage point of its own particular interests, and it strives to defend and expand the area of its own dominion. Behind the monolithic façade of totalitarianism, the plural pressures of professional bureaucratic power continue to find dynamic expression. They project into the future basic continuities which are all the more powerful because they have been embodied in institutional form.

One of the salient attributes of Soviet totalitarianism has been its ruthless determination in mobilizing human and material resources for the attainment of a dominating objective. In more specific terms, this has meant concentration on building the elements of military strength and constructing a heavy-industry base which would accelerate the rate of industrial growth and provide a modernized armament industry. This ruling priority has colored and affected every aspect of Soviet life. It has made the fulfillment of planned industrial targets the central preoccupation of every sector of the Party, police, and administrative apparatus. It has given the members of the managerial, technical, and scientific intelligentsia an increasingly significant role in the operational direction of the Soviet economy. It has resulted in a substantial increase in their prestige and in their access to the scarce material perquisites of Soviet society. It has also meant a general tightening of discipline and a corresponding strengthening of the repressive organs of the state to deal with the discontent and dissatisfaction generated by emphasis on a high rate of capital expansion. The unifying focus of the Soviet control system has been the harnessing of energies to serve the supreme purpose of building state power.

The techniques developed to enforce control represent a many-sided combination of indoctrination, incentives, and repression. The stress on indoctrination reflects the constant concern of the Soviet rulers with the problem of the loyalty of their subjects. All the resources of the Party, the Komsomol, the educational system, the instruments of mass communication, and the media of cultural life are utilized to instill devotion to the regime. Reliance is placed on the familiar totalitarian expedient of saturating the minds of the people with the propaganda themes which the regime is currently propagating. At the same time, the Soviet leadership seeks to preserve its monopoly of communication with its subjects by isolating them from the outside world and insulating them from exposure to any information which challenges the prevailing stereotypes of Soviet propaganda.

The substantive content of Soviet indoctrination is designed to induce the populace to identify itself with the regime and its leadership. In its effort to broaden its appeal to embrace all elements in Soviet society, the Kremlin employs a combination of patriotic and Marxist themes. Primitive nationalism and xenophobia are fused with the Communist faith in inevitable victory and the apocalyptic vision of a classless society. Speaking to their own people, the Communist leaders say in effect: "We live in the most progressive and democratic country in the world, the country in which the working class is enthroned in power. The outside capitalist world is decadent and disintegrating, while we advance from triumph to triumph. Under our leadership, the nation has been industrialized and transformed into a first-class power. Singlehandedly, we defeated the most formidable military machine in history — Hitler's Germany. The masses of the world look to us as an example, as a symbol of their hopes and aspirations, and as the agency of their liberation. The power of world Communism is growing. We have won a tremendous victory in China; Eastern Europe is bound to us by solid ties of friendship. We control the trade unions in France and Italy. Our strength is multiplying everywhere. We represent the wave of the future.

"We stand for peace and welfare. We should like to lighten the burden of sacrifices which we are forced to impose on our own people. We should welcome an opportunity to turn the energies of the nation towards tasks of peaceful reconstruction. But we cannot. We are surrounded by enemies. The capitalist masters of America are organizing a coalition against us. They threaten us with atom bombs. The destruction which they would visit on our people and cities would far exceed the dastardly atrocities of the Nazi barbarians. So we must continue to arm and make sacrifices to thwart their plans. We shall try to avoid war, but if they make war on us, we shall defeat them as we defeated the Nazis. Then the way will be open to the triumph of world Communism, and we shall begin to enjoy the fruits of our labors and usher in the classless society of our dreams."

In condensed, paraphrased form, this is the message which Soviet propaganda directs to the people. Varied in detail but constantly reiterated in its main themes, it beats upon the minds of the Soviet populace and even leaves its impress on those who think of themselves as enemies of the regime and deem themselves immunized against official propaganda. It exerts its maximum influence on successive generations of youth, on whom the regime depends to provide the *élan* which maintains the dynamic momentum of the system.

Through indoctrination the ruling group undertakes to breed a race of exemplary Soviet citizens who find "freedom" in conscious subordination to state purposes as they are formulated by the leadership. It insists on rigid orthodoxy in the ideological realm and unquestioning submission to the policies of the ruling group. The only officially approved outlet for fault-finding is the institution of "criticism and self-criticism," and this operates within rigidly prescribed limits fixed by state interests. Such ventilation of grievances as is permitted is consciously directed from above to give the leadership some index of popular dissatisfaction and of weaknesses in administration, to spur the bureaucracy to improve its performance, to give the masses a semblance of involvement in affairs of state, and to provide approved objects on which the dissatisfied can vent their wrath. Mass participation in criticism and in the elaborate network of elected soviets provides the popular façade of dictatorship. Soviet propaganda points to these engines of mass mobilization as final proof of the "democratic" character of the regime.

To the extent that indoctrination is effective, it conditions its victims to pour out their energies on behalf of the regime. But the Soviet leadership has found it expedient not to rely on indoctrination alone. Its qualified faith in the power of indoctrination is indicated by its tendency to put increasing reliance on extending the system of incentives and on strengthening the repressive machinery of the state.

The use of incentives as a technique of control has been strongly developed in recent decades. Material rewards, honorifics, and the lure of rapid promotion have been effectively employed to enlist the energetic and the ambitious in state service and to consolidate the loyalty of the elite to the regime. The system of income distribution and wage payments is designed to reward enterprise and productivity and to penalize sloth and inefficiency. Honorifics are freely awarded to outstanding workers; in some cases, these orders and awards carry substantial material perquisites. The Soviet system of compensation operates on two principles. In one of its aspects, it reflects the hierarchical structure of Soviet society and carefully grades payments in terms of skill, productivity, and responsibility. In another aspect, it takes on the character of a lottery and holds out impressive prizes for the innovator and the leading worker on the assumption that the existence of these outstanding prizes will serve as a lure and a spur to stimulate a general increase in efficiency and productivity.

The rapid rate of industrial growth in recent years has involved a high degree of upward social mobility for the Soviet-trained generation of administrative, technical, and scientific personnel. While this factor can be expected to decline in importance in the future, the regime has other resources at its disposal which it can utilize to create the same effect. One of the most ominous weapons in the totalitarian arsenal is the periodic use of the purge to accelerate mobility. The purge has at least three aims. It is designed to secure an apparatus which will be loyal to the leadership. It provides a flow of scapegoats for grievances which accumulate in the Soviet system. And it also keeps the gates of opportunity open for the coming generations whose devotion to the regime is crucial to its survival.

The Soviet system of power has been constructed around a functional rather than a hereditary elite. It is possible that the functional elite may take on hereditary characteristics, but as yet the process remains to be completed. The members of the elite can transmit opportunities to their descendants; they cannot guarantee that their heirs will inherit their status. The privileges of members of the elite inhere in the offices they occupy rather than in their persons. The rewards of high position are combined with great risks. There is constant circulation and no guarantee of permanency. The security of members of the elite depends on their ability to fulfill the demands which the leadership makes on them.

For most of the collective farmers and the mass of unskilled or semi-skilled workers, the Soviet system of incentives provides little more than a bare subsistence. The struggle to realize work quotas is a struggle for existence. The welfare services which the state furnishes in the form of educational opportunities, medical care, and social insurance are welcomed in so far as they are available, but even these are differentially utilized to reward so-called "leading workers" while leaving others with minimum protection. The brunt of the burden of industrialization and militarization is borne by the masses. In driving them to produce, the regime places heavier reliance on sanctions than on rewards.

In the Soviet armory of controls, repression plays a central role. Soviet society may be viewed as a continuum in which the enforced discipline which pervades the so-called "free" sector gradually shades into the extreme form of repression of the forced labor camp. The elements of compulsion which operate outside the forced labor camps exert a varying degree of pressure on virtually every Soviet citizen. The youths drafted for the State Labor Reserves are compelled to work for a number of years in the enterprises to which they are assigned and are subject to severe penalties if they abandon their jobs without official permission. The graduates of technical institutes and universities are subject to the disposition of superior authority and can be dispatched wherever their superiors see fit to send them. Labor operates under virtual military discipline. Travel is subject to severe restrictions. Certain categories of untrustworthy citizens are exiled to far places, and still others are denied access to the larger urban centers. The surveillance of the MVD extends into every major Soviet institution.

The atmosphere of mutual suspicion generated by such control gives a peculiar tone to Soviet social and business relations. The fear of denunciation breeds rigid orthodoxy, and a frank exchange of critical views becomes possible only among intimate, trusted friends. Even the many who manage to avoid any direct contact with the secret police live in its shadow and adjust their lives to the contingency that their words or acts may be subject to inspection and tale-bearing. The reliance on fear and repression as instruments of control has transformed the Soviet Union into a huge reformatory in which the primary difference between the forced labor camps and the rest of the Soviet Union is that inside the camps the regimen is much more brutal and humiliating.

The Soviet system of controls constitutes a complex pattern in which compulsion, incentives, and indoctrination each have their appointed place. The emphasis placed on one or another of these techniques varies with time and circumstance. The art of successful totalitarian dictatorship requires a capacity to gauge the endurance of the subject, to hold out a vista of hope and improvement when the situation threatens to become intolerable, to tap new sources of energy when the old are exhausted, to apply pressure when dangers are minimal, and to reverse course when catastrophe threatens. Stalin revealed himself as a past master of this type of manipulation. While never abandoning the substance of his authority and steadily extending his control of the key power positions in the Soviet state, he also demonstrated considerable skill in interrupting his steady march toward total power by periodic concessions and breathing spaces. By apparent reversals of policy, he gained time to consolidate his position and to reclaim support which earlier policies had alienated. He showed himself adept at diverting blame to his subordinates for mistakes and difficulties while reserving credit to himself for all major achievements and acts of clemency. He utilized alternating cycles of intensified repression and relative relaxation to entrench himself in power and to enlist the total energies of the nation in state service.

As Stalinism entered its mature phase of full-blown totalitarian development, its institutional characteristics tended to harden. The Party, police, military, and administrative apparatuses took on the character of rigid, bureaucratic hierarchies with the customary paraphernalia of titles, ranks, uniforms, and insignia associated with authoritarian political arrangements. The official ideology, which emphasized state service and was strongly infused with a nationalist content, congealed into a Procrustean conformity which brooked no challenge or criticism. Latter-day Stalinism sought to strengthen its foundations by invoking the traditional supports of authoritarianism — a conservative educational and family policy, an emphasis on the sanctity of legal commands and directives, and an arrangement with the Orthodox Church by which submission was purchased at the price of toleration of the practice of religious rites. Increasing stress was placed on the organic efficiency of the nation, on industrialization and militarization as a means of promoting it, and on a system of income distribution which was designed to contribute to it. The prerogatives of the elite were strengthened, and the power of the regime came to rest in the last analysis on the loyalty of the top layers of the Party, police, military, and administrative and industrial hierarchies.

Any effort to appraise the cohesiveness of this system must inevitably raise more questions than it can answer. It is obvious that the question of leadership is crucial. The role which Stalin discharged in maintaining a precarious balance among the different power structures of Soviet society is not easily filled. It remains to be seen whether Malenkov will be able to impose his authority on them and attain the position of undisputed supremacy which Stalin achieved. Under Stalin's aegis, his lieutenants worked together as a disciplined group for many years. It is possible that they may continue these working habits under Malenkov and that the unity of the ruling group will be maintained, particularly if its members feel themselves individually weak and collectively menaced by external danger. No outside observer is privy to the secrets of the Party Presidium, and the relationships among its members remain shrouded in mystery. But the historical experience with dictatorships suggests that the monolithic façade conceals a host of tensions and conflicts and that such rivalries are frequently most intense within the leadership group itself. If such rivalries find free expression, a purge of the ruling group would appear to be inevitable, and the reverberations of the struggle may be felt throughout Soviet society. The resulting disruption may serve as a powerful brake in checking the forward momentum of the Soviet regime.

The training of the Soviet leaders and their immersion in the Stalinist system of rule predispose them to utilize the pattern of controls that Stalin developed. Whether any one of them can manipulate the system with as great success as Stalin is another question. A weak successor may find himself confronted with autonomous centers of power in the Party, police, army, and administration which effectively resist coördination and discipline. Bureaucratic organizations have ways of developing wills and objectives of their own, and even the most skillful totalitarian Frankenstein may discover that the organizational monsters which he has nurtured can turn on their creator and destroy him.

While the death of Stalin points up possible divisive and disintegrative forces which may become manifest in the Soviet elite, it should not be forgotten that the members of the elite in the final analysis have a vested interest in the perpetuation of the Soviet system. They are, after all, its favored beneficiaries. While individual members may be alienated from the regime by particular experiences, as a functional group they identify with it. The regime turns for its basic support in three directions. It leans heavily on those who occupy the strategic positions in Soviet society. They include top administrative and managerial personnel, the senior officer corps, and the upper stratum of the artistic, literary, and scientific intelligentsia. In a somewhat wider sense, the administrative and managerial elite may be assumed to embrace plant directors and managers, chief engineers and technicians, directors of state farms and MTS, collective-farm chairmen, and even the workers' aristocracy of foremen, brigadiers, and leading Stakhanovites. In order to consolidate the support of these groups, who play key roles in the administrative structure, the Kremlin treats them as a privileged category, pays them well, and confers honor and prestige on them. It draws them into the Party and identifies them actively with Party affairs.

A second pillar of strength for the regime is the Party and, more especially, its inner core of functionaries for whom Party work is a full-time job which carries power and commands deference as well as material perquisites. The third basic strength of the regime is its repressive element, the officialdom of the MVD, whose authority extends into every corner of Soviet society, and who, like the Party functionaries, the officer corps, and the managerial elite, occupy a privileged status in Soviet society. It is not without significance that there have been relatively few defectors from the upper stratum of this privileged group.

The Grievances of the Elite

This is not to imply that members of the elite do not have their grievances and anxieties. The security of the totalitarian dictator is built on the insecurity of those who surround him. The threat of a purge is ever present, and even the highest Soviet dignitaries live in a milieu of surveillance and suspicion. There is always the fear that one may be toppled from the heights to the depths with dizzying swiftness, as the disappearance of Politburo member Voznesensky in 1949 bears witness.

The sources of anxiety of the members of the elite vary with their positions in the Soviet hierarchy. No sector of the elite is free from worry. Even the Soviet police organizations, whose task it is to watch others, are themselves subject to constant scrutiny and inspection through permeating Party controls. The top command of the MVD lives with the knowledge that even such powerful figures as Yagoda and Yezhov were eliminated in their time and that in both cases the disposal of the heads of the NKVD was accompanied by a purge of their entourage. Even though the secret police probably is the closest approximation to "a state within a state" which the Soviet system of government affords, the police officialdom is not immune from the anxiety that it creates for others. Its leading members become a tempting target for liquidation as they accumulate the unsavory secrets of the regime and build up the power which makes them a potential threat to the hegemony of the Soviet ruling group.

The Party apparatus shares the sense of insecurity which pervades the Soviet system. Enlarged responsibilities bring power, privileges, and perquisites, but they also entail burdens and hazards, with swift retribution for the first serious misstep. The functionary who wishes to survive and advance in the Party hierarchy must display a ruthless determination to meet the priorities which the regime establishes for him. He must possess an intuitive faculty which enables him to make a rapid adjustment to every change in the Party line and which sensitizes him to the precise configuration of power relationships within the Party. While the possession of these qualities contributes to a successful Party career, it does not necessarily guarantee it. Even the most adaptive Party careerist runs the risk of decapitation when the Party leadership seeks scape-goats for unanticipated difficulties or purges its senior leadership in order to create places for its younger cadres.

The circulation of the Party elite has both cohesive and corrosive consequences. It enlists the loyalty of those who are singled out for rapid advancement. It undermines the faith of those who feel their positions threatened. The aura of fear and apprehension created by the surveil-lance of the secret police penetrates the Party itself — not merely its rank-and-file but even its higher officialdom. No feature of the Soviet system is more widely resented, both in Party and non-Party circles, than the lack of trust which the system of institutionalized mutual suspicion sym-bolizes. Yet it has become an indispensable and integral part of the struc-ture of power on which the leadership depends to sustain its control of Soviet society. One of the strangest paradoxes of Soviet totalitarianism is that it cannot wholly trust even those upon whom it most strongly relies.

The officer corps of the armed forces shares this ambivalent status. Its material wants are relatively well cared for by the regime. It has been clothed in all the outer accoutrements of dignity and prestige — splendid uniforms, medals and orders, and special privileges which differentiate it from the rank-and-file. Yet its loyalty remains a subject of constant con-cern to the ruling group. Party and police controls permeate the armed forces. The professional officers, whether Party members or not, exercise their command responsibilities under the continuous surveillance of their *zampolits*, or Assistant Commanders for Political Affairs, as well as the plenipotentiaries of the Special Section of the MVD. While the great ma-jority of the cadre or professional officers probably adjust to these con-trols as an inescapable part of the environment in which they are com-pelled to function, this does not mean that control inspires affection. For-mer cadre officers of the Red Army who have escaped to the West express repeated resentment against both political officers and representatives of the secret police and assert that such attitudes are widely prevalent in the officer corps. The insecurity which such controls generate is a deter-rent to possible military conspiracy against the regime. It also leaves a residue of bitterness, frustration, and hostility that erodes the confidence of the officer corps and creates a gulf between it and the ruling group.

The administrative and economic bureaucracy is plagued by the same sense of insecurity which haunts other sections of the upper stratum of Soviet society. Like the army officers, the administrative, managerial, and technical elites are subject to Party and police supervision and inter-ference. The dilemmas which are peculiarly characteristic of the bureau-cratic and managerial apparatus arise out of its special responsibility for the fulfillment of planned economic goals. The overriding criterion in determining whether its members will survive and advance in the Soviet hierarchy is success in meeting or surpassing the targets of the plan. The harsh discipline of the plan creates its own unique hazards. The manager or bureaucrat who falls behind cannot point to extenuating circumstances, allegedly beyond his control, in order to justify his failure. As a result, Soviet management is under constant pressure to resort to a variety of "illegal" machinations in order to protect itself against the possibility of mishaps. While indulgence in such practices is often tolerated or overlooked by higher authorities as long as the substantive goals of the plan are fulfilled, the managers or bureaucrats who engage in them live with the constant knowledge that they are vulnerable to attack as law-breakers. They find themselves in an anomalous position where the choice appears to lie between violating the letter of the law and meeting the plan or obeying the detailed specifications of the law and failing to fulfill the plan. Either course involves risks, but on the whole, the first alternative presents fewer dangers than the second. Minor violations of regulations may be forgiven; nonfulfillment of the plan is a major disaster. The pressure to meet production targets is never ending, and the penalties of failure are drastic. The managerial and administrative elite must adjust to the strains which such pressures and penalties cause.

There are mitigating factors. Material rewards are substantial, and the perquisites and prestige of the higher-level bureaucrats, managers, and technical personnel are impressive. The skilled managerial and administrative elite is indispensable to the regime, and this factor contributes a certain measure of stability to its position. There is the work satisfaction to be obtained from professional achievement and pride in constructive accomplishments. Yet there remains a canker of fear and insecurity from which there is no escape. The dictatorship cannot show complete confidence even in those who contribute most to strengthen the basic material foundations of its power. This lack of trust on the part of the leadership acts as a corrosive force which weakens the attachment of the managerial and administrative elite to the regime.

The same pattern of insecurity infects the upper stratum of the scientific, professional, and cultural intelligentsia. Its members work under a compulsion to square their findings and their creative activities with "Party truths" as these are periodically reëvaluated by the Party leadership. For some branches of science, this may involve little more than a donning of protective camouflage in the form of quotations from the fathers of Marxist lore, claims of priority for Russian science, and deprecation of the achievements of the West. For other branches of science, such as genetics and some schools of psychology, the regime's intervention may amount to a death sentence. The patronage of the regime is richly available to subsidize scientific activities of demonstrated or purported usefulness in promoting its power and serving its immediate needs. It is not available to propagate the circulation of dangerous truths which conflict with state-imposed orthodoxies. The scientist or professional scholar who remains true to the code of his own discipline often faces a serious problem of conscience in meeting the demands which the regime makes on him. Survival dictates subservience, but the cost of subservience is frequently loss of self-respect, frustration, and a bottled-up resentment against the regime.

The cultural intelligentsia faces similar problems in even more intensified form. The elite among them — the leading writers, journalists, actors, musicians, and artists — are pampered with material privileges, but the price of the perquisites which they enjoy is absolute conformity to the regime's dictates. No sector of Soviet life is more jealously guarded by the ruling group than the ideological realm. Those who earn their livelihoods in this vineyard are richly rewarded if they are successful, but they also operate in an area of maximum danger. They must develop a chameleon-like capacity to reflect every changing shade in the Party line, and they must be prepared to lead the wolf pack or join the chorus of penitents when yesterday's orthodoxy becomes today's heresy. They must be able to produce ideas on order and gear their output to state purposes. The creative artists among them must suppress every heterodox thought and adjust their themes to the demands of the Party apparatus. The tensions generated by enforced conformity leave their mark. The stifling of spontaneous creative impulses not only makes art dull and official; it transforms the artist into a bitter, frustrated craftsman who loses his faith in the cause he serves. Official ideology breeds skepticism. As is true in so many areas of Soviet life, the ultimate source of disillusionment among many members of the cultural intelligentsia is their knowledge that the regime does not trust them.

This analysis of the strains and tensions which characterize the Soviet elite has stressed its insecurity, its sense of instability, and its feeling that it lacks the complete confidence of the top ruling group. The existence of these sources of dissatisfaction does not necessarily mean that the political cohesiveness of the Soviet regime is seriously threatened. Many members of the elite would probably welcome an alternative regime which ministered to their urge for security and stability. But as long as such an alternative is not available, the elite must make its way within the framework of the prevailing system.

Its members must balance the satisfying and unsatisfying experiences which attach to their status. They may bitterly resent the uncertainty of their positions, but they also find comfort in their privileges and perquisites, in the prestige which they enjoy, and in the very considerable responsibilities which they exercise. Some identify with the regime because they see no effective alternative, others because they are attracted by the prizes which the regime has to offer, and still others because they profoundly believe in its purposes. The motives of many may represent a complex amalgam of *all these strands*. Regardless of motivation, the members of the elite contribute their energies to sustain the power of the ruling group, and they become cogs in the system of controls with which the leadership maintains its supreme authority. As a group, they manifest the common human failing of adjusting themselves to the uncertainties and fears which they cannot avoid, and they live with the hope that they will be able to escape the drastic purges which have consumed some of their predecessors. Their loyalty to the regime may be qualified by inner reservations, but their devotion to duty maintains its momentum. In operational terms, they constitute the institutional expression of the regime's power, and they project its influence into every corner of the Soviet realm.

The existence of serious strains and dissatisfactions in Soviet society is documented by a variety of evidence of different degrees of value. The flow of criticism and self-criticism in the Soviet press as well as the testimony of Soviet *émigrés* yield revealing insights into the tensions which pervade the Soviet social structure. But the available data are far from complete, and the search for meaningful patterns resembles an effort to put an elaborate puzzle together when many key pieces are missing. There are real hazards involved in uncritical assumptions of precise identity of political attitudes between the Soviet *émigrés*, on the one hand, and the home population, on the other. Those who made the decision not to return to the Soviet Union at the end of the war or who have escaped since tend, on the whole, to reflect the views of that part of the Soviet population which is most negatively inclined toward the regime. The disposition of the *émigrés* to emphasize the darkest aspects of Soviet reality to the exclusion of such strengths as the system may possess is reinforced not only by their own unhappy experience under Soviet rule but also by an understandable zeal to acquaint the non-Communist world with those features of Soviet life which official Communist propaganda chooses to ignore or deny. Because the weight of *émigré* testimony is almost exclusively concerned with the vulnerabilities rather than the power of Soviet Communism, it has to be treated with discrimination. This does not mean that it does not possess great usefulness. Its utility lies, however, in the great variety of firsthand reports on specific Soviet experiences which it has produced rather than in the grand generalizations which some members of the emigration are prone to develop.

Problems of Loyalty and Disloyalty

Claims concerning the political loyalty or disloyalty of the Soviet populace run a startlingly wide gamut. At one extreme is the official line of Soviet propaganda with its insistence that the peoples of the Soviet Union are solidly identified with the regime. At the other extreme is the view propagated in some *émigré* circles that the Soviet peoples are completely alienated from the regime and that only the terror apparatus of the state prevents them from revolting.

Neither of these polar views carries conviction. While Soviet totalitarianism offers no precise yardsticks by which its political cohesiveness can be measured, the available evidence points to an intermediate range of speculation and surmise. The phenomena of political loyalty and disloyalty are not easily unraveled. They are not merely a reflection of external, objective circumstances and the life situations in which the Soviet citizen finds himself. The response to circumstances varies widely with differences in personality and diversity of reaction to the common indoctrination to which the Soviet populace is exposed. Different individuals occupying the same positions in Soviet society may balance the risks of disloyalty and the advantages of loyalty in widely divergent ways. The pattern of behavior of the Soviet citizen who finds himself totally enclosed and controlled by the Soviet system may change markedly when he is outside the reach of Soviet power or when he can freely choose an alternative system without danger to himself.

Some tentative hypotheses on the political cohesiveness of the Soviet system may be hazarded on the basis of material derived from interviews with former Soviet citizens and analysis of Soviet sources. Put in their baldest and most generalized form, these propositions may be summarized as follows:

(1) The political attitudes of different groups and individuals in Soviet society vary substantially, depending on the combination of affecting and disaffecting factors registered in their life situations and the degree to which they have or do not have a vested interest in the perpetuation of the regime.

(2) Political attitudes show marked variations over the age span, with indoctrination attaining its maximum effectiveness in the younger age range and with the Communist ruling group tending to anchor itself most firmly on the support of the oncoming youth formations.

(3) Political attitudes vary with national affiliations. The current tendency to emphasize the primacy of the Great Russians inspires resentment among the so-called "lesser" nationalities. National disaffection tends to be strongest in areas which have been recently incorporated into the Soviet Union, but it is by no means confined to such areas.

(4) Some policies of the regime command widespread approval even among those who deem themselves intransigent opponents of Communism, and other policies or institutional characteristics of the regime meet widespread disapproval even among those who have identified their fate with the survival of Communism.

(5) The behavior of many individuals and groups in Soviet society will show wide variations, depending on whether they feel the full impact of Soviet controls or whether they find themselves in a position where they can opt for a viable and more attractive alternative.

The first of these propositions stresses the influence of objective circumstances in shaping political attitudes. While it is obvious that the life situation of the individual is not an exclusive determinant of political attitudes, it is of basic importance. Indeed, in many cases the impact of objective factors may be decisive in determining the degree of loyalty to the regime. The elite categories of Soviet society by and large identify with the regime. Few defect, even when they have ample opportunity to do so. Despite the insecurity of their existence, they have a powerful vested interest in the perpetuation of the Soviet system, and they provide the motive power which keeps it going.

The disaffecting factors of Soviet life tend to concentrate most strongly at the lower end of the Soviet social scale. It is there that the burdens accumulate and the dissatisfactions are most intense. The millions who populate the forced labor camps or who have been the victims of other forms of repression have a definite interest in the destruction of the Soviet regime, though the situation in which they find themselves makes it impossible for them to make their hostility effective. If the repressed are excluded, the largest degree of dissatisfaction appears to be concentrated among the collective farmers. It is significant that when Soviet *émigrés* are asked to list the least desirable occupations in the Soviet Union, there is almost universal agreement in placing collective farming first. When they are also asked to indicate what features of the Soviet system they would abolish if they were free to do so, the collective-farm organizations are at the top of the list, together with secret police and Party controls. The exploitation of collective-farm labor, an accompaniment of the program of rapid industrialization, has left a residue of bitterness which is hidden, in the Soviet Union at least, behind an outward attitude of apathetic resignation. But the bitterness appears to be deep-rooted, and it is an important factor in weakening the fabric of Soviet unity.

In analyzing the regime's hold on the loyalty of collective farmers, important distinctions must be made between the collective farm's aristocracy and its rank-and-file, between older and younger collective farmers, and between the few relatively prosperous collective farms and the great bulk which provide their members with little more than a marginal existence. The collective-farm aristocracy enjoys material advantages which are not available to rank-and-file members and which are bitterly resented by them. It is bound to the regime by the modest privileges conferred upon it. It pays for its perquisites by serving as an outpost of the regime in the countryside.

Although the older generation of collective farmers has found it difficult if not impossible to reconcile itself to collective-farm existence, the newer generation has known no other form of agricultural holding and has had to make its way within the organizational framework in which it is confined. While the attitudes of the older generation are transmitted to youth, counterinfluences and counterincentives are also at work. The regime makes a special effort to train some of the more talented rural youths for skilled agricultural positions which lift their level of compensation above that of the average kolkhoznik. It absorbs a few of the more ambitious into the collective-farm aristocracy. To the extent that the regime is even partially successful in achieving this objective, it effects a cleavage between the generations and builds a nucleus of support within a social stratum which has traditionally been filled with hostility to the regime.

The Party leadership has also sought to enlist the loyalty of collective farmers by setting aside a few collective farms as showplaces of efficiency and prosperity in order to encourage others to attempt to duplicate their achievements. While this device has undoubtedly met with an enthusiastic response from the immediate recipients of governmental largesse, its effect on those who do not share in its benefits is much more dubious. For most rank-and-file collective farmers, the depressed living standards to which they are condemned and their feeling of being plundered and exploited are the decisive factors in alienating them from the regime.

Besides the collective farmers, there are other groups whose interest in the perpetuation of the Soviet system is low. While the regime commands a substantially higher degree of support among industrial labor than in the villages, here too important distinctions need to be drawn. The workers' aristocracy of foremen, skilled workers, and Stakhanovites provides the most reliable labor cadres of the dictatorship. The large group of unskilled and semiskilled labor is far less firmly attached to the regime. The office workers and other members of the lower stratum of government employees constitute a special case. While their material stake in the survival of the Soviet regime is small, the white-collar work in which they are engaged endows them with a certain feeling of superiority toward the mass of ordinary workers and collective farmers, and they frequently tend to identify with their superiors in the administrative hierarchy. Their grievances are a compound of low living standards and the pressure under which Soviet officialdom operates. Some of them, such as the teachers, are subjected to the special hazards which prevail in the ideological field. Their frustrations go largely unrelieved, and they succumb to the same mood of cowed resignation which permeates the mass of Soviet citizens.

The influence of objective circumstances on the formation of attitudes toward the regime is frequently of decisive significance, but other influences are also at work. Soviet totalitarianism has always been peculiarly sensitive to the problem of the generations, and it has concentrated its major indoctrination and propaganda efforts on enlisting the loyalty and devotion of youth. While these efforts have not enjoyed total success, it still appears to be true that indoctrination registers its maximum impact on the younger age groups and that the Communist leadership counts on youth to provide its firmest mass support.

Some of the testimony gathered from young ex-Soviet citizens, school teachers, and others who have had extensive contact with young people in the Soviet Union challenges this proposition. One teacher who had taught for nearly twenty-five years in Soviet schools insisted that the effectiveness of Communist indoctrination on Soviet youth was greatly exaggerated in the West. She pointed out that there was a great difference between the revolutionary ideology of the earlier Soviet period, which appealed to youth's idealistic and utopian instincts, and the official ideology of Stalinism, which insists on absolute, rigid conformity. The official ideology was dinned into the children day after day. Many, she claimed, became bored rather than imbued with it and turned for relief and escape toward literary, musical, athletic, and technical interests. Another Soviet *émigré*, himself a former Komsomol who had worked professionally with youth groups for many years, argued that it would be a mistake to assume that all Soviet children came off the Pioneer and Komsomol assembly lines as unthinking and unquestioning tools of the regime. Life contradicted official propaganda. Crowded conditions at home, food shortages, low living standards, the arrests of relatives and friends, compulsory labor service, the difficulty of obtaining a higher education when no stipends were available — these and other elements of daily experience planted skepticism and disbelief in the claims of propaganda touching on themes of Soviet life.

While these observations undoubtedly possess a measure of validity, at least for some part of Soviet youth, at the same time, when the question is put to Soviet *émigrés* as to who would fight to defend the Soviet regime in the event of war, the great majority agree that the mass of Soviet youth would be numbered among the defenders. Many support their answers by emphasizing the power of indoctrination and the strong pull of patriotic propaganda in cementing the allegiance of youth to the regime. Others stress the career opportunities open to youth who identify themselves with the regime. Still others point to the pressure of the terror and secret police apparatus in discouraging deviant behavior. Others emphasize the role of the army in engaging the loyalty of youth. They point out that while military discipline is stringent and while the caste privileges of the officers are resented by the rank-and-file, life in the army nevertheless represents an improvement over the collective farm for many peasant youths. Despite the contrary evidence provided by the occasional defector, the effect of army indoctrination and training is frequently to bring the rank-and-file soldiers closer to the regime rather than to alienate them from it. The power of the regime to bombard the minds of the young is perhaps its most formidable weapon. While loyalties may erode with experience and maturity, each new generation offers the ruling group a fresh opportunity to rebuild its mass support and to renew its life energies.

The political cohesiveness of the Soviet regime is also affected by nationality strains. There has been a widespread tendency in the political literature dealing with the Soviet system to assume that Soviet nationality policy constitutes one of the great strengths of the regime. This belief apparently survived the shock of the Great Purge of 1936–1938 when a substantial proportion of the top political and intellectual cadres of the national republics was liquidated. Another shock came during World War II when certain national republics proved themselves conspicuously less loyal than inhabitants of the Great Russian heartland. The dissolution of the Volga-German Autonomous Republic early in the war and the deportation of its population to the East provided one index of the regime's lack of confidence in the effectiveness of its nationality policy. In the course of the war, the regime also found it expedient to dissolve the binational autonomous republic of the Kabards and Balkars, as well as the Kalmyk, Chechen-Ingush, and Crimean autonomous republics. In these instances, the Soviet government frankly admitted that the minority nationalities had been disloyal. As *Pravda* put it in its issue of June 28, 1946, "Many Chechen and Crimean Tartars, at the behest of German agents, joined volunteer detachments organized by the Germans that fought in coöperation with the German troops against Red Army formations; likewise under German orders, they organized diversionist bands to fight the Soviet government behind the lines, and the bulk of the population of the Chechen-Ingush and Crimean Autonomous Soviet Socialist Republics failed to oppose actions of these traitors to the homeland."

Since the end of the war, there have been reports of anti-Soviet guerrilla activity in the Western Ukraine as well as large-scale deportations from this area and the border regions of the Baltic States and Bessarabia. Stalin's toast to the health of the Great Russian people at war's end was followed in due course by a campaign, with distinct anti-Semitic overtones, against "rootless cosmopolitans" and by an ideological offensive against the "remnants" of "bourgeois nationalism" in the minority republics. This offensive has not only infused Soviet patriotism with a chauvinistic Great Russian content; it has also emphasized the progressive, civilizing role of the Tsars in bringing the gifts of Great Russian culture to the minorities.

The treatment of Tsarist nationality policy by Soviet official historians has undergone a striking transformation. Painted at first in the darkest colors of oppression and exploitation, the policy was later defended as a lesser evil compared with the alternative of foreign conquest. The current campaign abandons the lesser-evil interpretation of Tsarist policy for a vigorous defense which stresses the positive advantages of incorporation in the Russian empire. In line with this thesis, the history of the national republics is being rewritten, and scholars involved in propagating outmoded versions have been condemned as "bourgeois nationalists" and severely rebuked or dismissed from their posts. The purge of "nationality deviationists" has already been accompanied by shakeups in the top command of the Party in the Azerbaidjan, Georgian, Kazakh, Turkmen, Uzbek, Moldavian, Karelo-Finnish, Esthonian, Latvian, and Belorussian republics.

These events, as well as the reports of representatives of the minority nationalities in the Soviet emigration, suggest that the political cohesiveness of the Soviet regime is still subject to severe nationality strains. This does not mean that the minority nationalities are at the point of revolt or that the regime has not had its successes in this area. Soviet *émigrés* belonging to national minorities whose development was retarded under the Tsars credit the Soviet regime with very positive achievements in the direction of racial equality, increased educational opportunities, and technological and industrial advance. But they also emphasize a darker side of Soviet nationality policy which is frequently overlooked. One of the most serious points of tension in the Soviet policy involves the position of the Soviet-trained native intelligentsia. Once these persons have been educated for administrative and other responsibilities, they aspire to real as well as formal authority, and they become increasingly restive under the rigid control exerted by the plenipotentiaries whom Moscow dispatches to supervise their activities. When they express their restiveness, they are charged with bourgeois-nationalist deviations, removed from office, and drastically punished. This phenomenon of incipient internal Titoism has been little noted, yet it would appear to be of considerable significance, and it constitutes an interesting counterpart to the difficulties encountered by Western imperial powers in dealing with the native intelligentsia in their colonies.

While the minority nationalities present problems for the regime, they are unlikely to become significant disruptive forces short of Soviet defeat in war. In normal circumstances, the power of the regime appears adequate to control the tensions which its nationality policy generates. Indeed, in some respects, the whole character of the nationality problem has been substantially altered by the impact of developments under Soviet rule. Mandatory shifts and exchanges of population and the vast migrations set in motion by industrialization have produced new mixtures of peoples in many of the national republics, with consequences for the future that cannot now be anticipated. The uniform pattern of indoctrination to which all Soviet youth is exposed may serve to mitigate even if it does not succeed in obliterating nationality consciousness. The common experiences of Soviet life provide new rallying points of unity and discontent which are superimposed on and may even transcend nationality loyalties. The Uzbek official in the MVD may feel closer to his Great Russian colleagues than to his own people whom he is appointed to watch. The Tadjik collective farmer may feel a greater kinship to the Russian collective farmers, whose grievances he shares, than to the local Tadjik officialdom who sit on his neck. The attitudes toward nationality which are being distilled in the retort of Soviet life are complex and permit no easy dogmatism. As long, however, as the regime continues to stress the primacy of the Great Russians, it can safely be predicted that "the lesser breeds" will feel resentment.

The complexity of the problem of political loyalty and disloyalty is emphasized by the fact that some policies of the Soviet leadership command widespread approval even among those hostile to the regime, while other policies or institutional characteristics meet widespread disapproval even among those who have identified their fate with the regime's survival. When Soviet *émigrés* are asked what features of the Soviet regime they would keep if they were free to build a new order in Russia, there is a surprising uniformity of response. Almost all choose free schools, free medical services, and other welfare features of the Soviet state. They tend to agree that the state ought to retain ownership and control of the basic industries and transportation and that it ought to guarantee employment. To the extent that such policies evoke approval even among those who are solidly opposed to the Soviet regime, it can be assumed that there are at least some features of the system which command widespread endorsement and which serve to build a tenuous bond of unity between leadership and people. Within limits, moreover, the regime can maneuver to relax tensions and broaden its area of consent. The NEP retreat, the modifications in the collectivization program in

1933, and the relaxation of the Great Purge toward the end of 1938 represent the kind of breathing space which is designed to revive hope and to avert total alienation. During World War II, hatred of the Nazis unleashed a genuine national upsurge of feeling which the Party leadership was shrewd enough both to stimulate and exploit. By opening the churches and tapping the wellsprings of national sentiment, the regime deepened its popular roots. The limited freedom permitted the Orthodox Church since the end of the war contributes toward the same end. This capacity to maneuver is an element of strength which should not be overlooked.

Interviews with former Soviet citizens disclose that, however great their hatred for the Communist regime may be, they continue to cherish a deep patriotic attachment to the homeland which they have abandoned. Many, indeed, reveal feelings of guilt at having left families or relatives behind and yearn for the day when they can again set foot on native soil. Their repudiation of Communism is combined with pride in the industrial and military achievements of the Soviet era, even though they attribute these accomplishments to the genius of the people rather than to the talents of the Soviet ruling group. The majority of Soviet *émigrés* unconsciously reflect the influence of their upbringing. The impact of years of Soviet rule is registered in widespread suspiciousness and fear, in a tendency to envisage problems in terms of black-and-white solutions, and in a predilection for authoritarian and paternalistic arrangements. The difficulty which the *émigrés* encounter in emancipating themselves from Soviet patterns of behavior and the continuing strength of their national consciousness suggest that these traits are even more characteristic of the mass of the home population. Despite the fact that identification with the Soviet system usually takes the form of passive accommodation rather than positive enthusiasm, the ability of the regime to command the loyalty of its subjects should not be minimized.

At the same time, there are institutional characteristics and policies of the system which arouse profound resentment even among those whose careers are linked with the survival of the regime. One of the striking impressions derived from interviews with former Party members and Party officials among the Soviet *émigrés* is the extent to which the atmosphere of fear which pervades Soviet society envelops the Party itself. No feature of the Soviet system is more widely hated — both in Party and in non-Party circles — than the arbitrary authority of the secret police. Yet the existence of the secret police is indispensable to the regime. It depends upon its specialists in terror to extirpate any thought of opposition or resistance. Paradoxically, the very power of the secret police is also a symbol of weakness. The resentment against the regime which it arouses and the widespread insecurity which it breeds undermine the loyalties of all parts of Soviet society and build a barrier between people and leadership which may become crucial in a period when the life of the regime is at stake.

The cohesiveness of the Soviet system also depends in considerable measure on the extent to which its subjects are presented with an opportunity to choose a more attractive alternative. Even those Soviet citizens who are most dissatisfied with the system under which they are compelled to live show little inclination toward martyrdom. Under ordinary conditions, their conduct tends to be adaptive. It is largely regulated by the desire to survive and improve their status in the only setting which is available to them. Not until they are given a choice of a different setting can the factor of rejection of the Soviet regime come into play.

Interviews with recent Soviet *émigrés* make clear that it was largely the accident of World War II or occupation duty after the war which made it possible for them to register their protest against the Soviet regime. Some frankly admitted that their eyes had not been opened until they found themselves abroad. Others who reported that they had harbored hostile sentiments toward the regime for many years were equally frank to admit that the position in which they found themselves inside the Soviet Union made it impossible for them to transform their sentiments into action. Most of these made no bones about the fact that they suppressed their resentment, were overtly pro-regime, and went through the motions of conformity in order to survive and make their way in Soviet society. Others referred to themselves as members of the so-called "inner migration" which sought refuge in a flight from politically dangerous activity and hid itself in inconspicuous niches far from the centers of authority. These qualities of cynical careerism and of apathetic resignation in the face of state power are in large part a product of the massive impact of Soviet repression with its pervasive net of informers and the omnipresent danger of arrest by the secret police and confinement in a forced labor camp. Soviet totalitarianism breeds a sense of aloneness, of isolation, and of suspiciousness in the individual. It is not a milieu congenial to the organization of large-scale conspiracies.

Indeed, most Soviet *émigrés* tend to discount the possibility or probability of the emergence of any organized or spontaneous revolutionary movement capable of unseating the Soviet regime in the near future. Most seem to agree that a mass uprising against the regime would be condemned to futility and bloody suppression. The weight of this testimony is all the more impressive since Soviet *émigrés* as a group ardently desire the downfall of the regime. In the light of the available evidence, it would appear that there is very little opportunity for the forces of internal opposition in the Soviet Union to organize and become effective, short of a major crisis of leadership which would give them a free field of action, or of Soviet defeat in war, in the course of which the Party and police controls of the regime break down.

Whether the death of Stalin will set forces in motion which lead to important modifications in the Soviet regime remains to be determined. In the first months after Stalin's death, the new regime initiated a series of measures which appeared to portend an easing of living standards for Soviet citizens, a "liberalization" of the dictatorship, and an alleviation of tension between East and West. Price cuts were put into effect for food and consumer goods. An amnesty was declared for minor offenders in prisons and forced labor camps. The release of the arrested Kremlin doctors was accompanied by a declaration that high secret police officials had fabricated evidence and abused their authority, that they had sought to stir up national animosities, and that the new leadership was prepared to guarantee the "constitutional" rights of its subjects against any form of arbitrary action. In the area of foreign policy, a marked change of line was evident. Anti-American propaganda was muted, and for the first time in a number of years, the Soviet press acknowledged the aid rendered by the Allies during the Second World War. In a statement to the Supreme Soviet on March 15, 1953, Malenkov declared, "At the present time there is no dispute or unresolved question that cannot be settled peacefully by mutual agreement of the interested countries. This applies to our relations with all states, including the United States of America." This announcement was soon followed by an East-West accord at the United Nations on the designation of a new Secretary-General, the conclusion of an agreement to exchange the sick and wounded in Korea, a Communist retreat on the issue of forcible repatriation of all prisoners, and the reopening of armistice negotiations in Korea.

Although the ultimate significance of these moves can be appraised only in the light of future developments, sanguine hopes that Soviet domestic and international policy will undergo fundamental revision do not appear to be warranted. In the perspective of Soviet historical development, the current peace campaign and the domestic concessions which accompany it must be viewed as a tactical maneuver designed to win the new regime a breathing space to consolidate its authority. During this period, the Kremlin can be expected to make every effort to quiet fears of Soviet aggression, to confuse and divide Western sentiment about long-term Soviet intentions, and to woo the support of its own subjects. Whether the present phase of defensive consolidation will be long-lasting will depend in considerable measure on the success which the new leadership enjoys in stabilizing its authority. If a successor emerges who gathers all the reins of power in his own hands and manipulates them with Stalin's dexterity, no significant changes in the character and goals of the Soviet regime are to be anticipated. If the successor is a weak figure or if the dictatorship is lodged in a divided committee, power may be diffused among the rival elite formations, and the competing aspirations of the Party, the police, the armed forces, and the bureaucracy may be suspended in an uneasy equilibrium or come into sharp conflict. While such a combination of circumstances may conceivably set the stage for an eventual transformation of Soviet totalitarianism into some type of constitutional order — what Mr. George F. Kennan has termed the "erosion" of despotism — the immediate prospects for such a development are not hopeful.

It is undoubtedly true that the Soviet regime could greatly broaden its popularity by slowing the tempo of industrialization and militarization, by devoting a larger part of its resources to the production of consumer goods, by abandoning collectivization of the peasantry, by imposing legal restraints on the secret police, and by stabilizing the position of its bureaucratic elites. There are forces in Soviet society which would warmly support such an evolution. The yearning for peace, security, and a rise in living standards is widespread among Soviet citizens. Substantial elements in the officer corps and the managerial, technical, and scientific intelligentsia would no doubt welcome liberation from police and Party controls; their aspirations center on achieving greater independence in performing their functions. With industrialization, the role of this sector of the elite has become increasingly significant. The imperatives of professional competence and solidarity drive toward the pluralization of functional authority.

But there are also important countervailing considerations. Stalin's successors are his best pupils, and they have risen to power by practicing the arts which he taught them. Their careers have been devoted to forging the weapons of totalitarianism, and the system with which they have identified themselves maintains its own dynamic momentum. The secret police and the Party apparatus, on which the regime depends to sustain its authority, have a vested interest in the perpetuation of their privileges and perquisites. The institutional pressures which they generate operate to preserve and consolidate the dictatorship. As long as the Kremlin leaders continue to see their future in terms of industrial and military might, they will probably persist in relying on totalitarian instruments to force the pace of industrialization. Those who possess absolute power do not part with it willingly. The governing formula of Soviet totalitarianism rests on a moving equilibrium of alternating phases of repression and relaxation, but its essential contours remain unchanged. The totalitarian regime does not shed its police-state characteristics; it dies when power is wrenched from its hands.

NOTES, BIBLIOGRAPHY, INDEX

NOTES

Chapter 1
The Seedbed of Revolution

1. George F. Kennan, "America and the Russian Future," *Foreign Affairs*, XXIX, no. 3 (April 1951), 365.
2. Quoted in B. H. Sumner, *Survey of Russian History* (2nd ed.; London, 1947), p. 68.
3. *Ibid.*, p. 67.
4. Cf. *ibid.*, p. 104.
5. K. P. Pobyedonostseff, *Reflections of a Russian Statesman* (London, 1898), pp. 27–28.
6. Henry Gifford, *The Hero of His Time* (London, 1950), p. vii.
7. V. G. Belinsky, *Selected Philosophical Works* (Moscow, 1948), p. 504.
8. Quoted in Gifford, p. 181.
9. James Mavor, *An Economic History of Russia* (London and Toronto, 1914), II, 592.
10. Quoted in Mavor, II, 469, 471.
11. *Ibid.*, p. 473.
12. George Vernadsky, *A History of Russia* (New York, 1944), p. 195.
13. Quoted in Sir John Maynard, *Russia in Flux* (London, 1946), p. 193.
14. *Ibid.*, p. 203.
15. G. T. Robinson, *Rural Russia under the Old Régime* (New York, 1949), p. 88.
16. *Ibid.*, p. 94.
17. *Ibid.*, p. 101.
18. A. A. Kornilov, *Krest'yanskaya Reforma* (Peasant Reform; St. Petersburg, 1905), pp. 250–251.
19. Robinson, pp. 109–110.
20. *Ibid.*, p. 108.
21. *Ibid.*, p. 144.
22. *Ibid.*, p. 162.
23. *Ibid.*, p. 182.
24. *Ibid.*, p. 183.
25. P. I. Lyashchenko, *History of the National Economy of Russia to the 1917 Revolution* (New York, 1949), p. 747.
26. Robinson, p. 194.
27. See V. I. Lenin, "Politicheskie Zametki" (Political Notes; 1908) in *Sochineniya* (Works; 3rd ed.; Moscow, 1935), XII, 123.
28. Lyashchenko, p. 462.
29. Quoted in Alfred Levin, *The Second Duma* (New Haven, 1940), pp. 183–184.
30. The herculean efforts of Peter the Great succeeded in building "a heavy industry, which in the end supplied all the ordnance requirements both of his army and of his navy; a rope, sail, and lumber industry which met all the needs of his navy, and a cloth industry which furnished uniforms for a large proportion of his troops" (B. H. Sumner, *Peter the Great and the Emergence of Russia* [New York, 1951], p. 164). This development was largely state sponsored or state stimulated, though ex-

tensive use was made of the capital of the merchant-traders of the day. By the time of Peter's death in 1725, Russian production of pig iron was probably larger than the English output (*ibid.*, pp. 165–166); by the middle of the eighteenth century, Russia was the world's largest producer of iron and copper. It was not until the end of the century that English production of iron caught up with that of Russia. See Witt Bowden, Michael Karpovich, and Abbott Payson Usher, *An Economic History of Europe since 1750* (New York, 1937), p. 301.

31. Lyashchenko, p. 338. The stagnation of Russian metallurgy was explained by a variety of factors. Protected against foreign competition by a tariff duty which amounted in 1822 to 600 per cent of the cost of pig iron, relying almost entirely on serf labor and adjusting its production targets to a limited domestic demand, the Ural iron industry had little or no incentive to modernize itself (*ibid.*).

32. *Ibid.*, pp. 490–491.

33. *Ibid.*, pp. 494, 502.

34. Bowden, Karpovich, and Usher, p. 607.

35. Lyashchenko, p. 560.

36. The oil industry lagged behind, and indeed the volume of production of petroleum dropped from 632 million *poods* (a *pood* equals 36 pounds avoirdupois) in 1900 to 561 million *poods* in 1913. In the same period, pig iron increased from 177 million to 283 million *poods*, iron and steel from 163 million to 246 million, coal from 1,003 million to 2,214 million, and cotton consumption from 16.1 million to 25.9 million (*ibid.*, p. 688).

37. *Ibid.*, p. 674.

38. *Ibid.*, p. 676.

39. Data quoted by the Soviet economic historian Lyashchenko indicate that in 1914, of the total basic stock capital of the eighteen major corporate banks, 42 per cent belonged to foreign capital. In 1916–17, the share of foreign capital in the mining industry was 90 per cent, in chemicals 50 per cent, in metal smelting and processing 42 per cent, in wood processing 37 per cent, and in textiles 28 per cent (pp. 708, 716). The significance of these figures should not be exaggerated. It remained true that in absolute terms Russian capital was far more important than foreign capital.

40. According to Lyashchenko (p. 527), "in 1895 only 15.9 per cent of Russia's workers were employed in small enterprises (employing 10 to 15 workers), while Germany had 31.5 per cent in that category; in the larger plants (over 500 workers) Russian industry employed 42 per cent and Germany only 15.3 per cent."

41. Lyashchenko, pp. 669–671.

42. *Ibid.*, p. 419.

43. Michael T. Florinsky, *The End of the Russian Empire* (New Haven, 1931), p. 169.

44. Bowden, Karpovich, and Usher, p. 609.

45. The "Credo," quoted in Mavor, II, 166.

Chapter 2

Bolshevism before 1917

1. Quoted in Nadezhda K. Krupskaya, *Memories of Lenin* (New York, 1930), II, 198.

2. Thomas G. Masaryk, *The Spirit of Russia* (London, 1919), II, 303.

3. Quoted in Bertram D. Wolfe, *Three Who Made a Revolution* (New York, 1948), p. 110. The precise language used by Marx was: "If Russia continues to pursue the path she has followed since 1861, she will lose the finest chance ever offered by history to a nation, and will undergo all the fatal vicissitudes of the capitalist regime." See *Perepiska K. Marksa i F. Engel'sa s Russkimi Politicheskimi Deyatelyami* (The

Correspondence of K. Marx and F. Engels with Russian Political Figures; 2nd ed.; Moscow, 1951), p. 221.

4. David Ryazanoff (ed.), *The Communist Manifesto of Karl Marx and Friedrich Engels* (New York, 1930), Marxist Library, vol. III, pp. 264–265. Engels, in the preface to the German edition of 1890, erroneously ascribed the translation of the Russian edition of 1882 to Vera Zasulich. See Ryazanoff's note in his edition of the *Manifesto*, p. 262.

5. *Ibid.*, p. 154.

6. Wolfe, p. 112.

7. *Sotsializm i Politicheskaya Bor'ba* (Socialism and the Political Struggle; 1883); *Nashi Raznoglasiya* (Our Differences; 1884); *K Voprosu o Razvitii Monisticheskogo Vzglyada na Istoriyu* (Toward the Development of the Monistic Conception of History; 1895).

8. Quoted in N. Popov, *Outline History of the Communist Party of the Soviet Union* (New York, 1934), I, 25; hereafter cited as *Outline History of the C.P.S.U.*

9. G. Plekhanov, *O Zadachakh Sotsialistov v Bor'be s Golodom v Rossii* (The Duty of the Socialists in the Struggle against Famine in Russia; Geneva, 1892), pp. 38–39.

10. See Lenin's pamphlet of 1894, *Chto Takoe "Druz'ya Naroda" i Kak Oni Voyuyut Protiv Sotsial-Demokratov?* (What the "Friends of the People" Are and How They Fight the Social-Democrats), reprinted in *Sochineniya*, I, 53–229.

11. G. Plekhanov, "Rech' na Mezhdunarodnom Rabochem Sotsialisticheskom Kongresse v Parizhe (14–21 Iyulya 1889 g.)" (Address at the International Socialist Workingmen's Congress, Paris, July 14–21, 1889 [The Second International]), reprinted in Plekhanov's *Sochineniya*, edited by D. Ryazanov (Works; Moscow–Petrograd, 1923), IV, 54.

12. Quoted in P. I. Lyashchenko, *History of the National Economy of Russia to the 1917 Revolution*, p. 432.

13. See "Chto Delat'?" (What Is to Be Done?), *Sochineniya*, IV, 402–411.

14. See Sergei Bulgakov's essay "Ot Marksizma k Idealizmu" in *Ot Marksizma k Idealizmu — Sbornik Statei (1896–1903)* (From Marxism to Idealism — Collection of Articles, 1896–1903; St. Petersburg, 1903).

15. See Wolfe, p. 282.

16. Lenin, "Dve Taktiki Sotsial-Demokratii v Demokraticheskoi Revolyutsii" (Two Tactics of Social-Democracy in the Democratic Revolution), *Sochineniya*, VIII, 40–41.

17. *Ibid.*, p. 104.

18. Quoted in Wolfe, p. 121.

19. Lenin, *Sochineniya*, VIII, 95–96.

20. Lenin's recipe for future action was summed up in the following quotation from *Two Tactics*: "The proletariat must carry to completion the democratic revolution by allying to itself the mass of the peasantry, in order to crush by force the resistance of the autocracy and to paralyze the instability of the bourgeoisie. The proletariat must accomplish the socialist revolution by allying to itself the mass of the semi-proletarian elements of the population in order to crush by force the resistance of the bourgeoisie and to paralyze the instability of the peasantry and the petty bourgeoisie" (*Sochineniya*, VIII, 96).

21. Lenin, "Otnoshenie Sotsial-Demokratii k Krest'yanskomu Dvizheniyu" (The Attitude of Social-Democracy toward the Peasant Movement), *Sochineniya*, VIII, 186.

22. Joseph Stalin, "The Foundations of Leninism," *Problems of Leninism* (11th ed., Moscow, 1940), p. 20.

23. "Chto Delat'?" *Sochineniya*, IV, 458.

24. *Ibid.*, p. 442.

25. *Ibid.*, p. 464.

26. In *What Is to Be Done?* Lenin provided a thinly disguised account of this and similar experiences. "A students' circle having no contacts with the old members of the movement, no contacts with circles in other districts, or even in other parts

of the same city . . . without the various sections of the revolutionary work being
in any way organized, having no systematic plan of activity covering any length of
time, establishes contacts with the workers and sets to work. The circle gradually ex-
pands its propaganda and agitation; by its activities it wins the sympathies of a rather
large circle of workers and of a certain section of the educated classes, which provides
it with money and from which the 'Committee' recruits new groups of young people
. . . its sphere of activities becomes wider . . . [its members] now establish contacts
with other groups of revolutionaries, procure literature, set to work to publish a local
newspaper, begin to talk about organizing demonstrations, and finally, commence open
hostilities (those open hostilities may, according to circumstances, take the form of
the publication of the first agitational leaflet, or the first newspaper, or the first demonstration). And usually the first action ends in immediate and wholesale arrests."

"The government . . ." Lenin went on, "managed to place its . . . *agents pro-*
vocateurs, spies and gendarmes in the required places. Raids became so frequent, affected such a vast number of people and cleared out the local circles so thoroughly
that the masses of the workers literally lost all their leaders, the movement assumed
an incredibly sporadic character, and it became utterly impossible to establish continuity and coherence in the work. The fact that the local active workers were hopelessly scattered, the casual manner in which the membership of the circles was recruited, the lack of training in and narrow outlook on theoretical, political and organizational questions were all the inevitable result of the conditions described above.
Things reached such a pass that in several places the workers, because of our lack
of stamina and ability to maintain secrecy, began to lose faith in the intelligentsia
and to avoid them; the intellectuals, they said, are much too careless and lay themselves open to police raids!" ("Chto Delat'?" *Sochineniya*, IV, 438–439).

27. Quoted in Wolfe, p. 156.
28. "Chto Delat'?" *Sochineniya*, IV, 170, 177.
29. *Ibid.*, p. 452.
30. *Ibid.*, p. 456.
31. In *What Is to Be Done?* he poured out his scorn on those who called for
"broad democracy" in party organization: "Broad democracy in party organization,
amidst the gloom of autocracy . . . is nothing more than a *useless and harmful toy.*
It is a useless toy because, as a matter of fact, no revolutionary organization has ever
practiced *broad* democracy, nor could it, however much it desired to do so. It is a
harmful toy because any attempt to practice the 'broad democratic principles' will
simply facilitate the work of the police in making big raids; it will perpetuate the
prevailing primitiveness, divert the thoughts of the practical workers from the serious
and imperative task of training themselves to become professional revolutionaries to
that of drawing up detailed 'paper' rules for election systems. Only abroad, where
very often people who have no opportunity of doing real live work gather together,
can the 'game of democracy' be played here and there, especially in small groups"
("Chto Delat'?" *Sochineniya*, IV, 468).
32. See "Kak Chut' Ne Potukhla 'Iskra'?" in *Sochineniya*, IV, 15–31.
33. Lenin, "Shag Vperëd, Dva Shaga Nazad" (One Step Forward, Two Steps
Back), *Sochineniya*, VI, 201. My italics.
34. Popov, *Outline History of the C.P.S.U.*, I, 111.
35. Quoted in Wolfe, p. 241.
36. Leon Trotsky, *Nashi Politicheskiya Zadachi* (Our Political Tasks; Geneva,
1904), p. 54.
37. At the London meeting of his faction, Lenin tried to undo the organizational
damage committed in 1903. Martov's Paragraph One of the Rules was replaced by
Lenin's formulation. The three central bodies set up by the Second Congress were
replaced by a single Central Committee, which appointed the Editorial Board of the
new central party paper, *Proletarii*. The Party Council was abolished.
38. Lenin, "Pobeda Kadetov i Zadachi Rabochei Partii" (The Victory of the
Kadets and the Tasks of the Workers' Party), *Sochineniya*, IX, 123.
39. Popov, *Outline History of the C.P.S.U.*, I, 184.

40. *Ibid.*, p. 186. Wolfe (p. 345), cites forty-six Bolsheviks.

41. According to Wolfe (p. 383), there were 91 Bolsheviks and 89 Mensheviks at the Congress. Stalin in his report on the Fifth Party Congress lists 92 Bolsheviks, 85 Mensheviks, 54 Bundists, 45 Poles, and 26 Latvians (*Protokoly Pyatogo S"ezda RSDRP* [2nd ed., Moscow, 1935], p. x). Popov (*Outline History of the C.P.S.U.*, I, 205) reports that the Congress "was attended by" 105 Bolsheviks, 97 Mensheviks, 57 Bundists, 44 Poles, and 29 Latvians. A. Bubnov, in his Party history in *Bol'shaya Sovetskaya Entsiklopediya* (Great Soviet Encyclopedia; 1930 ed., XI, 352), estimates the strength of the delegations within certain ranges: Bolsheviks, 81–90; Mensheviks, 80–85; Bundists, 54–56; Poles, 39–45; and Latvians, 25–26.

42. Stalin's remarks on this division, reported in the Protocols of the Fifth Congress, are of some contemporary interest: "In this connection one of the Bolsheviks (Comrade Aleksinsky, I think) jokingly remarked that the Mensheviks are a Jewish fraction and the Bolsheviks a genuinely Russian fraction; so it would seem not out of order for us Bolsheviks to hold a pogrom in the Party" (*Protokoly Pyatogo S"ezda RSDRP*, p. xii).

43. Quoted in Popov, *Outline History of the C.P.S.U.*, I, 232.

44. *Ibid.*, pp. 237–238.

45. Wolfe, p. 478.

46. Lenin, "Otnoshenie Sotsial-Demokratii k Krest'yanskomu Dvizheniyu" (The Attitude of Social-Democracy toward the Peasant Movement), *Sochineniya*, VIII, 182.

47. *Ibid.*, p. 186.

48. Lenin, "Stolypin i Revolyutsiya" (Stolypin and the Revolution), *Sochineniya*, XV, 221–227.

49. See Appendix IV, "Rezolyutsiya Vserossiiskoi Aprel'skoi Konferentsii R.S.-D.R.P. po Agrarnomu Voprosu" (Resolution of the All-Russian Conference of the RSDLP on the Agrarian Question) in Lenin, *Sochineniya*, XX, 615–616.

50. *Ibid.*, p. 616.

51. Lenin, "K. Lozungam" (On Slogans), *Sochineniya*, XXI, 33.

52. Lenin, "Nashi Zadachi i Sovet Rabochikh Deputatov" (Our Tasks and the Soviet of Workers' Deputies), *Sochineniya* (4th ed.; Moscow, 1949), X, 3.

53. *Vsesoyuznaya Kommunisticheskaya Partiya (B) v Rezolyutsiyakh i Resheniyakh S"ezdov, Konferentsii i Plenumov TsK (1898–1924)* (All-Union Communist Party [B] in Resolutions and Decrees of Congresses, Conferences, and Plenums of the Central Committee [1898–1924]), vol. I (4th ed.; Moscow-Leningrad, 1932), p. 64; hereafter cited as *VKP(b) v Rezolyutsiyakh*.

54. J. V. Stalin, "Rech' na Sobranii v Moskovskom Komitete RKP(b) po Povodu 50-letiya so Dnya Rozhdeniya V. I. Lenina" (Address at the meeting of the Moscow Committee of the RCP[b] in Connection with V. I. Lenin's Fiftieth Birthday), *Sochineniya* (Works; Moscow, 1946–), IV, 316–317.

55. Lenin, "O Boikote" (The Boycott), *Sochineniya*, X, 27. Later, in *Left-Wing Communism, an Infantile Disorder*, Lenin frankly admitted, "The boycott of the 'Duma' by the Bolsheviks in 1906 was . . . a mistake, although a small and easily remediable one" ("Detskaya Bolezn' 'Levizny' v Kommunizme," *Sochineniya*, XXV, 183).

56. Alfred Levin, *The Second Duma*, p. 70

57. See *ibid.* for a description of the work of the Duma.

58. A. E. Badayev, *Bol'sheviki v Tsarskoi Dume* (The Bolsheviks in the Tsarist Duma; Leningrad, 1929).

59. *Ibid.*, p. 86.

60. Lenin, in retrospect, insisted that "the right of nations to self-determination" was always understood to mean the right to secession. The evidence to sustain his view is meager.

61. Quoted in Solomon M. Schwarz, *The Jews in the Soviet Union* (Syracuse, 1951), p. 25.

62. *Ibid.*

63. *Ibid.*, p. 26.

64. *Ibid.*

65. *Ibid.*

66. Stalin, "Marksizm i Natsional'nyi Vopros," *Sochineniya*, II, 331–332.

67. Lenin, "Pis'mo S. G. Shaumyanu" (Letter to S. G. Shaumyan), *Sochineniya*, XVII, 90.

68. Lenin, "O Prave Natsii na Samoopredelenie" (The Right of Nations to Self-Determination), *Sochineniya*, XVII, 455.

69. The conference was actually held October 5–14, 1913. The August appellation was designed to mislead the Tsarist police.

70. *VKP(b) v Rezolyutsiyakh*, I, 238–240.

71. *Ibid.*, p. 239.

72. Stalin, "Marksizm i Natsional'nyi Vopros" (Marxism and the National Question), *Sochineniya*, II, 312–313.

73. Stalin, "Doklad po Natsional'nomu Voprosu" (Report on the National Question), *Sochineniya*, IV, 31–32.

Chapter 3

The Road to Power

1. Statistical Table 1 in A. Bubnov, "VKP(b)," *Bol'shaya Sovetskaya Entsiklopediya* (Great Soviet Encyclopedia; Moscow, 1930), XI, 531.

2. Popov, *Outline History of the C.P.S.U.*, I, 351.

3. V. P. Semennikov (ed.), *Nikolai II i Velikie Knyazya* (Nicholas II and the Grand Dukes; Moscow-Leningrad, 1925), p. 122.

4. For the origins of "Order Number One" see N. Sukhanov, *Zapiski o Revolyutsii* (Notes on the Revolution; St. Petersburg, 1919), I, 196–200.

5. V. V. Shulgin, *Dni* (Days; Belgrade, 1925), p. 179

6. These conditions included political amnesty; civil liberties; freedom to organize trade unions and to strike; abolition of all caste, religious, and national limitatons; replacement of the police by a people's militia; local self-government; the convocation of a constituent assembly; the protection of the military units which took part in the Revolution from loss of arms or removal from Petrograd; and the guarantee of general civil and political rights to soldiers on condition that they maintain strict military discipline in service (P. N. Milyukov, *Istoriya Vtoroi Russkoi Revolyutsii* [The History of the Second Russian Revolution; Sofia, 1921], I, Part 1, 47).

7. "The Provisional Government," wrote the War Minister Guchkov on March 22, 1917, "possesses no real power and its orders are executed only in so far as this is permitted by the Soviet of Workers' and Soldiers' Deputies, which holds in its hands the most important elements of actual power, such as troops, railroads, postal and telegraphic service. It is possible to say directly that the Provisional Government exists only while this is permitted by the Soviet of Workers' and Soldiers' Deputies. Especially in the military department it is possible now only to issue orders which do not basically conflict with the decisions of the above-mentioned Soviet" (A. Shlyapnikov, *Semnadtsatyi God* [The Year 1917; Moscow-Leningrad, 1925–1927], II, 236).

8. "Rezolyutsiya Vserossiiskogo Soveshchaniya Sovetov Rabochikh i Soldatskikh Deputatov" (Resolution of the All-Russian Conference of the Soviets of Workers' and Soldiers' Deputies) in N. Avdeyev (editor of vols. I and II), *Revolyutsiya 1917 g., Khronika Sobytii* (The Revolution of 1917, Chronicle of Events; 2nd ed.; Moscow, 1923–1926), I, 198.

9. "Manifesto of the Russian Social-Democratic Labour Party 'To All Citizens of Russia,'" in V. I. Lenin, *Collected Works* (London, 1929), XX, Book 2, 378. This edition of Lenin's works is hereafter cited as *CW*.

10. Popov, *Outline History of the C.P.S.U.*, I, 352.

11. *Ibid.*

12. L. Kamenev, "Without Secret Diplomacy," translated in Lenin, *CW*, XX(2), 380.

13. Stalin wrote a number of articles in a similar vein. "These articles," he acknowledged in 1924, "reflect certain waverings of the majority of our Party on the questions of peace and the power of the Soviets which occurred, as is known, in March and April 1917 . . . It is not surprising that Bolsheviks, scattered by Tsarism in prisons and places of exile, and just able to come together from different ends of Russia in order to work out a new platform, could not immediately understand the new situation. It is not surprising that the Party, in search of a new orientation, then stopped halfway in the questions of peace and Soviet power. The famous 'April Theses' of Lenin were needed before the Party could come out on the new road with one leap . . . I shared this mistaken position with the majority of the Party and renounced it fully in the middle of April, associating myself with the 'April Theses' of Lenin" (J. V. Stalin, *Na Putyakh k Oktyabryu* [On the Roads to October; Moscow-Leningrad, 1925], pp. viii–ix; quoted in W. H. Chamberlin, *The Russian Revolution 1917–1921* [New York, 1935], I, 115–116).

14. Lenin, *CW*, XX(1), 19.

15. *Ibid.*, p. 21.

16. *Ibid.*, p. 19.

17. Quoted in Chamberlin, I, 117.

18. Lenin, "Speech Delivered at a Caucus of the Bolshevik Members of the All-Russian Conference of the Soviets of Workers' and Soldiers' Deputies, April 17, 1917," *CW*, XX(1), 95–103.

19. E. H. Carr, *The Bolshevik Revolution, 1917–1923* (New York, 1951–1952), I, 81.

20. L. Kamenev, "Our Differences," translated in Lenin, *CW*, XX(2), 380–381.

21. Lenin, "Letters on Tactics," *CW*, XX(1), 119.

22. Lenin, "On the Tasks of the Proletariat in the Present Revolution," *ibid.*, p. 107.

23. "Letters on Tactics," *ibid.*, p. 119.

24. *Ibid.*, pp. 120–121.

25. Lenin, "On Dual Power," *ibid.*, p. 115.

26. Lenin, "The Tasks of the Proletariat in Our Revolution," *ibid.*, p. 133.

27. Lenin, "Report on the Political Situation and the Attitude Towards the Provisional Government, April 27, 1917," *ibid.*, p. 204.

28. A. V. Shestakov, "Krest'yanskie Organizatsii v 1917 godu" (Peasant Organizations in 1917) in V. P. Milyutin (ed.), *Agrarnaya Revolyutsiya* (The Agrarian Revolution; Moscow, 1928), II, 116–117.

29. See note 72 in Lenin, *CW*, XXI(1), 297.

30. See note 80, *ibid.*, p. 299.

31. Avdeyev, II, 242.

32. Chamberlin, I, 159.

33. See note 159 in Lenin, *CW*, XX(1), 375.

34. See note 49, *ibid.*, XXI(1), 291.

35. See *Protokoly Shestogo S"ezda RSDRP (b)* (Protocols of the Sixth Congress of the RSDLP [b] [August 1917]; Moscow, 1934), pp. 36–37.

36. Appendix 8, *ibid.*, p. 275.

37. Lenin, "One of the Fundamental Questions of the Revolution," *CW*, XXI(1), 167.

38. "The Political Situation," *ibid.*, p. 37.

39. "On Compromises," *ibid.*, p. 153.

40. "One of the Fundamental Questions of the Revolution," *ibid.*, p. 165.

41. Lenin, in his report of May 7 to the All-Russian Conference of the Party, said, "The government would like to see us make the first reckless step towards decisive action, as this would be to its advantage. It is exasperated because our party

has advanced the slogan of peaceful demonstration . . . The proletarian party would be guilty of the most grievous error if it shaped its policy on the basis of subjective desires when organisation is required. We cannot assert that the majority is with us; in this case our motto should be: caution, caution, caution" (*CW*, XXI [1], 279).

42. Chamberlin, I, 161; E. Burdzhalov, *Pervyi Vserossiiskii S″ezd Sovetov Rabochikh i Soldatskikh Deputatov* (First All-Russian Congress of Soviets of Workers' and Soldiers' Deputies; Moscow, 1938), p. 30.

43. For the Bolshevik version, see Stalin's Report on the Political Situation in *Protokoly Shestogo S″ezda RSDRP* (*b*), pp. 107–111.

44. During the Congress, Stalin, who delivered the political report, was asked for a more concrete definition of the relationships of the Party to the existing soviets. He replied as follows: "In so far as we are speaking of transferring power to the Central Executive Committee, this slogan is out-of-date . . . The fact that we propose to drop the slogan 'All Power to the Soviets' does not imply that we propose the slogan 'Down with the Soviets!' And, although we have dropped the former slogan, we have not even retired from the Central Executive Committee, despite the wretched role it has played during the last few weeks.

"The local soviets may still play a role, since they will have to defend themselves against the exactions of the Provisional Government, and we shall support them in this struggle . . . 'As to our attitude to the soviets in which we have the majority' — most friendly. May those Soviets live and grow in strength!" (*ibid.*, p. 118).

45. Lenin, "From a Publicist's Diary," *CW*, XXI(1), 144–145.

46. Leon Trotsky, *My Life* (New York, 1930), p. 289.

47. See Lenin, "On Compromises," *CW*, XXI(1), 153.

48. "To the Central Committee of the Russian Social-Democratic Labour Party," *ibid.*, pp. 137–138.

49. The great surge of Bolshevik strength did not develop until September. In the election to the Petrograd Municipal Duma on September 2, 1917, the Bolsheviks received 33 per cent of the votes as against 20 per cent in May. (See note 66 in Lenin, *CW*, XXI[1], 296.) Bolshevik resolutions carried the day for the first time in the Petrograd Soviet on September 13 and in the Moscow Soviet of Workers' Deputies on September 18. On October 8, Trotsky was elected President of the Petrograd Soviet. In the elections of the Moscow Municipal Duma, the Bolsheviks increased their vote from 11 per cent in July to 51 per cent in October (Chamberlin, I, 297). About the same time, Bolsheviks were also elected as chairmen both of the Moscow Soviet of Workers' Deputies and of the Moscow Provincial Soviet.

50. Quoted in Chamberlin, I, 281.

51. Before leaving, Trotsky fired "a little pistol shot" in the form of a declaration: "The Provisional Government, under the dictates of Kadet counter-revolutionaries and Allied imperialists, without sense, without force and without plan, drags out the murderous war, condemning to useless destruction hundreds of thousands of soldiers and sailors and preparing the surrender of Petrograd and the throttling of the Revolution . . . We, the delegation of Bolsheviks, say: we have nothing in common with this government of treason to the people and with this 'Council' of complicity in counter-revolution . . . All power to the Soviets! All land to the people! Long live an immediate, honest, democratic peace! Long live the Constituent Assembly!" (Leon Trotsky, *Sochineniya* [Works; Moscow, n.d.], III, Part 1, 323; for translation, see Chamberlin, I, 283–284).

52. Lenin, "The Bolsheviks Must Assume Power," *CW*, XXI(1), 221.

53. *Ibid.*, p. 222.

54. "Marxism and Uprising," *ibid.*, pp. 226, 228–229.

55. Those present at the meeting were Trotsky, Kamenev, Rykov, Nogin, Stalin, Sverdlov, Bubnov, Bukharin, Lomov, Kollontai, Dzerzhinsky, Uritsky, Joffe, Shaumyan, Sokolnikov, and Milyutin.

56. Leon Trotsky, *The History of the Russian Revolution* (New York, 1932), III, 133; hereafter cited as *History*.

57. *Protokoly Tsentral'nogo Komiteta RSDRP, Avgust 1917–Fevral' 1918* (Pro-

tocols of the Central Committee of the RSDLP, August 1917–February 1918; Moscow-Leningrad, 1929), p. 65; hereafter cited as *Protokoly TsK RSDLP*.

58. *Ibid.*

59. The decision to withdraw was made at the session of the Central Committee on October 18. Kamenev voted against the withdrawal and appended the following statement, addressed to the Central Committee, to the minutes of the meeting. "Dear Comrades: I think that your decision to withdraw from the very first session of the 'Soviet of the Russian Republic' predetermines the tactics of the Party during the next period in a direction which I personally consider quite dangerous for the Party. In submitting to the decision of the Party I at the same time request the comrades to relieve me of the duties in the representative bodies (CEC, etc.) and give me some other work" (*Protokoly TsK RSDRP*, pp. 90–91).

60. Lenin, "From a Publicist's Diary," *CW*, XXI(1), 254.

61. The letter, intended for distribution among the members of the Central Committee, the Moscow and Petrograd Committees, and the Bolshevik delegation in the Soviet, read in part: "To refrain from seizing power at present, to 'wait,' to 'chatter' in the Central Committee, to confine ourselves to 'fighting for the organ' (of the Soviet), to 'fighting for the Congress,' means to *ruin the revolution.*

"Seeing that the Central Committee has left *even without an answer* my writings insisting on such a policy since the beginning of the Democratic Conference, that the Central Organ is deleting from my articles references to such glaring errors of the Bolsheviks as the shameful decision to participate in the pre-parliament, as giving seats to the Mensheviks in the Presidium of the Soviets, etc., etc. — seeing all that, I am compelled to recognise here a 'gentle' hint as to the unwillingness of the Central Committee even to consider this question, a gentle hint at gagging me and at suggesting that I retire.

"I am compelled to *tender my resignation from the Central Committee,* which I hereby do, leaving myself the freedom of propaganda in *the lower* ranks of the party and at the Party Congress.

"For it is my deepest conviction that if we 'await' the Congress of Soviets and let the present moment pass, we *ruin* the revolution" ("The Crisis Has Matured," *CW*, XXI [1], 278).

62. For texts, see Lenin, *CW*, XXI (2), 65–70, 100–105.

63. Quoted in Trotsky, *History*, III, 137.

64. *Protokoly TsK RSDRP*, p. 99.

65. *Ibid.*, p. 101. It was at this meeting that a "politburo" was first created. The motion of Dzerzhinsky defined its purpose as that of "political guidance for the immediate future." Its membership consisted of Lenin, Zinoviev, Kamenev, Trotsky, Stalin, Sokolnikov, and Bubnov. There is no evidence that it played any role of importance in the insurrection. Trotsky comments: "This new institution . . . turned out [to be] completely impracticable. Lenin and Zinoviev were still in hiding; Zinoviev, moreover, continued to wage a struggle against the insurrection, and so did Kamenev. The political bureau in its October membership never once assembled, and it was soon simply forgotten — as were other organizations created *ad hoc* in the whirlpool of events" (*History*, III, 155).

66. *Protokoly TsK RSDRP*, pp. 104–108.

67. Zinoviev and Kamenev wrote: "The forces of the opponent are greater than they appear. Petrograd is decisive, and in Petrograd the enemies of the proletarian party have accumulated substantial forces: 5000 military cadets . . . also the staff, shock troops, Cossacks, a substantial part of the garrison, and very considerable artillery, which has taken up a position in fanlike formation around Petrograd . . . The proletarian party at the present time would have to fight under an entirely different interrelationship of forces than in the days of the Kornilov affair. At that time we fought together with the SR's, the Mensheviks, and to some extent, even with the adherents of Kerensky. Now, however, the proletarian party would have to fight against the Black Hundreds, plus the Kadets, plus Kerensky and the Provisional Government, plus the CEC (SR's and Mensheviks).

". . . In the biggest organizations (railroad unions, unions of post office and telegraph workers, etc.) . . . the influence of our Party is weak" (*ibid.*, p. 107).

68. *Ibid.*, pp. 103–104.

69. *Ibid.*, pp. 124–125.

70. Lenin, *CW*, XXI(2), 261.

71. "Letter to the Members of the Bolshevik Party," *ibid.*, p. 130.

72. "Letter to the Central Committee of the Russian Social-Democratic Labour Party," *ibid.*, pp. 133–137.

73. See *Protokoly TsK RSDRP*, p. 137.

74. *Ibid.*, pp. 128–129.

75. *Ibid.* In a session notable for its high temper, an added spark with future incendiary effects was provided by Trotsky's attack on Stalin's editorial note as "intolerable." Stalin replied by pleading the necessity for Party unity and announced his readiness to withdraw from the editorial board of *Rabochii Put'*. The Central Committee refused the tendered resignation and moved on to the next item on the agenda.

76. *Ibid.*, p. 141.

77. *Ibid.*, p. 124. The "military-revolutionary center" was created on October 29. The resolution of the Central Committee instructed the members of the center to join the Military Revolutionary Committee of the Soviet. According to Trotsky's account (*History*, III, 110), only Sverdlov was "brought in upon all important matters."

78. Trotsky, *ibid.*

79. "Resolutions of the Pre-Parliament," in James Bunyan and H. H. Fisher, *The Bolshevik Revolution, 1917–1918* (Stanford, California, 1934), pp. 91–92.

80. "The Proposal of Dan, Gotz, and Avxentiev," in Bunyan and Fisher, pp. 93–94.

81. Lenin, "Letter to the Members of the Central Committee," *CW*, XXI(2), 144–145.

82. *Protokoly TsK RSDRP*, pp. 142–143.

83. Trotsky, *Sochineniya*, III, Part 2, 55.

84. Bunyan and Fisher, p. 100.

85. No accurate count of the political affiliations of the delegates has been preserved. Non-Bolshevik estimates of the strength of the Bolshevik delegation run from 250 to 300. See Bunyan and Fisher, p. 110.

86. Trotsky, *History*, III, 307.

87. Bunyan and Fisher, p. 113.

88. *Ibid.*

89. "Proclamation of the Congress on the Assumption of Power," *ibid.*, p. 122.

90. Trotsky, *History*, III, 324.

91. The Congress also approved a decree transferring authority in the provinces to the Soviets and announced the abolition of capital punishment. The latter action, according to Trotsky, aroused Lenin's ire. "When he [Lenin] learned of this first legislative act his anger knew no bounds.

" 'This is madness,' he repeated. 'How can we accomplish a revolution without shooting? Do you think you can settle with your enemies if you disarm? What repressive measures have you then? Imprisonment? Who pays any attention to that in a time of bourgeois war when every party hopes for victory?'

"Kamenief [*sic*] tried to show that it was only a question of the repeal of the death penalty that Kerensky had introduced especially for deserting soldiers. But Lenin was not to be appeased.

" 'It is a mistake,' he repeated, 'an inadmissible weakness. Pacifist illusion . . .' He proposed changing the decree at once. We told him this would make an extraordinarily unfavorable impression. Finally some one said: 'the best thing is to resort to shooting when there is no other way.' And it was left at that" (Leon Trotzky, *Lenin* [New York, 1925], pp. 133–134).

92. According to Trotsky (*ibid.*, p. 132), the name originated in a conversation between Lenin and himself: " 'What name shall we use?' Lenin considered aloud. 'Not minister, that is a repulsive, worn-out designation.'

" 'We might say commissars,' I suggested, 'but there are too many commissars now. Perhaps chief commissar . . . No, "chief" sounds bad. What about people's commissars?' . . .

" 'People's commissars? As for me, I like it. And the government as a whole?'

" 'Council of People's Commissars?'

" 'Council of People's Commissars,' Lenin repeated. 'That is splendid. That smells of revolution.' "

93. Trotsky, *My Life*, p. 337.

94. Lenin, "Krest'yanskii Nakaz o Zemle" (The Peasants' Decree on the Land) in *Vtoroi Vserossiiskii S"ezd Sovetov R. i S.D.* (Second All-Russian Congress of Soviets of Workers' and Soldiers' Deputies [November 7–8, 1917]; Moscow-Leningrad, 1928), p. 73.

95. Lenin, "Will the Bolsheviks Retain State Power?" *CW*, XXI(2), 48.

96. See Oliver H. Radkey, *The Election to the Russian Constituent Assembly of 1917* (Cambridge, Massachusetts, 1950), p. 80; Chamberlin, I, 366.

97. See Lenin, "Vybory v Uchreditel'noe Sobranie i Diktatura Proletariata" (Elections to the Constituent Assembly and the Dictatorship of the Proletariat), *Sochineniya*, XXIV, 635.

98. *Sochineniya*, IV, 458.

Chapter *4*

The Dynamics of Power

1. Lenin, "O Prodovol'stvennom Naloge" (The Tax in Kind), *Sochineniya*, XXVI, 330.

2. Lenin, "Materials Relating to the Revision of the Party Programme," *CW*, XX(1), 343.

3. *CW*, XXI(2), 15–56.

4. "Grozyashchaya Katastrofa i Kak s Nei Borot'sya" (The Impending Catastrophe and How to Combat It), *Sochineniya*, XXI, 163–164.

5. "Will the Bolsheviks Retain State Power?" *CW*, XXI(2), 40.

6. *Ibid.*, p. 30.

7. *Ibid.*, p. 32.

8. *Ibid.*, p. 33.

9. *Ibid.*, p. 37.

10. "Ocherëdnye Zadachi Sovetskoi Vlasti," *Sochineniya*, XXII, 439–468.

11. *Ibid.*, pp. 445–446.

12. *Ibid.*, p. 447.

13. *Ibid.*, p. 448

14. *Ibid.*, p. 451.

15. *Ibid.*, p. 462.

16. "Doklad o Voine i Mire 7 Marta" (Report on War and Peace, March 7, 1918), *Sochineniya*, XXII, 324.

17. *Ibid.*, p. 327.

18. "Politicheskii Otchët Tsentral'nogo Komiteta R.K.P.(B.) 27 Marta" (Political Report of the Central Committee of the RCP[B], March 27, 1922), *Sochineniya*, XXVII, 244.

19. "O Prodovol'stvennom Naloge," *Sochineniya*, XXVI, 330.

20. E. H. Carr, *The Bolshevik Revolution 1917–1923*, II, 110.

21. It fell to Trotsky to provide a frank rationalization for the militarization of labor in the Soviet state. He declared, "We are now advancing towards a type of labour socially regulated on the basis of an economic plan which is obligatory for the whole country, i.e. compulsory for every worker. That is the foundation of socialism . . . And once we have recognized this, we thereby recognize funda-

mentally — not formally, but fundamentally — the right of the workers' state to send each working man and woman to the place where they are needed for the fulfillment of economic tasks. We thereby recognize the right of the state, the workers' state, to punish the working man or woman who refuse to carry out the order of the state, who do not subordinate their will to the will of the working-class and to its economic tasks . . . The militarization of labour in this fundamental sense of which I have spoken is the indispensable and fundamental method for the organization of our labour forces" (quoted in Carr, II, 215). The end of the Civil War and the introduction of the New Economic Policy were to postpone the application of Trotsky's logical theorem. By an ironic twist of history, it remained for Stalin to execute the program which his arch-enemy had adumbrated.

22. *VKP(b) v Rezolyutsiyakh*, I, 391–392.

23. Lenin, "K Chetyrëkhletnei Godovshchine Oktyabr'skoi Revolyutsii" (The Fourth Anniversary of the October Revolution), *Sochineniya*, XXVII, 29.

24. See Robert V. Daniels, "The Kronstadt Revolt of 1921: A Study in the Dynamics of Revolution," *The American Slavic and East European Review*, X, no. 4 (December 1951), 241–254.

25. "O Prodovol'stvennom Naloge," *Sochineniya*, XXVI, 348.

26. "O Chistke Partii" (On Purging the Party), *Sochineniya*, XXVII, 12.

27. "Doklad o Natural'nom Naloge 15 Marta" (Report on the Tax in Kind, March 15, 1921), *Sochineniya*, XXVI, 238.

28. "Politicheskii Otchët Tsentral'nogo Komiteta R.K.P.(B.) 27 Marta" *Sochineniya*, XXVII, 234. Lenin added on another occasion, "Those who find this work 'dull,' 'uninteresting,' and 'unintelligible,' those who turn up their noses, or become panic-stricken, or who become intoxicated with their own declamations about the absence of the 'previous elation,' the 'previous enthusiasm,' etc., had better be 'relieved of their jobs' and given a back seat, so as to prevent them from causing harm; for they will not or cannot understand the specific features of the present stage of the struggle" (Novye Vremena, Starye Oshibki v Novom Vide" [New Times and Old Mistakes in a New Guise], *Sochineniya*, XXVII, 10).

29. "Pyat' Let Rossiskoi Revolyutsii i Perspektivy Mirovoi Revolyutsii" (Five Years of the Russian Revolution and the Prospects of the World Revolution), *Sochineniya*, XXVII, 349.

30. For a very discerning treatment of the industrialization controversy, see Alexander Erlich, "Preobrazhenski and the Economics of Soviet Industrialization," *Quarterly Journal of Economics*, LXIV, no. 1 (February 1950), 57–88.

31. "The Tasks of Business Executives," *Problems of Leninism*, p. 365.

32. "The Results of the First Five-Year Plan," *ibid.*, pp. 409–410, 416–417.

33. "New Conditions — New Tasks in Economic Construction," *ibid.*, p 382.

34. For a more extended discussion of tightening labor discipline in the Soviet Union, see Solomon M. Schwarz, *Labor in the Soviet Union* (New York, 1952), pp. 86–129.

35. Stalin declared, "We must draw up wage scales that will take into account the difference between skilled labour and unskilled labour, between heavy work and light work . . . We cannot tolerate a situation where a railway locomotive driver earns only as much as a copying clerk . . .

"In every industry, in every factory, in every department of a factory, there is a leading group of more or less skilled workers who must first of all, and particularly, be retained in industry . . . These leading groups of workers are the chief link in production . . . We can retain them only by promoting them to higher positions, by raising the level of their wages, by introducing a system of payment that will give the worker his due according to qualification . . . In order to get skilled workers we must give the unskilled worker a stimulus and prospect of advancement, of rising to a higher position . . . The more boldly we do this the better" ("New Conditions — New Tasks in Economic Construction," *Problems of Leninism*, pp. 372–373).

36. See Raymond A. Bauer, *The New Man in Soviet Psychology* (Cambridge, Massachusetts, 1952).

37. See Ruth Widmayer, "The Communist Party and the Soviet Schools, 1917–1937" (doctoral dissertation, Harvard University, 1952).

38. See John N. Hazard (ed.) and Hugh W. Babb (trans.), *Soviet Legal Philosophy* (Cambridge, Massachusetts, 1951); also, Harold J. Berman, *Justice in Russia* (Cambridge, Massachusetts, 1950).

39. Stalin, "Politicheskii Otchët Tsentral'nogo Komiteta XVI S"ezdu VKP(b)" (Political Report of the Central Committee to the Sixteenth Congress of the All-Union CP[b]), *Sochineniya*, XII, 369–370.

40. "O Zadachakh Khozyaistvennikov" (The Tasks of Business Executives), *Sochineniya*, XIII, 41.

41. "On the Draft Constitution of the U.S.S.R.," *Problems of Leninism*, p. 586.

42. *Pravda*, June 9, 1934, p. 1.

43. J. Stalin, A. Zhdanov, and S. Kirov, "Zamechaniya po Povodu Konspekta Uchebnika po 'Istorii USSR' " (Remarks Concerning the Conspectus of a Textbook on "The History of the USSR"), *Istorik Marksist*, no. 1(53) (1936), pp. 5–6.

44. Translated in D. Fedotoff White, *The Growth of the Red Army* (Princeton, 1944), p. 413.

45. Quoted in John S. Curtiss and Alex Inkeles, "Marxism in the U.S.S.R. — The Recent Revival," *Political Science Quarterly*, LXI, no. 3 (September 1946), 358.

46. For English text of the speech, see "The Strategy and Tactics of World Communism," *House Doc.* 619; 80 Cong. 2 Sess. (Washington, 1948), pp. 168–178.

47. *Ibid.*, pp. 211–230.

48. See Stalin's toast at a Kremlin banquet on May 24, 1945, translated in Solomon Schwarz, *The Jews in the Soviet Union*, p. 72.

49. See N. S. Timasheff, "Religion in Russia, 1941–1950," in Waldemar Gurian (ed.), *The Soviet Union: Background, Ideology, Reality* (Notre Dame, 1951), pp. 153–194.

50. Nicholas S. Timasheff *The Great Retreat* (New York, 1946).

51. *My* (We; New York, 1952), p. 149.

Chapter 5

The Dictatorship of the Party in Theory and Practice

1. See speech by Marx in 1872 at the Congress of the International at The Hague, quoted in Karl Kautsky, *The Dictatorship of the Proletariat*, trans. H. J. Stenning (Manchester, n.d.), pp. 9–10; also, Engels' preface to the first English translation of Karl Marx, *Capital* (Chicago, 1906), p. 32.

2. See Karl Marx, "The Civil War in France" in his *Selected Works*, edited by V. Adoratsky (New York, n.d.), II, 475–527.

3. See V. I. Lenin, "Gosudarstvo i Revolyutsiya" (The State and Revolution), *Sochineniya*, XXI, 394–395.

4. *Protokoly TsK RSDRP, Avgust 1917–Fevral' 1918* (Protocols of the Central Committee of the RSDLP, August 1917–February 1918), pp. 149–150. At this meeting, the Bolshevik Central Committee adopted the following resolution: "In view of the fact that all previous negotiations have fully demonstrated that the compromisers are not aiming to form a unified Soviet Government but are trying to split the ranks of the workers and soldiers, to disrupt the Soviet Government, and to win over the Socialist-Revolutionaries of the Left to the policy of compromising with the camp of the bourgeoisie, the Central Committee resolves to allow Party members . . . to attend today's negotiations in which for the last time the Socialist-Revolutionaries of the Left will make a final attempt to form a so-called uniform [Socialist] government. [The Bolshevik delegates] must try to show the impossibility of such an attempt and the futility of further negotiations on the subject of forming a coalition government" (*ibid.*, pp. 155–156).

5. Quoted in Leon Trotsky, *The Stalin School of Falsification* (New York, 1937), pp. 110, 112.

6. *Protokoly TsK RSDRP*, p. 169.

7. *Ibid.*, p. 167.

8. Quoted in Trotsky, *The Stalin School of Falsification*, p. 114.

9. "Rech' o Rospuske Uchreditel'nogo Sobraniya na Zasedanii VTsIK 19(6) Yanvarya 1918 g." (Speech on the Dissolution of the Constituent Assembly, Delivered at a Meeting of the All-Russian CEC on January 6/19, 1918), *Sochineniya*, XXII, 184–187.

10. "Tezisy ob Uchreditel'nom Sobranii" (Theses on the Constituent Assembly), *Sochineniya*, XXII, 134.

11. *Tretii Vserossiiskii S"ezd Sovetov Rabochikh, Soldatskikh i Krest'yanskikh Deputatov* (Third All-Russian Congress of Soviets of Workers', Soldiers', and Peasants' Deputies [January 23–31, 1918]; St. Petersburg, 1918), p. 5.

12. "Doklad o Deyatel'nosti Soveta Narodnykh Komissarov 24(11) Yanvarya" (Report on the Activities of the Council of People's Commissars, January 11/24, 1918), *Sochineniya*, XXII, 207–208.

13. Text published in *Izvestiya*, no. 239, November 29/December 12, 1917, p. 1.

14. Trotsky, *Sochineniya*, III, Part 2, 138.

15. Reported in *Nash Vek* (Our Age; Petrograd), no. 21, December 23, 1917/January 5, 1918, p. 3.

16. "Otchët Tsentral'nogo Komiteta 18 Marta" (Report of the Central Committee, March 18, 1919), *Sochineniya*, XXIV, 120.

17. "O Prodovol'stvennom Naloge" (The Tax in Kind), *Sochineniya*, XXVI, 348.

18. Lenin, "The Revolt of the Left Socialist-Revolutionaries," *CW*, XXIII, 151.

19. Stalin, "The Foundations of Leninism," *Problems of Leninism*, p. 73.

20. *Ibid.*, pp. 74, 78.

21. "On the Problems of Leninism," *ibid.*, p. 135.

22. Joseph Stalin, *Mastering Bolshevism* (New York, 1937), p. 57.

23. Quoted in B. H. Sumner, *Peter the Great and the Emergence of Russia*, p. 162.

24. Stalin, "On the Draft Constitution of the U.S.S.R.," *Problems of Leninism*, pp. 578–579.

25. P. Katayan, "Svoboda Sobranii" (Freedom of Assembly), *Izvestiya*, August 6, 1936, p. 3.

26. Stalin, "Otvety Tovarishcham" (Replies to Comrades), *Bol'shevik*, no. 14 (July 1950), p. 6. This article has been translated in the *Current Digest of the Soviet Press*, II, no. 28 (August 26, 1950), 13; hereafter cited as *CDSP*.

27. "The Foundations of Leninism," *Problems of Leninism*, pp. 80–81.

28. Trotsky, *The Stalin School of Falsification*, p. 109.

29. *Protokoly TsK RSDRP*, p. 238.

30. *Ibid.*, p. 252.

31. *Sed'moi S"ezd Rossiiskoi Kommunisticheskoi Partii, Stenograficheskii Otchët* (Seventh Congress of the Russian Communist Party, Stenographic Report [December 5–9, 1919]; Moscow-Petrograd, 1923), p. 146.

32. "O 'Levom' Rebyachestve i o Melkoburzhuaznosti," *Sochineniya*, XXII, 503–528.

33. See Lenin, *Sochineniya*, XXIV, 749, note 35.

34. *Ibid.*, pp. 750–751.

35. E. Jaroslawski, *Aus der Geschichte der Kommunistischen Partei der Sowjetunion (Bolschewiki)* (Hamburg-Berlin, n.d.), II, 205.

36. Lenin, "Zaklyuchitel'noe Slovo po Dokladu Tsentral'nogo Komiteta 30 Marta" (Concluding Remarks on the Report of the Central Committee, March 30, 1920), *Sochineniya*, XXV, 112.

37. See Isaac Deutscher, *Soviet Trade Unions* (London-New York, 1950), p. 58.

38. "Krizis Partii," *Sochineniya*, XXVI, 94.

39. "Zaklyuchitel'noe Slovo po Otchëtu TsK RKP(B) 9 Marta" (Concluding

Remarks on the Report of the CC of the RCP[B], March 9, 1921), *Sochineniya,* XXVI, 227–228.

40. "Pervonachal'nyi Proekt Rezolyutsii X S"ezda R.K.P. o Sindikalistskom i Anarkhistskom Uklone v Nashei Partii" (First Draft of the Resolution Adopted by the Tenth Congress of the RCP on the Syndicalist and Anarchist Deviation in Our Party) in Lenin, *Sochineniya,* XXVI, 262, 264.

41. "Doklad ob Edinstve Partii i Anarkho-Sindikalistskom Uklone 16 Marta" (Speech of March 16, 1921 on Party Unity and the Anarcho-Syndicalist Deviation), *Sochineniya,* XXVI, 267.

42. "Pervonachal'nyi Proekt Rezolyutsii X S"ezda R.K.P. o Edinstve Partii" (First Draft of the Resolution Adopted by the Tenth Congress of the RCP on Party Unity) in Lenin, *Sochineniya,* XXVI, 259–261.

43. *Ibid.,* p. 261.

44. "O Chistke Partii" (On Purging the Party), *Sochineniya,* XXVII, 13.

45. Jaroslawski, II, 253.

46. *VKP(b) v Rezolyutsiyakh,* I, 536. Lenin in a speech at the Eleventh Congress reported that the motion failed by three votes. See "Zaklyuchitel'noe Slovo po Politicheskomu Otchëtu TsK RKP(B) 28 Marta" (Concluding Remarks on the Political Report of the CC of the RCP[B], March 28, 1922), XXVII, 268.

47. See Lenin, *Sochineniya,* XXVII, 495–496, note 2.

48. Jaroslawski, II, 245.

49. *Ibid.,* p. 247.

50. *Ibid.,* pp. 247–248.

51. "Politicheskii Otchët Tsentral'nogo Komiteta RKP(B) 27 Marta" (Political Report of the Central Committee of the RCP[B], March 27, 1922), *Sochineniya,* XXVII, 239.

52. *Sochineniya,* XXVII, 262.

53. *VKP(b) v Rezolyutsiyakh,* I, 538.

54. Appendix VI in Max Eastman, *Since Lenin Died* (London, 1925), pp. 146–149.

55. "Postanovlenie Politbiuro TsK RKP, Protiv Obostreniya Vnutripartiinoi Bor'by" (Decree of the Politburo of the CC of the RCP, Against Intensifying Intra-Party Strife), *Pravda,* December 18, 1923, p. 4.

56. Stalin, "Zaklyuchitel'noe Slovo po Politicheskomu Otchëtu Tsentral'nogo Komiteta" (Concluding Remarks on the Political Report of the Central Committee), *Sochineniya,* VII, 380.

57. Stalin, "Doklad ob Ocherëdnykh Zadachakh Partiinogo Stroitel'stva" (Report on the Immediate Tasks of Party Construction), *Sochineniya,* VI, 14–15.

58. *Ibid.,* pp. 44–45.

59. *VKP(b) v Rezolyutsiyakh,* I, 647–654.

60. *Trinadstatyi S"ezd Rossiiskoi Kommunisticheskoi Partii (Bol'shevikov), Stenograficheskii Otchët* (Thirteenth Congress of the Russian Communist Party [Bolshevik], Stenographic Report [May 23–31, 1924]; Moscow, 1924), pp. 166–167.

61. Stalin, "Zaklyuchitel'noe Slovo" (Concluding Remarks), *Sochineniya,* VI, 233.

62. Stalin, "Rech' na Plenume TsK i TsKK(b) 17 Yanvarya 1925 g." (Address at the Plenum of the CC and the CCC(b), January 17, 1925), *Sochineniya,* VII, 9–10.

63. Stalin, "Zaklyuchitel'noe Slovo po Politicheskomu Otchëtu Tsentral'nogo Komiteta," *Sochineniya,* VII, 388–389.

64. *XIV S"ezd Vsesoyuznoi Kommunisticheskoi Partii (b), Stenograficheskii Otchët* (Fourteenth Congress of the All-Union Communist Party [b], Stenographic Report [December 18–31, 1925]; Moscow-Leningrad, 1926), p. 186; hereafter cited as *XIV S"ezd VKP(b).*

65. *Ibid.,* pp. 165–166.

66. *Ibid.,* pp 274–275.

67. Stalin, *Sochineniya,* VII, 391.

68. "O Khozyaistvennom Polozhenii Sovetskogo Soyuza i Politike Partii" (On

the Condition of the Economy of the Soviet Union and Party Policy), *Sochineniya*, VIII, 146.

69. Trotsky, *My Life*, pp. 528–529.

70. Stalin, "O Merakh Smyagcheniya Vnutripartiinoi Bor'by" (On Measures for Lessening the Intra-Party Struggle), *Sochineniya*, VIII, 210–212.

71. Stalin, "Zaklyuchitel'noe Slovo po Dokladu 'O Sotsial-Demokraticheskom Uklone v Nashei Partii'" (Concluding Remarks on the Report "Concerning the Social-Democratic Deviation in Our Party"), *Sochineniya*, VIII, 350–354.

72. Stalin, "Mezhdunarodnoe Polozhenie i Oborona SSSR" (The International Situation and the Defense of the USSR), *Sochineniya*, X, 59.

73. Leon Trotsky, *The Real Situation in Russia*, translated by Max Eastman (New York, 1928), pp. 12, 14–15.

74. Trotsky, *My Life*, pp. 533–534.

75. *XV S"ezd Vsesoyuznoi Kommunisticheskoi Partii (b), Stenograficheskii Otchët* (Fifteenth Congress of the All-Union Communist Party [b], Stenographic Report [December 2–19, 1927]; Moscow-Leningrad, 1928), pp. 251–252; hereafter cited as *XV S"ezd VKP(b)*.

76. Stalin, "Politicheskii Otchët Tsentral'nogo Komiteta" (Political Report of the Central Committee), *Sochineniya*, X, 351.

77. *XV S"ezd VKP(b)*, pp. 1266–1267.

78. *Ibid.*, p. 1319.

79. Trotsky, *History*, III, 138.

80. Stalin, "O Pravoi Opasnosti v VKP(b)" (The Danger of the Right in the All-Union CP[b]), *Sochineniya*, XI, 236.

81. Stalin, "Ob Industrializatsii Strany i o Pravom Uklone v VKP(b)" (On the Industrialization of the Country and the Right Deviation in the All-Union CP[b]), *Sochineniya*, XI, 290.

82. Stalin, "Gruppa Bukharina i Pravyi Uklon v Nashei Partii" (The Bukharin Group and the Right Deviation in Our Party), *Sochineniya*, XI, 318–325.

83. Stalin, "O Pravom Uklone v VKP(b)" (On the Right Deviation in the All-Union CP[b]), *Sochineniya*, XII, 6–7.

84. *Ibid.*, pp. 103–104.

85. *Ibid.*, pp. 106–107.

86. "Zayavlenie TT. Tomskogo, Bukharina i Rykova v TsK VKP(b)" (Declaration by Comrades Tomsky, Bukharin, and Rykov to the CC of the All-Union CP[b]), *Pravda*, November 26, 1929, p. 2

87. L. M. Kaganovich's comment on the fall of Rykov was significant. In a speech before a Moscow Party gathering he declared, "Comrades, in a period of grandiose construction when the great questions of socialist construction are being decided in our land, can we . . . be satisfied with a Sovnarkom chairman who says that he executes the general line of the Party 'as much as and as best he can'? We cannot permit the slightest shade of doubt, the slightest cleavage between the Party and Soviet organs . . .

"From the Chairman of the Sovnarkom of this great land, there is demanded not only a recognition of the general line of the Party, but first and foremost an active struggle to carry it into effect. That we did not see on Rykov's part." L. M. Kaganovich, "Ob Itogakh Dekabr'skogo Ob"edinënnogo Plenuma TsK i TsKK VKP(b)" (On the Results of the December Joint Plenum of the CC and the CCC of the All-Union CP[b]), *Pravda*, December 30, 1930, p. 4.

88. Stalin, *Problems of Leninism*, pp. 515–516.

89. *History of the Communist Party of the Soviet Union (Bolsheviks), Short Course* (New York, 1939), p. 326; hereafter cited as *History of the CPSU*.

90. For lists see Boris Souvarine, *Staline: Aperçu historique du bolshévisme* (Paris, 1935), pp. 574–581, and Louis Fischer, *Men and Politics* (New York, 1941), pp. 433–439.

91. *History of the CPSU*, p. 347.

92. Stalin, *Mastering Bolshevism*, pp. 6–7.

93. *Ibid.*, p. 13.
94. *Ibid.*, p. 8.
95. *Ibid.*, p. 9.
96. See the Resolution of the Plenum of the Central Committee of January, 1938 in *VKP(b) v Rezolyutsiyakh*, vol. II (6th ed., 1941), pp. 671–677.

Chapter 6
The Growth of the Party Apparatus

1. See Appendix 8 in *Protokoly Shestogo S"ezda RSDRP(b)* (Protocols of the Sixth Congress of the RSDLP[b]), p. 275.
2. *XVI S"ezd Vsesoyuznoi Kommunisticheskoi Partii (bol'shevikov), Stenograficheskii Otchët* (Sixteenth Congress of the All-Union Communist Party [Bolshevik], Stenographic Report [June 26–July 13, 1930]; 2nd ed.; Moscow-Leningrad, 1931), p. 52; hereafter cited as *XVI S"ezd VKP(b)*.
3. *VKP(b) v Rezolyutsiyakh*, I, 353.
4. "Doklad Tsentral'nogo Komiteta 29 Marta 1920 g." (Report of the Central Committee, March 29, 1920), *Sochineniya*, XXV, 94.
5. *VKP(b) v Rezolyutsiyakh*, I, 407.
6. "Otchët o Rabote TsK za Period ot 9 do 10 Partiinogo S"ezda" (Report on the Work of the CC for the Period between the Ninth and Tenth Party Congresses), *Izvestiya Tsentral'nogo Komiteta Rossiiskoi Kommunisticheskoi Partii (Bol'shevikov)* (News of the Central Committee of the Russian Communist Party [Bolshevik]), no. 29 (March 7, 1921), p. 7. Hereafter this journal will be cited as *Izvestiya TsK*.
7. These included 325 at the center and regional level; 2,000 at the *guberniya* or provincial level; 8,000 at the *uezd* or county level, and another 5,000 full-time Party secretaries in the *volosts* or districts and in the larger industrial enterprises (*VKP[b] v Rezolyutsiyakh*, I, 560–561).
8. The first report — "Otchët Uchëtno-Raspredelitel'nogo Otdela" (Report of the Account and Assignment Section) in *Izvestiya TsK*, no. 22 (September 18, 1920), pp. 12–15.
9. "Otchët za God Raboty TsK RKP (s XI do XII S"ezda RKP)" (Report on a Year's Work by the CC of the RCP, from the Eleventh to the Twelfth Congress of the RCP), *Izvestiya TsK*, no. 4(52) (April 1923), p. 45.
10. During the year 1922, thirty-seven *guberniya* secretaries were removed or transferred by the central Party apparatus, and forty-two new "recommendations" were made for the post of secretary ("Vypolnenie Direktiv XI S"ezda Partii. Podbor Sekretarei Gubkomov i Obkomov" [Fulfillment of the Directives Issued by the Eleventh Party Congress. Selection of *Gubkom* and *Obkom* Secretaries], *Izvestiya TsK*, no. 3[51] [March 1923], p. 51).
11. The same report described the functions of *Uchraspred* as "detailed and attentive accounting of the commanding cadre of the Party; reassignment of Party forces to strengthen the most important provincial organizations; selection of organizers for Party work, review of the directors of *oblast, guberniya*, and *uezd* Party organizations and to a certain extent secretaries of cells; replacement of workers who did not measure up to the standards set forth by the Party Congress" ("Otchët Uchëtno-Raspredelitel'nogo Otdela. Obshchie Usloviya i Kharakter Raboty" [Report of the Account and Assignment Section. General Conditions and Character of Work], *ibid.*, p. 28).
12. "Organizatsionnyi Otchët Tsentral'nogo Komiteta RKP(b) 17 Aprelya 1923 g." (Organizational Report of the Central Committee of the RCP[b], April 17, 1923), *Sochineniya*, V, 212.
13. Quoted in Max Shachtman, *The Struggle for the New Course*, published in

one volume with his translation of Leon Trotsky's *The New Course* (New York, 1943), p. 159.

14. The functions of the Organization-Instruction Section, in the words of an official report, were: "to establish relations of the Central Committee with local organizations, in order to make possible daily study of the conditions of each organization and the activities going on in it; to strengthen the apparatus, bring about a vital link with the localities; to improve the conditions of information so they embrace and reflect the work of the localities; to draw nearer to the life and work of local organizations down to the lowest cells; to single out the most important industrial centers and establish a direct link with them, and, on this basis, to carry on planned work directed toward the strengthening and improvement of Party organizations, liquidation of disputes, [and] improvement of methods of general Party work" ("Otchët Organizatsionno-Instruktorskogo Otdela" [Report of the Organization-Instruction Section], *Izvestiya TsK*, no. 3[51] [March 1923], p. 3). Embraced in this somewhat ambiguous formulation was a major concentration of effort on the elimination of opposition activity in the localities and the transformation of the Party bureaucracy into a solid monolith of support for the General Secretary.

15. *Ibid.*, pp. 15–16.

16. The Siberian Bureau was headed by Yaroslavsky until 1922 and then by S. Kossior; the Far Eastern by Kubiak; the North Caucasus by Mikoyan; and the Turkestan (subsequently Central Asian) by Kuibyshev until 1922 and by Rudzutak later.

17. For a description of the Siberian case, see Robert V. Daniels, "The Left Opposition in the Russian Communist Party, to 1924" (doctoral dissertation, Harvard University, 1950), pp. 417–419.

18. See resolution of the Ninth Party Conference, September 1920, in *VKP(b) v Rezolyutsiyakh*, I, 415–416.

19. *VKP(b) v Rezolyutsiyakh*, I, 434.

20. *Ibid.*, p. 523.

21. *Ibid.*, p. 563.

22. *Ibid.*, p. 601.

23. *Dvenadtsatyi S"ezd Rossiiskoi Kommunisticheskoi Partii (Bol'shevikov) Stenograficheskii Otchët* (Twelfth Congress of the Russian Communist Party [Bolshevik], Stenographic Report [April 17–25, 1923]; Moscow, 1923), p. 122.

24. *XIV S"ezd VKP(b)*, p. 455.

25. *Ibid.*, p. 456.

26. Eastman, *Since Lenin Died*, pp. 81–82.

27. Sapronov, in the course of the debate at the Thirteenth Party Conference in 1924, reported that, while the opposition had elected 36 per cent of the delegates at the *raion* conferences in the Moscow *guberniya*, its representation at the *guberniya* conference was only 18 per cent. "If the opposition," he continued, "lost 18 per cent between the *raion* conference and the *guberniya* conference, then I pose the question: of how many votes was the opposition deprived in the workers' cells by the pressure of the apparatus, when these votes went to the *raion* conference?" ("XIII Konferentsiya RKP(b), Rech' Tov. Sapronova," *Pravda*, January 22, 1924, p. 4).

Sapronov's charge that the opposition had been defrauded of a majority in Moscow probably cannot be documented, but there is plentiful testimony to verify the steam-roller tactics of the troika. Bukharin, soon to become closely associated with Stalin, provided an authoritative description in a speech at a Moscow Party meeting toward the end of 1923: "As a rule, putting the matter to a vote takes place according to a method that is taken for granted. The meeting is asked: 'Who is against?' and inasmuch as one fears more or less to speak up against, the appointed candidate finds himself elected secretary of the bureau of the group" (quoted in Schachtman, pp. 172–173). Aided by such tactics, the *apparatchiki* were everywhere triumphant, and the Thirteenth Conference registered a complete rout of the opposition.

28. See Aleksandrov (pseud.), *Kto Upravlyaet Rossiei?* (Who Rules Russia?; Berlin [1933?]), pp. 111–113.

29. *Ibid.*, pp. 114, 119–121.

30. Stalin, "Trotskizm ili Leninizm?" (Trotskyism or Leninism?), *Sochineniya,* VI, 324–357.

31. See Aleksandrov, p. 137; also, *XIV S"ezd VKP(b),* p. 484.

32. See Uglanov's statement at the Fourteenth Congress, *XIV S"ezd VKP(b),* p. 193.

33. *Ibid.,* p. 524.

34. In dealing with the opposition, Stalin resorted to the strategy of divide and conquer. Part of the opposition was left in its place. Zinoviev remained in the Politburo; Evdokimov, one of Zinoviev's lieutenants, was reëlected to the Central Committee and even given new posts as a secretary of the Central Committee and member of the Orgburo, though he did not long retain these new dignities. Bakayev, another Zinoviev follower, was returned to the Central Control Commission. Other oppositionists felt the full lash of Stalin's displeasure, though the penalties imposed at this stage of the struggle were comparatively mild. At the same time, Stalin took the precaution of purging the Leningrad Party organization of Zinoviev supporters. At a special Party conference in February 1926 a Stalinist apparatus was installed in Leningrad. Kirov, operating as Stalin's proconsul, presided over the purge and became the new head of the Leningrad Party organization. Thus, the only firm core of organizational strength which remained to Zinoviev and Kamenev was cut out from under them.

35. For a more optimistic judgment of the bloc's prospects see Ruth Fischer, *Stalin and German Communism* (Cambridge, Massachusetts, 1948), pp. 537–572.

36. Trotsky, *My Life,* p. 521.

37. Quoted in Souvarine, *Staline,* p. 445.

38. See Stalin, "O Pravoi Opasnosti v VKP(b)" (On the Danger of the Right in the All-Union CP[b]), *Sochineniya,* XI, 222–238.

39. Souvarine, p. 447.

40. See Molotov's Organizational Report in *XIV S"ezd VKP(b),* p. 81.

41. *Ibid.,* p. 89.

42. Aleksandrov, pp. 106–108.

43. *XV S"ezd VKP(b),* p. 114.

44. *Ibid.,* pp. 114–115.

45. *XVI S"ezd VKP(b),* p. 81.

46. The speech "Ob Apparate TsK VKP(b)" (On the Apparatus of the Central Committee of the All-Union CP[b]) was printed in *Partiinoe Stroitel'stvo* (Party Construction), no. 2(4) (February 1930), pp. 9–13.

47. *XVI S"ezd VKP(b),* p. 83.

48. *XVII S"ezd Vsesoyuznoi Kommunisticheskoi Partii (b) Stenograficheskii Otchët* (Seventeenth Congress of the All-Union Communist Party [b], Stenographic Report [January 26–February 10, 1934]; Moscow, 1934), pp. 561–562, 672, 676. The republic, *oblast,* and *krai* secretariats were similarly organized, except that the Industrial and Transport Sections were combined and a Soviet and Trade Section replaced the Political-Administrative and Planning-Finance-Trade Sections.

49. "O Reorganizatsii Kul'tpropa TsK VKP(b)" (On the Reorganization of the *Kul'tprop* of the Central Committee of the All-Union CP[b]), *Partiinoe Stroitel'stvo,* no. 11 (June 1935), p. 47.

50. At the same time, a Soviet Control Committee was also established to replace the old Commissariat of Workers' and Peasants' Inspection. The Soviet Control Committee later became the Ministry of State Control.

51. *XVII S"ezd VKP(b),* p. 674.

52. Stalin, "Report on the Work of the Central Committee to the Seventeenth Congress of the C.P.S.U.(B.)" in *Problems of Leninism,* p. 516.

53. When the carnage was over, out of a total of 139 Central Committee members and candidates elected at the Seventeenth Party Congress, twenty-two carried over to membership in the Central Committee in 1939 and two remained as candidates. Among the twenty-two were Stalin, Andreyev, Beria, Voroshilov, Zhdanov, Lazar Kaganovich, Kalinin, Mikoyan, Molotov, Khrushchëv, Shvernik, all eleven of

whom were members of the Politburo circle; Bulganin, who was elected a candidate member in 1946; Poskrebyshev, the head of Stalin's personal secretariat; M. M. Kaganovich, the brother of Lazar; Manuilsky, the Comintern expert; Litvinov, the Commissar of Foreign Affairs; Losovsky, a trade-union expert; Budënny, the Civil War cavalry hero; Mekhlis, the head of the Political Administration of the Red Army; and a few others of lesser significance. It is perhaps not too fantastic to suggest that this narrow group of survivors of the Purge also included the chief executioners.

54. *The Land of Socialism Today and Tomorrow: Reports and Speeches at the Eighteenth Congress of the Communist Party of the Soviet Union* (*Bolshevik*) (Moscow, 1939), p. 202.

55. *Ibid.*, p. 207.

56. *Ibid.*, p. 205.

57. *XVIII S"ezd Vsesoyuznoi Kommunisticheskoi Partii* (*b*) *Stenografícheskii Otchët* (Eighteenth Congress of the All-Union Communist Party [b], Stenographic Report [March 10–21, 1939]; Moscow, 1939), p. 670; hereafter cited as *XVIII S"ezd VKP(b)*.

58. *The Land of Socialism Today and Tomorrow*, pp. 204–205.

59. *Ibid.*, p. 212.

60. *Ibid.*, p. 471.

61. *Ibid.*, p. 460.

62. G. M. Malenkov, "O Zadachakh Partiinykh Organizatsii v Oblasti Promyshlennosti i Transporta" (Concerning the Tasks of Party Organizations in the Sphere of Industry and Transport), *Partiinoe Stroitel'stvo*, no. 4–5 (February–March 1941), p. 13.

63. "O Zadachakh Partiinykh Organizatsii v Oblasti Promyshlennosti i Transporta, Rezolyutsiya po Dokladu Tov. Malenkova, Prinyataya XVIII Vsesoyuznoi Konferentsiei VKP(b)" (Concerning the Tasks of Party Organizations in the Sphere of Industry and Transport, Resolution on the Report of Comrade Malenkov Adopted by the Eighteenth All-Union Conference of the All-Union CP[b]), *ibid.*, p. 151.

64. For a remarkably ingenious effort at reconstruction, see Louis Nemzer, "The Kremlin's Professional Staff: The 'Apparatus' of the Central Committee, Communist Party of the Soviet Union," *American Political Science Review*, XLIV, no. 1 (March 1950), 64–85.

65. *Moskovskii Bol'shevik*, February 2, 1949, p. 6.

66. For verification, see *Sovetskaya Estoniya* (Soviet Esthonia), August 19, 1949.

67. See *Pravda*, October 7, 1952, p. 2.

68. Stalin, *Mastering Bolshevism*, p. 36.

69. See *XIV S"ezd VKP(b)*, p. 81.

Chapter 7

Party Organization, Activities, and Problems

1. "Ustav Kommunisticheskoi Partii Sovetskogo Soyuza" (The Rules of the Communist Party of the Soviet Union), *Pravda*, October 14, 1952, p. 2.

2. *Ibid.*

3. *Ibid.*, p. 1.

4. *Ibid.*, p. 2.

5. *Ibid.*

6. *Ibid.*

7. *Pravda*, October 17, 1952, p. 1.

8. See N. M. Pegov, "Doklad Mandatnoi Kommissii XIX S"ezda VKP(b)" (Report of the Mandate Commission of the Nineteenth Congress of the All-Union CP[b]), *Pravda*, October 9, 1952, p. 6. At the Eighteenth Party Congress (1939),

Stalin stated that there were 113,060 primary Party organizations in existence (*The Land of Socialism Today and Tomorrow*, p. 38). The report of the Mandate Commission at the Nineteenth Party Congress claims that 237,245 organizations were added between 1939 and 1952. This would make a total of 350,304.

9. See *Sovetskaya Estoniya*, August 19, 1949.

10. Nemzer, "The Kremlin's Professional Staff," *American Political Science Review*, XLIV (March 1950), 65.

11. See *Voprosy Partiino-Organizatsionnoi Raboty* (Questions of Party Organizational Work; Moscow, 1948), p. 41.

12. *Ibid.*, pp. 42–45.

13. *Ibid.*, p. 7.

14. *Ibid.*, pp. 11–12.

15. See F. Yakovlev, "O Partiinom Uchëte" (Concerning Party Records), *Bol'shevik*, no. 12 (June 1951), pp. 47–52.

16. *Ibid.*, p. 49.

17. Nemzer, *American Political Science Review*, XLIV, 68.

18. *Pravda*, October 14, 1952, p. 2.

19. See *Voprosy Partiino-Organizatsionnoi Raboty*, pp. 26, 29.

20. *Ibid.*, p. 30.

21. *Ibid.*, pp. 4–5.

22. See S. Kurdin, "Rukovodstvo Priëmom v Ryady Partii i Vospitanie Molodykh Kommunistov" (Supervision of Admission to Party Membership and the Training of Young Communists), *Bol'shevik*, no. 23 (December 1951), pp. 48–53.

23. See *Voprosy Partiino-Organizatsionnoi Raboty*, pp. 18–19.

24. *Pravda*, October 14, 1952, p. 2.

25. "Partiinaya Rabota v Sovetskikh Uchrezhdeniyakh" (Party Work in Soviet Institutions), *Bol'shevik*, no. 14 (July 1951), pp. 12, 13.

26. Stalin, *Mastering Bolshevism*, pp. 44–46.

27. *Pravda*, October 6, 1952, p. 8.

28. *Socialism Victorious* (A collection of the most important reports and speeches delivered at the Seventeenth Party Congress) (New York, n.d.), p. 179.

29. V. Verkhovsky, "Uluchshat' Metody Rukovodstva" (Improve the Methods of Management), *Pravda*, April 8, 1950, p. 2.

30. See "Report by Comrade M. D. Bagirov at 18th Congress of Azerbaidzhan Communist Party on the Work of the Azerbaidzhan Communist Party Central Committee," *Bakinskii Rabochii* (The Baku Worker), May 26, 1951, pp. 1–6, as translated in *CDSP*, III, no. 24 (July 28, 1951), 11.

31. L. Slepov, "O Bol'shevistskom Metode Rukovodstva Khozyaistvennymi Organami" (The Bolshevik Method of Managing Economic Agencies), *Bol'shevik*, no. 2 (January 1951), p. 55. Translated in *CDSP*, III, no. 6 (March 24, 1951), 11.

32. Bagirov, p. 5.

33. *Pravda*, October 6, 1952, p. 5.

34. G. Airyan, "Ser'eznye Nedostatki v Podbore i Vospitanii Kadrov" (Serious Deficiencies in the Selection and Training of Cadres), *Pravda*, January 25, 1952, p. 2.

35. Harry Schwartz, "Crime Wave Hits Stalin's Old Home," *New York Times*, February 6, 1952, p. 12. See also, "Meeting of Tbilisi City Party Organization *Aktiv*," *Zarya Vostoka* (Dawn of the East; Tbilisi), January 27, 1952, p. 2, as translated in *CDSP*, IV, no. 7 (March 29, 1952), pp. 5–7.

36. See *Informatsionnoe Soveshchanie Predstavitelei Nekotorykh Kompartii v Pol'she v Kontse Sentyabrya 1947 goda* (Informational Conference of Representatives of Certain Communist Parties in Poland at the End of September 1947; Moscow, 1948), p. 145.

37. G. Vyunov, "Administrativno-Khozyaistvennyi Podkhod k Rabote" (An Administrative and Economic Approach to Work), *Pravda*, March 3, 1950, p. 4.

38. V. Yakhnevich, "Pravil'no Sochetat' Politicheskuyu i Khozyaistvennuyu Rabotu" (The Correct Combining of Political and Managerial Work), *Pravda*, March 20, 1950, p. 2.

39. Stalin, *Mastering Bolshevism*, pp. 27–28.
40. Drawing by A. Bazhenov in *Krokodil*, no. 7 (March 10, 1951), p. 5.
41. *Pravda*, October 6, 1952, p. 5.

Chapter 8

The Composition and Social Structure of the Party

1. G. M. Malenkov, "Otchëtnyi Doklad Tsentral'nogo Komiteta VKP(b) XIX S"ezdu Partii" (Report of the Central Committee of the All-Union CP[b] to the Nineteenth Party Congress), *Pravda*, October 6, 1952, p. 7.
2. *VKP(b) v Rezolyutsiyakh*, I, 299.
3. *Ibid.*, pp. 370–371.
4. Lenin, "O Chistke Partii" (On Purging the Party), *Sochineniya*, XXVII, 12.
5. Three categories were established to provide differential conditions of eligibility to Party membership: (1) workers and Red Army men who were workers or peasants, (2) peasants (except Red Army men) and artisans not exploiting the labor of others, (3) other (office employees, etc.). Candidates in the first and second categories were to be admitted on the recommendation of three members with a Party standing of at least three years. Candidates in the third category required the recommendation of five members with a Party standing of at least five years. For those in the first category, the minimum candidate stage was fixed as six months, for the second category one year, and for the third category two years. Regardless of their social position, former members of other parties required the recommendation of five Party members of not less than five years' standing and could only be admitted with the approval of a provincial Party committee.

At the Fourteenth Party Congress in December 1925 the Party Rules were again revised to provide additional preferential advantages for workers at the bench. The first category of workers and Red Army men of worker or peasant origin was subdivided into two groups: (1) industrial workers permanently engaged as wage earners at physical work, and (2) non-industrials and Red Army men of worker, peasant, or farm labor origin. Industrial workers were to be admitted into the Party on the recommendation of two members of not less than one year's standing, while the remaining groups in the first category required two recommendations from Party members of not less than two years' standing. Persons in the second category were to be admitted on the recommendation of three Party members of not less than two years' standing, while persons of the third category continued to require five recommendations from Party members of not less than five years' standing.
6. See V. V., "Rost Partii v Pervom Polugodii 1932 g." (Party Growth in the First Half of 1932), *Partiinoe Stroitel'stvo* (Party Construction), no. 21 (November 1932), pp. 46–48.
7. *Ibid.*, p. 48.
8. Khataevich, "O Sostoyanii i Rabote Partiinoi Yacheiki v Derevne" (On the Condition and Work of the Party Cell in the Village), *Bol'shevik*, no. 3–4(19–20) (February 1925), pp. 74–86.
9. See Ya. Paikin, "Kommunisty-Krest'yane Belorusskoi Derevni" (Communist Peasants in the Belorussian Village), *Bol'shevik*, no. 17 (September 15, 1929), pp. 70 ff.
10. Of these, 20 per cent were eliminated as "alien elements" or for "connections with alien elements," 9.2 per cent for various criminal offenses such as embezzlement and bribery, 6.4 per cent for refusal to enter a kolkhoz, 3.6 per cent for hiding grain surpluses, 4.6 per cent for performance of religious rites and anti-Semitism, and the remainder for various miscellaneous reasons ("Vypolnim Vazhneishee Reshenie Partii" [We Shall Carry Out the Most Important Decision of the Party], *Bol'shevik*, no. 18 [September 30, 1929], p. 6).

11. V. Vlasov, "Rost i Kachestvennoe Ukreplenie Ryadov Partii" (The Increase and Qualitative Strengthening of the Party's Ranks), *Partiinoe Stroitel'stvo*, no. 16 (August 1932), p. 7.

12. See Table 9 in Bubnov, "VKP(b)," *Bol'shaya Sovetskaya Entsiklopediya*, XI, 534.

13. Vlasov, *Partiinoe Stroitel'stvo*, no. 16 (August 1932), p. 5. A study limited to the largest industrial enterprises, where the Party organizations were strongest, reported the following percentages as of April 1, 1931: oil, 20.5 per cent; leather, 19.8; metalworking, 17.3; chemical, 16.3; textile 14.2; paper, 13.1; wood, 12.5; transport, 10.8; ore-mining, 8.7; coal, 8.6; and electrical energy, 7.5 (G. Peskarev, "Dinamika Rosta i Problema Regulirovaniya Sostava Partii" [The Dynamics of Growth and the Problem of Regulating the Composition of the Party], *Partiinoe Stroitel'stvo*, no. 17 [September 1931], p. 38).

14. See book review by V. Anichkov, "P. Zaslavsky, 'Partrabota na Krupnykh Stroitel'stvakh,' Ogiz, Moskovskii Rabochii, 1931 g., str. 64" (P. Zaslavsky, "Party Work in Large Industries," Ogiz, Moscow Worker, 1931, 64 pp.), *Partiinoe Stroitel'stvo*, no. 13 (July 1931), p. 69.

15. "XVI S"ezd VKP(b) v Tsifrakh" (Sixteenth Congress of the All-Union CP[b] in Figures), *Partiinoe Stroitel'stvo*, no. 13–14 (July 1930), p. 30; *XV S"ezd VKP(b)*, p. 1107.

16. Vlasov, *Partiinoe Stroitel'stvo*, no. 16 (August 1932), p. 5.

17. V. Vlasov, "Za Uluchshenie Sostava Natsorganizatsii" (For Improvement in the Composition of National Organizations), *Partiinoe Stroitel'stvo*, no. 19–20 (October 1930), p. 21.

18. Vlasov, *Partiinoe Stroitel'stvo*, no. 16 (August 1932), p. 9.

19. *Bol'shaya Sovetskaya Entsiklopediya* (1930 ed.), XI, 541.

20. See A. Serebrennikov, "O Priëme Intelligentsii v Partiyu" (On the Acceptance of Intelligentsia into the Party), *Partiinoe Stroitel'stvo*, no. 6(8) (March 1930), pp. 32–35.

21. M. Ryutin, "Rukovodyashchie Kadry VKP(b)" (Leading Cadres of the All-Union CP[b]), *Bol'shevik*, no. 15 (August 15, 1928), p. 27.

22. See Table 18 in *Bol'shaya Sovetskaya Entsiklopediya*, XI, 542.

23. *XVII S"ezd VKP(b)*, p. 675.

24. The categories of the purged included so-called "passive elements" whose politico-ideological training was deficient, "class-alien and hostile elements" who concealed their social origin in applying for admission to the Party, "double-dealers" who hid their real views from the Party, "violators of the iron discipline of the Party," "degenerates" who were accused of softness toward the bourgeoisie and *kulaks*, "moral degenerates" whose misbehavior undermined the prestige of the Party, and "careerists," "self-seekers," and "bureaucratic" elements who utilized their privileges as Party members for their own ends.

25. *VKP(b) v Rezolyutsiyakh*, II, 635–636, 638, 641.

26. *Ibid.*, pp. 671–677.

27. Stalin, "New Conditions — New Tasks in Economic Construction," *Problems of Leninism*, p. 378–380.

28. *Ibid.*, pp. 566–567.

29. Thus, the district committee of the Gorky region reported that out of 602 candidates enrolled between November 1936 and November 1938, 208 were engineering-technical personnel, 312 were workers, and the rest belonged to other categories. See I. Shishkin, "Luchshikh Lyudel v Partiyu Lenina-Stalina" (Better People for Membership in the Party of Lenin and Stalin), *Partiinoe Stroitel'stvo*, no. 23 (December 1, 1938), p. 40. Djashi's report for the Georgian organization at the Eighteenth Party Congress in 1939 gave the following breakdown for the more than 26,000 members and candidates admitted since November 1, 1936: workers, 35.6 per cent; collective farmers, 18.3 per cent; and employees, 42.8 per cent (*XVIII S"ezd VKP [b]*, p. 577). His speech also made clear that the Party was pursuing a vigorous drive to enlist the rural intelligentsia and administrators in the Party, and

impressive figures were cited on the number of agronomists, teachers, doctors, chair-men of village soviets, chairmen of collective farms, and brigadiers who were listed on the Party rolls. Similar statistics were adduced by other speakers. Cheplakov of the Azerbaidjan Party analyzed the candidate group in that republic as composed of 25.5 per cent workers, 30 per cent collective farmers, and 44.5 per cent intelli-gentsia (*ibid.*, p. 548).

30. Stalin, "Report on the Work of the Central Committee to the Eighteenth Congress of the C.P.S.U.(B.)," *Problems of Leninism*, pp. 663, 665.

31. *The Land of Socialism Today and Tomorrow*, pp. 181, 183.

32. I. Kiryushkin, "Pouchitel'nye Uroki" (Instructive Lessons), *Pravda*, April 22, 1942, p. 3.

33. *Socialism Victorious*, pp. 217–218.

34. *Ibid.*, p. 213.

35. F. Chivirev, "K Voprosu o Rabote s Kommunistami-Odinochkami" (On the Question of Work with Single Communists), *Partiinoe Stroitel'stvo*, no. 14 (July 1935), p. 30.

36. *The Land of Socialism Today and Tomorrow*, p. 244.

37. *Socialism Victorious*, p. 205.

38. V. Egorov, "Za Stalinskoe Vydvizhenie Partkadrov" (For the Stalinist Pro-motion of Party Cadres), *Partiinoe Stroitel'stvo*, no. 13 (July 1, 1937), p. 40.

39. "O Rabote Partiinykh Organizatsii sredi Zhenshchin" (On the Work of Party Organizations among Women), *Bol'shevik*, no. 1 (January 1951), p. 11. There were substantial variations in the regional pattern. In the Ivanovo region with its large number of female textile operatives, women composed 30 per cent of the Party organization in 1937, but this proportion was far from characteristic of the Soviet Union as a whole (I. Nosov, "Uchëba Partiinogo Aktiva" [Training the Party *Aktiv*], *Partiinoe Stroitel'stvo*, no. 1 [January 1, 1937], p. 34). In an article entitled "Some Conclusions after the Purge of the Central-Asian Party Organization," Ya. Peters wrote, "The Central Committees of the national Communist Parties . . . show little interest in these questions [concerning the role of women], and in their apparatuses it is impossible to find any data about the participation of women in Party work or about the admission of women into the Party or the government — in fact, any material whatsoever about work among women. This field is completely forgotten and neglected" ("Nekotorye Vyvody iz Chistki Sredne-Aziatskoi Partor-ganizatsii," *Bol'shevik*, no. 3 [February 15, 1935], p. 31).

40. Out of 2,049 secretaries elected in 1937 by primary Party organizations in the Moscow area, 300 or 14.6 per cent were women. In the Ivanovo region in the same year 13.7 per cent of the secretaries and 17.7 per cent of the *partorgs* were women (A. Bogomolov, "Vybory Partorganov v Moskovskoi Organizatsii" [Election of Party Organs in the Moscow Organization], *Partiinoe Stroitel'stvo*, no. 11 [June 1, 1937], p. 13; L. Kovalëv, "Bol'shevistskaya Proverka Snizu" [Bolshevik Verification from Below], *ibid.*, p. 23). In the Leningrad elections in 1938, 18 per cent of the secretaries chosen were women (M. Sokolov, "Partiinye Massy Proveryayut Svoikh Rukovoditelei" [The Party Masses Check on Their Leaders], *Partiinoe Stroitel'stvo*, no. 10 [May 15, 1938], p. 35).

41. *XVIII S"ezd VKP(b)*, p. 149.

42. Ya. Peters, p. 23.

43. Solomon M. Schwarz, *The Jews in the Soviet Union*, p. 302.

44. See Rudzutak's report to the Seventeenth Congress in *XVII S"ezd VKP(b)*, p. 287.

45. See S. Freiberg, "Iz Praktiki Raboty s Partiinym Aktivom" (From experience in Work with the Party *Aktiv*), *Partiinoe Stroitel'stvo*, no. 10 (May 1935), p. 26.

46. *XVIII S"ezd VKP(b)*, p. 149.

47. See Malenkov's report, *ibid.*, p. 148.

48. *Ibid.*

49. *The Land of Socialism Today and Tomorrow*, pp. 238–239.

50. *Ibid.*, p. 239.

51. By a Central Committee decree of August 19, 1941, such applicants could be received into the Party on the endorsement of three Party members of one year's standing. By a later decree (December 9, 1941), the candidacy stage for these applicants was reduced to three months. These decrees are summarized in "Voprosy Chlenstva v VKP(b), po Dokumentam i Tsifram za 30 Let" (Questions of Membership in the All-Union CP[b], According to Documents and Figures for Thirty Years), *Partiinaya Zhizn'* (Party Life), no. 20 (October 1947), p. 82.

52. P. Pospelov, "Partiya Lenina-Stalina — Rukovodyashchaya i Napravlyayushchaya Sila Sovetskogo Obshchestva" (The Party of Lenin and Stalin Is the Leading and Directing Force of Soviet Society), *Bol'shevik*, no. 20 (October 30, 1947), p. 37.

53. *Informatsionnoe Soveshchanie Predstavitelei Nekotorykh Kompartii v Pol'she v Kontse Sentyabrya 1947 goda* (Informational Conference of Representatives of Certain Communist Parties in Poland at the End of September 1947), p. 144.

54. *Pravda*, October 9, 1952, p. 6.

55. "Report by Comrade M. D. Bagirov at 18th Congress of Azerbaidzhan Communist Party on the Work of the Azerbaidzhan Communist Party Central Committee," *Bakinskii Rabochii* (The Baku Worker), May 26, 1951, pp. 1–6, translated in *CDSP*, III, no. 24 (July 28, 1951), 9.

56. M. Shamberg, "Nekotorye Voprosy Vnutripartiinoi Raboty" (Certain Questions on Intra-Party Work), *Partiinoe Stroitel'stvo*, no. 4 (February 1946), p. 28.

57. S. Kurdin, "Rukovodstvo Priëmom v Ryady Partii i Vospitanie Molodykh Kommunistov" (Supervision of Admission to Party Membership and the Training of Young Communists), *Bol'shevik*, no. 23 (December 1951), p. 50.

58. "Report of the Party Central Committee of Kazakhstan to the Fifth Congress of the Kazakhstan Communist Party," *Kazakhstanskaya Pravda* (Alma-Ata), December 16, 1951, pp. 1–6, translated in *CDSP*, IV, no. 15 (May 24, 1952), 13. The only notable divergence from this trend was Baku where 56.3 per cent of those admitted as members and candidates in 1950 were reported as workers while only 25.3 per cent were classified as engineers, technicians, and persons of other specialties. This ratio was markedly atypical (Bagirov, *CDSP*, III [July 28, 1951], 9).

59. "Shiroko Razvernut' Politicheskuyu Rabotu v Derevne" (For the Widespread Development of Political Work in Rural Areas), *Bol'shevik*, no. 6 (March 1947), p. 6.

60. Bagirov, *CDSP*, III (July 28, 1951), 9.

61. *Partiinaya Zhizn'*, no. 5 (March 1948), p. 11.

62. See Malenkov's speech to the Nineteenth Party Congress, *Pravda*, October 6, 1952, p. 5.

63. "O Rabote Partiinykh Organizatsii sredi Zhenshchin" (On the Work of Party Organizations among Women), *Bol'shevik*, no. 1 (January 1951), p. 11.

64. Shamberg, p. 28.

65. *Bol'shevik*, no. 1 (January 1951), p. 11.

66. See the report of the Mandate Commission to the Nineteenth Party Congress, *Pravda*, October 9, 1952, p. 6.

67. "O Rabote Partiinykh Organizatsii sredi Zhenshchin," *Bol'shevik*, no. 1 (January 1951), p. 17.

68. Shamberg, p. 28.

69. See *XVIII S"ezd VKP(b)*, p. 149, and the report of the Mandate Commission to the Nineteenth Party Congress, *Pravda*, October 9, 1952, p. 6.

70. G. F. Aleksandrov, "Nas Osenyaet Velikoe Znamya Lenina-Stalina" (The Great Banner of Lenin and Stalin Shields Us), *Bol'shevik*, no. 1 (January 1947), p. 14.

71. *Ibid.*

72. *XVIII S"ezd VKP(b)*, p. 148.

73. Report of the Mandate Commission, *Pravda*, October 9, 1952, p. 6.

74. As an indication of its increased hold on the intelligentsia, the Party in 1947 listed among its members 148,000 engineers, 24,000 agronomists and other agricultural specialists, almost 40,000 physicians, and 80,000 teachers (G. F. Aleksandrov, *Bol'shevik*, no. 1 [January 1947], p. 14).

Chapter *9*

The Komsomol—Youth under Dictatorship

1. These are the figures supplied by N. Mikhailov, then first secretary of the Komsomol, in his report to the Nineteenth Party Congress, *Pravda*, October 7, 1952, p. 6.

2. The observations reported here are based both on a consultation of official Soviet publications and on a series of interviews with some fifty Soviet defectors and non-returners who were at one time members of the Pioneers and Komsomol. The interviews took place in Western Germany and Austria during the summer and fall of 1949. The great majority of those interviewed had left the Soviet Union during World War II; a small minority consisted of recent defectors from the Red Army and the Soviet Military Government in Germany. For a general treatment of the attitudes of Soviet non-returners and defectors, see Merle Fainsod, "Controls and Tensions in the Soviet System," *American Political Science Review*, XLIV, no. 2 (June 1950), 266–282.

3. Quoted in Klaus Mehnert, *Youth in Soviet Russia* (London, 1933), p. 49.

4. *Bol'shaya Sovetskaya Entsiklopediya* (Great Soviet Encyclopedia; 1930 ed.), XI, 635–638.

5. For a copy of this resolution, see VKP(b), *O Komsomole i Molodëzhi* (On the Komsomol and Youth; Moscow, 1938), p. 76. This volume is a valuable collection of the most important Party resolutions on the Komsomol for the period up to 1938.

6. Mehnert, p. 53.

7. *Bol'shaya Sovetskaya Entsiklopediya*, XI, 638.

8. *Ibid.*, p. 640.

9. *Ibid.*, pp. 645–649; also VKP(b), *O Komsomole i Molodëzhi* (On the Komsomol and Youth), pp. 80–82.

10. Mehnert, pp. 60–61.

11. *Bol'shaya Sovetskaya Entsiklopediya*, XI, 649.

12. *Ibid.*, pp. 649–650.

13. *Ibid.*, p. 649.

14. *Ibid.*, pp. 653–654.

15. See Mehnert, *passim*.

16. *Ibid.*, p. 91.

17. Julian Towster, *Political Power in the USSR* (New York, 1948), p. 140; also "Dvadtsatiletie Komsomola" (Twenty Years of the Komsomol), *Partiinoe Stroitel'stvo* (Party Construction), no. 16 (August 15, 1938), pp. 52–59.

18. A. A. Andreyev, "Kommunisticheskoe Vospitanie Molodëzhi i Zadachi Komsomola" (The Communist Education of the Youth and the Tasks of the Komsomol), *Partiinoe Stroitel'stvo*, no. 9 (May 1936), p. 10.

19. *Ibid.*

20. A. V. Kosarëv, "O Perestroike Raboty Komsomola" (On the Reorganization of Komsomol Work), *Partiinoe Stroitel'stvo*, no. 14 (July 1935), p. 8.

21. Towster, p. 140.

22. See the attack in the editorial "Vyshe Bol'shevistskuyu Bditel'nost' Komsomol'tsev" (Raise the Bolshevistic Vigilance of the Komsomol), *Partiinoe Stroitel'stvo*, no. 18 (September 1937), p. 8.

23. See for example, D. Smirnov, "Perestroika Raboty v Komsomole" (Reshaping the Work of the Komsomol), *Partiinoe Stroitel'stvo*, no. 12 (June 15, 1937), pp. 23–27. See also P. Vershkov, "Sovetskoi Molodëzhi — Leninsko-Stalinskoe Vospitanie" (A Leninist-Stalinist Education for Soviet Youth), *Partiinoe Stroitel'stvo*, no. 7 (April 1, 1938), pp. 28–33, where some typical expulsion figures are cited. In the Komsomol organization of Georgia, 1,577 persons were excluded in the third

quarter of 1937, of whom 1,182 were denounced as "hostile elements." In the Omsk region, during the same period, 1,101 Komsomols were excluded, of whom 731 were denounced as "hostile elements and double-dealers."

24. See Vershkov, *ibid.*, p. 28.

25. *Sobranie Postanovlenii i Rasporyazhenii Pravitel'stva SSSR* (Collection of Decrees and Ordinances of the Government of the USSR), 1940, no. 27, sect. 637; 1940, no. 29, sect. 698.

26. *Vedomosti Verkhovnogo Soveta SSSR* (Official Journal of the Supreme Soviet of the USSR), 1940, no. 37.

27. Towster, p. 140.

28. See A. N. Shelepin, "Doklad Mandatnoi Komissii XI S"ezda VLKSM" (Report of the Mandate Commission, Eleventh Congress of the All-Union Leninist Communist League of Youth), *Molodoi Bol'shevik* (Young Bolshevik), no. 8 (April 1949), p. 67.

29. See for examples the following articles: V. Ershov, "Ne Isklyuchat' Ogul'no, a Vospitat' (Ob Oshibke Kemerovskogo Obkoma Komsomola)" (Do Not Exclude Without Foundation, but Educate [On the Mistakes of the Kemerovo Regional Committee of the Komsomol]), *Molodoi Bol'shevik*, no. 21 (November 1949), pp. 39–43; resolutions of the Second Plenum of the Komsomol Central Committee, "O Roste Ryadov VLKSM Sverdlovskoi Oblastnoi Komsomol'skoi Organizatsii" (On the Growth in the Ranks of the All-Union LCLY in the Sverdlovsk Regional Komsomol Organization) and "O Rabote Komsomol'skoi Organizatsii Stalingradskogo Traktornogo Zavoda Imeni F. Dzerzhinskogo" (On the Work of the Komsomol Organization in the F. Dzerzhinsky Tractor Factory in Stalingrad), *Molodoi Bol'shevik*, no. 1 (January 1950), pp. 33–44; "O Stile Raboty Molotovskogo Obkoma Komsomola" (On the Style of Work of the Molotov Regional Committee of the Komsomol), *Molodoi Bol'shevik*, no. 9 (May 1950), pp. 30–37.

30. N. A. Mikhailov, "Nepreryvno Uluchshat' Rabotu s Komsomol'skimi Kadrami" (For Constant Improvement in the Work with Komsomol Cadres), *Molodoi Bol'shevik*, no. 15 (August 1952), p. 4.

31. N. A. Mikhailov, "O Roste Ryadov VLKSM" (On the Growth in the Ranks of the All-Union LCLY), *Molodoi Bol'shevik*, no. 3 (February 1951), p. 5.

32. E. N. Medynsky, *Narodnoe Obrazovanie v SSSR* (Public Education in the USSR; Moscow, 1947), p. 32.

33. For recent descriptions of Pioneer activities, see *Kommunisticheskoe Vospitanie v Sovetskoi Shkole: Sbornik Statei* (Communist Education in the Soviet School: Collection of Articles; Moscow, 1950), II, 313–336.

34. For a recent description of this ceremony, see *ibid.*, pp. 322 ff. The celebration is attended by all the Pioneers of the school, their leaders, teachers, the school director, and honored guests. The assembly hall is decorated with portraits of Lenin and Stalin. The Pioneers march into the hall in quasi-military formation. One of the honored guests, an old Party member, presents each initiate, arrayed in his new uniform, with his red kerchief, his Pioneer badge, and his membership card. As the presentation is made, the symbolism of kerchief and badge is explained. The three corners of the triangularly folded kerchief stand for Party, Komsomol, and Pioneer, pillars of the Soviet state. The badge is decorated with a red flag on which are the hammer and sickle and a camp fire of five logs burning with three flames. The five logs represent the continents of the earth; the three flames symbolize the Third International with its promise of the future world revolution. The new recruits are greeted with the slogan, "To battle for Lenin and Stalin — be ready!" Rendering the Pioneer salute, they reply in the slogan emblazoned on the Pioneer badge, "Always ready!" The ceremony is concluded with speeches, recitations, and songs designed to impress the initiates with their new estate.

35. See the revised rules adopted at the Eleventh Congress of the Komsomol, April 6, 1949. They are reprinted in full in *Molodoi Bol'shevik*, no. 9 (May 1949), pp. 19–24.

36. *Ibid.*, pp. 19–20.

37. *Ibid.*, pp. 20–24.

38. See N. A. Mikhailov, "Otchët TsK VLKSM XI S"ezdu" (Report of the Central Committee of the All-Union LCLY to the Eleventh Congress), *Molodoi Bol'shevik*, no. 8 (April 1949), p. 36.

39. The membership of these bodies is listed in *Molodoi Bol'shevik*, no. 9 (May 1949), pp. 25–26.

40. Shelepin, *Molodoi Bol'shevik*, no. 8 (April 1949), pp. 66–72.

41. Mikhailov, *ibid.*, p. 27.

42. *Ibid.*, p. 29.

43. *Young Communists in the USSR*, trans. Virginia Rhine (Washington, 1950), p. 19.

44. For descriptions of Komsomol relationships to Dosarm and Dosflot, see Major-General V. Golovkin, "Komsomol i Dosarm" (Komsomol and Dosarm), *Molodoi Bol'shevik*, no. 22 (November 1949), pp. 31–35, and Rear Admiral I. Golubev-Monatkin, "Komsomol i Dosflot" (Komsomol and Dosflot), *Molodoi Bol'shevik*, no. 14 (July 1950), pp. 35–39.

45. In the course of his remarks to the Nineteenth Party Congress, Mikhailov, then Komsomol leader, reminded Komsomols in the countryside that they had a special obligation to guard collective-farm property, and he called upon them to report immediately to higher authorities when they encountered irregularities (*Pravda*, October 7, 1952, p. 6).

46. See D. G. Popov, "Rabota Komsomol'skoi Organizatsii v Shkole" (The Work of Komsomol Organizations in the School) in *Kommunisticheskoe Vospitanie v Sovetskoi Shkole: Sbornik Statei* (Communist Education in the Soviet School: Collection of Articles), II, 289.

47. *Young Communists in the USSR*, p. 7.

48. *Ibid.*, p. 16.

49. *Ibid.*, p. 77.

50. *Ibid.*, p. 76.

51. Strenuous efforts have been made in recent years to strengthen Komsomol membership in rural areas. By April 1949, according to Soviet figures, there were 2,200,000 Komsomols in the countryside (*Pravda*, April 5, 1949). As the kolkhoz merger movement gathered momentum in 1950, the Komsomol Central Committee launched a campaign to establish Komsomol units in each one of the new amalgamated farms. In February 1951 Mikhailov announced that the task had been accomplished by 116 *oblast, krai*, and republic organizations, though he also indicated that there were "hundreds" of collective farms into which the Komsomol had not yet penetrated (*Molodoi Bol'shevik*, no. 3 [February 1951], p. 7).

52. Frederick C. Barghoorn, *The Soviet Image of the United States* (New York, 1950), p. 268.

53. *Young Communists in the USSR*, p. 77.

54. *Ibid.*

55. *Ibid.*

56. *Ibid.*, p. 79.

57. *Ibid.*, p. 80.

58. *Ibid.*, p. 11.

59. *Molodoi Bol'shevik*, no. 8 (April 1949), p. 25.

60. See the resolutions of the Second Plenum of the Komsomol Central Committee on the growth of the Komsomol organization in the Sverdlovsk Region and the work in the Stalingrad Tractor Factory, cited earlier, *Molodoi Bol'shevik*, no. 1 (January 1950), pp. 33–44.

Chapter 10

The Party Command—Politburo and Presidium

1. *Protokoly TsK RSDRP, Avgust 1917–Fevral' 1918* (Protocols of the Central Committee of the RSDLP, August 1917–February 1918), pp. 100–101.

2. For a description of the incident, see Lenin, "Politicheskii Otchët Tsentral'nogo Komiteta RKP(b) 27 Marta" (Political Report of the Central Committee of the RCP[b], March 27, 1922), *Sochineniya,* XXVII, 247–251.

3. *Ibid.,* p. 257.

4. *XV S"ezd VKP(b),* p. 108.

5. *VKP(b), v Rezolyutsiyakh,* II, 100–102.

6. Lenin, "Luchshe Menshe, da Luchshe" (Better Less, but Better), *Sochineniya,* XXVII, 413.

7. *VKP(b) v Rezolyutsiyakh,* II, 275–276.

8. Quoted in Fischer, *Stalin and German Communism,* p. 436.

9. Kuibyshev's father was an army officer and his mother a teacher. As a youth he attended a military school and spent a year at the St. Petersburg Academy of Military Medicine, from which he was excluded in 1906 for subversive political activity. From that point on he became a professional revolutionary. Ordjonikidze came from a family of small gentry and was trained as a *feldsher,* or medical assistant. Molotov was born in a family of merchant clerks and interspersed his career as a revolutionary organizer with study at the St. Petersburg Polytechnic Institute. Both Ordjonikidze and Molotov were particularly close to Stalin. Ordjonikidze, a fellow Georgian, was an intimate associate of Stalin in the days of his obscurity in the Caucasus. Molotov, a later acquisition, began his career as a *fides Achates* in 1917 and continued to discharge that role until Stalin's death.

10. See F. Beck and W. Godin, *Russian Purge and the Extraction of Confession* (New York, 1951), p. 212.

11. Quoted in Walter Duranty, *Stalin & Co.* (New York, 1949), pp. 201–202.

12. Published in *Pravda,* March 8, 1950, p. 4. See also, "O Nekotorykh Voprosakh Organizatsionno-Khozyaistvennogo Upravleniya Kolkhozov" (Several Questions on Organizational-Economic Direction of Kolkhozes), *Pravda,* April 25, 1950, p. 2.

13. *Pravda,* August 26, 1952, p. 2.

14. *Pravda,* October 17, 1952, p. 1.

15. See *The Report of the Royal Commission Appointed under Order in Council P.C. 411 of February 5, 1946, to Investigate . . . Communication by Public Officials . . . of Secret . . . Information to Agents of a Foreign Power, June 27, 1946* (Ottawa, 1946).

16. See Stalin's letter to Colonel Razin of February 23, 1946, translated in Byron Dexter, "Clausewitz and Soviet Strategy," *Foreign Affairs,* XXIX, no. 1 (October 1950), 44. For the original text, see "Otvet Tov. Stalina na Pis'mo Tov. Razina" (Comrade Stalin's Reply to the Letter of Comrade Razin) in *Bol'shevik,* no. 3 (February 1947), pp. 6–8.

17. Stalin, *Mastering Bolshevism,* p. 11.

18. "Pis'mo T. Ivanova i Otvet T. Stalina" (The Letter of Comrade Ivanov and Comrade Stalin's Reply), *Bol'shevik,* no. 4 (February 15, 1938), p. 14.

19. Lenin, "Otchët Tsentral'nogo Komiteta 18 Marta" (Report of the Central Committee, March 18, 1919), *Sochineniya,* XXIV, 122.

20. From Stalin's speech "The Task of Business Executives" delivered February 4, 1931, and reprinted in his *Problems of Leninism,* pp. 365–366.

21. From a preëlection speech of February 7, 1946, to the voters in the Leningrad electoral district printed in *Pravda,* February 8, 1946, p. 2.

22. See letter to Colonel Razin in Byron Dexter, p. 44.

23. *The Soviet-Yugoslav Dispute* (London–New York, 1948), p. 36.

24. *Ibid.*, p. 51.
25. Stalin, "Ekonomicheskie Problemy Sotsializma v SSSR," *Bol'shevik*, no. 18 (September 1952), pp. 17–18; for translation, see *CDSP*, supplementary issue, IV, no. 36 (October 18, 1952), 20; also available in English in pamphlet form published by International Publishers, New York, 1952.
26. *Ibid.*, p. 19.
27. *Pravda*, October 6, 1952, p. 3. My italics.
28. *Bol'shevik*, no. 18 (September 1952), p. 19.

Chapter *11*

Constitutional Myths and Political Realities

1. *Vtoroi Vserossiiskii S″ezd Sovetov R. i S.D.* (Second All-Russian Congress of Soviets of Workers' and Soldiers' Deputies), p. 79.
2. Radkey, *The Election to the Russian Constituent Assembly of 1917*, p. 80.
3. Bunyan and Fisher, *The Bolshevik Revolution, 1917–1918*, p. 375.
4. *Ibid.*, p. 378.
5. *Ibid.*, p. 385.
6. *Tretii Vserossiiskii S″ezd Sovetov Rabochikh, Soldatskikh i Krest'yanskikh Deputatov* (Third All-Russian Congress of Soviets of Workers', Soldiers' and Peasants' Deputies), p. 5.
7. *Ibid.*, p. 85.
8. *Ibid.*, pp. 93–94.
9. The richest source on the history of the drafting of the 1918 Constitution is G. S. Gurvich, *Istoriya Sovetskoi Konstitutsii* (History of the Soviet Constitution; Moscow, 1923). This volume contains the texts of all proposals which were submitted to the committee and provides a revealing analysis of the debates within the drafting group.
10. Quoted in James Bunyan, *Intervention, Civil War, and Communism in Russia, April–December 1918* (Baltimore, 1936), p. 502.
11. *Ibid.*, pp. 502, 504.
12. See Stanley W. Page, "Lenin, the National Question and the Baltic States, 1917–19," *The American Slavic and East European Review*, VII, no. 1 (February 1948), 15–31.
13. Stalin, "Ob Ukrainskoi Rade" (On the Ukrainian Rada), *Sochineniya*, IV, 15.
14. "Sovet Narodnykh Komissarov ob Ukraine" (The Council of People's Commissars on the Ukraine), *Pravda*, no. 198, November 24/December 7, 1917, p. 3.
15. Yu. V. Klyuchnikov and A. V. Sabanin, *Mezhdunarodnaya Politika Noveishego Vremeni v Dogovorakh, Notakh i Deklaratsiyakh* (International Politics of Modern Times in Treaties, Notes, and Declarations; Moscow, 1925–1929), III(1), 22.
16. See W. R. Batsell, *Soviet Rule in Russia* (New York, 1929), p. 217.
17. Stalin, "Organizatsionnyi Otchët Tsentral'nogo Komiteta RKP(b) 17 Aprelya 1923 g." (Organizational Report of the Central Committee of the RCP[b], April 17, 1923), *Sochineniya*, V, 231.
18. See Batsell, pp. 232–235.
19. Stalin, "Vystuplenie na Soveshchanii po Sozyvu Uchreditel'nogo S″ezda Tataro-Bashkirskoi Sovetskoi Respubliki" (Address at the Conference on the Convocation of a Constituent Congress of the Tatar-Bashkir Soviet Republic), *Sochineniya*, IV, 87.
20. According to Batsell, p. 235, about 60 per cent of the original membership of the Communist Parties of Bokhara and Khorezm was composed of clergy and merchants. At the Tenth Party Congress in 1921, Safarov, an Old Bolshevik who had visited Turkestan, reported seeing the following notice in a small town of Turkestan: "Since divine service today is being performed . . . by a Communist

priest, all members of the Communist Party are invited to the service" (*Protokoly Desyatogo S"ezda RKP[b]* [Moscow, 1933], p. 195).

21. Lenin, "Kriticheskie Zametki po Natsional'nomu Voprosu" (Critical Remarks on the National Question), *Sochineniya*, XVII, 146.

22. Quoted in Batsell, p. 117.

23. Lenin, "Zaklyuchitel'noe Slovo po Dokladu o Partiinoi Programme 19 Marta" (Concluding Remarks on the Report Concerning the Party Program, March 19, 1919), *Sochineniya*, XXIV, 155.

24. *VKP(b) v Rezolyutsiyakh*, I, 456–457. Translated in Schwarz, *The Jews in the Soviet Union*, p. 37.

25. Stalin, "Politika Sovetskoi Vlasti po Natsional'nomu Voprosu v Rossii" (Policy of the Soviet State on the National Question in Russia), *Pravda*, October 10, 1920; reprinted in *Sochineniya*, IV, 358.

26. Stalin, "O Politicheskikh Zadachakh Universiteta Narodov Vostoka" (On the Political Tasks of the University of the Peoples of the East), *Sochineniya*, VII, 138; quoted in Schwarz, *The Jews in the Soviet Union*, pp. 38–39.

27. Stalin, "Marksizm i Natsional'nyi Vopros" (Marxism and the National Question), *Sochineniya*, II, 343.

28. Stalin, "Doklad po Natsional'nomu Voprosu 29 Aprelya 1917 g." (Report on the National Question, April 29, 1917), *Sochineniya*, III, 55.

29. *XIV S"ezd VKP(b)*, pp. 881–882.

30. For text of treaty see Batsell, pp. 246–247.

31. *VKP(b) v Rezolyutsiyakh*, I, 456.

32. *Devyatyi Vserossiiskii S"ezd Rabochikh, Krest'yanskikh, Krasnoarmeiskikh i Kazach'ikh Deputatov, Stenograficheskii Otchёt* (Ninth All-Russian Congress of Workers', Peasants', Red Army and Cossacks' Deputies, Stenographic Report [December 22–27, 1921]; Moscow, 1922), p. 299; Carr, *The Bolshevik Revolution 1917–1923*, I, 389.

33. See Batsell, p. 276.

34. *VKP(b) v Rezolyutsiyakh*, I, 593.

35. Stalin, "Doklad o Natsional'nykh Momentakh v Partiinom i Gosudarstvennom Stroitel'stve" (Report on the National Factors in Party and State Construction), *Sochineniya*, V, 244–245.

36. "Chetvёrtoe Soveshchanie TsK RKP(b) s Otvetstvennymi Rabotnikami Natsional'nykh Respublik i Oblastei, Zaklyuchitel'noe Slovo" (Fourth Conference of the Central Committee RCP[b] with Officials of the National Republics and *Oblasts*, Concluding Remarks), *Sochineniya*, V, 335–336.

37. "Politika Sovetskoi Vlasti po Natsional'nomu Voprosu" (Policy of the Soviet State on the National Question), reprinted in *Sochineniya*, IV, 353–354.

38. "Tov. Kaganovichu i Drugim Chlenam PB TsK KP(b)U" (To Comrade Kaganovich and Other Members of the Politburo of the Central Committee of the CP[b] of the Ukraine), *Sochineniya*, VIII, 149–154.

39. *Ibid.*, p. 152.

40. *Ibid.*

41. Andrei Y. Vyshinsky, *The Law of the Soviet State* (New York, 1948), p. 122.

42. Stalin, "On the New Constitution" in *Problems of Leninism*, p. 571.

43. *Ibid.*, pp. 578–579.

44. *Ibid.*, p. 589.

45. *Konstitutsiya (Osnovnoi Zakon) Soyuza Sovetskikh Sotsialisticheskikh Respublik* (Constitution [Fundamental Law] of the Union of Soviet Socialist Republics; Moscow, 1947), p. 4.

46. N. N. Polyansky, "The Soviet Criminal Court as a Conductor of the Policy of the Party and the Soviet Regime," *Vestnik Moskovskogo Universiteta* (Moscow University Herald), no. 11 (November 1950), pp. 125–139, condensed and translated in *CDSP*, IV, no. 6 (March 22, 1952), 10.

47. For evidence see Solomon Schwarz, *The Jews in the Soviet Union*, pp. 351–364.

48. Vyshinsky, p. 610.

49. *Zasedaniya Verkhovnogo Soveta SSSR, Tret'ya Sessiya, 20–25 Fevralya 1947 g., Stenograficheskii Otchët* (Sessions of the Supreme Soviet of the USSR, Third Session, February 20–25, 1947, Stenographic Report; Moscow, 1947), p. 311.

50. *Ibid., Pervaya Sessiya, 12–19 Marta 1946 g.* (First Session, March 12–19, 1946; Moscow, 1946), pp. 345–346.

51. Vyshinsky, p. 722.

52. See the editorial, "Vybory v Verkhovnyi Sovet SSSR i Zadachi Agitatsionno-Propagandistskoi Raboty" (Election to the USSR Supreme Soviet and the Problems of Agitation and Propaganda Work), *Kul'tura i Zhizn'*, January 11, 1950, p. 1, as summarized and translated in *CDSP*, II, no. 3 (March 4, 1950), 10–11.

53. "Soobshchenie Tsentral'noi Izbiratel'noi Komissii po Vyboram v Verkhovnyi Sovet SSSR ob Itogakh Vyborov 12 Marta 1950 goda i Personal'nom Spiske Deputatov" (Statement of the Central Election Commission on the Election to the USSR Supreme Soviet, on the Results of the Election of March 12, 1950, and the Individual List of Deputies), *Pravda*, March 15, 1950, p. 1.

54. "Velichestvennaya Demonstratsiya Edinstva Sovetskogo Naroda" (A Majestic Demonstration of the Unity of the Soviet People), *Pravda*, March 14, 1950, p. 1.

55. For an example of such action, see P. K. Ignatov, "From a Deputy's Memoirs," *Oktyabr'* (October), no. 1 (January 1950), pp. 138–154. Excerpts from this are translated in *CDSP*, II, no. 9 (April 15, 1950), 3–10.

56. *Ibid.*, p. 7.

57. Stalin, "On the Problems of Leninism" in *Problems of Leninism*, p. 149.

58. "Foundations of Leninism," *ibid.*, p. 36.

59. I. P. Trainin and I. D. Levin (eds.), *Sovetskoe Gosudarstvennoe Pravo* (Soviet State Law; Moscow, 1948), p. 437.

Chapter 12

The Control of the Bureaucracy

1. Stalin, "On the Problems of Leninism," *Problems of Leninism*, p. 135.

2. See for example, I. I. Evtikhiev and V. A. Vlasov, *Administrativnoe Pravo SSSR* (Administrative Law of the USSR; Moscow, 1946), part I, pp. 3–143.

3. Lenin, "Pyat' Let Rossiiskoi Revolyutsii i Perspektivy Mirovoi Revolyutsii" (Five Years of the Russian Revolution and the Prospects of the World Revolution), *Sochineniya*, XXVII, 353.

4. For text of this speech, see "O Zadachakh Partiinykh Organizatsii v Oblasti Promyshlennosti i Transporta" (On the Tasks of Party Organizations in the Spheres of Industry and Transport), *Partiinoe Stroitel'stvo* (Party Construction), no. 4–5 (February–March 1941), pp. 9–33.

5. *Sbornik Zakonov* (Collection of Laws; Moscow, 1945), vol. II, 1933–1944, p. 41.

6. For a brief description of their operation, see I. P. Trainin and I. D. Levin (eds.), *Sovetskoe Gosudarstvennoe Pravo* (Soviet State Law), pp. 435–436.

7. See *Vedomosti Verkhovnogo Soveta SSSR*, no. 10(419), March 28, 1946.

8. This and the following table have been adapted from tables reproduced in Trainin and Levin, pp. 391–392. The statistics, however, have been brought up to date.

9. For a complete list as of 1946, see Evtikhiev and Vlasov, pp. 28–29. This list has been translated by John Hazard in Fritz Morstein Marx (ed.), *Foreign Governments* (2nd ed.; New York, 1952), p. 475.

10. Descriptions of the internal organization and assignment of functions within ministries were published from time to time in the collections of Administrative Orders and Decrees issued by the Council of Ministers of the USSR and the various

union republics (*Sobranie Postanovlenii i Rasporyazhenii Soveta Ministrov Soyuza Sovetskikh Sotsialisticheskikh Respublik* or *RSFSR*, cited hereinafter as *Sob. Post. SSSR* and *Sob. Post. RSFSR* respectively). For some typical examples, see *Sob. Post. SSSR*, 1941, no. 15, on the organizational structure of the People's Commissariat of Machine Construction; *Sob. Post. RSFSR*, 1946, no. 7, on the organization of the Ministry of State Control; *Sob. Post. RSFSR*, 1947, no. 11, on the organization of the Ministry of Light Industry. These publications are no longer publicly circulated.

11. Some of the more important enterprises in the field may be directly attached for supervisory purposes to the union-republic ministry at the center, but this is not the typical pattern.

12. See *Zasedaniya Verkhovnogo Soveta SSSR, Pervaya Sessiya, 12–19 Iyunya 1950 g., Stenograficheskii Otchët* (Sessions of the Supreme Soviet of the USSR, First Session, June 12–19, 1950, Stenographic Report; Moscow, 1950), p. 345; hereafter cited as *Verkh. Sov. SSSR*, with the relevant session given in abbreviated form.

13. *Verkh. Sov. SSSR*, 2 Sess., March 6–12, 1951 (Moscow, 1951), p. 366.

14. See E. Lokshin, "Normirovanie Raskhoda Syr'ya i Materialov v Proizvodstve" (The Allocation of Resources and Materials in Industry), *Planovoe Khozyaistvo* (Planned Economy), no. 6 (November–December 1950), pp. 86–94, *passim*.

15. See *Sob. Post. SSSR*, 1941, no. 2, for a detailed organizational breakdown.

16. A. Kursky, *The Planning of the National Economy of the U.S.S.R.* (Moscow, 1949), pp. 182–183.

17. Mekhlis, "Tridtsat' Let Sotsialisticheskogo Gosudarstvennogo Kontrolya" (Thirty Years of Socialist State Control), *Pravda*, April 9, 1949, p. 6.

18. *Pravda*, October 6, 1952, p. 7.

19. *Ibid.*, p. 4.

20. Kursky, p. 162.

21. This discussion of financial controls draws heavily on N. N. Rovinsky, *Gosudarstvennyi Byudzhet SSSR* (The State Budget of the USSR; Moscow, 1951), and N. N. Rovinsky (ed.), *Finansovoe Pravo* (Financial Law; Moscow, 1946).

22. *Verkh. Sov. SSSR*, 2 Sess., March 6–12, 1951, pp. 361–363.

23. For a recent article on the history of this ministry, see Mekhlis, *Pravda*, April 9, 1949, pp. 5–6.

24. *Verkh. Sov. SSSR*, 2 Sess., March 6–12, 1951, p. 288.

25. See for example, A. Sivakov, "Ob Odnom Sudebnom Dele" (Concerning a Certain Legal Case), *Izvestiya*, January 3, 1950, p. 3.

26. Quoted in Berman, *Justice in Russia*, p. 81.

27. Decree translated in Meisel and Kozera, *Materials for the Study of the Soviet System*, pp. 404–405.

28. *Ibid.*, pp. 407–408.

29. For recent examples, see speech by Comrade A. I. Mgeladze, "Report of the Georgian Communist Party Central Committee," *Zarya Vostoka*, September 16, pp. 2–6; September 17, pp. 2–4; and September 18, 1952, pp. 2–4, as condensed and translated in *CDSP*, IV, no. 41 (November 22, 1952), 8–10; "Producer of Inferior Goods Punished," *Izvestiya*, November 19, 1952, p. 4, and "A Case of Padding," *Vechernyaya Moskva*, November 22, 1952, p. 4, both translated in *CDSP*, IV, no. 47 (January 3, 1953), 16–17; also "Deliberate Violator of Collective Farm Statutes," *Izvestiya*, December 14, 1952, p. 4, translated in *CDSP*, IV, no. 50 (January 24, 1953), 12–13, and A. Iushin, "Outlandish Behavior of Khabarovsk Prosecutor's Office," *Izvestiya*, December 18, 1952, p. 2, translated in *CDSP*, IV, no. 51 (January 31, 1953), 21.

30. Quoted in Gsovski, *Soviet Civil Law*, I, 874.

31. Quoted in Berman, p. 65.

32. For a description of the work of the Commission, see Evtikhiev and Vlasov, pp. 41–44.

33. For a succinct summary of the work of the Ministry of Labor Reserves, see A. E. Pasherstnik, *Pravo na Trud* (The Right to Work; Moscow, 1951), pp. 125 ff.

34. *Ibid.*, p. 131.

35. Quoted in Gsovski, I, 144.

Chapter *13*

Terror as a System of Power

1. Lenin, "Doklad o Deyatel'nosti Soveta Narodnykh Komissarov 24(11) Yanvarya 1918 g." (Report on the Activities of the Council of People's Commissars, January 11/24, 1918), *Sochineniya*, XXII, 208.

2. "Vse na Bor'bu s Denikinym" (All Out for the Fight against Denikin), *Sochineniya* (4th ed.), XXIX, 417.

3. *Ibid.*, pp. 415, 417.

4. Stalin, "Beseda s Inostrannymi Rabochimi Delegatsiyami" (Interview with Foreign Workers' Delegations), *Sochineniya*, X, 234.

5. "The present-day wreckers and diversionists, the Trotskyites," declared Stalin in 1937, "are mostly Party people with a Party card in their pocket, and consequently people who formally are not alien to us . . . Their advantage lies in the fact that holding a Party card and pretending to be friends of the Soviet power they tricked our people *politically*, misused their confidence, did their wrecking work furtively, and disclosed our secrets of state to the enemies of the Soviet Union" (Stalin, *Mastering Bolshevism*, pp. 18–20).

6. *Ibid.*, pp. 26–27.

7. *The Land of Socialism Today and Tomorrow*, p. 44.

8. *Ibid.*, p. 45.

9. Stalin, "Otvet Tov. A. Kholopovu" (Reply to Comrade A. Kholopov), *Pravda*, August 2, 1950, p. 2.

10. Lenin, "Zapiska F. E. Dzerzhinskomu" (Note to F. E. Dzerzhinsky), *Sochineniya*, XXII, 126.

11. The Cheka was assigned the following functions:

"1. To persecute and liquidate all attempts and acts of counterrevolution and sabotage all over Russia, no matter what their origin.

"2. To hand over to the Revolutionary Tribunal all counterrevolutionaries and saboteurs and work out measures of struggle against them.

"3. The Commission is to make preliminary investigations only in so far as that may be necessary for suppression . . .

". . . The Commission is to watch the press, sabotage, etc. of the Right Socialist-Revolutionaries, saboteurs, and strikers. Sanctions [to be enforced] — confiscation, confinement, deprivation of food cards, publication of lists of enemies of the people, etc." The text of the decree was printed in *Pravda*, December 18, 1927, p. 2.

12. "Ko Vsem Sovetam na Mestakh" (To All the Local Soviets), *Izvestiya*, no. 252, December 15/28, 1917, p. 5.

13. Meisel and Kozera, *Materials for the Study of the Soviet System*, p. 44.

14. *Pravda*, no. 33(259), February 10/23, 1918, p. 1.

15. Translated in Bunyan and Fisher, *The Bolshevik Revolution, 1917–1918*, p. 577.

16. *Izvestiya*, April 13, 1918, p. 3.

17. See Chamberlin, *The Russian Revolution*, II, 56.

18. *Izvestiya*, September 29, 1918, p. 5.

19. Quoted in "Information on Russia," *Senate Document* 50, 67 Cong., 1 Sess. (Washington, 1921), p. 64.

20. The Chekist Latsis in a pamphlet entitled Two Years of Battle on the Internal Front (*Dva Goda Bor'by na Vnutrennem Fronte* [Moscow, 1920], p. 75), acknowledged 8,389 executions by the Cheka in twenty provinces of Central Russia during 1918 and the first seven months of 1919. A report of the Ukrainian Cheka for 1920 listed 3,879 executions, of which 1,418 occurred in Odessa alone. On the basis of these scattered official data (which, it can be assumed, did not exaggerate

the carnage), an estimate that the victims of the Red Terror during the Civil War period reached at least 50,000 would appear to be conservative (for corroboration, see Chamberlin, I, 73–76). It is not unlikely that this record was matched by equally sanguinary achievements on the part of the Whites.

21. Minutes of the Conference, translated in Bunyan and Fisher, pp. 580–581.

22. *Ibid.*, p. 580.

23. Quoted in Chamberlin, II, 79.

24. The resolution read: "The Congress considers that at present the consolidation of Soviet power within and without makes it possible to narrow the extent of the activity of the Cheka and its organs, reserving for the judicial organs the struggle against violations of the laws of the Soviet republics.

"Therefore the Congress of Soviets charges the presidium of VTsIK to review at the earliest date the statute of the Cheka and its organs in the sense of reorganizing them, of restricting their competence, and of strengthening the principles of revolutionary legality" (*Devyatyi Vserossiiskii S"ezd Sovetov Rabochikh, Krest'yanskikh, Krasnoarmeiskikh i Kazach'ikh Deputatov, Stenograficheskii Otchët* [Ninth All-Russian Congress of Soviets of Workers', Peasants', Red Army and Cossacks' Deputies, Stenographic Report], p. 254; for a translation, see Carr, *The Bolshevik Revolution, 1917–1923*, I, 180).

25. For translation of text of decree, see Batsell, *Soviet Rule in Russia*, pp. 606–609.

26. *Ibid.*, pp. 317–318.

27. Translated, *ibid.*, pp. 609–610.

28. Lenin, "Pis'mo D. I. Kurskomu po Voprosu o Terrore" (Letter to D. I. Kursky on the Question of Terror), *Sochineniya*, XXVII, 296.

29. See David J. Dallin and Boris I. Nicolaevsky, *Forced Labor in Soviet Russia* (New Haven, 1947), pp. 170–177.

30. For a not very reliable description of OGPU organization during the period by a former member, see Georges Agabekov, *OGPU, the Russian Secret Terror* (New York, 1931), pp. 255–277.

31. Quoted in Dallin and Nicolaevsky, p. 173.

32. Michael Farbman, *After Lenin* (London, 1924), p. 134.

33. For an example, see Anton Ciliga, *The Russian Enigma* (London, 1940), pp. 156–157. The memoirs of ex-prisoners of the OGPU during this period testify to mass arrests of the so-called "gold-hoarders." Ciliga reported, "In the Leningrad prison I was particularly shocked by the treatment reserved for those who were accused of hoarding gold. At that time, people throughout Russia were arrested on suspicion of possessing gold and precious objects . . . After . . . tortures, those who had any gave it up. The Industrialization Fund grew richer by a hundred or two hundred million roubles throughout the U.S.S.R.; but as the arrests were made in a haphazard way, as a rule on denunciations, most of those who were tortured did not possess any gold, but instead lost their health if not their life."

34. Sidney and Beatrice Webb, *Soviet Communism: A New Civilisation?* (London, 1936), II, 553.

35. Soltz quoted by the Webbs, II, 556.

36. Reported in *Izvestiya*, March 12, 1933, p. 2.

37. This is the figure cited by the Webbs, II, 589. Dallin and Nicolaevsky (pp. 212–213), claim that almost 300,000 prisoners were employed at the peak. At the conclusion of the project it was announced that 12,484 prisoners had been amnestied and the sentences of 59,516 others had been reduced (see the Webbs, II, 591).

38. For an example, see the Webbs, II, 591–594.

39. See *Izvestiya*, July 11, 1934, p. 1.

40. See Ciliga, *The Russian Enigma*.

41. *Ibid.*, p. 283.

42. Stalin, *Problems of Leninism*, p. 542.

43. "Ob Obshchestve Starykh Bol'shevikov" (Concerning the Society of Old Bolsheviks), *Partiinoe Stroitel'stvo* (Party Construction), no. 11 (June 1935), p. 47.

44. *VKP(b) v Rezolyutsiyakh*, II, 635.

45. "Uroki Politicheskikh Oshibok Saratovskogo Kraikoma" (The Lessons of the Political Errors of the Saratov *Krai* Committee), *Partiinoe Stroitel'stvo*, no. 15 (August 1935), p. 6.

46. "Glavnye Uroki Proverki Partiinykh Dokumentov" (The Main Lessons of the Verification of Party Credentials), *Partiinoe Stroitel'stvo*, no. 2 (January 25, 1936), p. 12.

47. See *VKP(b) v Rezolyutsiyakh*, II, 635–641.

48. See the report of the Mandate Commission in *XVII S"ezd VKP(b)*, p. 303; also, "Za Individual'nyi — Protiv Gruppovogo Priëma v Partiyu" (For Party Membership on an Individual Rather than a Group Basis), *Partiinoe Stroitel'stvo*, no. 10 (May 20, 1936), p. 3.

49. See Stalin, *Mastering Bolshevism*, p. 10.

50. *Report of Court Proceedings, the Case of the Trotskyite-Zinovievite Terrorist Centre, Heard before the Military Collegium of the Supreme Court of the USSR, August 19–24, 1936* (Moscow, 1936).

51. Quoted in Fedotoff White, *The Growth of the Red Army*, pp. 385–386.

52. *Report of Court Proceedings in the Case of the Anti-Soviet "Bloc of Rights and Trotskyites"* (Moscow, 1938), p. 777.

53. Beck and Godin, *Russian Purge and the Extraction of Confession*, p. 106.

54. For text see *VKP(b) v Rezolyutsiyakh*, II, 671–677.

55. For examples see V. Kudryavtsev, "Razbor Apellyatsii v Leninskom Raione" (Review of Appeals in the Leninsk *Raion*), *Partiinoe Stroitel'stvo*, no. 8 (April 15, 1938), pp. 34–38, and "Za Bol'shevistskii Razbor Apellyatsii" (For a Bolshevik Review of Appeals), *Partiinoe Stroitel'stvo*, no. 13 (July 1, 1938), pp. 42–44.

56. See Alexander Weissberg, *The Accused* (New York, 1951), chap. xiv, pp. 418–427.

57. Beck and Godin, p. 38.

58. *The Land of Socialism Today and Tomorrow*, p. 191.

59. *Ibid.*, p. 198.

60. See John Scott, *Behind the Urals* (Boston, 1942), pp. 195–196.

61. For accounts of survivors, see *The Dark Side of the Moon* (New York, 1947), and Jerzy Gliksman, *Tell the West* (New York, 1948).

62. For a list of the classifications used in NKVD arrests in the Baltic States, see A. K. Herling, *The Soviet Slave Empire* (New York, 1951), pp. 79–81.

63. See Elinor Lipper, *Eleven Years in Soviet Prison Camps* (Chicago, 1951), pp. 279, 281–282.

64. See Herling, pp. 71–78, and Lipper, pp. 278–279.

65. *Vedomosti Verkhovnogo Soveta SSSR* (Official Journal of the Supreme Soviet of the USSR), no. 11, 1941.

66. *Ibid.*, no. 37, 1941.

67. See Evtikhiev and Vlasov (eds.) *Administrativnoe Pravo SSSR* (Administrative Law of the USSR), pp. 191–192.

68. For official confirmation as to the border guards, see S. S. Studenikin, V. A. Vlasov, and I. I. Evtikhiev, *Sovetskoe Administrativnoe Pravo* (Soviet Administrative Law; Moscow, 1950), pp. 278–279.

69. As the report of the Canadian investigation of Soviet espionage makes clear, the Foreign Administration directed one of a number of parallel Soviet intelligence undercover systems in Canada. The organization actually exposed in Canada was under the control of Red Army Military Intelligence. "While Gouzenko's evidence and the documents establish the existence of the N.K.V.D. organization in Canada," the Commission reported, "we have been unable to ascertain the extent of its infiltration and the identity of its Canadian or other agents. We have, however, sufficient evidence to show that the N.K.V.D. system is parallel to, but entirely independent of and quite distinct from the military espionage network" (*The Report of the Royal Commission . . . June 27, 1946*, p. 23). Within the Soviet Mission at Ottawa, there were at least five separate channels of communication with Moscow. The Ambassador sent his reports to the Commissariat for Foreign Affairs; the Commercial Counselor reported

to the Commissariat for Foreign Trade; the Military Attaché communicated with the Director of Military Intelligence in Moscow; the NKVD section dispatched its messages to NKVD headquarters in Moscow; and the Political Section, which was charged with transmitting political directives to Canadian Communists as well as with Party work in the Embassy, was directly responsible to the Party Central Committee in Moscow (*ibid.*, pp. 12–13, 28–29).

70. Beck and Godin, p. 76.
71. *Ibid.*, pp. 75–76.
72. *Ibid.*, p. 70.
73. Weissberg, pp. 318–319.
74. Dallin and Nicolaevsky, p. 86.
75. *Gosudarstvennyi Plan Razvitiya Narodnogo Khozyaistva*, American Council of Learned Societies Reprint: Russian Series no. 30 (Baltimore, n.d.).
76. Voznesensky, "Khozyaistvennye Itogi 1940 goda i Plan Razvitiya Narodnogo Khozyaistva SSSR na 1941 god" (The Economic Results for 1940 and the Plan of Development of the National Economy of the USSR for 1941), *Pravda*, February 19, 1941, p. 2.
77. See the careful article by Naum Jasny, "Labor and Output in Soviet Concentration Camps," *The Journal of Political Economy*, LIX, no. 5 (October 1951), 409–410.
78. *Ibid.*, p. 413.
79. See, for example, Book One entitled "Soviet Gold" in Vladimir Petrov, *It Happens in Russia* (London, 1951); Lipper, *passim*; and Jasny, "Labor and Output in Soviet Concentration Camps," p. 419.
80. Dallin and Nicolaevsky, p. 137.
81. This estimate is based on the careful analysis of Mr. Naum Jasny in "Labor and Output in Soviet Concentration Camps."
82. Dallin and Nicolaevsky, p. 88.

Chapter *14*

The Party and the Armed Forces

1. "Decree on the Equalization of Rights of All Serving in the Army," translated in Meisel and Kozera (eds.), *Materials for the Study of the Soviet System*, pp. 37–38.
2. Quoted in Erich Wollenberg, *The Red Army* (London, 1938), p. 41.
3. Translation in Bunyan and Fisher, *The Bolshevik Revolution, 1917–1918*, p. 568.
4. Quoted in Chamberlin, *The Russian Revolution*, II, 26.
5. Leon Trotsky, *Kak Vooruzhalas' Revolyutsiya (na Voennoi Rabote)* (How the Revolution Armed Itself [on War Service]; Moscow, 1923–1925), I, 14; hereafter cited as KVR.
6. Bunyan and Fisher, p. 567.
7. Trotsky, KVR, I, 15.
8. *Ibid.*, p. 314.
9. Decree translated in Bunyan, *Intervention, Civil War, and Communism in Russia, April–December 1918*, p. 275.
10. *Ibid.*, p. 276.
11. Wollenberg, p. 42.
12. Trotsky, KVR, I, 310.
13. *Ibid.*, p. 28.
14. Quoted in Wollenberg, pp. 157–158.
15. Trotsky, KVR, I, 63–64.

16. Fedotoff White, *The Growth of the Red Army*, p. 51.
17. Trotsky, *KVR*, I, 145.
18. *Ibid.*, p. 17.
19. Quoted in Fedotoff White, p. 53.
20. Trotsky, *KVR*, I, 17.
21. *Ibid.*, p. 159.
22. *Ibid.*, p. 151.
23. See decree translated in Wollenberg, p. 255.
24. *Ibid.*, p. 256.
25. See Trotsky's decree issued August 5, 1918, translated in Wollenberg, p. 71.
26. *Ibid.*, pp. 70–71.
27. Trotsky, *KVR*, I, 174; for translation, see Bunyan, p. 273.
28. Fedotoff White, p. 51.
29. *Ibid.*, p. 58.
30. Trotsky, *KVR*, I, 18; translated in Bunyan and Fisher, p. 571.
31. Fedotoff White, p. 62.
32. Quoted, *ibid.*, p. 63.
33. Cited, *ibid.*, p. 91.
34. Trotsky, *KVR*, II(2), 126; for a translation see Fedotoff White, p. 99.
35. Resolution quoted in Fedotoff White, p. 86.
36. Quoted, *ibid.*, pp. 90–91.
37. Lenin, "Rech' pri Zakrytii S"ezda 23 Marta" (Address at the Conclusion of the Congress, March 23, 1919), *Sochineniya*, XXIV, 176.
38. Lenin, "Doklad o Deyatel'nosti Soveta Narodnykh Komissarov 22 Dekabrya" (Report on the Activities of the Council of People's Commissars, December 22, 1920), *Sochineniya*, XXVI, 26.
39. Quoted in Fedotoff White, p. 194.
40. *Protokoly Devyatogo S"ezda RKP(b)* (Protocols of the Ninth Congress of the RCP[b] [March–April, 1920]; Moscow, 1934), p. 451.
41. *Protokoly Desyatogo S"ezda RKP(b)* (Protocols of the Tenth Congress of the RCP[b]), p. 619.
42. Fedotoff White, p. 266.
43. *Ibid.*, p. 261.
44. Wollenberg, p. 177.
45. Fedotoff White, p. 201.
46. *Ibid.*, p. 213.
47. *Ibid.*, p. 206.
48. *Ibid.*, p. 234.
49. *Ibid.*, pp. 235–236.
50. *Ibid.*, p. 250.
51. *Ibid.*, p. 260.
52. Quoted *ibid.*, p. 202.
53. *Finansy SSSR za XXX Let (1917–1947)* (The Finances of the USSR for Thirty Years, 1917–1947; Moscow, 1947), pp. 170, 180.
54. *Ibid.*, p. 180.
55. *The Land of Socialism Today and Tomorrow*, p. 275.
56. *XVIII S"ezd VKP(b)*, p. 274.
57. *The Land of Socialism Today and Tomorrow*, p. 292.
58. Fedotoff White, p. 379.
59. *Ibid.*, p. 420.
60. See *ibid.*, p. 402.
61. A. I. Zaporozhets, *O Perestroike Raboty Politorganov i Partiinykh Organizatsii Krasnoi Armii* (On Reorganizing the Work of the Political Organs and Party Organizations in the Red Army; Moscow, 1941), p. 9.
62. *The Land of Socialism Today and Tomorrow*, p. 298.
63. Fedotoff White, p. 357.
64. Colonel V. Kraskevich, "Pervichnaya Partorganizatsiya v Krasnoi Armii"

(The Primary Party Organization in the Red Army), *Partiinoe Stroitel'stvo* (Party Construction), no. 12 (June 1943), p. 40.

65. *XVIII S"ezd VKP(b)*, p. 276.

66. Wollenberg, pp. 182–183.

67. *Pravda*, October 10, 1952, p. 5.

Chapter 15

Controls and Tensions in the Soviet Factory

1. "Vsem Partiinym Organizatsiyam, Vsem Chlenam Partii. Postanovlenie TsK VKP(b) o Merakh po Uporyadocheniyu Upravleniya Proizvodstvom i Ustanovleniyu Edinolichiya" (To All Party Organizations, All Party Members. Decree of the CC of the All-Union CP[b] on Measures for Regulating the Management of Industry and Instituting One-Man Control), *Pravda*, September 7, 1929, p. 1.

2. David Granick, *Plant Management in the Soviet Industrial System* (doctoral dissertation to be published by Columbia University Press), p. 127.

3. *Ibid.*

4. *Ibid.*

5. L. M. Kaganovich in his report to the Congress concentrated his fire on the organizational confusion and the lack of accountability which the functional system produced. Citing the case of the Mytishchy Railway Car Works, Kaganovich stated: "There we have all the symptoms of bureaucratic routine methods of managing the works, *viz.*, the functional system in the structure of the apparatus and the over-staffing. The factory management is split up into 14 departments in which 367 people are employed. In addition, there are 234 office employees in the various shops. The total number of workers employed at these works is 3,832, so that the office staff represents 16 per cent of the total number of workers employed. In addition to the director there is an assistant technical director, an assistant director of the supply department, an assistant director of workers' supply, a production department, a preparatory production department, a chief engineer's department, technical control department, planning and economic department, a staff department, a special department, a department for the supervision of fulfillment of decisions, a central bookkeeping department, a commercial department, which is subdivided into two sub-departments, namely: finance sub-department and sub-department for supplies and sales, a general manager's department, stores department, building department, and workers' supply department. . . .

"In most cases works directors have no direct contact with the chiefs of the shops; the only contact they have with them is through the functional departments . . .

"If the chief of the shop has to apply to the management when he wants anything done, he has to apply to various departments: he has to apply to the Hiring and Discharge Department if it is a matter concerning workers; to the Energetics Bureau of the Machine Department if it is a matter of fuel; to the Supplies Department if it is a matter concerning materials; to the Preparatory Production Department if it is a matter of drawings; to the Production Department and Planning and Economic Department if it is a matter concerning the program of output; to the Wages and Economic Section if it is a matter concerning rates of pay and output, etc.

"This functional system leads directly to the position that a director is relieved of the duty of directly guiding the work of the shops and occupies himself with giving general orders" (*XVII S"ezd VKP[b]*, pp. 534–535).

6. A. Arakelian, *Industrial Management in the USSR*, translated by Ellsworth L. Raymond (Washington, 1950), p. 123.

7. See David Granick, "Initiative and Independence of Soviet Plant Management," *The American Slavic and East European Review*, X, no. 3 (October 1951),

191–201; Joseph S. Berliner, "The Informal Organization of the Soviet Firm," *The Quarterly Journal of Economics*, LXVI (August 1952), 342–365; Alexander Vucinich, *Soviet Economic Institutions* (Stanford, California, 1952), pp. 43–50.

8. See Malenkov's speech at the Nineteenth Party Congress, *Pravda*, October 6, 1952, p. 7.

9. See Isaac Deutscher, *Soviet Trade Unions*; Solomon M. Schwarz, *Labor in the Soviet Union*.

10. See Gregory Bienstock, Solomon M. Schwarz, and Aaron Yugow, *Management in Russian Industry and Agriculture* (London–New York, 1944), p. 43.

11. *Trud*, May 11, 1949, p. 2.

12. See John Scott, *Behind the Urals*, pp. 34–36.

13. N. G. Aleksandrov, E. I. Astrakhan, S. S. Karinsky, and G. K. Moskalenko, *Zakonodatel'stvo o Trude* (Labor Legislation; Moscow, 1947), pp. 242–256.

14. Berman, *Justice in Russia*, pp. 264–265.

15. See Berliner's article and Granick, "Initiative and Independence of Soviet Plant Management."

Chapter 16

Controls and Tensions in Soviet Agriculture

1. Quoted in Lazar Volin, *A Survey of Soviet Russian Agriculture* (Washington, n.d.), Agriculture Monograph 5, p. 14.

2. Lenin, "Doklad o Rabote v Derevne" (Report on Work in the Rural Districts), *Sochineniya*, XXIV, 161.

3. *Ibid.*, pp. 167–168.

4. Lenin, "Doklad o Natural'nom Naloge 15 Marta" (Report on the Tax in Kind, March 15, 1921), *Sochineniya*, XXVI, 246; quoted in Carr, *The Bolshevik Revolution, 1917–1923*, II, 291.

5. Stalin, "The Right Deviation in the C.P.S.U.(B.)," *Problems of Leninism*, p. 289.

6. "Report on the Work of the Central Committee to the Seventeenth Congress of the C.P.S.U.(B.)," *ibid.*, p. 503.

7. Volin, p. 15.

8. Stalin, "Problems of Agrarian Policy in the U.S.S.R.," *Problems of Leninism*, p. 315.

9. The following account by a village Communist conveys the flavor of the period: "When we were told of collectivization . . . I liked the idea. So did a few others in our village, men like me, who had worked in the city and served in the Red Army. The rest of the village was dead set against it and wouldn't even listen to me. So my friends and I decided to start our own little co-operative farm, and we pooled our few implements and land. You know our peasants. It's no use talking to them about plans and figures; you have to show them results to convince them. We knew that if we could show them that we earned higher profits than before, they would like it and do as we did.

"Well, we got going. Then, one day, an order comes from the Klin party committee that we had to get 100 more families into our little collective. We managed to pull in about a dozen. And, believe me, this was not easy. It needed a lot of coaxing and wheedling. But no coaxing could get us even one more family. I went to Klin and explained the situation to the party committee. I begged them to let us go ahead as we started and I promised them, if they did, to have the whole village in the collective by next year. They wouldn't listen to me. They had orders from Moscow, long sheets saying how many collectives with how many members they had to show on their records. That was all. They told me that I was sabotaging collectivization and that unless I did as I was told I would be thrown out of the party and disgraced forever. Well, I knew that I couldn't get our people in, unless I did what I heard others were doing, in other words, forced them . . . I called a village meeting and I told the people that they had to join the collective, that these were Moscow's orders, and if they didn't, they would be exiled and their property taken away from them. They all signed the paper that same night, every one of them. Don't ask me how I felt and how they felt. And the same night they started to do what the other villages of the U.S.S.R. were doing when forced into collectives — to kill their livestock. They had heard that the government would take away their cattle as soon as they became members of a collective.

"I took the new membership list to the committee at Klin, and this time they were very pleased with me. When I told them of the slaughter of cattle and that the peasants felt as though they were being sent to jail, they weren't interested. They had the list and could forward it to Moscow; that was all they cared about. I couldn't blame them, they were under orders as well as I was.

". . . In our village as well as elsewhere, even though the peasants had formally joined the collectives, they wouldn't work and went on killing the cows and chickens" (Markoosha Fischer, *My Lives in Russia* [2nd ed.; New York-London, 1944], pp. 49–51).

10. V. S. Mertsalov, *Tragediya Rossiiskogo Krest'yanstva* (The Tragedy of the Russian Peasantry; "Posev," n.d.), p. 39.

11. "Golovokruzhenie ot Uspekhov," *Pravda*, March 2, 1930, p. 1; reprinted in Stalin's *Sochineniya*, XII, 191–199.

12. Volin, p. 18.

13. *Ibid.*, p. 19.

14. Winston S. Churchill, *The Hinge of Fate* (Boston, 1950), p. 498.

15. See Table 30 in Naum Jasny, *The Socialized Agriculture of the USSR* (Stanford, California, 1949), p. 793.

16. As Lazar Volin points out (p. 37), "In the aggregate, kolkhoz deliveries to the state and payments in kind to MTS constituted 26 percent of their bumper grain crop in 1937 and 31 and 34 percent, respectively, of the smaller crops in 1938 and 1939. During 1935–37, an average of 68 percent of the meat and animal fats, 45 percent of the milk, and 53 percent of the wool produced collectively went to the state. No statistics are available for subsequent years, but the proportion was doubtless larger, because . . . deliveries have been based on total or tillable kolkhoz acreages since 1940 and not on the area to be seeded to crops or on the number of livestock."

17. For text of the decree, see Gsovski, *Soviet Civil Law*, II, 475–483.

18. For text, see *ibid.*, pp. 484–486.

19. Jasny, *The Socialized Agriculture of the USSR*, p. 398.

20. For text, see Gsovski, II, 487–497.

21. *Ibid.*, p. 488.

22. *Ibid.*, p. 491.

23. *Ibid.*, p. 492.

24. *Sob. Post. SSSR*, 1946, nos. 13 and 14.

25. "K Novym Pobedam Kolkhoznogo Stroya!" (On to New Victories of Kolkhoz Construction!), *Pravda*, September 19, 1947, p. 1.

26. *Sotsialisticheskoe Zemledelie* (Socialist Agriculture), September 11, 1948, cited in Volin, p. 32.

27. A. Andreyev, "Speech at the Eighteenth Congress of the C.P.S.U.(B.)," *The Land of Socialism Today and Tomorrow*, p. 254; also, A. Andreyev, "Stalin i Kolkhoznoe Krest'yanstvo" (Stalin and the Kolkhoz Peasantry), *Bol'shevik*, no. 24 (December 1949), p. 78.

28. Melnikov, "Report of Central Committee of Communist Party (of Bolsheviks) of the Ukraine," *Pravda Ukrainy*, September 25, 1952, pp. 1–5, as translated and condensed in *CDSP*, IV, no. 41 (November 22, 1952), 24.

29. Harry Schwartz, *Russia's Soviet Economy* (New York, 1950), p. 421.

30. P. P. Pyatnitsky, *Organizatsiya, Oplata i Distsiplina Truda v Kolkhozakh* (Organization, Compensation, and Labor Discipline in the Kolkhozes; Moscow, 1951), p. 35.

31. "Trëkhletnii Plan Razvitiya Obshchestvennogo Kolkhoznogo i Sovkhoznogo Produktivnogo Zhivotnovodstva (1949–1951 gg.)" (Three-Year Plan for the Development of the Kolkhoz Communal and State Farm Livestock Industry, 1949–1951), *Sotsialisticheskoe Zemledelie,* April 19, 1949, p. 1.

32. *XVIII S"ezd VKP(b),* p. 117; for translation, see *The Land of Socialism Today and Tomorrow,* pp. 259–260.

33. "Protiv Izvrashchenii v Organizatsii Truda v Kolkhozakh," *Pravda,* February 19, 1950, pp. 4–5; translated in *CDSP,* II, no. 9 (April 15, 1950), 12.

34. Andreyev's letter translated in *CDSP,* II (April 15, 1950), 14–15.

35. Volin, p. 30.

36. *CDSP,* II (April 15, 1950), 12.

37. *Pravda,* October 6, 1952, p. 4.

38. See D. Brezhnev, "V Novykh Usloviyakh" (Under New Conditions), *Izvestiya,* August 26, 1950, p. 2.

39. N. S. Khrushchëv, "O Stroitel'stve i Blagoustroistve v Kolkhozakh" (On Building and Improvements on the Collective Farms), *Pravda,* March 4, 1951, pp. 2–3; translated in *CDSP,* III, no. 7 (March 31, 1951), 13–16.

40. Translated, *CDSP,* III (March 31, 1951), 16.

41. "Report by Comrade G. A. Arutyunov on Work of Armenian Communist Party Central Committee," *Kommunist* (Organ of the Armenian Communist Party), March 21, pp. 1–6; condensed translation in *CDSP,* III, no. 21 (July 7, 1951), 3–4.

42. *Pravda,* October 6, 1952, p. 5.

43. *Gsovski,* II, 459–460.

44. *Ibid.,* p. 461.

45. See Pyatnitsky, p. 34.

46. Volin, p. 31.

47. Quoted in Volin, p. 32.

48. Volin, p. 53.

49. *Pravda,* September 29, 1952, p. 2.

50. Pyatnitsky, pp. 6–7.

51. *Ibid.,* pp. 50–51.

52. *Ibid.,* p. 53.

53. *Ibid.,* pp. 51–52.

54. Volin, p. 46.

55. *Ibid.,* p. 60.

56. V. Ovchinnikova, "Kolkhoznyi Trudoden' za 20 Let" (Twenty Years of the Collective-Farm Workday), *Voprosy Ekonomiki* (Problems of Economics), no. 8 (August 1951), p. 75; condensed translation in *CDSP,* IV, no. 6 (May 22, 1952), 5.

57. Melnikov, "Report of Central Committee of Communist Party (of Bolsheviks) of the Ukraine," *Pravda Ukrainy,* September 25, 1952, pp. 1–5, as condensed and translated in *CDSP,* IV, no. 41 (November 22, 1952), 23.

58. Stalin, "Ekonomicheskie Problemy Sotsializma v SSSR," *Bol'shevik,* no. 18 (September 1952), p. 50; translation in *CDSP,* supplementary issue, IV, no. 36 (October 18, 1952), 20.

59. *Ibid.*

60. Volin, p. 68.

61. Vucinich, *Soviet Economic Institutions,* p. 115.

62. *Ibid.,* p. 123.

63. *Ibid.,* p. 116.

64. N. S. Khrushchëv, "Organizatsionno-Khozyaistvennoe Ukreplenie Kolkhozov — Zalog Dal'neishego Moshchnogo Pod"ema Sel'skogo Khozyaistva" (Organizational-Economic Strengthening of the Collective Farms — Guarantee of Further Mighty Advance in Agriculture), *Sotsialisticheskoe Zemledelie,* February 8, 1951, p. 3; translated in *CDSP,* III, no. 7 (March 31, 1951), 9.

65. Vucinich, p. 67.

66. *Ibid.*

67. *CDSP*, III (March 31, 1951), 10.

68. *Ibid.*

69. I. Benediktov, "MTS v Bor'be za Novyi Pod"em Sotsialisticheskogo Sel'skogo Khozyaistva" (The Machine-Tractor Stations in the Struggle for a New Advance in Socialist Agriculture), *Bol'shevik*, no. 5 (March 1951), p. 17.

70. K. Zhukov, "O Partiino-Politicheskoi Rabote v MTS" (On Party-Political Work in the Machine-Tractor Stations), *Bol'shevik*, no. 5 (March 1951), p. 54.

71. See Khrushchëv in *CDSP*, III (March 31, 1951), 8.

72. V. Yarantsev, "Po Sledam Reshenii Kraiispolkoma" (Tracking Down the Decisions of the Territorial Executive Committee), *Izvestiya*, September 1, 1951, p. 2.

73. "Na Strazhe Interesov Obshchestvennogo Khozyaistva Kolkhozov" (Guarding the Interests of the Communal Economy of Collective Farms), *Pravda*, April 19, 1952, p. 1; translation in *CDSP*, IV, no. 16 (May 31, 1952), 30.

74. See the editorial, "Uluchshat' Normirovanie Truda v Kolkhozakh" (Improve the Computation of Labor Norms on Collective Farms), *Sotsialisticheskoe Zemledelie*, January 10, 1952, p. 1.

75. Khrushchëv in *CDSP*, III (March 31, 1951), 8–9.

76. "Report by Comrade M. D. Bagirov at 18th Congress of Azerbaidzhan Communist Party on the Work of the Azerbaidzhan Communist Party Central Committee," *Bakinskii Rabochii* (The Baku Worker), May 26, 1951, pp. 1–6; condensed translation in *CDSP*, III, no. 24 (July 28, 1951), 5.

BIBLIOGRAPHY

This bibliography does not include all works consulted. Only those cited in the text are listed.

1. PRIMARY SOURCES

PARTY CONGRESSES AND CONFERENCES

Protokoly Pyatogo S"ezda RKP(b) (Protocols of the Fifth Congress of the Russian Social-Democratic Labor Party). Held May–June 1907. 2nd ed. Moscow: Partizdat TsK VKP(b) (Party Publishers for the Central Committee of the All-Union Communist Party [Bolshevik]), 1935.

Protokoly Shestogo S"ezda RSDRP(b) (Protocols of the Sixth Congress of the RSDLP[b]). Held in August 1917. Moscow: Partiinoe Izdatel'stvo (Party Publishers), 1934.

Sed'moi S"ezd Rossiiskoi Kommunisticheskoi Partii, Stenograficheskii Otchët (Seventh Congress of the Russian Communist Party, Stenographic Report). Held December 5–9, 1919. Moscow–Petrograd: Gosudarstvennoe Izdatel'stvo (State Publishing House), 1923.

Protokoly Devyatogo S"ezda RKP(b) (Protocols of the Ninth Congress of the RCP[b]). Held in March–April 1920. Moscow: Partiinoe Izdatel'stvo, 1934.

Protokoly Desyatogo S"ezda RKP(b) (Protocols of the Tenth Congress of the RCP[b]). Held in March 1921. Moscow: Partiinoe Izdatel'stvo, 1933.

Dvenadtsatyi S"ezd Rossiiskoi Kommunisticheskoi Partii (Bol'shevikov), Stenograficheskii Otchët (Twelfth Congress of the Russian Communist Party [Bolshevik], Stenographic Report). Held April 17–25, 1923. Moscow: Krasnaya Nov', 1923.

Trinadtsatyi S"ezd Rossiiskoi Kommunisticheskoi Partii (Bol'shevikov), Stenograficheskii Otchët (Thirteenth Congress of the Russian Communist Party [Bolshevik], Stenographic Report). Held May 23–31, 1924. Moscow: Krasnaya Nov', 1924.

XIV S"ezd Vsesoyuznoi Kommunisticheskoi Partii (b), Stenograficheskii Otchët (Fourteenth Congress of the All-Union Communist Party [b], Stenographic Report). Held December 18–31, 1925. Moscow–Leningrad: Gosudarstvennoe Izdatel'stvo, 1926.

XV S"ezd Vsesoyuznoi Kommunisticheskoi Partii (b), Stenograficheskii Otchët (Fifteenth Congress of the All-Union Communist Party [b], Stenographic Report). Held December 2–19, 1927. Moscow–Leningrad: Gosudarstvennoe Izdatel'stvo, 1928.

XVI S"ezd Vsesoyuznoi Kommunisticheskoi Partii (b), Stenograficheskii Otchët (Sixteenth Congress of the All-Union Communist Party [b], Stenographic Report). Held June 26–July 13, 1930. 2nd ed. Moscow–Leningrad: Ogiz, Moskovskii Rabochii (Moscow Worker), 1931.

XVII S"ezd Vsesoyuznoi Kommunisticheskoi Partii (b), Stenograficheskii Otchët (Seventeenth Congress of the All-Union Communist Party [b], Stenographic Report). Held January 26–February 10, 1934. Moscow: Partizdat, 1934.

Socialism Victorious. A collection of the most important reports and speeches delivered at the Seventeenth Party Congress. New York: International Publishers, n.d.

XVIII S"ezd Vsesoyuznoi Kommunisticheskoi Partii (b), Stenograficheskii Otchët (Eighteenth Congress of the All-Union Communist Party [b], Stenographic Report). Held March 10–21, 1939. Moscow: Ogiz, Gosudarstvennoe Izdatel'stvo Politicheskoi Literatury (State Publishing House for Political Literature), 1939.

The Land of Socialism Today and Tomorrow. Reports and Speeches at the Eighteenth Congress of the Communist Party of the Soviet Union (Bolsheviks). Moscow: Foreign Languages Publishing House, 1939.

Informatsionnoe Soveshchanie Predstavitelei Nekotorykh Kompartii v Pol'she v Kontse Sentyabrya 1947 goda (Informational Conference of Representatives of Certain Communist Parties in Poland at the End of September 1947). Moscov: Ogiz, 1948.

PARTY RESOLUTIONS AND DECREES

Vsesoyuznaya Kommunisticheskaya Partiya (B) v Rezolyutsiyakh i Resheniyakh S"ezdov, Konferentsii i Plenumov TsK (1898–1939) (All-Union Communist Party [B] in Resolutions and Decrees of Congresses, Conferences, and Plenums of the Central Committee, 1898–1939). 2 vols. Volume I, 1898–1924, 4th ed. Moscow–Leningrad: Partiinoe Izdatel'stvo, 1932. Volume II, 1925–1939, 6th ed. Moscow–Leningrad: Politizdat pri TsK VKP(b) (Political Publishers of the CC of the All-Union CP [b]), 1941.

VKP(b). *O Komsomole i Molodëzhi* (On the Komsomol and Youth). A collection of decisions and decrees of the Party concerning the youth, 1903–1938. Moscow: Izd. TsK VLKSM, Molodaya Gvardiya (Publishing House of the Central Committee of the All-Union Leninist Communist League of Youth, Young Guard), 1938.

MINUTES OF THE PARTY CENTRAL COMMITTEE

Protokoly Tsentral'nogo Komiteta RSDRP, Avgust 1917–Fevral' 1918 (Protocols [Minutes] of the Central Committee of the Russian Social-Democratic Labor Party, August 1917–February 1918). Moscow–Leningrad: Gosudarstvennoe Izdatel'stvo, 1929.

PARTY CENSUS

TsK VKP (b), Statisticheskii Otdel (Central Committee, All-Union Communist Party [b], Statistical Department), compilers. *Sotsial'nyi i Natsional'nyi Sostav VKP(b), Itogi Vsesoyuznoi Partiinoi Perepisi 1927 goda* (Social and National Composition of the All-Union CP[b], Results of the All-Union Party Census for 1927). Moscow–Leningrad: Gosizdat (State Publishing House), 1928.

PROCEEDINGS OF THE CONGRESS OF SOVIETS AND THE SUPREME SOVIET

Vtoroi Vserossiiskii S"ezd Sovetov R. i S.D. (Second All-Russian Congress of Soviets of Workers' and Soldiers' Deputies). Held November 7–8, 1917. Moscow–Leningrad: Gosudarstvennoe Izdatel'stvo, 1928.

Tretii Vserossiiskii S"ezd Sovetov Rabochikh, Soldatskikh i Krest'yanskikh Deputatov (Third All-Russian Congress of Soviets of Workers', Soldiers', and Peasants' Deputies). Held January 23–31, 1918. St. Petersburg: Priboi, 1918.

Devyatyi Vserossiiskii S"ezd Sovetov Rabochikh, Krest'yanskikh, Krasnoarmeiskikh i Kazach'ikh Deputatov, Stenograficheskii Otchët (Ninth All-Russian Congress of Soviets of Workers', Peasants', Red Army, and Cossacks' Deputies, Stenographic Report). Held December 22–27, 1921. Moscow: Izdanie VTsIK (Publication of the All-Union Central Executive Committee), 1922.

Zasedaniya Verkhovnogo Soveta SSSR, Pervaya Sessiya, 12–19 Marta 1946 g., Stenograficheskii Otchët (Sessions of the Supreme Soviet, First Session, March 12–19, 1946, Stenographic Report). Moscow: Izdanie Verkhovnogo Soveta SSSR (Publication of the Supreme Soviet of the USSR), 1946.

—— *Tret'ya Sessiya, 20–25 Fevralya 1947 g.* (Third Session, February 20–25, 1947). Moscow: Izdanie Verkhovnogo Soveta SSSR, 1947.

—— *Pervaya Sessiya, 12–19 Iyunya 1950 g.* (First Session, June 12–19, 1950). Moscow: Izdanie Verkhovnogo Soveta SSSR, 1950.

—— *Vtoraya Sessiya, 6–12 Marta 1951 g.* (Second Session, March 6–12, 1951). Moscow: Izdanie Verkhovnogo Soveta SSSR, 1951.

CONSTITUTIONAL DOCUMENTS, TREATIES, LAWS, DECREES AND COURT PROCEEDINGS

Aleksandrov, N. G., E. I. Astrakhan, S. S. Karinsky, and G. K. Moskalenko. *Zakonodatel'stvo o Trude* (Labor Legislation). Moscow: Yuridicheskoe Izdatel'stvo Ministerstva Yustitsii SSSR (Juridical Publishing House for the Ministry of Justice of the USSR), 1947.

Gosudarstvennyi Plan Razvitiya Narodnogo Khozyaistva SSSR na 1941 god (State Plan of Development of the National Economy of the USSR for 1941). American Council of Learned Societies Reprint: Russian Series no. 30. Baltimore: Universal Press, n.d.

Klyuchnikov, Yu. V., and A. V. Sabanin (eds.). *Mezhdunarodnaya Politika Noveishego Vremeni v Dogovorakh, Notakh i Deklaratsiyakh* (International Politics of Modern Times in Treaties, Notes, and Declarations). 3 parts. Moscow: Izdanie Litizdata NKID (Publishers of Literature for the People's Commissariat for Foreign Affairs), 1925–1929.

Konstitutsiya (Osnovnoi Zakon) Soyuza Sovetskikh Sotsialisticheskikh Republic (Constitution [Fundamental Law] of the Union of Soviet Socialist Republics). Moscow: Izdanie Verkhovnogo Soveta SSSR, 1947.

Report of Court Proceedings in the Case of the Anti-Soviet "Bloc of Rights and Trotskyites." Moscow: People's Commissariat of Justice of the USSR, 1938.

Report of Court Proceedings, the Case of the Trotskyite-Zinovievite Terrorist Centre, Heard before the Military Collegium of the Supreme Court of the USSR, August 19–24, 1936. Moscow: People's Commissariat of Justice of the USSR, 1936.

Sbornik Zakonov SSSR i Ukazov Prezidiuma Verkhovnogo Soveta SSSR (Collection of Laws of the USSR and Decrees of the Presidium of the Supreme Soviet of the USSR). Vol II, 1938–1944. 2nd ed. Moscow: Izdanie Verkhovnogo Soveta SSSR, 1945.

Sobranie Postanovlenii i Rasporyazhenii Pravitel'stva SSSR (Collection of Decrees and Ordinances of the Government of the USSR).

Sobranie Postanovlenii i Rasporyazhenii Soveta Ministrov Russkoi Sotsialisticheskoi Federativnoi Sovetskoi Respubliki (Collection of Administrative Orders and Decrees of the Council of Ministers of the Russian Socialist Federative Soviet Republic).

Sobranie Postanovlenii i Rasporyazhenii Soveta Ministrov Soyuza Sovetskikh Sotsialisticheskikh Respublik (Collection of Administrative Orders and Decrees of the Council of Ministers of the Union of Soviet Socialist Republics).

Vedomosti Verkhovnogo Soveta SSSR (Official Journal of the Supreme Soviet of the USSR).

2. BOOKS AND PAMPHLETS

Agabekov, Georges. *OGPU, the Russian Secret Terror.* Translated by Henry W. Bunn. New York: Brentano's, 1931.

Aleksandrov (pseud.). *Kto Upravlyaet Rossiei?* (Who Rules Russia?). Berlin: Parabola [1933?].

Arakelian, A. *Industrial Management in the USSR.* Translated by Ellsworth L. Raymond. Washington: Public Affairs Press, 1950.

Avdeyev, N. (ed. of vols. I and II), Vera Vladimirovna (ed. of vols. III and IV), and K. Ryabinsky (ed. of vol. V). *Revolyutsiya 1917 g., Khronika Sobytii* (The Revolution of 1917, Chronicle of Events). 5 vols. Moscow: Gosudarstvennoe Izdatel'stvo, 1923–1926.

Badayev, A. E. *Bol'sheviki v Tsarskoi Dume* (The Bolsheviks in the Tsarist Duma). Leningrad: Priboi, 1929.

Bajanov, Boris. *Avec Staline dans le Kremlin.* Paris: Les Editions de France, 1930.

Barghoorn, Frederick C. *The Soviet Image of the United States.* New York: Harcourt, Brace and Company, 1950.

Batsell, Walter Russell. *Soviet Rule in Russia.* New York: The Macmillan Company, 1929.

Bauer, Raymond A. *The New Man in Soviet Psychology.* Cambridge: Harvard University Press, 1952.

Beck, F., and W. Godin. *Russian Purge and the Extraction of Confession.* Translated by Eric Mosbacher and David Porter. New York: The Viking Press, 1951.

Belinsky, V. G. *Selected Philosophical Works.* Moscow: Foreign Languages Publishing House, 1948.

Berman, Harold J. *Justice in Russia.* Cambridge: Harvard University Press, 1950.

Bienstock, Gregory, Solomon M. Schwarz, and Aaron Yugow. *Management in Russian Industry and Agriculture.* London and New York: Oxford University Press, 1944.

Bol'shaya Sovetskaya Entsiklopediya (Great Soviet Encylopedia). 65 vols. Moscow: Aktsionernoe Obshchestvo Sovetskaya Entsiklopediya (The Soviet Encyclopedia Joint–Stock Company), 1926–1939.

Bowden, Witt, Michael Karpovich, and Abbott Payson Usher. *An Economic History of Europe since 1750.* New York: American Book Company, 1937.

Bulgakov, Sergei. *Ot Marksizma k Idealizmu — Sbornik Statei (1896–1903)* (From Marxism to Idealism — A Collection of Articles, 1896–1903). St. Petersburg: Tovarishchestvo Obshchestvennaya Pol'za (Society for the Public Weal), 1903.

Bunyan, James. *Intervention, Civil War, and Communism in Russia, April–December 1918.* Baltimore: The Johns Hopkins Press, 1936.

Bunyan, James, and H. H. Fisher. *The Bolshevik Revolution, 1917–1918.* Stanford: Stanford University Press, 1934.

Burdzhalov, E. *Pervyi Vserossiiskii S"ezd Sovetov Rabochikh i Soldatskikh Deputatov* (The First All-Russian Congress of Soviets of Workers' and Soldiers' Deputies). Moscow: Ogiz, Gosudarstvennoe Izdatel'stvo Politicheskoi Literatury, 1938.

Carr, E. H. *The Bolshevik Revolution, 1917–1923.* 3 vols. New York: The Macmillan Company, 1951–53.

Chamberlin, W. H. *The Russian Revolution, 1917–1921.* 2 vols. New York: The Macmillan Company, 1935.

Churchill, Winston S. *The Hinge of Fate.* Boston: Houghton Mifflin Company, 1950.

Ciliga, Anton. *The Russian Enigma.* London: George Routledge and Sons, 1940.

Dallin, David J., and Boris I. Nicolaevsky. *Forced Labor in Soviet Russia.* New Haven: Yale University Press, 1947.

Daniels, Robert V. "The Left Opposition in the Russian Communist Party, to 1924." Doctoral dissertation, Harvard University, 1950.

The Dark Side of the Moon. New York: Charles Scribner's Sons, 1947.

Deutscher, Isaac. *Soviet Trade Unions.* London and New York: Royal Institute of International Affairs, 1950.

Duranty, Walter. *Stalin & Co.* New York: William Sloane Associates, 1949.

Eastman, Max. *Since Lenin Died.* London: The Labour Publishing Company, 1925.

Evtikhiev, I. I., and V. A. Vlasov. *Administrativnoe Pravo SSSR.* (Administrative Law of the USSR). Moscow: Yuridicheskoe Izdatel'stvo Ministerstva Yustitsii SSSR, 1946.

Farbman, Michael. *After Lenin.* London: Leonard Parsons, 1924.

Finansy SSSR za XXX Let (1917–1947) (The Finances of the USSR for Thirty Years, 1917–1947). Moscow: Gosudarstvennoe Finansovoe Izdatel'stvo SSSR (State Financial Publishing House of the USSR), 1947.

Fischer, Louis. *Men and Politics.* New York: Duel, Sloan and Pearce, 1941.

Fischer, Markoosha. *My Lives in Russia.* 2nd ed. New York and London: Harper & Brothers, 1944.

Fischer, Ruth. *Stalin and German Communism*. Cambridge: Harvard University Press, 1948.

Florinsky, Michael T. *The End of the Russian Empire*. New Haven: Yale University Press, 1931.

Gifford, Henry. *The Hero of His Time*. London: Edward Arnold & Co., 1950.

Gliksman, Jerzy. *Tell the West*. New York: The Gresham Press, 1948.

Granick, David. *Plant Management in the Soviet Industrial System*. Doctoral dissertation to be published by Columbia University Press.

Gsovski, Vladimir. *Soviet Civil Law*. 2 vols. Ann Arbor: University of Michigan Law School, 1948.

Gurian, Waldemar (ed.). *The Soviet Union: Background, Ideology, Reality*. Notre Dame, Indiana: University of Notre Dame Press, 1951.

Gurvich, G. S. *Istoriya Sovetskoi Konstitutsii* (History of the Soviet Constitution). Moscow: Izdanie Sotsialisticheskoi Akademii (Socialist Academy Publication), 1923.

Hazard, John N. (ed.). *Soviet Legal Philosophy*. Translated by Hugh W. Babb. Cambridge: Harvard University Press, 1951.

Herling, A. K. *The Soviet Slave Empire*. New York: Wilfred Funk, 1951.

History of the Communist Party of the Soviet Union (Bolsheviks) Short Course. New York: International Publishers, 1939.

"Information on Russia." *Senate Document* 50, 67th Congress, 1st Session. Washington: Government Printing Office, 1921.

Jaroslawski, E. (Yaroslavsky, Emilian). *Aus der Geschichte der Kommunistischen Partei der Sowjetunion (Bolschewiki)*. 2 vols. Hamburg-Berlin: Carl Hoym Nachfolger, n.d.

Jasny, Naum. *The Socialized Agriculture of the USSR*. Stanford: Stanford University Press, 1949.

Kautsky, Karl. *The Dictatorship of the Proletariat*. Translated by H. J. Stenning. Manchester: The National Labour Press, n.d.

Kommunisticheskoe Vospitanie v Sovetskoi Shkole: Sbornik Statei (Communist Education in the Soviet School: Collection of Articles). Vol. II. Moscow: Izdatel'stvo Akademii Pedagogicheskikh Nauk RSFSR (Publishing House for the Academy of Pedagogic Sciences of the RSFSR), 1950.

Kornilov, A. A. *Krest'yanskaya Reforma* (Peasant Reform). St. Petersburg: P. P. Gershunin and Co., 1905.

Krupskaya, Nadezhda K. *Memories of Lenin*. 2 vols. New York: International Publishers, 1930.

Kursky, A. *The Planning of the National Economy of the U.S.S.R.* Moscow: Foreign Languages Publishing House, 1949.

Latsis, M. Ya. *Dva Goda Bor'by na Vnutrennem Fronte* (Two Years of Battle on the Internal Front). Moscow: Gosudarstvennoe Izdatel', 1920.

Lenin, Vladimir Ilyich. *Collected Works*. Vols XX and XXI. London: Martin Lawrence, Ltd., 1929. Vol. XXIII, New York: International Publishers, 1945.

———— *Sochineniya* (Works). 30 vols. 3rd ed. Moscow: Partizdat TsK VKP(b), 1935.

———— *Sochineniya* (Works). 35 vols. 4th ed. Moscow: Gosudarstvennoe Izdatel'stvo Politicheskoi Literatury, 1941–1951.

Levin, Alfred. *The Second Duma*. New Haven: Yale University Press, 1940.

Lipper, Elinor. *Eleven Years in Soviet Prison Camps*. Chicago: Henry Regnery Co., 1951.

Lorimer, Frank. *The Population of the Soviet Union: History and Prospects*. Geneva: League of Nations, 1946.

Lyashchenko, P. I. *History of the National Economy of Russia to the 1917 Revolution*. New York: The Macmillan Co., 1949.

Marx, Karl. *Capital*. 3 vols. Chicago: Charles H. Kerr & Co., 1906–1909.

———— *Selected Works*. Edited by V. Adoratsky. 2 vols. New York: International Publishers, n.d.

Masaryk, Thomas G. *The Spirit of Russia*. 2 vols. London: Allen & Unwin, 1919.

Mavor, James. *An Economic History of Russia*. 2 vols. London and Toronto: J. M. Dent & Sons, 1914.

Maynard, Sir John. *Russia in Flux*. London: Victor Gollancz, 1946.

Medynsky, E. N. *Narodnoe Obrazovanie v SSSR* (Public Education in the USSR). Moscow: Gos. Uchebno-Pedagog. Izd-vo Ministerstva Prosveshcheniya RSFSR (State Educational-Pedagogical Publishing House for the Ministry of Education of the RSFSR), 1947.

Mehnert, Klaus. *Youth in Soviet Russia*. London: Allen & Unwin, 1933.

Meisel, James H., and Edward S. Kozera (eds.). *Materials for the Study of the Soviet System*. Ann Arbor: The George Wahr Publishing Co., 1950.

Mertsalov, V. S. *Tragediya Rossiiskogo Krest'yanstva* (The Tragedy of the Russian Peasantry). Posev, n.d.

Milyukov, P. N. *Istoriya Vtoroi Russkoi Revolyutsii* (History of the Second Russian Revolution). 3 parts. Sofia: Russo-Bulgarian Publishers, 1921–1924.

Milyutin, V. P. (ed.). *Agrarnaya Revolyutsiya* (The Agrarian Revolution). Vol. II. Moscow: Izdatel'stvo Kommunisticheskoi Akademii (Publishing House for the Communist Academy), 1928.

Morstein Marx, Fritz (ed.). *Foreign Governments*. 2nd ed. New York: Prentice-Hall, 1952.

Pasherstnik, A. E. *Pravo na Trud* (The Right to Work). Moscow: Izdatel'stvo Akademii Nauk SSSR (Publishing House for the Academy of Sciences of the USSR), 1951.

Perepiska K. Marksa i F. Engel'sa s Russkimi Politicheskimi Deyatelyami (Correspondence of K. Marx and F. Engels with Russian Political Figures). 2nd ed. Moscow: Gosudarstvennoe Izdatel'stvo Politicheskoi Literatury, 1951.

Petrov, Vladimir. *It Happens in Russia*. London: Eyre & Spottiswoode, 1951.

Plekhanov, G. B. *O Zadachakh Sotsialistov v Bor'be s Golodom* (The Duty of the Socialists in the Struggle against Famine in Russia). Geneva: Sotsial'-Demokrat, 1892.

——— *Sochineniya*. Edited by David Ryazanov. 24 vols. Moscow-Petrograd: Gosudarstvennoe Izdatel'stvo, 1923–1927.

Pobedonostsev, K. P. (Pobyedonostseff). *Reflections of a Russian Statesman*. Translated by Robert C. Long, London: Grant Richards, 1898.

Popov, N. *Outline History of the Communist Party of the Soviet Union*. 2 vols. New York: International Publishers, 1934.

Pyatnitsky, P. P. *Organizatsiya, Oplata i Distsiplina Truda v Kolkhozakh* (Organization, Compensation, and Labor Discipline in the Kolkhozes). Moscow: Izdatel'stvo Akademii Nauk SSSR, 1951.

Radkey, Oliver H. *The Election to the Russian Constituent Assembly of 1917*. Cambridge: Harvard University Press, 1950.

The Report of the Royal Commission Appointed under Order in Council P.C. 411 of February 5, 1946, to Investigate the Facts Relating to and the Circumstances Surrounding the Communication, by Public Officials and Other Persons in Positions of Trust, of Secret and Confidential Information to Agents of a Foreign Power. June 27, 1946. Ottawa: Edmond Cloutier, 1946.

Robinson, Geroid T. *Rural Russia under the Old Régime*. New York: The Macmillan Co., 1949.

Rovinsky, N. N. (ed.). *Finansovoe Pravo* (Financial Law). Moscow: Yuridicheskoe Izdatel'stvo Ministerstva Yustitsii SSSR, 1946.

——— *Gosudarstvennyi Byudzhet SSSR* (The State Budget of the USSR). Moscow: Gosfinizdat (State Financial Publishing House), 1951.

Ryazanov, David (Ryazanoff) (ed.). *The Communist Manifesto of Karl Marx and Friedrich Engels*. Marxist Library, vol. III. New York: International Publishers, 1930.

Schwartz, Harry. *Russia's Soviet Economy*. New York: Prentice-Hall, 1950.

Schwarz, Solomon M. *The Jews in the Soviet Union.* Syracuse: Syracuse University Press, 1951.
———— *Labor in the Soviet Union.* New York: Frederick A. Praeger, 1952.
Scott, John. *Behind the Urals.* Boston: Houghton Mifflin Co., 1942.
Semennikov, V. P. (ed.). *Nikolai II i Velikie Knyazya* (Nicholas II and the Grand Dukes). Moscow-Leningrad: Gosudarstvennoe Izdatel'stvo, 1925.
Shabad, Theodore. *Geography of the USSR.* New York: Columbia University Press, 1951.
Shachtman, Max. *The Struggle for the New Course.* Published in one volume with his translation of Leon Trotsky's *The New Course.* New York: New International Publishing Co., 1943.
Shlyapnikov, A. G. *Semnadtsatyi God* (The Year 1917). 3 vols. Moscow-Leningrad: Gosudarstvennoe Izdatel'stvo, 1925–1927.
Shulgin, V. V. *Dni* (Days). Belgrade: M. A. Suvorin and Co., 1925.
Souvarine, Boris. *Staline: Aperçu historique du bolshévisme.* Paris: Librairie Plon, 1935.
The Soviet-Yugoslav Dispute. London-New York: Royal Institute of International Affairs, 1948.
Stalin, Joseph (Stalin, I. V.). *Mastering Bolshevism.* New York: Workers Library Publishers, 1937.
———— *Na Putyakh k Oktyabryu* (On the Roads to October). Moscow-Leningrad: Gosudarstvennoe Izdatel'stvo (State Publishing House), 1925.
———— *Problems of Leninism.* 11th ed. *Moscow*: Foreign Languages Publishing House, 1940.
———— *Sochineniya* (Works). 13 vols. Moscow: Ogiz, Gosudarstvennoe Izdatel'stvo Politicheskoi Literatury (State Publishing House for Political Literature), 1946–.
"The Strategy and Tactics of World Communism." *House Document* 619, 80th Congress, 2nd Session. Washington: Government Printing Office, 1948.
Studenikin, S. S., V. A. Vlasov, and I. I. Evtikhiev. *Sovetskoe Administrativnoe Pravo* (Soviet Administrative Law). Moscow: Gosudarstvennoe Izdatel'stvo Yuridicheskoi Literatury (State Publishing House for Juridical Literature), 1950.
Sukhanov, Nik. *Zapiski o Revolyutsii* (Notes on the Revolution). St. Petersburg: Z. I. Grzhevin, 1919.
Sumner, B. H. *Peter the Great and the Emergence of Russia.* New York: The Macmillan Co., 1951.
———— *Survey of Russian History.* 2nd ed. London: Duckworth, 1947.
Timasheff, Nicholas S. *The Great Retreat.* New York: E. P. Dutton & Company, 1946.
Towster, Julian. *Political Power in the USSR.* New York: Oxford University Press, 1948.
Trainin, I. P., and I. D. Levin (eds.). *Sovetskoe Gosudarstvennoe Pravo* (Soviet State Law). Moscow: Yuridicheskoe Izdatel'stvo Ministerstva Yustitsii SSSR, 1948.
Trotsky, Leon (Trotzky). *The History of the Russian Revolution.* 3 vols. New York: Simon and Schuster, 1932.
———— *Kak Vooruzhalas' Revolyutsiya* (*na Voennoi Rabote*) (How the Revolution Armed Itself [on War Service]). 3 vols. Moscow: Vysshyi Voennyi Redaktsionnyi Sovet (Supreme Military Editorial Board), 1923–1925.
———— *Lenin.* New York: Minton, Balch & Co., 1925.
———— *My Life.* New York: Charles Scribner's Sons, 1930.
———— *Nashi Politicheskiya Zadachi* (Our Political Tasks). Geneva: Izd. Rossiiskoi Sotsial'-Demokraticheskoi Partii (Russian Social-Democratic Labor Party Publishing House), 1904.
———— *The Real Situation in Russia.* Translated by Max Eastman. New York: Harcourt, Brace and Co., 1928.
———— *Sochineniya* (Works). 21 vols. Moscow: Gosudarstvennoe Izdatel'stvo, 1924–1927.

——— *The Stalin School of Falsification.* Translated by John G. Wright. New York: Pioneer Publishers, 1937.

Vernadsky, George. *A History of Russia.* New York: New Home Library, 1944.

Volin, Lazar. *A Survey of Soviet Russian Agriculture.* Agriculture Monograph 5. Washington: United States Department of Agriculture, n.d.

Voprosy Partiino-Organizatsionnoi Raboty (Questions of Party-Organizational Work) Moscow: Ogiz, 1948.

Vucinich, Alexander. *Soviet Economic Institutions.* Stanford: Stanford University Press, 1952.

Vyshinsky, Andrei Y. *The Law of the Soviet State.* Translated by Hugh W. Babb. New York: The Macmillan Co., 1948.

Webb, Sidney and Beatrice. *Soviet Communism: A New Civilisation?* 2 vols. London: Longmans, Green and Co., 1936.

Weissberg, Alexander. *The Accused.* New York: Simon and Schuster, 1951.

White, D. Fedotoff. *The Growth of the Red Army.* Princeton: Princeton University Press, 1944.

Widmayer, Ruth. "The Communist Party and the Soviet Schools, 1917–1937." Doctoral dissertation, Harvard University, 1952.

Wolfe, Bertram D. *Three Who Made a Revolution.* New York: The Dial Press, 1948.

Wollenberg, Erich. *The Red Army.* Translated by Claud W. Sykes. London: Secker & Warburg, 1938.

Young Communists in the USSR. Translated by Virginia Rhine. Washington: Public Affairs Press, 1950.

Zamyatin, E. I. *My* (We). New York: Chekhov Publishing House, 1952.

Zaporozhets, A. I. *O Perestroike Raboty Politorganov i Partiinykh Organizatsii Krasnoi Armii* (On Reorganizing the Work of the Political Organs and Party Organizations in the Red Army). Moscow: Voennoe Izdatel'stvo Narodnogo Komissariata Oborony Soyuza SSR (Military Publishing House for the People's Commissariat for the Defense of the USSR), 1941.

3. JOURNALS AND NEWSPAPERS

American Political Science Review:

Fainsod, Merle. "Controls and Tensions in the Soviet System." XLIV, no. 2, June 1950.

Nemzer, Louis. "The Kremlin's Professional Staff: The 'Apparatus' of the Central Committee, Communist Party of the Soviet Union." XLIV, no. 1, March 1950.

The American Slavic and East European Review:

Daniels, Robert V. "The Kronstadt Revolt of 1921: A Study in the Dynamics of Revolution." X, no. 4, December 1951.

Granick, David. "Initiative and Independence of Soviet Plant Management." X, no. 3, October 1951.

Page, Stanley W. "Lenin, the National Question and the Baltic States, 1917–19." VII, no. 1, February 1948.

Bol'shevik, theoretical organ of the Central Committee of the All-Union Communist Party (b):

Aleksandrov, G. F. "Nas Osenyaet Velikoe Znamya Lenina-Stalina" (The Great Banner of Lenin and Stalin Shields Us). No. 1, January 1947.

Andreyev, A. "Stalin i Kolkhoznoe Krest'yanstvo" (Stalin and the *Kolkhoz* Peasantry). No. 24, December 1949.

Benediktov, I. "MTS v Bor'be za Novyi Pod'em Sotsialisticheskogo Sel'skogo Khozyaistva" (The Machine-Tractor Station in the Struggle for a New Advance in Socialist Agriculture). No. 5, March 1951.

Khataevich, M. "O Sostoyanii i Rabote Partiinoi Yacheiki v Derevne" (On the Condition and Work of the Party Cell in the Village). No. 3–4(19–20), February 1925.

Kurdin, S. "Rukovodstvo Priëmom v Ryady Partii i Vospitanie Molodykh Kommunistov" (Supervision of Admission to Party Membership and the Training of Young Communists). No. 23, December 1951.

"O Rabote Partiinykh Organizatsii sredi Zhenshchin" (On the Work of Party Organizations among Women). No. 1, January 1951.

"Otvet Tov. Stalina na Pis'mo Tov. Razina" (Comrade Stalin's Reply to the Letter of Comrade Razin). No. 3, February 1947.

Paikin, Ya. "Kommunisty-Krest'yane Belorusskoi Derevni" (Communist Peasants in the Belorussian Village). No. 17, September 15, 1929.

"Partiinaya Rabota v Sovetskikh Uchrezhdeniyakh" (Party Work in Soviet Institutions). No. 14, July 1951.

Peters, Ya. "Nekotorye Vyvody iz Chistki Sredne-Aziatskoi Partorganizatsii" (Some Conclusions after the Purge of the Central-Asian Party Organization). No. 3, February 15, 1935.

"Pis'mo T. Ivanova i Otvet T. Stalina" (The Letter of Comrade Ivanov and Comrade Stalin's Reply). No. 4, February 15, 1938.

Pospelov, P. "Partiya Lenina-Stalina — Rukovodyashchaya i Napravlyayushchaya Sila Sovetskogo Obshchestva" (The Party of Lenin and Stalin is the Leading and Directing Force of Soviet Society). No. 20, October 30, 1947.

Ryutin, M. "Rukovodyashchie Kadry VKP(b)" (Leading Cadres of the All-Union CP[b]). No. 15, August 15, 1928.

"Shiroko Razvernut' Politicheskuyu Rabotu v Derevne" (For the Widespread Development of Political Work in Rural Areas). No. 6, March 1947.

Slepov, L. "O Bol'shevistskom Metode Rukovodstva Khozyaistvennymi Organami" (The Bolshevik Method of Managing Economic Agencies). No. 2, January 1951.

Stalin, J. (I. V. Stalin). "Ekonomicheskie Problemy Sotsializma v SSSR" (Economic Problems of Socialism in the USSR). No. 18, September 1952.

———— "Otvety Tovarishcham" (Replies to Comrades). No. 14, July 1950.

"Vypolnim Vazhneishee Reshenie Partii" (We Shall Carry Out the Most Important Decision of the Party). No. 18, September 30, 1929.

Yakovlev, F. "O Partiinom Uchëte" (Concerning Party Records). No. 12, June 1951.

Zhukov, K. "O Partiino-Politicheskoi Rabote v MTS" (On Party-Political Work in the Machine-Tractor Stations). No. 5, March 1951.

Current Digest of the Soviet Press, New York, N. Y.
Foreign Affairs:

Dexter, Byron. "Clausewitz and Soviet Strategy." XXIX, no. 1, October 1950.

Kennan, George F. "America and the Russian Future." XXIX, no. 3, April 1951.

Istorik Marksist (Marxist Historian):

Stalin, J. (Stalin, I.), A. Zhdanov, and S. Kirov. "Zamechaniya po Povodu Konspekta Uchebnika po 'Istorii SSSR'" (Remarks Concerning the Conspectus of a Textbook on "The History of the USSR"). No. 1 (53), 1936.

Izvestiya (News), central government organ, Moscow.

Izvestiya Tsentral'nogo Komiteta Rossiiskoi Kommunisticheskoi Partii (B) (News of the Central Committee of the Russian Communist Party [B], renamed *Izvestiya Tsentral'nogo Komiteta Vsesoyuznoi* [All-Union] *Kommunisticheskoi Partii (B)* with issue no. 1(122), January 1926:

"K Voprosu o Natsional'nom Sostave RKP" (On the Question of the National Composition of the RCP). No. 7–8(55–56), September 1923.

"Otchët o Rabote TsK za Period ot 9 do 10 Partiinogo S"ezda" (Report on the Work of the Central Committee for the Period between the Ninth and Tenth Party Congresses). No. 29, March 7, 1921.

556 Bibliography

"Otchët Organizatsionno-Instruktorskogo Otdela" (Report of the Organization-Instruction Section). No. 3(51), March 1923.

"Otchët Uchëtno-Raspredelitel'nogo Otdela" (Report of the Account and Assignment Section). No. 22, September 18, 1920.

"Otchët Uchëtno-Raspredelitel'nogo Otdela. Obshchie Usloviya i Kharakter Raboty" (Report of the Account and Assignment Section. General Conditions and Character of Work). No. 3(51), March 1923.

"Otchët za God Raboty TsK RKP (s XI do XII S"ezda RKP)" (Report on a Year's Work by the Central Committee of the Russian Communist Party [from the Eleventh to the Twelfth Congress of the RCP]). No. 4(52), April 1923.

"Vypolnenie Direktiv XI S"ezda Partii. Podbor Sekretarei Gubkomov i Obkomov" (Fulfillment of the Directives Issued by the Eleventh Party Congress. Selection of *Gubkom* and *Obkom* Secretaries). No. 3(51), March 1923.

The Journal of Political Economy:

Jasny, Naum. "Labor and Output in Soviet Concentration Camps." LIX, no. 5, October 1951.

Krokodil, Soviet humorous publication.

Kul'tura i Zhizn' (Culture and Life), journal of the Agitation and Propaganda Department of the Central Committee of the All-Union Communist Party.

Molodoi Bol'shevik (Young Bolshevik), Komsomol journal:

Ershov, V. "Ne Isklyuchat' Ogul'no, a Vospitat' (Ob Oshibke Kemerovskogo Obkoma Komsomola)" (Do Not Exclude without Foundation, but Educate [On the Mistakes of the Kemerovo Regional Committee of the Komsomol]). No. 21, November 1949.

Golovkin, Major-General V. "Komsomol i Dosarm" (Komsomol and Dosarm). No. 22, November 1949.

Golubev-Monatkin, Rear Admiral I. "Komsomol i Dosflot" (Komsomol and Dosflot). No. 14, July 1950.

Mikhailov, N. A. "Nepreryvno Uluchshat' Rabotu s Komsomol'skimi Kadrami" (For Constant Improvement in the Work with Komsomol Cadres). No. 15, August 1952.

———— "O Roste Ryadov VLKSM" (On the Growth in the Ranks of the All-Union Leninist Communist League of Youth). No. 3, February 1951.

———— "Otchët TsK VLKSM XI S"ezdu" (Report of the Central Committee of the All-Union LCLY to the Eleventh Congress). No. 8, April 1949.

"O Rabote Komsomol'skoi Organizatsii Stalingradskogo Traktornogo Zavoda Imeni F. Dzerzhinskogo" (On the Work of the Komsomol Organization in the F. Dzerzhinsky Tractor Factory in Stalingrad). No. 1, January 1950.

"O Roste Ryadov VLKSM Sverdlovskoi Oblastnoi Komsomol'skoi Organizatsii" (On the Growth in the Ranks of the All-Union LCLY in the Sverdlovsk Regional Komsomol Organization). No. 1, January 1950.

"O Stile Raboty Molotovskogo Obkoma Komsomola" (On the Style of Work of the Molotov Regional Committee of the Komsomol). No. 9, May 1950.

Shelepin, A. N. "Doklad Mandatnoi Komissii XI S"ezda VLKSM" (Report of the Mandate Commission, Eleventh Congress of the All-Union LCLY). No. 8, April 1949.

Moskovskii Bol'shevik, journal of the Moscow Regional and City Party Committees.

Nash Vek (Our Age), Petrograd.

New York Times.

Partiinaya Zhizn' (Party Life), journal of the Party Central Committee; successor to *Partiinoe Stroitel'stvo:*

"Voprosy Chlenstva v VKP(b), po Dokumentam i Tsifram za 30 Let" (Questions of Membership in the All-Union CP[b], According to Documents and Figures for Thirty Years). No. 20, October 1947.

Partiinoe Stroitel'stvo (Party Construction), journal of the Party Central Committee; successor to *Izvestiya TsK*:

Andreyev, A. A. "Kommunisticheskoe Vospitanie Molodëzhi i Zadachi Komsomola" (The Communist Education of the Youth and the Tasks of the Komsomol). No. 9, May 1936.

Anichkov, V. "P. Zaslavsky, 'Partrabota na Krupnykh Stroitel'stvakh,' Ogiz, Moskovskii Rabochii, 1931 g., str. 64" (P. Zaslavsky, "Party Work in Large Industries," Ogiz, Moscow Worker, 1931, 64 pp.). No. 13, July 1931.

Bogomolov, A. "Vybory Partorganov v Moskovskoi Organizatsii" (Election of Party Organs in the Moscow Organization). No. 11, June 1, 1937.

Chivirev, F. "K Voprosu o Rabote s Kommunistami-Odinochkami" (On the Question of Work with Single Communists). No. 14, July 1935.

"Dvadtsatiletie Komsomola" (Twenty Years of the Komsomol). No. 16, August 15, 1938.

Egorov, V. "Za Stalinskoe Vydvizhenie Partkadrov" (For the Stalinist Promotion of Party Cadres). No. 13, July 1, 1937.

Freiberg, S. "Iz Praktiki Raboty s Partiinym Aktivom" (From Experience in Work with the Party *Aktiv*). No. 10, May 1935.

"Glavnye Uroki Proverki Partiinykh Dokumentov" (The Main Lessons of the Verification of Party Credentials). No. 2, January 25, 1936.

Kaganovich, Lazar. "Ob Apparate TsK VKP(b)" (On the Apparatus of the CC of the All-Russian CP[b]). No. 2(4), February 1930.

Kosarëv, A. V. "O Perestroike Raboty Komsomola" (On the Reorganization of Komsomol Work). No. 14, July 1935.

Kovalëv, L. "Bol'shevistskaya Proverka Snizu" (Bolshevik Verification from Below), No. 11, June 1, 1937.

Kraskevich, Colonel V. "Pervichnaya Partorganizatsiya v Krasnoi Armii" (The Primary Party Organization in the Red Army). No. 12, June 1943.

Kudryavtsev, V. "Razbor Apellyatsii v Leninskom Raione" (Review of Appeals in the Leninsk *Raion*). No. 8, April 15, 1938.

Malenkov, G. M. "O Zadachakh Partiinykh Organizatsii v Oblasti Promyshlennosti i Transporta" (On the Tasks of Party Organizations in the Spheres of Industry and Transport), No. 4–5, February–March 1941.

Nosov, I. "Uchëba Partiinogo Aktiva" (Training the Party *Aktiv*). No. 1, January 1, 1937.

"O Reorganizatsii Kul'tpropa TsK VKP(b)" (On the Reorganization of the *Kul'tprop* of the Central Committee of the All-Union CP[b]). No. 11, June 1935.

"O Zadachakh Partiinykh Organizatsii v Oblasti Promyshlennosti i Transporta, Rezolyutsiya po Dokladu Tov. Malenkova, Prinyataya XVIII Vsesoyuznoi Konferentsiei VKP(b)" (Concerning the Tasks of Party Organizations in the Spheres of Industry and Transport, Resolution on the Report of Comrade Malenkov Adopted by the Eighteenth Conference of the All-Union CP[b]). No. 4–5, February–March 1941.

"Ob Obshchestve Starykh Bol'shevikov" (Concerning the Society of Old Bolsheviks). No. 11, June 1935.

Peskarev, G. "Dinamika Rosta i Problema Regulirovaniya Sostava Partii" (Dynamics of Growth and the Problem of Regulating the Composition of the Party). No. 17, September 1931.

Serebrennikov, A. "O Priëme Intelligentsii v Partiyu" (On the Acceptance of Intelligentsia into the Party). No. 6(8), March 1930.

"XVI S"ezd VKP(b) v Tsifrakh" (Sixteenth Congress of the All-Union CP[b] in Figures). No. 13–14, July 1930.

Shamberg, M. "Nekotorye Voprosy Vnutripartiinoi Raboty" (Certain Questions on Intra-Party Work). No. 4, February 1946.

Shishkin, I. "Luchshikh Lyudei v Partiyu Lenina-Stalina" (Better People for Membership in the Party of Lenin and Stalin). No. 23, December 1, 1938.

Smirnov, D. "Perestroika Raboty v Komsomole" (Reshaping the Work of the Komsomol). No. 12, June 15, 1937.

Sokolov, M. "Partiinye Massy Proveryayut Svoikh Rukovoditelei" (The Party Masses Check on Their Leaders). No. 10, May 15, 1938.

"Uroki Politicheskih Oshibok Saratovskogo Kraikoma" (The Lessons of the Political Errors of the Saratov *Krai* Committee). No. 15, August 1935.

Vershkov, P. "Sovetskoi Molodëzhi — Leninsko-Stalinskoe Vospitanie" (A Leninist–Stalinist Education for Soviet Youth). No. 7, April 1, 1938.

V. V. "Rost Partii v Pervom Polugodii 1932 g." (Party Growth in the First Half of 1932). No. 21, November 1932.

Vlasov, V. "Rost i Kachestvennoe Ukreplenie Ryadov Partii" (The Increase and Qualitative Strengthening in the Party's Ranks). No. 16, August 1932.

Vlasov, V. "Za Uluchshenie Sostava Natsorganizatsii" (For Improvement in the Composition of National Organizations). No. 19–20, October 1930.

"Vyshe Bol'shevistskuyu Bditel'nost' Komsomol'tsev" (Raise the Bolshevik Vigilance of the Komsomol). No. 18, September 1937.

"Za Bol'shevistskii Razbor Apellyatsii" (For a Bolshevik Review of Appeals). No. 13, July 1, 1938.

"Za Individual'nyi — Protiv Gruppovogo Priëma v Partiyu" (Party Membership on an Individual Rather than a Group Basis). No. 10, May 20, 1936.

Planovoe Khozyaistvo (Planned Economy), *Gosplan* journal:

Lokshin, E. "Normirovanie Raskhoda Syr'ya i Materialov v Proizvodstve" (The Allocation of Resources and Materials in Industry). No. 6, November–December 1950.

Political Science Quarterly:

Curtiss, John S., and Alex Inkeles. "Marxism in the U.S.S.R. — The Recent Revival." LXI, no. 3, September 1946.

Pravda (Truth), organ of the Party Central Committee and Moscow Regional Committee of the Party.

The Quarterly Journal of Economics:

Berliner, Joseph S. "The Informal Organization of the Soviet Firm." LXVI, no. 3, August 1952.

Erlich, Alexander. "Preobrazhenski and the Economics of Soviet Industrialization." LXIV, no. 1, February 1950.

Sotsialisticheskoe Zemledelie (Socialist Agriculture), organ of the Ministry of Agriculture.

Sovetskaya Estoniya (Soviet Esthonia).

Trud (Labor), organ of the All-Union Central Council of Trade-Unions.

Voprosy Ekonomiki (Problems of Economics), organ of the Institute of Economics, Academy of Sciences of the USSR:

Ovchinnikova, V. "Kolkhoznyi Trudoden' za 20 Let" (Twenty Years of the Collective Farm Workday). No. 8, August 1951.

INDEX